IMPORTANT

HERE IS YOUR REGISTRATION CODE TO ACCESS MCGRAW-HILL PREMIUM CONTENT AND MCGRAW-HILL ONLINE RESOURCES

To obtain 30-day trial access to premium online resources for both students and instructors, you need THIS CODE. Once the code is entered, you will be able to use the web resources.

Access is provided for examination purposes only to assist faculty in making textbook adoption decisions.

If the registration code is missing from this examination copy, please contact your local McGraw-Hill representative for access information.

If you have adopted this textbook for your course, contact your local representative for permanent access

To gain access to these online resources

1. **USE** your web browser to go to: www.mhhe.com/motives

2. **CLICK** on "First Time User"

3. **ENTER** the Registration Code printed on the tear-off bookmark on the right

4. After you have entered your registration code, click on "Register"

5. **FOLLOW** the instructions to setup your personal UserID and Password

6. **WRITE** your UserID and Password down for future reference. Keep it in a safe place.

If your course uses WebCT or Blackboard, you'll be able to use this code to access the McGraw-Hill content within your online course. Contact your system administrator for details.

REGISTRATION CODE

4CVT–AGJ8–MQTP–MGFM–QM3Y

The McGraw-Hill Companies

 Higher Education

Thank you, and welcome to your McGraw-Hill Online Resources.

0-07-322049-3 T/A MILLER: MOTIVES FOR WRITING, 5/E

MOTIVES FOR WRITING

MOTIVES FOR WRITING

FIFTH EDITION

ROBERT KEITH MILLER

University of St. Thomas

Boston   Burr Ridge, IL   Dubuque, IA   Madison, WI   New York
San Francisco   St. Louis   Bangkok   Bogotá   Caracas   Kuala Lumpur
Lisbon   London   Madrid   Mexico City   Milan   Montreal   New Delhi
Santiago   Seoul   Singapore   Sydney   Taipei   Toronto

The McGraw·Hill Companies

 Higher Education

Published by McGraw-Hill, an imprint of The McGraw-Hill Companies, Inc., 1221 Avenue of the Americas, New York, NY 10020. Copyright © 2006, 2003, 1999, 1995, 1992, by The McGraw-Hill Companies, Inc. All rights reserved. No part of this publication may be reproduced or distributed in any form or by any means, or stored in a database or retrieval system, without the prior written consent of The McGraw-Hill Companies, Inc., including, but not limited to, in any network or other electronic storage or transmission, or broadcast for distance learning.

2 3 4 5 6 7 8 9 0 DOC/DOC 0 9 8 7 6

SET   ISBN-13: 978-0-07-322070-3
         ISBN-10: 0-07-322070-1

BOOK   ISBN-13: 978-0-07-322050-5
         ISBN-10: 0-07-322050-7

Vice president and Editor-in-chief: *Emily Barrosse*
Publisher: *Lisa Moore*
Sponsoring editor: *Christopher Bennem*
Developmental editor: *Bennett Morrison*
Marketing manager: *Lori DeShazo*
Production editor: *Melanie Field*
Production supervisor: *Tandra Jorgensen*
Design manager: *Violeta Díaz*
Interior designers: *Susan Breitbard, Linda Robertson, and Ellen Pettengell*

Cover designer: *Violeta Díaz*
Photo research coordinator: *Alexandra Ambrose*
Photo researcher: *Judy Mason*
Art editor: *Ayelet Arbel*
Compositor: *Thompson Type*
Typeface: *11/12 Bembo*
Printer and binder: *RR Donnelley, Crawfordsville*

Cover image: © *Ryoichi Yotsumoto/Images.com/Corbis*

Text and photo credits begin on page 691 and constitute an extension of the copyright page.

LIBRARY OF CONGRESS CATALOGING-IN-PUBLICATION DATA

Motives for writing / [compiled by] Robert Keith Miller.—5th ed.
   p. cm.
  Includes index.
  ISBN 0-07-298286-1
  1. College readers. 2. Report writing—Problems, exercises, etc. 3. English language—rhetoric—Problems, exercises, etc. I. Miller, Robert Keith.

PE1417.M65 2005
808'.0427–dc22   20050414502

The Internet addresses listed in the text were accurate at the time of publication. The inclusion of a Web site does not indicate an endorsement by the author or McGraw-Hill, and McGraw-Hill does not guarantee the accuracy of the information presented at these sites.

www.mhhe.com

Contents

2 WRITING TO REPORT INFORMATION   97

3 WRITING TO EXPLAIN INFORMATION   173

4 WRITING TO EVALUATE SOMETHING 241

5 WRITING TO ANALYZE IMAGES 303

Core Text: The Story of an Hour, KATE CHOPIN 394
> An American writer of the late nineteenth century tells what happens during the hour that passes from the time a woman is told that her husband was killed in an accident and when she learns that he is still alive.

Feminine Double Consciousness in Kate Chopin's "The Story of an Hour,"
ANGELYN MITCHELL 397
> A scholar who frequently works with minorities uses feminist theory to argue that the protagonist in Chopin's story had been oppressed by marriage.

Fatal Self-Assertion in Kate Chopin's "The Story of an Hour,"
LAWRENCE I. BERKOVE 403
> A scholar who has read Mitchell rejects feminist interpretations of the story and argues that the protagonist is profoundly selfish.

Core Text: Book of Genesis, Chapter 9 411
> This part of the Bible focuses on what happened to Noah after the great flood and how he came to place a curse upon a member of his own family.

Noah's Nakedness and the Curse of Canaan: A Case of Incest?,
FREDERICK W. BASSETT 413
> A theologian argues that understanding the idiomatic meaning of language in the Old Testament leads to concluding that a serious sin is conveyed by apparently simple words: seeing the "nakedness" of one's father.

The Curse That Never Was, GENE RICE 420
> An African American scholar argues that analyses such as Bassett's have been used to justify slavery and that the story of the curse upon Canaan "may well be the most misunderstood and abused passage in the Bible. . . ."

Companion Text: Psalm 87 429
> One of the texts cited by Rice is reprinted here—a psalm that shows Africans treated with respect.

Core Text: The Bill of Rights 431
> The first ten amendments to the Constitution—collectively known as the Bill of Rights, because they establish how the civil liberties of Americans must be respected by the government—are reprinted here because they are open to various interpretations and often provide the basis for court rulings, such as the two that follow.

Groh v. Ramirez: A Majority Decision, JOHN PAUL STEVENS 433
> A senior member of the Supreme Court concludes that the rights guaranteed by the Fourth Amendment had been violated in a specific case.

8 WRITING TO INSPIRE OTHERS   521

9 WRITING TO AMUSE OTHERS   569

10 WRITING TO EXPERIMENT WITH FORM   609

APPENDIX: DOCUMENTING SOURCES AND AVOIDING PLAGIARISM   665

Readings Arranged by Subject and Theme

Education

Environment

Ethics and Morality

Family

Gender Issues

Health and Wellness

Identity

Language and Learning

Popular Culture

Preface

The fifth edition of this book continues to reflect my experience that helping students to discover and fulfill their motives for writing will help
them to write well. As its title suggests, *Motives for Writing* emphasizes the importance of the writer's purpose—the reason for composing and the goals the
writer seeks to achieve. Understanding these motives—or aims of discourse as
they are sometimes described in theory—contributes to effective communication. Moreover, an emphasis on motive helps students to develop the active
minds that are essential for making sense of the world and conveying that
sense to others. *Motives for Writing* encourages students to develop these skills
by studying, analyzing, and responding to a diverse collection of readings organized by purpose.

In addition to illustrating ten motives for writing, the readings provide
examples of different writing styles and patterns of arrangement. Although
the readings vary in length—with the longer, more challenging selections
concentrated toward the end of most chapters—they all address issues that are
likely to inspire good class discussion. Of the 78 selections, 38 are new in the
fifth edition. The choices have resulted in a collection that is both rhetorically
and culturally diverse. The writers included in this edition discuss diversity in
terms of race, gender, geography, religion, social class, and sexual orientation;
and their works include personal essays, feature articles, documented arguments, and critical assessments. Many of these pieces have not been previously
anthologized. I have nevertheless retained a number of familiar pieces both
because they have proven records as classroom favorites and because I wanted
to spare instructors the necessity of undertaking an entirely new class preparation. Gloria Naylor, Annie Dillard, Martin Luther King, Jr., George Orwell,
and Alice Walker are a few of the authors represented by well-known works.

Each of the ten chapters focused on motive begins with an introduction
that discusses why writers choose to pursue that purpose and what readers expect when given a work that promises to fulfill the motive in question. These
introductions also explain how writers fulfill those expectations, and offer
guidelines for students when planning an essay of their own. One guideline is
to consider audience, and each chapter introduction discusses how students
should take their audience into account when writing. These introductions
each conclude with a new feature to this edition: a clear summary of tips for
reading and writing with the chapter motive in mind.

The book itself opens with a longer introduction, "Writing for Your Life."
It shows how motive intersects with other elements of the rhetorical situation, such as audience and context, so that students can understand that writing involves more than one concern. "Writing for Your Life" also discusses

strategies for invention, arrangement, and revision so that students will be better able to fulfill their goals as writers. It concludes with advice about style, so that students can understand additional principles for effective writing, and an introduction to the conventions of academic discourse so that they will be prepared to write for academic audiences.

Experience shows that the aims of discourse can be pursued by different means, and discussions of planning and drafting—both in the general introduction and in the chapter introductions—encourage writers to choose the methods that work best for them. The entire book reflects the conviction that different writers work in different ways, and the same writer may work well using different approaches at different times. I have seen in my classrooms that providing students with choices can enable them to overcome the difficulties that writers encounter. Mindful of these difficulties, I have tried to keep the book's rhetoric as simple and direct as possible and to choose readings that speak to a diverse range of students.

To support the readings, an extensive apparatus accompanies each selection. Head notes provide information about authors and the context in which their work originally appeared—and, in many cases, insights into their motivation for writing or the writing process they follow. Although some "Questions for Discussion" are designed to gauge reading comprehension, most raise concerns that invite readers to think about what they have read and to formulate their own responses. Every reading is also followed by three "Suggestions for Writing." Moreover, the apparatus for each selection includes links making connections with other selections within the book, as well as directing students to additional resources in print and online. Individual readers may well identify other questions, links, and suggestions; I did not attempt to exhaust the possibilities of any piece. My goal was simply to encourage thoughtful responses to reading, and I believe that such responses, when encouraged, can take any number of directions. The apparatus for each piece concludes with a reference to the book's Web site, where students can access additional information. The development of this Web site responds to the increasing role of technology in supporting the teaching of writing.

Although the organization of *Motives for Writing* emphasizes the importance of recognizing and fulfilling a specific purpose, the book includes features designed to help instructors to use the book in courses that are organized according to other principles. For example, an alternative table of contents groups selections on related topics for users interested in pursuing a particular subject or theme. In addition, the book also includes an Index to the Readings by Rhetorical Strategy ("or mode").

A word here about the rhetorical modes: This book takes the position that writing seldom involves conforming to a fixed pattern, that a single piece usually involves several modes, and that no mode is limited to any one motive. In other words, I present the modes as means for generating ideas when pursuing different aims—not as models to which writers should make their thoughts conform. I believe that instruction based on fixed patterns of arrangement can turning writing into an exercise that bears little relationship to the way writers write in the world beyond the classroom. Patterns such as narration, comparison, and definition are more likely to grow out of the act of writing than to be imposed at the outset as a framework to which writers must be subordinate. Because the modes can be useful for instructors and students who wish to focus on organization, I include discussion of them in the introductions to Chapters 3, 4, and 7. However, the text as a whole presents arrangement as one of the writer's tools, not an end in itself.

In this spirit, the text also includes frequent reminders that motive is not an end in itself, and there are occasions when writers have more than one motive when writing, just as they may draw upon more than one mode to fulfill a certain motive. For example, writers may need to report information before setting out to explain it, or they may need to evaluate something as part of writing to persuade.

New to the Fifth Edition

When preparing this edition, I had the benefit of advice from excellent reviewers. Although reviewers reported that they liked the material in the general introduction, "Writing for Your Life," they asked me to introduce breaks that would make what was then fifty pages of text easier to assign and to digest. In response, I shortened the introduction by moving material on documenting sources to an appendix that now includes a model student paper. I introduced more art, so that there would be more visual breaks. And I added five sets of exercises, the placement of which signifies where instructors may conclude when assigning part of the introduction. Moreover, most of these exercises provide students with the opportunity to write short papers early in the course.

I used the following criteria when selecting new readings: the clarity with which a piece fulfilled one of the motives which are discussed in the book, the quality of a writer's prose, the timeliness of the material, and the extent to which a piece could deepen students' understanding of cultural diversity. Some of the new selections address topics from popular culture that are especially likely to appeal to students. These include an inside view of the gambling industry, an explanation of how to alter photographs, an evaluation of gossip magazines, and an argument on reforming college sports. I know, from my own classroom experience, that providing students with accessible readings on topics that are familiar to them can easily generate good class discussion. But I also believe in the importance of helping students to think critically about material that they might not be inclined to read on their own, and I know that students can be engaged by this challenge by teachers committed to the importance of critical reading and thinking. So the fifth edition also includes selections that call for discussion so that students can better understand what may initially seem unrelated to their own experience or values. For example, Chapter 1 now includes a piece in which a writer explores how his search for the perfect aftershave has shaped his identity, Chapter 2 includes an investigative report on how the outsourcing of American jobs appears from the point of view of those working for such a company in India, and Chapter 7 includes an argument on behalf of allowing openly gay and lesbian citizens to serve in the U.S. military. These are among the new selections from which students can learn when guided to explore their responses in a college writing course. And since the book as a whole includes more material than a teacher can reasonably assign in a single semester, instructors are free to assign the pieces that seem most appropriate for their own students and course goals.

Like the readings as a whole, the new selections vary in length, and I have once again considered gender, race, and location as factors when making choices. The new selections come from all regions of the country. When considering race, I encourage students to consider the extent to which race is a social construction. When considering gender, I was especially interested in showing how men and women can write both in keeping with gender expectations and in defiance of those conventions. Accordingly, the book includes a new selection in which a woman evaluates gossip magazines and a man discusses why he admired Johnny Cash—to cite two of the new selections in Chapter 4. But the book also shows that a man can care passionately about finding the perfect scent and that a woman can be in a position to demand reform in the sports programs at Division I schools. The book even includes a piece written by a woman who used to be a man—a biologist who briefly discusses what it means to be transgendered in an interview that accompanies her work in Chapter 3.

Positioned next to "Writing to Analyze Images" (a well-received chapter that was new to the fourth edition), a new chapter "Writing to Analyze Texts" is designed to help students make the connection between reading closely and writing thoughtfully about what has been read. Although the importance of critical reading, thinking, and writing informs the book as a whole, this new chapter makes the connection explicit. It includes three "core texts," which are texts that lend themselves to diverse interpretations: "The Story of an Hour" by Kate Chopin, Chapter 9 of the Book of Genesis, and the Bill of Rights. Each of these core texts is followed by two scholarly but nevertheless accessible responses, thus demonstrating how literary scholars, theologians, and judges must read carefully and then become active participants in determining the meaning of what they have read. Instructors assigning this chapter will give students experience in developing skills they are likely to need in courses across the curriculum and to see that there is no single way of reading a text that is the correct way. Meaning is constructed by readers through their thoughtful engagement with texts. Well established though this idea is in literary theory, it is often a revelation for students who have reached college convinced that education means supplying correct answers and repeating the opinions of their instructors. Seeing how texts can inspire significantly different responses worthy of being taken seriously can be liberating for such students—and for instructors who don't want to read a set of papers each of which has the same tidy thesis.

After adding this new chapter, I made some changes in the book's structure. "Writing to Inspire Others," formerly called "Writing to Move" has been moved after "Writing to Persuade Others" instead of being placed immediately before it. The close relationship between persuasion and pathos is retained, but the new sequence provides at the book's heart an unbroken series of motives that are commonly pursued in academic discourse: "Writing to Report Information," "Writing to Explain Information," "Writing to Evaluate Something," "Writing to Analyze Images," "Writing to Analyze Texts," and "Writing to Persuade Others." This sequence is then followed by a series of literary motives: "Writing to Inspire Others," "Writing to Amuse Others," and "Writing to Experiment with Form." "Writing to Understand Experience"—which can also be classified as "literary," (although some theorists would call it experiential) continues to be the opening chapter, because the material in it speaks to where students are most likely to be at the beginning of a writing course, and a good book, like a good teacher, begins with where students are, not with where they might arrive.

Another change is the addition of new component of the apparatus supporting the reading selections. Each chapter now includes at least one "Companion Text"—a short selection that provides additional information about one of the principal readings. Two of these "Companion Texts" are interviews with the authors; another provides an update on the increasing popularity of cell phones. Others include documents relevant to the reading in which they are placed such as the letter to which Martin Luther King, Jr. was responding when writing "Letter from Birmingham Jail" and the Defense Department's official policy on homosexuality in the military, a policy popularly known as "Don't Ask, Don't Tell," which is challenged by one of the arguments in "Writing to Persuade Others." Each of these—which range from a personal narrative about dating one of the authors included in the book to historical background on the European exploitation of Africa—has a brief introduction and is set off visually from the reading that it supplements.

Finally, the fifth edition now includes a newly designed appendix which discusses why it is important to document sources and why plagiarism is a problem. This appendix includes examples of both MLA and APA parenthetical and bibliographical citations. Additional entries can be found on the book's Web site: www.mhhe.com/motives. A student paper using MLA-style documentation concludes the appendix and also provides a model of an argument arranged according to the principles of classical rhetoric.

Acknowledgments

In completing this edition of *Motives for Writing*, I have accumulated many debts. I want to thank the following authors for communicating with me about their work, giving me information that enriched the apparatus: Marilyn Scheil, Gloria Naylor, Rick Marin, Catherine Dold, YiLing Chen-Josephson, Dara Moskowiz, Annie Bourneuf, Angelyn Mitchell, Lawrence I. Berkove, Sally Jenkins, and Melissa S. Embser-Herbert. Elizabeth Hoier of the National Museum in Stockholm was very helpful when I needed to identify the Morisot and the Rembrant alluded to by John Berger in an essay that is new to this edition.

At the University of St. Thomas, I am grateful for support from my colleague and friend Erika Scheuruer, who shared with me her experience in teaching the book and cheered me whenever I fretted about deadlines. Andy J. Leet, the administrative assistant for the English department, was always helpful and good humored when I turned to him with requests for photocopying, scanning—and, most frequently—helping me to sort out problems with accessing and transmitting information electronically. David Doody, my research assistant, and a fine writer, consistently demonstrated creativity and good judgment when I was searching for new selections. And my students provided clear responses when I tested these new readings—in addition to helping me see what worked best in the book and where changes would be useful.

When planning this edition, I benefited from advice from the following reviewers: Jenifer Fennell, Minneapolis Community and Technical College; Lynée Gaillet, Georgia State University; Wendy Hesford, Ohio State University; Rebecca Hewett, California State University, Bakersfield; Ann Ross, California State University, Dominguez Hills; Amy Rust, California State University, Dominguez Hills; Lisa Schneider, Columbus State Community College; Jennifer Spiegel, Grand Canyon University; Penny Tschantz, University of Tennessee; James Van Sickle; Grand Valley State University; Lucy Wilcox, University of North Carolina, Wilmington; and Sandra Young, Sacred Heart University.

Tom Briggs, my copyeditor, helped me to see numerous ways in which my prose could be more concise and precise. He also raised thoughtful queries that prompted me to see more clearly what I wanted to communicate. Melanie Field, my production editor, kept track of the many pieces of this book as they moved from one part of the country to another, and did everything she could to make sure that the book was published in a timely manner despite working with an author who likes to hold on to a manuscript as long as he can get away with it. In this work, she was supported by David Staloch at McGraw-Hill, with whom I was glad to work again because of his expertise and never-failing courtesy. Marty Granahan was once again a model of efficiency and good humor when supervising the work of securing permissions, and I want to thank Robyn Renahan for her work in locating copyright holders and negotiating agreements with them. Carole Quandt read page proofs with careful attention. Judy Mason and Alex Ambrose located the photographs used in the book, providing me with a wonderful selection of images to choose among. Designers Susan Breitbard, Ellen Pettengell, and Violeta Díaz deserve credit for the book's appearance and thanks for making numerous adjustments in response to my vision of the book. Finally I want to thank Ben Morrison, the quick-witted, deeply knowledgeable, and ever resourceful developmental editor who worked with me on every stage of this project. He always made time for me, consistently gave excellent advice, and even laughed at my jokes.

MOTIVES FOR WRITING

Introduction
Writing for Your Life

Writing can change your life. It can help you deepen your understanding of yourself as well as achieve the goals you set for yourself. It can help you make sense of the information that assaults you every day and present ideas so that others will take you seriously. And it can broaden your world by enabling you to communicate effectively with people you have never met.

Despite the tremendous advantages of writing well, many people persuade themselves that they can never learn to write, because they believe that writing is a talent they were denied at birth. People who think in these terms are unlikely to write well, because they lack the motivation to take their writing seriously. It is true that some people learn to write more easily than others because they have a certain aptitude for it or because they have been encouraged by parents, friends, or good teachers. But to a large extent writing is a skill that can be learned by anyone willing to take the trouble. Believe that you will fail, and you are likely to fail. Believe that you can succeed, and you will have begun to succeed. It will certainly take time and effort to write successfully, for writing involves hard work; but you will find that this investment will pay rich dividends.

You probably know more about writing than you realize, but you may not know how to apply that knowledge to accomplish the full range of writing you need to do. You may have been discouraged by assignments that seemed unrelated to your interests and goals. If so, you probably wondered, "Why?" and, when you finished, "So what?" What you sensed was that real writing is done for a real purpose: Someone has a motive for writing—a motive stronger than simply wanting to complete an assignment. There are, as you will see, many motives for writing. Whatever the specific motive may be, however, writers write because they understand that writing is a way to satisfy a purpose that is important to them.

This book takes the position that successful writing begins with having a motive for writing and understanding how that motive can be fulfilled. The ten chapters that follow this introduction discuss a number of these motives and show how various writers have realized them: to understand experience, to report information, to explain information, to evaluate something, to analyze images, to analyze texts, to persuade others, to inspire others, to amuse others, and to experiment with form. Recognizing, through reading, the motives of other writers can help you discover your own sense of what you hope to accomplish when you write and so understand the principles likely to help you succeed.

■■■■■ UNDERSTANDING YOUR RHETORICAL SITUATION

Any act of writing involves five elements that together form what is called the rhetorical situation:

- Author
- Audience
- Purpose
- Topic
- Context

As writers pursue different motives, they emphasize certain elements of the rhetorical situation over others. Writing about personal experience focuses mainly on satisfying the needs of the writer. Persuading, inspiring, and amusing others focus mainly on eliciting appropriate responses from the audience. Although reporting and interpreting information, evaluating something, and analyzing images or texts satisfy the writer's needs and require the writer to think about the reader's needs, they all focus to varying degrees on the subject matter or topic. Whatever your emphasis, though, you can seldom lose sight of any of these elements of the rhetorical situation for long.

Author

Some writers do their best work in the early morning, others at night. Some need a quiet place, and others write happily with music playing and friends wandering around the room. In short, different writers write best in different environments. To the extent that your time and circumstances permit, you should choose the environment that allows you to be most productive.

Although writers have different habits and write in different ways, all good writers have at least one common characteristic: They are active readers. As readers, they are constantly acquiring new information, much of which they may never use, although some of it will help them write. To put it simply: The more you know, the more you have to say, and the easier it is to discover ideas when writing.

But good writers are also readers in another sense: They are critical readers of their own work. When they write—and especially when they revise—they consider their work not only from their own point of view (by asking, for example, "Have I said what I wanted to say?") but also from the point of view of readers (by asking, for example, "Is this point clear?"). Such writers understand that writing is a form of communication.

One way of thinking about the variety of possible transactions between writers and readers is to envision them on a scale ranging from the personal and private at one end to the impersonal and public at the other, with additional motives brought into play as you move from the private toward the public. This is not to say that any one type of writing is necessarily better than another, just different. Successful writing calls on the writer's ability to analyze the rhetorical situation and make appropriate adjustments.

Audience

A good sense of audience is one of the most important factors in writing well. Inexperienced writers often write as if they do not really expect anyone else to read what they have written. There are, without question, times when writers write solely for their own benefit, putting on paper words they have no intention of sharing with others; but most writing involves communicating with other people. The "others" with whom we communicate can range from a single individual, whom we may or may not know, to a large group that includes people we have never even met. When addressing an unfamiliar audience, beware of being ethnocentric—of assuming that your nation or cultural group is at the center of human affairs. Realize that readers from other regions may not be receptive to your ideas. And don't make the mistake of thinking that all your readers are exactly like you. In a large audience, they may come from different socioeconomic strata, from different ethnic groups, and from different geographic regions. At least half of them may be of a different gender. Your readers may also differ in ways that are not readily apparent. A large audience, or even a small one, can include readers who differ in religious faith, political affiliation, and sexual orientation. As a general rule, your writing will benefit if you are aware of how readers differ, for this awareness can help you avoid questionable generalizations and other language that has the potential to exclude or offend. (For additional information about cultural differences, see Chapter 6, pages 382–386.)

You can see how audiences differ if you think about a time when you wrote an essay explaining something to your fellow students but also had to turn it in to a professor. Had you not had to turn it in, you might have used different language or different examples. Your peers and your teacher could need to know different things; or your peers could need their information more urgently than your teacher does. You must decide carefully how much information to give each audience, what order to put it in, and what to leave out.

Whoever these "others" may be, however, they are your readers; you must engage their attention and help them understand what you have to say. One strategy for reaching these readers is to identify with them as much as possible—to become as much like them as you can, to put yourself in their shoes, to see through their eyes. Identifying with readers in this way requires imagination. To some extent, of course, you always construct your audience imaginatively, even when you write for a particular person you believe you know well—your English teacher, for instance. Because there is much about that audience you do not know, you must create to some extent an image of it. If you present yourself as a credible, well-intentioned writer, your readers are likely to be willing to accept this imaginative creation and play whatever role is required of them.

In most rhetorical situations, you can appeal to your audience by honoring the following principles:

- When planning and drafting, try to imagine more than one type of audience. Imagining different audiences can help you choose appropriate topics—topics that will interest both you and your readers. If you are writing for a particular audience, especially one with power and expertise, you may benefit from constructing another audience in your mind, one with which you feel comfortable. Doing so can help you draft the first (and often most difficult) version of the work at hand because you won't feel intimidated.

- When revising early drafts of your work, keep your real audience clearly in mind. Ask yourself if you have failed to provide any information your readers will need to understand what you are trying to convey. Similarly, ask yourself if you have dwelt too long on any point, providing information you can safely assume your readers already know.

- Whoever your readers may be, recognize their values and needs, and do not rely too much on their patience and cooperation. If readers find that they have to work unnecessarily hard, or if they feel that a writer is underestimating their knowledge or intelligence, they will often stop reading, even if the material is important.

Purpose

A writer's *purpose* is essentially the same as a writer's *motive;* both terms are used to describe what a writer hopes to accomplish. The benefit of having a clear sense of purpose is obvious: You are much more likely to accomplish your objective if you know what it is. When you are reading other people's writing, a good way to understand purpose is to ask yourself why the writer chose to approach a topic one way rather than another. For example, when reading a humorous essay, you might immediately recognize that the writer's motive was to amuse, but you might enrich your understanding of the essay by considering why someone would *want* to be amusing on this topic.

This book identifies a number of motives for writing, each of which will be discussed individually in the chapters that follow this general introduction. Keep in mind, however, that writing often reveals an interplay among various motives. For example, although the primary purpose of an argument may be to persuade readers to accept some belief or undertake some action, an argument might easily include paragraphs devoted to informing, amusing, or inspiring readers. Having more than one purpose is fine as long as one purpose does not conflict with another in the same work. As a general rule, however, you should try to make one purpose prevail within any one work, for this will help make the work unified and coherent.

Topic

Although the terms *subject* and *topic* often are used interchangeably, a distinction can be made between them. *Subject* often is used to describe the general area that a writer has considered; *topic* identifies the specific part of that subject that the writer has discussed. Writers often begin with a subject and then narrow it down to a topic suitable for the work (and audience) they have in mind. If you are interested in writing about the Second World War, for example, you could not hope to discuss more than a small part of this subject in a four- or five-page essay. The subject contains many possible topics, and you might decide to write about the attack on Pearl Harbor or the firebombing of Tokyo—both of which topics might be narrowed even further. Decisions about how much to include depend on for whom you are writing (and why) as well as on the length appropriate for the context.

By narrowing a subject to a specific topic, you focus attention on something you want your readers to see in detail. To use an analogy: If you are watching a football game from a seat high up in a large stadium, you have a very large field of view, much of which is totally irrelevant to the game— thousands of spectators, the curve of the bleachers, the pitch of the ramps, and so on. Unless you find some way to narrow that field of view, you will be distracted by these irrelevancies, and you will not be able to get a clear view of exactly what is happening on the field. Binoculars will help immensely, for you can train them on the players, and the binoculars will magnify the images of the players so you can see more details of each play. However, to see the players clearly, you have to adjust the focus of the binoculars. Just as you have too large a field of view from the top of the stadium, you may at first target too large an area to write about; and as you proceed, you may discover that you are most interested in a much smaller part of it. Thus, just as you would at the ball game, you must shut out some details and focus on others.

Finally, a good topic will lead to your saying something worth saying. Some topics have been written about so extensively that you may find it difficult to communicate something that your readers do not already know. A writer with an original topic, or a topic about which something new can be said, has a head start on maintaining readers' interest. Because choosing a topic is such an important part of writing well, additional advice on how to do it is included later in this introduction.

Context

Writing is also influenced by the particular event or circumstance that prompted it—what is called the *context* for writing. Writing an essay in class, for example, may be very different from writing an essay out of class to be turned in next week—even though the author, audience, purpose, and topic remain the same. Or suppose you want to write a letter to a friend. If you are a thoughtful writer, your tone will reflect what you know of your friend's state of mind, even though the basic elements of the rhetorical situation remain the same: A light letter full of jokes might not be appropriate if you know that your friend has just sustained a serious loss. A sense of context helps writers satisfy these conventions.

When considering the context for a specific work, you can benefit from thinking about *time*. A college professor, for example, may expect more from an essay written near the end of her course than she did from one written early in the term. You can also benefit from considering what writing specialists sometimes call *climate*—whatever is happening in the world of the writer and the audience when the writing takes place. Just as both readers and writers may be influenced by temperature (as when working in a room that is either too hot or too cold) and weather (especially when the weather is unusually severe, as would be the case, for example, when reading or writing in a community suffering from drought or flood), they may also be influenced by current political, economic, and social events. A recent crime wave or an international political crisis, for instance, may be on many people's minds. Experienced writers often consider such events when choosing a topic and deciding how to present it. On some occasions, readers might be glad to be distracted from an oppressive climate; on others, they may question the wisdom of a writer who seems altogether oblivious of current events.

In short, any document that you compose for others to read should be informed by your purpose, your audience, and your context. Even when you are confident about your purpose, remember to think clearly about your audience, imagining what this audience expects from you and considering the context in which the transaction between writing and reading will take place. Moreover, you must have a clearly focused topic that is suitable for your purpose, audience, and context. Remember that you are the author of any text with your name on it. Draw upon your strengths, and think critically about all aspects of your work.

EXERCISE 1

Write approximately five hundred words in response to one of the following questions:

1. Have you ever tried to figure out how to please a specific teacher and then written with that goal primarily in mind? How did you learn what that audience would welcome, and how did you feel about sub-ordinating your own thoughts and language in an effort to please?

2. If you had free choice, what purpose or motive for writing would give you the most pleasure to pursue, and why?

3. How does it feel to be studying at the school you attend? How would you describe the context and climate in which your writing will be read this year?

■▨■▨■ PREPARING TO WRITE

How do writers go about meeting the demands we have just discussed? The answer is that there are about as many ways as there are writers; everyone has his or her own process. Generally speaking, however, every successful writing process includes *planning, drafting, revising,* and *editing,* even though the writer may sometimes be engaged in all of these activities at once. That is, there is no predetermined order in which these activities must occur, no obligation to complete one activity before beginning another. When we write, we loop back and forth over our own mental tracks, rethinking, rearranging, restating, and researching. We may not complete one loop before we're off in another direction, on another loop. And we don't necessarily begin at the beginning; sometimes, we finish at the beginning. Writing, in short, is a fairly chaotic process. Still, we do know something about it.

Finding a Topic

Writers need something to write about, and finding a topic can be the most difficult part of the process. Writing often goes best when we can write about something we are vitally interested in and know a good deal about; some-times, however, we are required to write on a topic dictated by someone else or by circumstances. In that case, the preliminary work becomes deciding what to say about that topic. Regardless of whether we have chosen the topic or have had it imposed on us, however, we must decide what to include and what to leave out. We must also settle on the order in which to present our material. Some of this work may go on informally while we are actually doing other things, but some of it is more deliberately structured, as in the lists we may make to help us to schedule and to remember various responsibilities.

So how do we know what we want to write about? Conventional wisdom tells new writers, "Write what you know" or "Write about what you enjoy." This can be sound advice, but it's unhelpful if you're not sure what you know or why what you enjoy would interest other readers. Moreover, there will be many occasions when you are expected to demonstrate that you have learned about a topic through research—even if you initially feel uncertain about that topic.

For most of us, a choice of topic is seldom entirely free, and for everyone, the topic for writing derives directly from the rhetorical situation. In this way, college writing is not really very different from writing on the job. In college writing, the choice of a topic is conditioned by the courses in which the writer is enrolled—by the academic discipline as well as the dictates of the professor. In the working world, the topic depends on the constraints of employment—the employer's attitudes and requirements, as well as the needs of clients and customers. Insofar as we have choices, we are well advised to follow our interests, keeping in mind that our topic should be appropriate for our audience, our purpose, and our context.

Consider the full rhetorical situation in which you are writing: Precisely what do you hope to accomplish, and what information do you need to do so? Ask yourself who will read your writing, bearing in mind that your audience may be larger than it seems: You might write a memo to your boss, but your boss may decide to distribute it to other people in the company. Remember also the context for writing: You may have a topic you want to bring to the attention of your boss, but the time isn't right. You may have to wait for a more opportune occasion. In the meantime, you have to find something else to say.

Chaotic Processes

Ways of exploring a subject fall rather naturally into two groups: chaotic processes and structured processes. Among the chaotic processes for exploring subjects are those that rely on the subconscious knowledge we all have. They are time-tested techniques for encouraging that kind of knowledge to surface so that we can impose order on it. Depending on your inclination and your topic, two of these techniques—*brainstorming* and *freewriting*—may be interchangeable; the other technique, *mapping,* places ideas in spatial relationships to each other. You may already be familiar with these methods; if they have worked for you in the past, by all means continue to use them. If you've never tried them, you may find them useful. But if they don't work for you, try something else, perhaps some of the structured processes described on pages 11–16.

Brainstorming   A time-honored way to increase creativity and productivity is to get a small group of people together for unstructured discussion—a process called *brainstorming;* but it can also be used successfully by one person looking for ideas about a subject. It involves listing everything that occurs to you (or that others say) about the idea as fast as possible in a limited period of time. You can do it over and over, checking your list at the end of each spurt of intensive thinking.

To try it out, get a pen or pencil and a sheet of paper, and set a clock or timer for fifteen minutes. Concentrate on your subject. Ask yourself what you know about it, and jot down your answers. As ideas come to the surface, jot them down as fast as you can. Don't worry about spelling or sequence or anything except putting ideas on paper. And don't worry about whether your answers seem worthwhile; you can evaluate them later. The point is to get as many thoughts as you can on paper. If you keep your mind working, a good idea may come only after a dozen that you'll reject later. Stop when the timer goes off, and take a few minutes to look over your jottings. Mark ideas you find useful or interesting. (Colored markers ease the task of grouping those that seem to go together.) If you think you still don't have enough to go on, you can brainstorm again, perhaps focusing on one of the ideas you wrote down or taking a new direction; but give yourself a rest between sessions.

Freewriting   Like brainstorming, *freewriting* is done nonstop, occurs intensely for a short time, and is done without worrying about audience. Although freewriting will produce much that is unusable, it can also produce much that will be surprisingly important, attesting to the notion that our subconscious minds contain enormous amounts of valuable information. Freewriting is a way to get some use out of this information, and it may very well give us a focus for the rest of our work on the subject. Sometimes, when we find a topic through brainstorming, freewriting unlocks a wealth of ideas about that topic.

Some writers like to think informally about an idea before they put pen to paper; others simply like to begin and see what comes out. Both approaches are fine. When you begin writing, don't worry if you can't think of something to write. Just write anything; it doesn't matter what it is or whether it makes sense. Don't stop for any reason—to figure out how to spell a word, to choose between two terms, or for any other reason. Don't worry if you find yourself straying from your guide sentence at the top of the page. The new direction may be useful. When the time you set for this exercise has passed, stop writing and look at what you have. If you find a good idea, you may be able to develop it as you draft and revise.

Journaling   Keeping a journal allows you to record in detail, for your own benefit, whatever you have in mind. Unlike a diary, which is used simply to record meetings and events, a journal is more personal and reflective, focusing on how a writer reacts to experience. A journal is less likely to note what the writer ate for breakfast than it is to discuss how the writer responded to a novel, a sunset, or a quarrel. Many writers find this kind of writing highly satisfying.

Journals can be designed in different ways with different motives in mind. The two most common types are the *personal journal* and the *reading journal*. In a personal journal, you write primarily about yourself and your world. Personal journals can be a useful resource when you are preparing to write essays that focus on your own experience—as in Chapter 1, "Writing to Understand Experience." In a reading journal, you focus on responses to what you are reading—including summaries of difficult assignments that you may want to review when preparing for an exam, as well as reactions to what you have read: what you liked, disliked, or wanted to learn more about. Reading journals are an excellent resource when you are preparing to undertake college writing assignments, such as "Writing to Report Information" (Chapter 2),

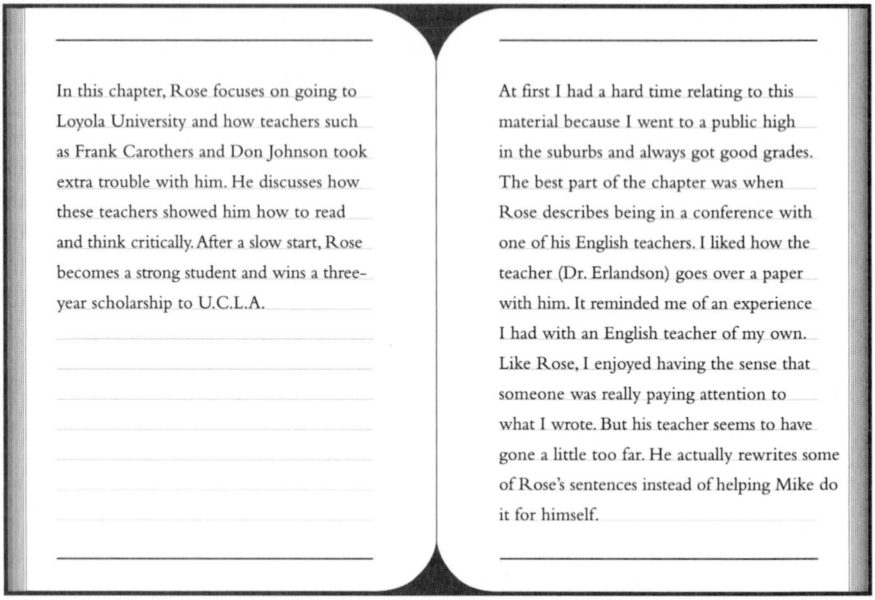

In this chapter, Rose focuses on going to Loyola University and how teachers such as Frank Carothers and Don Johnson took extra trouble with him. He discusses how these teachers showed him how to read and think critically. After a slow start, Rose becomes a strong student and wins a three-year scholarship to U.C.L.A.

At first I had a hard time relating to this material because I went to a public high in the suburbs and always got good grades. The best part of the chapter was when Rose describes being in a conference with one of his English teachers. I liked how the teacher (Dr. Erlandson) goes over a paper with him. It reminded me of an experience I had with an English teacher of my own. Like Rose, I enjoyed having the sense that someone was really paying attention to what I wrote. But his teacher seems to have gone a little too far. He actually rewrites some of Rose's sentences instead of helping Mike do it for himself.

FIGURE 1. Double-entry reading journal, in which summaries are kept on one page and responses on another.

"Writing to Explain Information" (Chapter 3), "Writing to Analyze Texts" (Chapter 6), and "Writing to Persuade Others" (Chapter 7). An additional benefit of a reading journal is that writing about what you read increases your likelihood of retaining what you learned. If you are interested in experimenting with a reading journal, you could begin by keeping one devoted to your reading this quarter or semester. For an example, see Figure 1.

No matter how much experience a writer may have, it is not unusual to feel, at times, that "there's nothing to write about." Most people know more than they realize, and reviewing the entries in either a personal journal or a reading journal can often help writers recall events and ideas that they had somehow lost sight of—thus generating topics for further writing.

Because we write journals for ourselves, we can write quickly without worrying about what someone else might think of us. So unless you are keeping a journal that you wish to share with someone or that you are required to submit for evaluation, do not allow concerns about audience to interfere with the free flow of ideas. You are writing for the audience you know best of all: yourself.

By keeping a journal in which you write daily, you can protect yourself from the anxiety some people feel when they have to write. The more writing you do, the more natural it becomes to write. Another advantage is that you can explore responses to what has happened or what you have read—

personal responses that you would be reluctant to discuss with anyone, believing them too trivial, too personal, or too confusing. Journal writing can be a form of freewriting, with one sentence leading to another in ways that you had not anticipated when you began to write. When you are writing for yourself in this way, some entries will be stronger than others. But it would be a mistake to try to edit yourself as you write, attempting to write a consistent series of well-crafted passages, each of the same length. Do not worry about grammar or punctuation or spelling. And do not worry about wandering off the point. Although you will not want your journal writing to be point*less,* the point can be anything you want it to be when you are your own audience.

Mapping   *Mapping* (sometimes called *clustering* or *webbing*) is a way of visually analyzing the parts of a subject. Write the subject in the middle of your paper and circle it. From the edges of the circle, draw lines radiating outward to nodes labeled to represent the main parts of the subject. Repeat this process for each of those nodes until you have exhausted all the information you have. You will notice that some parts generate several levels, whereas others do not, and that the interrelationships between parts of the idea are easy to see in this kind of graphic. Consider Figure 2 (on page 12), but note that it is only an example and that no two maps look alike.

Brainstorming, freewriting, and mapping can be used together to bring some order to the chaotic information that surfaces from the unconscious. Try pulling some of the related ideas that surfaced during a brief brainstorming session into a single statement; jot the statement down at the top of a sheet of paper you can use for freewriting. When you are through freewriting, look at what you have produced and try to map related ideas. This activity will focus your efforts to find the vein of gold in a pile of earth.

Structured Processes

Structured processes are conscious ways to encourage thinking along specific lines. People have been using these techniques successfully for centuries. In classical times, Aristotle provided numerous ways to get below the surface of a subject. These were called *topoi,* from which our word *topic* is derived. In the twentieth century, the philosopher Kenneth Burke offered an alternative way to explore a subject by using five elements he called the *pentad.* A related method, *journalists' questions,* lists six aspects of a subject; and *varying perspectives* offers at least nine ways to view a subject.

Classical Topics   It is often useful to look at a subject from the perspectives originally developed by Aristotle to help generate ideas. Aristotle proposed asking certain questions to define what something is and others to compare and contrast it with other things. Additional questions help writers examine possible relationships: cause, antecedent, contraries, contradictions. Questions about circumstances explore matters of possibility and factuality. And questions

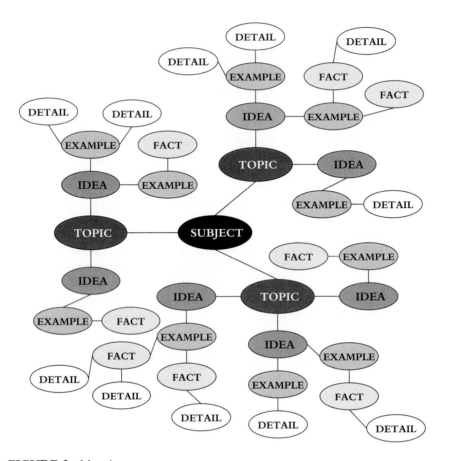

FIGURE 2. Mapping.

about testimony—authority, statistics, maxims, law, examples—can help writers support their points.

Originally designed as ways to discover proofs in persuasive writing, Aristotle's topics provided a foundation for the work of many other rhetoricians and have played an important role in education for more than two thousand years. One advantage of these topics is that they remind us to consider both the general qualities and the particular features of a given subject. At least one of Aristotle's questions should always be appropriate, whatever we want to write about. The answers we give help us decide what we want or need to say.

Aristotle identified thirty-two topics, and few people are able to keep them all in mind. But without memorizing a long list of topics, you can still benefit from classical rhetoric by asking yourself a series of questions when you prepare to write. These questions can help you not only to generate ideas when you feel stymied but also to narrow and focus a subject so that you can choose an appropriate topic:

- Should I provide an *example* of what I mean?
- Should I *divide* this subject into parts, discuss each separately, or focus on a single part?
- Can I *classify* this subject by putting it within categories?
- Would it be useful to *narrate,* or provide a brief story?
- Would it be appropriate to see this subject as a *process* and explain how it takes place?
- Should I explain what *caused* this subject or what its *effects* will be?
- Should I *define* what I mean?
- Should I *describe* the features of my subject?
- Should I *compare* my subject with something similar or *contrast* it to something with which it might be confused?

Providing the answers to these questions has led some people to think that writing needs to be organized along the lines that the topics suggest. You may have already studied a book that taught you how to write a "description" or a "definition." Such assignments have a certain value, but it is much like the value that practicing scales has for a musician. Outside of classes in composition, a writer is unlikely to wake up some morning and decide, "Today, I am going to write an essay of comparison and contrast." Writers are much more likely to begin with a motive or subject and then decide on a plan that best suits what they want to say. When you use classical topics or questions derived from them, think of them as a way to get started rather than as a pattern of organization that you are bound to follow.

The Pentad Kenneth Burke believed that neither reading nor writing can be passive. Burke's pentad explains how this active response takes place and provides a useful means for generating ideas for writing. Burke defined five elements that are always present to some degree in a piece of writing:

- Scene
- Purpose
- Act
- Agent
- Agency

For instance, a writer may concentrate attention on a particular locale in a particular moment in time; these are a part of what Burke calls *scene.*

Similarly, a writer may choose to emphasize a *purpose*—that is, a motive, rationale, or reason; a goal, aim, or objective; an intention or design; or a mission or cause. And, of course, the writer may choose to focus on an event, an *act,* which may involve not only examining something that happens but also delving into the meaning of the event. Sometimes, a writer chooses to spotlight an *agent,* which may be a person but may also be a force or a power or a catalyst for producing an event. The other element the writer may examine is *agency*—an instrument that causes something, the mechanism or vehicle by which something is accomplished.

But even if a writer has emphasized one element of the pentad, you should be able to find the others if you look for them. Burke's own analogy may help you understand how these various elements are related to one another. He compared them to the five fingers on a hand—separate but ultimately joined. Tracing down one finger will help you make a path to another. We can, of course, cross our fingers or clench them together. Similarly, we can consider any element of the pentad in combination with any other to establish a relationship (what Burke called a *ratio*) among the elements. And these relationships expand meaning. For instance, an act can be examined in its relationship to the scene, agent, agency, and purpose, just as the scene can be examined in relationship to the act, agent, agency, and purpose; and so on. These expanded perspectives from which to view the subject matter are useful to writers as well as readers. They help us understand more fully and more clearly what we mean to say as well as what some other writer meant us to know.

For example, suppose the subject is hot weather. We can examine what people do and how they feel in hot weather, when and where hot weather occurs, what the world looks like when it is hot, what causes hot weather, how hot weather develops, and what purpose it serves. And as Burke argued, we will discover the most if we view each of these parts of the pentad in relation to every other part (the ratios). This method has been used to analyze all kinds of subjects and to reveal how the elements of which a subject is composed relate to each other. What happens, for example, when we see the act in relation to the scene? We can look at what people do (act) in certain cultures (scene) when it is hot. Or we can examine how people (agents) respond to hot weather in the South and in the North or how we lived with hot weather before air conditioning (agency).

If you think about the pentad in this way, your understanding of an event changes as you combine and recombine the elements. This leads to Burke's idea that the pentad is enriched and expanded by considering the combinations in the context of social concerns and economic processes. For example, when thinking about hot weather and preparing to write about it, you might consider whether the weather seems to be growing warmer in your region, what factors could be responsible for climate change, who benefits from those factors, and who is most likely to suffer from them.

How, then, can the pentad help you as a writer? If you use it as a tool to analyze what others have written, you will discover that you have much to say about that piece. But you can also use it as a means of writing something entirely on your own. Burke himself described the pentad as "a generating principle." Suppose you have been asked to write about a significant personal experience. Once you have identified that experience (or act, in Burke's terms), you have to decide where to begin your essay, how much to include, and what points to emphasize. In one case, the pentad might lead you to discover the importance of scene, and much of the essay you write will then focus on how the scene contributed to the act. In another instance, you may realize that you want to emphasize the means by which an act was done or the agents who committed it.

Journalists' Questions   Journalists' questions are similar to Burke's pentad, but they do not incorporate the relationships to the same extent. They look only at *who* did *what* to whom, *when* and *where,* and *why* and *how.* Journalists often try to convey much of this information early in a news story so their audience can grasp the heart of the story immediately. Here, for example, is the opening paragraph of a front-page story in the *New York Times* on August 18, 2001:

> Detroit, Aug. 17—The Ford Motor Company said today that it was eliminating 5,000 salaried jobs in North America and planned to reduce production this fall, the latest sign that the auto industry may no longer be able to prop up the stumbling American economy.

Notice how much information the reader is given in these few words:

- *Who?* Ford Motor Company. Most American readers are familiar with the name of this company and what it manufactures. The "who" in this case is a major U.S. corporation.

- *What?* "Said today that it was eliminating 5,000 salaried positions and planned to reduce production this fall." The "what" is a significant job cut and a reduction in the number of vehicles produced.

- *When?* "Today" refers to August 17, the date the story was filed. Readers on the eighteenth, when the story was published, would understand that "when" was "yesterday."

- *Where?* Most American readers know that the major U.S. automobile companies are headquartered in Detroit. But the "where" is also established by the name of the city in which the story was filed, which is indicated immediately before the date. And the jobs being cut are in North America.

- *Why?* Ford's announcement is "the latest sign that the auto industry may no longer be able to prop up the stumbling American economy." Now we understand why the story is news. Although the loss of 5,000 jobs at Ford is significant in itself, this information indicates that the auto industry as a whole is in trouble and that the American economy is at risk.

- *How?* "Salaried workers" establishes that white-collar jobs will be eliminated and that the jobs of workers in manufacturing and assembly are not immediately at risk. Additional jobs are likely to be lost, however, once production is reduced.

Readers of the story that followed could expect to learn more answers to all of these questions. *How* will Ford decide which jobs to eliminate? To *what* extent will production be reduced? *Why* did the company get into financial trouble? *Where* are the plants that are most likely to be affected?

Journalists' questions work well for exploring almost any kind of subject, and by answering each of them, you can discover interesting material for writing. Although not all the questions will be suitable for every subject, this method almost always generates useful material.

Varying Perspectives   Another way to explore a subject is based on the particle-wave-field theory of physics. Scientists and others who are most comfortable with empirical information often find this technique more helpful than the less structured ones. *Varying perspectives* involves thinking of a subject as something in a stable state (static), as something that changes over time and through space (dynamic), and as something that exists in relationship to other things (relational). Within each of these contexts, this method also involves seeing a subject as a single entity, as a member of a group or class, and as part of a larger system. Thus, a single rose (static, single entity), say, is part of a class of objects called plants (static, class). Plants are part of a larger system of biology (static, system). That single rose might change over time from a bud (static, single), to a full-blown blossom, to a husk, and finally, to a berrylike object (single, dynamic) containing seeds. Those seeds are part of the seasonal cycle of renewal (single, relational). We can thus construct a matrix that gives us several different perspectives from which to examine a rose.

Dealing with Writer's Block

It is easy to get sidetracked in your writing at this point. You may even talk yourself into a case of writer's block. You know what you are going to write about, and you know what the main points are, but you just can't seem to begin writing. There's that empty computer screen or piece of blank paper staring back at you. How do you overcome writer's block? Many of the techniques useful for exploring ideas are also useful for getting over this snag, but you should consider, too, whether you are trying to write in a setting conducive to doing good work. You may be tensing up simply because you are trying to work in the wrong place, or in the wrong clothes, or at the wrong time.

Make yourself as comfortable as you can, but don't get so comfortable that you will fall asleep. Fish out your favorite sweatshirt, loosen your belt, clear your desk, sharpen your pencils or start your computer, provide yourself with a stack of paper or some fresh disks, arrange the lighting, set a snack nearby, and sit down. Take up a pencil, or place your fingers on the keys, and begin to freewrite. At this point, it doesn't matter what you write. You are just breaking through your block. As soon as your ideas are flowing freely, you can begin to be more conscious of what you are saying and how the pieces fit together. Perhaps the section you are working on isn't very congenial at that

"Where do you come up with your rationalizations for not writing?"

moment. So start on something else. You don't have to begin at the begin-ning; you can begin with something that will flow easily for you and fit it into the whole later on. This method is called *chunking*. Writers begin with a piece of writing they feel comfortable working on and develop that piece as far as it needs to go. Then they set it aside and take up another piece, some-times at the same sitting, sometimes not. When all the pieces are done, writers fit them into a whole, linking them with appropriate transitional material and providing introductions and conclusions.

If you are particularly susceptible to writer's block, it may be a good idea to do what Ernest Hemingway used to do by ending each writing session at a point at which you feel sure you know what will come next. That way you can pick up quickly where you left off. Other things you can do to stave off writer's block include talking into a cassette recorder and then transcribing what you have dictated, rereading material you have already written, writing on the backs of old drafts so that you don't really have a blank sheet of paper, writing on small pieces of paper so as not to be intimidated by a large one, writing e-mail to friends to exercise your writing muscles, writing in a jour-nal, or using a special pen or pencil—one that has already been used to craft a number of completed compositions or feels especially good in your hand. If none of these techniques helps, try anything you think will help. Exercise, ride your bicycle, go for a walk, wash dishes, shovel snow, or do some other physical task that requires little concentration but during which a good idea may come to you if you keep your mind receptive. You will come back to writing refreshed. If that doesn't seem fruitful, put the idea of writing aside for the time being; go to a movie, watch television for an hour, read a couple of chapters of a novel. But be alert for ways you may be fooling yourself out of, rather than into, writing. If you find a way to overcome a block, remember it and use it whenever you need it, much as baseball players wear lucky socks or eat certain meals before games.

As you write more and more, you will acquire a variety of techniques to help you get over writing blocks. Some writers keep files of interesting material they find while reading for pleasure, just as they do when they are actually researching. Others keep a journal in which they record ideas and perceptions that may be useful in the future. When you feel like writing, you can go to this material to find a subject to explore, and you can consult it for help when you are stuck.

Arranging Ideas

How can you arrange your ideas in an effective sequence? Some writers find it helpful to make an outline or to list the order in which they will present their main points. Others prefer going wherever the writing takes them. Even when they prepare an outline, they end up not following it. There is nothing intrinsically wrong with that; writing is, after all, one of the best ways to learn, and you will generally wind up with something that can be reworked into a worthwhile piece of prose. Writing often takes its own shape as you do it, and plans developed beforehand often need to be reconsidered. That's all right, too. Planning and drafting can occur over and over until you feel that you have said exactly what you intended. The point is that some kind of organization needs to be evident in the writing when it is completed, whether or not the plan for it was there from the beginning.

Some writers work one way on one project and a different way on the next. The important thing to understand about planning is that your plans are not contracts. They can easily be changed during drafting and revision. So there's no single, correct way to plan that will work every time you write. Any plan that works for you—and produces an arrangement that works for your audience—is the correct one for that particular writing activity. With that in mind, let's look at a number of different methods.

Outlines

There are several kinds of outlines, each of which might suit a different kind of project or a different kind of writer. Some outlines are exceedingly detailed, presenting almost as much information as the completed project will. Others are very sketchy, offering only a general indication of where to go next. The kind you need depends on a combination of your discipline, your project, and your process. But if you find that your readers frequently comment that they can't follow what you're writing about, you probably need to make your outline a little more detailed. Or when you finish drafting, you may need to outline your draft meticulously and compare the "before" outline with the "after" one. At the least, you will see where you need to revise heavily, and you may even be able to chart where the revision should go. Conversely, if your readers tell you that your writing seems mechanical and predictable, you need to loosen up a little. Making your outline less formal may be one way to go about it.

Lists and Jottings

The most informal kind of outline is a list you jot down on a scrap of paper or keep in your head. It may be as informal as listing two or three points you don't want to forget. Such a list for a paper on, say, hunting elephants for ivory might look like this:

> health hazards
> economic consequences
> poaching
> U.S. trade policy
> popularity of ivory in Asia
> endangered species
> effects on other animals

Nothing is indicated about other points you may plan to include, nor is anything noted about the order in which the points will appear, although you can easily add numbers once you decide on the sequence you think will be best. Furthermore, as your plan evolves, you may find that some items on your list are not appropriate; if so, just ignore them. This kind of outline is for you alone, and you don't need to worry about making it more comprehensive if it does the job for you. Many students find this kind of outline helpful in taking essay examinations because it is brief enough to occupy a small space and doesn't take much time to produce. But it can be suitable for other occasions as well.

Here is a somewhat more detailed list for the same writing project:

1. Place in endangered species lists
   a. Reasons, locations
2. Place in environmental chain
   a. Above and below in food chain
   b. Relationship to other animals
   c. Meaning for humans
3. Who hunts ivory
   a. Licensed hunters
   b. Poachers
4. Human impact
   a. Physical dangers of elephant hunting
      —From elephants
      —From authorities
   b. Health hazards
      —Food-related—rotting meat, malnutrition
      —Ivory-related—elephant anthrax

Formal Outlines

A formal outline for the same paper would indicate the relationships between main points and details more clearly than a list:

Thesis: Hunting elephants for ivory has two negative effects: It causes environmental damage, and it is dangerous to humans.

I. Environmental effects
   A. Endangered species
      1. Reasons
      2. Locations
   B. Place in environmental chain
      1. Relationship of elephant to other animals
         a. Effect on food chain
         b. Maintenance of grasslands
      2. Importance of elephant for humans
II. Human impact
   A. Physical dangers of elephant hunting
      1. Unpredictability of elephants
      2. Crackdown by governments on poachers
   B. Health hazards
      1. Carcasses left to rot
      2. Elephant anthrax
         a. Conditions for infecting humans
         b. Locations of the disease

Notice that the formal outline is a graphic representation of the paper and that it is balanced and complete. For this reason, some people insist that if there is an item 1, there must be an item 2, or if there is an item A, an item B must follow. Actually, there is no hard-and-fast rule, but common sense suggests that if there is, say, no item 2 to accompany item 1, either the writer has not pursued the subject far enough, or the main heading and subheading can be combined. For example, if there were only a human disease issue and no consideration of geography in point 2 under "Health hazards," the idea could be expressed as "2. Elephant anthrax dangerous to humans." Beginning with uppercase roman numerals, a formal topic outline relies on indented uppercase letters of the alphabet, Arabic numbers, lowercase letters, Arabic numbers in parentheses, and so on to reflect various levels of relationships. Each topic should be grammatically parallel with other topics on the same level.

Any topic outline can easily be turned into a sentence outline by stating all points as sentences. A sentence outline has the advantage of helping writers be specific. For instance, "B. Health hazards" could become "B. Elephant hunting poses health hazards."

Formal outlines can be developed as plans for writing, as tools for revision, or as guides for readers. Most writers need flexibility in the plans they make to guide their writing, because the human mind often develops new insights during drafting. If you do make a formal outline before you write, review it when drafting to see whether you have lost sight of any points you intended to make and if you need to incorporate new points that have occurred to you. You may find that you are satisfied with the direction your writing has taken. But you could see ways to improve your organization.

Nutshells, Abstracts, and Capsules

Another way to bring some order to writing is to use a summary paragraph (sometimes called a *nutshell, abstract,* or *capsule*). Consider this paragraph, for example:

> Under the microscope we can see that blood is composed of a watery fluid called plasma, in which certain formed elements are suspended. The formed elements are different types of cells—red blood cells, white blood cells and platelets. —Louis Faugeres Bishop

It is easy to imagine how we could use this paragraph as a nutshell for organizing a paper. The first group of paragraphs following this one could describe red blood cells—what they look like, how they are made, what their parts are; the next group of paragraphs might offer the same kind of information about white blood cells; and the final paragraphs could describe platelets. That is, indeed, how Bishop developed this piece of writing, and the technique works well for many situations.

Classic Oration

The classic pattern for presenting information was in full use at least two thousand years ago, and that pattern continues to be useful today, especially in writing to persuade. People who gathered to listen to the great orators of classical times generally knew that, right after they had been exhorted to pay attention, they would get background information on the subject, followed by a clear statement of what issues would be addressed and what position the speaker would take. Then they could expect information that would confirm the speaker's point and refute the opposing viewpoint. And finally, they usually expected a summary of what had been said and sometimes even a call to act on it. (A variation in the sequence could draw attention to a particular part of the oration and thereby divert attention from another part.) In other words, a classic oration had the following outline:

- *Introduction:* Gain the attention and confidence of your audience, and indicate what problem you will address.
- *Statement of issues, facts, or circumstances:* Give the relevant background information, and describe present conditions.
- *Proof of the case:* Establish your own position and why you believe it.
- *Refutation of opposing viewpoints:* State the objections and any complications; then show why these points should not trouble the audience.
- *Conclusion:* Sum up, highlight important points, point out future directions, and call for action.

Originally developed for oral presentations, this sequence became well established because nearly everyone used the same pattern or some variation of it—thus making it easy for listeners to follow the speech. And if the sequence varied, the listeners could depend on their experience to know which part they were listening to. Even today, we often expect presentations to follow this familiar pattern.

EXERCISE 2

1. Choose a subject and freewrite on it for fifteen minutes. Review what you generate, highlighting or underlining ideas about which you can write in more detail. Then arrange these ideas into either an outline or a list.

2. Write an essay of two to three pages in which you describe how you have usually organized your papers and how well readers have responded to your organization. Consider whether you always use the same kind of plan or whether you experiment with different plans. If readers have ever found your writing difficult to follow, what issues have they raised with you?

■ ■ ■ ■ DRAFTING, REVISING, AND EDITING

Once we have an idea of what we want to write about and how we want to arrange our ideas, we may begin *drafting*, writing ideas down in a sequence that allows for their development. Here is where the "looping back" (or recursive) nature of the writing process is most readily apparent. We may draft several pages to discover what we want to say and then throw out all but two or three sentences. Or if we are more confident of what we mean to say, we may draft several pages before we are interrupted. Then, when we come back to the writing, we may start out by revising what we have written, or we may find ourselves starting over—but we'll save the writing we're not using because it may be useful later. We may also draft a part of the writing we feel most comfortable about first to warm up our brains in an effort to hit our intellectual stride for the more difficult parts. It doesn't matter if the piece of writing we do first will go near the end. We'll put it where it belongs when we have a clearer vision of the shape of what we're saying.

When we've developed these pieces of writing, we can weave them together—a process we may have begun earlier. If we begin to see gaps that we have to fill with new writing, we're doing part of our job as writers. And if we haven't already done so, we have to find a way to begin and a way to conclude. We may have been *revising* all along, reshaping sentences that disappoint us as soon as we see them and rearranging paragraphs when we are only midway through our initial draft. But when we can see the whole composition, we can move into a different kind of revising, testing everything we say against what we have already said and what will come later to seek the greatest possible clarity and coherence.

Unlike revising, which often generates new writing, *editing* is primarily devoted to polishing what we have already written. When editing, we look for ways to tighten our prose, eliminating wordy constructions and unnecessary repetition. We also check our grammar, punctuation, and spelling. Many writers treat editing as the final stage in their writing process; they recognize that there is no point in perfecting material they may eliminate during revision. Others find comfort in fixing errors when they are briefly stymied at an earlier point in the process (instead of stopping work altogether), but their work is also likely to benefit from additional editing when they reach the end of the writing process.

Although there's no set order to the parts of the writing process, we obviously can't revise what was never written; and we've completed all the other parts of the process when we do final proofreading. It is therefore within the boundaries defined by finding a topic and proofreading the final copy that the writing process occurs.

Drafting

Drafting means writing a preliminary version of a work that you will later revise. That is, it means getting your ideas on paper (or screen) so that you can work with them. If you think of drafting as "writing the paper," you put yourself at risk. Thinking in these terms can lead to writer's block by making drafting seem excessively important. And if you think drafting means "writing," you may be less likely to appraise your work critically before preparing another version of it. Drafting is simply one of the stages of the writing process, and experienced writers usually compose more than one draft of what they write.

Unlike planning and revision—both of which can be undertaken at various times throughout a busy day—drafting usually requires a block of uninterrupted time. If you have twenty minutes free between classes, you can brainstorm or refine a paragraph or two that are already drafted. But when you are ready to write the first draft of a paper, you should set aside at least two or three hours when you can give your undivided attention to this work. You may finish your draft much sooner, but knowing that you have a few hours at this point in the writing process will help you avoid feeling tense. Providing yourself with adequate time for drafting can also protect you from being forced to stop prematurely just as your ideas start to flow.

You may be thinking, "Doesn't this guy know how busy I am? Where can I ever find two or three hours to draft a paper?" The answer is that busy people can usually find time to do the things they genuinely want or need to do—even if it means getting up earlier, staying up later, or putting another activity aside. But no one expects you to invest a whole afternoon in everything you draft. You will probably spend more time on some projects than on others because some are more important to you. And as you become a more experienced writer, you may find that you need less time for drafting. Because experienced writers expect to revise their work, they often draft quickly, aware that they are composing only a preliminary version of their work.

Recognizing that writing a good introduction can be difficult, some writers draft by beginning in the middle and compose an introduction only after they have drafted several pages. But other writers draft most comfortably after they have composed an introduction that pleases them, and there are even writers who need to write a good title before they can draft with any ease. Such writers like the sense of direction they obtain from a title or an introduction, for a good title or introduction often reveals a writer's thesis. Follow the procedure that seems best suited to you.

Discovery Drafts

Alert and energetic, you are generating lots of ideas. It's all right to let them flow; write them down as fast as you can. Writers frequently begin with only a general idea of what they want to say, and they simply let the ideas flow naturally until they have figured out what point or points they really want to make. If you write without any kind of formal plan, letting your ideas flow and take shape as you set them down, you are producing a *discovery draft,* an extended piece of freewriting in which you try to stick to a topic. For this kind of draft, the end is usually signaled by the discovery of the point you want your essay to make or of unexpected material to support that point.

The important thing to remember is that the discovery draft is only a beginning, a way to let ideas find their own shape; ultimately, you will have to identify the most effective plan inherent in the draft and reshape it with this plan in mind. In other words, a discovery draft can help you define the main point of the paper you are planning and generate related material, making it easier for you to then write a more focused draft or to arrange your ideas into a plan that will guide your next draft.

Identifying Your Main Point or Thesis

Drafting should normally lead to identifying a main point or thesis. A thesis is usually stated early in a piece of writing, probably in the first paragraph or two (or the first chapter of a book), and repeated later. However, because writers continue to think about ideas as they write, the thesis with which a writer begins may not be the thesis that governs the completed work. In other words, writers often begin drafting with a main point in mind, only to find that the thesis has changed as the work proceeded. Don't be alarmed if you think your thesis is changing or if you cannot identify a clear thesis in your draft; clarifying your thesis is something you can take care of later.

Neither writing nor reading would be much fun if all writers had to work the same way. Although classical rhetoric emphasized the need to follow predetermined patterns, modern rhetorical theory gives writers much more freedom. Thus, writers may state the main point early in an essay and restate it in the conclusion, or they may engage the attention of readers by experimenting with introductions that at first seem unrelated to the topic. Moreover, writers are not always bound to a single main point. Sometimes, particularly in a long piece, a writer will develop two or more main points. And sometimes, a writer may not even have a thesis as that concept is usually understood. When writing to understand experience, for example, a writer may unify the work by a search for meaning rather than by a central idea that can be stated in a sentence or two.

You should recognize, however, that writing without either a thesis or a clearly defined goal can leave readers feeling confused. When you read a piece that seems pointless, you may feel that you missed something. As a reader, you may be willing to go back and reread; but as a writer, you should recognize that some readers are not going to take the time. So if you are writing without a thesis, be sure to consider the expectations of your audience. You should also consider your motive for writing: Writing to understand experience or to experiment with form may not need a thesis, but writing for other motives, such as to evaluate or to persuade, will. In sum, ask yourself whether you are following a strategy suitable for your rhetorical situation.

Developing Your Ideas

By itself, even a well-crafted thesis statement will not suffice to make your readers understand what you have to say. Readers resist taking in new information unless you can support your thesis with details and examples, provide support for any other claims you make, and link new ideas to information already familiar to your audience.

Details help readers to picture what you have in mind. Consider the following paragraph from Edward Abbey's "Death Valley." (Abbey is considered one of the most important writers who focused on environmental issues in the late twentieth century.) In this passage, he has just stopped at a gas station in the middle of the valley on a morning when the temperature is already 114 degrees:

> Sipping cold drinks, we watch through the window a number of desert sparrows crawl out of the grills of the parked automobiles. The birds are eating tourists—bugs and butterflies encountered elsewhere and smashed, baked, annealed to the car radiators. Like the bears of Yellowstone, the Indians of Arizona, and roadside businessmen everywhere, these birds have learned to make a good thing off passing trade. Certainly they provide a useful service; it's a long, hot climb out of here in any direction, and a clean radiator is essential.

Where an inexperienced writer might have settled for writing, "We were glad to get something cold to drink when we were in Death Valley, because we felt like we were in the middle of nowhere," Abbey efficiently describes a scene that helps readers to imagine that they are there with him—conveying a relationship between the natural world and the people who drive through it. We learn that there are birds in Death Valley, what kind of birds they are, how difficult it must be for them to survive, and how nature seems to be able to accommodate at least some of the incursions of humans. As readers, we can be pleased that Abbey was a trained observer of the natural world who paid close attention to what he saw and heard. In many cases, your own observations will provide the details you need to develop your ideas; in others, however, you will need to find the supporting details through research and close reading.

This brief excerpt from Abbey also contains elements of Kenneth Burke's pentad, one of the strategies discussed earlier in this chapter for generating ideas (see pages 13–15). The *scene* is a gas station/store in Death Valley in the morning; the *act* is the eating of bugs and butterflies; the *agents* are the birds; the *agency* is the cars that have brought the insects into the valley; and the *purpose* is survival. But if we can see all this, it is because of Abbey's descriptive detail. The bugs aren't simply somewhere outside the window; they are "smashed, baked, annealed to the car radiators." The birds must be small if they can crawl in and out of the grills to reach the radiators, and, as already noted, they must be hungry if they are willing to go to the trouble. There are only two additional details that we might wonder about: What kind of cold drink was Abbey sipping (was it a beer or a Diet Pepsi?), and whom does that "we" include?

Note also that Abbey attempts to link his material to what readers may already be able to visualize by comparing the birds to "the bears of Yellowstone, the Indians of Arizona, and roadside businessmen everywhere." Even readers who have never visited the American West should be able to grasp the comparison to "roadside businessmen everywhere." Annie Dillard, in an essay that appears in Chapter 10, "Writing to Experiment with Form" (pages 627–630), uses a similar strategy when describing a meal she ate on a trip through the Amazon watershed:

> Lunch, which was the second and better lunch we had that day, was hot and fried. There was a big fish called doncella, a kind of catfish, dipped whole in corn flour and beaten egg, then deep fried. With our fingers we pulled off soft fragments of it from its sides to our plates, and ate; it was delicate fish-flesh, fresh and mild. Someone found the roe, and I ate of that too—it was fat and stronger, like egg yolk, naturally enough, and warm.

In this short paragraph, we learn not only what Dillard had for lunch but also how it was prepared, how it was eaten, and how it tasted. Moreover, references to "catfish" and "egg yolk" give readers who have never eaten a meal like this a sense of how it tasted.

In addition to using details about a specific scene or experience to develop their ideas, writers also use *examples*. Consider the following example from "Levi's," an essay by Marilyn Schiel that appears in Chapter 1, "Writing to Understand Experience" (pages 55–58).

> Mothers stayed home. Unlike dads, mothers didn't work. Mothers made the beds, cooked the meals, cleaned the house, baked the cook-

ies, tended the garden, squeezed the clothes through the wringer-washer, hung washed clothes to dry on lines strung through the basement, ironed everything—including sheets and towels—scrubbed the floors while kneeling on pink rubber pads, walked seven blocks pulling an empty Red-flyer wagon to buy groceries, struggled seven blocks home with a week's worth of carefully budgeted supplies, and picked out clothes for their children to wear.

In this case, Schiel lists a series of examples illustrating the responsibilities of a stay-at-home mother with young children in the 1950s (as well as using some details, such as the references to "pink rubber pads" and "an empty Red-flyer wagon"). And by listing all these examples in a single sentence, she demonstrates that the claim that "mothers didn't work" was ironic. The examples make it clear that mothers worked very hard even if they were not earning a paycheck.

Use details and examples to develop your own ideas as you draft.

Revising

Revising distinguishes writing from speaking: Revision affords the writer a second (or third, or tenth) chance to get the meaning right. One professional writer explains that he always produces a "zero draft," a draft that is even rougher than a first draft. Only then can he get down to the business of writing as he reshapes those rough ideas into the first of many drafts. Many writers feel that they aren't writing when they're drafting; they're writing only when they're revising.

Good writers can often be distinguished from poor writers by their attitude toward revision. Good writers don't expect to get it right the first time; poor writers assume that they have. As we have seen, writing is a dynamic, unpredictable process: It doesn't begin with planning and then proceed systematically through drafting, revising, editing, and proofreading. Each of these activities can occur or recur at any moment during the production of a finished piece of prose. You may even get an idea you want to include in your paper just as you are typing the final words of the final draft. If that happens, don't be discouraged; and above all, don't throw that good idea away. Just work it into your paper and produce another final copy. Conversely, you may know from the very first moment you set pencil to paper what the final words of your piece will be. Go ahead and write them down. Let them stay there throughout your whole effort as a beacon to aim for. There's no right or wrong way to go about the process of writing, but revision should be part of whatever process works best for you.

Revising involves considerably more than fixing the spelling and punctuation before you pass your writing on to a reader. It is easier to understand what revising is if we break the word into its parts: *re,* meaning "again," and *vising,* meaning "seeing." Revising is seeing again, taking another look. Even though writers often do some revising as they draft, revision is most productive when something written days or weeks ago can be viewed with "new" eyes, almost as another person would see it. (Days and weeks are desirable incubation periods for writing, but writers do not always have that luxury. It is often possible, however, to let writing incubate overnight.) When you revise in this way, if you are alert and keep your audience in mind, you will notice parts that are unclear, inaccurately phrased, poorly organized, or inadequately explained.

Think of revision as reentering the writing on at least three different levels—appraising the content, checking the organization, and refining the style—to see what works and what might need changing.

Appraising Content

On the first or deepest level, you can look at whether you have conveyed the proper meaning, done what you promised readers you would do, provided support, and focused clearly on your main point. You can use several techniques to reenter and review your writing at this level. One good way to see whether you have said what you intended to say is to read your manuscript aloud and pretend to be your own audience. If it helps, try to read your writing as if you were the person you most admire. You may immediately see where you have gone astray. You can also do the same exercise pretending that you have just received the manuscript in the mail.

Another technique is to ask the following questions:

- Have I stressed the important issues?
- Have I made sure my point is clear?
- Have I backed all claims with evidence?
- Is my evidence credible?
- Have I dealt fairly with my audience?
- Did I promise anything that I could not deliver?
- Have I accounted for any objections that might be raised?
- Has my attitude been appropriate? Have I been honest and direct, or do I seem glib or apologetic?

Revision at this level is not merely a way to fix problems that you can see on the page. It is also a way to identify where you need to say more. Play the audience role again, this time looking for what is not said. Are there any points that have not been made that should have been? Would an example make a point clearer? Are there any unexplored consequences or loose ends? Is anything that readers may not understand taken for granted?

Checking Organization

When you have answered these questions as best you can, you are ready to move on to a closer examination of structure, considering the sequence in which you arranged your ideas. You may already have cut some sentences that didn't seem to fit and decided to move others to different paragraphs. But since your first level of revision may have led to major changes, including the addition of new material, you should now focus on your essay's structure.

Did you follow your outline or depart from it? If you departed from your outline, is it because drafting generated unexpected ideas that you believe are important and wish to retain somehow? Or did you simply get off track? Do you need to delete any paragraphs? Combine any? Split others up? Shift them around? Do you still need to develop your ideas with new paragraphs? If so, where would they go? Have you provided transitions so that each paragraph seems to follow from the one that precedes it?

Pay particular attention to the first and last paragraphs. A good introductory paragraph will capture the attention of readers and provide them with a sense of where the work is going. A good conclusion will draw the work together. While every paragraph should be helping to fulfill the writer's motive and be directly related to the topic in question, the introductory and concluding paragraphs are those for which readers have the clearest expectations. Body paragraphs develop a main idea, but readers usually expect the idea itself—and a sense of why that idea is worth reading about—to be established in the paragraphs that are easiest to see at a glance: those that are not surrounded by other paragraphs because they appear at the beginning or at the end.

Although writers sometimes begin by drafting a strong introduction or conclusion, they may find that these paragraphs no longer fit the essay they have written. You can't be altogether sure what you are introducing until you have written what you want to introduce. And revision could also lead you to decide that you have begun before the beginning or ended after the ending. For instance, you may get off to a slow start and write a paragraph or two that add little to the paper; in this case, you may find that the second or third paragraph provides the best beginning. Similarly, you may sometimes ramble on a bit after you have said what you needed to say; in this case, the conclusion of your paper may be buried somewhere before the point at which you stopped writing.

If you discover that you need to write a new introduction, you could try starting with a nutshell paragraph (see page 21) that states the major points the following paragraphs will discuss. But for variety, try beginning with an anecdote, example, quotation, unusual detail, or statement of the problem you hope to resolve. If you find that you need a conclusion, you can restate or summarize your major points. But this strategy often works best for long papers during which readers might lose sight of an idea. Repeating key points may be unnecessary in a short work, and it may leave some readers feeling as if you doubt their intelligence. When trying to write an effective conclusion, you can often benefit from asking yourself, "Why have I told you all this?" or, as a reader might put it, "So what?" Thinking along these lines may lead you to take one last step that will make the significance of your paper clear. Another effective strategy is to repeat an element found in the introduction, thus framing the work with two paragraphs that seem related to each other. You can also try rephrasing your thesis or asking your readers to undertake an action that seems appropriate.

Improving Unity and Coherence

Even if an essay is well organized in term of the sequence in which you have arranged your paragraphs, there may be other gaps in your organization. If you were thinking and writing quickly when drafting, you may have made leaps in thought that are clear to you but will not be clear to readers. Look closely at the arrangement of sentences in each paragraph, and determine if each sentence leads logically to the sentence that follows. You may discover sentences that do not belong in the paragraphs in which they appear because they are unrelated to the main idea of these paragraphs. In a *unified* paragraph, every sentence in that paragraph relates to its main idea. Similarly, you may find a paragraph in which every sentence relates to the main idea of the paragraph, but the sentences are not arranged in a meaningful pattern. In a *coherent* paragraph, each sentence leads logically to the next. In other words, a paragraph can be unified without being coherent. To improve the coherence of a paragraph, you may need to rearrange the sentences it already contains, add new sentences that help link the existing sentences together, or add transitional expressions (such as "for example" or "on the other hand") to clarify how a sentence relates to what has immediately preceded it.

You can also improve coherence through repetition—focusing on one idea and going back to it repeatedly—and by association—linking new information to a previously established idea.

The following paragraph by Peter Stark, from a work included in Chapter 2, illustrates both repetition and association. Boldface has been added here to help you see how repetition contributes to coherence, and underling has been added to help you see examples of association.

> But those who understand **cold** know that even as it <u>deadens</u>, it offers perverse <u>salvation</u>. <u>Heat</u> is a <u>presence</u>: the rapid **vibrating of molecules. Cold** is an <u>absence</u>: the damping of the **vibrations.** At absolute zero, minus 459.67 degrees Fahrenheit, **molecular** motion ceases altogether. It is this **slowing** that converts gases to **liquids, liquids** to **solids,** and renders **solids** harder. It **slows** <u>bacterial growth</u> and <u>chemical reactions</u>. In the human <u>body</u>, **cold** shuts down **metabolism.** The <u>lungs</u> take in **less oxygen,** the heart pumps **less blood. Under** <u>normal temperatures</u>, this would produce **brain** damage. But the <u>chilled</u> **brain,** having **slowed** its own **metabolism,** needs far less **oxygen**–rich **blood** an can, **under** the <u>right circumstances</u>, <u>survive</u> intact.

Stark uses repetition by repeating *cold, liquids, solids, less, oxygen, blood, under,* and *metabolism* as well as by using words that are very similar: *vibrating/vibrations, molecules/molecular,* and *slowing/slows/slowed.* He uses association by linking closely related concepts and images: *cold/heat, deadens/salvation/survive, presence/absence, bacterial growth/chemical reactions, body/lungs/brain,* and *normal temperatures/right circumstances* as well as by using a word closely associated with cold: *chilled.*

EXERCISE 3

Demonstrate your skills in revising paragraphs for unity and coherence by (1) arranging all of the following sentences into a sequence that would be easy for readers to understand, (2) dividing the rearranged sentences into two paragraphs, and (3) developing these two paragraphs by adding at least one new sentence to each.

> While he was overseas, Dimitri felt embarrassed about being unable to speak Greek or any other language besides English. His parents were fluent in English when they moved to the United States, and they did not speak Greek at home while Dimitri was growing up. In high school, he studied French for three years, but he never became fluent in that language. During the summer between his junior and senior year, he accompanied his parents on a trip to visit relatives in Greece. He was only three years old when his family moved to this country. When planning what courses to take in college, Dimitri considered continuing to study French, but he eventually decided to learn Spanish. Proud to be an American, Dimitri could see that Spanish is an important language within the United States. His cousins could speak English and at least one other language in addition to Greek. In fact, Spanish was spoken in what is now the United States before English was introduced. His motivation was poor. Demographics indicate that Spanish will become even more widely spoken in the United States in the future. He studied a foreign language only because doing so was a requirement at his school. His cousins explained that knowing different languages made it possible to have different kinds of ideas. There are similarities in French and Spanish grammar, so the work he had done in French would help him get started in Spanish.

Refining Style

After studying the structure of your work as a whole, as well as the unity and coherence of your paragraphs, check to see whether individual sentences can be improved. Here are a few basic guidelines:

- Vary the length of your sentences. If too many sentences are short, your writing will seem choppy. If too many sentences are long, your readers may grow weary or impatient. A mixture of lengths usually works best; but note that short sentences are more emphatic than long ones, so use short sentences to make key points.

- Vary the structure of your sentences. If too many sentences follow a subject-verb-object pattern, your writing may seem monotonous. Try beginning with an adverb, a phrase, or a subordinate clause. Check the rhythm of your sentences by reading them aloud and listening carefully to how they sound.

- Check for wordiness and repetition. If your sentences are often described as "too long," your problem may be wordiness, which refers to redundancy, padding, and clutter. Look for unnecessary repetition. See also whether you can reduce wordiness by eliminating qualifiers and intensifiers such as *rather, very*, and *quite*. Look for phrases such as *in the event that, on the part of, it seems to me that, as a matter of fact, in view of,* and *the point that I am trying to make,* and see whether you can phrase them more precisely or delete them.

- Use the active voice, which means making the grammatical subject of a sentence the same as the doer of the action: "I broke your bowl" (active), as opposed to "Your bowl was broken by me" (passive). Note that the passive voice is wordier and also allows a writer to duck responsibility, thus reducing clarity: "Your bowl was broken." As a general rule, use the passive voice only if the receiver of an action is more important than the doer or if the doer is unknown.

- Rework your sentences so that the verb reflects an action rather than a state of existence. For instance, write, "Eating rich desserts makes you fat" instead of "Getting fat is often the result of eating rich desserts." In general, avoid using an abstract subject with a linking verb and an abstract complement. Instead of saying, "Overeating is a leading cause of weight gain," say, "Overeating makes you fat."

- Make sure that elements that should be parallel are parallel. That is, use the same pattern and the same grammatical forms to express words, phrases, and clauses that have the same function and importance—for example, "I have learned how much water I am using when I wash my car, water the lawn, or take a shower."

- Check your sentences for clichés and jargon. *Clichés* are those tired expressions that show up in your paper without your having thought about them, such as *at the crack of dawn* or *hitting the books. Jargon* is language specific to a particular group or field. If you find yourself writing about "font managers" and "scalable outlines," for example, you had better be sure that your audience consists only of computer experts; other readers would be grateful for simpler language.

EXERCISE 4

Rework the following sentences so that they no longer have the weaknesses in style outlined in the preceeding checklist.

1. In today's fast-paced society, professional success is often the result of the skill of being able to write well.

2. There is a computer on the desk of almost any professional person, and this technology means that whoever has access to it is expected to be able to write clear e-mail messages, access information efficiently, and often composing proposals and other documents.

3. Although it is possible to succeed without writing well, no one likes to look badly educated or stupid in the workplace.

4. When e-mails circulate among various departments, a poor writer often sticks out like a sore thumb.

5. A meeting to review expectations for writing in the workplace has been scheduled for 7:00 A.M., and attendance is expected to be mandatory.

6. This meeting will take the form of a workshop that will be led by staff members who acquired good writing skills when they were in college, and these members of our organization will provide hands-on assistance for those employees who seem to be having difficulty being able to communicate with effectiveness and succinctly.

7. Don't think that college is the chance of a lifetime for learning to write, and you failed to take advantage of what was offered to you on a silver platter; plans have been made to offer you a golden opportunity for catching up on what we thought you already knew when we hired you.

8. Since we never make mistakes, and we did hire you, it is obvious that you must have the ability to write well within the inner reaches of your personal self.

9. You should bring a pen and paper with you. You will be expected to write during the workshop. You will be required to share your writing with others. You will also receive feedback and input about your writing.

10. In the event that ill health or an emergency in your family keeps you from coming to work tomorrow, you can access your writing assignment by clicking on human resources that can be found on the company's home page. You will then be able to circulate what you have written to a group that will include the leaders of tomorrow's workshop as well as your supervisors. An assessment of your writing as well as of your attendance will be included in your next performance review, but do not be alarmed, because we at the company always have your best interests at heart, and we would never want you to feel under any pressure or regretful that you did not study harder in college. Of course, economic conditions may necessitate the implementation of policy changes at some future time, and we cannot guarantee that your position will never be needed to be eliminated.

Editing

When you believe that you have said what you want to say the way you want to say it, you are ready to edit your paper. Check your grammar. Make sure that each sentence is complete. Check each subject–verb pair to make sure that they agree. Correct dangling modifiers (words or phrases that do not logically modify the sentence elements with which they are placed) and shifts in tense, person, or tone. Look for instances of mixed metaphors (a combination of metaphors that cannot be easily pictured) and faulty predication (the use of a predicate that does not fit the subject with which it is used). Make sure that all your pronouns clearly refer to their antecedents.

Pay attention to spelling, mechanics, and punctuation. If you are using a computer, this is the time to run your spell checker. But don't expect a computer program to identify every problem. If you used *there* when you needed *their,* or mistyped *fro* (as in *to and fro*) instead of *for,* your spell checker is unlikely to notice. Honor standard conventions for such issues as when to use a comma and whether to italicize a title.

Be careful about the final appearance of your paper. First impressions are just as important in writing as they are in social relationships. But don't confuse good typing with good writing. A beautifully printed essay on thick, expensive paper may be a pleasure to see and hold, but what ultimately matters is what you have written and how well you have written it. Consider the presentation of your final draft as a symbol rather than a disguise. It should look good because it is good.

Peer Review

Comments from well-disposed, thoughtful readers can help you gain a new perspective on what you have written. You can begin to recognize your own developing maturity as a writer when you are able not only to accept and profit from constructive criticism but also to seek it out. Professional writers seldom rely on their own judgment alone. They test what they have written by having others read it—family, friends, colleagues, professional editors—to determine whether the writing communicates what the writer intended or needed to say. And very often, these early readers make suggestions that help the writer produce a more effective text.

Whenever possible, move beyond your circle of family and friends by sharing drafts with classmates who are working on the same assignment. When peer review is undertaken by a group of people in the same writing situation, the advice given is especially likely to be helpful. For example, if you are writing a paper about a text you studied in class, other readers of this book will be well equipped to respond to what you have written. Peer review by friends who have not read the book in question may alert you to problems in organization and sentence structure but not to a misunderstanding of the text you are discussing. Moreover, members of an in-class writing group will be familiar with the assignment sheet and the instructor's evaluation criteria. If peer review is not a scheduled part of a course you are taking, see if you can meet outside of class with two or three other students. And if this is not possible, make sure that readers outside the class—such as a friend or a writing center tutor—understand the assignment behind the draft you are asking them to review.

Peer review can be beneficial at almost any point in the writing process. Some writers like to share early drafts to see how their topic and purpose appeal to readers. Others like to make all the improvements they can on their own before soliciting responses from peers. One advantage to using peer review early in the writing process is that you get a sense of how readers are likely to respond to your material before you invest a lot of time and energy in it; another is that you may get helpful advice about how to develop and organize your ideas. An advantage to using peer review late in the writing process is that your readers are less likely to identify problems of which you are already aware and that you are capable of fixing. Moreover, readers can see that you have taken your project seriously. On the other hand, if you have taken a work through several drafts and edited it with care, you may be reluctant to make substantial changes recommended by your reviewers even if these changes would be beneficial. And if you submit a very rough draft for peer review, readers might think that you are wasting their time. When to use peer review should be determined by your own needs as a writer as well as by the expectations and resourcefulness of your peers. The manner in which you present your work to them will influence how helpful they will be to you. And you may find that you want to benefit from peer review at more than one stage in your writing process.

Getting Useful Responses

If you pass a draft to a reader or a group of readers and say nothing more than, "Here it is; let me know what you think," you may be putting an unfair burden on others. Without any guidance or orientation from you, they have to figure out what you are trying to accomplish and what kind of help would be most useful for you. Make your own early readers understand that you are not just looking for praise. Be frank with them about anything that concerns you, and direct their attention specifically to those points of concern, but also be open to comments on things you have not considered.

You can significantly increase your chance of getting real help if you introduce your draft to readers with an orientation composed along the following lines.

Explain Your Purpose   Tell your readers exactly what you are trying to accomplish in this essay. If you have a thesis, tell them what it is and how you have tried to support it. If you are working without a thesis, explain why that is and where you see yourself heading.

Identify Your Strengths   Tell your readers what parts of your draft you like. Doing so will help them help you build upon what you are already doing well. It will also help them understand that there are some aspects of your draft that you want to preserve.

Identify Your Concerns   If you have studied your draft, you are likely to have some concerns about it—for example, "I am worried about the unity and coherence of my paragraphs," "I ran out of ideas and worry that I have not developed my paper enough," or "I didn't know how to end this paper. I'd be especially grateful for help with my conclusion." Instead of keeping your concerns to yourself, get them out in the open. Doing so draws attention to the areas that worry you. This strategy focuses the attention of readers and can generate specific advice within a limited amount of time.

An orientation like this one can be given orally when you are working in a writing group. Or it can be written up as a cover letter when you are giving a draft to someone who will read your work elsewhere.

Because writing is so intimately bound up with who we are, we all feel that we put ourselves at risk when we show our writing to others. From its earliest flowering as the private, interior, and highly specific expression of the young child, communication becomes increasingly public until it reaches the impersonal and distant stage most often represented by academic discourse. As we learn to risk showing our writing to others, we mature as writers, but we never really lose the fear that someone may think us fools or idiots. Cynthia Ozick refers to this feeling of risk when she says that writing is "an act of courage." And Barbara Mellix says, "Each experience of writing was like standing naked and revealing my imperfection, my 'otherness.'" So it is understandable if a writer feels hurt or defensive when his or her writing elicits something other than a totally favorable response. Writing is intensely personal. We offer the world a part of ourselves, and we don't want to be rejected. But it is important to overcome undue sensitivity if you want to write well. Be honest with others and encourage others to be honest with you. You may find yourself wincing every now and again when criticism is directed at your work, and you may get some unhappy looks when you offer criticism to others. But pleasure in a job well done ultimately outweighs any aches along the way.

Giving Useful Responses

When you review someone's writing, do not think you are being kind if you ignore problems you see. Tactful, constructive criticism is always appropriate; personal attacks never are. Consider how you felt when you submitted work for peer review. Were you disappointed when no one offered any useful advice? Upset when someone came on too strong? Or grateful when you got clear responses from readers who were taking the trouble to give you some real help?

Respond to the Writer's Concerns Pay close attention to how a writer presents his or her work, and be sure to offer the kind of help requested. If a writer asks for help with organization and you respond by discussing punctuation, you are talking past each other rather than having a real conversation about the work in question. When offering criticism, be specific but kind. That means responding in a friendly voice and framing your comments as personal responses rather than as final verdicts. If you say, "I have trouble following the second half of your paper because I don't see how it relates to your thesis," you are offering a personal response. But if you say, "The organization is poor throughout the second half of your essay, and those pages have nothing to do with your thesis," you are offering a final verdict. Because other reviewers may have different responses, you would be wise—and kind—to speak only for yourself. It is important to treat others with respect, but you are failing to respect the responsibility you have been given if you overlook major problems in order to seem polite.

Praise Almost every writer welcomes praise, and people who invite you to read their work may feel anxious about how you will respond. Look for parts of the draft that you can praise sincerely. Explain why you like them.

Ask Permission You may discover problems in the draft that the writer has not identified as concerns. Instead of plunging in and telling the writer more than he or she may be prepared to hear, ask if you can talk about other issues that concern you. Most writers will respond affirmatively when asked, but the asking shows that you are being respectful and helps make subsequent discussion safe for all concerned.

EXERCISE 5

Write two to three pages in response to one of the following options, envisioning the instructor who has assigned this book as your audience.

1. If you have ever been part of a writing group that did not give you helpful peer review, explain what went wrong, and discuss how you or your teacher could have made that group function more effectively.

2. Many writers form peer review groups that meet outside of school, in settings such as a coffee shop or a member's home. Some of these groups continue to meet for years. If you were to create a writing group of your own, how big would it be, how would you select its members, how frequently would it meet, where would it convene, and what guidelines would it follow?

■■■■ WRITING PAPERS IN ACADEMIC DISCIPLINES

Writing for college courses often demands that you honor specific conventions determined by your purpose, audience, and context (see pages 3–6). Scholars use the phrase *academic discourse* to describe the kind of formal writing done for college courses by students who need to sound thoughtful and well informed. Academic discourse is also used by college professors when they present papers at professional conferences and submit articles to scholarly journals. What college professors consider to be successful examples of academic discourse is shaped by the conventions of their own discipline. These conventions vary from one discipline to another.

When writing academic discourse, you will benefit from following the writing process described earlier in this chapter, by planning, drafting, revising, and editing (see pages 7–37) before you submit a final product for evaluation. But as you move through this process, you must pay close attention to your assignment and make sure you satisfy your instructor's expectations. The audience and the context determine your topic and purpose, as well as how you need to present yourself. For instance, your political science instructor might expect you to demonstrate an objective attitude rather than a partisan one in a report summing up the results of a recent session of Congress. Your diction and tone will influence how you sound—whether you seem biased or fair-minded, timid or confident, casual or professional. For example, your physics professor might wonder if you know what you are talking about if you substitute the word *doughnut* for the technical term *torus* in a report on fusion reaction; *doughnut* is the wrong level of language for this context, even though it can mean *torus* and might be used in an informal conversation between physicists.

Moreover, writing a formal paper in the sciences often requires a pattern of organization that is inappropriate for writing in the humanities. Thus, a paper reporting the results of research in psychology might begin with a summary (or abstract) and then move on to separate sections devoted to research methods, results, and implications. A paper interpreting a work of English literature, in contrast, is unlikely to open with an abstract or include a section on research methodology.

In addition to including essays written for a nonacademic audience of thoughtful adults—such as those in Chapter 1, "Writing to Understand Experience," and Chapter 9, "Writing to Experiment with Form"—this book also includes examples of academic discourse from several disciplines. You will find these examples included in Chapters 2–7. Although the nature of academic discourse changes from one discipline to another, it can also vary within a specific discipline. For example, a paper written for oral presentation at a scholarly conference may be less formal than the revised version of that paper subsequently submitted for publication. And different journals within a field may have different editorial policies; one might publish only articles that are research based, whereas another might welcome a personal narrative describing a classroom practice or an essay reflecting on an issue being debated by scholars in that discipline.

Addressing the full extent to which academic discourse can vary is beyond the scope of this introduction. Nevertheless, you can make appropriate writing decisions if guided by the following advice.

Studying Literature Published in Your Discipline

The textbooks you are assigned in a college course often can give you a sense of the style of writing used in that discipline. And your instructor might distribute examples of successful papers written by other students. But one of the best ways to understand the nature of academic discourse in a specific field is to study periodical literature published in the discipline you are studying.

Because so much information is now available online through the World Wide Web, many students limit themselves to downloading material from it. Excellent sources can be found this way, but they may appear alongside sources that are unreliable. To visit the Web is to visit a world where all sorts of voices try to claim your attention. The democratic nature of the Web is part of its appeal: There is no governing body of scholars or editors determining who gets to have space on the Web. So a search for information on the Web can lead you to a site created by scholars at a major university or to one slapped together by a ten-year-old. This is good news for the ten-year-old, who gets a chance at being heard. But sorting through all the possibilities available on the Web can be time-consuming—and potentially misleading when you need to make decisions about academic discourse. The Web sources that you downloaded may be shorter than comparable articles published in print, and they are almost certainly going to be arranged differently because of the nature of the medium: A print source can be read from start to finish, with each section leading logically to the next. A Web source is likely to make different kinds of information available through links that can be clicked on at different times, making both the nature of the text and the experience of reading it less sequential.

The easiest way to search for material on the Web is to use a search engine such as Google. Many people have found Google to be so useful that they have fallen into the habit of using it as their primary means for obtaining information. Although a search engine like this can help you to locate dozens (and often hundreds) of sites, scholarly information can be buried under numerous sites put together quickly or designed to push a specific agenda. For college-level research, you will often need to supplement the use of a well-designed search engine by turning to electronic databases available through your college or university. These databases can be accessed through systems such as these:

- *Expanded Academic ASAP:* Provided by *InfoTrac,* this service provides full-text retrieval of articles from 709 of the 1,260 journals it covers. It is a good place to begin.

- *ERIC:* Indexing articles and conference papers in all areas of education, *ERIC* can be accessed online through many college libraries.

- *FirstSearch:* Covering dozens of databases, *FirstSearch* provides electronic access to more than 10 million articles.

- *PsycINFO:* Also available through college libraries, *PsycINFO* provides abstracts of articles in psychology as well as citations that will identify how you can find the full text of these articles.

- *Medline:* Indexing more than seven thousand journals in medicine and biology, *Medline* can be a useful supplement to *PsycINFO*.

- *MLA Bibliography:* Essential for research in English and American literature, the *MLA Bibliography* indexes books as well as articles. It too can be accessed through most college libraries.

Familiarity with these systems will help you when completing research assignments, and many of the "Suggestions for Writing" that appear at the end of each selection in Chapters 1–10 invite you to do some research. In some cases, you will be able to obtain the entire text of an article when you use an electronic index, an option called "full-text retrieval." Often, however, you will need to consult the periodicals housed in your library, either in bound volumes or on microform, in order to get the text of the articles you have located. (For additional information on research, see pages 104–105.)

Unlike the World Wide Web, which publishes an enormous range of material, much of which is nonacademic, electronic indexes will direct you to examples of academic discourse that have been carefully selected and edited for publication. But if you just want to get a sense of how academic discourse sounds in your field, you can reserve these indexes for occasions when you need to locate material on a specific topic and, instead, undertake a much simpler exercise: Go to the periodical room in your college or university library and browse among the current issues on display. Then choose three or four from your field, and read the first few pages of several articles, paying attention to their tone and diction. You are likely to find that different writers have different voices, even when working within the conventions of academic discourse. But you are also likely to find consistency in diction, documentation, and organization. When you note that an article is divided into subsections, examine what these divisions reveal about the pattern of organization and the issues writers in that discipline are expected to address.

Consulting Handbooks

You may already own—or be able to acquire easily—a writing handbook composed for college students that covers grammar, spelling, punctuation, documentation, and mechanics, as well as discussing the writing process. A handbook of this kind provides a useful resource when you need to get clear answers to questions about such issues as capitalization, italics, abbreviations, and the correct use of verbs and pronouns. A good handbook is also likely to furnish an introductory guide for formatting papers and documenting source material. Just as you can benefit from keeping a reliable dictionary on or near your desk, you can also benefit from keeping a writing handbook close at hand long after completing the course for which you purchased it.

But if you want to master academic discourse in a specific field, you should also have access to a handbook especially designed for writers in that field. These handbooks include:

American Chemical Society. *The ACS Style Guide: A Manual for Authors and Editors.* 2nd ed. Washington: Amer. Chem. Soc., 1998.

American Institute of Physics. *AIP Style Manual.* 4th ed. New York: Amer. Inst. of Physics, 1990.

American Mathematical Society. *A Manual for Authors of Mathematical Papers.* Rev. ed. Providence: Amer. Mathematical Soc., 1990.

American Medical Association. *American Medical Association Manual of Style.* 9th ed. Baltimore: Williams, 1997.

American Psychological Association. *Publication Manual of the American Psychological Association.* 5th ed. Washington: Amer. Psychological Assn., 2001.

Associated Press. *The Associated Press Stylebook and Libel Manual.* Rev. ed. Reading: Perseus, 1998.

The Chicago Manual of Style. 15th ed. Chicago: U of Chicago P, 2003.

Council of Biology Editors. *Scientific Style and Format: The CBE Manual for Authors, Editors, and Publishers.* 6th ed. New York: Cambridge UP, 1994.

Gilbaldi, Joseph. *MLA Handbook for Writers of Research Papers.* 6th ed. New York: Modern Language Assn., 2003.

Harvard Law Review. *A Uniform System of Citation.* 16th ed. Cambridge: Harvard Law Review, 1996.

Linguistic Society of America, *LSA Bulletin,* Dec. issue, annually.

Turabian, Kate L. *A Manual for Writers of Term Papers, Theses, and Dissertations.* 6th ed. Chicago: U of Chicago P, 1996.

United States Geological Survey. *Suggestions to Authors of the Reports of the United States Geological Survey.* 7th ed. Washington: GPO, 1991.

United States Government Printing Office. *Style Manual.* Washington: GPO, 2000.

Each of these handbooks addresses a number of issues, including information on document design and the documentation of sources. Among the most widely consulted are *The Chicago Manual of Style,* which is used by editors at numerous journals and publishing companies; *The MLA Handbook for Writers of Research Papers,* which sets forth the conventions that students in English courses are expected to follow when citing sources; and the *Publication Manual of the American Psychological Association,* which describes the format, organization, and documentation guidelines for writing in the social sciences.

Documenting Research

Because many of the "Suggestions for Writing" that follow the reading selections in *Motives for Writing* encourage you to do research—and because your instructor will almost certainly expect you to document your research—an introduction to the key components of MLA style and APA style are included as an appendix (see pages 667–676). These are the two documentation styles most frequently used in college writing assignments.

Commonly Asked Questions

When you are getting ready to submit a college paper for evaluation, one of the following questions may occur to you. The answer may appear on your assignment sheet, or your instructor may answer in class or by e-mail. The responses provided below, however, can help you to make appropriate decisions on your own.

Do I Need a Title Page?

Different instructors have different expectations, so you would be wise to learn if the instructor for whom you are writing a paper has a preference. But the Modern Language Association does not require a title page, recommending instead that students place all the information that would appear on such a page on the first page of the paper (see Figure 3). The American Psychological Association does recommend the use of a title page (see Figure 4), which can be modified if you are writing a paper for any course in which the instructor requires a title page. (*The Chicago Manual of Style* advises editors how to design the title page of a book, but it does not address how to submit a college paper.)

Does It Matter What Font I Use or How Large My Margins Are?

Academic papers should have a clear, professional appearance. Use a standard font such as Courier or Times New Roman, and avoid unusual fonts like Script or Gothic. Font size should be neither too small to be easily readable nor so large that you end up looking as if you were trying to fill space. An 11- or 12-point font is usually acceptable.

In both MLA-style and APA-style papers, set your margins for one inch at the top and bottom of each page and on both sides of the text. The page number appears at the right margin, one-half inch from the top.

In addition, be sure to double-space your paper. Double-spacing helps readers follow your text and allows room for writing comments.

Can I Use the First Person?

The most likely answer is a clear "probably." Like any other writing decision, choosing whether to write in the first person should be informed by your purpose, topic, audience, and context. Doing so is natural when writing to understand experience (Chapter 1). And the first person can also be useful when fulfilling the other motives for writing discussed in this book. For example, you will find that Eric Schlosser and Elizabeth Kolbert use the first person to some extent when writing to report information (see Chapter 2),

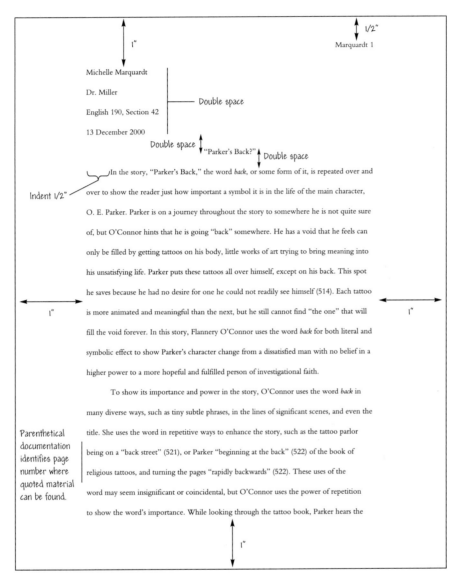

FIGURE 3. First page of an MLA-style paper.

because it helps readers see how they obtained the information in question—as when they interviewed people. A restaurant review like Dara Moskowitz's "The Sad Comedy of Really Bad Food" (Chapter 4) also uses the first person appropriately: Readers expect the reviewer to tell them what food she ate and what she thought of the service. And in arguments such as "Letter from

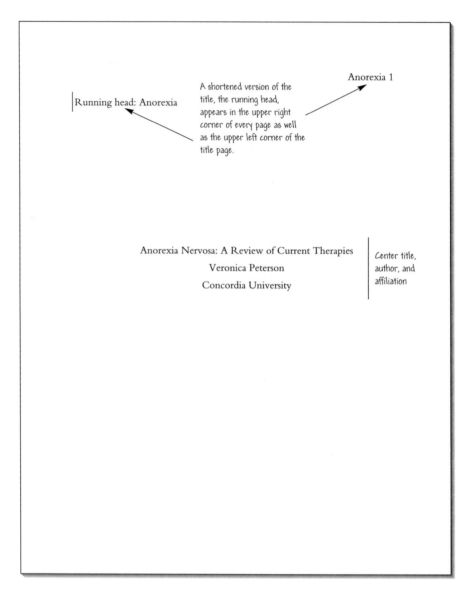

Anorexia 1

Running head: Anorexia

A shortened version of the title, the running head, appears in the upper right corner of every page as well as the upper left corner of the title page.

Anorexia Nervosa: A Review of Current Therapies

Veronica Peterson

Concordia University

Center title, author, and affiliation

FIGURE 4. APA-style title page.

Birmingham Jail" (Chapter 7), personal experience is a key source, so once again the use of the first person is appropriate.

As a rule, *I* sounds friendlier and less stuffy than *one*. But it should not be overused. One reason instructors sometimes discourage the use of the first person is that inexperienced writers include phrases such as "I think," "I feel," or "I believe" in dozens of sentences when the information is redundant: If it is your paper, your audience will assume that the ideas in it are your own. Nevertheless, these phrases can play a useful role in helping you to distinguish your own views from the views of others you are including in your work: "Although John Anderson argues that the Electoral College should be abolished, I believe that we should retain it." When you use the first person in drafting, consider, when revising, whether each use is justified and if any can be omitted.

If you find yourself in a writing situation in which you have been told not to use the first person, you can avoid it from the moment you begin the draft. But you might find it easier to use the first person when drafting and then delete it when revising. Although this practice may seem like extra work, it can help you to draft quickly and to convey your thoughts in your own voice. And that voice may still linger in the paper once you delete the first person. If you draft as if you were a faceless member of some impersonal organization, you may end up sounding unnecessarily dry and remote.

■▦■▦■ A FINAL NOTE

Additional advice about writing is provided in the introductions to each of the following ten chapters. Do not be overwhelmed by the advice in these introductions or in the introductory material you have just read. No one expects you to become a perfect writer by the end of the semester. Writing well is a lifelong challenge. The immediate challenge, the one confronting you in the weeks ahead, is to understand the principles that can help you become the best writer you can be. Although these principles can be studied in the abstract, they are best understood through examples and practice. If you want to write well, you must be prepared to write often and to appraise your work critically. You must also be prepared to read often and to think critically about what you read. The essays and articles collected in this book offer you an opportunity to exercise your reading and thinking skills, and they will introduce you to authors and topics you may want to read more of in the future.

Writing to Understand Experience

1

When you write to understand experience, you do not settle for simply recording what has happened to you. Instead, you draw upon that record to examine the significance of what happened. The writers in this chapter draw upon memories to help them understand who they are, how they became that way, what they like, or what they want. Because they are writing about their own lives, they all use the first person—as you are likely to do when you write about your own experience. But although they are writing about themselves, they are not writing for themselves alone. They are also writing to share their experience with readers. Writing to understand experience thus achieves at least two goals: Writers come to a better understanding of themselves, and readers come to understand experience different from their own.

In addition to generating reflections about the past, writing to understand experience can also prompt writers to reflect on what their present lives are like: what they enjoy, dislike, or fear. In this chapter, essays such as "Levi's" by Marilyn Schiel and "Life with Father" by Itabari Njeri illustrate how writers sometimes seek to understand the past. Others, like "Grub" by Scott Russell Sanders and "Lavender" by André Aciman, move back and forth between the past and the present, using the past to understand what is happening in the present. Like these writers, you will usually have a range of options when writing to understand experience.

GAINING PERSPECTIVE

When choosing a topic, recognize that writing to understand experience requires effort. During or immediately after an experience, we seldom know what its implications will be or why we acted in a particular way. Distance—the passage of time—is essential. Distance enables Itabari Njeri, for example, to understand why her father was often angry and sometimes brutal. Writing about a current romance may allow you to vent your feelings, but you could easily find yourself unable to move beyond the expression of these feelings. You might, however, write successfully about a former romance if you have the distance necessary to understand it and the discipline to make the effort. Writing to understand experience relies on thought and reflection more than on emotion and confession. Thinking can be difficult when your heart is full.

Your motive for such thinking and writing is to discover something rather than to report something you knew before you began to write. The act of writing will generate insight. Do not suppose, however, that writing to understand experience means finding a truth that is conveniently stored somewhere in your head, some secret knowledge that, once uncovered, will explain everything you want to understand. Writing often leads to new perceptions. If you write thoughtfully about experience, you will be constructing knowledge as you proceed.

As you prepare to write about experience, remember that you can achieve a unique perspective. No one else can know exactly what you know. What you discover and how much you tell are your choice, though. Take some risks, but do not think that you have to confess all. What ultimately matters is the degree of insight you achieve through writing and the clarity with which you convey that insight to readers—not the degree to which you reveal your personal life. To a large extent, the topic matters less than what you do with it.

As an essay like Marilyn Schiel's "Levi's" suggests, a thoughtful writer can write meaningfully about a topic as apparently simple as a pair of used jeans. Most people would think, "What could be simpler than that?" And inexperienced writers might not even consider writing on such a topic, because they have convinced themselves that writers need extraordinary material in order to be interesting. But interest is something the writer creates. Some writers are capable of making the extraordinary seem boring; others help us see what is wonderful about the ordinary. In Schiel's hands, the memory of a pair of jeans becomes a vehicle for understanding her life. With a good eye for detail, Schiel helps readers to visualize triple-roll cuffs with sidewalk burns, real pockets marked with metal rivets, and a difficult-to-manage button fly. But by the time we finish the essay, we can see what Schiel was like, what her brother was like, and what her mother was like. We also come away understanding something of what it meant to grow up in the 1950s. Another writer could address much more personal material without reaching a better understanding of experience.

GETTING STARTED

Although some people are more reflective than others, most people spend at least some time trying to figure out reasons for the things they have done or felt. For instance, suppose you do not drink alcohol, and this principle normally governs your conduct. But at a party one evening, you decide to take a drink that someone offers you. Then you have another. You lose control of yourself, feel ill the next morning, and wonder why you engaged in behavior you carefully avoided in the past. You may also wonder who saw you when the alcohol had taken effect and what they thought of you. Attempting to answer such questions can motivate writing to understand experience.

The answer to the first question, "Why did I do it?" may lead you to make discoveries about yourself by looking inward and examining your feelings and ideas. Marilyn Schiel illustrates this approach as she writes to express why acquiring a pair of blue jeans was so important to her when she was a little girl. The answer to the second question, "Who saw me do it?" may lead you to understand experience by seeing yourself through the eyes of others. Scott Russell Sanders uses the second approach when, as he is leaving a restaurant, he speculates about another customer:

> She might figure me for a carpenter, noticing my beard, the scraggly hair down over my collar, my banged-up hands, my patched jeans, my flannel shirt the color of the biscuits I just ate, my clodhopper boots. Or maybe she'll guess mechanic, maybe garbageman, electrician, janitor, maybe even farmer.

In addition to trying to see yourself as others see you, you can move beyond yourself by focusing on how something (or someone) has helped make you the person you are or led you to do something that you might not have done. In this chapter, Gloria Naylor explores how her understanding of language evolved through experience, and Rick Marin explores an aspect of contemporary culture that he wants to avoid. You might also look for parallels between what you encounter in the world around you and how you perceive yourself. Annie Dillard engages in this kind of exploration when she reflects on an unexpected experience with a weasel while she is out for a walk, as does André Aciman when exploring the meaning of his relationship to aftershave.

Search through your memories to find experiences that have made you the way you are. Perhaps you can pull them together to show, for instance, how you developed an interest in art or how travel made you more tolerant of other people's customs. Or you might explore why you have lost interest in something that once mattered to you or why you have grown away from a person to whom you were once close.

Another possibility is to explore the significance of behavior with which you are content. For example, if you enjoy getting up earlier than most people, you might explore how early rising affects you. This is the approach Rick Marin takes when he discusses why he is glad to keep clear of delivery rooms. Alternatively, you might write about a habit you would like to change. Have your friends complained that you always interrupt them? You might want to explore that behavior to see when you began doing it, why you do it, and what it says about you.

For other ideas, look at the beginnings of the essays in this chapter. For example, Scott Russell Sanders tells us that he was inspired by a newspaper report that "Indiana leads the nation in fat." Perhaps your own reading—of a newspaper, magazine, or novel, or an essay in this chapter—will prompt reflections that inspire you to write to understand experience. Or you may find inspiration in a film, play, or television program that provokes a strong personal response.

Conversations, too, may generate topics for essays about experience. If you've ever said something you later regretted or played a conversation over in your mind, you may have the beginnings of an essay. Gloria Naylor's essay, for example, can be traced back to a kind of conversation—the first time she heard a disturbing term spoken to her with contempt. When you talk to a friend about some event that has left you feeling uneasy, you may discover that you have more to say than you realized. The give-and-take of conversation may lead to a clearer understanding of what you are talking about. Consider writing to understand experience as a way to continue such a conversation— or even to initiate it.

CONSIDERING AUDIENCE

When writing to understand experience, you are an important part of your own audience. If you do not come to understand the experience you have chosen to write about, people who read what you write are unlikely to understand it either. Accordingly, you can benefit from considering audience on two levels at different points in the writing process.

When drafting and then rereading what you draft, ask yourself if you understand what you are trying to convey. Remember that you are seeking to understand experience, not merely to report it. Is your writing leading you to an insight that you did not have when you began—or, at least, enriching your understanding of what occurred? If so, there is a good chance that the audience with whom you later share your work will find it meaningful. At this point in the writing process, when you are your own audience, be as truthful as you can be. When revising, you can eliminate information that you decide is too personal to share with other readers, but allowing this information to surface as you draft can help you discover what you want your essay to communicate.

When drafting, be careful to avoid insincerity and a conclusion designed to please others. For example, if you spent a week doing service work in a culture other than your own, it might be tempting to conclude that this experience made you a "better person," or that you "learned to be grateful for what you have," or that "poor people are warm-hearted, and they taught you what is really important in life." If you were addressing an audience that sponsored your trip, conclusions such as these might generate polite applause. The problem is that thousands of writers have said the same thing. Now is the time to consider whether you are telling the truth or merely saying what you think others want to hear. If you really have become a "better person," what is the precise nature of the change and how is it demonstrated in your daily life? If you are still more or less the same person who went off on the trip, but you really did have a meaningful experience while you were away from home, what pulled you back into your normal routines? And if, deep down, you hated the week you spent on service work, this might be time to be frank instead of pious. You cannot communicate the truth to others if you are afraid to communicate it to yourself.

Of course, an essay is not a journal entry. As you revise your essay with other readers in mind, you need to consider whether you have disclosed more than you wish or whether you need to say more. If you have not already done so, it is important to consider whether other readers will be able to follow what you have drafted. Make sure that events unfold in an understandable sequence so that readers can understand what happened when. Check also whether others will be able to identify the people who appear in your essay. It is easy, when drafting, to leap ahead in time or to mention the names of people whom you do not identify because you know what happened when and who various people are. When revising, clarify anything that readers may have difficulty following.

Stories from experience have the potential to appeal to a large audience. What happens to people can be the subject of both gossip and great literature. No matter how egocentric a person may seem to be, almost everyone has some degree of interest in learning what happened to others. But when writing for an audience other than yourself, you need to consider whether your material will hold people's attention. Those who are close to you may be willing to hear anything you care to share, but an audience that is not confined to your family or friends will expect you to address a topic that is an issue in lives other than your own and to say something significant about it. Perhaps you have noted in conversation how some people interrupt at the earliest opportunity to either change the subject or to tell a story from their own experience that they think is similar to what you have been disclosing. In a conversation, you can assert yourself by saying that you had not finished. But when writing, you need to use your time wisely. Readers are likely to stay with you if they sense that you are telling the truth about something that matters, but they also may turn to other material if they sense that you are insincere or long-winded.

FOCUSING AND ARRANGING IDEAS

Essayists usually focus on something specific because they are working on a small canvas. In this chapter, Marilyn Schiel focuses on a pair of blue jeans, Scott Russell Sanders on a meal, Itabari Njeri on her father, Rick Marin on how new fathers are expected to behave, Gloria Naylor on a word, Annie

Dillard on an encounter with a wild animal, and André Aciman on his quest for the perfect aftershave.

You are more likely to write in depth and say something meaningful when you have discussed a specific topic and remained focused on it. Consider, for example, how much Annie Dillard conveys about encountering a weasel while out for a walk one evening. An essay of similar length that tried to address all the animals she has seen would lack the depth and intensity she achieves in "Living like Weasels."

But having a clear focus does not mean that you must limit yourself to a single memory in an essay about experience. Recording one memory can sometimes lead to another. When this happens, you should feel free to tie one memory to another. Writing to understand experience can become a voyage of self-discovery that takes you far away from where you began. A short essay, however, does not afford room for every memory that occurs to you. If you find yourself wanting to move from one memory to another, ask yourself if they are closely related or if you are being lured away from your original focus by material that might best be saved for another occasion. (If they are not closely related, you might jot the extra one in your journal or notebook to use another time.)

Two of the works in this chapter demonstrate how writers can include more than one memory without losing their focus. In "Life with Father," Itabari Njeri records several closely related memories of her father as she seeks to understand the experience of growing up in the same apartment with him. More ambitiously, André Aciman weaves together a series of memories, from different locations and different stages of his life, to make sense of his lifelong quest for the perfect cologne—a topic that could seem frivolous if not handled with care.

In an essay of your own, you might start in the middle of a story—if the middle provides an opening that will attract the readers' attention—and then go back to the beginning before finishing with the conclusion. There is no single method of organization that works all the time. But if you are new to writing or worried about keeping your ideas organized, take your lead from Marilyn Schiel and Annie Dillard, both of whom arrange events in chronological order as they try to understand the nature of these events.

Moreover, keep in mind three principles when planning how to share a memory with readers:

- Give readers a clear indication of where your memories are located in time.

- Remember that your own experience is different from the experiences of your audience. References to people or places that seem clear to you may not be clear to readers. When you prepare to revise what you have drafted, read as if you are a member of your audience, and clarify any references that seem unclear.

- Whether you are writing chronologically or moving backward and forward in time for dramatic effect, save a strong scene for the ending so that your essay does not trail off after reaching an early climax.

You may already have used writing to understand experience, or you may have convinced yourself long ago that writing about your personal experience is something you want to avoid. If you are uncomfortable writing about yourself, you can write meaningfully about the experiences of other people if you have been paying attention to lives other than your own. For example, you could write to enrich your understanding of someone you know well by writing about that person's character or behavior, as Marilyn Schiel does when writing about her mother or Itabari Njeri does when writing about her father. Both of these writers also write about themselves, but you could choose to focus exclusively on another person. Consider also how Gloria Naylor focuses on the use of language and how Rick Marin explores his response to cultural expectations. In both cases, we get a sense of the writers' values, yet the focus is not on the writers themselves but on parts of the world in which they live.

Once again, don't assume that an essay about experience must be deeply personal. Some of the best essays examine life from a distance. If you watch television talk shows, you may get the misguided impression that discussion of experience must deal with sexual abuse, dysfunctional families, or chemical dependency. An inexperienced writer who attempts to discuss such intimate material may subsequently regret what she or he has revealed to others. Remember that an evocative essay can be written about nothing more intimate than a pair of Levi's or a walk by a pond. You are the best judge of what is significant to you, and you are ultimately responsible for what you decide to share with others. The challenge is to convey significant experience—be it large or small—without embarrassing yourself or your readers.

TIPS FOR READING AND WRITING TO UNDERSTAND EXPERIENCE

When Reading

- Identify the understanding the writer is trying to convey.
- Determine what led to this understanding.
- Consider whether the understanding seems genuine or insincere.
- Reflect on whether the experience offers any insights into lives other than the writer's.

When Writing

▪ Make sure that you have chosen a topic about which you have something meaningful to say, preferably something you want to discover through writing about experience.

▪ Ask yourself whether you can adequately discuss this topic without embarrassing yourself or your audience.

▪ Include sufficient detail so that readers can understand what happened and to whom it happened.

▪ Make sure that readers will be able to tell what happened when.

▪ When reviewing what you draft, make sure that you are conveying an understanding of experience, not just reporting something that happened.

▪ Reflect on whether the understanding you have achieved is sincere or whether you are simply telling others what you think they want to hear.

▪ Make sure that your final draft is focused by eliminating nonessential details.

LEVI'S

Marilyn Schiel

In "Levi's," Marilyn Schiel paints a picture of the past that focuses on a pair of blue jeans. Think about how the clothes people wear help determine what acts they perform—what they can and cannot do. As you read, ask yourself why the Levi's were so important to Schiel. What would they enable her to do? If you have seen reruns of such TV series as Leave It to Beaver *or* Father Knows Best, *you have some knowledge of American values in the fifties and early sixties. Draw on what you know of that era so that you can locate Schiel's memoir in a context of time and place.*

"Levi's" was first published in 1992 when Schiel was a high school English teacher in Stevens Point, Wisconsin. Looking back at this essay in 2004, Scheil—who is now retired and living in Utah—wrote, "I've always believed I had no thoughts deeper than curb water . . . [but] digging around in the muck of curb water can be fun and sometimes turn up unexpected bits and pieces of the past to revisit. Examining those small, but for some reason memorable, moments of our lives helps us understand not only what we've done, but who we are. Oh sure, the major traumas of our lives help define us, but those apparently insignificant moments that stick in our memory tell us who we are, too. Too often we overlook the 'small stuff.' After all, it seems so unimportant." To other writers, she offers the following advice: "Keep it simple, keep it honest, and keep it going!" And on a more personal note, she adds, "I'm glad I had a chance to pick up these old pants, shake them out and share them with my family. My brother died unexpectedly just three months after I wrote the essay. He'd had a chance to read it. He knew then, as I'd always known . . . how much I loved him."

They weren't boot cut, or spiked leg, or 501. They weren't stone washed, or acid bleached, or ice black. They weren't Guess, or Zena, or Jordache. They were just blue jeans—old, worn Levi's.

My ten-year-old brother wore blue jeans. I wore slacks. In summer, cotton pastel pants with embroidered bunnies or ducks. In winter, grey corduroys with girl-pink flannel lining. I wanted to wear blue jeans.

As a five-year-old I didn't understand the difference between cause and coincidence. My brother's jeans meant he could wander his two-wheel bike blocks from home after school; he could, with a crew of blue-jeaned boys, build a tree house in the oak in the vacant lot next door; he could carry a BB gun all the way to the cemetery to shoot at squirrels. I had to be content triking my embroidered bunnies up and down the driveway; I had to settle for building domino houses on the living room floor; I could shoot only caps at imaginary black-hatted cowboys in the basement. I wanted to wear blue jeans.

But little girls in my 1950 world didn't wear blue jeans. Big girls didn't wear them either. Big girls didn't even wear pastel cotton slacks or winter corduroys. At least my mother, the big girl I knew best, didn't. When the family gathered for breakfast, seven days a week sharp at 7:30, Mom was already in uniform, a shirtwaist dress garnished with a colored, beaded necklace that matched clip-on earrings. By the 1960s June Cleaver may have been an anachronism, but in the early 1950s she lived at my house.

Mothers stayed home. Unlike dads, mothers didn't work. Mothers made the beds, cooked the meals, cleaned the house, baked the cookies, tended the garden, canned the vegetables, squeezed the clothes through the wringer-washer, hung washed clothes to dry on lines strung through the basement, ironed everything—including sheets and towels—scrubbed the floors while kneeling on pink rubber pads, walked seven blocks pulling an empty Red-flyer wagon to buy groceries, struggled seven blocks home with a week's worth of carefully budgeted supplies, and picked out the clothes their children would wear. My brother got blue jeans. I got embroidered bunnies.

Then, in 1953, my world changed. Elvis took us all to Heartbreak Hotel; Eisenhower brought us home from Korea; and my mother went to work. The hardware store Dad bought pulled Mom from the home to the business. Her transition from the breadbaker to a breadwinner taught my mother that women, big or little, didn't have to wear embroidered bunnies anymore.

The change was more evolutionary than revolutionary. She still wore the housewife uniform—but now she wore it to work. She still did the laundry, but now with an automatic washing machine and electric dryer. We still ate breakfast together at 7:30, but now cereal and milk replaced eggs and bacon. The ironing went out every Tuesday night to a house on the hill behind the railroad tracks and came back folded every Wednesday evening. And as a business-woman, my mother discovered that sometimes function was more important than fashion, at least for little girls.

Those old, worn Levi's of my brother's met the expectations of the advertisements. They survived an entire season of his hard wear and, unlike most of his clothes, were outgrown before worn out. And as mother used to say about anything that might be salvaged for use, "These old pants still have a little life left in them."

Not only did they have some life left in them, but they were going to give that life to me. A year earlier they would have been boxed with other we-don't-want-them-anymore clothes for the "naked children" of some foreign country I'd never heard of or, if the postage wasn't too expensive, shipped off to my poor cousins in South Dakota. With her newfound economic acumen and with her slowly evolving awareness of a woman's place, my mother looked at those blue jeans differently than she would have the year before. Maybe she looked at me a little differently, too.

"Marilyn, come here," she called from my brother's room. That in itself tripped anticipation. Now that Bob was approaching adolescence, his room held the mystery earned of secrecy. The door to his room was open; my mother leaned over the bed folding and sorting boy-clothes. Shirts in one stack, pants in another, worn to see-through-thin garments in still a third pile. But smoothed out full length along the edge of Bob's bed were a pair of old, worn Levi's.

"Here, try these on." She held them up against my seven-year-old middle. "I think these will fit you if you roll up the legs."

And fit they did, more like a gunnysack than a glove, but they were blue jeans and they were my brother's—and they were now mine. Cinched tightly with an Indian-beaded belt scrounged from my brother's dresser, the chamois-soft denim bunched in unplanned pleats at my waist. No more sissy elastic for me. Triple-roll cuffs still scuffed the ground by my shoe heels when I walked—my excuse for the swaggering steps those Levi's induced. After a time side-walk burns frayed the bottom edge, finally denoting my singular ownership. Metal rivets marked the pockets and seam overlaps. Gone were the telltale girl-white overstitching outlines. And those pockets. Real pockets. Not that patch pocket pretend stuff of girl-pants, but deep inside pockets of white, soft, gather-in-my-fist material that could be pulled inside out in search of the dis-appeared dime.

But those Levi's marked more than my move from little-girl clothes to big-brother clothes. Indeed, they were the only hand-me-downs ever handed down. Instead, those old ratty pants marked my move to freedom, freedom from the conventional girl-stuff my mother had so carefully fostered only one year earlier. Maybe my mother—who was learning the difference between roofing nails and wood screws, who was learning to mix paint in the vise-gripping shake-machine bolted to the floor in the back room of the hardware store, who would later teach me to cut glass, make keys, and clean Surge milk pumpers—wanted me to know what she was learning about women's work and men's work. I don't know. I just know that those Levi's—old, worn, with a difficult-to-manage button fly—meant the world to me, at least the limited world offered by my neighborhood.

The next summer I got my first two-wheeled bike, a full-size, blue, fat-tire Schwinn off the store's showroom floor. It was mother who convinced Dad that I didn't need training wheels. "If you want her to learn to ride, put her on it and let her ride." Oh, I dented the fenders some that summer and suffered some scars from the inescapable tip-overs, but I learned to ride as well as the boys. And by the end of the summer, Mom was packing peanut butter sandwiches for me to take on fishing expeditions down at the Chip-pewa River below the railroad trestle.

Along with the traditional dolls and play cookware, Christmas Eve brought   15
chemistry kits and carpenter tools. Even my brother acknowledged my new-found worldliness. Better than any gift were the after-school hours spent help-ing him rebuild an old auto engine in the basement. I didn't do much, but watching him work and occasionally fetching wrenches taught me where pis-tons went and what they did, and that my big brother didn't mind having me around.

By junior high, I had my own .22. Our family Sundays in the fall found three of us in the woods searching for squirrel. My brother elected to hunt a more dangerous game, senior high school girls. Dad wore that goofy brown billed hat with cold-weather earflaps; I wore wool side-zipping slacks from the juniors department at Daytons, topped by a crew-neck matching sweater—style in a seventh-grade girl mattered even in the woods; Mom wore a turtle-neck under one of Dad's wool shirt-jacs pulled out to hang over her blue jeans—old, worn Levi's.

QUESTIONS FOR DISCUSSION

1. How does Schiel characterize her mother in this piece? What causes her mother to change? Does Schiel approve of this change?
2. Why did Schiel want to wear jeans when she was a little girl? What details in this essay help you understand her point of view?
3. The first three sentences in this essay begin with the same two words, and the fourth provides only a minor variation. What is the effect of paragraph 1? Do you note any other examples of repetition in this essay? What does repetition contribute to the essay as a whole?
4. Consider the third sentence in paragraph 5. What is the effect of conveying so much information in a single sentence?
5. In the last glimpse of herself that she provides, Schiel remembers wearing a pair of slacks from a fashionable department store rather than the jeans that once meant so much to her. What is this meant to show?

SUGGESTIONS FOR WRITING

1. Remember a favorite possession that you had when you were young. Write about that item in enough detail for readers to understand why it mattered to you.
2. Write about a time when you were denied the chance to do something because other people considered it unsuitable for your gender.
3. Write about how a difference in gender enriched or complicated your relationship with a sibling, friend, or colleague.

▌ LINKS

▪ Within the Book

Like Schiel, several other writers in this book challenge gender expectations. If this subject interests you, see "Tough Break" (pages 148–153) and "Women's Brains" (pages 214–219).

■ Elsewhere in Print

Downey, Lynn, Jill Novach Lynch, and Kathleen McDonough. *This Is a Pair of Levi's Jeans: The Official History of the Levi's Brand.* San Francisco: Levi, 1997.

Dru, Ricki. *The First Blue Jeans.* New York: Contemporary, 1987.

Friedan, Betty. *The Feminine Mystique.* 1963. New York: Dell, 1984.

Goodwin, Doris Kearns. *Wait Till Next Year: A Memoir.* New York: Simon, 1997.

Harris, Alice. *The Blue Jean.* New York: Powerhouse, 2002.

Kaledin, Eugenia. *Daily Life in the United States, 1940–1959: Shifting Worlds.* Westport: Greenwood, 2000.

Layman, Richard, ed. *American Decades, 1950–1959.* Detroit: Gale, 1994.

■ Online

www.mhhe.com/motives

Click on "More Resources" then "Writing to Understand Experience."

■ ■ ■

GRUB

Scott Russell Sanders

Distinguished Professor of English at Indiana University, where he has taught since 1971, Scott Russell Sanders is also a contributing editor to Audubon. *The author of many books and essays, he has been awarded fellowships from the Guggenheim Foundation, the National Endowment for the Arts, and the Lily Endowment, among many other awards. When describing his writing process, he observes: "Of the sentences that come to me, I wait for the one that utterly convinces me, then I wait for another and another, each building upon all that went before and preparing for all that follows, until, if I am patient and fervent and lucky enough, the lines add up to something durable and whole."*

Sanders often writes about family and community, which are among the issues you will find in the following essay. As you read it, be alert for what Sanders comes to understand as he reflects upon why he is eating an unhealthy breakfast. If you are surprised that a writer could discover something about himself by considering why he eats "slithery eggs and gummy toast," ask yourself if what you eat and where you eat it says anything about who you are.

The morning paper informs me that, once again, Indiana leads the nation in fat. The announcement from the Centers for Disease Control puts it less bluntly, declaring that in 1989 our state had the highest percentage of over-weight residents. But it comes down to the same thing: on a globe where hunger is the rule, surfeit the exception, Indiana is first in fat.

I read this news on Saturday morning at a booth in Ladyman's Cafe, a one-story box of pine and brick wedged between the Christian Science Reading Room and Bloomington Shoe Repair, half a block from the town square. It is a tick after 6 A.M. My fellow breakfasters include a company of polo-shirted Gideons clutching Bibles, a housepainter whose white trousers are speckled with the colors of past jobs, two mechanics in overalls with "Lee" and "Roy" stitched on their breast pockets, three elderly couples exchanging the glazed stares of insomniacs, and a young woman in fringed leather vest and sunglasses who is browsing through a copy of *Cosmopolitan*. Except for the young woman and me, everyone here is a solid contributor to Indiana's lead in fat. And I could easily add my weight to the crowd, needing only to give in for a few weeks to my clamorous appetite.

I check my belt, which is buckled at the fourth notch. Thirty-two inches and holding. But there are signs of wear on the third and second and first notches, tokens of earlier expansions.

The lone waitress bustles to my booth. "Whatcha need, hon?" Her permed hair is a mat of curls the color of pearls. Stout as a stevedore, purple

under the eyes, puckered in the mouth, she is that indefinite age my grandmother remained for the last twenty years of her long life.

"What's good today?" I ask her.

"It's all good, same as every day." She tugs a pencil from her perm, drums
ringed fingers on the order pad. Miles to go before she sleeps. "So what'll it
be, sugar?"

I glance at the smudgy list on the chalkboard over the counter. Tempted
by the biscuits with sausage gravy, by the triple stack of hotcakes slathered in
butter, by the twin pork chops with hash browns, by the coconut cream pie
and glazed doughnuts, I content myself with a cheese omelet and toast.

"Back in two shakes," says the waitress. When she charges away, a violet
bow swings into view among her curls, the cheeriest thing I have seen so far
this morning.

I buy breakfast only when I'm on the road or feeling sorry for myself.
Today—abandoned for the weekend by my wife and kids, an inch of water in
my basement from last night's rain, the car hitting on three cylinders—I'm
feeling sorry for myself. I pick Ladyman's not for the food, which is indifferent, but for the atmosphere, which is tacky in a timeless way. It reminds me of
the truck stops and railroad-car diners and jukebox cafés where my father
would stop on our fishing trips thirty years ago. The oilcloth that covers the
scratched Formica of the table is riddled with burns. The seat of my booth
has lost its stuffing, broken down by a succession of hefty eaters. The walls,
sheathed in vinyl for easy scrubbing, are hung with fifty-dollar oil paintings
of covered bridges, pastures, and tree-lined creeks. The floor's scuffed linoleum
reveals the ghostly print of deeper layers, material for some future archaeolo-
gist of cafés. Ceiling fans turn overhead, stirring with each lazy spin the odor
of tobacco and coffee and grease.

There is nothing on the menu of Ladyman's that was not on the menus I
remember from those childhood fishing trips. But I can no longer order from
it with a child's obliviousness. What can I eat without pangs of unease, knowing
better? Not the eggs, high in cholesterol, not the hash browns, fried in oil, not
the fatty sausage or bacon or ham, not the salty pancakes made with white flour
or the saltier biscuits and gravy, not the lemon meringue pies in the glass case,
not the doughnuts glistering with sugar, not the butter, not the whole milk.

Sipping coffee (another danger) and waiting for my consolatory breakfast, I read the fine print in the article on obesity. I learn that only thirty-two
states took part in the study. Why did the other eighteen refuse? Are they embarrassed? Are they afraid their images would suffer, afraid that tourists, knowing the truth, would cross their borders without risking a meal? I learn that
Indiana is actually tied for first place with Wisconsin, at 25.7 percent overweight, so we share the honors. For Wisconsin, you think of dairies, arctic
winters, hibernation. But Indiana? We're leaders in popcorn. Our hot and
humid summers punish even the skinny, and torture the plump. Why us?
There's no comment from the Indiana Health Commissioner. This gentleman, Mr. Woodrow Myers, Jr. (who is now on his way to perform the same

office in New York City), weighed over three hundred pounds at the time of his appointment. He lost more than a hundred pounds in an effort to set a healthy example, but has since gained most of it back. He doesn't have much room to talk.

My platter arrives, the waitress urging, "Eat up, hon," before she hustles away. The omelet has been made with processed cheese, anemic and slithery. The toast is of white bread that clots on my tongue. The strawberry jelly is the color and consistency of gum erasers. My mother reared me to eat whatever was put in front of me, and so I eat. Dabbing jelly from my beard with a paper napkin as thin as the pages of the Gideons' Bibles, I look around. At six-thirty this Saturday morning, every seat is occupied. Why are we all here? Why are we wolfing down this dull, this dangerous, this terrible grub?

It's not for lack of alternatives. Bloomington is ringed by the usual necklace of fast food shops. Or you could walk from Ladyman's to restaurants that serve breakfast in half a dozen languages. Just five doors away, at the Uptown Cafe, you could dine on croissants and espresso and quiche.

So why are we here in these swaybacked booths eating poorly cooked food that is bad for us? The answer, I suspect, would help to explain why so many of us are so much bigger than we ought to be. I sniff, and the aroma of grease and peppery sausage, frying eggs and boiling coffee jerks me back into the kitchen of my grandparents' farm. I see my grandmother, barefoot and bulky, mixing biscuit dough with her blunt fingers. Then I realize that everything Ladyman's serves she would have served. This is farm food, loaded with enough sugar and fat to power a body through a slogging day of work, food you could fix out of your own garden and chicken coop and pigpen, food prepared without spices or sauces, cooked the quickest way, as a woman with chores to do and a passel of mouths to feed would cook it.

"Hot up that coffee, hon?" the waitress asks.

"Please, ma'am," I say, as though answering my grandmother. On those fishing trips, my father stopped at places like Ladyman's because there he could eat the vittles he knew from childhood, no-nonsense grub he never got at home from his wife, a city woman who had studied nutrition, and who had learned her cuisine from a Bostonian mother and a Middle Eastern father. I stop at places like Ladyman's because I am the grandson of farmers, the son of a farm boy. If I went from booth to booth, interviewing the customers, most likely I would find hay and hogs in each person's background, maybe one generation back, maybe two. My sophisticated friends would not eat here for love or money. They will eat peasant food only if it comes from other countries—hummus and pita, fried rice and prawns, liver pâté, tortellini, tortillas, tortes. Never black-eyed peas, never grits, never short ribs or hush puppies or shoofly pie. This is farm food, and we who sit here and shovel it down are bound to farming by memory or imagination.

With the seasoning of memory, the slithery eggs and gummy toast and rubbery jam taste better. I lick my platter clean.

15

Barely slowing down as she cruises past, the waitress refills my coffee once more, the oil-slicked brew jostling in the glass pot. "Need anything else, sugar?"

My nostalgic tongue wins out over my judgment, leading me to say, "Could I get some biscuits and honey?"

"You sure can."

20

The biscuits arrive steaming hot. I pitch in. When I worked on farms as a boy, loading hay bales onto wagons and forking silage to cows, shoveling manure out of horse barns, digging postholes and pulling barbed wire, I could eat the pork chops and half a dozen eggs my neighbors fed me for breakfast, eat corn bread and sugar in a quart of milk for dessert at lunch, eat ham steaks and mashed potatoes and three kinds of pie for supper, eat a bowl of hand-cranked ice cream topped with maple syrup at bedtime, and stay skinny as a junkyard dog. Not so any longer. Not so for any of us. Eat like a farmer while living like an insurance salesman, an accountant, a beautician, or a truck driver, and you're going to get fat in a hurry. While true farmers have always stored their food in root cellars and silos, in smoke shacks and on canning shelves, we carry our larders with us on haunches and ribs.

The Gideons file out, Bibles under their arms, bellies over their belts.

With the last of my biscuits I mop up the honey, thinking of the path the wheat traveled from Midwestern fields to my plate, thinking of the clover distilled into honey, of grass become butter, the patient industry of cows and bees and the keepers of cows and bees. Few of us still work on the land, even here in Indiana. Few of us raise big families, few of us look after herds of animals, few of us bend our backs all day, few of us build or plow or bake or churn. Secretaries of Agriculture tell us that only four percent of our population feeds the other ninety-six percent. I have known and admired enough farmers to find that a gloomy statistic.

I am stuffed. I rise, stretch, shuffle toward the cash register. The woman in the fringed vest looks up from her *Cosmopolitan* as I pass her booth. She might figure me for a carpenter, noticing my beard, the scraggly hair down over my collar, my banged-up hands, my patched jeans, my flannel shirt the color of the biscuits I just ate, my clodhopper boots. Or maybe she'll guess mechanic, maybe garbageman, electrician, janitor, maybe even farmer.

I pluck a toothpick from a box near the cash register and idly chew on it   25
while the waitress makes change. "You hurry back," she calls after me.

"I will, ma'am," I tell her.

On the sidewalk out front of Ladyman's, I throw my toothpick in a green trash barrel that is stenciled with the motto "Fight Dirty." I start the car, wincing at the sound of three cylinders clapping. I remember yesterday's rainwater shimmering in the basement, remember the house empty of my family, who are away frolicking with relatives. Before letting out the clutch, I let out my belt a notch, to accommodate those biscuits. Thirty-three inches. One inch closer to the ranks of the fat. I decide to split some wood this morning, turn the compost from the right-hand bin to the left, lay up stones along the edge of the wildflower bed, sweat hard enough to work up an appetite for lunch.

QUESTIONS FOR DISCUSSION

1. Why is Sanders eating breakfast in a restaurant? Why has he chosen Lady-man's when he could be dining on "croissants and espresso and quiche"?
2. Why is it that Sanders hesitates to eat food he enjoys? How has his life changed since he was a young man?
3. The essay begins with what turns out to be an exaggeration about Indiana. Why do you think Sanders waits for several paragraphs before reporting more about the study first cited in paragraph 1?
4. What role does the waitress play in this essay? How does she help Sanders enjoy a bad meal?
5. Consider the description of himself that Sanders provides in paragraphs 3 and 24. Why is it misleading? What is the woman reading *Cosmopolitan* unlikely to realize?

SUGGESTIONS FOR WRITING

1. Are there any foods you enjoy even though you know they aren't good for you? Of all the things you eat, is there any food you are most likely to eat when you are alone? Write an essay about eating that will help you to understand something about yourself.
2. Visit a place that reminds you of your past. Write a description of it that will make readers understand what you see and feel when you visit there.
3. Spend some time in a coffee shop or café, recording in a journal what you witness there. Then write an essay exploring how you felt in that place and what factors contributed to that feeling.

■ **LINKS**

■ Within the Book

In "The Sad Comedy of Really Bad Food" (pages 266-269), Dara Moskowitz shows how a professional food critic writes about a restaurant.

■ Elsewhere in Print

Critzer, Greg. *Fat Land: How Americans Became the Fattest People on Earth.* Boston: Mariner, 2004.

Mamet, David. *The Cabin: Reminiscence and Diversion.* New York: Turtle Bay, 1992.

Sanders, Scott Russell. *The Country of Language.* Minneapolis: Milkweed, 1999.

■ **Elsewhere in Print (continued)**

————. *The Force of Spirit.* Boston: Beacon, 2000.

————. *Hunting for Hope: A Father's Journey.* Boston: Beacon, 1998.

————. *The Paradise of Bombs.* Athens: U of Georgia P, 1987.

————. *Secrets of the Universe.* Boston: Beacon, 1991.

■ **Online**

www.mhhe.com/motives

Click on "More Resources" then "Writing to Understand Experience."

■ ■ ■

THE MEANINGS OF A WORD

Gloria Naylor

Born and raised in New York City and a graduate of Brooklyn College, Gloria Naylor was inspired to write fiction after reading Toni Morrison's The Bluest Eye *in 1971, the first novel that she had read by an African-American woman and a work that she has described as "so painfully eloquent that it becomes a song." Since then, she has done graduate work in African-American studies at Yale University and has taught at the University of Pennsylvania, Princeton University, and Brandeis University, among other schools. Her novels include* The Women of Brewster Place *(1982), which won the American Book Award in 1983. She is also the founder of a multimedia production company, One Way Productions, dedicated to presenting positive images of black cultures.*

Naylor recognizes that terms such as black *and* white *are problematic and in a lecture at Yale stated, "To be black or white in America is nothing but a political construct." In the following selection, first published by the* New York Times Magazine, *Naylor explores how language is constructed and used by focusing on a term that is usually associated with racial prejudice. As she does so, drawing upon childhood memories, she shows how the meaning of a term depends on the rhetorical situation in which it appears: who is using the word, in what context, for what purpose, and to what audience.*

Language is the subject. It is the written form with which I've managed to keep the wolf away from the door and, in diaries, to keep my sanity. In spite of this, I consider the written word inferior to the spoken, and much of the frustration experienced by novelists is the awareness that whatever we manage to capture in even the most transcendent passages falls far short of the richness of life. Dialogue achieves its power in the dynamics of a fleeting moment of sight, sound, smell and touch.

I'm not going to enter the debate here about whether it is language that shapes reality or vice versa. That battle is doomed to be waged whenever we seek intermittent reprieve from the chicken and egg dispute. I will simply take the position that the spoken word, like the written word, amounts to a nonsensical arrangement of sounds or letters without a consensus that assigns "meaning." And building from the meanings of what we hear, we order reality. Words themselves are innocuous; it is the consensus that gives them true power.

I remember the first time I heard the word "nigger." In my third-grade class, our math tests were being passed down the rows, and as I handed the papers to a little boy in back of me, I remarked that once again he had re-

ceived a much lower mark than I did. He snatched his test from me and spit
out that word. Had he called me a nymphomaniac or a necrophiliac, I couldn't
have been more puzzled. I didn't know what a nigger was, but I knew that
whatever it meant, it was something he shouldn't have called me. This was
verified when I raised my hand, and in a loud voice repeated what he had
said and watched the teacher scold him for using a "bad" word. I was later to
go home and ask the inevitable question that every black parent must face—
"Mommy, what does 'nigger' mean?"

And what exactly did it mean? Thinking back, I realize that this could
not have been the first time the word was used in my presence. I was part of
a large extended family that had migrated from the rural South after World
War II and formed a close-knit network that gravitated around my maternal
grandparents. Their ground-floor apartment in one of the buildings they
owned in Harlem was a weekend mecca for my immediate family, along with
countless aunts, uncles, and cousins who brought along assorted friends. It
was a bustling and open house with assorted neighbors and tenants popping
in and out to exchange bits of gossip, pick up an old quarrel or referee the
ongoing checkers game in which my grandmother cheated shamelessly. They
were all there to let down their hair and put up their feet after a week of labor
in the factories, laundries, and shipyards of New York.

Amid the clamor, which could reach deafening proportions—two or   5
three conversations going on simultaneously, punctuated by the sound of a
baby's crying somewhere in the back rooms or out on the street—there was
still a rigid set of rules about what was said and how. Older children were sent
out of the living room when it was time to get into the juicy details about
"you-know-who" up on the third floor who had gone and gotten herself
"p-r-e-g-n-a-n-t!" But my parents, knowing that I could spell well beyond
my years, always demanded that I follow the others out to play. Beyond sexual
misconduct and death, everything else was considered harmless for our young
ears. And so among the anecdotes of the triumphs and disappointments in the
various workings of their lives, the word "nigger" was used in my presence,
but it was set within contexts and inflections that caused it to register in my
mind as something else.

In the singular, the word was always applied to a man who had distinguished himself in some situation that brought their approval for his strength,
intelligence or drive:

"Did Johnny really do that?"

"I'm telling you, that nigger pulled in $6,000 of overtime last year. Said
he got enough for a down payment on a house."

When used with a possessive adjective by a woman—"my nigger"—it
became a term of endearment for husband or boyfriend. But it could be more
than just a term applied to a man. In their mouths it became the pure essence
of manhood—a disembodied force that channeled their past history of struggle
and present survival against the odds into a victorious statement of being: "Yeah,
that old foreman found out quick enough—you don't mess with a nigger."

In the plural, it became a description of some group within the commu- *10*
nity that had overstepped the bounds of decency as my family defined it: Parents who neglected their children, a drunken couple who fought in public,
people who simply refused to look for work, those with excessively dirty
mouths or unkempt households were all "trifling niggers." This particular circle could forgive hard times, unemployment, the occasional bout of depression—they had gone through all of that themselves—but the unforgivable sin
was lack of self-respect.

A woman could never be a "nigger" in the singular, with its connotation
of confirming worth. The noun "girl" was its closest equivalent in that sense,
but only when used in direct address and regardless of the gender doing the
addressing. "Girl" was a token of respect for a woman. The one-syllable word
was drawn out to sound like three in recognition of the extra ounce of wit,
nerve or daring that the woman had shown in the situation under discussion.

"G-i-r-l, stop. You mean you said that to his face?"

But if the word was used in a third-person reference or shortened so that
it almost snapped out of the mouth, it always involved some element of communal disapproval. And age became an important factor in these exchanges. It
was only between individuals of the same generation, or from an older person
to a younger (but never the other way around), that "girl" would be considered a compliment.

I don't agree with the argument that use of the word "nigger" at this social
stratum of the black community was an internalization of racism. The dynamics were the exact opposite: The people in my grandmother's living room
took a word that whites used to signify worthlessness or degradation and rendered it impotent. Gathering there together, they transformed "nigger" to signify the varied and complex human beings they knew themselves to be. If the
word were to disappear totally from the mouths of even the most liberal of
white society, no one in that room was naïve enough to believe it would disappear from white minds. Meeting the word head-on, they proved it had absolutely nothing to do with the way they were determined to live their lives.

So there must have been dozens of times that the word "nigger" was spoken *15*
in front of me before I reached the third grade. But I didn't "hear" it until it
was said by a small pair of lips that had already learned it could be a way to
humiliate me. That was the word I went home and asked my mother about.
And since she knew that I had to grow up in America, she took me in her lap
and explained.

QUESTIONS FOR DISCUSSION

1. What two motives led Naylor to become a writer?
2. How does Naylor describe her family background? Why is it relevant to
   the question she is exploring in this essay?

3. How many different meanings of *nigger* does Naylor provide in this essay? Why is it that the word can be understood only in the context in which it is used and the inflection with which it is spoken? What elements of the situation described in paragraph 3 alerted Naylor to the use of a "bad word" before the teacher confirms that she had been insulted?
4. What does Naylor mean when she writes that some people consider the use of *nigger* by blacks to be "an internalization of racism"? Why does she believe that it shows the opposite?
5. Consider the final paragraph of this essay. What does the last sentence imply?
6. This essay has also been published under the title "Mommy, What Does 'Nigger' Mean?" When preparing this edition of *Motives for Writing,* the book's author consulted with Naylor. She told him that either title was acceptable to her and generously allowed him to choose the title that he thought most appropriate for students. Did he make the right choice?

SUGGESTIONS FOR WRITING

1. Identify another word that can be either insulting or affectionate depending on how it is used. Explore what the varied meanings of your term reveal about the people who use it.
2. According to an expression known to many children, "Sticks and stones can break your bones, but words can never hurt you." Is this true? Write an essay exploring the extent to which words can cause injury.
3. Write an essay focused on a lesson about language you learned as a child and whether you have chosen to honor that lesson as an adult.

▌ **LINKS**

▪ **Within the Book**

Racism is also the focus of selections by Stuart Taylor, Jr. (pages 476–479), Martin Luther King, Jr. (pages 488–501 and 535–538).

▪ **Elsewhere in Print**

Montgomery, Maxine Lavon, ed. *Conversations with Gloria Naylor.* Oxford: UP of Mississippi, 2004.
Naylor, Gloria. *Bailey's Café.* New York: Harcourt, 1992.
———. *Linden Hills.* New York: Ticknor, 1985.
———. *Mama Day.* New York: Ticknor, 1988.
———. *The Women of Brewster Place.* New York: Viking, 1982.
Pemberton, Gayle. *The Hottest Water in Chicago: On Family, Race, Time, and American Culture.* Boston: Faber, 1992.

■ **Elsewhere in Print (continued)**

Tsesis, Alexander. *Destructive Messages: How Hate Speech Paves the Way for Harmful Social Movements.* New York: New York UP, 2002.

■ **Online**

www.mhhe.com/motives

Click on "More Resources" then "Writing to Understand Experience."

■ ■ ■

LIFE WITH FATHER

Itabari Njeri

A graduate of the Columbia University School of Journalism, Itabari Njeri (born Jill Stacy Moreland) is a contributing editor at the Los Angeles Times Magazine. *In 1990, she won the American Book Award for her memoir* Every Good-Bye Ain't Gone: Family Portraits and Personal Escapades. *Although she has worked as a professional actress and singer as well as a journalist, she is best known for writing memoirs. When discussing the impulse to write about experience, in an interview for* Contemporary Authors, *she said: "To impose order on the chaos of memory is a universal impulse fueling the desire to write autobiography. But first and foremost, I wanted to illuminate the beauty, pain, and complexity of a particular piece of the African diaspora, a piece central to the American experience. I wanted to tell the truth and make it sing."*

Njeri discusses both race and singing in the following selection. The scene is a Harlem apartment during the early 1960s—a time when African Americans were struggling for civil rights. The scene thus includes not only the apartment but also the era in which the author was growing up. As you read this account of family conflict, think about how racial prejudice in the world beyond the apartment can help account for the personal conflicts that happened within it.

Daddy wore boxer shorts when he worked; that's all. He'd sit for hours reading and writing at a long, rectangular table covered with neat stacks of *I. F. Stone's Weekly, The Nation, The New Republic,* and the handwritten pages of his book in progress, *The Tolono Station and Beyond.* A Mott's applesauce jar filled with Teacher's scotch was a constant, and his own forerunner of today's wine coolers was the ever-present chaser: ginger ale and Manischewitz Concord grape wine in a tall, green iced-tea glass.

As he sat there, his beer belly weighing down the waistband of his shorts, I'd watch. I don't know if he ever saw me. I hid from him at right angles. From the bend of the hallway, at the end of a long, dark, L-shaped corridor in our Harlem apartment, it was at least thirty feet to the living room where my father worked, framed by the doorway. I sat cross-legged on the cold linoleum floor and inspected his seated, six-foot-plus figure through a telescope formed by my forefinger and thumb: bare feet in thonged sandals, long hairy legs that rose toward the notorious shorts (I hated those shorts, wouldn't bring my girlfriends home because of those shorts), breasts that could fill a B cup, and a long neck on which a balding head rested. Viewed in isolation, I thought perhaps I'd see him clearer, know him better.

Daddy was a philosopher, a Marxist historian, an exceptional teacher, and a fine tenor. He had a good enough voice to be as great a concert artist as

John McCormack, one of his favorites. The obstacles to that career couldn't have been much greater than the ones he actually overcame.

The state of Georgia, where my father grew up, established its version of the literacy test in 1908, the year he was born. If you substituted Georgia for Mississippi in the story that Lerone Bennett Jr. relates in *Before the Mayflower: A History of Black America,* the main character could easily have been my father: A black teacher, a graduate of Eton and Harvard, presents himself to a Mississippi registrar. The teacher is told to read the state constitution and several books. He does. The registrar produces a passage in Greek, which the teacher reads. Then another in Latin. Then other passages in French, German, and Spanish, all of which the teacher reads. The registrar finally holds up a page of Chinese characters and asks: "What does this mean?" The teacher replies: "It means you don't want me to vote."

Apocryphal, perhaps, but the tale exemplified enough collective experi-　5
ence that I heard my father tell virtually the same story about a former Morehouse College classmate to a buddy over the phone one afternoon. At the punchline, he fell into a fit of laughter, chuckling hard into a balled fist he held at his mouth. Finally, he said, "Fred, I'll have to call you back," then fell back on the bed, in his boxer shorts, laughing at the ceiling.

He claimed he burst out laughing like this once in a class at Harvard. A law professor, discussing some constitutional issue in class, singled out my father and said, "In this matter, regarding men of your race—".

"Which race is that?" my father boomed, cutting him off, "the 50 yard or the 100?" But it seemed to me he always related that particular tale with a sneer on his lips.

He'd been at Harvard studying law on a postdoctoral scholarship from 1942 to 1943. After receiving his Ph.D. in philosophy from the University of Toronto ten years earlier, he had headed toward the dust bowls others were escaping in the mid-1930s and became the editor of a black newspaper, the *Oklahoma Eagle,* in Tulsa. He eventually returned to academia and by 1949 was the head of the philosophy department at Morgan State University in Baltimore. That's where he met my mother, a nurse many years his junior.

My mother—who commits nothing to paper, speaks of the past cryptically, and believes all unpleasantries are best kept under a rug—once leaked the fact that she and my father took me to a parade in Brooklyn when I was about three. We were standing near the arch at Grand Army Plaza when he suddenly hauled off and punched her in the mouth, with me in her arms. My mother, a very gentle and naive woman, said the whole thing left her in a state of shock. My father had never been violent before.

They separated, and I seldom saw my father again until my parents re-　10
united when I was seven. We moved into my father's six-room apartment on 129th Street, between Convent Avenue and St. Nicholas Terrace. It was certainly far more spacious than the apartment I'd lived in with my mother on

St. James Place in Brooklyn. The immediate neighborhood was an attractive, hilly section of Harlem, just a few blocks from City College. All things considered, I hated it. More precisely, I hated my father, so I hated it all.

Because of his past leftist political affiliations, Daddy had lost his government and university jobs. Now, out of necessity but also desire, he decided to devote his time to teaching younger people. He wanted to reach them at a stage in their lives when he felt he could make a difference. He joined the faculty of a Jersey City high school and began teaching journalism, history, and English. He also taught English at night to foreign-born students at City College. His students, I came to learn, loved him; his daughter found it hard to. I made the mistake of calling him Pop—once. He said, "Don't ever call me that again. If you don't like calling me Daddy, you can call me Dr. Moreland."

Once, my mother deserted me, leaving me alone with him. She went to Atlanta for several weeks with my baby brother to tend my ailing Grandma Hattie, my father's mother. Since I hadn't known this man most of my seven years on the planet, and didn't like him much now that I did, I asked him if I could stay around the corner with a family friend, Aunt Pearl. "If she asks you to stay, fine. But don't ask her," he told me. Naturally I asked her.

When he asked me if I had asked her, I hesitated. But I was not a child inclined to lie. So I said, "I don't want to lie. I asked her." I got a beating for that, a brutal beating with a belt that left welts and bruises on my legs for months.

My father felt children should be hit for any infraction. Further, they should be seen and not heard, speak only when spoken to, etc. From the day he hit me, the latter became my philosophy, too. I never consciously decided to stop speaking to my father, but for the next ten years, I rarely initiated a conversation with him. Later he would tell me, "You were a very strange child."

But if I would not accept him as a father, my curiosity would not let me   15
deny him as a teacher. One day, a question about the nature of truth compelled a thaw in my emotional cold war—nothing less could have. Truth changes, a classmate in the seventh grade had insisted that day. It is constant, I argued, and went to my father for confirmation.

People's perceptions change, I explained. New information debunks the lies of the past, but the truth was always there. And I told my father what I had told my mostly white classmates in a Bronx junior high school at the height of the civil rights movement: Black people were always human beings worthy of the same rights other Americans enjoyed, but it took hundreds of years of a slave system that dehumanized the master as well as the slave and a social revolution before most white Americans would accept that truth.

My father turned from his worktable, took off his glasses, with their broken right temple piece, and released a long and resonant "Yesssss." And then he spoke to me of a rational cosmos and what Lincoln had to do with Plato. When our philosophical discussion ended, we each went to our separate corners.

My father had a beaten, black upright piano in the parlor, badly out of tune. But its bench was a treasure of ancient sheet music: Vincent Youman's "Through the Years," with a picture of Gladys Swarthout on the frayed cover. And I loved the chord changes to "Spring Is Here."

I ventured from the sanctuary of my blue-walled room one summer afternoon, walking down the long hallway toward the kitchen, then stopped abruptly. I heard my father in the kitchen several feet away; he was making an ice-cream soda, something as forbidden to him as alcohol since he was a diabetic. I heard the clink of a metal spoon against a glass as he sang, "For I lately took a notion for to cross the briny ocean, and I'm off to Philadelphia in the morning." It was an Irish folk song made famous by John McCormack. I backed up. Too late. He danced across the kitchen threshold in his boxer shorts, stopped when he spotted me in the shadows, then shook his head. He smiled, lifted one leg and both arms in a Jackie Gleason "and away we go" motion, then slid off.

Minutes later he called me. "Jill the Pill, you know this song!" I knew all the songs and wrote down the words to "Moon River" for him. Then he asked me to sing it. I was always ready to sing, even for my father. 20

He sat on the edge of his bed with the lyrics in his hand as I sang. When I finished the phrase "We're after the same rainbow's end, waitin' round the bend, my huckleberry friend," my daddy looked at me and said what others would tell me years later but with far less poetry: "My girl, you have the celestial vibration." And then he asked me to sing it again and told me it was "wonderful." Then I left him.

For days, maybe weeks, a tense calm would reign in the apartment. Then, without warning, the hall would fill with harsh voices. My father stood in the narrow, shadowy space hitting my mother. "Put it down," he yelled. "Put it down or I'll . . ."

My mother had picked up a lamp in a lame effort to ward off his blows. His shouting had awakened me. I'd been sick in bed with the flu and a high fever. When he saw me open my bedroom door he yelled, "Get back in your room." I did, my body overtaken by tremors and the image of my mother branded on my eyeballs. I swore that I would never let anyone do that to me or to anyone else I had the power to help. I had no power to help my mother. It was an oath with terrible consequences, one I'd have to disavow to permit myself the vulnerability of being human.

I know my father's fury was fueled by his sense of insignificance. He felt himself to be an intellectual giant boxed in by mental midgets. Unlike Ralph Ellison, Paul Robeson, or Richard Wright°—all contemporaries and acquaintances of my father's—he was never acknowledged by the dominant culture

---

°*Ralph Ellison:* American novelist (1914-1994) best known for *The Invisible Man* (1952). *Paul Robeson:* American singer, actor, and political activist (1898-1976). *Richard Wright:* American writer (1908-1960), best known for *Native Son* (1940).

whose recognition he sought. He could be found, Ellison once told me, pontificating in Harlem barbershops, elucidating the dialogues of Plato for a captive audience of draped men, held prone, each with a straight-edge razor pressed against his cheek.

My father's unreconciled identities—the classic schizophrenia of being black and an American, the contradictions of internalizing whole the cultural values of a society that sees you, when it sees you at all, as life in one of its lower forms—stoked his alcoholism. And since my father at once critiqued the society that denied him and longed for its approbation, he lived with the pain-filled consciousness of one who knows he is a joke. I think sometimes he laughed the hardest, so often did I stumble upon him alone, chuckling into his balled fist at some silent, invisible comedian.

When his drunken rages ended, he slept for days, spread out on the bed wearing only his boxer shorts. I watched him on those days, too, daring to come closer, safe with the knowledge that Morpheus° held him. I examined his face, wondering who he was and why he was. As I watched, he'd lift his head off the pillow, then fall back muttering: "Truth and justice will prevail."

QUESTIONS FOR DISCUSSION

1. Njeri opens her essay with a vivid description of her father sitting in his underpants and drinking scotch out of an applesauce jar. What do the details in this opening reveal, and how do they prepare for the essay that follows?
2. What makes Daddy laugh in paragraphs 4–6? Is the laughter good-humored?
3. Njeri records that she hated Daddy and "would not accept him as a father." Does she succeed in making this response understandable to you as a reader? What personal factors kept the two in "separate corners"?
4. Consider Njeri's discussion of the family violence she witnessed and experienced as a child. What does she understand now that she is an adult?
5. Does Njeri seem at all reconciled with the past she is recalling? Were you led to feel any sympathy for her father?
6. How do you interpret the concluding line, "'Truth and justice will prevail'"? What does this belief say about Njeri's father? Does it have any additional significance for writers trying to understand experience?

SUGGESTIONS FOR WRITING

1. Njeri's father tells her, "You were a very strange child." Think about times when your behavior seemed strange to others, even though it made perfect sense to you. Write about one such time so that readers can understand what the people around you failed to grasp at the time.

°*Morpheus:* In Greek mythology, one of the children of Sleep.

2. When she was in junior high school, Njeri believed, "perceptions change
   [. . .]. New information debunks the lies of the past, but the truth was always there." Write about a person toward whom your own perceptions
   have changed as you have grown more mature. Describe that person as
   you initially saw him or her, and then record what you have since come to
   understand.
3. Write an essay about how you have determined your race and how this
   racial identity has influenced your life.

■ LINKS

■ Within the Book

Martin Luther King, Jr.'s "Letter from Birmingham Jail" (pages 488–501) provides background that can help you understand the father's anger in Njeri's
essay.

■ Elsewhere in Print

Ellison, Ralph. *Invisible Man.* 1952. New York: Vintage, 1995.
hooks, bell. *Yearning: Race, Gender, and Cultural Politics.* Boston: South End,
    1990.
Njeri, Itabari. *Every Good-Bye Ain't Gone: Family Portraits and Personal
    Escapades.* New York: Times, 1990.
————. *The Last Plantation: Color, Conflict, and Identity: Reflections of a New
    York Black.* Boston: Houghton, 1997.
————. *Sushi and Grits: The Challenge of Diversity.* New York: Random, 1993.
West, Cornel. *Race Matters.* Boston: Beacon, 1993.
Wright, Richard. *Black Boy: A Record of Childhood and Youth.* 1945. New York:
    Harper, 1998.

■ Online

www.mhhe.com/motives
Click on "More Resources" then "Writing to Understand Experience."

■ ■ ■

COUNT ME OUT OF THE HARD LABOR, PLEASE

Rick Marin

Born in Toronto, Rick Marin is a senior writer for Newsweek *who used to write (under another name) an advice column about men for a major women's magazine. He is also a regular contributor to the* New York Times, *which published the following article in 2004, a year after Marin married the author of an advice book for women. In "Count Me Out of the Hard Labor, Please," he focuses on why he did not want to be in the delivery room when his wife was giving birth to their first child, and he locates his concerns within cultural expectations that he finds questionable.*

Marin is best known for a work in which he focuses on his life as a single man: Cad: Confessions of a Toxic Bachelor. *When discussing his life as a writer, he observes: "Without a deadline I would produce nothing. Journalism is excellent training, but expository writing is very different from a narrative. I wanted my memoir,* Cad, *to read like a novel and had to unlearn many habits of the fifteen years in newspapers and magazines. Like don't give away the ending at the beginning. But writing is rewriting. Wait, let me rephrase that. . . ." One of the women who dated Marin responds to* Cad *on pages 79–80, providing an example of how Marin's work can provoke strong responses.*

A few months into the pregnancy, my wife informed her doctor that I'd just as soon skip the delivery-room bit, and that I had her blessing.

"Oh, he'll be there," the obstetrician instructed, in her take-no-prisoners tone. "He wouldn't want to miss it."

And that was that. The doctor dismissed my reservations—a combination of squeamishness and an urge to rebel against the whole "we're pregnant" culture—as casually as she might dismiss a craving for Pickles Garcia ice cream. I had no say in the matter.

Whose fatherhood is this, anyway?

Open *Us Weekly* or *The Star* and notice how celebrity dads are squeezed out of the picture as their wives' bellies swell. Before she gave birth in January, the 172-pound Kate Hudson was everywhere, worshiped like some latter-day fertility icon, the Venus of Wilshiredorf.

But Chris Robinson, Ms. Hudson's husband, and Chris Martin, married to another new mother, Gwyneth Paltrow, seem to have had their rock-star mojo sapped by pram-pushing duty for ever yummier mummies. Guy Ritchie, one of the mas macho directors around, strollers Madonna's little ones to play dates with a cabala bracelet on his wrist.

This from the Guy who made "Snatch"?

At our first birthing class, I made a crack about how I had tried to get out of it, but the doctor wouldn't let me. No laughs. You could hear crickets chirping. I stopped short of tapping an imaginary microphone and asking, "Is this thing on?" But I got the message: Such heresies are not to be uttered.

The instructor asked the husbands, "Who better to coach a mother through this ordeal than the one who knows her best, who she's closest to?" Ilene and I—who feel like the oldest and most immature couple in the room—looked at each other and agreed there was only one person for the job: her yoga teacher.

Surely the last person a woman wants relaxing her in the throes of child-   10
birth is her *husband.* Isn't he the one she's cursing out like a sailor for getting her into this in the first place?

Dr. Fernand Lamaze, the Frenchman who developed the class's "he-he-he" breathing and relaxation techniques in the 1950's, referred to the mother's birthing coach as a monitrice—a word whose feminine suffix, I thought, suggested he did not have the father in mind. But I held my tongue, took a "deep, cleansing breath" and laid off the Insensitive Guy routine.

I'm not saying we should go back to the dark ages when a man's place was boozing at a corner bar and nursing a fistful of cigars while the mother of his child endured the agonies of labor. (Am I?) But these days he's not even allowed to pace in the waiting room. Attendance in the delivery room has become mandatory. As if only a craven weirdo wouldn't jump at the chance to witness what, in the "Friends" finale, Chandler described as "one disgusting miracle." You've got to be right in there, stirrup-side, severing the umbilical cord with one hand and wielding a video camera with the other.

Speaking of zooming camera lenses, it occurs to me that my fear of the delivery room might date to 1985, when I was forced to see "Bring On the Night," the documentary about the making of Sting's first album. The footage of Trudie Styler giving birth to their first child haunts me to this day.

Some men swear cutting the umbilical cord is the greatest moment of their lives, though I've yet to meet one who bragged of biting it off. The more delicate fellows ask if it would be O.K. if they just hang back, maybe by the mother's head, supplying ice chips and massage, then suddenly find themselves pressed into active duty. That happened to A. J. Jacobs, an editor at *Esquire,* when his first was born three months ago.

"The doctors want you to go right up to the front lines," he said, still   15
traumatized. "My advice is, when the ob-gyn says, 'You're going to want to see this,' you probably aren't going to want to see it."

There is an alternative, Mr. Jacobs suggested. *The Know-It-All* (Simon & Schuster), his coming memoir of reading every volume of the *Encyclopaedia Britannica,* includes the following passage on a ritual last recorded in the Basque country during the 1950's, called couvade, "the ancient custom of the father taking to bed during the birth of his child and simulating the symptoms of labor":

"In its extreme form, the mother goes back to work as soon as possible, often the same day, and waits on the father. Its social function seems to emphasize the role of the father in reproduction."

At last, the role of the father defined not as mere helpmeet, drone or coach, but as . . . a guy in a beret pretending to be pregnant.

"No offense to the Basques," Mr. Jacobs said. "But couvade just seems sad, a desperate cry for attention. The mom is getting all the glory for creating a human life, so the dad says, 'Hey look at me! I can contort *my* face too!'"

But I understand the impulse. For the past few months, I've been going around saying, "I'm pregnant." With heavy irony, I announce, to appalled stares: "Oh, sure, she's *carrying* the baby. But I'm the one with the issues: weight gain, mood swings, decorating the nursery."   20

Irony or no, this is a classic case of sympathetic pregnancy, also known as Couvade Syndrome. And the "Hey, look at me!" impulse only gets worse, I'm told, once the baby is born.

This sad cry for attention is the core satirical gag of "The Stepford Wives." The first time around, in the 70's, "Stepford" played on fears of a feminized future. In the remake, set in the present, women have lapped men in the gender-equality race. They run the show, literally. Nicole Kidman is president of a TV network until she's packed off to Stepford, Conn., where men command their womenfolk with gilded remote controls.

But you know they're not going to get away with it. This is Nicole Kidman they're dealing with. We all know who really controls the remote. Even on Father's Day, it's tuned to the Maternity Channel. The movie has it backward. A far more chilling remake would been "The Stepford Husbands."

As for the delivery room, "Oh, I'll be there," he said, in a robotic tone. "I wouldn't want to miss it."

Doctor's orders.   25

COMPANION TEXT   *I Dated Rick Marin*

This is an excerpt from an article published on February 27, 2003, in Salon, *an on-line magazine.*

Imagine this nightmare scenario: As a young reporter in New York—a fact checker, actually, if you want to be technical about it—you hook up with a divorced, older writer. It's a messy, booze-filled affair, because at the time, yours always were. [. . .] He makes you nervous—he's so much smoother, more urbane, more established than you are—and you wonder what he's doing with you. But he also laughs at your jokes, praises your looks, has flattering predictions about your career. You figure that maybe babes his own age aren't interested in him because he's not that cute. In fact, to friends who haven't met him, you say he looks like Bart's glasses-wearing, asthmatic friend Milhouse on "The Simpsons."

So gingerly, once, you hint at future hookups, some continuity. He looks at you like you have two heads. Then, he starts answering your calls erratically—nothing, nothing, and just as you're about to fade away, a phone call. Confused, you pursue, pursue, pursue—until you're humiliated and just sick of yourself. When you run into him months later in front of Banana Republic, his eyes dart around like he's a rodent trying to escape. You feel guilty, ashamed; you leave him alone. And then you forget about him.

Until six years after, that is. That's when you find out that, while all this time you've been trying to repress the memory of your yucky, low-point-of-life misdirected affection, Milhouse has been reveling in the memories. Maybe not of you, personally, but of other girls like you, girls who had sex too quickly and then called a lot, girls who thought that when he said he was interested in them, he actually was. In fact, your old flame has been thinking of himself as quite the chick magnet, the rascal, the Casanova. How do you know? Because your former lover is Rick Marin, and he's just published his memoir, "Cad: Confessions of a Toxic Bachelor." . . .

There is an argument to be made that what makes Rick a cad is not what he did, but that he wrote about it. "I was a critic, I was a takedown artist, a master of finding fault," he writes of his stint as a TV critic at the *Washington Times*. On a basic level, he's taken the same approach to his sex life, and that of his partners, selling them out for a book-and-movie deal. No one escapes his acid tongue. He lavishes a string of choice adjectives on his ex-wife: "petulant," "inscrutable," "troubled," "weird." And heaps scornful prose on girls who did nothing wrong but have the bad sense to sleep with him, girls like "the chubby speech therapist in L.A. who flopped around the Sunset Marquis hot tub like a manatee."

Cad? Hmm. Maybe there's a better word.

Sandy M. Fernandez

QUESTIONS FOR DISCUSSION

1. Marin's essay incorporates references to celebrities in the news when he published this piece. Do these references make his work seem dated? Or does his material still seem timely?
2. By using phrases such as "take–no–prisoners tone," Marin implies that he is one of the few men resisting what he calls "the whole 'we're pregnant' culture." How do you respond to this exaggeration as a reader?
3. In paragraph 12, Marin raises the question "Am I?" within parentheses. What does this question reveal or accomplish?
4. What does Marin's discussion of couvades contribute to this essay? How would the piece change if it was omitted?
5. Just before concluding this work, Marin discusses a remake of a movie that involves men having unnatural control over their wives. Is this discussion relevant to his topic?
6. How seriously do you think Marin expects readers to take him?

SUGGESTIONS FOR WRITING

1. Review a selection of current magazines that focus on the lives of celebrities and then write an essay about how pregnancy is now being featured.
2. Read what Sandy Fernandez reports on pages 79–80 about her experience with Marin, and then write an essay focused on how this information affects your response to "Count Me Out of the Hard Labor, Please." As you do so, consider whether it is best to judge a work simply on its own or whether it is useful to know about the author's background.
3. Write an essay in which you explore your own experience or expectations for pregnancy or childbirth.

LINKS

■ Within the Book

The public presentation of what have come to be called "celebrities" is also discussed by YiLing Chen-Josephson in "Sweet and Lowdown" (pages 258–264).

■ Elsewhere in Print

Bleiden, Larry, and Irene Zutzell. *I'll Never Have Sex with You Again!: Tales from the Delivery Room.* New York: Fireside, 2002.

Brockenbrough, Martha. *It Could Happen to You: Diary of a Pregnancy and Beyond.* Kansas City: Andrews, 2002.

Cancellaro, Cecelia A. *Pregnancy Stories: Real Women Share the Joys, Fears, Thrills, and Anxieties of Pregnancy from Conception to Birth.* Oakland: New Harbinger, 2001.

Levin, Ira. *The Stepford Wives.* New York: Harper, 2004.

Marin, Rick. *CAD: Confessions of a Toxic Bachelor.* New York: Hyperion, 2003.

Savage, Beverly, and Diana Simkin. *Preparation for Birth: The Complete Guide to the Lamaze Method.* New York: Ballantine, 1987.

■ Online

www.mhhe.com/motives

Click on "More Resources" then "Writing to Understand Experience."

■ ■ ■

LIVING LIKE WEASELS

Annie Dillard

One of our country's most respected writers and the winner of a Pulitzer Prize for nonfiction, Annie Dillard teaches at Wesleyan University in Connecticut. In many of her works, she seeks to understand how close attention to nature can contribute to the development of a spiritual life. She has also written about the nature of writing. In "Write Till You Drop," she states: "The writer knows her field—what has been done, what could be done, the limits—the way a tennis player knows the court. And like that expert, she, too, plays the edges. That is where the exhilaration is. She hits up the line. In writing she can push the edges. Beyond this limit, here the reader must recoil." As you read the following selection, be alert for ways Dillard "plays the edges," and if you find that she goes beyond your limits as a reader, be prepared to explain why. Be alert also for what she comes to understand about life by looking a wild animal in the eye.

A weasel is wild. Who knows what he thinks? He sleeps in his underground den, his tail draped over his nose. Sometimes he lives in his den for two days without leaving. Outside, he stalks rabbits, mice, muskrats, and birds, killing more bodies than he can eat warm, and often dragging the carcasses home. Obedient to instinct, he bites his prey at the neck, either splitting the jugular vein at the throat or crunching the brain at the base of the skull, and he does not let go. One naturalist refused to kill a weasel who was socketed into his hand deeply as a rattlesnake. The man could in no way pry the tiny weasel off, and he had to walk half a mile to water, the weasel dangling from his palm, and soak him off like a stubborn label.

And once, says Ernest Thompson Seton—once, a man shot an eagle out of the sky. He examined the eagle and found the dry skull of a weasel fixed by the jaws to his throat. The supposition is that the eagle had pounced on the weasel and the weasel swiveled and bit as instinct taught him, tooth to neck, and nearly won. I would like to have seen that eagle from the air a few weeks or months before he was shot: Was the whole weasel still attached to his feathered throat, a fur pendant? Or did the eagle eat what he could reach, gutting the living weasel with his talons before his breast, bending his beak, cleaning the beautiful airborne bones?

I have been reading about weasels because I saw one last week. I startled a weasel who startled me, and we exchanged a long glance.

Twenty minutes from my house, through the woods by the quarry and across the highway, is Hollins Pond, a remarkable piece of shallowness, where I like to go at sunset and sit on a tree trunk. Hollins Pond is also called Murray's Pond; it covers two acres of bottomland near Tinker Creek with six inches of water and six thousand lily pads. In winter, brown-and-white steers stand in the middle of it, merely dampening their hooves; from the distant shore they look like miracle itself, complete with miracle's nonchalance. Now, in summer, the steers are gone. The water lilies have blossomed and spread to a green horizontal plane that is terra firma to plodding blackbirds, and tremulous ceiling to black leeches, crayfish, and carp.

This is, mind you, suburbia. It is a five-minute walk in three directions to rows of houses, though none is visible here. There's a 55-mph highway at one end of the pond, and a nesting pair of wood ducks at the other. Under every bush is a muskrat hole or a beer can. The far end is an alternating series of fields and woods, fields and woods, threaded everywhere with motorcycle tracks—in whose bare clay wild turtles lay eggs.

So. I had crossed the highway, stepped over two low barbed-wire fences, and traced the motorcycle path in all gratitude through the wild rose and poison ivy of the pond's shoreline up into high grassy fields. Then I cut down through the woods to the mossy fallen tree where I sit. This tree is excellent. It makes a dry, upholstered bench at the upper, marshy end of the pond, a plush jetty raised from the thorny shore between a shallow blue body of water and a deep blue body of sky.

The sun had just set. I was relaxed on the tree trunk, ensconced in the lap of lichen, watching the lily pads at my feet tremble and part dreamily over the thrusting path of a carp. A yellow bird appeared to my right and flew behind me. It caught my eye; I swiveled around—and the next instant, inexplicably, I was looking down at a weasel, who was looking up at me.

Weasel! I'd never seen one wild before. He was ten inches long, thin as a curve, a muscled ribbon, brown as fruitwood, soft-furred, alert. His face was fierce, small and pointed as a lizard's; he would have made a good arrowhead. There was just a dot of chin, maybe two brown hairs' worth, and then the pure white fur began that spread down his underside. He had two black eyes I didn't see, any more than you see a window.

The weasel was stunned into stillness as he was emerging from beneath an enormous shaggy wild rose bush four feet away. I was stunned into stillness twisted backward on the tree trunk. Our eyes locked, and someone threw away the key.

Our look was as if two lovers, or deadly enemies, met unexpectedly on an overgrown path when each had been thinking of something else: a clearing blow to the gut. It was also a bright blow to the brain, or a sudden beating of brains, with all the charge and intimate grate of rubbed balloons. It emptied our lungs. It felled the forest, moved the fields, and drained the pond; the world dismantled and tumbled into that black hole of eyes. If you and I looked at each other that way, our skulls would split and drop to our shoulders. But we don't. We keep our skulls. So.

He disappeared. This was only last week, and already I don't remember what shattered the enchantment. I think I blinked, I think I retrieved my brain from the weasel's brain, and tried to memorize what I was seeing, and the weasel felt the yank of separation, the careening splashdown into real life and the urgent current of instinct. He vanished under the wild rose. I waited motionless, my mind suddenly full of data and my spirit with pleadings, but he didn't return.

Please do not tell me about "approach-avoidance conflicts." I tell you I've been in that weasel's brain for sixty seconds, and he was in mine. Brains are private places, muttering through unique and secret tapes—but the weasel and I both plugged into another tape simultaneously, for a sweet and shocking time. Can I help it if it was a blank?

What goes on in his brain the rest of the time? What does a weasel think about? He won't say. His journal is tracks in clay, a spray of feathers, mouse blood and bone: uncollected, unconnected, loose-leaf, and blown.

I would like to learn, or remember, how to live. I come to Hollins Pond not so much to learn how to live as, frankly, to forget about it. That is, I don't think I can learn from a wild animal how to live in particular—shall I suck warm blood, hold my tail high, walk with my footprints precisely over the prints of my hands?—but I might learn something of mindlessness, something of the purity of living in the physical senses and the dignity of living without bias or motive. The weasel lives in necessity and we live in choice, hating necessity and dying at the last ignobly in its talons. I would like to live as I should, as the weasel lives as he should. And I suspect that for me the way is like the weasel's: open to time and death painlessly, noticing everything, remembering nothing, choosing the given with a fierce and pointed will.

I missed my chance. I should have gone for the throat. I should have lunged for that streak of white under the weasel's chin and held on, held on through mud and into the wild rose, held on for a dearer life. We could live under the wild rose wild as weasels, mute and uncomprehending. I could very calmly go wild. I could live two days in the den, curled, leaning on mouse fur, sniffing bird bones, blinking, licking, breathing musk, my hair tangled in the roots of grasses. Down is a good place to go, where the mind is single. Down is out, out of your ever-loving mind and back to your careless senses. I remember muteness as a prolonged and giddy fast, where every moment is a feast of utterance received. Time and events are merely poured, unremarked, and ingested directly, like blood pulsed into my gut through a jugular vein. Could two live that way? Could two live under the wild rose, and explore by the pond, so that the smooth mind of each is as everywhere present to the other, and as received and as unchallenged, as falling snow?

We could, you know. We can live any way we want. People take vows of poverty, chastity, and obedience—even of silence—by choice. The thing is to stalk your calling in a certain skilled and supple way, to locate the most tender and live spot and plug into that pulse. This is yielding, not fighting. A weasel

15

doesn't "attack" anything; a weasel lives as he's meant to, yielding at every moment to the perfect freedom of single necessity.

I think it would be well, and proper, and obedient, and pure, to grasp your one necessity and not let it go, to dangle from it limp wherever it takes you. Then even death, where you're going no matter how you live, cannot you part. Seize it and let it seize you up aloft even, till your eyes burn out and drop; let your musky flesh fall off in shreds, and let your very bones unhinge and scatter, loosened over fields, over fields and woods, lightly, thoughtless, from any height at all, from as high as eagles.

QUESTIONS FOR DISCUSSION

1. What do you think Dillard means when she writes, "A weasel is wild"? What does it mean to be "wild," and what is attractive about "the wild"?
2. Consider the story of the weasel that is borne aloft by an eagle and eaten in the air. What does this example reveal about weasels, and why is Dillard using it?
3. The setting of this essay isn't some remote forest, but rather a small pond in a suburb. "There's a 55-mph highway at one end of the pond, and a nesting pair of wood ducks at the other," writes Dillard. "Under every bush is a muskrat hole or a beer can." Why is this setting significant?
4. What does Dillard hope to learn from nature? Why is she attracted to the weasel that looks her in the eye?
5. According to Dillard, "Down is a good place to go, where the mind is single. Down is out, out of your ever-loving mind and back to your careless senses." In what sense—or senses—is she using "down," "single," and "careless"?
6. In her conclusion, Dillard urges readers "to grasp your one necessity and not let it go." Is this advice you are prepared to follow? How can you tell when it's wise to let something go or essential to hold on "wherever it takes you"?

SUGGESTIONS FOR WRITING

1. Write about an animal that you have observed closely; focus on what draws you to this animal.
2. Write an essay exploring your relationship to nature—whether it be hiking in a wilderness area or stepping over blades of grass springing up between the cracks of a city sidewalk.
3. What is your own "single necessity"—the desire that would be the most difficult for you to abandon? Write an essay that would help other people understand why this desire is so important to you.

LINKS

■ Within the Book

For another example of Dillard's work, see "The Deer at Providencia" (pages 627–630).

■ Elsewhere in Print

Dillard, Annie. *An American Childhood.* New York: Harper, 1987.
———. *Holy the Firm.* New York: Harper, 1977.
———. *Pilgrim at Tinker Creek.* 1974. New York: Harper, 1988.
———. *Teaching a Stone to Talk: Expeditions and Encounters.* New York: Harper, 1982.
King, Carolyn M. *Natural History of Weasels and Stoats.* Ithaca: Comstock, 1989.
Seton, Ernest Thompson. *Trail of an Artist-Naturalist: The Autobiography of Ernest Thompson Seton.* New York: Scribner, 1940.
———. *Wild Animals I Have Known.* 1898. Toronto: McClellan, 1996.

■ Online

www.mhhe.com/motives

Click on "More Resources" then "Writing to Understand Experience."

■ ■ ■

LAVENDER

André Aciman

Born in Alexandria, Egypt—one of the great cities of the ancient world—André Aciman has lived in France and Italy, as well in the United States, where he attended Harvard and went on to teach comparative literature at Princeton, Bard, and the Graduate Center of the City University of New York. A contributor to the New York Times *and* The New Yorker *among other periodicals, he originally published "Lavender" in the* Harvard Review. *Although he could not have assumed that his original audience would share his obsession with fragrance, he could have safely assumed that they would be attentive readers who may have benefited from foreign travel.*

If you are inclined to think that there is something strange about taking a keen interest in aftershave and holding onto old bottles of it, consider whether you or someone close to you has ever followed an interest or developed a collection that is unusual in some respect. Doing so can help prepare you for reading the following work, which is the first part of a three-part essay. If this piece interests or puzzles you, you might enjoy reading the full text of Aciman's essay by going to www.mhhe.com/motives and clicking on "More Resources" then "Writing to Understand Experience."

Life begins somewhere with the scent of lavender. My father is standing in front of a mirror. He has just showered and shaved and is about to put on a suit. I watch him tighten the knot of his necktie, flip down his shirt collar, and button it up. Suddenly, there it is, as always: lavender.

I know where it comes from. An elaborately shaped bottle sits on the dresser. One day, when I'm having a very bad migraine and am lying on the living room sofa, my mother, scrambling for something to take my mind off the pain, picks up the bottle, unscrews the cap, and dabs some of its contents onto a handkerchief, which she then brings to my nose. Instantly, I feel better. She lets me keep the handkerchief. I like to hold it in my fist, with my head tilted slightly back, as if I'd been punched in a fistfight and were still bleeding—or the way I'd seen others do when they were feeling sick or crushed and walked about the house taking occasional sniffs through crumpled handkerchiefs in what looked like last-ditch efforts to avoid a fainting spell. I liked the handkerchief, liked the secret scent emanating from within its folds, liked smuggling it to school and taking furtive whiffs in class, because the scent brought me back to my parents, to their living room, and into a world that was so serene that just inhaling its scent cast a protective cloud around me. Smell lavender and I was sheltered, happy, beloved. Smell lavender and in came good thoughts—about life, about those I loved, about me. Smell lavender and, no matter how far from each other, we were all gathered in one warm, snug room stuffed with pillows, close to a crackling fire, with the patter of rain outside to remind us our lives were secure. Smell lavender and you couldn't pull us apart.

My father's old cologne can be found the world over. I have only to walk into a large department store and there it is. Half a century later it looks exactly the same. I could, if I were prescient enough and did not want to risk walking into a store one day and not finding it, purchase a tiny bottle and keep it somewhere, as a stand-in for my father, for my love of lavender, or for that fall evening when, as an adolescent, I'd gone with my mother to buy my first aftershave lotion, but couldn't make up my mind and retuned alone the next evening after school, happy to discover, among so many other things, that a man could use shaving as an excuse for wearing perfume.

I was baffled to find there were so many scents on the world, and even more baffled to find my father's scent among them. I asked the salesman to let me sample my father's brand, mispronouncing its name on purpose, overdoing my surprise as I examined its slanted shape as though it were a stranger whom I had hailed in error, knowing that the bottle and I were on intimate terms at home, that if it knew every twist my worst migraines took—as I knew every curve on its body—it knew of my imaginary flights from school in Mother's handkerchief, knew more about my fantasies than I dared know myself. And yet, in the shop that was about to close that day and whose owner was growing ever more impatient with my inability to choose, I felt mesmerized by something new, something at once dangerous and enticing, as though these numberless bottles, neatly arranged in stacks around the store, held the promise of nights out in large cities where everything from the buildings, lights, faces, foods, places, and the bridges I'd end up crossing made the world ever more desirable, if only because I too, by virtue of this or that potion, had become desirable—to others, to myself.

I spent an hour testing bottles. In the end I bought a lavender cologne, but   5
not my father's. After paying and having the package gift-wrapped, I felt like I'd been handed a birth certificate or a new passport. This would be me—or me as long as the bottle lasted. Then we'd have to look into the matter again.

Over time, I discovered all kinds of lavenders. There were light, ethereal lavenders; some were mild and timid, others lush and overbearing, some tart, as if picked from the field and left to parch in large vats of vinegar; others were overwhelmingly sweet. Some lavenders ended up smelling like an herb garden; others, with hints of so many spices, were blended beyond recognition.

I experimented with each one, purchased many bottles, not just because I wanted to collect them all or was searching for the ideal lavender—the hidden lavender, the ur-lavender that superseded all other lavenders—but because I was eager to either prove or disprove something I suspected all along: that the lavender I wanted was none other than the one I'd grown up with and would ultimately turn back to once I'd established that all the others were wrong for me. Perhaps the lavender I wanted was basic lavender. Ordinary lavender. Papa's lavender. You go out into the world to acquire all manner of habits and learn all sorts of languages, but the one tongue you neglect most is the one you've spoken at home, just as the customs you feel most comfortable with are those you never knew were customs until you saw others practice completely different ones and realized you didn't quite mind your own, though you'd strayed so far now that you probably no longer knew how to practice them. I collected every fragrance in the world. But my scent—what was *my* scent? Had I ever had a *scent?* Was there going to be one scent only, or would I want all of them?

What I found after purchasing several aftershave lotions was that they would all lose their luster, like certain elements in the actinide series that have a brief radioactive life before turning into lead. Some smelled too strong, or too weak, or too much of such and such and not enough of this or that. Some failed to bring out something essential about me; others suggested things that weren't in me at all. Perhaps finding fault with each fragrance was also my way of finding fault with myself, not just for choosing the wrong fragrance each time, or for even thinking I needed a fragrance in the first place, but for believing that the blessings conferred by cologne could ever bring about the new life I yearned for.

And yet, even as I criticized each fragrance, I found myself growing attached to it, as though something that had less to do with the fragrances themselves than with that part of me that had sought them out and been seduced by them and finally blossomed because of them should never be allowed to perish. Sometimes the history of provisional attachments means more to us than the attachments themselves, the way the history of a love affair stirs more love than the affair itself. Sometimes it is in blind ritual and not faith that we encounter the sacred, the way it is habit, not character, that makes us who we are. Sometimes the clothes and scents we wear have more of us in them than we do ourselves.

The search for ideal lavender was like the search for that part of me that needed nothing more than a fragrance to emerge from the sleep of thousands. I searched for it the way I searched for my personal color, or for a brand of cigarettes, or for my favorite composer. Finding the right lavender would finally allow me to say, "Yes, this is me. Where was I all this time?" Yet, no sooner is the scent purchased, than the me who was supposed to emerge—like the us who is about to emerge when we buy new clothes, or sign up for a magazine that seems so thoroughly right for us, or purchase a membership to a health club, or move to a new city, or discover a new faith and practice new rituals with new congregants among whom we make new friends—this me turns out to be, of course, the one we'd always wished to mask or drive away. What did I expect? Different scent, same person.

Over the past thirty-five years I have tried almost all the colognes and aftershave lotions that perfume manufacturers have concocted. Not just lavenders, but pine, chamomile, tea, citrus, honeysuckle, fern, rosemary, and smoky variations of the most rarefied leathers and spices. I liked nothing more than to clutter my medicine cabinet and the entire rim of my bathtub with bottles two and three deep, each vial like a tiny, unhatched effigy of someone I was, or wished to be, and, for a while, thought I'd finally become. Scent A: purchased in such and such year, hoping to encounter happiness. Scent B: purchased while scent A was almost finished; it helped me abandon A. C, marking sudden fatigue with B. D was a gift. Never liked it; wore it to make the giver happy, stopped using it as soon as she was gone. Comes E, which I loved so much that I eventually purchased F, along with nine of its sibling scents made by the same house. Yet F managed to make me tire of E and its isotopes. Sought out G. Disliked it as soon as I realized that someone I hated loved it. Then H. How I loved H! Stayed with H for years. They don't make it any longer, should have stocked up on it. But then, much as I loved it, I had stopped using it long before its manufacturer discontinued it. Back to E, which I had always liked. Yes, definitely E. Until I realized there had always been something slightly off, something missing about E. I stopped using it again. Of the woman who breezed through my life and, in the ten days I knew her, altered me forever, all I remember is her gift. I continued to wear the fragrance she'd given me as a way of thinking she'd be back soon enough. Now, twenty years later, all that's left of her is a bottle that reminds me less of her than of the lover I once was.

I have thrown many things away in life. But aftershave bottles, never. I take these bottle wherever I move, the way the ancients traveled with their ancestral masks. Each bottle contains part of me, a formaldehyded me, the genie of myself. One could, as in an Arabian tale, rub each bottle and summon up an older me. Some, despite the years, are still alive, though not a thing they own or wear is any longer in my possession; others have even died or grown so dull I want nothing more to do with them; I've forgotten their phone number, their favorite song, their furtive wishes. I take up an old scent and, suddenly, I remember why this scent always reminds me of the most ardent days of my life—ardent not because they were happy times, but because I had spent so much time thirsting for happiness that, in retrospect, some of that imagined happiness must have rubbed off and scented an entire winter, casting a happy film over days I've always known I'd never wish to relive. And as I hold this bottle, which seems more precious than so many things, I begin to think that one day someone I love—particularly someone I love—will happen along and open it and wonder what this scent could possibly have meant to me. What was it I'd wished to keep alive all these years? This is the scent of early spring when they called to say things had gone my way. This of an evening with my mother, when she came to meet me downtown and I thought how old she looks—now I realize she was younger by ten years than I am today. This the night of the A-minor. "And this?" they'll want to ask. "How about this one?"

Fragrances linger for decades, and our loved ones may remember us by them, but the legend in each vial clams up the moment we're gone. Our genie

Testing fragrances to find the right scent.

speaks to no one. He simply watches as those he's loved open and investigate. He's dying to scream with the agony of ten Rosetta stones begging to be heard across the centuries. "This was the day I discovered pleasure. And this— how couldn't any of you know?—this was the night we met, standing outside Carnegie Hall after a concert, and how simply one thing led to another, and afterward, when it rained, we had waited a while under the cantilever, both reluctant to leave, having found a pretext in rain, strangers starting to talk, making a quick dash into a nearby coffee shop—deplorable coffee, damp shoes, wet hair, surly foreign waiter mumbling Unspeakanese when we tipped him kindly—and sat and spoke of Mahler and *The Four Quartets*,° and no one would have guessed, not even us, we'd end up together in a studio on the Upper West Side." But the voice cannot be heard. To die is to forget you ever lived. To die is to forget you loved, or suffered, or got and lost things you wanted. Tomorrow, you say to yourself, I won't remember anything, won't remember this face, this knee, this old scar, or the hand that wrote all this.

The bottles are stand-ins for me. I keep them the way the ancient Egyptians kept all of their household belongings: for that day when they'd need them in their afterlife. To part with them now is to die before my time. And yet, there are times when I think there should have been many, many other

---

°*Mahler:* Gustav Mahler (1860–1911), Austrian composer best known for his symphonies. *The Four Quartets* (1943): A major work by the poet T. S. Eliot (1888–1965).

bottles there—not just bottles I lost or forgot about, but bottles I never owned, bottles I don't even know exist and, but for a tiny accident, might have given an entirely different scent to my life. There is a street I pass by every day, never once suspecting that in years to come it will lead to an apartment I still don't know will be mine one day. How can I not know this—isn't there a science?

Conversely, there are places I bid farewell to long before knowing I must   *15*
leave, places and people whose disappearance I rehearse not just to learn how to live without them when the time comes but to put off their loss by foreseeing it a bit at a time beforehand. I live in the dark so as not to be blinded when darkness comes. I do the same with life, making it more conditional and provisional than it already is, so as to forget that one day . . . one day my birthday will come around and I won't be there to celebrate it.

It is still unthinkable that those who caused us the greatest pain and turned us inside out could at some point in time have been totally unknown, unborn to us. We might have crossed them in numberless places, given them street directions, opened a door for them, stood up to let them take their seat in a crowded concert hall, and never once recognized the person who would ruin us for everyone else. I'd be willing to shave years from the end of my life to go back and intercept that evening under a cantilever when we both put our coats over our heads and rushed through the rain after coffee and I said, almost without thinking, I didn't want to say goodnight yet, although it was already dawn. I would give years, not to unwrite this evening or to rewrite it, but to put it on hold and, as happens when we bracket off time, be able to wonder indefinitely who I'd be had things taken another turn. Time, as always, is given in the wrong tense.

The walls of the Farmaceutica of Santa Maria Novella in Florence are lined with rows of tiny drawers, each of which contains a different perfume. Here I could create my own scent museum, my own laboratory, my imaginary Grasse, the perfume capital of France, with all of its quaint *ateliers* and narrow lanes and winding passageways linking one establishment to the next. My scent museum would even boast its own periodic table, listing all the perfumes in my life, beginning, of course, with the first, the simplest, the lightest—lavender, the hydrogen of all fragrances—followed by the second, the third, the fourth, each standing next to the other like milestones in my life, as though there were indeed a method to the passage of time. In the place of helium (He, atomic number 2) I'd have Hermès, and in the place of lithium (Li, 3) Liberty; Bernini would replace beryllium (Be, 4), Borsari boron (B, 5), Carven carbon (C, 6), Night nitrogen (N, 7), Oynx oxygen (O, 8), and Floris fluorine (F, 9). And before I know it my entire life could be charted by these elements alone: Arden instead of argon (Ar, 18), Knize instead of potassium (K, 19), Canoë for calcium (Ca, 20), Guerlain for germanium (Ge, 32), Yves Saint Laurent for yttrium (Y, 39), Patou for platinum (Pt, 78), and, of course, Old Spice for osmium (Os, 76).

As in Mendeleyev's° periodic table, one could sort these scents in rows and categories: by herbs; flowers; fruits; spices; woods. Or by places. By people. By loves. By the hotels where this or that soap managed to cast an unforgettable scent over this or that great city. By the films or foods or clothes or concerts we've loved. By perfumes women wore. Or even by years, so that I could mark the bottles as my grandmother would when she labeled each jar of marmalade with her neat octogenarian's cursive, noting on each the fruit and the year of its make—as though each scent had its own *werkeverzeichnis*° number. Aria di Parma (1970), Acqua Amara (1975), Ponte Vecchio (1980).

The aftershaves I used at eighteen and at twenty-four, different fragrances, yet located on the same column: a voyage to Italy is what they shared in common. Me at sixteen and me at thirty-two: twice the age, yet still nervous when calling a woman for the first time; at forty I couldn't solve the calculus problems I didn't understand at twenty; I had reread and taught *Wuthering Heights* so many times, but the scenes I remember best at forty-eight were those retained from my very first reading at twelve, four "generations" earlier. Me at 14, 18, 22, 26—life retold in units of four. Me at 21, 26, 31, 36, of fives. The folio method, the quarto method, the octavo—in halves, in fourths, by eighths. Life arranged in Fibonacci's sequence: 8, 13, 21, 34, 55, 89. Or in Pascal's: 4, 10, 20, 35, 56. Or by primes:° 7, 11, 13, 17, 19, 23, 29, 31. Or in combinations of all three: I was handsome at twenty-one, why did I think I wasn't; I had so much going for me at thirty-four, why then was I longing to be who I'd been at seventeen? At seventeen, I couldn't wait to be twenty-three. At twenty-three, I longed to meet the girls I'd known at seventeen. At fifty-one, I'd have given anything to be thirty-five, and at forty-one was ready to dare things I was unprepared for at twenty-three. At twenty, thirty seemed the ideal age. At eighty, will I manage to think I'm half my age? Will there be summer in the snow?

Time's covenants are all warped. We live Fibonacci lives: three steps forward, two steps back, or the other way around: three steps forward, five back. *20* Or in both directions simultaneously, in the manner of spiders or of Bach's crab canons, spinning combinations of scents and elective affinities in what turns out to be an endless succession of esters and fragrances that start from the simplest and fan out to the most complex: one carbon, two carbons, three carbons: six hydrogens, eight hydrogens, ten . . . $C_3H_6O_2$, ethyl formate; $C_4H_8O_2$, ethyl acetate; $C_5H_{10}O_2$, ethyl propionate; $C_5H_{10}O_2$, methyl butanoate (which has an apple aroma); $C_5H_{10}O_2$, propyl ethanoate (pear

---

°*Mendeleyev:* Dimitri Ivanovich Mendeleyev (1834–1907), Russian chemist who was largely responsible for developing the system through which chemicals are classified and analyzed.
°*werkeverzeichnis:* a meticulous catalog of words.
°*Fibonacci's sequence:* an infinite sequence of numbers in which each term is the sum of the two that preceded it (named after the Italian mathematician Leonardo Fibonacci). *Pascal's sequence:* a sequence of numbers from the triangle of binominal coefficients developed by the French philosopher and mathematician Blaise Pascal. *Primes:* the sequence of numbers that cannot be factored into smaller numbers.

aroma); $C_6H_{12}O_2$, ethyl butyrate; $C_7H_{14}O_2$, ethyl valerate (banana); $C_8H_{10}NO_2$, methyl anthranilate (grape); $C_9H_{10}O_2$, benzylyl ethanoate (peach); $C_{10}H_{12}O_2$, ethyl phenylethanoate (honey); $C_{10}H_{20}O_2$, octyl ethanoate (orange–apricot); $C_{11}H_{22}O_2$, ethyl decanoate (cognac); $C_9H_6O_2$, coumarin (lavender). Say lavender and you have a scent, a chain, a lifetime.

And here lay Mendeleyev's genius. He understood that, though he could plot every element, many elements hadn't been discovered yet. So he left blank spaces on his table—for missing elements to come—as though life's events were cast in so orderly and idealized a numerical design that, even if we ignored when they'd occur or what effect they might have, we could still await them, still make room for them before their time. Thus, I too look at my life and stare at its blind spots: scents I never discovered; bottles I haven't stumbled on and don't know exist; selves I haven't been but can't claim to miss; pockets in time I should have lived through but never did; people I could have met but missed out on; places I might have visited, gotten to love and ultimately lived in, but never traveled to. They are the blank tiles, the "rare-earth" moments, the roads never taken.

QUESTIONS FOR DISCUSSION

1. In his opening paragraph, Aciman implies that his earliest memory is associated with scent. What is your own earliest memory?
2. Although Aciman refers to his father's cologne, he never identifies the brand. Why do you think he made this writing decision?
3. When making his first independent visit to a store with a wide selection of aftershave and cologne, Aciman found the experience "dangerous and enticing." What do you think he means by this?
4. In paragraph 10, Aciman writes: "The search for ideal lavender was like the search for that part of me that needed nothing more than a fragrance to emerge from the sleep of thousands." What kind of a search is this? How do you interpret a phrase like "the sleep of thousands"?
5. Aciman develops a habit of acquiring a new scent just before he has finished with the scent he has been most recently using. Does this kind of behavior compare with anything you have done or witnessed?
6. Consider Aciman's reflections on aging in paragraph 19. What kind of factors could make someone feel discontented with whatever age he or she happens to be?
7. How effective is Aciman's use of Mendeleyev's periodic table? Why do you think Aciman is drawn to the idea of "blank spaces"?

SUGGESTIONS FOR WRITING

1. Write an essay about a fragrance that is especially important to you, exploring how that fragrance first entered your life and what associations you have with it.

2. Write an essay about how the way you shop reflects your values or identity. Consider whether you shop to confirm how you already see yourself or to transform how you wish to be seen by others.
3. Aciman compares his used bottles of aftershave to "ancestral masks" that he takes with him wherever he moves no matter what else he discards. Write an essay focused on whatever you would most want to carry with you if forced to move suddenly—like a refugee, or a person whose house is on fire.

LINKS

■ Within the Book

In "Levi's" (pages 55–58), Marilyn Schiel also explores how identity can be influenced by something a person acquires.

■ Elsewhere in Print

Aciman, André, *False Papers.* New York: Picador, 2001.
————. *Letters of Transit: Reflections on Exile, Identity, and Loss.* New York: New Press, 2000.
————. *Out of Egypt.* New York: Riverhead, 1996.
————. *The Proust Project.* New York: Farrar, 2004.
Moran, Jan. *Fabulous Fragrances: A Guide to Prestige Perfumes for Women and Men.* Avenel: Crescent, 2000.
Silvester, Hans. *Lavender: Fragrances of Provence.* New York: Abrams, 2004.
Susskind, Patrick. *Perfume.* New York: Vintage, 2001.

■ Online

www.mhhe.com/motives

Click on "More Resources" then "Writing to Understand Experience."

2

Writing to Report Information

Ask yourself whether, in the course of a single week, you do any of the following: ask directions, consult the telephone directory, look something up in a book, read a newspaper, check gasoline prices, or listen to a weather report. All these efforts to acquire data are things people do routinely to negotiate the pathways of their world. This task is becoming both easier and more challenging as a result of technology. Today, we have almost instant electronic access to vast reserves of data. But to keep from being overwhelmed by the data we acquire and to avoid overwhelming others when we report to them, we need to learn how to sort, select, and arrange data—and thereby turn data into information.

Data in this sense means unorganized, unconstructed bits and pieces. Billions of them. Information is constructed out of data by a particular person or group of people with particular concerns they wish to communicate. So information always involves a rhetorical situation. The challenge is to transform data into information by furnishing a context and a social purpose.

To understand the nature of data, you must be able to distinguish among facts, inferences, and opinions. *Facts* are independently verifiable events, statistics, and statements: The Arkansas River runs southwest from central Colorado into Kansas; Enron filed for bankruptcy protection on December 2, 2001; genetic engineering has produced square tomatoes. *Inferences* are reasonable suppositions drawn from facts. For example, if Office Tiger—about which Katherine Boo wrote in an article in this chapter—went from having 100 employees in 1998 to approximately 3000 employees in 2004, then it seems likely that this company will continue to grow in the years ahead. So data also consist of inferences. Finally, an *opinion* is a belief that may or may not be accurate but that nevertheless exists and must therefore be taken into account by those who report information. For example, you might think that it would be wise to invest in Office Tiger or that Office Tiger is doing a disservice to American workers. Facts and inferences could support either of these opinions. Whether an opinion is reliable matters a great deal in some rhetorical situations—in writing to evaluate, for example, or writing to persuade (which are discussed in other chapters). But right or wrong, an opinion becomes data once it is shared with others. No longer yours alone, it becomes one of those random bits and pieces with which others must cope.

Our main concern in this chapter is with the way we draw on data to transfer information from one mind to another. Although this is a very complex process—one that has been studied at length by psychologists, neurologists, and communication specialists—there is agreement that the most powerful way to transfer information from one mind to another is through language. Our concern here is specifically with written language.

GUIDELINES FOR REPORTING INFORMATION

Reading for information is very different from reading to enter imaginatively into another person's life or to reflect at length about ideas. When people read for information, they appreciate having clear signals from the author that alert them to the most important points and give them the opportunity to skim the rest. They also appreciate having some idea of the scope of the article and the reasons they are expected to read it.

Writing that reports information need not always have a thesis. A newspaper article, after all, rarely has a thesis, but the lack of one does not mean that it consists of random pieces of data. It is still arranged in a pattern so that readers can make sense of it. Business reports, too, frequently consist simply of narratives of what has happened or of text that exists mainly to link numbers in some meaningful way. In this chapter, Peter Stark relies on narrative to report on the nature and treatment of hypothermia. Katherine Boo also uses narrative when she reports how two Americans founded a company based in India and tells the story of one employee's background. But many reports benefit from having a clear thesis stated early on. At the end of his opening paragraph in "Jefferson and the Environment," Peter Ling introduces what he will set out to prove: Jefferson's "botanical and agricultural ideas have had the most visible, widespread and long-lasting impact for good or ill." After discussing these ideas, Ling reinforces his thesis by concluding that we can learn from Jefferson's mistakes and act "to reduce the damage of the great President's environmental legacy."

Philosopher H. Paul Grice provides four rules to guide the transfer of information so clear communication takes place, and to help writers decide what to tell and how to tell it when reporting information. In Grice's scheme, reporters of information should observe the rules of quantity, quality, relevance, and manner.

To observe the *rule of quantity,* you need to give your readers just enough information—but no more—so they can understand what you want them to know, so there are no gaps to impede their understanding, and so they do not drown in data. An example may help. In "The American Flavor Industry,"

Eric Schlosser mentions several chemical plants at which aromas for processed food are created: International Flavors & Fragrances, Givaudan, Haarmann & Reimer, Takasago, Flavor Dynamics, Frutarom, and Elan Chemical. He also notes that there are "dozens" of such companies in New Jersey and indicates that other companies exist elsewhere. He chooses, however, to report about his visit to one of these companies.

The *rule of quality* dictates that you give correct, accurate information. Because those who report information must observe the rule of quantity as well as quality, they should use the best material at their disposal. When determining which material is of the best quality, they should consider whether examples and sources are reliable and representative. They may discover sensational material that could capture the attention of their audience but reject it because they cannot verify its accuracy. Readers, however, are also responsible for appraising the quality of the information they receive. Some reporters are more reliable than others, and most use inferences and opinion as well as facts—which means that readers must distinguish the kind of information they are receiving and decide whether they can trust it. Although Schlosser reports a visit to only one flavor company, International Flavors & Fragrances, he helps his audience to understand that this example is of good quality by noting that IFF is "the world's largest flavor company" and that it has developed the aromas for "famous, widely advertised products ranging from potato chips to antacids."

The *rule of relevance* means that readers get the information the writer promises and are not distracted by unrelated material. If you are reading about the fast-food industry, you might expect information on how flavors are manufactured, but you would not expect to read several paragraphs about how to cook with tofu. When reporting about International Flavors & Fragrances, Schlosser establishes the relevance of this example by noting that, while there, he saw "a french fryer identical to those I'd seen at innumerable fast-food restaurants." And he concludes his report with a reference to the artificial aroma of grilled hamburger. The references to french fries and hamburger make his visit to IFF relevant to his discussion of McDonald's.

Finally, the *rule of manner* means that accurate information is presented clearly and plausibly. Schlosser's report is plausible because he includes expert testimony from sources inside the industry he is investigating and recognizes that artificially created flavors can be appealing—demonstrating that he is not one-sided. Moreover, the information he reports is presented clearly, without sarcastic commentary. Thus, the rule of manner requires a credible reporter framing information so that readers can understand it. This is not determined simply by the reporter's being self-confident—although that contributes to credibility—but also by the reporter's demonstrating his or her own fair-mindedness and ability to distinguish fact from opinion.

Implicit in Grice's four rules is a point that should be emphasized: Writers transfer information most effectively when they help readers connect it to something they already know. For example, Peter Ling opens "Jefferson and the Environment" with information about Jefferson that is likely to be familiar to readers and then goes on to provide information that is less widely known. And Katherine Boo places a reference to Home Depot, a chain of stores familiar to many Americans, at the beginning of a report in which she takes readers behind closed doors on the other side of the world.

CONSIDERING AUDIENCE

When observing the rules of quantity, quality, relevance, and manner (see pages 98–99), writers motivated to report information must consider that many readers have relatively short attention spans. News media in the United States frequently give important stories only brief attention in order to save time and space for advertisements and gossip about celebrities. A major speech by a prominent leader, for example, may be reduced to a single sound bite. Moreover, the increasing popularity of cable stations that keep stories short and entertaining has encouraged the networks to dumb down their coverage as well.

There is reason to believe, however, that many people would welcome more extensive information. When the FCC conducted public hearings during 2004, hundreds of citizens showed up to demand a higher level of news coverage. And the circulation enjoyed by periodicals such as the *New York Times,* the *Los Angeles Times,* the *Wall Street Journal, Harpers, The Atlantic,* and *The New Yorker* shows that many Americans want detailed information about what is going on in the world.

When you are writing to report information, you may have a clear sense of audience. For example, if your audience consists of the instructor for a specific class, and the assignment calls for you to demonstrate how much you have learned about a certain topic, you can proceed to write at length and in depth. If you are writing for a larger and more diverse audience, however, you need to consider how much detail you can include without losing the attention of your readers. When making this decision, you can benefit from imagining a range of potential readers—from those who are satisfied by a thirty-second story on Fox News to those who welcome a twenty-thousand-word feature story in *The New York Times Magazine.* Whoever reads your paper is likely to fall somewhere within this continuum.

Recognizing that readers tend to have a limited attention span when it comes to digesting information (even though different readers have different limits) should help you to focus and organize what you write. Ask yourself:

- What are the most important points I want to convey while people are still paying attention?
- How can I arrange these points in a sequence likely to hold the attention of my readers?

- What strategies can I use to keep attention as long as I need it? For example, would one example be more engaging than another? Would an anecdote dramatize the information I want to communicate? Can I use language to engage attention—either by selecting vocabulary best suited for readers who have a certain level of education or by making stylistic choices (such as varying sentence length and structure) to keep readers reading?

As a rule, however, you should treat readers with respect and be willing to put faith in them. If you misjudge how much information your audience can take in, it is better to err on the side of generosity rather than parsimony. In other words, when in doubt give more, not less. Readers can then choose to skim some paragraphs rather than read them attentively, but they will nevertheless note that you took the trouble to report in depth. Readers may be bored if you overwhelm them with more information than they can handle, but they are likely to feel insulted if you come across as someone who assumes that they are not capable of learning much. No one wants to be boring or to be bored. But to insult or feel insulted causes greater damage to effective communication.

USING APPROPRIATE LANGUAGE

Students are often advised to couch all their information in neutral, precise, objective language, because informing is supposed to be evenhanded; but that does not mean draining all the life out of your prose. Overly scientific and informative writing sounds as if it were produced by a machine. As the clear, direct prose of Peter Stark reveals, you can report information and still let your own personality show through. Presenting information while conveying a human voice helps readers remain interested in the information without devaluing it.

If you are to offer the appropriate information, reporting requires you to pay special attention to the interests and abilities of your audience. When you write for general readers, you should not expect them to understand specialized vocabulary and advanced concepts, and it is usually your responsibility to select a topic that will interest your readers and present it in an appealing way. Consider the following excerpt from a college textbook for an introductory course in astronomy:

> Based on his determination that the sun was much larger than the earth, Aristarchus proposed that the sun was at rest and the earth moved around it in a yearly orbit. This *heliocentric* (sun-centered) model was opposed to the prevailing *geocentric* (earth-centered) model. The concept of a heliocentric universe was immediately challenged. If the earth moved in an orbit, the stars would appear

to shift relative to one another, depending on the position of the earth in its orbit. This phenomenon, called *parallax,* was not observed. Aristarchus' reply to this objection was that the stars must be extremely far away, making any parallax shifts too small to notice.
—*Thomas Michael Corwin and Dale C. Wachowiak,* The Universe: From Chaos to Consciousness

The authors considered their audience. They did not talk down to their readers but recognized that vocabulary may be a problem. They described *parallax,* a fairly difficult concept, using simple, clear language.

Compare that passage with one from Gilbert E. Satterthwaite's *Encyclopedia of Astronomy,* which also describes parallax but is directed to more sophisticated readers:

The angle subtended at a heavenly body by a baseline of known length, usually designated P or π. It is of course directly related to the distance; the word has therefore come to be used by astronomers as synonymous with distance.

The baseline used for nearer objects, such as the members of the solar system, is the equatorial radius of the earth; parallaxes determined on this basis are termed *geocentric parallaxes.* . . . For more distant objects, the baseline used is the semimajor axis of the Earth's orbit; these are termed *heliocentric parallaxes.*

Satterthwaite's discussion goes on to discuss in considerable detail various kinds of parallaxes, but he can assume that his readers are motivated to read his discussion and have the knowledge to understand fine points—a different audience from Corwin and Wachowiak's.

SUMMARIZING AND SYNTHESIZING INFORMATION

As you transform data into information, you need to know how to summarize and synthesize.

To *summarize* is to condense: Summaries report the main points—and only the main points—of something you have heard, read, or witnessed. For example, here are the first three paragraphs of a story that appeared in the *New York Times* on July 26, 1998:

Murder in the United States has been dropping dramatically for years, to the lowest level since the modern crime wave began in the 1960's. But this encouraging decline has masked a fundamental fact—that there is no such thing as an American murder rate.

In fact, there are sharp regional differences in homicide, with the South having by far the highest murder rate, almost double that of the Northeast, a divergence that has persisted for as long as records have been kept, starting in the 19th century. The former slaveholding states of the old Confederacy all rank in the top 20 states for murder, led by Louisiana, with a rate of 17.5 murders per 100,000 people in 1996. The 10 states with the lowest homicide rates are in New England and the northern Midwest, with South Dakota's the lowest at 1.2 murders per 100,000 people.

Experts note, in addition, that much of the disparity in murder rates between the South and other sections of the country stems from a difference in the character of Southern homicide. In the South, many murders are of a personal and traditional nature: a barroom brawl, a quarrel between acquaintances or a fight between lovers. Elsewhere, homicides usually begin with another crime, like a robbery gone bad, and typically involve strangers.

Summarizing these paragraphs means understanding what they mean and restating in your own words the points you consider important. Here's a summary of the passage:

The murder rate in the United States is highest in the South, where almost twice as many murders are committed as in other regions. Southern murders are also more personal than those committed elsewhere.

This summary reduces the passage to approximately one-seventh of its original length. Statistics have been left out, and references to Louisiana, South Dakota, the Midwest, and New England have also been omitted, as have data about the declining murder rate for the nation as a whole and examples of the background behind many murders in the South. The summary is accurate, but its utility would depend on the audience, context, and purpose. Some readers might require more detail, such as an explanation of "personal," and a writer with those readers in mind would summarize the passage differently. Remember that your audience, context, and purpose determine what kind of information you report and how much of it you expect readers to need.

To *synthesize* is to put data of different kinds together in meaningful ways. This means creating information by sorting through data, identifying relationships, and presenting them in a coherent pattern. When you are summarizing, you are usually working with data from a single source. When you are synthesizing, you are drawing together data from many different sources. When writing about Thomas Jefferson, Peter Ling draws on what he has learned about Jefferson and agricultural practices in the South during Jefferson's lifetime by citing Jefferson's journal and his *Notes on the State of Virginia* (1787) among other eighteenth-century sources. But he also draws on an 1878 report by John Wesley Powell and a 1995 piece about American grasslands by Richard Manning.

OBTAINING DATA

Although writing to report information does not necessarily require you to gather more knowledge than you already have, there may be times when you lack adequate knowledge to finish your paper. Research can provide you with additional data. If you have ever wondered, for example, how food is prepared in a fast-food restaurant, you might consider doing some field research—touring a local facility, asking questions of employees—and then writing an informative, behind-the-scenes report. To obtain data for her article, Elizabeth Kolbert interviewed an entrepreneur whom she observed in two different settings, visited one of the schools his company had set up, and spoke with students there. Or if you are interested in writing a piece like Tim Rogers's profile of Vivian Villarreal, one of the best women pool players in the United States, you might interview that person and perhaps his or her associates.

When interviewing someone, always do some preliminary research so you will be able to ask knowledgeable questions. Schedule the interview in advance, and prepare a list of questions that are specific enough to find out what you need to know but that allow the interviewee enough latitude to be comfortable. Try to memorize your questions so you can talk naturally with this person, without having to stop to find and read one of the questions you wrote down. And if you want to use a tape recorder, always ask your interviewee's permission to do so.

For many topics, however, you will need to consult published material. Many guides to research are in print, and you will also find a chapter on how to do research in most composition handbooks. Teaching in detail the research strategies available for writers is beyond the scope of this introduction, but you should be aware of some basic principles:

- Research is not limited to long, formal papers with lengthy bibliographies, such as a ten-page "research paper" due at the end of the semester. Writers often need to consult sources when working on shorter assignments prompted by a number of different motives for writing.

- A good research strategy involves consulting different kinds of sources, including electronic databases, books and articles, and sometimes government documents and personal interviews. Don't get discouraged if you can't find a book on your topic in your local library or if the periodicals you need have been checked out by someone else. You may be able to get the information elsewhere.

- Writers who use sources should be careful to remain in control of their material and not let their paper become a collection of undigested data from which the writer's own voice has disappeared.

- Information that comes from sources should be documented appropriately. (Handbooks published by the Modern Language Association and the American Psychological Association, among other groups, provide guidance. See page 41.)

The fastest, most efficient way to do research today is by electronic searching. Thanks to Google and other search engines, many writers now turn to the World Wide Web for information, and much useful information can be obtained there. (See page 39.) Serious research almost always requires moving beyond the Web, however. Most college and university libraries thus provide tools for searching online databases that can help you locate material that does not appear on the Web. *Expanded Academic ASAP,* one of the databases provided by InfoTrac, indexes articles from approximately 1260 journals; the full text of articles can be obtained electronically from 709 of them—a feature called "full-text retrieval." *Academic Search Premier* is another helpful tool. Although it allows for searching many of the same journals that can be located through *Expanded Academic ASAP, Academic Search Premier* indexes other titles as well. Either of these services can help you to obtain reliable data, and one may be more helpful than another, depending on what you need to find for a specific project. When you have access to both, try using both.

For information in scholarly publications, you will need to consult a specialized index. Articles about psychology, for example, can be located by searching the electronic database of *PsycINFO.*

Being able to obtain the full text of an article electronically is convenient. You can quickly determine if the source is likely to help you and print out a copy of anything that looks promising. Often this can be done without even going to the library. But remember that libraries continue to house important collections that should not be ignored simply because working elsewhere is more convenient. For example, an article for which you discover a citation (but cannot access the full text electronically) might prove to be the source that is the most helpful for you and thus well worth the effort of visiting the library in person in order to read or photocopy it there.

You can also locate books electronically in your own library and in other college and university libraries (and some municipal ones). If you do locate a book held in the collection of a library other than your own, you can usually request that it be sent to you through interlibrary loan. Moreover, some books are available in electronic format, so you may be able to download an appropriate text from a personal computer. Consult your reference librarian for more information about what research tools are available in this rapidly changing branch of information science.

Whatever research strategies you use and whatever resources are available to you, remember that obtaining data is only one part of the process of reporting information. Do not allow the quest for data to become an end in itself. As we have seen, data become useful as they are transformed into information. To transform data, you must allow yourself plenty of time for writing and revising.

TIPS FOR READING AND WRITING ABOUT INFORMATION

When Reading

■ Assess the quality of the information provided.

■ Consider whether the quantity of information is too little, too much, or appropriate.

■ Consider whether all of the information included in the work is relevant to the writer's topic and purpose.

■ Reflect on whether the author inspires confidence.

■ Determine what the author's original audience was and how you may differ from that audience.

■ If you find your attention wandering, ask if it is because of the topic, the way the writer is presenting it, or some factor unrelated to the work itself.

When Writing

■ Choose a topic that matters to you and that you think you can make matter to others.

■ Make sure the information you obtain is accurate and current.

■ Consider how much information your audience is capable of digesting; then emphasize the information you most want to convey.

■ Be careful to distinguish fact from opinion and inference.

■ Make sure you use language that your audience can understand.

■ Emphasize your topic, not your personal response to the topic.

■ When reviewing what you draft, think about including examples or narratives that would dramatize information readers may not be eager to digest.

AS FREEZING PERSONS RECOLLECT THE SNOW—FIRST CHILL, THEN STUPOR, THEN THE LETTING GO

Peter Stark

Peter Stark is a travel writer who specializes in writing about adventures in cold climates. In a review of Stark's Driving to Greenland: Arctic Travel, Nordic Sport, and Other Ventures into the Heart of Winter, *a critic for* Kirkus Reviews *describes Stark as a "daredevil writer" who "brings you to places you never dreamed of going, takes all the lumps, and gets you home safe and sound." You will get a sense of how Stark takes readers on well-guided adventures through the following selection, which was first published in 1997 by* Outside *magazine, to which Stark is a regular contributor. In that publication, the article was subtitled: "The Cold Hard Facts of Freezing to Death." As you read, be alert for any "facts" that Stark reports. But also consider how he uses narration to locate these facts within a story designed to hold the attention of readers.*

When your Jeep spins lazily off the mountain road and slams backward into a snowbank, you don't worry immediately about the cold. Your first thought is that you've just dented your bumper. Your second is that you've failed to bring a shovel. Your third is that you'll be late for dinner. Friends are expecting you at their cabin around eight for a moonlight ski, a late dinner, a sauna. Nothing can keep you from that.

Driving out of town, defroster roaring, you barely noted the bank thermometer on the town square: minus 27 degrees at 6:36. The radio weather report warned of a deep mass of arctic air settling over the region. The man who took your money at the Conoco station shook his head at the register and said he wouldn't be going anywhere tonight if he were you. You smiled. A little chill never hurt anybody with enough fleece and a good four-wheel-drive.

But now you're stuck. Jamming the gearshift into low, you try to muscle out of the drift. The tires whine on ice-slicked snow as headlights dance on the curtain of frosted firs across the road. Shoving the lever back into park, you shoulder open the door and step from your heated capsule. Cold slaps your naked face, squeezes tears from your eyes. You check your watch: 7:18. You consult your map: A thin, switchbacking line snakes up the mountain to the penciled square that marks the cabin.

Breath rolls from you in short frosted puffs. The Jeep lies cocked sideways in the snowbank like an empty turtle shell. You think of firelight and saunas and warm food and wine. You look again at the map. It's maybe five or six miles more to that penciled square. You run that far every day before breakfast. You'll just put on your skis. No problem.

There is no precise core temperature at which the human body perishes   5
from cold. At Dachau's cold-water immersion baths, Nazi doctors calculated
death to arrive at around 77 degrees Fahrenheit. The lowest recorded core
temperature in a surviving adult is 60.8 degrees. For a child it's lower: In 1994,
a two-year-old girl in Saskatchewan wandered out of her house into a minus-
40 night. She was found near her doorstep the next morning, limbs frozen
solid, her core temperature 57 degrees. She lived.

Others are less fortunate, even in much milder conditions. One of Europe's worst weather disasters occurred during a 1964 competitive walk on a
windy, rainy English moor; three of the racers died from hypothermia, though
temperatures never fell below freezing and ranged as high as 45.

But for all scientists and statisticians now know of freezing and its physiology, no one can yet predict exactly how quickly and in whom hypothermia
will strike—and whether it will kill when it does. The cold remains a mystery, more prone to fell men than women, more lethal to the thin and well
muscled than to those with avoirdupois,° and least forgiving to the arrogant
and the unaware.

The process begins even before you leave the car, when you remove your
gloves to squeeze a loose bail back into one of your ski bindings. The freezing
metal bites your flesh. Your skin temperature drops.

Within a few seconds, the palms of your hands are a chilly, painful 60 degrees. Instinctively, the web of surface capillaries on your hands constricts,
sending blood coursing away from your skin and deeper into your torso. Your
body is allowing your fingers to chill in order to keep its vital organs warm.

You replace your gloves, noticing only that your fingers have numbed   10
slightly. Then you kick boots into bindings and start up the road.

Were you a Norwegian fisherman or Inuit hunter, both of whom frequently work gloveless in the cold, your chilled hands would open their surface capillaries periodically to allow surges of warm blood to pass into them
and maintain their flexibility. This phenomenon, known as the hunter's response, can elevate a 35-degree skin temperature to 50 degrees within seven
or eight minutes.

Other human adaptations to the cold are more mysterious. Tibetan Buddhist monks can raise the skin temperature of their hands and feet by 15 degrees through meditation. Australian aborigines, who once slept on the
ground, unclothed, on near-freezing nights, would slip into a light hypother-
mic state, suppressing shivering until the rising sun rewarmed them.

You have no such defenses, having spent your days at a keyboard in a
climate-controlled office. Only after about ten minutes of hard climbing, as
your body temperature rises, does blood start seeping back into your fingers.
Sweat trickles down your sternum and spine.

°*avoirdupois:* French for "excess weight."

By now you've left the road and decided to shortcut up the forested mountainside to the road's next switchback. Treading slowly through deep, soft snow as the full moon hefts over a spiny ridgetop, throwing silvery bands of moonlight and shadow, you think your friends were right: It's a beautiful night for skiing—though you admit, feeling the minus-30 air bite at your face, it's also cold.

After an hour, there's still no sign of the switchback, and you've begun to worry. You pause to check the map. At this moment, your core temperature reaches its high: 100.8. Climbing in deep snow, you've generated nearly ten times as much body heat as you do when you are resting.

As you step around to orient map to forest, you hear a metallic pop. You look down. The loose bail has disappeared from your binding. You lift your foot and your ski falls from your boot.

You twist on your flashlight, and its cold-weakened batteries throw a yellowish circle in the snow. It's right around here somewhere, you think, as you sift the snow through gloved fingers. Focused so intently on finding the bail, you hardly notice the frigid air pressing against your tired body and sweat-soaked clothes.

The exertion that warmed you on the way uphill now works against you: Your exercise-dilated capillaries carry the excess heat of your core to your skin, and your wet clothing dispels it rapidly into the night. The lack of insulating fat over your muscles allows the cold to creep that much closer to your warm blood.

Your temperature begins to plummet. Within 17 minutes it reaches the normal 98.6. Then it slips below.

At 97 degrees, hunched over in your slow search, the muscles along your neck and shoulders tighten in what's known as pre-shivering muscle tone. Sensors have signaled the temperature control center in your hypothalamus, which in turn has ordered the constriction of the entire web of surface capillaries. Your hands and feet begin to ache with cold. Ignoring the pain, you dig carefully through the snow; another ten minutes pass. Without the bail you know you're in deep trouble.

Finally, nearly 45 minutes later, you find the bail. You even manage to pop it back into its socket and clamp your boot into the binding. But the clammy chill that started around your skin has now wrapped deep into your body's core.

At 95, you've entered the zone of mild hypothermia. You're now trembling violently as your body attains its maximum shivering response, an involuntary condition in which your muscles contract rapidly to generate additional body heat.

It was a mistake, you realize, to come out on a night this cold. You should turn back. Fishing into the front pocket of your shell parka, you fumble out the map. You consulted it to get here; it should be able to guide you back to the warm car. It doesn't occur to you in your increasingly clouded and panicky mental state that you could simply follow your tracks down the way you came.

And after this long stop, the skiing itself has become more difficult. By the time you push off downhill, your muscles have cooled and tightened so dramatically that they no longer contract easily, and once contracted, they won't relax. You're locked into an ungainly, spread-armed, weak-kneed snowplow.

Still, you manage to maneuver between stands of fir, swishing down *25* through silvery light and pools of shadow. You're too cold to think of the beautiful night or of the friends you had meant to see. You think only of the warm Jeep that waits for you somewhere at the bottom of the hill. Its gleaming shell is centered in your mind's eye as you come over the crest of a small knoll. You hear the sudden whistle of wind in your ears as you gain speed. Then, before your mind can quite process what the sight means, you notice a lump in the snow ahead.

Recognizing, slowly, the danger that you are in, you try to jam your skis to a stop. But in your panic, your balance and judgment are poor. Moments later, your ski tips plow into the buried log and you sail headfirst through the air and bellyflop into the snow.

You lie still. There's a dead silence in the forest, broken by the pumping of blood in your ears. Your ankle is throbbing with pain and you've hit your head. You've also lost your hat and a glove. Scratchy snow is packed down your shirt. Meltwater trickles down your neck and spine, joined soon by a thin line of blood from a small cut on your head.

This situation, you realize with an immediate sense of panic, is serious. Scrambling to rise, you collapse in pain, your ankle crumpling beneath you.

As you sink back into the snow, shaken, your heat begins to drain away at an alarming rate, your head alone accounting for 50 percent of the loss. The pain of the cold soon pierces your ears so sharply that you root about in the snow until you find your hat and mash it back onto your head.

But even that little activity has been exhausting. You know you should *30* find your glove as well, and yet you're becoming too weary to feel any urgency. You decide to have a short rest before going on.

An hour passes. At one point, a stray thought says you should start being scared, but fear is a concept that floats somewhere beyond your immediate reach, like that numb hand lying naked in the snow. You've slid into the temperature range at which cold renders the enzymes in your brain less efficient. With every one-degree drop in body temperature below 95, your cerebral metabolic rate falls off by 3 to 5 percent. When your core temperature reaches 93, amnesia nibbles at your consciousness. You check your watch: 12:58. Maybe someone will come looking for you soon. Moments later, you check again. You can't keep the numbers in your head. You'll remember little of what happens next.

Your head drops back. The snow crunches softly in your ear. In the minus-35-degree air, your core temperature falls about one degree every 30 to 40 minutes, your body heat leaching out into the soft, enveloping snow. Apathy at 91 degrees. Stupor at 90.

You've now crossed the boundary into profound hypothermia. By the time your core temperature has fallen to 88 degrees, your body has abandoned the urge to warm itself by shivering. Your blood is thickening like crankcase oil in a cold engine. Your oxygen consumption, a measure of your metabolic rate, has fallen by more than a quarter. Your kidneys, however, work overtime to process the fluid overload that occurred when the blood vessels in your extremities constricted and squeezed fluids toward your center. You feel a powerful urge to urinate, the only thing you feel at all.

By 87 degrees you've lost the ability to recognize a familiar face, should one suddenly appear from the woods.

At 86 degrees, your heart, its electrical impulses hampered by chilled *35* nerve tissues, becomes arrhythmic. It now pumps less than two-thirds the normal amount of blood. The lack of oxygen and the slowing metabolism of your brain, meanwhile, begin to trigger visual and auditory hallucinations.

You hear jingle bells. Lifting your face from your snow pillow, you realize with a surge of gladness that they're not sleigh bells; they're welcoming bells hanging from the door of your friends' cabin. You knew it had to be close by. The jingling is the sound of the cabin door opening, just through the fir trees.

Attempting to stand, you collapse in a tangle of skis and poles. That's OK. You can crawl. It's so close.

Hours later, or maybe it's minutes, you realize the cabin still sits beyond the grove of trees. You've crawled only a few feet. The light on your wristwatch pulses in the darkness: 5:20. Exhausted, you decide to rest your head for a moment.

When you lift it again, you're inside, lying on the floor before the woodstove. The fire throws off a red glow. First it's warm; then it's hot; then it's searing your flesh. Your clothing has caught fire.

At 85 degrees, those freezing to death, in a strange, anguished paroxysm, *40* often rip off their clothes. This phenomenon, known as paradoxical undressing, is common enough that urban hypothermia victims are sometimes initially diagnosed as victims of sexual assault. Though researchers are uncertain of the cause, the most logical explanation is that shortly before loss of consciousness, the constricted blood vessels near the body's surface suddenly dilate and produce a sensation of extreme heat against the skin.

All you know is that you're burning. You claw off your shell and pile sweater and fling them away.

But then, in a final moment of clarity, you realize there's no stove, no cabin, no friends. You're lying alone in the bitter cold, naked from the waist up. You grasp your terrible misunderstanding, a whole series of misunderstandings, like a dream ratcheting into wrongness. You've shed your clothes, your car, your oil-heated house in town. Without this ingenious technology you're simply a delicate, tropical organism whose range is restricted to a narrow sunlit band that girds the earth at the equator.

And you've now ventured way beyond it.

There's an adage about hypothermia: "You aren't dead until you're warm and dead."

At about 6:00 the next morning, his friends, having discovered the stalled   45
Jeep, find him, still huddled inches from the buried log, his gloveless hand shoved into his armpit. The flesh of his limbs is waxy and stiff as old putty, his pulse nonexistent, his pupils unresponsive to light. Dead.

But those who understand cold know that even as it deadens, it offers perverse salvation. Heat is a presence: the rapid vibrating of molecules. Cold is an absence: the damping of the vibrations. At absolute zero, minus 459.67 degrees Fahrenheit, molecular motion ceases altogether. It is this slowing that converts gases to liquids, liquids to solids, and renders solids harder. It slows bacterial growth and chemical reactions. In the human body, cold shuts down metabolism. The lungs take in less oxygen, the heart pumps less blood. Under normal temperatures, this would produce brain damage. But the chilled brain, having slowed its own metabolism, needs far less oxygen-rich blood and can, under the right circumstances, survive intact.

Setting her ear to his chest, one of his rescuers listens intently. Seconds pass. Then, faintly, she hears a tiny sound—a single thump, so slight that it might be the sound of her own blood. She presses her ear harder to the cold flesh. Another faint thump, then another.

The slowing that accompanies freezing is, in its way, so beneficial that it is even induced at times. Cardiologists today often use deep chilling to slow a patient's metabolism in preparation for heart or brain surgery. In this state of near suspension, the patient's blood flows slowly, his heart rarely beats—or in the case of those on heart–lung machines, doesn't beat at all; death seems near. But carefully monitored, a patient can remain in this cold stasis, undamaged, for hours.

The rescuers quickly wrap their friend's naked torso with a spare parka, his hands with mittens, his entire body with a bivy sack. They brush snow from his pasty, frozen face. Then one snakes down through the forest to the nearest cabin. The others, left in the pre-dawn darkness, huddle against him as silence closes around them. For a moment, the woman imagines she can hear the scurrying, breathing, snoring of a world of creatures that have taken cover this frigid night beneath the thick quilt of snow.

With a "one, two, three," the doctor and nurses slide the man's stiff, curled   50
form onto a table fitted with a mattress filled with warm water which will be regularly reheated. They'd been warned that they had a profound hypothermia case coming in. Usually such victims can be straightened from their tortured fetal positions. This one can't.

Technicians scissor with stainless-steel shears at the man's urine-soaked long underwear and shell pants, frozen together like corrugated cardboard. They attach heart-monitor electrodes to his chest and insert a low-temperature electronic thermometer into his rectum. Digital readings flash: 24 beats per minute and a core temperature of 79.2 degrees.

The doctor shakes his head. He can't remember seeing numbers so low. He's not quite sure how to revive this man without killing him.

In fact, many hypothermia victims die each year in the process of being rescued. In "rewarming shock," the constricted capillaries reopen almost all at once, causing a sudden drop in blood pressure. The slightest movement can send a victim's heart muscle into wild spasms of ventricular fibrillation. In 1980, 16 shipwrecked Danish fishermen were hauled to safety after an hour and a half in the frigid North Sea. They then walked across the deck of the rescue ship, stepped below for a hot drink, and dropped dead, all 16 of them.

"78.9," a technician calls out. "That's three-tenths down."

The patient is now experiencing "afterdrop," in which residual cold close to the body's surface continues to cool the core even after the victim is removed from the outdoors. 55

The doctor rapidly issues orders to his staff: intravenous administration of warm saline, the bag first heated in the microwave to 110 degrees. Elevating the core temperature of an average-size male one degree requires adding about 60 kilocalories of heat. A kilocalorie is the amount of heat needed to raise the temperature of one liter of water one degree Celsius. Since a quart of hot soup at 140 degrees offers about 30 kilocalories, the patient curled on the table would need to consume 40 quarts of chicken broth to push his core temperature up to normal. Even the warm saline, infused directly into his blood, will add only 30 kilocalories.

Ideally, the doctor would have access to a cardiopulmonary bypass machine, with which he could pump out the victim's blood, rewarm and oxygenate it, and pump it back in again, safely raising the core temperature as much as one degree every three minutes. But such machines are rarely available outside major urban hospitals. Here, without such equipment, the doctor must rely on other options.

"Let's scrub for surgery," he calls out.

Moments later, he's sliding a large catheter into an incision in the man's abdominal cavity. Warm fluid begins to flow from a suspended bag, washing through his abdomen, and draining out through another catheter placed in another incision. Prosaically, this lavage operates much like a car radiator in reverse: The solution warms the internal organs, and the warm blood in the organs is then pumped by the heart throughout the body.

The patient's stiff limbs begin to relax. His pulse edges up. But even so the jagged line of his heartbeat flashing across the EKG° screen shows the curious dip known as a J wave, common to hypothermia patients. 60

"Be ready to defibrillate," the doctor warns the EMTs.°

For another hour, nurses and EMTs hover around the edges of the table where the patient lies centered in a warm pool of light, as if offered up to the sun god. They check his heart. They check the heat of the mattress beneath

---

°*EKG:* electrocardiogram.
°*EMT:* emergency medical technician.

him. They whisper to one another about the foolishness of having gone out alone tonight.

And slowly the patient responds. Another liter of saline is added to the IV. The man's blood pressure remains far too low, brought down by the blood flowing out to the fast-opening capillaries of his limbs. Fluid lost through perspiration and urination has reduced his blood volume. But every 15 or 20 minutes, his temperature rises another degree. The immediate danger of cardiac fibrillation lessens, as the heart and thinning blood warm. Frostbite could still cost him fingers or an earlobe. But he appears to have beaten back the worst of the frigidity.

For the next half hour, an EMT quietly calls the readouts of the thermometer, a mantra that marks the progress of this cold-blooded protoorganism toward a state of warmer, higher consciousness.

"90.4 . . ."

"92.2 . . ." 65

From somewhere far away in the immense, cold darkness, you hear a faint, insistent hum. Quickly it mushrooms into a ball of sound, like a planet rushing toward you, and then it becomes a stream of words.

A voice is calling your name.

You don't want to open your eyes. You sense heat and light playing against your eyelids, but beneath their warm dance a chill wells up inside you from the sunless ocean bottoms and the farthest depths of space. You are too tired even to shiver. You want only to sleep.

"Can you hear me?" 70

You force open your eyes. Lights glare overhead. Around the lights faces hover atop uniformed bodies. You try to think: You've been away a very long time, but where have you been?

"You're at the hospital. You got caught in the cold."

You try to nod. Your neck muscles feel rusted shut, unused for years. They respond to your command with only a slight twitch.

"You'll probably have amnesia," the voice says.

You remember the moon rising over the spiky ridgetop and skiing up toward it, toward someplace warm beneath the frozen moon. After that, nothing—only that immense coldness lodged inside you. 75

"We're trying to get a little warmth back into you," the voice says.

You'd nod if you could. But you can't move. All you can feel is throbbing discomfort everywhere. Glancing down to where the pain is most biting, you notice blisters filled with clear fluid dotting your fingers, once gloveless in the snow. During the long, cold hours the tissue froze and ice crystals formed in the tiny spaces between your cells, sucking water from them, blocking the blood supply. You stare at them absently.

"I think they'll be fine," a voice from overhead says. "The damage looks superficial. We expect that the blisters will break in a week or so, and the tissue should revive after that."

If not, you know that your fingers will eventually turn black, the color of bloodless, dead tissue. And then they will be amputated.

But worry slips from you as another wave of exhaustion sweeps in. Slowly *80* you drift off, dreaming of warmth, of tropical ocean wavelets breaking across your chest, of warm sand beneath you.

Hours later, still logy and numb, you surface, as if from deep under water. A warm tide seems to be flooding your midsection. Focusing your eyes down there with difficulty, you see tubes running into you, their heat mingling with your abdomen's depthless cold like a churned-up river. You follow the tubes to the bag that hangs suspended beneath the electric light.

And with a lurch that would be a sob if you could make a sound, you begin to understand: The bag contains all that you had so nearly lost. These people huddled around you have brought you sunlight and warmth, things you once so cavalierly dismissed as constant, available, yours, summoned by the simple twisting of a knob or tossing on of a layer.

But in the hours since you last believed that, you've traveled to a place where there is no sun. You've seen that in the infinite reaches of the universe, heat is as glorious and ephemeral as the light of the stars. Heat exists only where matter exists, where particles can vibrate and jump. In the infinite winter of space, heat is tiny; it is the cold that is huge.

Someone speaks. Your eyes move from bright lights to shadowy forms in the dim outer reaches of the room. You recognize the voice of one of the friends you set out to visit, so long ago now. She's smiling down at you crookedly.

"It's cold out there," she says. "Isn't it?"   *85*

QUESTIONS FOR DISCUSSION

1. What assumptions has Stark made about the social class of skiers and the people most likely to be reading this piece when it was first published?
2. What kinds of people are especially at risk of freezing to death?
3. What mistakes are made by the character Stark invented for this article? Could any of them have been avoided?
4. How can hypothermia be treated? Under what circumstances can someone suffering from profound hypothermia have any chance of surviving?
5. Stark reports "the cold hard facts of freezing to death" within a narrative that traces what happens to a character exposed to severe cold overnight. How effective is this strategy? Did it influence the extent to which you were willing to trust the information he is reporting?

SUGGESTIONS FOR WRITING

1. Write an essay reporting how you were treated for a sports injury. Research medical literature on your injury and indicate whether other methods of treatment could have been used in your case.

2. Consider the risks that people face when engaging in a sport or other activity of interest to you. Write a report in which you alert readers to these risks.
3. Research heat exhaustion and report how people can protect themselves from the effects of prolonged exposure to extreme heat.

LINKS

▨ Within the Book

For a woman's view of the outdoors, see "Living like Weasels" by Annie Dillard (pages 82–85).

▨ Elsewhere in Print

Blumberg, Mark S. *Body Heat: Temperature and Life on Earth.* Cambridge: Harvard UP, 2002.

Cobb, Norma, and Charles Sasser. *Arctic Homestead: The True Story of One Family's Survival and Courage in the Alaskan Wilds.* New York: St. Martin's, 2000.

Gisolfi, Carl V., and Francisco Mora. *The Hot Brain: Survival, Temperature, and the Human Body.* Cambridge: MIT, 2000.

Janowsky, Chris, and Gretchen Janowsky. *Survival: A Manual That Could Save Your Life.* Boulder: Paladin, 1986.

Stark, Peter. *Driving to Greenland: Arctic Travel, Nordic Sport, and Other Ventures into the Heart of Winter.* New York: Lyons, 1994.

———. *Last Breath: The Limits of Adventure.* New York: Ballantine, 2002.

———, ed. *Ring of Ice: True Tales of Adventure, Exploration, and Arctic Life.* New York: Lyons, 2000.

———, and Steven M. Krauzer. *Winter Adventure: A Complete Guide to Winter Sports.* New York: Norton, 1995.

▨ Online

www.mhhe.com/motives

Click on "More Resources" then "Writing to Report Information."

■ ■ ■

JEFFERSON AND THE ENVIRONMENT

Peter Ling

Although best known as one of the nation's founders and its third president, Thomas Jefferson was also an amateur scientist who took a keen interest in experimenting with different ways of improving the environment. Ironically, as Peter Ling shows in the following article, several of Jefferson's ideas have ultimately had a harmful effect on land management within the United States. To prepare yourself to understand the issues in question, you might benefit from reflecting on the extent to which you believe that humans can control what happens to the environment.

Ling first published "Jefferson and the Environment" in a 2004 issue of History Today, *an American magazine for readers who enjoy learning about history but are not necessarily professional historians. Born and educated in England, Ling teaches American studies at the University of Nottingham. The author of books on the role of the automobile in the United States and the influence of Martin Luther King, Jr., in the struggle for civil rights, Ling explained his approach to history for* Contemporary Authors: *"The car book was prompted by an aversion to theories of technological determinism, the protest book by a reaction against protest accounts that stress the leaders." Accordingly, "Jefferson and the Environment" can be read not just as "history" but as a response to an ongoing problem.*

Over two centuries since his presidency, most Americans still feel that Thomas Jefferson deserves not just his memorial on the Mall in Washington, D.C., but to have his face carved gigantically into the face of Mount Rushmore. Every year, tourists flock to the Virginian's elegant mansion of Monticello and hear their guides describe Jefferson's many talents as architect, botanist, inventor and violinist, not to mention politician. Jefferson himself listed three achievements for posterity: drafting the Declaration of Independence, securing freedom of religion under the law, and founding the University of Virginia. Of these, most people know simply the first. But arguably his botanical and agricultural ideas have had the most visible, widespread and long-lasting impact, for good or ill.

Those who know that Jefferson was America's third president (1801–9) would probably add the Louisiana Purchase (1803) from Napoleonic France, a measure which doubled the size of the United States by securing a claim to the trans-Mississippi West. He is also remembered for commissioning two army officers, Meriwether Lewis and William Clark, to explore the new territory, especially the Missouri valley, in search of an easy pathway to the Pacific.

Jefferson retains a wide appeal in America. Historically-minded Westerners see the Lewis and Clark expedition as marking the opening up of their region to pioneer settlement. Old-style Southerners, on the other hand, like to highlight his (and James Madison's) defense of states' rights against federal power in the 1790s. Republicans who believe in limited government venerate Jefferson for coining the phrase "that government which governs least governs best," while radicals equally gleefully quote Jefferson's sanguine response to the French Revolution: "the tree of liberty must be refreshed from time to time with the blood of patriots and tyrants. It is its natural manure."

The main source of posthumous criticism has been the clash between Jefferson's immortal declaration that "all men are created equal and are endowed by their Creator with certain inalienable rights" and his actual conduct as a slave-owning planter. Revelations about his intimate relationship with one of his slaves, Sally Hemings, seemingly confirmed by DNA tests on their descendants, have further deepened the controversy surrounding Jefferson and race. Little, however, has been said about Jefferson's environmental legacy.

Jefferson was one of the leading American figures in the Enlightenment, which sought to place the whole of experience under the scrutiny of reason or science. This scientific outlook is amply documented in his many notebooks recording detailed observation, and the environmental consequences of that approach are first evident in his work as a plantation owner. To understand its legacy, however, it is also useful to know a little about the farming practices from which he broke away. By Jefferson's time, tobacco cultivation was well established as the Virginian road to wealth and power. To cope with the soil-depleting effects of tobacco, planters had adopted a "land-rotation system." In the first year of cultivation, the raw land, still littered with stumps, roots and girdled trees, was planted with maize or beans or both. If the cleared land proved fertile, tobacco was then grown for as many as three successive years. Thereafter, the preferred crop would be maize, intercropped with beans, for a further three years, with perhaps a final crop of wheat or rye before the field was abandoned for as much as twenty years. During this long "fallow," a secondary succession of plants—grasses, shrubs, pines, even hardwoods—restored a measure of fertility. When planters noted this second-growth forest, they knew that it was safe to bring the land back into cultivation. It was a system that required almost perpetual land clearance. Planters had to have some land growing tobacco to produce a cash crop because of their reliance on mercantile credit and because the labor-intensive land-rotation system depended on the maintenance of a large slave labor force.

Jefferson was not satisfied with current farming practices. Spurred partly by the relatively poor fertility of his own land along the Rivanna River, his reforming impulse was deepened when he heard the many adverse comments made about the Virginian landscape. Almost all visitors whether from Europe or the more mixed, arable farmlands of the middle and northern colonies complained about the unkempt fields of the region: dying trees and stumps, hummocked fields (due to the need to "hill" tobacco), maize entangled with beans, and areas seemingly left to go "wild." It all smacked of poor husbandry, they commented, indicative perhaps of the disaffected mentality of the slaves.

By the 1780s, Southern agricultural reformers such as John Taylor of Caroline were urging change. Fields should be put in good order from the start by removing stumps and other rubbish that might prevent effective ploughing. Land rotation should be displaced by more continuous cultivation, sustained by fertilizers such as Plaster of Paris and animal manure. Jefferson's agricultural analogy regarding the benefits of the French Revolution reflects the fact that he advocated these new scientific farming methods: he defended the divine rite of manuring.

Yet this Enlightenment-inspired imposition of order on the unkempt farm landscape was environmentally devastating. The more intensive clearing and tilling of fields accelerated the loss of soil nutrients to the processes of wind and rain erosion. Sediment core samples from Chesapeake estuaries reveal sharp increases in sedimentation rates and pollen accumulation in the late eighteenth and early nineteenth centuries. Both are consistent with increased soil erosion due to the intensification of farming. Jefferson was aware of the problem, and tried to mitigate it by what we would term contour ploughing on his hilly estate. After heavy summer rains in 1795, he wrote:

> I imagine we never lost more soil than this summer. It is moderately estimated at a year's rent.

His faith in the superiority of a rationalist order, however, obscured the need to adapt production goals to sustainable environmental parameters. He held to the illusion that the land could be changed to suit human designs much as he changed and developed his house at Monticello. This dream of progress leached into the larger agricultural development of America, thanks in part to Jefferson's colossal influence.

A key part of that influence was promoting the transplantation of flora and fauna. The French philosopher Abbé Renaud had popularized the idea that living creatures transplanted from Old World to New would not flourish but degenerate. In his most extensive published work, the *Notes on the State of Virginia,* (1787), Jefferson was at pains both to refute the claim, and at the same time to introduce nonindigenous animals and plants that might help American farmers to prosper. Among the crops he championed was upland rice, which he hoped might replace the type of rice grown on the large slave plantations of coastal South Carolina and Georgia. He experimented with African, European and Asian species and enjoyed some success with the upland varieties.

He was similarly determined to promote olive cultivation, but his efforts *10* at Monticello met with little success. Persistent experiments in Georgia and South Carolina were equally disappointing, and yet even in his dotage in the mid-1820s, Jefferson refused to acknowledge that this tree of the semi-arid Mediterranean would not grow well along America's southeastern seaboard. So blind was his enthusiasm for exotic sources of cooking oil, such as the olive and sesame, that he ignored the potential of the native American crop, maize, and that of peanuts, a plant which had been introduced by African slaves. Jefferson was equally keen to transplant species from one part of North

America to another. His largely unsuccessful attempts to grow sugar maple trees at Monticello testify to that determination, and also to his refusal to heed the tree's preference for higher, cooler locales than his Blue Ridge estate.

Jefferson's fields and gardens at his retirement home of Poplar Forest contained hop clover, hemp, bent grass and winter vetch from England; alfalfa from the Mediterranean; Guinea corn and sesame from Africa; Nanking cotton from Asia; field peas, sainfoin, and turnips from Europe; sulla grass from Malta. His buffalo or Kentucky clover came from the inland grasslands of the Ohio Valley. All his prized orchard fruits—apples, pears, cherries and peaches—were introduced from abroad. His zeal for the importation of non-local plants both underlies and explains his notion that the huge tracts of territory west of the Mississippi could serve as a natural reserve for the Native American tribes. He expected the transplanted tribes to develop into farmers; an odd notion, given that many of them had agricultural practices whose adoption had enabled the early eastern seaboard colonists to survive. Jefferson's reserve idea ultimately enabled his successors to expedite land development east of the Mississippi via a policy of Indian removal.

Jefferson gave priority to development in a profoundly agrarian rather than industrial way. He deplored cities as "sores on the body politic" and celebrated the "cultivators of the earth" as "the most valuable citizens." A virtuous citizenry, which Jefferson considered essential to a republican form of government, was most reliably constituted of yeoman farmers he believed. Their preponderance within America's growing population was guaranteed, in his words, "as long as there shall be vacant lands in any part of America." An enormous act of erasure was implicit within that term "vacant lands," but leaving this aside, Jefferson's political economy rested on the principle of a fairly general access to land. It was a principle that underpinned the powerful "homesteading" ideal that attracted thousands of immigrants to nineteenth-century America. Jefferson's most enduring legacy in environmental terms, however, was not simply the acquisition of the trans-Mississippi West via the Louisiana Purchase; it was his contribution to the development of the key means of promoting its sale: the rectilinear castral survey, as prescribed in the Land Ordinance of 1785, sometimes referred to as the Jeffersonian grid.

He supported the application of navigational principles of latitude and longitude to impose order on the uncharted land, and thus facilitate its commodification and sale. Subdividing the navigational lines into township boxes of thirty-six square miles, surveys segmented the land into 640-acre tracts, quartered into 160-acre sections, and then requartered to achieve the minimum 40-acre parcel of land. Subsequent land law commonly regarded 160 acres or a quarter section as sufficient to sustain a homestead or yeoman farm. This abstract approach ignored the ecology of the land. As Richard Manning points out in his reflections on America's lost grasslands (1995), the grid system conceived of the land as "a blank slate needing only lines, plows, and bags of European seeds."

Born of a unique set of conditions, each ecosystem has its own specific plant community, but such particularities had no place within the Jeffersonian

American farmland divided in rectangles (a pattern that follows from the Jeffersonian grid).

grid. The latter's limitations were famously highlighted by John Wesley Powell's 1878 report on the arid lands of the West. He insisted that the 1862 Homestead Act's sale and distribution of public lands had created a carpet of 160-acre rectangles of land that could not sustain agriculture in an area defined by access to limited water supplies. Settlement, Powell insisted, must adapt to the arid conditions: with smaller, intensively cultivated plots in the low proportion of land where irrigation was feasible and much larger ranches of typically 2,560 acres for grazing elsewhere. Overall, Powell wanted settlement to conform to the land, but a snapshot of the American West today, with its straight irrigation canals and rectangular parcels running like tiles to the horizon, confirms his failure in displacing the Jeffersonian grid.

Equally the result of the Jefferson legacy, most of the animals and plants raised within those rectangles today are non-native species. In the 1880s, more docile, easier to fatten, shorthorn cattle from the British Isles began to replace the Spanish-derived, long-horned steers, which had predominated on the open range. As products of a much wetter climate, the shorthorn breeds preferred leafy plants, known as forbs, and so they congregated in coulées, streambeds, and draws, and selectively overgrazed the land to dirt. Even their grazing of grasses was destructive. Thus whereas native elk and deer leave the indigenous blue-stem wheat grass alone during the summer and only dig out its tuft of leaves from the winter snow, shorthorn cattle eat it indiscriminately in the growing season, slowing its root growth pattern and diminishing a potential winter food supply.

15

After several catastrophic winters in the late 1880s proved that the new herds were unable to find sufficient winter forage, ranchers began raising winter-feed crops, such as alfalfa and other imported exotic grasses. In this oft-repeated cycle, new fauna debilitated the native flora and encouraged the introduction of alien flora, not only in the West, but in the Midwest, too, where 70 percent of the grain now goes to feed livestock. As a cash crop, cattle encouraged ranchers to practice ruthless predator control, killing bears, bob-cats and mountain lions. Elk, bison, antelope, and deer numbers were sharply reduced also, because while not predators, they were competitors for grazing. Man became the prime, and often blind, regulator of the environment.

Jefferson was the proud holder of a patent for a mould-board plough. This enabled deeper ploughing, which, he wrote to Charles Wilson Peale in 1813, was "the recipe for every good thing in farming." Jefferson's plough would have been unable to cut through the dense root system of the prairie grasslands, but subsequent inventors developed steel ploughs that did so. By that stage, Abraham Lincoln, who idolized Jefferson, had presided over a Republican-dominated Congress that passed the 1862 Homestead Act, appro-priated funds for a U.S. Department of Agriculture (USDA), and allocated public lands to support both railroad construction and a college system to teach farmers to farm scientifically. Collectively, the grid, the sale of public lands on the expectation that they would raise commodities that would jus-tify the railroads, and the development of a federal department and an educa-tional system wedded to the scientific exploitation of natural resources completed the Jeffersonian onslaught on the land.

The new agricultural institutions encouraged the continuing introduc-tion of non-native species. Richard Manning points to the work of Frank Meyer of the USDA's Bureau of Plant Industry, who, as a result of four plant-hunting expeditions between 1905 and 1918, single-handedly introduced 2,500 plants from Europe, Siberia and China. Meyer was interested especially in plants that would flourish in areas of low rainfall. The exotic plants he found, however, had characteristics that enabled them to dominate their new surroundings in ways reminiscent of their human immigrant counterparts. Chinese chestnuts, for instance, had developed immunity to a type of blight found in their homeland, but when Meyer's specimens brought that same blight with them to America, it devastated the native American varieties that had no such immunity.

Meyer also introduced crown vetch, a nitrogen-fixing forb that grows on disturbed sites, and crested wheat grass, a grass able to withstand hard grazing. Both species seemed remedies to the overgrazing problems produced by the introduction of shorthorn cattle. Planted extensively alongside roadside cuts, however, crown vetch spread rapidly at the expense of native prairie grasses. Commercial crested wheat grass seed became available in 1929, just as the Dust Bowl and the Great Depression forced the abandonment of many wheat farms. At the USDA's urging, and at a subsidized price, much of the aban-doned land was seeded with crested wheat grass and it continued to be the plant of choice under the federal Conservation Reserve Program for many years. As a result, crested wheat grass—and nothing but crested wheat grass—grows for miles on America's high plains. Unlike native species, the new grass does not cure—that is, it has no nutritional value in winter. In recent winters, this has produced the ghoulish spectacle of mule deer, elk and antelope starving to death in endless fields of grass. Crested wheat grass has also been implicated in the sharp decline in the Great Plains' native bird population.

Many more exotic species have invaded the American grassland accidentally, unwittingly transported by the processes of exchange that have always been fundamental to Western expansion. The most successful show a characteristic rapid growth on disturbed soil. The flow of motor traffic ensures that roadside verges offer a perpetual seedbed for such plants and since the roads follow the Jeffersonian grid, so do these weeds. What was once an abstract line on a map has now been inscribed in vegetation across the land. And if Jefferson's fabled pursuit of happiness requires Americans to go off-road, the alien grasses soon follow, initiating a policy of herbicidal containment that has its own malign effects. 20

It might be argued that Jefferson himself is not historically culpable, that these are unintended consequences, the product of processes of which he and his contemporaries had no knowledge. But they did flow from a will to power that is inherent in Enlightenment rationalism, and Jefferson certainly shared that impulse. They were also inherent in a philosophy of expropriation that Jefferson celebrated when he declared that he wished to shake off "the dead hand of the past" and guarantee the world in "usufruct" to the living. Neither the quest for power over nature nor the preoccupation with the planet's yield to the present (what is casually referred to as "growth") has abated. We, unlike Jefferson, know the consequences, so we cannot exonerate ourselves except by acting to reduce and repair the damage of the great President's environmental legacy.

QUESTIONS FOR DISCUSSION

1. What does Ling accomplish by beginning his article with a list of Jefferson's accomplishments?
2. Ling does not introduce his focus on Jefferson and the environment until the end of paragraph 4. Should he have done so sooner?
3. According to Ling, what motivated Jefferson to become an agricultural reformer?
4. What has been the lasting impact of Jefferson's attitude toward the environment?
5. In your opinion, who has benefited from the Jeffersonian approach to farming, and who has suffered?
6. Consider Ling's concluding paragraph. Based on what has led up to it, how fair is this paragraph, and how well does it function as a conclusion?

SUGGESTIONS FOR WRITING

1. Identify a nonnative species that is now commonly found in your state. Research the effect this species has had on the environment, and report what you discover.
2. Research agricultural policies that could "repair the damage of the great President's environmental legacy"; then write a report summarizing the changes that could be implemented.
3. Discover the context in which Jefferson made the remark Ling quotes in paragraph 3: "the tree of liberty must be refreshed from time to time with the blood of patriots and tyrants. It is its natural manure." Without seeking to justify or condemn this opinion, write a report that summarizes what Jefferson could have known about the French Revolution at the time he made this remark.

LINKS

■ Within the Book

To understand another way in which Jefferson has had a lasting effect on the United States, see "The Declaration of Independence" (pages 481–484).

■ Elsewhere in Print

Bernstein, R. B. *Thomas Jefferson.* New York: Oxford UP, 2003.
Cochrane, Willard. *The Development of American Agriculture.* Minneapolis: U of Minnesota P, 1993.
Cronon, William. *Uncommon Ground: Toward Reinventing Nature.* New York: Norton, 1996.
Doyle, William. *The French Revolution.* New York: Oxford UP, 2001.
Jackson, Donald. *Thomas Jefferson and the Stony Mountains: Exploring the West from Monticello.* Urbana: U of Illinois P, 1981.
Ling, Peter. *America and the Automobile.* Manchester: Manchester UP, 1990.
———. *Martin Luther King, Jr.* New York: Routledge, 2002.
Manning, Richard. *Grassland: The History, Biology, Politics, and Promise of the American Prairie.* New York: Penguin, 1995.
Onuf, Peter. *Jeffersonian Legacies.* Charlottesville: U of Virginia P, 1993.

■ Online

www.mhhe.com/motives

Click on "More Resources" then "Writing to Report Information."

■ ■ ■

THE AMERICAN FLAVOR INDUSTRY

Eric Schlosser

Eric Schlosser is the author of Fast Food Nation, *which has been described as "a groundbreaking work of investigation and cultural history, likely to transform the way America thinks about the way it eats." Discussing what motivated him to do the research for this book, he told an interviewer, "I'm not a radical vegetarian, although I have a lot of respect for vegetarians and I think a lot of their arguments are very compelling. I came to this project as a person who has eaten enormous amounts of fast food and as a person who has probably eaten more hamburgers than any other type of food." "The American Flavor Industry" is an excerpt from Schlosser's book. It was published in a 2001 issue of* The Atlantic, *to which Schlosser is a regular contributor. Read primarily by college-educated men and women,* The Atlantic *has been published since 1857. Each issue includes well-regarded analyses of social and political concerns, fiction, and poetry, as well as reviews of books and movies.*

The french fry was "almost sacrosanct for me," Ray Kroc, one of the founders of McDonald's, wrote in his autobiography, "its preparation a ritual to be followed religiously." During the chain's early years french fries were made from scratch every day. Russet Burbank potatoes were peeled, cut into shoestrings, and fried in McDonald's kitchens. As the chain expanded nationwide, in the mid-1960s, it sought to cut labor costs, reduce the number of suppliers, and ensure that its fries tasted the same at every restaurant. McDonald's began switching to frozen french fries in 1966—and few customers noticed the difference. Nevertheless, the change had a profound effect on the nation's agriculture and diet. A familiar food had been transformed into a highly processed industrial commodity. McDonald's fries now come from huge manufacturing plants that can peel, slice, cook, and freeze two million pounds of potatoes a day. The rapid expansion of McDonald's and the popularity of its low-cost, mass-produced fries changed the way Americans eat. In 1960 Americans consumed an average of about eighty-one pounds of fresh potatoes and four pounds of frozen french fries. In 2000 they consumed an average of about fifty pounds of fresh potatoes and thirty pounds of frozen fries. Today McDonald's is the largest buyer of potatoes in the United States.

The taste of McDonald's french fries played a crucial role in the chain's success—fries are much more profitable than hamburgers—and was long praised by customers, competitors, and even food critics. James Beard loved McDonald's fries. Their distinctive taste does not stem from the kind of potatoes that McDonald's buys, the technology that processes them, or the restaurant equipment that fries them: other chains use Russet Burbanks, buy their french fries from the same large processing companies, and have similar fryers in their restaurant kitchens. The taste of a french fry is largely determined by the cooking oil. For decades McDonald's cooked its french fries in a mixture of about seven percent cottonseed oil and 93 percent beef tallow. The mixture gave the fries their unique flavor—and more saturated beef fat per ounce than a McDonald's hamburger.

In 1990, amid a barrage of criticism over the amount of cholesterol in its fries, McDonald's switched to pure vegetable oil. This presented the company with a challenge: how to make fries that subtly taste like beef without cooking them in beef tallow. A look at the ingredients in McDonald's french fries suggests how the problem was solved. Toward the end of the list is a seemingly innocuous yet oddly mysterious phrase: "natural flavor." That ingredient helps to explain not only why the fries taste so good but also why most fast food—indeed, most of the food Americans eat today—tastes the way it does.

Open your refrigerator, your freezer, your kitchen cupboards, and look at the labels on your food. You'll find "natural flavor" or "artificial flavor" in just about every list of ingredients. The similarities between these two broad categories are far more significant than the differences. Both are man-made additives that give most processed food most of its taste. People usually buy a food item the first time because of its packaging or appearance. Taste usually determines whether they buy it again. About 90 percent of the money that Americans now spend on food goes to buy processed food. The canning, freezing, and dehydrating techniques used in processing destroy most of food's flavor—and so a vast industry has arisen in the United States to make processed food palatable. Without this flavor industry today's fast food would not exist. The names of the leading American fast-food chains and their best-selling menu items have become embedded in our popular culture and famous worldwide. But few people can name the companies that manufacture fast food's taste.

The flavor industry is highly secretive. Its leading companies will not divulge the precise formulas of flavor compounds or the identities of clients. The secrecy is deemed essential for protecting the reputations of beloved brands. The fast-food chains, understandably, would like the public to believe that the flavors of the food they sell somehow originate in their restaurant kitchens, not in distant factories run by other firms. A McDonald's french fry is one of countless foods whose flavor is just a component in a complex manufacturing process. The look and the taste of what we eat now are frequently deceiving—by design.

THE FLAVOR CORRIDOR

The New Jersey Turnpike runs through the heart of the flavor industry, an industrial corridor dotted with refineries and chemical plants. International Flavors & Fragrances (IFF), the world's largest flavor company, has a manufacturing facility off Exit 8A in Dayton, New Jersey; Givaudan, the world's second-largest flavor company, has a plant in East Hanover. Haarmann & Reimer, the largest German flavor company, has a plant in Teterboro, as does Takasago, the largest Japanese flavor company. Flavor Dynamics has a plant in South Plainfield; Frutarom is in North Bergen; Elan Chemical is in Newark. Dozens of companies manufacture flavors in the corridor between Teaneck and South Brunswick. Altogether the area produces about two thirds of the flavor additives sold in the United States.

The IFF plant in Dayton is a huge pale-blue building with a modern office complex attached to the front. It sits in an industrial park, not far from a BASF plastics factory, a Jolly French Toast factory, and a plant that manufactures Liz Claiborne cosmetics. Dozens of tractor-trailers were parked at the IFF loading dock the afternoon I visited, and a thin cloud of steam floated from a roof vent. Before entering the plant, I signed a nondisclosure form, promising not to reveal the brand names of foods that contain IFF flavors. The place reminded me of Willy Wonka's chocolate factory. Wonderful smells drifted through the hallways, men and women in neat white lab coats cheerfully went about their work, and hundreds of little glass bottles sat on laboratory tables and shelves. The bottles contained powerful but fragile flavor chemicals, shielded from light by brown glass and round white caps shut tight. The long chemical names on the little white labels were as mystifying to me as medieval Latin. These odd-sounding things would be mixed and poured and turned into new substances, like magic potions.

I was not invited into the manufacturing areas of the IFF plant, where, it was thought, I might discover trade secrets. Instead I toured various laboratories and pilot kitchens, where the flavors of well-established brands are tested or adjusted, and where whole new flavors are created. IFF's snack-and-savory lab is responsible for the flavors of potato chips, corn chips, breads, crackers, breakfast cereals, and pet food. The confectionery lab devises flavors for ice cream, cookies, candies, toothpastes, mouthwashes, and antacids. Everywhere I looked, I saw famous, widely advertised products sitting on laboratory desks and tables. The beverage lab was full of brightly colored liquids in clear bottles. It comes up with flavors for popular soft drinks, sports drinks, bottled teas, and wine coolers, for all-natural juice drinks, organic soy drinks, beers, and malt liquors. In one pilot kitchen I saw a dapper food technologist, a middle-aged man with an elegant tie beneath his crisp lab coat, carefully preparing a batch of cookies with white frosting and pink-and-white sprinkles. In another pilot kitchen I saw a pizza oven, a grill, a milk-shake machine, and a french fryer identical to those I'd seen at innumerable fast-food restaurants.

In addition to being the world's largest flavor company, IFF manufactures the smells of six of the ten best-selling fine perfumes in the United States, including Estée Lauder's Beautiful, Clinique's Happy, Lancôme's Trésor, and Calvin Klein's Eternity. It also makes the smells of household products such as deodorant, dishwashing detergent, bath soap, shampoo, furniture polish, and floor wax. All these aromas are made through essentially the same process: the manipulation of volatile chemicals. The basic science behind the scent of your shaving cream is the same as that governing the flavor of your TV dinner.

"NATURAL" AND "ARTIFICIAL"

Scientists now believe that human beings acquired the sense of taste as a way   10
to avoid being poisoned. Edible plants generally taste sweet, harmful ones bitter. The taste buds on our tongues can detect the presence of half a dozen or so basic tastes, including sweet, sour, bitter, salty, astringent, and umami, a taste discovered by Japanese researchers—a rich and full sense of deliciousness triggered by amino acids in foods such as meat, shellfish, mushrooms, potatoes, and seaweed. Taste buds offer a limited means of detection, however, compared with the human olfactory system, which can perceive thousands of different chemical aromas. Indeed, "flavor" is primarily the smell of gases being released by the chemicals you've just put in your mouth. The aroma of a food can be responsible for as much as 90 percent of its taste.

The act of drinking, sucking, or chewing a substance releases its volatile gases. They flow out of your mouth and up your nostrils, or up the passageway in the back of your mouth, to a thin layer of nerve cells called the olfactory epithelium, located at the base of your nose, right between your eyes. Your brain combines the complex smell signals from your olfactory epithelium with the simple taste signals from your tongue, assigns a flavor to what's in your mouth, and decides if it's something you want to eat.

A person's food preferences, like his or her personality, are formed during the first few years of life, through a process of socialization. Babies innately prefer sweet tastes and reject bitter ones; toddlers can learn to enjoy hot and spicy food, bland health food, or fast food, depending on what the people around them eat. The human sense of smell is still not fully understood. It is greatly affected by psychological factors and expectations. The mind focuses intently on some of the aromas that surround us and filters out the overwhelming majority. People can grow accustomed to bad smells or good smells; they stop noticing what once seemed overpowering. Aroma and memory are somehow inextricably linked. A smell can suddenly evoke a long-forgotten moment. The flavors of childhood foods seem to leave an indelible mark, and adults often return to them, without always knowing why. These "comfort foods" become a source of pleasure and reassurance—a fact that fast-food chains use to their advantage. Childhood memories of Happy Meals, which come with french fries, can translate into frequent adult visits to McDonald's. On average, Americans now eat about four servings of french fries every week.

The human craving for flavor has been a largely unacknowledged and unexamined force in history. For millennia royal empires have been built, unexplored lands traversed, and great religions and philosophies forever changed by the spice trade. In 1492 Christopher Columbus set sail to find seasoning. Today the influence of flavor in the world marketplace is no less decisive. The rise and fall of corporate empires—of soft-drink companies, snack-food companies, and fast-food chains—is often determined by how their products taste.

The flavor industry emerged in the mid-nineteenth century, as processed foods began to be manufactured on a large scale. Recognizing the need for flavor additives, early food processors turned to perfume companies that had long experience working with essential oils and volatile aromas. The great perfume houses of England, France, and the Netherlands produced many of the first flavor compounds. In the early part of the twentieth century Germany took the technological lead in flavor production, owing to its powerful chemical industry. Legend has it that a German scientist discovered methyl anthranilate, one of the first artificial flavors, by accident while mixing chemicals in his laboratory. Suddenly the lab was filled with the sweet smell of grapes. Methyl anthranilate later became the chief flavor compound in grape Kool-Aid. After World War II much of the perfume industry shifted from Europe to the United States, settling in New York City near the garment district and the fashion houses. The flavor industry came with it, later moving to New Jersey for greater plant capacity. Man-made flavor additives were used mostly in baked goods, candies, and sodas until the 1950s, when sales of processed food began to soar. The invention of gas chromatographs and mass spectrometers—machines capable of detecting volatile gases at low levels—vastly increased the number of flavors that could be synthesized. By the mid-1960s flavor companies were churning out compounds to supply the taste of Pop Tarts, Bac-Os, Tab, Tang, Filet-O-Fish sandwiches, and literally thousands of other new foods.

The American flavor industry now has annual revenues of about $1.4 billion. Approximately 10,000 new processed-food products are introduced every year in the United States. Almost all of them require flavor additives. And about nine out of ten of these products fail. The latest flavor innovations and corporate realignments are heralded in publications such as *Chemical Market Reporter, Food Chemical News, Food Engineering,* and *Food Product Design.* The progress of IFF has mirrored that of the flavor industry as a whole. IFF was formed in 1958, through the merger of two small companies. Its annual revenues have grown almost fifteenfold since the early 1970s, and it currently has manufacturing facilities in twenty countries.   *15*

Today's sophisticated spectrometers, gas chromatographs, and headspace-vapor analyzers provide a detailed map of a food's flavor components, detecting chemical aromas present in amounts as low as one part per billion. The human nose, however, is even more sensitive. A nose can detect aromas present in quantities of a few parts per trillion—an amount equivalent to about 0.000000000003 percent. Complex aromas, such as those of coffee and roasted meat, are composed of volatile gases from nearly a thousand different chemicals.

The smell of a strawberry arises from the interaction of about 350 chemicals that are present in minute amounts. The quality that people seek most of all in a food—flavor—is usually present in a quantity too infinitesimal to be measured in traditional culinary terms such as ounces or teaspoons. The chemical that provides the dominant flavor of bell pepper can be tasted in amounts as low as 0.02 parts per billion; one drop is sufficient to add flavor to five average-size swimming pools. The flavor additive usually comes next to last in a processed food's list of ingredients and often costs less than its packaging. Soft drinks contain a larger proportion of flavor additives than most products. The flavor in a twelve-ounce can of Coke costs about half a cent.

The color additives in processed foods are usually present in even smaller amounts than the flavor compounds. Many of New Jersey's flavor companies also manufacture these color additives, which are used to make processed foods look fresh and appealing. Food coloring serves many of the same decorative purposes as lipstick, eye shadow, mascara—and is often made from the same pigments. Titanium dioxide, for example, has proved to be an especially versatile mineral. It gives many processed candies, frostings, and icings their bright white color; it is a common ingredient in women's cosmetics; and it is the pigment used in many white oil paints and house paints. At Burger King, Wendy's, and McDonald's coloring agents have been added to many of the soft drinks, salad dressings, cookies, condiments, chicken dishes, and sandwich buns.

Studies have found that the color of a food can greatly affect how its taste is perceived. Brightly colored foods frequently seem to taste better than bland-looking foods, even when the flavor compounds are identical. Foods that somehow look off-color often seem to have off tastes. For thousands of years human beings have relied on visual cues to help determine what is edible. The color of fruit suggests whether it is ripe, the color of meat whether it is rancid. Flavor researchers sometimes use colored lights to modify the influence of visual cues during taste tests. During one experiment in the early 1970s people were served an oddly tinted meal of steak and french fries that appeared normal beneath colored lights. Everyone thought the meal tasted fine until the lighting was changed. Once it became apparent that the steak was actually blue and the fries were green, some people became ill.

The federal Food and Drug Administration does not require companies to disclose the ingredients of their color or flavor additives so long as all the chemicals in them are considered by the agency to be GRAS ("generally recognized as safe"). This enables companies to maintain the secrecy of their formulas. It also hides the fact that flavor compounds often contain more ingredients than the foods to which they give taste. The phrase "artificial strawberry flavor" gives little hint of the chemical wizardry and manufacturing skill that can make a highly processed food taste like strawberries.

A typical artificial strawberry flavor, like the kind found in a Burger King strawberry milk shake, contains the following ingredients: amyl acetate, amyl butyrate, amyl valerate, anethol, anisyl formate, benzyl acetate, benzyl isobutyrate, butyric acid, cinnamyl isobutyrate, cinnamyl valerate, cognac essen-

20

tial oil, diacetyl, dipropyl ketone, ethyl acetate, ethyl amyl ketone, ethyl butyrate, ethyl cinnamate, ethyl heptanoate, ethyl heptylate, ethyl lactate, ethyl methylphenylglycidate, ethyl nitrate, ethyl propionate, ethyl valerate, heliotropin, hydroxyphenyl-2-butanone (10 percent solution in alcohol), α-ionone, isobutyl anthranilate, isobutyl butyrate, lemon essential oil, maltol, 4-methylacetophenone, methyl anthranilate, methyl benzoate, methyl cinnamate, methyl heptine carbonate, methyl naphthyl ketone, methyl salicylate, mint essential oil, neroli essential oil, nerolin, neryl isobutyrate, orris butter, phenethyl alcohol, rose, rum ether, γ-undecalactone, vanillin, and solvent.

Although flavors usually arise from a mixture of many different volatile chemicals, often a single compound supplies the dominant aroma. Smelled alone, that chemical provides an unmistakable sense of the food. Ethyl-2-methyl butyrate, for example, smells just like an apple. Many of today's highly processed foods offer a blank palette: Whatever chemicals are added to them will give them specific tastes. Adding methyl-2-pyridyl ketone makes something taste like popcorn. Adding ethyl-3-hydroxy butanoate makes it taste like marshmallow. The possibilities are now almost limitless. Without affecting appearance or nutritional value, processed foods could be made with aroma chemicals such as hexanal (the smell of freshly cut grass) or 3-methyl butanoic acid (the smell of body odor).

The 1960s were the heyday of artificial flavors in the United States. The synthetic versions of flavor compounds were not subtle, but they did not have to be, given the nature of most processed food. For the past twenty years food processors have tried hard to use only "natural flavors" in their products. According to the FDA, these must be derived entirely from natural sources—from herbs, spices, fruits, vegetables, beef, chicken, yeast, bark, roots, and so forth. Consumers prefer to see natural flavors on a label, out of a belief that they are more healthful. Distinctions between artificial and natural flavors can be arbitrary and somewhat absurd, based more on how the flavor has been made than on what it actually contains.

"A natural flavor," says Terry Acree, a professor of food science at Cornell University, "is a flavor that's been derived with an out-of-date technology." Natural flavors and artificial flavors sometimes contain exactly the same chemicals, produced through different methods. Amyl acetate, for example, provides the dominant note of banana flavor. When it is distilled from bananas with a solvent, amyl acetate is a natural flavor. When it is produced by mixing vinegar with amyl alcohol and adding sulfuric acid as a catalyst, amyl acetate is an artificial flavor. Either way it smells and tastes the same. "Natural flavor" is now listed among the ingredients of everything from Health Valley Blueberry Granola Bars to Taco Bell Hot Taco Sauce.

A natural flavor is not necessarily more healthful or purer than an artificial one. When almond flavor—benzaldehyde—is derived from natural sources, such as peach and apricot pits, it contains traces of hydrogen cyanide, a deadly poison. Benzaldehyde derived by mixing oil of clove and amyl acetate does not contain any cyanide. Nevertheless, it is legally considered an artificial flavor and sells at a much lower price. Natural and artificial flavors are now manufactured at the same chemical plants, places that few people would associate with Mother Nature.

A TRAINED NOSE AND A POETIC SENSIBILITY

The small and elite group of scientists who create most of the flavor in most of the food now consumed in the United States are called "flavorists." They draw on a number of disciplines in their work: biology, psychology, physiology, and organic chemistry. A flavorist is a chemist with a trained nose and a poetic sensibility. Flavors are created by blending scores of different chemicals in tiny amounts—a process governed by scientific principles but demanding a fair amount of art. In an age when delicate aromas and microwave ovens do not easily co-exist, the job of the flavorist is to conjure illusions about processed food and, in the words of one flavor company's literature, to ensure "consumer likeability." The flavorists with whom I spoke were discreet, in keeping with the dictates of their trade. They were also charming, cosmopolitan, and ironic. They not only enjoyed fine wine but could identify the chemicals that give each grape its unique aroma. One flavorist compared his work to composing music. A well-made flavor compound will have a "top note" that is often followed by a "dry-down" and a "leveling-off," with different chemicals responsible for each stage. The taste of a food can be radically altered by minute changes in the flavoring combination. "A little odor goes a long way," one flavorist told me.

In order to give a processed food a taste that consumers will find appealing, a flavorist must always consider the food's "mouthfeel"—the unique combination of textures and chemical interactions that affect how the flavor is perceived. Mouthfeel can be adjusted through the use of various fats, gums, starches, emulsifiers, and stabilizers. The aroma chemicals in a food can be precisely analyzed, but the elements that make up mouthfeel are much harder to measure. How does one quantify a pretzel's hardness, a french fry's crispness? Food technologists are now conducting basic research in rheology, the branch of physics that examines the flow and deformation of materials. A number of companies sell sophisticated devices that attempt to measure mouthfeel. The TA.XT2i Texture Analyzer, produced by the Texture Technologies Corporation, of Scarsdale, New York, performs calculations based on data derived from as many as 250 separate probes. It is essentially a mechanical mouth. It gauges the most-important rheological properties of a food—bounce, creep, breaking point, density, crunchiness, chewiness, gumminess, lumpiness, rubberiness, springiness, slipperiness, smoothness, softness, wetness, juiciness, spreadability, springback, and tackiness.

Some of the most important advances in flavor manufacturing are now occurring in the field of biotechnology. Complex flavors are being made using enzyme reactions, fermentation, and fungal and tissue cultures. All the flavors created by these methods—including the ones being synthesized by fungi—are considered natural flavors by the FDA. The new enzyme-based processes are responsible for extremely true-to-life dairy flavors. One company now offers not just butter flavor but also fresh creamy butter, cheesy butter, milky butter, savory melted butter, and super-concentrated butter flavor, in liquid or powder form. The development of new fermentation techniques, along with new techniques for heating mixtures of sugar and amino acids, have led to the creation of much more realistic meat flavors.

The McDonald's Corporation most likely drew on these advances when it eliminated beef tallow from its french fries. The company will not reveal the exact origin of the natural flavor added to its fries. In response to inquiries from *Vegetarian Journal,* however, McDonald's did acknowledge that its fries derive some of their characteristic flavor from "an animal source." Beef is the probable source, although other meats cannot be ruled out. In France, for example, fries are sometimes cooked in duck fat or horse tallow.

Other popular fast foods derive their flavor from unexpected ingredients. McDonald's Chicken McNuggets contain beef extracts, as does Wendy's Grilled Chicken Sandwich. Burger King's BK Broiler Chicken Breast Patty contains "natural smoke flavor." A firm called Red Arrow Products specializes in smoke flavor, which is added to barbecue sauces, snack foods, and processed meats. Red Arrow manufactures natural smoke flavor by charring sawdust and capturing the aroma chemicals released into the air. The smoke is captured in water and then bottled, so that other companies can sell food that seems to have been cooked over a fire.

The Vegetarian Legal Action Network recently petitioned the FDA to 30 issue new labeling requirements for foods that contain natural flavors. The group wants food processors to list the basic origins of their flavors on their labels. At the moment vegetarians often have no way of knowing whether a flavor additive contains beef, pork, poultry, or shellfish. One of the most widely used color additives—whose presence is often hidden by the phrase "color added"—violates a number of religious dietary restrictions, may cause allergic reactions in susceptible people, and comes from an unusual source. Cochineal extract (also known as carmine or carminic acid) is made from the desiccated bodies of female *Dactylopius coccus Costa,* a small insect harvested mainly in Peru and the Canary Islands. The bug feeds on red cactus berries, and color from the berries accumulates in the females and their unhatched larvae. The insects are collected, dried, and ground into a pigment. It takes about 70,000 of them to produce a pound of carmine, which is used to make processed foods look pink, red, or purple. Dannon strawberry yogurt gets its color from carmine, and so do many frozen fruit bars, candies, and fruit fillings, and Ocean Spray pink-grapefruit juice drink.

In a meeting room at IFF, Brian Grainger let me sample some of the company's flavors. It was an unusual taste test—there was no food to taste. Grainger is a senior flavorist at IFF, a soft-spoken chemist with graying hair, an English accent, and a fondness for understatement. He could easily be mistaken for a British diplomat or the owner of a West End brasserie° with two Michelin stars. Like many in the flavor industry, he has an Old World, old-fashioned sensibility. When I suggested that IFF's policy of secrecy and discretion was out of step with our mass-marketing, brand-conscious, self-promoting age, and that the company should put its own logo on the countless products that bear its flavors, instead of allowing other companies to enjoy the consumer loyalty and affection inspired by those flavors, Grainger politely disagreed, assuring me that such a thing would never be done. In the absence of public credit or acclaim, the small and secretive fraternity of flavor chemists praise one another's work. By analyzing the flavor formula of a product, Grainger can often tell which of his counterparts at a rival firm devised it. Whenever he walks down a supermarket aisle, he takes a quiet pleasure in seeing the well-known foods that contain his flavors.

Grainger had brought a dozen small glass bottles from the lab. After he opened each bottle, I dipped a fragrance-testing filter into it—a long white strip of paper designed to absorb aroma chemicals without producing off notes. Before placing each strip of paper in front of my nose, I closed my eyes. Then I inhaled deeply, and one food after another was conjured from the glass bottles. I smelled fresh cherries, black olives, sautéed onions, and shrimp. Grainger's most remarkable creation took me by surprise. After closing my eyes, I suddenly smelled a grilled hamburger. The aroma was uncanny, almost miraculous—as if someone in the room were flipping burgers on a hot grill. But when I opened my eyes, I saw just a narrow strip of white paper and a flavorist with a grin.

QUESTIONS FOR DISCUSSION

1. Schlosser claims that approximately "90 percent of the money that Americans now spend on food goes to buy processed food." What is "processed food," and why do you think Americans eat so much of it?
2. What factors determine how we taste the food we eat?
3. What is the difference between "natural" and "artificial" flavor?
4. Consider paragraph 20. What is the rhetorical effect of listing so many chemicals in a single paragraph?
5. Why do vegetarians have reason to be concerned about the flavor industry?
6. What effect has this article had upon your appetite? Are you likely to make any changes in your diet?

°*West End brasserie:* A small restaurant serving beer and wine; located, in this case, within a fashionable part of London.

SUGGESTIONS FOR WRITING

1. Write an essay explaining why you choose the foods you most frequently buy.
2. Research the food plan at your college or university, and explain how dieticians select the offerings that are available to you on campus.
3. Find out what preservatives are most commonly used in processed food, and explain what effect, if any, they have on human health.

LINKS

■ Within the Book

To help you understand why Americans buy certain foods, see "Please, Please, You're Driving Me Wild" by Jean Kilbourne (pages 313–326).

■ Elsewhere in Print

Brenner, Joël Glenn. *The Emperors of Chocolate: Inside the Secret Worlds of Hershey and Mars.* New York: Random, 1999.

Brownell, Kelly D., and Katherine Battle Horgen. *Food Fight: The Inside Story of the Food Industry, America's Obesity Crisis, and What We Can Do about It.* New York: McGraw, 2003.

Kroc, Ray, and Robert Anderson. *Grinding It Out: The Making of McDonald's.* 1977. New York: St. Martin's, 1990.

Nestle, Marion. *Food Politics: How the Food Industry Influences Nutrition and Health.* Berkeley: U of California P, 2003.

Risch, Sara J., and Chi-Tango Ho. *Flavor Chemistry: Industrial and Academic Research.* Washington, DC: American Chemical Soc., 2000.

Schlosser, Eric. *Fast Food Nation.* Boston: Houghton, 2001.

Teranishi, Roy, Emily L. Wick, and Irwin Hornstein, eds. *Flavor Chemistry: Thirty Years of Progress.* New York: Kluwer, 1999.

■ Online

www.mhhe.com/motives

Click on "More Resources" then "Writing to Report Information."

■ ■ ■

UNCHARTERED TERRITORY

Elizabeth Kolbert

Elizabeth Kolbert is a staff writer and political correspondent for The New Yorker, *a weekly magazine much respected for the quality of fiction and poetry it publishes as well as for its feature articles on various aspects of contemporary culture.* The New Yorker *published the following selection in 2000. In this piece, Kolbert reports on a charter school she visited in New Jersey—one of close to forty states that are experimenting with charter schools in response to widespread concern about the quality of public education. These schools are publicly funded but usually operate under rules and requirements that differ from those of public schools. Although the laws governing such schools vary from state to state, these semiprivate schools receive "charters" (or contracts to operate) when they set out achievement goals and measurements that are approved by local officials. These charters can be revoked when a school fails to fulfill its goals. Some charter schools have been recognized for excellence; others have been closed because of mismanagement. Traditionally, charter schools have been run by not-for-profit groups. In "Unchartered Territory," Kolbert reports on a company that runs a chain of schools for profit—hence her title.*

Before you read it, think about what you liked and disliked about your own elementary school education. Then, as you read, consider what the school Kolbert describes is trying to accomplish and whether your own experience makes you sympathetic to the objectives and methods in question.

Anacostia, in southeastern Washington, D.C., is poor in most of the familiar ways. Much of the housing is decrepit, too many of the storefronts sell liquor or cash checks, and every few blocks there's a mural depicting, in exaggeratedly cheerful colors, happy, purposeful activity. To walk the neighborhood's streets and see any kind of commercial possibility takes a forceful and none too fastidious imagination. To look at its schools and see a promising new business opportunity takes a vision like Steven Wilson's.

Wilson is a lanky forty-one-year-old with prominent cheekbones and close-cropped hair that sticks out in different directions, perhaps as a fashion statement or perhaps just as an accident of physiognomy. His background in education is slight. He has never taught in a school, or administered one, and his formal training is limited to a few courses he took when he was an undergraduate at Harvard. Four years ago, he founded a company called Advantage Schools, and the year after that the company opened its first venture, a charter school on the east side of Phoenix. Like the charter-school movement in general, Advantage has expanded at a dizzying pace. It now has fifteen schools: New ones opened this fall in Detroit; in Benton Harbor, Michigan; and in

Fairburn, Georgia. A sixteenth, which is under development and scheduled to open next summer, will be in Anacostia. Within two years, Wilson hopes to be running thirty schools, almost all of them in inner-city neighborhoods.

I first met Wilson last spring, in the Manhattan offices of U.S. Trust. The bank is one of Advantage's backers, and, along with several major venture-capital firms, including Chase Capital and Kleiner Perkins Caufield & Byers, it has helped finance the company to the tune of more than sixty million dollars. Wilson was late to arrive, having just come from a meeting where he was seeking yet more financing. After we shook hands, we were shown into a conference room, where a plate of exquisite little cookies had been set out. As we drank the bank's coffee from gold-rimmed china cups, Wilson told me he thought that one of the reasons so many urban schools had failed was a misplaced emphasis on equity. A lot of public-school administrators, he said, subscribe to the notion that "the only kind of change that's good is change that affects every child equally"—an idea that he labeled "appalling," since "if you applied that test you'd never do anything."

Wilson argues that fostering competition among schools is a good way to get results—"People like to try different things and get a chance to demonstrate that their way is more effective," he says—and that fostering capitalism is even better. While most charter schools are not aimed at turning a profit, there is nothing to prevent enterprising businessmen from running them with that goal in mind. Wilson's goal is to run his schools in such a way that roughly one out of every five dollars spent on them goes toward operating his company.

Wilson is not the first to try to make money off the failures of the public 5 schools, and he may not, in the end, be the best positioned to succeed at it, but his strategy is, in many ways, the most logical. Advantage's plan is to offer a low-cost education to the poor and, by exploiting the most recent educational reforms, get taxpayers to finance the entire enterprise. When it suits him, Wilson can speak as eloquently as the next guy about society's obligation to needy students; in a recruitment brochure for teachers, for example, Advantage urges them to "join the revolution" and "help save the next generation of urban youth." At the same time, Wilson is quite clear about the core of his ambition. "I'm an entrepreneur," he told me.

Last spring, I spent several days sitting in on classes at Golden Door, an elementary school that Advantage operates in Jersey City. The school is housed in a brand-new faux-Federalist building with arched windows and the simulacrum of a clock tower out front. Jersey City constructed the building, ostensibly as a community center, and now leases it to the company. It sits across the street from a huge parking garage and just a few blocks away from the local elementary school, P.S. 37. Eighty percent of the children who attend Golden Door are eligible for the federal school-lunch program, meaning that those from a family of three, for example, have a household income of less than twenty-seven thousand dollars.

One morning, I arrived at the school in time for a second-grade reading lesson. The teacher, Brian Stiles, told the students to get out their textbooks; he himself picked up what appeared to be a huge spiral notebook. "Find lesson seventy-eight," Stiles told the class. "Touch column one. Word one is 'seagulls.' What word?" He snapped his fingers.

"Seagulls!" the students answered, in unison.

"Seagulls are birds that are seen around the ocean," Stiles went on. "They are sometimes called gulls. Word two is 'elevator.' What word?" He snapped his fingers again.

"Elevator!"   10

"Read, spell, read 'elevator.' Get ready." He snapped his fingers.

"Elevator. E-l-e-v-a-t-o-r. Elevator."

"Elevator! Beautiful. Everybody, word three is 'surface.' What word?" Another snap of the fingers.

"Surface!"

"Read, spell, read 'surface.' Get ready." He snapped his fingers.   15

"Surface. S-u-r-f-a-c-e. Surface."

After some more spelling and vocabulary words—"pirates," "instant," "handkerchief"—the children turned to a reading-comprehension lesson. Stiles was still working from his notebook. He asked a student to read from the text.

"You're going to read about big storm clouds," the student said. "Here are facts about clouds: Clouds are made up of tiny drops of water."

"Everybody, I want you to look at that fact," Stiles said. "The fact is that clouds are made up of tiny drops of water. Everybody say that fact. Get ready."

He snapped his fingers.   20

"Clouds are made up of tiny drops of water."

Stiles had another student continue to read. "In clouds that are very high, the water drops are frozen."

"Everybody, where are the clouds that have frozen water drops?" He snapped his fingers.

"High!"

Much like a fast-food franchise, an Advantage school comes as a package,   25
and to sign on with the company is, at least in theory, to accept this package in a McMuffin to McFlurry sort of way. Advantage students, whether they live in Kalamazoo or Newark, are required to wear uniforms (maroon on top, khaki on the bottom), to pass through the halls silently, in single file, and to obey the rules posted in every classroom: "Follow directions the first time they are given"; "Get attention the right way"; "Don't work ahead." The company issues a twenty-page Code of Civility, which lists ten Keys to Success, beginning with Responsibility and ending with True Friendship, by way of Perseverance and Truth, and it expects students to pledge, in writing, to adopt them. The curriculum is the same in all the schools and so, almost to the letter, are the teaching methods.

"Teachers have been socialized in schools of education, and taught to apply their own creativity to a problem," Wilson once told me, when I asked how he had arrived at Advantage's pedagogical program. "That's nice up to a point, but the idea that we should have tens of thousands of teachers all around the country trying to stumble upon the best way to teach reading to a first grader is kind of psychotic, right?"

The system that Advantage uses to teach reading is known as Direct Instruction. The system is also used for math, and was developed some thirty-five years ago at the University of Illinois by Siegfried Engelmann, an advertising executive who became interested in education after conducting research on how often kids needed to hear a slogan before they memorized it. A typical reading lesson, like the one about clouds, consists of a series of questions that the teacher poses and the students answer in unison, often repeating what they have just been told. There is rarely any doubt about what constitutes the right answer.

In Stiles's class, every time there was a break in the lesson the kids began chatting and pestering one another and rifling through their desks, stalling for time. To maintain order, Stiles used a system of warnings and punishments recorded on a wall hanging at the back of the class. The hanging had little clear-plastic pockets, each containing a student's name and several squares of construction paper in different colors. At the beginning of each day, Stiles told me, the green square was out front in every pocket. When someone misbehaved, the yellow square came forward—I saw this happen to one girl who refused, several times, to follow directions—and then, after still more infractions, the blue one, and, finally, the red would be moved to the front. Later, I saw the same wall hanging in the other classrooms I visited at Golden Door; it, too, I learned, was mandated by Advantage, as part of what the company calls its Classroom Positive Management Systems.

Stiles, who is thirty-six, has been working at Golden Door since it opened, in trailers, two years ago. Before that, he was a buyer for men's sportswear, a job he quit because he found it unsatisfying. He seemed like a nice enough person, and also probably a competent teacher, but since so much of what he did was scripted it was hard for me to tell. At the end of the reading class, Stiles showed me his notebook, and I saw that the entire lesson had been printed out for him, including the cues for when to snap his fingers.

Over the last eight years, thirty-six states have amended their education laws 30 to make the creation of charter schools possible. This legislation has been supported by groups that favor privatizing government services, like the Heritage Foundation, and, in a more grudging sort of way, by some teachers' unions, like the National Education Association—and by politicians on the right and also by many on the left. Al Gore, who said in his speech at the Democratic Convention that he would never "go along with any plan that would drain taxpayer money away from our public schools and give it to private schools in the form of vouchers," has backed charter-school legislation, and so has George W. Bush.

The sudden rush to embrace charter schools could be described as either the most dramatic development in educational reform since desegregation or as an essentially conservative effort to forestall real change. In contrast to vouchers, charter schools are supposed to expand families' options wholly within the existing public-school framework. A charter school is a public school that, thanks to a special dispensation—or charter—from the state, operates outside the jurisdiction of the local school district. Such a school cannot teach the Gospels, but for the most part it can ignore the local union contracts. It is free to develop its own curriculum and code of conduct.

Already, some two thousand charter schools have opened, enrolling about half a million students. The vast majority of these schools are operated by local nonprofit organizations, and the educational theories that guide them are as various as the communities they serve—which, according to charter-school advocates, is precisely the point. There are charter schools that stress "traditional values," charter schools that emphasize "project-based learning," charter schools that have an Afrocentric curriculum, charter schools that focus on community service, and charter schools for the performing arts. The notion behind the movement as a whole is that parents and teachers should be allowed to innovate (Advantage, of course, operates on the opposite theory), and that from the process of coming together to create a school a heightened sense of purpose will emerge, producing better educational results. Whether this notion is, in any rigorous way, true is impossible to know at this point, and the answer may remain unknowable. Charter schools are, in effect, a series of social-science experiments for which no control groups have been established.

Each student who attends a charter schools brings with him an allotment of public-school aid, which is diverted from the regular public-school system in the area. The sum varies from state to state and, in some states, from district to district, with high expenditure-per-pupil districts, like White Plains, New York, paying as much as $11,609 dollars for each student, and low-expenditure states, like Kansas, paying as little as $3,820. (Jersey City pays $9,251.) The states specify how much money the schools will get, but they don't dictate how the money should be spent, or even whether it needs to be expended on students. Ideally, Wilson hopes to use fifteen percent of the money he gets to pay for services, like accounting and equipment leasing, that are provided by his company's central staff. He plans to take another seven percent straight off the top, as a "management fee" for Advantage.

Most states do not allow commercial enterprises to hold charters directly, but Advantage gets around this by finding local groups that will run a school on paper while in practice turning operations over to the company. This arrangement can work out extremely well, as it has in Jersey City, where Advantage has teamed up with the mayor, Bret Schundler, who is an outspoken advocate of school choice. It can, however, also work out disastrously, as it did in Albany, where in 1999 the company opened a school in partnership with a local chapter of the Urban League. An investigation into the chapter suggested that the group's president had misapplied nearly ninety thousand dollars

COMPANION TEXT *Charter School Results Repeatedly Delayed*

Since the original publication of "Uncharted Territory" in 2000, educators and policy makers have continued to consider whether charter schools are beneficial to students. The following press release points to the most recent research available at the time this book went to print.

Washington, D.C. (August 17, 2004)—The 2003 National Assessment of Educational Progress (NAEP) in math and reading, which was publicly released in November 2003, included the first-ever nationally representative sample of charter schools, but the federal government has repeatedly delayed public reporting of the NAEP charter school achievement results. These are among the findings of a report released today by the American Federation of Teachers, which was able to obtain and examine the NAEP charter school data. . . .

The 2003 NAEP charter school achievement data originally were scheduled for release in January 2004. After numerous delays, NAEP is scheduled to officially release the data in December 2004. In the meantime, the NAEP results (often called the "gold standard" in education data) from the charter school sample are effectively unavailable to educators, parents, and public policy makers.

Furthermore, the authorities responsible for NAEP plan to accompany the charter school achievement data with an analysis that adjusts the results. Not only is such an analysis unprecedented in NAEP's history, but NAEP is also prohibited from officially reporting its results in this fashion.

The AFT analysis of the NAEP charter school achievement data (which is presented in the same way NAEP results are typically reported) shows that charter school students mostly underperform and sometimes score about as well as regular public school students. Researchers at the AFT were able to unearth the NAEP charter school achievement data by using the Web-based NAEP Data Tool, a difficult, if not impossible, task for a layperson. (Detailed achievements results are available at www.aft.org.)

"The government's first obligation to the public was to release the NAEP charter school results, just like it does with other NAEP results," said Bella Rosenberg, an author of the AFT report. "Repeatedly delaying that report for the sake of packaging the results with an official explanation tarnishes NAEP's gold-standard reputation."

The repeated delays in releasing NAEP charter school achievement data are especially disturbing because one of the sanctions for schools that persistently fail to make adequate yearly progress (AYP) under the federal No Child Left Behind Act (NCLB) is restructuring as a charter school. Many schools across the country are already in this predicament.

American Federation of Teachers

in school aid. Over the summer, the Urban League and Advantage severed their relationship, and the whole fiasco has been widely described as a case study of how not to put together a charter school.

Advantage has its headquarters in Boston, in a suite of spare, loft-like of- 35 fices near North Station. When I visited recently, the company was in the midst of trying to hire a chief financial officer, and Wilson had gathered his top staff for a search meeting. He sat on one side of a long table, next to the company's president, Geoffrey Swett, who joined Advantage after running a chain of dialysis centers, and across from its vice-president for human resources, Thomas Saltonstall, who worked previously at a rival dialysis company. An executive headhunter was participating in the meeting via speaker-phone.

Six candidates were being considered for the C.F.O. job, and the group at the table went through them one by one, with the goal of narrowing the field. Instead, the meeting seemed to go in reverse, so that the one candidate who, at the start, had been on the verge of being dropped from the list wound up back in the running. There was a lot of discussion about what kind of background made the most sense for Advantage—was it experience in a regulated industry or experience in retail?—but Wilson's overriding concern, it seemed, was drive. "There's only two categories: energy generator or energy absorber," he said at one point. "There's no in-between. It's a binary thing." At another point, he observed, "The last thing we want is someone who brings in this culture of complaining. That is just radioactive." Several of the candidates, according to the headhunter, were a little shaky on Advantage's business plan, and wanted more information about it. No one around the table seemed to find this disconcerting.

Advantage is Wilson's third startup company—an impressive statistic even in the current business climate. He started his first company when he was twenty-one, dropping out of college in order to do so. The company marketed a kind of technology known as data-acquisition systems, which connect computers to instruments that measure things like light or pressure or temperature. A few years later, he sold that company and immediately started a new one, to develop control systems for automated-process plants. This second company, according to Wilson, achieved its goals technically but not financially. "I've experienced very modest success and more substantial failure," he told me. "I probably shouldn't reveal that."

In explaining why he believes it is possible to run schools that are better than the regular public schools but also cost less to operate, Wilson likes to say that a typical large urban district spends at least forty percent of its budget on administration alone. This purported waste is essential not just to his calculations but to those of the entire for-profit public-school industry, which has received a huge boost from charter-school legislation. In a recent, unrelentingly sunny report on the industry's future, analysts at Merrill Lynch asserted that only about half of what is spent on regular public K-12 education is spent in the classroom. "We can't think of another service industry that exists where fifty percent of the money is spent outside of where the service is rendered," they wrote.

These figures may correspond to what many taxpayers suspect about administrative costs, but the experts in public-school financing I spoke with all described them as far off the mark. They noted that while it was possible to classify costs like counseling and school buses as administrative or, alternatively, as money spent outside the classroom, this does not make them any less essential. "Is there money to be made here?" asked Jim Wyckoff, an associate professor at the State University of New York in Albany who has conducted an extensive study of New York State public-school financing. "There might be. But is a lot of it going to come from what is typically called administration? I doubt it."

At the moment, Advantage is not showing a profit; the funding it's getting from Chase and Kleiner Perkins is going toward easing the deficits at its schools. In this lack of profitability Advantage is no different from its rivals; with revenues of two hundred and twenty million dollars, for example, Edison Schools, the largest of the for-profit school companies, lost forty-nine million last year. In Boston, I was told that various economies of scale would allow Advantage to operate in the black when it reached its target of thirty schools; a few weeks later, Wilson told me that on the basis of more recent figures he believed the company *could* begin to see a return much sooner than that, perhaps as early as this year—but because the company will put that money toward opening new schools it will almost immediately go back into the red. One of the great discoveries of contemporary capitalism, of course, is that it is possible to become very rich without ever coming up with a business plan that actually works, and one of the reasons Advantage was looking for a new C.F.O. was to begin the process of preparing for an initial public offering. This, I was told, could happen at any time.

40

There is no lunchroom at Golden Door; the students take their meals in the classroom, under the supervision of a teacher. The ostensible rationale for this practice is that meals are part of the educational program—students will be learning while they eat. In one class I visited, I watched some third graders grapple with pizza. The food, courtesy of the federal school-lunch program, arrived in large quilted bags of the sort used by Domino's deliverymen. The students picked up trays, collected their slices, along with a cup of juice and an orange, and then went back to their desks. While they were eating, they chatted, held burping contests, and examined Pokémon cards. One student was using a utensil as some sort of catapult. "If I see you doing that again, you will not get a spoon," the teacher, a middle-aged woman, told him. When the kids were done, they dumped their trash in the garbage, stacked their trays, and went off to recess, leaving stray bits of paper on the floor. After they left, I asked the teacher what the educational objective of this particular lunch hour had been. "Supposedly, they're learning to speak quietly," she said, and shrugged.

Whatever its heuristic value, Golden Door's lunch policy obviously makes good financial sense. The school did not have to build a cafeteria, and now it does not have to maintain it, or heat it, or clean it. Instead of hiring aides, it simply asks teachers to give up half of their own lunch hour to keep order.

Other elements of the school's program are similarly equivocal. Advantage places a great deal of emphasis on basic skills; in Brian Stiles's class, for example, I saw a schedule for second graders. It showed them spending three and a half hours a day on Direct Instruction in reading, writing, and spelling, and another hour on Direct Instruction in math, which left just over ninety minutes to be divvied up, according to a complicated weekly rotation, among gym, Spanish, science, art, music, and history. Missing almost entirely from the schedule were the exercises in self-expression and discovery typically associated with elementary school: the illustrated reports that get tacked on the walls, or the scraggly seedlings groping toward the windows. In Stiles's classroom, there were some simple cutouts of hot-air balloons hanging from the ceiling; these were the only student-made decorations in the room, and he told me it had been difficult, given the rigors of the curriculum, to find the time to make them.

Advantage's emphasis could reflect a pedagogical decision about what skills matter most in life or, just as plausibly, an economic calculation. The pledge that Advantage makes when it launches a new school is that, over five years, the standardized-test results of virtually every student will improve, though by how much varies substantially according to how well, or how badly, the student scored initially. (According to figures provided to me by the company, reading scores at Golden Door last year did improve significantly for the youngest children but much less so for older children.) Since it's very difficult to measure progress on intangibles like creativity or independent thinking, in a school that is run as a business it probably doesn't make much sense to devote a whole lot of resources to them.

As for Direct Instruction, Wilson and other Advantage executives told me   *45* that the method had been chosen because it was demonstrably the most effective. In its literature, the company asserts that research has "overwhelmingly supported the superiority of DI over all other programs," a claim that, to say the least, exaggerates the supporting data. At the same time, Advantage's reliance on Direct Instruction follows altogether logically from the company's efforts to keep salary costs down. Most of the teachers I met at Golden Door were inexperienced, and a few told me that they had tried to get jobs in public-school systems but, for one reason or another, had been unable to do so. Direct Instruction leaves so little to the teacher's discretion that classroom experience, not to say talent or imagination, seems almost beside the point. "Advantage could train a monkey," one teacher told me.

When I asked Wilson about what I saw as the ambiguity of the company's educational model, he told me that it was "no different, really, from that of any other school, because every school has limited resources, has a budget." In terms of the quality of education, he said he did not believe that Advantage had made any meaningful sacrifices in its efforts to economize. "Frankly, some programs are just much, much more efficient, even though people don't like to hear that word in education."

I talked to dozens of students at Golden Door about their experiences, and when word got around that I was a reporter more kids sought me out, eager to relate their stories. A few of the kids had complaints. One serious-looking fifth grader told me that she missed the regular public school she used to attend. "The other school had more activities and projects and trips," she said, adding that she had once won a prize for a project on a woman she admired. Many more, though, said they were happy. Another fifth grader, with pigtails, told me, "I love this school. I was about to stay back, and this school gave me another chance."

Over and over again, kids talked about violence they had seen, or even participated in, at their previous schools, and how much more secure they felt at Golden Door. "I like this school because they have rules about not touching the other kids," one girl told me. "I feel more protected." Last spring, Golden Door had enough room to admit only one new class of kindergartners. Posted near the main entrance was a roster of children who had been wait-listed; a hundred and eighty-one names were on it.

Wilson doesn't pretend that the program he is providing for students in Jersey City and in Detroit is one that would hold much appeal in wealthier districts like Summit or Bloomfield Hills. "We shouldn't be struggling to find one approach that's right for everybody," he told me. "The needs of our urban students resulting from their backgrounds and their previous educational and social deprivations in some cases are very different from the needs of the son or daughter of an affluent suburban parent."

If one considers the public schools a primary institution of democracy, it *50* is hard not to be discomfited by this separate-but-not-altogether-equal philosophy. Everything that I saw in Advantage's Boston office—the emphasis on drive and risk-taking and innovation—reflected a corporate culture that was fundamentally at odds with the cookie-cutter, don't-work-ahead design of its schools. Answering on command and respecting authority are not entrepreneurial virtues, though they do have a place farther down the economic order. It struck me as not insignificant that, while Advantage schools serve mostly black and Hispanic kids, everyone I met in the corporate headquarters, except for a single receptionist, was white.

Yet dwelling on this discomfort may itself be a luxury: The choice that parents in the inner city are confronting is not one about abstract ideals, or even about the appropriate role of profit in public education; it is a choice for the most part between dysfunctional public schools and some alternative— any alternative. And if these parents choose to send their kids to Advantage, if only because they feel that the kids will be safer there, who, in the end, can blame them?

QUESTIONS FOR DISCUSSION

1. What accounts for the rapid rise of charter schools? What kinds of problems are they meant to address?
2. Consider the references to "exquisite little cookies" and "gold-rimmed china cups" in paragraph 3. What do these details convey to you?
3. Do you agree that fostering competition among schools is a good way to improve the quality of such schools?
4. Consider the reading lesson described in paragraphs 7–24. Would you want your child to be taught by this method?
5. How typical of charter schools are the schools run by Advantage?
6. In paragraph 36, Kolbert quotes Steven Wilson: "There's only two categories: energy generator or energy absorber [. . .]. There's no in-between." When you read classifications such as "energy generator" and "energy absorber," what kind of people come to mind? Do you agree that all people can be placed in one of these two categories?
7. Based on the information in this article, what is your opinion of Steven Wilson and the schools for which his company is responsible?

SUGGESTIONS FOR WRITING

1. Write a report on classroom practices and homework assignments in a class you have taken within the last two years.
2. Research the state of public education in a major American city, and report what you learn about facilities and instruction.
3. Research charter schools and find a school that seems admirable. Write about what that school is doing right.

▌ **LINKS**

▪ **Within the Book**

For information about how children are treated in another culture, see "In Japan, Nice Guys (and Girls) Finish Together" (pages 187–190).

▪ **Elsewhere in Print**

Finn, Chester E., Jr., Bruno V. Manno, and Gregg Vanourek. *Charter Schools in Action: Renewing Public Education.* Princeton: Princeton UP, 2000.

Freire, Paolo. *Pedagogy of the Oppressed.* Trans. Myra Bergman Ramos. 1970. New York: Continuum, 2000.

Hassel, Bryan C. *The Charter School Challenge: Avoiding the Pitfalls, Fulfilling the Promise.* Washington, DC: Brookings Inst., 1999.

Hill, Paul Thomas, et al. *Charter School's Accountability in Public Education.* Washington, DC: Brookings Inst., 2002.

■ **Elsewhere in Print (continued)**

Rose, Mike. *Lives on the Boundary: The Struggles and Achievements of America's Underprepared*. New York: Free, 1989.

Rosenblatt, Louise. *Literature as Exploration*. 1938. New York: MLA, 1996.

Schorr, Jonathan. *The Promise of the Inner City Charter School*. New York: Ballantine, 2002.

■ **Online**

www.mhhe.com/motives

Click on "More Resources" then "Writing to Report Information."

■ ■ ■

TOUGH BREAK

Tim Rogers

The following selection illustrates a kind of report frequently undertaken by journalists and freelance writers: the profile of an individual. Profiles usually combine description and narration to convey a sense of what makes someone distinctive or newsworthy. In this case, Tim Rogers focuses on a successful woman—one of the best women billiard players in the country. As you read, be alert for how he attempts to engage the attention of readers and how he combines information with personal impressions. Note how he sounds in this piece, and consider whether his manner might be different if he were writing about a man or a well-known athlete.

Rogers is a Dallas-based writer who first published "Tough Break" in American Way, *the in-flight magazine of American Airlines. After you have read this piece, you might also consider the assumptions it makes about audience—what kind of people are likely to be reading an in-flight magazine and what expectations they have as they browse through one.*

Vivian has gone to call her mother, which seems an odd thing for a grown woman to do on a date, especially when it's a long-distance call from a bar pay phone. I hope it's not a sign the night is going badly. To be honest, I don't recall if the word *date* actually came up all that often in our phone conversations. Maybe the word I used was closer to *interview.* The dinner we just shared must have gone to my head. Vivian, truth be told, has come to San Francisco for the Connelly National Nine Ball Championship of women's pool. The twenty-nine-year-old is currently ranked the third-best woman player in the world by the Women's Professional Billiard Association. She won the championship last year, and hopes to repeat. I have come for Vivian. While I'm currently not ranked in the world standings, whenever I play my roommate, Joe, I usually win. I only hope Vivian will be my pool partner for the night, that she'll carry me for a few games. That, and I aim to find out what happens when long hair and manicured nails get mixed up with balls and sticks and other implements generally reserved for men.

Just as I begin to think Vivian's been gone too long, she walks into the room. She explains that when she's on the road for a tournament, she always calls home to let the folks in San Antonio know she's safe. She takes a seat next to me, against a wall, in a row of red vinyl chairs—the sort you'd find in a gas station. Then I relax, because I know I've got Vivian Villarreal, arguably the best woman pool player in the world, right where I want her: in a bar, where no one recognizes her, waiting to play a game of pool.

Our names sit below six others on a chalkboard, so I have time to size up this place called Paradise Lounge. A three-piece jazz band is going pretty good

in the next room. Hanging lamps cast light over the pool tables; people standing back from them are only lit from the waist down, their faces hidden in
the shadow and smoke above. A guy in leather pants has the table Vivian and I
are waiting to play on. Between shots, he talks about motorcycles. A woman
in black stretch-pants wobbles around telling anyone who will listen, "Someone just spilled my WHOLE DAMN DRINK!"

Leather Pants loses to a guy with a red beard—by the looks of it, he eats
well. At some point during Red Beard's game, Vivian becomes impatient.
When it ends, and there's a brief pause before the next name on the list steps
up, Vivian slides out of her chair and asks the room a rhetorical question:
"Who's next?"

She hands me her lipstick, strides up to the table, and has the balls racked   5
before anyone can stop her. As she picks out a stick—before she's even taken
her first shot—Red Beard turns to me: "Is she in town for the tournament?"

I quickly pocket the lipstick.

"Tournament?" I ask. "What tournament?" *That walk,* I think. *He could
tell just by the way she walked to the table.*

"There's a women's professional nine-ball tournament in town."

"You don't say."

Then Red Beard breaks, doesn't sink anything, and Vivian takes over. She   10
has a fast hard stroke. She's often ready for the next shot before the balls have
stopped rolling and recovered from her last shot. She runs the table in maybe
two minutes.

Red Beard doesn't look like he's accustomed to women beating him. He
preempts the next name on the chalkboard and racks for Vivian, who breaks
with an explosion that sends the cue ball leaping off the felt. Heads turn.
While she's busy running the table again, Red Beard and I watch.

"Looks like she's ready to bet some money," he tells me over the jazz.
"Does she ever bet?"

"Bet?" I ask.

Over dinner, Vivian told me about a night in a San Antonio bar a few
years back. She was playing for $1,000 a game. Even after she ran nine racks
in a row, the man she was playing didn't know when to give up. Vivian went
home with $25,000.

"Um, no," I inform Red Beard. "As a matter of fact, I don't think she   15
does bet."

Vivian also told me that gambling—never hustling, which involves dishonesty, misrepresenting your talent; only simple betting—is part of her past.
But I wasn't entirely convinced. Neither is Red Beard—about the betting or
the tournament, because he lures Vivian to an empty table, without saying a
word, by setting up a diamond-shaped nine-ball rack.

Nine ball, you see, is a *contest;* whereas eight ball, what drunk men in
smoky bars play, is merely an *amusement.* In eight ball, or stripes and solids,
you smack your balls around in any order. Your opponent smacks his balls
around. Then, whoever finishes hacking first goes for the eight.

In nine ball, both players shoot at the same balls, sinking them in numerical order, one through nine. And, so long as you strike the proper ball first, the nine ball may be sunk any time, either by a combination shot or a carom. Which means the game of nine ball requires control, strategy. It's the difference between fishing and fly-fishing, between checkers and chess.

So Red Beard trades nine-ball games with Vivian. It turns out he can handle a stick—at least on a bar table—and Vivian chats him up between shots, learning his name is Ron. She starts to draw attention to herself, the way she has of shooting hard and generally not missing much. Leather Pants and a few others have formed an audience in the shadows.

Meanwhile, I slouch a little lower in my vinyl chair and wonder if I'll   20
ever get a chance to play pool with Vivian. I'm afraid I've been relegated to the role of lipstick holder.

Just south of the Bay Bridge, a pool hall called The Great Entertainer comes to life around noon. It is here that the best women pool players from around the world have gathered for the National Championship. The place resembles a warehouse with a high ceiling and exposed concrete columns. Jazz plays over the sound system, while regulars shoot pool outside the tournament area. From behind black drapes comes periodic applause.

At the front counter, a man with a cue-stick case slung over his shoulder asks for a ticket to the tournament. "You mean to the girlie show?" the cashier behind the counter jokes, demonstrating that at least one employee has yet to get in touch with his inner, nurturing side. His term of endearment also suggests that he hasn't had a look yet behind the black curtains.

Vivian and the rest of the girlie show, sometimes known as the Women's Professional Billiard Association, have gotten two strange notions into their heads: First, physics and linear algebra can't distinguish between the sexes. Friction, inertia—all that stuff seems to work for the women. When they hit a ball, they expect it to roll.

Their second notion (and here their male counterparts really seem to disagree): Pool is just a game. In a sport still dominated by pinkie rings and testosterone, ideas like these are nothing short of radical. Maybe even a little dangerous.

For one thing, they lead to an awful lot of hugging. Before tournament   25
play begins, Vivian runs into the two women in the world currently ranked above her, Loree Jon Jones and Robin Bell. Vivian knows she'll likely have to beat one or both of these women to take home first place and the $7,500 that goes with it. One expects tension, icy stares, and cold greetings; but instead, they make with the warm fuzzies. The display seems appropriate for one of those *Unsolved Mysteries* long-lost twin-sister reunion episodes, but a little surprising for professional pool players.

"The men would be kneeing each other in the groin," observes a silver-haired gentleman in a double-breasted blazer. Robert Byrne, a trick-shot legend and author of best-selling pool instruction books, says the women go about things a little differently "because the men come up from the hustling background, where it's you against the world, and you're playing for your supper, and it's a vicious world out there when you're on the road. The women don't come from that kind of background. . . . You look at the women, and then you look at the men: The women make the men look like the war in Bosnia. It's ego gone wild. It's territorial aggression. It's power-seeking. It's back-stabbing."

"The men are just interested in gambling and winning money from each other," says Vivian. "We have come together as a . . . [she struggles for the right word] family. We are all friends, and we want the sport to grow. Selfishness will only get you so far. . . . That's why we're not affiliated anymore with the men."

The women decided they'd had enough in 1992. Previously, the men and women marketed their tournaments together, but the guys always insisted on acting like, well, like *guys*. So last year, the WPBA started organizing its own events.

"When we separated from the men," Vivian says, "they never, ever thought that we could make it without them. But we're so successful now. The women never used to be close to the men as far as prize money. But now, there are about four of us who are making *more* money than them."

As recently as 1990, the women had only two events they could call their own, in which only women played. In 1993, that number jumped to fourteen, one more tournament than the men played. Prize money topped $440,000, and of the top five money-winners—men and women—three were women. Excluding endorsements, this means Vivian made about $35,000 last year playing pool. And in 1994, the WPBA landed its first corporate sponsor: Gordon's gin and vodka proclaiming "the fun, refreshing mixability of Gordon's is a perfect fit." 30

But don't get the wrong idea. Gordon's didn't get involved with women's pool for family values. They know the women can flat-out shoot.

It's almost midnight behind the black curtains at The Great Entertainer, and Vivian is playing her fifth match of the day, tearing through the one-loss bracket. Tomorrow, ESPN shows up to tape the finals, and she wants to be there. But she's already lost one match in a double-elimination tournament. It has played out the way the seedings said it should: Across the table from Vivian, noticeably not looking for hugs, stands Robin Bell.

A guy with a Heineken in his hand watches Vivian from the bleachers. She just ran the first rack in a race to nine games, and he's lost his patience. "I don't even think she's a girl," he mutters. "Even the way she walks is like a man. It's hell on your ego."

Vivian's father taught her how to play pool at Mollie's, her grandmother's San Antonio bar. He also taught her how to walk. He would make her practice walking in heels, back and forth in the living room, while he gave pointers from the couch. "If they had such a thing as a school for walking," he would tell her, "I'd send you."

It's the same walk that Ron must have noticed at the Paradise Lounge before he went to trading nine-ball games with her on that bar table. But the bar table was like a small, wet quilt compared to what Vivian has to work with 35 now. The tournament tables are almost twice as big as most bar tables, and the cloth is so fast that the balls slide like they're on ice. Players describe good tables as "tight"; these are the tightest.

Into the fifth game, Vivian has her stroke going. It's the stroke that the other women all talk about. No matter how difficult the shot—it could be a full-table combination with a match tied at eight—Vivian always takes two practice strokes and shoots. She works so quickly that other women say they can't watch her shoot while they're playing her. It throws them off, takes them out of their own rhythm.

And then there's the break. Going into the fifteenth game, now past midnight, the match is tied at seven games each. Spectators have switched from beer to coffee. Earlier in the match, Vivian was breaking conservatively, holding back so she wouldn't send balls flying off the table. But she won the last two games and looks confident. She chalks up and lets loose.

Most players use one cue stick for breaks and another for play. They don't want to risk shattering their good shooting sticks, which often run thousands of dollars. Vivian isn't most players. She breaks with a $15,000 custom-made Omega, with nice touches like inlaid eighteen-karat gold, silver, and mastodon ivory.

It was at a tournament in Chicago that she fell in love with the stick. A rep from Omega told her she could practice with it before a match, and after she ran a few racks without missing a shot, Vivian said she wanted to finish the tournament with it. Her coach tried to stop her; it usually takes a player anywhere from six months to a year to get used to a new stick. Vivian didn't listen, and won the tournament, becoming the top-ranked woman in the world at the time. That convinced the Omega folks to sign her up for endorsements, with part of the deal being Vivian's custom-made cue.

The stick, the walk, the stroke—Vivian looks as if she's too much for *40* Robin Bell to handle tonight. Vivian plays out the fifteenth game with precision, drawing the cue ball back for a perfect leave on the nine. With this game behind her, she'll need one more to finish the race to nine games, and then it's back to the hotel for some rest. Tomorrow, the lights and ESPN.

And then she does the unthinkable. She misses. She misses the straight-in shot on the nine. It rolls, seems to trip on its own yellow stripe, and rattles around in the mouth of the corner pocket. It just stops and seems to peer over the edge. And Bell finishes it off. And goes on to win the next game after sinking the five ball in a pocket she wasn't even aiming for. But it doesn't matter. Slop counts, and Bell wins the match.

Vivian has got to be kicking herself for the fourth game, much earlier in the match, when her honesty might have cost her the tournament. She fouled on a safe, failing to drive a ball to a rail. She was nice enough to point this out to Bell, who hadn't noticed. Someone in the stands said a man would never have done that, pointed out a mistake to an opponent. With ball in hand, Bell promptly set the cue down for a two-nine combo, lined it up, and knocked it down. Vivian's mistake was Bell's game.

Vivian will return tomorrow for the finals, but she'll watch from the bleachers. For now, she gives Robin Bell a congratulatory hug, signs a few autographs, and takes her father's walk through the black curtains.

I did finally get to play pool with Vivian. We eventually left the Paradise Lounge that night and headed to a place called the Bus Stop. Ron recommended it, told us to "Tell 'em Ron sent ya." And, "Oh, boy, they're going to just looove you."

Vivian, again, got to the table a few names before her turn, and this time   45
we played partners. At some point in our first game, one of our opponents, a guy with his short sleeves rolled up, asked if Vivian was in town for the nine-ball tournament. Vivian ran the table that game and the next.

I got my chance to shoot in game three. We had two balls left on the table, plus the eight, and the other guys had just scratched. I put the cue right where I wanted it. Lining up my shot, though, I discovered my heart literally racing, which got me to feeling a bit foolish, and I think it threw me off. Plus the table—you know, it wasn't real tight.

I sank our two balls and muffed the eight. We lost.

As we got up to leave, Vivian told me I played well. But Short Sleeves wasn't done with us. "What?" he said. "You guys lose *one game,* and you leave?"

"The tournament," I said. "She's got to get up early."

Like Vivian's father, mine taught me to shoot pool, too (obviously, he   50
didn't do as good a job as Vivian's dad). And my father gave me this piece of pool-shooting advice, which I shared with Vivian outside the Bus Stop: "Always leave them wanting more." And I handed her the lipstick.

QUESTIONS FOR DISCUSSION

1. At the beginning of his article, Rogers pretends that he is having a date with Vivian Villarreal and draws attention to her long hair and manicured nails. How would you describe his tone? Do you think it is appropriate?
2. In the world of professional billiards, what is the difference between gambling and hustling?
3. How does Rogers respond to the needs of readers who know little about billiards? Where does he include specific data about the sport?
4. How does the behavior of women professional billiard players differ from that of their male counterparts?
5. Drawing on the information reported in this article, how would you describe Vivian Villarreal?

SUGGESTIONS FOR WRITING

1. Interview a woman athlete in a sport that interests you, and report on how she trains, what support she receives, what obstacles she has overcome, and what goals she has for the future.

2. Gather data on athletic programs at your school or in a nearby school district; then report on how well sports for men and women are funded and how those funding decisions are made.
3. Research how women have managed to succeed in a profession traditionally dominated by men, such as law or medicine. Report what you learn.

LINKS

■ Within the Book

Rogers' article shows a woman succeeding in a game traditionally associated with men. In "The Deer at Providencia" (pages 627–630), Annie Dillard is the only woman in a group of North American travelers to the Amazon watershed.

■ Elsewhere in Print

Cahn, Susan K. *Coming On Strong: Gender and Sexuality in Twentieth-Century Women's Sport.* New York: Free, 1994.

Fields, Sally K. *Female Gladiators: Gender, Law, and Contact Sports in America.* Urbana: U of Illinois P, 2004.

Lee, Jeanette, and Adam Scott Gershenson. *The Black Widow's Guide to Killer Pool: Become the Player to Beat.* New York: Three Rivers, 2000.

McCumber, David. *Playing off the Rail: A Pool Hustler's Journey.* New York: Random, 1996.

Messner, Michael A. *Taking the Field: Women, Men and Sports.* Minneapolis: U of Minnesota P, 2002.

Sandoz, Joli, and Joby Winans, eds. *Whatever It Takes: Women on Women's Sports.* New York: Farrar, 1999.

Smith, Lissa, ed. *Nike Is a Goddess: The History of Women in Sports.* New York: Atlantic Monthly P, 1988.

■ Online

www.mhhe.com/motives

Click on "More Resources" then "Writing to Report Information."

■ ■ ■

THE BEST JOB IN TOWN

Katherine Boo

The following article is an excerpt from a longer article first published in a 2004 issue of The New Yorker. *It focuses on an issue of growing concern to many Americans: how jobs once done within the United States are now being done overseas. In a practice know as "outsourcing," American companies hire workers in foreign countries to do jobs that would require higher wages if filled within the United States. If you buy an "American" product, you might note on the label that it was manufactured overseas. But you may not be aware of how workers in other countries are now providing a range of banking, insurance, and other services that involve access to data that many people consider "private." As you read "The Best Job in Town," you will find that it offers an inside view of a company based in India—a view that includes the perspective of the American owner of this company as well as that of an Indian employee.*

A graduate of Columbia University, Katherine Boo has written for Washington Monthly, *the* Washington Post, The Atlantic, *and* The New Yorker. *She specializes in investigative reporting about the lives of people who are socially disadvantaged, and she currently works as a senior fellow for the New America Foundation. In addition to winning a Pulitzer Prize for public service, Boo was awarded a MacArthur Fellowship in 2003. A MacArthur Fellowship is sometimes called "the genius award" because of the requirements specified by the philanthropist who endowed it. When announcing Boo's award, the MacArthur Foundation stated, "Among the most influential journalists writing about contemporary social conditions, Boo's reportage is characterized by its expansive research, elegant presentation, and empathy for her subjects."*

One Monday this spring, a forty-three-year-old salesclerk at the Home Depot in Plano, Texas, scribbled some updates onto an old résumé and took it to his local copy shop. To his education and work history—a bachelor's degree in industrial engineering and technology, service in the U.S. Marine Corps—he added a recent moonlighting job as a handyman and a new "career objective." Ten minutes later, in southern India, a middle-aged Hindu man in a cavernous workplace began to type the Home Depot clerk's words. A prevailing fiction in the Indian office was that the dozens of "document specialists" doing American work didn't actually register the content of the résumés, funeral programs, pro-se lawsuits, and erotic manifestos sent to them over broadband from store counters with "While-U-Wait" signs. Rather, the document specialists were to type, format, proofread, and zap things back while maintaining an exquisite blankness of mind. But American résumés, as much as American erotica, caused an inconvenient upwelling of emotion. "To secure a position at a company that would utilize my skills and provide an opportunity for advancement": row upon row of typing Indians recognized the Plano clerk's yearning as their own.

The typists were new, entry-level employees at a prominent firm in the sprawling coastal city of Chennai—still "wet behind the ears," as Americans would say, or so they'd been informed during a company crash course on Western ways. Their narrow cubicles were lodged on the sixth floor of a pink stucco building whose lobby possessed, in addition to a purposeless set of turnstiles and a statue of the Hindu god Ganesh, solid evidence that even plastic rhododendrons will wilt in extreme heat. Most of the workers had been born in Chennai and would, in all likelihood, die there. Still, from their workstations they could imagine, not unreasonably, that they were seeing a bit of the world. Their employer, a company named Office Tiger, did the work not just of an American copy-shop chain but of seven of the twelve biggest banks on Wall Street—confidential labor carried out in unmarked rooms with film-covered windows, closed-circuit cameras, and electronic security so unforgiving that as the typist finished the résumé from Plano three bankers, accidentally locked in a nearby room, were frantically pounding on a door. Office Tiger also performed work for a Big Four accounting agency, several white-shoe Northeastern law firms, an insurance conglomerate, two large publishing concerns, a Madison Avenue advertising agency, global management consultancies, and other enterprises whose identities were not divulged to workers of the résumé-typing rank.

The document specialists, all college graduates, earned roughly a tenth of what they would have commanded for this work in the U.S., and less, too, than they would have been paid in some call centers. But it was the possibility that one could rise up from a lowly position that had made Office Tiger one of the city's status employers, a firm whose workers were so pleased by their affiliation that they put it on their wedding invitations, just below their fathers' names. A foreign notion—that jobs should be distributed on the basis of merit—was amending the rules of a society where employment had for millennia been allotted by caste, and great possibilities abounded. A clerk who today did a bang-up job of formatting the work history of a part-time handyman in Plano might be an adjunct investment banker by year's end.

Chennai, the capital of the state of Tamil Nadu, was at one time an agglomeration of fishing hamlets near the Bay of Bengal—a mile-wide spit of sand upon which seventeenth-century British traders imposed the name Madras. As the imperialists built forts and seaside promenades, the less refined aspects of colonialism sharpened the Tamil-speaking locals' preference for their indigenous culture. This now vast community—the fourth-largest city in India, after Delhi, Mumbai, and Calcutta—was, until recently, a willfully anti-cosmopolitan place. If the Calcuttan post-colonial ideal was outward-looking, intellectual, and romantic, like the heroes of Satyajit Ray films, Chennaians rated hard work over lofty thought, science over poetizing, and humility over everything else. Though most Chennai residents were Hindu, violence against the city's Muslim minority was relatively rare. Discord between rich and poor was similarly muted—perhaps because the city's élites tended to leave ostentation to the peacocks, which (along with goats, water buffalo, auto-rickshaws, roosters, and homeless families) beautified the roadsides.

For centuries, the Western world knew this city, if at all, through a group   *5* of unpresumptuous tradesmen: weavers who rendered the colorful, comfortable madras plaid that has long outfitted the gentries of Cornwall and Nantucket. This "better cheape" cloth, as one seventeenth-century British trader described it, provided the city with an economic base until the late twentieth century, when tariffs and global competition brought many power looms to a standstill. Some former weavers earned renown for a more macabre kind of trading: as one of the international black market's primary sources of human kidneys. Other citizens, though, turned to more renewable resources for economic survival. Capitalizing on their celebrated work ethic, on a dozen practical-minded local universities, and on the ability of the élites to speak, in addition to Tamil, the clipped and elegant English of their colonizers, Chennaians developed the sort of forward-looking economy that many of America's post-manufacturing cities still struggle to achieve. "Better cheape" Western business is Chennai's new niche.

Schoolgirls here maintain a picturesque ancient tradition—entwining their braids, morning and night, with fragrant jasmine flower. The perfume is particularly welcome lately, as constant road construction, unprecedented automotive pollution, and a three-year drought have created a stench that the vanilla candles in the new wi-fi coffeehouses cannot mask. Flower fields have given way to steel-and-glass buildings, which, despite continuous exposure to sun in one of the world's least temperate climates, have become a status essential. The glass in these office towers is blue and black and silver, and its impenetrability seems at first to be a consequence of the city's blinding sun. The refraction is partly by design. American uneasiness about outsourcing—an issue in the current Presidential campaign—has turned Chennai into a secretive city, where the American back-office presence, everywhere felt, is almost nowhere stated. Although American companies with Picassos in their foyers and Corbusier chairs in reception still dispatch work to South Asia office buildings fronted by beggars and spavined cattle, the company names have been deleted from phone books, Web sites, and corporate entryways. The American International School in Chennai, which serves children of American executives and diplomats, recently doubled in size. It wears no sign on its gate.

The British were drawn to India as a physical place: a repository of precious raw materials from which the natives might be parted, and a locus of beauty and mystique. The new American attachment is not physical but conceptual—the lure of cheap, smart, pliable labor. Among Chennai's janitors and security guards, as well as its bankers, the need for discretion about that labor is understood. Even the ephemera of the United States offshoring debate becomes front-page news here; many of Chennai's young professionals now know the names John Kerry, Lou Dobbs, Benedict Arnold, and Timothy Platt—the latter the proprietor of a U.S.-based Web site called yourjobisgoingtoindia.com, which is as closely followed in Chennai as it is in Silicon Valley. Fascination with the American controversy is more bemused than fearful. Chennaians in general believe that what they call "outsource hoopla" has already redounded to their favor, alerting a wider audience of executives and stockholders to the benefits of wage arbitrage.

Some American companies, such as Ford, have been manufacturing in the region for years, working to capture a piece of a potentially vast consumer market. But now non-factory, professional employment is surging. Among the white-collar options available to Chennai's college graduates are work for Verizon, Bank of America, Hewlett-Packard, Citibank, Visa, MasterCard, and Electronic Data Systems, a Plano-based tech company founded by the free-trade opponent Ross Perot, which recently announced a layoff of fifty-two hundred U.S. employees.

One indicator of Chennai's new corporate mass is the recently opened Park Hotel, where a glass of Chablis costs nearly as much as the monthly salary of the low-caste busboy who spirits away the empties. Situated near a faded mural of Mahatma Gandhi, bare-chested and bent into his walking stick, the hotel features Texas barbecue, "appletinis," and, to ease executive stress, poolside chaises in cabanas. One spring evening, a tense Indian doing Harley-Davidson work sat in one such cabana, promising his ten-year-old daughter, whom he was "raising by cell phone," that on his day off he would take her to a theme park called M.G.M. Dizzee World. The initials M.G.M. are for the park's founder, M. G. Muthu, who made his first fortune introducing the city's growing middle class to American-style installment plans. Now he is educating working parents about expensive American antidotes to guilt—roller coasters and Seven Dwarfs-like characters resembling incarnations of Vishnu.

The Americanization of Chennai has been so swift and—save inside the Park Hotel—so quiet that many of its citizens do not yet grasp the change in their cultural and literal landscape. An animation company makes cartoons seen by American children on Saturday mornings. Radiologists read American MRIs, clerks adjudicate patients' insurance claims, and programmers automate Medicaid eligibility for an entire Midwestern state. Chartered accountants complete U.S. tax returns while underwriters certify U.S. mortgages. And within Office Tiger's pink building aspiring financiers analyze American firms that are ripe for corporate takeover in a place they call Wall Street East. *10*

One afternoon in late March, Office Tiger's wiry thirty-three-year-old co-C.E.O. stood at his desk, surrounded by luggage, receiving from Manhattan the news that his firm had just landed Wall Street investment bank No. 8—a half-a-million-dollar "starter" contract. "There are a few liability issues still

Indian employees focused on their computers.

outstanding, but basically we're good to go," an underling on a speakerphone said. She anticipated a doubling of the contract within the year. "The only tricky thing is that we've got to get the employees hired and ready in three weeks." "Three weeks," the C.E.O. repeated; he was pleased but also harried. Executives of a Fortune 10 company would be descending on the office the following day, but he had decided he would have to miss the visit: officials of a Fortune 5 company were awaiting him the same morning in Bangalore, a thirty-five-minute plane ride away.

The co-C.E.O. is Joseph Sigelman; the other co-C.E.O. is Randy Altschuler, also thirty-three. Their enterprise, Office Tiger, is named not for the fauna of the East but for the mascot of Princeton University, where they met in the cafeteria their freshman year and became best friends. Joe and Randy, middle-class boys who had attended, respectively, St. Ann's in Brooklyn and Manhattan's Hunter College High School, were the kind of Princetonians who sough entrée into student government, not the eating clubs. They shared abstemiousness and obsessive work habits (if you dined most nights on applesauce that you kept in your dorm room, you saved money and gained an extra hour to invest in your medieval-history paper) that since college days have become a selling point.

After Harvard Business School and jobs at Lazard Frères, Goldman Sachs, Deutsche Bank, and the Blackstone Group, in 1998 the friends gave up a combined annual income of half a million dollars and the experience of hearing

Paris doormen say, "Welcome back to the Ritz, Mr. Sigelman," in order to pursue an idea born in a late-night fit of pique. It had become apparent to them that not every typist and copyist working the midnight shift in their investment banks—the moonlighting actor, the artist with the ring in his nose—was putting his heart, soul, and syntactical memory into completing the PowerPoint presentations that needed to be done, perfectly, by morning. Randy began to speculate that workers overseas might invest more care in the menial jobs that Manhattanites seemed not to relish. Joe, who had been introduced to Madras on a family vacation when he was twelve, thought that some of its underemployed citizens might be grateful indeed. "You met people in factories or running the elevator who had the intelligence and spirit to do so much more," he remembered. "We thought, why not release that talent?"

The Indian government gave them a ten-year "tax holiday." American and British venture capitalists gave them seventeen million dollars for the startup, only a sliver of which they had to spend on labor. (Tamil Nadu's per-capita income equates to thirty-six U.S. dollars a month.) Their first "office" was a sheet-metal shed. Former business-school classmates gossiped that Joe and Randy had cracked from the stress of investment-banking and run off to an ashram. Initially, ashram life would have rendered a better return. "We had virtually no business," Randy recalled, "because at the time people thought it was crazy to be sending work to India. So we had a hundred people sitting in a room and we'd get one fax a day to type. When the fax came through, it was like a five-alarm fire—we'd all fall over each other trying to get it done, and we always, always fucked it up." But this slow start turned out to be profitable. During the mutual-reassurance sessions common to foundering enterprises, Joe and Randy got to know their employees better than they ordinarily might have. All were college educated. A third possessed postgraduate or doctoral degrees. Randy returned to New York to establish the American side of the business and, from a small office overlooking a Dunkin' Donuts, pressed his former Wall Street colleagues to give the Indian workers a trial run at higher-end labor.

Six years later, the Manhattan banks that Randy and Joe abandoned still have odes to "thrift" in their marble lobbies, but those banks also have rows of capacious, upholstered, untenanted cubicles. Almost twenty percent of the jobs on Wall Street have disappeared in the last three years. Office Tiger recently doubled its staff, to sixteen hundred and fifty workers, and will nearly double in size again by year's end, on the strength of "judgment-dependent services": equity analysis, legal research, and accounting jobs that pay an annual salary of up to a hundred thousand dollars in the United States and between ten and twenty percent of that in Chennai. *15*

"Anything else?" Joe asked the subordinate who had informed him of investment bank No. 8. He ran his hand anxiously through his sandy hair—he had a reservation on the night's last flight. Well, actually, the colleague said, representatives of an investment bank in London wanted in. "They've just got to get the regulatory approvals, see how much of their work they can take offshore."

"All right, that's good. Is that it?"

Well, actually, the woman said, since he was traveling to the U.S. and London later this month, it might be nice if he stopped in to see some Office Tiger employees who were doing on-site analysis at another investment bank. Joe was momentarily nonplussed; he'd forgotten that his Tigers were in-house there.

"I mean, it's not essential," the subordinate said. "Only, if you had time it would be a nice show of support . . ."

"I get it, I'll do it—sweet idea. Anything else?"   20

Well, actually, there was another impending new contract. "It's been fast-tracked, they want to go live with a pilot."

Salomon Brothers° in its heyday received five hundred job applications a month. Office Tiger sometimes receives fifteen hundred applicants a day, many of them accompanied by parents who pray as their sons and daughters take one test after another in the hope of earning an interview with the beautiful, ruthlessly efficient human-resources executive in black pajamas, who does her work in the reception area, behind a thin glass wall. As Joe returned one more phone call—a cautious executive from Germany, which is experiencing an outsourcing backlash, too—the narrow hallway outside the firm's door grew crowded with the survivors of that testing. They sat in plastic chairs, heads in hands, awaiting their face-to-face encounters.

"Mercy, how do you think you did on the proofreading test?" the human-resources goddess, whose name is Sudha, asked one such survivor, who was perched on the edge of her seat.

"I found it quite easy," responded Mercy, fatally. Her score was eight-five. Joe and Randy seek workers like themselves—the type haunted fifteen years later by the single question botched on the college aptitude test, and game to perform even dull tasks, with, to use the local term, "full sincerity." A minute later, another applicant was warming the chair.

"Hindu culture tends to be gentle, forgiving of shortcomings, which is   25 not exactly the Wall Street ethos," Joe said. Though he trains his workers intensively, cultural miscommunications remain. Not long ago, Office Tiger accidentally hand-delivered to the American consul Joe's underwear, which had been sent to him by his mother. Soon after, during a fast-turnaround project, Joe offended his staff by waving rupee notes—incentive—in front of their noses. He has given up trying to reprogram the hotel coffee-shop pianist, who, having realized that Joe is perhaps the only Jew in Chennai, routinely

---

°*Salomon Brothers:* A major financial company that helped finance U.S. military expenses during the Second World War and occupied a million square feet of trading space during the stock market boom of the 1990s.

serenades him with "Hava Nagila" when he sits down to lunch, even when his companion is a Kuwaiti investor. But after Joe and Randy hired a former Coast Guard petty officer named Lonnie Sapp—a veteran of semi-pro football, a graduate of Connecticut's Trinity College, and almost certainly Chennai's only six-foot-four-inch African-American—to manage the workforce a smoothness settled over the operation, even without the grease of government bribes. (The Princetonians say that they won't pay them.) Cost-saving improvements percolated up from the production level. Satisfied clients begat more clients. And, by the time Randy and Joe turned thirty and outsourcing had become a term of art, they were undermining many of the assumptions that Americans try to nurture while watching their nation's jobs go overseas.

One false assumption had been that only the manufacture of goods, not the provision of services, could be exported. Another, supported most recently by the U.S. Department of Labor, is that the number of American jobs lost to outsourcing is minuscule. But Labor statisticians rely on the corporations to link their domestic downsizing to work they now send abroad—a connection that some corporate leaders are loath to make. Other analyses suggest that the number of American jobs lost to this phenomenon will soon reach a million, as the Indian and Chinese back-office sectors expand by thirty percent a year. Indian analysts foresee outsourcing in biotech research, pharmaceuticals, architecture, and the law. Although many economists believe that this global transition is mutually beneficial—that an economy is better off specializing in areas where it is relatively more productive and importing in areas where it is not—a study by the University of California at Berkeley identifies fourteen million American jobs at risk in the near term. The latest consolation is that, since many outsourced jobs are low-end and mechanistic, Americans are now being liberated to use their exceptional skills as innovators and entrepreneurs. Being tactful, the Tigers pretend to agree. What is the advantage of pointing out that the country of Salman Rushdie and Amartya Sen may not, in fact, be creatively impaired? The résumés and credit-repair leaflets spewing into the copy shop from Texas are less diplomatic. They intimate that some Americans have been "freed up" to do nothing productive whatsoever.

An Office Tiger manager concluded a phone call that required an American accent and began to help one of his document specialists decipher a five-page scrawled submission. "The supervisor called plaintiff gay, child molester, pedophile, and other malicious things": he slowly made out the words. "'Pedophile' misspelled here," the typist noted quietly, in order not to disturb the concentration of her colleagues. "It's not 'p-h-e-d-o . . .'"

"And he obviously didn't mean to write 'viscous,'" the manager said. "It should be 'The vicious rumors that were spread . . .'"

"And in the next sentence that's 'hostile work environment.'"

"Hostile work environment" was not a concept that Joe and Randy had thought to introduce in cultural training, but the document specialists quickly learned it on the job. The phrase evoked very little recognition.

30

As Joe prepared to leave for the airport, a worker appeared at his office door—a slight twenty-six-year-old with a wispy mustache and a smile half the size of his face. In Indian-run workplaces, hierarchies are often too strict for such unannounced visits. Here, employees drop by constantly; they are mesmerized by Joe. As Joe greeted him, his eyes settled on the younger man's collar. "Harish," he admonished. "That's why they put the buttons there—for you to use them." In his boss's wake, Harish stood buttoning and beaming, as if he'd been named employee of the year.

Seriously behind schedule now, Joe skipped to the front of the security gantlet at the entrance to the firm, where the pocketbooks and backpacks of departing workers were being searched to prevent the theft of Western corporate secrets. (The investigations that day turned up "Who Moved My Cheese?" and the Indian edition of *Cosmopolitan*.) "The outsourcing backlash?" Joe was saying. To him, it was political entertainment, music for Presidential campaigns. "In the real world, it's inexorable. This is radical global change, and it is going to happen more and more, not just because the labor in developing countries is cheaper but because the work is often done better. Businesses will have to outsource to stay competitive, and eventually the American public will get used to it. Look, that's what a free market is all about."

Joe passed the applicants awaiting interviews, lost time in a balky elevator, and recovered that time by racing through the twilight to the Taj Hotel, a few hundred yards from Office Tiger, where he has been living for the past five years. His route was through a back alley, where he dodged a succession of two-wheelers, three or four passengers astride. Some of the riders were his employees, hastening to work at the start of the American business day. "It kills me," he said, shaking his head. "Their brains are their careers, but I can't get any of them to wear a helmet." He stopped momentarily in his hotel room, where the liveried workers who deliver his meals often petition him, sometimes successfully, for jobs. At the airport, flight attendants were waiting to hand him his ticket and escort him onto the plane. Despite a philosophical commitment to what he calls "lavatory class" travel, Joe is regularly bumped to first class. The flight attendants, it recently dawned on him, might want to be Tigers, too.

His collar properly buttoned now, the cheerful worker named Harish Kumar, who not long ago took pleasure in sewing his own clothes, stood in the front of a white-walled classroom. The room's chief decoration was a flyer stating the criminal consequences of insider trading. Ten middle-aged students wearing electronic-security cards around their necks held their fingers over computer keyboards; they did not want to miss a word. The students were known as Office Tiger "candidates"—the two percent of applicants who had been, provisionally, hired. The job of Harish (known as Harry to American clients and Employee No. 489 to electronic security) was to teach them the Western business tools and mores they would need to survive a six-month probation period and become full-fledged Tigers. Much of the previous week had been devoted to the consequences of revealing proprietary information and engaging in securities fraud—subjects that Joe and Randy had instructors teach until they saw fear in candidates' eyes. Now, following a vigorous discussion of spreadsheets, Harish turned to a practical problem. "Let us ready ourselves," he told his students, "to make an organizational chart using PowerPoint."

Leaning his gaunt frame over the keyboard, Harish tapped until a giant green box was projected onto a white wall. He tapped the keyboard again: two smaller boxes materialized beneath the large one, and then four more boxes, smaller still. Then he laid out the problem to be solved. In most organizations there is one "boss box" and many subordinate ones. "Now, can you make all of them perfectly align?"

When New Yorkers like Joe apologize for speaking quickly, Indians smile. They speak faster—especially when working for companies like Office Tiger, where a third of all work assignments must be sent back to the United States within an hour. Harish's speech is truly rapid, because before his candidates graduate to permanent status they're expected to master two dozen subjects—among them securities regulations, Western manners, and Manhattan investment-banking slang. "Verygood, verynice," Harish now complimented one of the classroom's better box-aligners, allowing his "r"s to roll in his enthusiasm, though it violated the conventions of American pronunciation. "And, of course, you can draw the connectors this way, drag-and-drop," he said, demonstrating. "But is it the most efficient way? No. It is too slow. Remember, very often the banker is going to make all sorts of changes. You will want to accommodate him, and quickly."

In his curriculum, Harish wastes no time discussing wage differentials or the asymmetry of the power relationship. Among his students, the colonial resonances are not ignored; they're understood. Upon consideration, the students will argue that, since America is globalization's great hegemon, it's an advantage to work for Americans directly, instead of for Indian-owned companies like Infosys or Wipro, where U.S. work is also done. Tigers can learn from Joe's perfectionism, from his preference for J.C. Penney ties, from his imperviousness to fatigue, and from his wry self-deprecation—useful, they note, in softening the effect of a command. On the rare occasion that Joe gets angry, his workers sometimes forget to register the cause, engaged as they are in studying the technique. "Joe is our Harvard Business School," Harish says. "We watch his energy and aggression and try to learn."

To explain the yearning that brought them to Office Tiger, Harish and his students invariably use the same word: "exposure." In its Indian sense, "exposure" means not publicity or vulnerability but contact with the world beyond Chennai. After three years at Office Tiger, Harish is still occasionally jarred by dislocation. When Wall Streeters call and say, "Hey, Harry, what's up?"—as they do, often—the wrong picture always pops into his mind. What's up is a rotating metal fan on the low Styrofoam ceiling of the room where he sleeps, on the floor, beside his father, mother, brother, and grandmother. The ceiling fan's hum is a baseline to Harish's late-night puzzling about the virtual world he now inhabits.

"I am afraid I was born a quirky and curious boy," Harish says. "Like Harry Potter, you could say, without glasses." Globalization has given him a work life rich in riddles. Why do Americans speak of the "end" of a show called "Friends," when in India it runs in perpetuity, serving as a more effective instructor than anyone at Office Tiger on the subject of the American vernacular? Is it really a compliment to say of someone, "She is dynamite"? The words themselves make Harish shudder. "We'll have to pay through the nose" and "He jumped down my throat" make him wince. More pleasant in its mysteriousness is "couch potato." There was, when he first came to Office Tiger, the expression "just hang loose until tomorrow," but he hasn't heard that one in a while. In the outsourcing business, a sudden surge in clients is called an "escalation"—a word that warns of seven-day workweeks. Office Tiger has been escalating for nearly two years now, the growth of its Wall Street research operations fueled by regulatory reforms that came (along with criminal actions and billion-dollar legal settlements) when United States banks were caught manipulating their research in order to boost the profits of favored clients. Companies now send junior-analyst and research jobs to Office Tiger not just because it is cheaper but also because it is nine thousand miles from Wall Street temptations. Harish has been granted full exposure. Now it's home with which he struggles to make contact.

The neighborhood where Harish has lived all his life is named Triplicane, and was once an ancient fishermen's village. It is today so densely populated that some travel guides mistake it for a slum. Harish's house is off the main road, in an alley of jasmine peddlers, Muslim shop workers, and Hindu priests. He rises around 5:30 A.M., mounts his rusted bike, and rides to work, startling the neighborhood parrots and the buffalo that lug the milkmen's wares. His passage doesn't rouse the beggar children, who have learned his recently acquired belief that direct handouts to the poor encourage sloth. At work, he trains his candidates, takes ten minutes or so for lunch in the office pantry, and trains some more. At seven-thirty in the evening, when it's 9 A.M. in New York, he confers with the American banking clients for whom he tailors his training, to insure that he is emphasizing the right skills. And then he turns to a slew of computer-programming challenges that may show management his greater gifts. He often goes home after midnight.

On his concrete threshold in Triplicane, as on others in the neighborhood, is an intricate chalk design known as a *kolam*. His grandmother, who is seventy-nine, draws it there each morning, in the Hindu hope of keeping catastrophe safely out in the streets. At night, from her mat, she listens for her grandson, sometimes cupping a hand around an elaborately bejeweled ear. The ear adornment was the custom in the village where she was born, a place where the tigers were real and said to devour boys in one go, not bit by bit each workday. She is the first at the door when her grandson rings the bell. He leaves his new square-toed lace-ups at the threshold, swallows a few spoonfuls of rice to silence protests about his declining weight, and joins his extended family on the floor. It is then that his grandmother, if not Harish, can sleep.

"Harish? There are a hundred here like him," the human-resources goddess once observed in passing. To Harish, that's no slight, it's heaven. The office is crammed with smart young people who speak freely and are as open to ideas as he is. It is what he imagines an American college dorm might be like, and in it he has shed the shyness of childhood. Though the money he earns is welcome, he is sometimes at a loss as to how to spend it. "For instance, when I wanted a computer for my parents' home it was simpler to gather discarded parts and make it myself," he said. Since becoming a Tiger, he has made a single significant outlay: to help his parents retire. Every month now, he hands them his paycheck, and when he needs another button-down shirt he has to ask them. Usually, they say yes.

In Hindu families, to acknowledge the gifts of a child too early is to put him at risk—to provoke the evil eye. So Harish's father put away an accidental tape recording he had made of his firstborn and did not listen to it for years. Harish's parents had been trying to record Hindu devotional songs from the All India Radio station when their son, eleven months old, grew incensed at their inattention. He began to shriek, and in their exasperation at the now-botched recording the parents didn't immediately recognize the content of the baby's cries. In Tamil, he was saying, "I want my ABCs."

As smart as the child might have been, they worried how he would intersect with the world. The family was of the education-revering Brahmin caste, but the parents were too poor for the mother to fulfill her expected role of staying home and tutoring Harish and his younger brother and sister. She worked instead as a clerk in a government office, her intelligence never rewarded. Her husband worked across town, in another government office, and Harish grew up in his own imagination—a world of Isaac Asimov and astronauts and the ships that he could see dropping anchor in the Bay of Bengal, if he chose a certain seat by a certain window in his schoolroom and trained his peripheral vision just so.

In that schoolroom, he was a failure, flunking math, science, and geography year after year. In sports, he was fast but too small. His solace was "The Harish Book of Records and News": a brown-paper chapbook in which he drew intricate sketches of Gandhi and pasted newspaper clippings. Like other boys, he was drawn to cricket stars and advertisements for films like "Godzilla Fights King Monster." He also collected reports of improbable talent. There was the Delhi boy who set a record by belching ninety-one times in a single minute, and a legless man who swam from Italy to Sicily, and a Chinese dentist who popped his patients' teeth out by pressing his fingers on their necks. Harish longed to find his own unconventional ability, because by the time he

45

reached the age of twelve his teachers had concluded that higher education was not in his future.

His parents, anguished at their own child-rearing deficiencies, couldn't summon the anger to beat him for his academic failure. So he exacted his own punishment. He ran to the Bay of Bengal marina, where he regularly played cricket with the boys he called his "batch." Sitting apart on the sand, he made a stark accounting. Having squandered advantages that his parents had sacrificed to give him, he would try to accept his mediocrity with grace. At sixteen, he left school. After a stint as a magician for children's parties—"Of course, there was no magic to my mind reading," he said, "just the tricks of psychology and logic"—he enrolled in a computer-training course.

A society with far more bright aspirants than promising jobs inevitably becomes an over-credentialled one. The institutions from which the young amass certificates and ribbons are sometimes rigorous, sometimes fraudulent, but all have rousing names. Harish's school was called, simply, Brilliant. There were programming languages to learn and independent explorations to launch, and, when his curiosities took him beyond the lesson plan, his new teachers did not object. Some days, there were no teachers at all. On one such morning, Harish rose to help his classmates get through an exercise in accounting. An administrator happened by, registered a smart, coherent presence at the head of the classroom, and hired the boy, age seventeen, as faculty.

"My colleagues were much older and more learned than I, but it was such a rich time, sitting there like a pet, being fed what they knew," Harish said. In turn, he enriched seven years' worth of subsequent Brilliant scholars. Now, after insuring that no other Tiger will see him being "over-prideful," he will tap for a second on his keyboard and bring up an American Web site that lists the holders of Microsoft Office Master Instructor certification. The site reports that the United States has seven hundred master instructors, Yugoslavia has five, and Oman and Botswana three each. India has just one: Harish.

In the classrooms of his childhood, he had tried to imagine what it would feel like to be on one of the ships moving out of the bay. When a colleague at Brilliant made the leap to Office Tiger and encouraged Harish to come, too, he saw himself as finally aboard. For other Tigers, there were other metaphors, but the sense of movement after decades of socioeconomic stasis was the same. Harish's friend Vidhya, who is twenty-five, heady with her rise from reception to sell-salaried senior management, bought her parents not just freedom from their jobs but a house—a gesture so expansive that her parents chose to overlook her new stilettos. Other parents cringed to hear the children they had raised on Gandhian notions of national self-sufficiency faking American accents into their cell phones. But most accepted the air-conditioning units nonetheless, and few could help feeling pleasure. Those parents had had dreams of ships themselves.

Harish, usually lighthearted, was sobered by the fact that the hopes of some trainees would be thwarted in his classroom. The ultimate goal of his teaching was something that Joe and Randy called "foolproofing." In a *50* company that offered judgment-dependent services, clients needed to believe that those judgments were routine, culturally uninflected, idiosyncrasy-free—that ten people confronted with the same data set would rank ten different utility companies the same way. As adroit as Harish was at the front of the classroom, it was after class that he excelled. That's when he studied data from intricate programs he'd invented that analyzed keyboard strokes in training and alerted him to students falling behind. These tools were an extension of his peripheral vision—a means of discerning the person sitting in the corner, miserably lost. Alone with his data, he was excited to find consistent error: those who made the same category of mistake repeatedly were the ones he knew how to help. But wild variations in performance depressed him. "The data analysis is convincing on this point," he said. Erratic, unfocused students, the ones like him in his pre-computing days, were those who would not make the cut.

When Harish tried to explain his inventions, he made them sound modest, self-therapeutic—fiddlings of a restless wit. There was something else at work too, something that resisted both old-fashioned Hindu acceptance and his new peers' enthusiasm for meritocracy, with its bright distinctions between those who are capable and those who are not. Improbability was, after all, his stock in trade. If he wrote the right programs, taught his classes in the clearest and most effective way, he wondered, why shouldn't all his batch win? . . .

The beach where Harish wandered one Saturday night contained roughly the same number of kite sellers and beggar children as it had when he was a twelve-year-old failure, but neon signs promoting bank loans and washing machines had altered the quality of the light. The quality of the air, too, was appreciably different, owing to a traffic jam fifty yards away. Harish would have mourned this transformation more if he hadn't been rethinking the concept of place. Lately, he considered community less a function of roads and roofs and teashops than of imagination. Even the solid presence of his grandmother could dematerialize at the late-night ring of his cell phone, the urgent summons of American clients. And while his parents rolled their eyes at the constant needs of the world beyond Chennai, Harish saw the calls as tidings of cultural integration, more niches for curious boys.

He had just seen the film "The Lord of the Rings," which had prompted him to reflect on Asimov and the rest of his science-fiction and fantasy canon. "Now I can hardly think of those books as fiction anymore," he said. "So many new things have been happening, and what just last year seemed impossible is now not. What I think instead is how lucky I am to have been born into this strange, right time. In these last years, we've found that New York and Chennai can do the same things—that we almost are the same thing. Already, we are half of the time in New York, just our bodies are left behind." In such hybrid lives, he knew, some parts of one's culture disappear. But among the vanished elements might be caste discrimination and religious bigotry—things Harish longed to see go. "So much of globalization is, I think, mischaracterized and misunderstood. It is because of this trend that there will come a

A street scene in India showing two sides of contemporary culture there.

day when there are no boundaries, no castes or divides between Muslims and Hindus or Christians—a day when, indeed, there will be no nations at all! Indian time? New York time? They are passing phenomena, in my opinion. Soon we will all share one time zone—or, really, there will be no time at all."

There was already, in his life, no time. He had been working like mad for his American clients. There was a programming job that outside contractors had said they'd need three months to complete. Harish did it on his own in sixty hours. "It was just intuitive, a three-day stunt," he said, modestly. "I have no big theories, but some problems I can solve from the bottom up." Such efficiency-minded innovation was a Tiger trademark, and helped explain why, over five years, only a single American company had, after a trial run at Office Tiger, opted out. (The exception was a New York firm that, battered by the events of September 11th, decided not to traumatize workers further by sending their jobs offshore.)

The constant expansion required new macros, databases, quality-control systems, and information systems—so many inventions, so urgently needed, that Harish didn't always consider their implications. For instance, the system he'd created to help candidates see and correct their data-entry errors had now mutated into a tool that helped executives identify and remove imperfect "permanent" workers. But, at the end of long days of inventing and foolproofing and universalizing the judgments of others, Harish preferred to dwell on his own recent performance evaluation, which described his contribution as "phenomenal."

55

"Whatever I accomplish, I forget, because I am thinking about the next thing," Harish said. So he focused not on his employers' praise—"a source of inspiration," "role model," "strong intellectual curiosity," "loyal to O.T."—but on future possibilities. If he worked to improve his communication skills and written English, he would be "groomed to handle supervisory activities." This faith in his future as an employee was particularly welcome, as he was feeling a bit inadequate at home. . . .

Competition is good, Harish told himself, and change too, whether or not it feels so at first. He tried to concentrate on a new class of trainees—men and women who were just beginning to learn the meaning of "What's up?" and other American puzzles, and all of whom he wanted to see win. It was far too early for them to learn that their yearning word, "exposure," had another, disquieting definition.

He was tired and had developed a wracking cough—Chennai's polluted air, he said, though family members gently suggested a work schedule antithetical to human health. "I know, it is unlike me," he said on the Friday of election week. "But I am in need of a break." He left his cubicle at eight instead of midnight, waiting patiently in a queue for his backpack to be searched and reassurances made to American businesses that, populist politics notwithstanding, the corporate *omertà* was intact.

Riding his bike home, he could smell the sea but did not stop. Fewer Chennaians were coming to the beach these days. Many of those with televisions were at home watching soap operas, like "The Bold and the Beautiful." Some without televisions had recently been deprived of the shore as well, the government having increased parking fees from five rupees to fifty. The beggar children were left with few prospects to importune. Amusement-park workers turned the handcranks of empty Ferris wheels as much out of habit as of hope.

On a previous evening's visit, Harish had turned away from the calls of vendors and children to stare into the expanse of the bay. It was the most beautiful time of the evening—the light faint enough to obscure the empty Coke cans and cigarette butts yet sufficient, still, to cast a shine on the sea. "The perfect time and place for thinking about one's life and future, the moment when a person feels free," he had said. But, by May, free thinking about the future seemed less appealing than a spell of thinking nothing at all. This was the burden of trained peripheral vision: sometimes a man noticed what he might have been happier to miss. There were ships that anchored in the bay only briefly, and other ships that sailed right through.

60

QUESTIONS FOR DISCUSSION

1. In her opening paragraph, Boo uses the phrase "prevailing fiction" to describe the belief that workers do not notice the content of the documents they process. What kind of factors could prompt employers to misjudge

what these employees experience, and why might employees hesitate to disrupt this misperception?

2. What does Boo reveal about the history of Chennai? Is there a connection between this history and what is now happening there?

3. In paragraph 8, Boo describes Texas billionaire and former presidential candidate Ross Perot as a "free-trade opponent." What does "free-trade" mean, and why is it significant that Perot opposes it?

4. How has the American presence in Chennai affected the quality of life there?

5. Why do you think that American companies and other organizations operating in Chennai try not to draw attention to their locations?

6. What do you think of Joe Siegelman, the co-founder of Office Tigers? How is your opinion shaped by the information Boo reports about him?

7. Consider paragraphs 27–29. What do they imply about literacy?

8. When editing Boo's article for this book, the author and editor considered stopping at the end of paragraph 39 but then decided to include most of Boo's material about Harish Kumar even though it made the piece longer than some readers might like. Was this a good decision? How would your response to this piece change if you did not learn about Harish?

9. What does Harish's experience say about the nature of intelligence and "hybrid lives"?

SUGGESTIONS FOR WRITING

1. Research one of the American corporations that has outsourced jobs through Office Tiger and then write an essay in which you report what you learned about that firm. Consider its nature, size, and power, as well as how it presents itself to both stockholders and the general public.

2. What industry has suffered the greatest job loss in your state in the last five years? Write a report in which you establish the size of that loss and the impact on the local economy.

3. Imagine that you have been invited to give a twenty-minute presentation about American culture for an audience consisting of job applicants at Office Tiger. Write the speech that conveys the information you believe this audience most needs to know.

LINKS

▪ Within the Book

In "Bet on It" (pages 201–202), Gary Riven provides an inside view of another American company.

▪ Elsewhere in Print

Das, Gurcharan. *India Unbound: The Social and Economic Revolution.* New York, Anchor, 2002.

Davies, Paul. *What's With This India Business?* London: Brealey, 2004.

Forster, E. M. *A Passage to India.* 1924. New York: Harvest, 1965.

Greaver, Michael. *Strategic Outsourcing.* New York: American Management Assn., 1999.

Lacity, May, et al. *Global Information Technology Outsourcing.* Hoboken: Wiley, 2001.

Linder, Jane. *Outsourcing for Radical Change.* New York, Amacom, 2004.

Robinson, Marcia, and Ravi Kalakota. *Offshore Outsourcing.* Atlanta: Mivar, 2004.

▪ Online

www.mhhe.com/motives

Click on "More Resources" then "Writing to Report Information."

▪ ▪ ▪

3

Writing to Explain Information

Is there a connection between gender and intelligence? Why did an ancient people abandon beautiful homes that they had built with care? Why do many people gamble in casinos? To answer such questions requires you to explain information so you can help people understand what something means, what causes it to happen, and what its consequences are. In other words, you must explain information to reveal what is not readily apparent to others. Because information can legitimately be viewed in more than one way, different writers can come to significantly different conclusions. Explanation is an essential skill for making sense of the world around us.

When we explain, we need to analyze or classify information, examine causes and consequences, and define concepts by distinguishing them from other, similar ones. We may also need to paraphrase, which means taking someone else's words and translating them into words of our own that can be more easily understood by our audience. Any of these ways of explaining information can be used independently or in combination with any of the others.

Suppose you are asked on a midterm exam in earth science to explain why there is a big desert between the Sierra Nevada and the Rockies. You could begin by describing what a desert is. You might then note some of the implications of that description: "Only a few, very hardy plants that have adapted well to going without water can grow in deserts, and animals that require large supplies of water, such as mammals, generally avoid deserts." All you will have done to this point is report information. This step is often necessary before you can explain information, because gaps in your readers' knowledge may hinder them from understanding what you wish to convey.

But once you begin to address *why* the area became a desert, you have moved from reporting to explaining. Alternatively, if you convey *how* animals can adapt successfully to living in such a harsh environment, you are also offering an explanation. Similarly, you would be explaining information if, instead of simply listing the animals living in the desert, you placed these animals into different categories (or classes) based on different strategies for survival. You would be explaining, too, if you defined a concept about which people might disagree. For example, although most readers would agree that "a desert is a place where there is very little annual rainfall," they may not agree about the meaning of more abstract terms such as *environmentalist*. Hence the need for strategies such as definition, classification, and analysis when you write to explain rather than to report. You will find examples of all these strategies in this chapter.

The principal difference between interpreting and explaining is the difference between knowing something and understanding it. If you were to simply describe a perfectionist named Evelyn by showing what she looks like and how she behaves, your readers would learn something about her, but they would not understand why she is the way she is. To promote an understanding of Evelyn, you would need to explain her background—considering, for example, the way she was treated by her parents as a child. You would be *reporting* if you presented information without reasons but *explaining* if you identified the reasons underlying that information.

Although explaining information is different from reporting information, you will find that writers often choose to do both in a single piece. Writers who are primarily interested in reporting may include brief explanations for some of the information they are conveying. And, as noted earlier, writers who are primarily interested in explaining may need to report information before they can interpret it. For example, if you review "The Best Job in Town" in Chapter 2, you will find that Katherine Boo focuses on reporting information about a specific company, its founders, and some of its employees. Although she suggests some reasons to account for why this company has been successful and why people are eager to work there, she devotes much more attention to providing information from which readers can draw their own conclusions. Stephen Jay Gould, whose work appears in this chapter, reports information about nineteenth-century science primarily to explain how reputable scientists can come to erroneous conclusions. Similarly, Catherine Dold offers some background information about the Anasazi before focusing on why these people disappeared. Like writers such as these, you may need to combine reporting and explaining in an essay of your own. The challenge, as in any kind of writing, is to remain mindful of your primary purpose—or motive for writing. If you are asked to explain something, make sure that you are helping your audience to understand your subject, not just gain information about it. Your aim is to change the way readers view the subject, not just to increase their knowledge of it.

Once you have identified a tentative topic, you should test your choice before proceeding. Ask yourself: "Will I be explaining something that my readers probably do not understand?" If the answer is yes, then you know that you are about to engage in meaningful communication. You are now ready to give some additional thought to what the readers you envision are like.

CONSIDERING AUDIENCE

Writers who are motivated to explain information have an advantage over writers who must confine themselves to reporting it. Since more than one explanation is possible for any set of data, writing to explain allows for flexibility. And because people like to know how and why things work, there is a large audience for explanations. Even when people believe they already understand the significance of information, they can be engaged by an explanation that suggests a new way of thinking.

When you are writing to explain, you must make sure that your audience is familiar with the information or situation you have chosen to discuss. In some cases, you may write for an audience that has as much information as you do—maybe even more. For example, when writing a paper for a college professor who presumably is an expert on the topic you are addressing, you can focus your energy on explaining rather than reporting. But if you have reason to believe that your audience may lack background in the area you wish to discuss, then you must provide it—usually at the beginning of your work, so that the information then leads to an explanation of its significance. Similarly, you should be careful to explain any terms with which your audience may be unfamiliar—as Wes Pitts does in "Photo Exorcism."

Sometimes you can simply ask an audience how much it knows about the topic you plan to discuss. For example, in a college writing class, you might be writing with your classmates in mind and have the opportunity to work in small groups or discuss your projects with the class as a whole. This could also be the case when you are collaborating with other students in a science lab and planning to write about the significance of your results. If you envision a larger audience—say, the student body of your campus—then you must remember that your audience will be diverse in terms of age, gender, and other factors (see pages 3–4). Rather than guess what most students know or do not know, you can conduct an informal survey by mentioning your project to various people whom you encounter on campus or online each week and see how much they already seem to know about your topic. Having short conversations of this sort offers another benefit: You may find that people do not know much about your topic but are interested in learning about it. Or you may find that people seem disinterested. When this happens, you may decide to choose another topic—or resolve to work harder at capturing attention for a topic that is important to you even if it is not immediately important to others.

Many readers are drawn to articles that teach them how to do something. An engaging manner—one that makes readers feel as if they are being addressed by someone who is friendly—can be helpful when writing explanations of this kind. In "Photo Exorcism," for example, Wes Pitts uses both the first and second person when discussing how to use photo software to change images. He assumes that most readers already know how to use a camera and have on hand pictures that include individuals they no longer wish to remember. These are reasonable assumptions given the popularity of photography and the frequency with which relationships break down, Pitts then goes on to explain specific steps for altering images. By doing so, he is using a social situation (breaking up) to enliven a discussion that could be purely technical. Even readers who would never consider altering a photograph to remove an individual no longer in favor can be engaged by Pitt's strategy—a strategy that you can easily use in an essay of your own if you want to hold the attention of readers: Locate your explanation within a situation that is amusing or likely to inspire some other emotional response.

When writing to explain, be careful not to insult the intelligence of your readers. There is no reason to teach anyone over the age of six how to make a peanut-butter-and-jelly sandwich, but you could reasonably expect to find adult readers interested in learning how to make bread or organic peanut butter from scratch. A basic principle for writing to explain information, therefore, is to consider how much your audience knows and how you can build on that knowledge to teach something it is unlikely to know but may benefit from knowing.

Another principle to bear in mind when considering audience is whether your readers may be inclined to resist what you wish to explain. If you are writing about the gambling industry, as Gary Rivlin does in "Bet on It," you can safely assume that many readers will take at least some interest in the results of your work because gambling is a widespread social phenomenon and associated in the popular imagination with excitement. To write about a subject like sexuality, as Joan Roughgarden does, is more challenging. Even though we live in a culture in which sexuality is often emphasized, many people are understandably squeamish when it comes to learning the details of who is doing what to whom—hence the popularity of such euphemisms as "sleeping together" and "the birds and the bees." Popular magazines may never lose money printing articles explaining how to improve one's love life, but explanations of this sort are unlikely to be graphic. To actually explain what birds and bees are up to—or mammals in the case of Roughgarden's article— you need to have an audience that is reasonably sophisticated. There is no reason to follow Roughgarden's lead and write an explanation about sexuality, but you can benefit from following her approach to audience: Be direct, not coy; sound professional without seeming stuffy; and provide ample evidence to support a conclusion that an audience may initially be inclined to resist.

PLANNING YOUR ESSAY

One useful way to prepare for writing explanation is to review your topic to see what its main divisions are and then list the subtopics that develop those main points. In making decisions like these, you are analyzing. *Analysis* is a systematic way of thinking about a subject so as to divide it into the elements of which it is made. This analysis must be done consistently on some logical basis.

The opposite of analysis is *classification,* a thinking process whereby you consider a number of diverse items or pieces of information, looking for ways to group this bit with that and establish some order. As with analysis, you must have some logical basis for a classification—some principle by which you decide which things go in each group. Suppose you have a bin full of used T-shirts to sell. You need to price them, but putting a price tag on each shirt is time-consuming. So you make a sign that says:

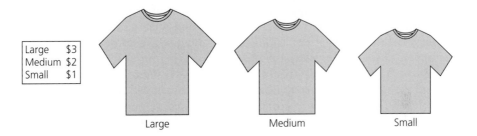

or one that says:

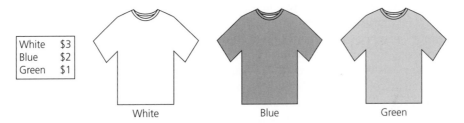

But you should not make one that says:

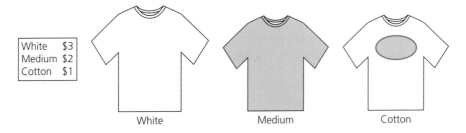

Using more than one basis for classification creates confusion: How much does a white, medium-sized cotton T-shirt cost?

To take another example, suppose you look at an automobile and note that it has wheels, a body, a motor, a transmission, and so on; you have analyzed the automobile by dividing it into parts. Or you can look at all those parts lying on the garage floor and figure out that this part belongs to the motor, that one to the transmission, and so on—that's classification. Analysis involves taking things apart, and classification involves putting them together.

Within this chapter, Joan Roughgarden's "Same-Sex Sexuality" provides an example of classification. She writes about mammals, one of the classes of animals, and then focuses on specific species of mammals—each of which is another class. She also points to two classes of primates: the prosimians and the anthropoids. And when reviewing scientific research on animal sexuality, she classifies scientists as "neutralists" and "adaptationists."

Another widely used approach for interpreting information is called *cause-and-effect analysis,* a strategy writers use to explain what has caused something to happen or what happens as the result of a cause. To some extent, all the writers in this chapter use cause-and-effect analysis. In "What Happened to the Anasazi?" for example, Catherine Dold discusses a theory about what caused the disappearance of the Native American people known for the elaborate cliff dwellings they constructed at Mesa Verde and other sites in the West. And in "Bet on It," Gary Rivlin explains what has caused slot machines to become more popular, especially with Americans over the age of fifty-five. Although he focuses on causes, his conclusion indicates an effect as well.

Cause-and-effect analysis can be undertaken in a number of ways. But if you are writing a short essay, you may find it helpful to focus on either causes or effects. You will often find that you can interpret information by using either causes or effects to focus an analysis of the same subject. An essay on terrorism, for example, could focus on what causes terrorists to commit mass murder—as they did when destroying the twin towers of the World Trade Center in 2001. You might prefer, however, to focus on the effects of terrorism or the effects of a specific act—as in an essay on what happened as the result of terrorists seizing commercial aircraft and flying them into the World Trade Center. The charts on page 179 may help you see how very different essays are generated by the same subject depending on what kind of analysis you use. As you develop essays along these lines, you can explore different causes or different effects in separate paragraphs—although some causes or effects will need more than one paragraph to explain.

Process analysis provides another way to explain information. When writers focus on "process," they are attempting either to explain how something has been or could be changed (such as the process through which contaminated rivers have been purified) or to teach how something can be undertaken by readers (such as how to catch a fish). In this chapter, Wes Pitts uses process analysis to explain how readers can alter digital photographs. And Gary Rivlin uses process analysis when explaining how slot machines are designed to appeal to growing numbers of gamblers.

Definition often plays an important role in writing to explain information. If you are writing about terrorism, you may need to distinguish it from conventional warfare. In an essay included in this chapter, Nicholas Kristof

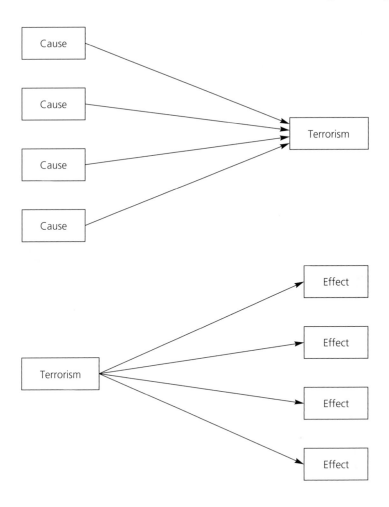

defines the meaning of *wa* in Japanese culture. Other writers might devote an entire essay to defining a complex or frequently misunderstood term.

To define what you mean by a word or phrase that requires explanation, you must go beyond quoting a dictionary definition, for quoting by itself is simply reporting information already constructed by others. To compose your own definition of a problematic term, you can proceed as follows:

- Trace its origin and show how its meaning has evolved.
- Contrast it with whatever it might be confused with.
- Use negation to clarify what it does *not* mean.
- Provide examples.

When you read the essays in this chapter, you may identify a number of terms that require explanation, because they could mean different things to different people. How, for example, would you define *feminist, victim,* or *free speech?* Or consider some of the words that appear in public policy debates. Explaining the meaning of *multicultural,* for example, can be not only a useful service in itself but also an important preliminary for other motives for writing— such as writing to evaluate or writing to persuade.

In short, when you get ready to explain information for others, make a realistic appraisal of who your readers are, what they know, and what they need to be told. Remember that when you write to explain information, you are making a conscious effort to help readers make sense of it. You are assuming the role of teacher rather than reporter. As you assume this responsibility, arrange your ideas in a pattern that will help readers understand them.

TIPS FOR READING AND WRITING EXPLANATIONS

When Reading

- Consider whether the author has defined any terms that are necessary for communicating the material in question.
- Think about how similar you are to the audience for which the explanation was originally composed.
- Ask whether you have gained a new understanding of a topic, not just additional information about it.
- Consider whether the explanation offered by the writer is the only plausible one or whether other explanations are possible.
- Reflect on how the writer's explanation can help you think clearly and be open to new ideas about the topic in question.

When Writing

- Choose a topic that your audience does not yet fully understand and about which it would be willing to learn.
- Make sure that you provide readers with any background information that they will need to understand your explanation.
- Explain what you want that audience to grasp.
- Even when you believe that you know more about your topic than your audience and more than you can convey within a single essay or article, be sure to treat readers with respect.
- Organize your ideas in a pattern that will make them easy to follow.
- If an alternative explanation for your information is conceivable, convey that to readers while emphasizing why you believe your own explanation is credible.

PHOTO EXORCISM

Wes Pitts

Have you ever thrown away a photograph because it reminded you of a painful relationship? Or wished that you could alter one that had a disturbing element but was otherwise important to you? Through contemporary technology, amateur photographers can now easily alter images in ways that surpass what professionals were able to accomplish in old-fashioned darkrooms. The results of this technology can please the eye—as Wes Pitts explains in "Photo Exorcism." But they may also become deceptive if presented as historically accurate images of the past.

A graduate of the University of California at Santa Cruz, Wes Pitts is online editor for Outdoor Photographer *and* PCPhoto, *the latter of which published the following article in 2003. As you read it, be alert to how Pitts tries to hold the attention of readers and to avoid confusing people who lack his expertise.*

We've all had relationships that simply didn't work, so we cut our losses and moved on. But what about all of those smiley photos that are now merely thorny reminders of her puzzling inability to recognize just how lucky she was?

I have a friend whose refrigerator is covered with photos that have been diced and dissected with common scissors, leaving her grinning face next to an empty hole where "that jerk" used to be. It's a rather crude approach to rewriting history, but it's effective nonetheless.

There's a better way. Using photo software, we can remove the offending visage from otherwise treasured photos with relative ease. And we can get results far superior to the old scissor technique.

Original photo.

Woman at left side of original removed.

Instead of leaving glaring holes, we can remove unwanted persons from our photos and replace them with parts of the background. Or, we can quickly crop the photo to get rid of unsightly exes near the edge of the frame. Here's how.

In our first example (see page 181), we have a photo of a group of friends and couples. It's a nice shot of the group overall, the type of shot that's likely to be a favorite, if it wasn't for that woman with too much baggage to ever truly appreciate us. Fortunately, she's at the left edge of the group, so we can simply crop the photo tightly to remove her. We used Jasc Paint Shop Pro 8 (www.jasc.com) for our example, but most photo-imaging software has the same or similar tools. If the person you wish to remove is conveniently placed at the edge of the picture, as in this case, just use your software's Crop tool to draw around the people you want to keep in the photo.

When cropping, try to keep your composition balanced. In this case, to remove the woman on the left, we had to crop in close on the man next to her, which made the composition look a little uneven. So, we also cropped in close to the man on the right side of the frame, to keep the amount of space around our subjects even on both sides. Voilà—no more traitorous backstabber! (see photo above)

Woman at center of original removed.

That was pretty simple to do, but what if the persona non grata is in the center of your photograph? While it's a bit more complicated, you'll still be able to remove him or her more swiftly and cleanly from the photo than you did from your relationship.

Start by examining the image. If parts of the two of you are overlapping or embracing, it will be more complicated than if not. Look for background areas that you can use to copy and paste over the ex. In our second example, we wanted to remove the lady in the center of the photo. Fortunately, we re-alized that we could eliminate her by simply sliding the couple at her left on top of her.

To do this, we started by creating a selection around the couple that we'd use to cover the unwelcome presence. Again, we used Jasc Paint Shop Pro 8, but any photo software that supports layers will work for this technique. Using the Freehand selection tool (you could also use the Magnetic Lasso if avail-able in your software), we carefully drew a selection around the couple.

Drawing selections can be tricky. We've found that the best approach is to take your time and try to draw the best selection possible, then switch the se-lection tool mode to Additive or Subtractive as necessary to refine the selec-tion. Spend a little more time cleaning up the edge of the selection by adding or removing parts in this way, and you'll eventually get a clean outline.

10

Normally, you might choose to feather your selection—that is, to soften the selection's edge. In this case, though, because we'd be moving the couple to slightly overlap with the rest of the group, we chose not to do this, instead opting to clean up the edge later.

We selected the couple and the area to the left of them, all the way to the edge of the frame. Next, we used the Cut and Paste commands to copy them from the background layer and place them in a new layer on top of the background. Then we moved them to the right to cover the girl about whom momma had warned us, slightly overlapping the couple on top of the rest of the group.

Satisfied with the results so far, we flattened the image (meaning that we combined this layer with the background). Now we used the Crop tool to eliminate the empty space that resulted from moving the couple to the center of the image (see photo on page 183).

All that was left was a quick clean-up of the edge between the group and the couple we had moved to forever conceal the proof of our misguided infatuation. We created another selection around the overlap, feathered the selection by a few pixels, and then applied a soft blur effect to the selection to smooth out the jagged edge. We also used the Clone (or Rubber Stamp) tool to clean up some areas in the background.

Another way to handle edge clean-up is to work on the area before flat- _15_ tening the image. Use the Eraser tool set with a soft edge and drag the tool along the edge to smooth it.

If you're not comfortable doing this freehand, you can use a selection mask to protect the areas you don't want to soften. Select the entire layer and reduce the selection's size by a few pixels (look for a Contract or similar command under the Selection menu). Next, use the Invert Selection command to reverse the selection so that the edge is unmasked and, finally, feather the selection by a few pixels. Now you can use the Eraser tool freely without worrying about accuracy.

That's all there is to it. While it takes a little more time and practice than the traditional scissor technique, the results are much better. It's as if she was never "in the picture." Now, if we could just get her to drop that palimony suit. Is there software for that, too?

Six Quick Tips for Star-Crossed Photos

1. If you know your relationship is destined to smash upon the rocky shores of heartache, keep that in mind when posing for photographs in the first place. Try to position your future ex near the edge of the frame, where he or she will be easy to remove later with a simple crop.

2. Photos of people embracing are the hardest to "correct." With that in mind, if you're seeing a relationship counselor, try to avoid gestures of affection when being photographed.

3. If you're looking at your mate when the photo is taken, you'll be looking at nothing once he or she is gone. So, always look at the camera and smile like nothing's wrong.

4. When taking photos at family reunions or with your buddies from college, get some shots of you and the group without the ball and chain in them. That way, you won't have to bother with doctoring the photo at all.

5. When you don't have advance notice of impending doom, you're stuck with what you've got. If all else fails and you can't find a way to remove him or her from the shot, you can always cut and paste your current companion's face on top of your ex. Just don't show that to your new squeeze or you might have to do it all over again.

6. Use this technique in other applications as well. Sports team portraits, social club event photos and family gatherings are all occasions when it might be appropriate or necessary to remove someone from a photo.

QUESTIONS FOR DISCUSSION

1. How effective is Pitt's decision to use failed relationships as a way to explain how to alter photographs? What does this decision say about his sense of audience? What assumptions does he make about gender, age, class, and sexual orientation?

2. At what points in his explanation does Pitts show that he is aware that readers may be unfamiliar with the language used by photographers who alter images?

3. What is the purpose of paragraph 2? How does it contrast with the rest of this article?

4. How does Pitts present himself within this piece? What kind of person seems behind the voice you hear in "Photo Exorcism"?

5. How useful is the list of "quick tips" with which Pitts concludes his explanation?

6. What are the social and political implications of being able to alter photographs?

SUGGESTIONS FOR WRITING

1. Write an essay explaining how the techniques explained by Pitts could be used unethically.

2. Think about why so many people take so many photographs. Write an essay focused on the role of photography in fostering and establishing personal identity.

3. Teach an audience composed of your peers how to do something at which you are skilled.

■ **LINKS**

■ **Within the Book**

For an analysis of how historically important photographs were composed, see Barbie Zelizer's "Conveying Atrocity in Image" (pages 359–369).

■ **Elsewhere in Print**

Barthes, Roland. *Camera Lucida*. Trans. Richard Harris. New York: Hill, 1982.

Bivins, Thomas. *Moral Distinctions in Journalism, Advertising, and Public Relations.* Hillsdale: Erlbaum, 2003.

Eismann, Katrin, Sean Duggan, and Tim Grey. *Real World Digital Photography.* Upper Saddle River: Peachpit, 2003.

George, Gregory. *Digital Photography: Top 100 Simplified Tips and Tricks.* New York: Wiley, 2003.

Grey, Tim. *Color Confidence: The Digital Photographer's Guide to Color Management.* Alameda: Sybex, 2004.

Sontag, Susan. *On Photography.* 1977. New York: Picador, 2003.

■ **Online**

www.mhhe.com/motives

Click on "More Resources" then "Writing to Explain Information."

■ ■ ■

IN JAPAN, NICE GUYS
(AND GIRLS) FINISH TOGETHER

Nicholas D. Kristof

A Phi Beta Kappa graduate of Harvard who went on to study law as a Rhodes Scholar at Oxford University, Nicholas D. Kristof writes for the New York Times *and was bureau chief for their Tokyo office when he first published the following piece in 1997.*

While observing the behavior of Japanese children, Kristof was struck by how these children seemed less competitive than American children of the same age. The "information" that he wishes to interpret in this case is quite simple: Japanese children who were attending a birthday party for his son were too polite, at first, to win at playing a game of musical chairs. To interpret this information, however, Kristof needs to understand differences in cultural values. As you read, be alert for the reasons the author offers as he attempts to explain the behavior he witnessed.

My intention, honest, was not to scar these Japanese kids for life. I just wanted to give them a fun game to play.

It was the fifth birthday party last year for my son Gregory, and he had invited all his Japanese friends over from the Tokyo kindergarten that he attended. My wife and I explained the rules of musical chairs, and we started the music.

It was not so awful for the Japanese boys. They managed to fight for seats, albeit a bit lamely. But the girls were at sea.

The first time I stopped the music, Gregory's 5-year-old girlfriend, Chitose-chan, was next to him, right in front of a chair. But she stood politely and waited for him to be seated first.

So Gregory scrambled into her seat, and Chitose-chan beamed proudly   5
at her own good manners. Then I walked over and told her that she had just lost the game and would have to sit out. She gazed up at me, her luminous eyes full of shocked disbelief, looking like Bambi might after a discussion of venison burgers.

"You mean I lose because I'm polite?" Chitose-chan's eyes asked. "You mean the point of the game is to be rude?"

Well, now that I think of it, I guess that is the point. American kids are taught to be winners, to seize their opportunities and maybe the next kid's as well. Japanese children are taught to be good citizens, to be team players, to obey rules, to be content to be a mosaic tile in some larger design.

One can have an intelligent debate about which approach is better. The Japanese emphasis on consideration and teamwork perhaps explains why Japan has few armed robbers but also so few entrepreneurs. The American emphasis on winning may help explain why the United States consistently racks up Olympic gold medals but also why its hockey players trashed their rooms in Nagano.

The civility that still lingers in Japan is the most charming and delightful aspect of life here today. Taxi drivers wear white gloves, take pride in the cleanliness of their vehicles, and sometimes give a discount if they mistakenly take a long route. When they are sick, Japanese wear surgical face masks so they will not infect others. The Japanese language has almost no curses, and high school baseball teams bow to each other at the beginning of each game.

One can go years here without hearing a voice raised in anger, for when Japanese are furious, they sometimes show it by becoming incredibly formal and polite. Compared with New York, it's rather quaint.   10

The conundrum is that Japan is perhaps too civilized for the 1990s. To revive its economy, mired in a seven-year slump, the country now needs an infusion of economic ruthlessness, a dose of the law of the jungle. Japan desperately needs to restructure itself, which is to say that it needs to create losers—companies need to lay off excess workers, Mom-and-Pop rice shops need to be replaced by more efficient supermarkets and failing banks need to go bankrupt.

But Japan is deeply uncomfortable with the idea of failures or losers. The social and economic basis of modern Japan is egalitarianism, and that does not leave much room for either winners or losers. In Japan, winning isn't everything, and it isn't the only thing; in elementary schools it isn't even a thing at all.

When Gregory and his brother Geoffrey went to Sports Day at their Japanese kindergarten, everybody told us that this was the big event of the year. So my wife and I went to cheer, but it wasn't really necessary. There were three-legged races and team basketball shoots and all kinds of games, but somehow at the end of the day no one won and no one lost. There were no blue ribbons, no prizes for the fastest runner, no cheers for the best basketball shooter, or anything else; instead, every child got a small prize.

The point of Sports Day was not to divide students by recognizing individual excellence but to unite them by giving them a shared experience. Likewise, schools do not normally break up children into "fast reading classes" and "slow reading classes," because that would stigmatize the slower ones. During recess or phys ed, there is no system of having a few captains take turns picking teams, because the last-picked might be upset; instead kids divide by class or by the Japanese equivalent of alphabetical order. When drama teachers select a play to perform, they choose one in which there is no star, just a lot of equal parts—which makes for first-rate student harmony and second-rate drama.

Of course, competition is inevitable in any society, and in Japan it is introduced in junior high schools, when children must compete intensely to pass high school and college entrance examinations. But the emphasis remains on "wa," or harmony, on being one with the group.   15

Ask a traditional Japanese housewife what she wants for her child, and you will sometimes hear an answer like: "I just want my kid to grow up so as not to be a nuisance to other people." Hmmm. Not a dream often heard in America.

Even in business, the obsession with egalitarian wa goes to astonishing lengths. One Tokyo bank executive told me how he envied the Japanese subsidiary of Citibank, which waives certain fees for customers who keep a large minimum balance. That would never be tolerated in a Japanese bank, he said, because it would be regarded as discriminatory against the poor. Likewise, he said, his bank cannot easily close unprofitable branches in remote areas, because then it would be criticized for abandoning the people there.

The emphasis on wa perhaps arises because 125 million Japanese, almost half of America's population, are squeezed into an area the size of California. How else could they survive but with a passion for protocol and a web of picayune rules dictating consideration for others? If 125 million Americans were jammed into such a small space, we might have torn each other to shreds by now.

Building teamwork in Japan starts from birth. When our third child, Caroline, was born in Tokyo last fall, the hospital explained that the mothers were to nurse their babies all together in the same room at particular meal times. So on her first day of life, Caroline was effectively told to discipline her appetites to adjust to a larger scheme with others.

This civility and egalitarianism shape just about every aspect of life. When the Japanese translation of a book that my wife and I wrote was published, we were pleased that the first reviews were positive. But we were frankly surprised when every single Japanese review was positive, and I remarked on that to a Japanese friend. "Oh, that's the only kind of book review there is in Japan," he explained. "There are no bad book reviews. Just nice ones." 20

And insipid ones, of course. Indeed, Japan itself is so polite as to be a bit bland, rather like "Mr. Rogers' Neighborhood" on a national scale. And of course Mr. Rogers' Neighborhood was never known for its hustle or economic vibrancy.

So now, Japan is trying to become nastier. Workers are being pushed out of their jobs, occasionally even laid off. Employees are no longer being automatically promoted by seniority. Pay differentials are widening. Companies are becoming more concerned with efficiency and share prices, less concerned with employee welfare.

All this will make Japan a more prosperous country but perhaps a less civil one. The changes certainly rub against the grain here, particularly of older people.

They rub just a bit against my grain, too. I bought a long scroll of calligraphy with the character "wa" in hopes that my kids will learn harmony instead of clubbing each other over toys. Yet, on the other hand, I still want them to win—at musical chairs and everything else.

That is getting tougher, because young Japanese are adapting to greater 25 competition, and they seem to be a bit more aggressive and individualist than their parents. Some young Japanese are even getting pretty good at musical chairs.

And little Chitose-chan, Gregory's girlfriend—well, she may be polite, but don't underestimate her generation's ability to catch on quickly. Thirty minutes after the game of musical chairs, Chitose-chan and her friend Naoko-chan got into an argument over a party favor. Chitose-chan slugged Naoko-chan in the mouth and grabbed the toy.

Perhaps that's globalization.

QUESTIONS FOR DISCUSSION

1. At the beginning of his essay, Kristof notes that Japanese girls seem less competitive than Japanese boys. Assuming that this information is accurate, how do you interpret it?
2. According to Kristof, "Japan is deeply uncomfortable with the idea of failures or losers." What information does he provide to support this interpretation?
3. Consider Kristof's description of Sports Day. How does it compare with your own experience in sports? How would you feel if you were participating in an athletic competition organized along the lines described by Kristof?
4. What does *wa* mean? Have you ever seen it practiced by American children?
5. On the basis of what he witnessed at his son's birthday party, what kind of future does Kristof envision for Japan?

SUGGESTIONS FOR WRITING

1. Spend an afternoon or evening in the company of American children, observing their behavior closely and taking notes if necessary. Then write an essay in which you offer your interpretation of the behavior you witnessed.
2. Observe a group of your peers when they are competing with each other. Based on what you witness, explain whether competition is beneficial.
3. Consider how your co-workers relate to one another on the job. Then write an essay explaining conduct that enhances or interferes with efficient performance in the workplace.

LINKS

■ Within the Book

"If You Are What You Eat, Then What Am I?" by Geeta Kothari (pages 640–648) provides another example of what happens when different cultures intersect.

■ Elsewhere in Print

Benjamin, Gail R. *Japanese Lessons: A Year in a Japanese School through the Eyes of an American Anthropologist and Her Children.* New York: New York UP, 1998.

Gudykunst, William B., and Tsukasa Nishida. *Bridging Japanese/North American Differences.* Thousand Oaks: Sage, 1994.

Heinrich, Amy Vladeck. *Currents in Japanese Culture: Translation and Transformations.* New York: Columbia UP, 1997.

Kristof, Nicholas, and Sheryl WuDunn. *Thunder from the East: Portrait of a Rising Asia.* New York: Knopf, 2000.

Okakura, Kakuzo. *The Book of Tea.* 1906. Introd. Liza Dalby. Boston: Tuttle, 2000.

Whiting, Robert. *You Gotta Have Wa.* New York: Macmillan, 1989.

Yarmuda, Haru. *Different Games, Different Rules: Why Americans and Japanese Misunderstand Each Other.* New York: Oxford UP, 1997.

■ Online

www.mhhe.com/motives

Click on "More Resources" then "Writing to Explain Information."

■ ■ ■

WHAT HAPPENED TO THE ANASAZI?

Catherine Dold

Some of the most beautiful houses in our country were built almost a thousand years ago by the Anasazi, an Indian tribe that briefly flourished in the Southwest when Europe was still climbing out of the Dark Ages. The ruins of these houses, which were often built into the sides of cliffs (as shown by the illustration on page 196), have inspired consider-able speculation about the fate of this vanished tribe. The following article explains how scholars are interpreting recent findings at archeological digs in the area. As you read, remember that you are reading about an ancient people struggling to survive during desperate times.

Catherine Dold lives in Boulder, Colorado. Formerly a senior editor at Audubon *magazine, she has also written for* Smithsonian, Discover, *and the* New York Times *in addition to being a staff writer for the National Resources Defense Council. When dis-cussing her life as a science writer, Dold emphasizes that she is "constantly learning." To illustrate this point, she provided the following example in the fall of 2004: "I recently interviewed an archeologist who found the oldest house in Colorado. He took me up to the mesa-top site, showed me the telltale ring of rocks, and explained it all to me so well that I could nearly see the people who once lived there. It was almost like having my own personal graduate seminar in archaeology."*

Life in the southwestern corner of Colorado can be difficult in the best of times. Rainfall is scarce, making growth hard even for the scrubby sage-brush and tough piñon and juniper trees that dot the arid land. In summer the heat is oppressive on the flatlands, and only slightly more tolerable on top of the flat, high mesas that jut above the horizon. Winter is not much better.

Chapin Mesa, one of the largest features in the area, dominates the land-scape and the imagination. Tucked away within its hidden canyons are the famous cliff dwellings built long ago by the Anasazi Indians. Sheltered by enormous natural overhangs, each village is a dense cluster of brick-walled rooms stacked two or three stories high, fronted by sunny plazas. Tiny win-dows in some rooms yield glimpses of paintings on inside walls; subterranean gathering rooms—called kivas—feature benches and elaborate ventilation systems. Everything is constructed of reddish–gold sandstone, which seems to glow in the unforgiving southwestern sun. Magnificent as these homes were, however, the Anasazi lived in them for fewer than a hundred years. For some unknown reason, they completely abandoned the area around A.D. 1300. Today, most of the cliff dwellings are preserved in Mesa Verde National Park, and every summer throngs of visitors ponder the mysterious departure of the Anasazi. Drought, warfare, and the harsh environment are all cited as possible explanations.

But another, deeper mystery lies just a dozen or so miles west of Mesa Verde, in an area known as Cowboy Wash, a broad, flat floodplain in the shadow of Sleeping Ute Mountain. A century and a half before the abandonment of Mesa Verde, Cowboy Wash was home to another group of people, probably Anasazi as well. Recently archeologists discovered several piles of human bones at the site. These bones, they say, show clear evidence of cannibalism. What's more, they maintain that this find does not represent an isolated incident. In the last few years, at least 30 nearby digs have yielded similar evidence of humans eating humans. Some archeologists speculate, naturally, that only people forced to desperate measures by starvation in this harsh environment would resort to cannibalism. The excavators of Cowboy Wash, however, propose a new theory. The cannibalism that occurred there, they say, was an act of prehistoric terrorism.

Traditionally, the Anasazi have been portrayed as peaceful farmers who quietly tended their corn and bean crops. Archeological records indicate that they occupied the Four Corners area—the juncture of present-day Colorado, Utah, Arizona, and New Mexico—from the beginning of the first millennium to around 1300. During that time they developed complex societies, farming methods, and architectural styles, culminating in life among the cliff dwellings. But recent work hints that the Anasazi world was far more turbulent than suspected.

The clues come from an archeological dig conducted by Soil Systems, 5 Inc., a private consulting firm in Phoenix, Arizona. Under contract to the Ute Mountain Ute Tribe, SSI excavated several ruins in the Cowboy Wash area so the tribe could relocate any ancient human remains before the launch of a new irrigation project. The site where the bones were found, a dwelling known as 5MT10010, is believed to have been occupied between the years 1125 and 1150. It includes three pit structures, the roofed, semi-sunken rooms typical of Anasazi homes at that time, as well as other rooms and trash heaps known as middens. Some 15 to 20 people, divided into three households, probably lived there.

The telltale bones were found scattered about the floors of two of the pit structures. In one, known as Feature 3, SSI archeologists found more than 1,100 bones and bone fragments, including shoulder blades, skulls, vertebrae, ribs, arm bones, hand and foot bones, and teeth. Nearly all were broken. Most were found in a heap at the bottom of an air shaft. In the other pit structure, Feature 13, the bones were found scattered on the floor and in side chambers.

"This was in no way a burial," says Patricia Lambert, a bioarcheologist from Utah State University in Logan who was hired to analyze the bones. "There was no reverence for these remains." Lambert's job was to try to reconstruct complete skeletons from the fractured pieces and decipher the clues left behind. "It was a big puzzle," she says. "The elements were all mixed together and broken." Many bones, particularly large leg bones, were missing. Eventually Lambert established that at least five people had been disposed of at Feature 3—three adult males, one adult female, and an 11-year-old child. Two children were found in the other pit structure, one a 7-year-old, the other 14.

Evidence of trauma was not hard to find. Most of the bones were broken, and many looked scraped and scorched. The marks looked like those left on the bones of large game animals after butchering. According to many archeologists, the presence of such marks on human bones is a clear indication of cannibalism. Someone who is planning to eat a human body part, the theory goes, would naturally prepare it in the same manner as he would an elk or a deer. And that is exactly what Lambert found.

"I found cut marks at muscle attachment sites, such as where the femur is attached to the hipbone," she says. "It's pretty clear they were disarticulating the body, cutting tendons and soft tissues that connect various parts." The cut marks occur when cutting tools slip and strike bone instead of tissue, she explains, and they cannot be mistaken for the gnawing marks an animal might leave. The relatively pristine condition of the bones is yet another clue. If the flesh had been left to rot away rather than being deliberately removed, says Lambert, the bones would be discolored and pitted instead of white, smooth, and dense. And some bones look as though they were broken open so the nutritious marrow could be extracted. They bear the complex fractures that occur in living bone—not the simple, smooth fractures of decaying bone. Moreover, they show flake scars, the marks that are left when a hammering tool chips bone.

Perhaps most disturbing was the evidence of burning and cooking—even   *10*
a mere summation of it, 850 years after the fact, is enough to make one queasy: Some bones appear to have been browned by heat exposure when they were still covered with flesh, and the skulls of both children in Feature 13 were obviously burned. "The burning clearly happened while the head was intact," says Lambert. "The back of the cranial vault was down around the coals, and the flames licked up and browned the side and blackened the back. Sometime later the head was taken apart—we found the pieces in two separate piles. They were putting the head on the fire. They were not incinerating it, but they did put it on there long enough to have cooked the brains.

"I can't say that they were eating these people, but they were certainly processing them in a way that suggests they were," says Lambert.

The victims and alleged perpetrators also left behind a few other clues. In one pit structure, archeologists found a set of tools, including two axes, that might have been used to butcher the bodies. "Sort of like leaving a calling card," muses archeologist Brian Billman, project director for SSI. Not only were cooking pots, ladles, and lids left behind, but so were tools, beads, and some jewelry. Leaving behind such valuables suggests that the sites were suddenly abandoned, says Billman, and sediment deposits on top of the bones and pots provide clues that the homes remained vacant. Furthermore, three other sites in the immediate area yielded the same type of remains, from the same time period: human bones irreverently scattered about deserted homes.

The evidence, Billman concludes, all points to an outbreak of cannibalism designed to terrorize and intimidate a group of people, most likely some foreigners who posed competition for scarce food resources. "It was a time of severe drought, as well as social and political upheaval," he says. "People were moving into new areas and mixing up alliances." Billman believes that people from about 60 miles south moved into Cowboy Wash and replaced the local community, as evidenced by several pots found there bearing the style of a more southern culture. But the immigrants' arrival apparently did not sit well with the local Anasazi.

"We think that certain groups in the Mesa Verde area, out of desperation, then turned to a strategy of warfare and cannibalism. One or more of the communities in this area decided on this as a political strategy, to push the new groups back out of the area and give themselves more resources. Plus, the message would be delivered to other communities that 'You'd better not mess with us.' It would so terrorize people that they would never think of messing with you." The carnage was indeed extensive. Billman estimates that between 60 and 100 people lived in the nine dwellings at Cowboy Wash. In the four dwellings he has excavated so far, he turned up the remains of 24 people.

Billman says two distinct patterns of human remains at several suspected cannibalism sites support his terrorism theory. In one pattern, which was also observed at Cowboy Wash, human remains were scattered on floors and the dwellings abandoned soon after. In the other, remains were not left lying about but were dumped into trash pits or unused rooms. Billman thinks the first pattern occurred in victims' homes, where they were cut up and consumed. The second pattern occurred in sites belonging to the perpetrators, who continued to use their homes after processing the bodies. "At the Mancos Canyon site, which is only 12 miles from Cowboy Wash, 30 to 40 people were found in trash dumps. They might have been people who were taken back to that village and consumed there." Likewise, the meat-laden leg bones missing from Cowboy Wash were probably carried off to be eaten later at secondary sites. At any rate, that is what Billman suspects, based on how hunters typically handle large game.

At least half the suspected incidents of cannibalism at the sites he reviewed occurred around 1150. "We call this an 'outbreak' of cannibalism. It looks like before this there was a very low level of cannibalism, then with this severe drought and social turmoil a few groups turned to terroristic violence." By the early 1200s, he notes, climatic conditions were back to normal and there were very few incidents of cannibalism. Around this time, too, the inhabitants of Mesa Verde moved from the pueblos on top of the mesa to the cliff dwellings in the sheltered cliff alcoves, a move some say was taken because the cliff dwellings were more easily defended.

Researchers have proposed other motivations for the alleged cannibalism, but they just don't fit the scenario, he adds. If the perpetrators had been goaded by hunger, he says, they would have been more likely to leave the area

Cliff Place, constructed A.D. 1209–1270s, has 250 rooms and 23 kivas.

and search for food rather than resort to such drastic measures. Hunger-induced cannibalism typically occurs in groups that are trapped, such as the Donner party, which was caught by a snowstorm in the Sierra Nevada in 1846. The people of the Cowboy Wash site had no such constraints. And besides, most of the victims appear to have been done away with in one fell swoop—not a prudent use of resources if you're starving.

Christy Turner, a bioarcheologist at Arizona State University in Tempe, agrees with the terrorism theory but thinks the explanation for it is even more complex. Anasazi culture bears signs of trade with Mexico, such as copper bells, macaws, and corn. During this time central Mexico was in social turmoil, says Turner, and hundreds of cults sprang up. Some members may have fled north, bringing not only distinctive trade goods but, possibly, flesh-eating rituals too. Plenty of evidence for such rituals occurs in historical accounts and in the archeological record of central Mexico, says Turner, and the practice was often used to intimidate neighboring tribes. Another possibility is that cannibalism might have developed independently—but for similar reasons—in the Four Corners region. It may, for example, be linked to a strategy for social control by inhabitants of Chaco Canyon, a New Mexico community of several thousand Anasazi that lay some 80 miles south of Mesa Verde. Chaco Canyon was a hub of Anasazi culture, and many scholars think it had great political and social influence over outlying communities.

The details of that particular scenario are sketchy, and Turner, who is at work on a book about the subject, won't elaborate. But Billman doesn't think the evidence supports that theory. He contends that the major outbreak of cannibalism actually occurred *after* Chaco Canyon was abandoned in the 1140s. Moreover, nobody knows where the former residents of Chaco Canyon went. Billman thinks it more likely that the victims at Cowboy Wash came from the Chuska Mountains, some 60 miles south of the site. What both hypotheses share, however, is the idea that neighboring groups were using cannibalism as a terrorist strategy to drive out competition for scarce resources.

There is no shortage of speculation on the causes of the suspected canni-   20
balism. But do the bones really tell a tale of cannibalism? With no eyewitnesses, can anyone really be sure of what happened at Cowboy Wash eight and a half centuries ago?

"How do you tell that a person committed a murder when nobody saw it?" asks Tim White, a physical anthropologist at the University of California at Berkeley. "Evidence." White has closely examined the bones found at Mancos Canyon, and both he and Turner have proposed criteria that they say must be met to make a finding of cannibalism. Among them are cut marks, burn patterns, broken bones, and "pot polish," the way sharply fragmented bone gets rounded by rattling around in a pot of boiling water. "The question we need to ask is, Do people prepare other mammals in this fashion in this culture? Because humans are large animals. If you find that the patterning matches, then that becomes evidence," says White.

Turner, Billman, and others agree that, by these criteria, evidence from many southwestern sites, including Cowboy Wash, clearly indicates cannibalism. But Peter Bullock, a staff archeologist at the Museum of New Mexico in Santa Fe, is not ready to convict. He says that basing such studies on animal-butchering practices biases the results toward a consumption conclusion and fails to consider human motivations. Bones could end up being scraped, shattered, and scorched as a result of warfare, mutilation, or burial practices, he says. As an example, Bullock cites human remains recovered from the Battle of Little Bighorn, where General George Custer and his troops were slain. "The results looked pretty similar to this cannibalism stuff, but we know from historical accounts that no cannibalism took place," he says. Kurt Dongoske, an archeologist employed by the Hopi, agrees. "To say that these disarticulated remains have been cannibalized is a real stretch."

"We've got folks who are processing humans in exactly the same way they process animals and we're supposed to believe that the end result was not consumption?" White asks incredulously. "Why does it look exactly like consumption?"

Native American representatives are silent on the matter. A spokesman for the Ute Mountain Ute Tribe, on whose land the Cowboy Wash bones were found, declined to comment either on that site or on the possibility of any incidents of cannibalism among the Anasazi. The tribe also refused to allow outsiders to visit the excavated site or to view the bones. Their reaction is understandable, some say. How would other people feel if scientists dug up bodies at Arlington National Cemetery and declared the soldiers cannibals? Not surprisingly, Park Service brochures handed out at Mesa Verde make no mention of the possibility of cannibalism either. The bones will eventually be reburied by a Ute religious leader.

"We can't get the meat from the hand into the mouth," concedes Billman. "But there is now a possibility that we may be able to do that. One of the last things that was done on our site—once the hearth had gone cold and was filled with ash—was someone squatted down in the hearth and defecated." A preliminary analysis of the coprolite, as the preserved specimen is called, indicates that its owner's last meal was almost entirely animal protein. Determining just what type of animal—elk, deer, or human—the protein came from will be the job of Richard Marlar, a professor of molecular biology at the University of Colorado at Denver. He heard about the Cowboy Wash coprolite and offered to analyze its contents.

It might seem that Marlar could just look for human blood or cells in the coprolite, but humans often shed their own intestinal cells in feces. So he will test for the presence of myoglobin, a protein found in human skeletal muscle but not in the intestines. He will dissolve samples of the coprolite in a buffer solution and then add antibodies that recognize myoglobin. If myoglobin is present, reactions with the antibodies will tint the solution. Marlar also plans to test residues from cooking vessels found at the site.

Although such tests have been routinely used to identify bison, antelope, and human blood at archeological sites, no one has used the technique yet to address the question of humans eating humans. But Marlar predicts that it "could really answer if cannibalism occurred, once and for all." And, if the test is positive, archeologists will have even more reason to speculate on scenarios about social turmoil in the Southwest. Of course, if the test is negative, the case is still not closed. The abundance of evidence points to cannibalism among the Anasazi. But without clear historical records, the precise reason for that cannibalism—if it occurred—will probably never be known.

QUESTIONS FOR DISCUSSION

1. What are the traditional explanations for the disappearance of the Anasazi? If scholars confirm evidence that the Anasazi practiced cannibalism, how would that information help us understand the past?
2. What evidence has led investigators to believe that there was an outbreak of cannibalism near Mesa Verde some 850 years ago?
3. Are there any circumstances under which eating human flesh could be morally justifiable?
4. Where does Dold indicate that claims of cannibalism have not yet been entirely proven? What does she achieve by doing so?
5. How would you describe the tone of this article? How respectful is Dold of the culture she is interpreting?
6. In the years that have passed since the Anasazi disappeared, has warfare become more civilized or less so?

SUGGESTIONS FOR WRITING

1. Do research on the art and architecture of the Anasazi. Then write an essay interpreting what these artistic achievements reveal about Anasazi culture.
2. In paragraph 17, Dold mentions the Donner party—a group of white settlers who practiced cannibalism when they were stranded by a snowstorm while traveling to California. Research how this trip was planned, and write an essay explaining what went wrong.
3. Taken from their original sites, Native American objects—and even the remains of human bodies—are held in the collections of many American museums. Write an essay explaining why some of these holdings have become controversial.

LINKS

■ Within the Book

In "The Pentagon's Secret Stash" (pages 372–377), Matt Welch discusses contemporary behavior that is hard for many Americans to understand.

▪ Elsewhere in Print

Billman, Brian, and Gary M. Feinman, eds. *Settlement Pattern Studies in the Americas.* Washington, DC: Smithsonian, 1999.

Ferguson, William M. *The Anasazi of Mesa Verde and the Four Corners.* Niwot: U of Colorado P, 1996.

Goldman, Laurence, ed. *The Anthropology of Cannibalism.* Westport: Bergin, 1999.

Noble, David Grant. *Understanding the Anasazi of Mesa Verde and Hovenweep.* Santa Fe: Ancient City P, 1985.

———. *Ancient Ruins of the Southwest.* Flagstaff: Northland, 2000.

Turner, Christy G., II, and Jacqueline Turner. *Man Corn: Cannibalism and Violence in the Prehistoric American Southwest.* Salt Lake City: U of Utah P, 1999.

▪ Online

www.mhhe.com/motives

Click on "More Resources" then "Writing to Explain Information."

▪ ▪ ▪

BET ON IT

Gary Rivlin

As recently as forty years ago, gambling was associated primarily with cities such as Las Vegas and Reno and with racetracks where it was legal to bet on the horses and dogs (in addition to illegal betting conducted through "bookies," many of whom had ties to organized crime). Now—through state lotteries and the proliferation of casinos—gambling has become a major industry. A large source of revenue in this industry is the slot machine, which provides one of the easiest ways to gamble. In "Bet on It," Gary Rivlin explains why the slot machine has become both popular and profitable.

A graduate of Northwestern University, Rivlin writes primarily about business issues, especially those involving technology. His writing has earned him the Carl Sandburg Award for Nonfiction, the Gold Medallion Award from the California Bar Association, and the Gerald Loeb Award for Distinguished Business and Financial Journalism. The author of a book on Bill Gates, he has published in Fortune, Newsweek, Wired, *and the* New York Times Magazine, *in which the following article appeared in the spring of 2004. As you prepare to read it, you might reflect on a quotation that Rivlin has above his desk, for it helps explain his motive for writing: "The nonfiction writer's greatest task is to state complex social issues in human terms impossible to ignore."*

When Anthony Baerlocher makes his monthly visit to the Atlantis Casino Resort in Reno, Nev., he always starts with a ritual he calls "taking inventory," walking several laps around the casino's sprawling 32,000-square-foot gambling floor and noting which machines sit unloved, vainly burping out their come-hither sounds, and which machines have captured players' attention. The Atlantis is home to more than 1,400 slot machines, but so vivid is the mental snapshot that Baerlocher, 35, carries in his head that he immediately registers the presence of a new machine on the floor. Although Baerlocher is a trained mathematician, his interest is far from academic. He is the chief game designer for the country's largest maker of slot machines, International Game Technology of Reno. At the first sign of a new slot machine from a competitor, he goes into action. "Give me 30 minutes and $60," he says, "and I can tell you pretty much anything you want to know about another company's machine."

At 8 P.M. on a warm midsummer's night, Baerlocher watched a woman dressed in green polyester pants and a yellow-and-white-striped short-sleeved top play a slot machine he designed called "The Price Is Right." At first, the woman's body language was noncommittal: she stood half-turned from the game, as if no more than mildly curious about the outcome of her wager. "Price" is what slot pros call "a cherry dribbler," a machine that dispenses lots of small payouts while it nibbles at your stash rather than biting off large chunks of it. "You want to give the newbie lots of positive reinforcement—to keep 'em playing," Baerlocher told me. As if on cue, the woman hit a couple of small jackpots and took a seat. "Gotcha," Baerlocher said softly under his breath.

Baerlocher also watched players nearby at another machine he designed for I.G.T., "Wheel of Fortune." I.G.T. is to the slot industry as Microsoft is to computer software, and no product contributes more to I.G.T.'s bottom line than what industry insiders simply call "Wheel." How big is it? In its 14-year lifetime, "Madden N.F.L. Football," from Electronic Arts, has made roughly $1 billion, making it one of the most successful home video games ever produced. "Wheel of Fortune," by contrast, takes in more than a billion dollars each year.

As in the televised game show, there is an actual wheel, which spins whenever a player reaches the bonus round, on average once in every 42 plays. The presence of the wheel allows the slot machine to employ one of the most powerful feints in the slot designer's arsenal: the near miss. When a contestant spins the wheel on the game show and it stops one or two spots past the $1,000 mark—that's a near miss. The slot machine version of "Wheel," like many of I.G.T.'s most popular slots, is designed to produce these near misses, lots of them: though the wheel is divided into 22 pie slices of equal size, the odds are weighted so that a player is likely to land on some wedges far more often than on others.

After a couple of minutes, an older woman, dressed in a sparkly pink _5_ sweatsuit ensemble, reached the bonus round. She groaned when the wheel nudged past the "250 times bet" wedge and landed on "10 times bet." Her male companion cried out, "Honey, you were so close!" Baerlocher's starchy mien melted away, revealing an amused smile. "You can see it on their faces every time," he said. "They feel they came _soooo_ close. They're ready to try it again, because next time they're going to get it."

Baerlocher shook his head and laughed in a way that suggested he never gets bored witnessing this moment. He is among a cadre of people inside I.G.T.'s giant slots factory who study addiction—though unlike their counterparts in academia, of course, he and his colleagues work on the promotion side of things. He is so devoted to the slot machine that he has one in the front room of his town house, in the hills above Reno, and a second one downstairs in his den. We lingered another minute or so, long enough to watch the lady in pink slip another $20 into the machine, confident that this time the wheel wouldn't make those extra couple of clicks.

Nearly 40 million Americans played a slot machine in 2003, according to an annual survey of casino gambling conducted by Harrah's Entertainment. Every day in the United States, slot machines take in, on average, more than $1 billion in wagers. Most of that money will be paid back to players, but so great is the "hold" from slot machines that collectively the games gross more annually than McDonald's, Wendy's, Burger King and Starbucks combined. All told, North American casinos took in $30 billion from slots in 2003—an amount that dwarfs the $9 billion in tickets sold in North American movie theaters that year. Pornography, the country's second most lucrative form of adult entertainment, doesn't come close, either: experts estimate that Americans spend at most $10 billion a year on live sex shows, phone sex and porn in various media from cable to DVD to video and the Internet. Is it any wonder that Baerlocher's boss, Joe Kaminkow, I.G.T.'s head of design and product development, likes to say that he's in the business of creating "beautiful vaults"?

Although it has frequently been controversial—Fiorello La Guardia and Earl Warren are among those who have made headlines crusading against it—the slot machine has traditionally enjoyed little status in the world of casino gambling. Slots were where the wives of the high rollers sat, killing time with buckets of coins. But revenues from the games have grown exponentially over the past few decades, according to Bill Eadington, director of the Institute for the Study of Gambling and Commercial Gaming at the University of Nevada, Reno, and now the slot machine is the undisputed king of the casino. Craps, blackjack and roulette—which once defined organized gambling—are going the way of tuxedos and diamonds inside the modern-day casino, where the standard dress these days tends toward polyester and athletic wear. Accounting for more than $7 out of every $10 of gambling revenues in casinos across the United States, the once lowly slot machine is the top earner even in glitzy palaces along the Las Vegas strip.

Not only have slots been capturing an expanding share of business on gambling floors across the country—grabbing an ever greater "share of wallet," as industry insiders put it; they have also played a crucial role in expanding the footprint of casino gambling in the United States. Where casinos were legal in just 2 states at the end of the 1980's, today they are legal in more than 30—a trend that the slot machine, so easy to learn to play and seemingly harmless, has no doubt helped fuel. "It's the slot machine that drives the industry today," says Frank J. Fahrenkopf Jr., head of the American Gaming Association. While craps, roulette and baccarat are outlawed in roughly half the states that permit casino gambling, slot machines are widely viewed as a politically palatable solution for elected officials seeking to raise revenues—the casino equivalent, critics say, of a gateway drug. And the trend is far from exhausted: Maryland, Massachusetts, Ohio, Pennsylvania, Alabama and Kentucky are among the states that have recently considered installing slots at racetracks to generate needed tax revenue.

Fahrenkopf is reportedly paid in seven figures to praise all things casino, *10* but he can't seem to help taking a poke at the slot machine. He views the transition from table games to slots as symptomatic of the dumbing down of American life. Playing craps means learning a complex set of rules. Blackjack may be easy to learn, but it still requires skill and concentration, and it's not uncommon for the novice player to feel stupid in front of strangers. "I don't know if it's the education system, or maybe it's that we as a society have gotten intellectually lazy," says Fahrenkopf, who headed the Republican National Committee under Ronald Reagan. "But people would rather just sit there and push a button." When I asked one elderly man to explain the allure of playing slots, he replied, "I don't have to think."

Slot machines are in fact for those well into the second half of life. Manufacturers design games primarily for women over 55 with lots of time and disposable income, and casinos near retirement communities in and around places like Phoenix and San Diego operate small fleets of jitneys that shuttle back and forth to assisted-living centers. As a come-on, one casino advertises free oxygen-tank refills for its players, and heart defibrillators are increasingly becoming standard equipment inside casinos. If a good portion of the younger set today is hooked on video games, it seems that the over-60 crowd has its own similarly hypnotic fixation. "For older people, it's a safe environment," Baerlocher says. "There are cameras and security guards everywhere. You can go to one place and shop and eat and be in a crowd even if you don't know anybody." As one old Las Vegas hand put it, the country's casinos are now providing "day care for the elderly."

The archetypal slot machine was invented in 1899 by Charles Fey, a German immigrant, in San Francisco. But most modern-day slot machines bear little resemblance to the familiar one-armed bandit with its three reels spinning behind a pane of glass and mechanically click-click-clicking into position with each pull of a lever. Today's slot machines feature well-choreographed illusions designed to hide a fundamental truth: at heart they're really nothing more than computers whose chips randomly cycle through hundreds of thousands of numbers every second. A player's fate is determined almost the instant play begins. But to simply display a long string of numbers on a computer screen, along with an accounting of the money won or lost, would hardly prove entrancing.

That said, the computer chip at a slot machine's core does account in part for the exploding popularity of slots—it means flexibility for game designers. The physical size of the spinning reels in most of yesterday's mechanical machines typically limited them to 22 stops and just over 10,000 possible combinations. Computer technology lets game makers weight the reels so that winning big occurs as infrequently as, say, one in 46 million plays (the odds of hitting the big multimillion-dollar jackpot on "Wheel of Fortune"). The increased odds make possible today's huge jackpots, which reach into the millions of dollars on some machines. You can double your wager on a hand of blackjack or win 35 times your bet on a single spin of the roulette wheel, but only the slot machine gives you the hope of turning a few dollars into a seven- or eight-figure payoff.

Still, to maintain a sense of suspense in games that are over the moment they start, to increase what Baerlocher and his fellow game designers call "time on device," I.G.T. spends $120 million each year and employs more than 800 designers, graphic artists, script writers and video engineers to find

Older people enjoying a "safe environment."

ways to surround the unromantic chips with a colorful matrix of sounds, chrome, garishly-painted glass and video effects, which include the soothing images of famous people, from Bob Denver (the actor who played Gilligan on "Gilligan's Island") to Elizabeth Taylor, many of whom receive hundreds of thousands, if not millions, of dollars to lend their identities to the machines. The traditional pull-handle, if it exists at all, is nothing more than a vestigial limb; most players now press a button to start the reels, often virtual, spinning. Many slot machines don't even pay out coins but issue "credits" on a paper receipt to be redeemed at the cashier's cage. Slot makers have found that their customers don't miss handling money—coins are heavy and dirty, after all— and stereo speakers can project the simulated yet satisfying ping and clink of cascading cash. "We basically mixed several recordings of quarters falling on a metal tray and then fattened up the sound with the sound of falling dollars," says Bill Hecht, I.G.T.'s top audio engineer, when describing one of the audio files he programs into a machine.

Founded in 1981, I.G.T. dominated the expanding casino slot machine 15
industry until the mid-90's, when video slot machines suddenly appeared. WMS Gaming, based in Illinois, was the first company to cash in on these new machines in the United States. (The marriage of slot machines and video games was first consummated in Australia.) Their popularity took I.G.T. by surprise. Bob Bittman, who was then the company's chief designer, confesses that by 1999 he and his fellow executives were anxious. The company's stock

had fallen precipitously, and Bittman recognized that he was hardly the one to turn things around. "I wasn't left-brain enough—or do I mean right brain?" says Bittman, who remains on I.G.T.'s board. That's when the company decided to hire a talented young game designer, Joe Kaminkow, to lead them into this jazzed-up new world.

Kaminkow began college thinking he would someday work as a TV weatherman, but soon his ambitions veered toward game making. He was a co-founder of a pinball-design firm in his 20's, and after he and his partner sold the company to Sega, the video-game giant, Kaminkow spent the next seven years overseeing that company's U.S.-based pinball operations.

Kaminkow knew virtually nothing about slot machines when he took the reins of I.G.T.'s design and product-development division. Yet five years later, the company has reasserted its supremacy in the slot machine industry. The majority of I.G.T.'s most popular games—"The Munsters," for example, or "The Price Is Right"—now feature virtual reels spinning on video monitors, touch screens and, in the bonus rounds, video clips. The company has been so profitable during Kaminkow's tenure that if you bought $10,000 worth of stock in I.G.T. and Microsoft in the month of his arrival, January 1999, the I.G.T. shares would be worth more than $70,000 today and the Microsoft shares about $6,000. "I'm not worthy of being mentioned in the same paragraph as Joe Kaminkow," says Brooke Dunn, who had been Kaminkow's equivalent at Shuffle Master, a Las Vegas–based company that made a short-term foray into the slots business. Jerald Seelig, general manager of A.C. Coin and Slot, which occasionally creates machines in tandem with I.G.T., says, "History will certainly show he's one of the guys who changed the industry forever." . . .

Among the first things Kaminkow did when he arrived in Reno in 1999 was spend as much time in the local casinos as he could learning more about the games he was now responsible for designing. "I'd feed a twenty into a machine, and it'd be gone in two minutes," he recalls. The word he uses to describe the experience is not suitable for a family newspaper. The problem, he decided, wasn't the vanishing $20—taking people's money, after all, is the whole purpose of these beautiful vaults—but the speed with which it disappeared. He instructed his mathematicians to design most of I.G.T.'s new video games so that the typical player would get at least 15 or 20 minutes on a machine before needing to reach into her purse for another bill. He also wanted games that paid more frequent, smaller payouts.

Inside I.G.T. they call it "Joe's $20 test." One of the first games released on Kaminkow's watch was based on the old television sitcom "I Dream of Jeannie." It was Kaminkow who pioneered slots based on old TV shows; he chose "Jeannie" as his first, he says, because "every woman wanted to be Jeannie" (played by Barbara Eden), and every man wanted—paraphrasing Kaminkow—to get to know Eden's character intimately. The "Jeannie" machine, which made its debut in 2000, included the show's big-band theme song, Eden's voice (on small payouts you sometimes hear her say, "I can do so much more for thee, master") and reel icons tied to the show: a bejeweled thin-necked bottle, a space capsule splashing into water and so on. And when you have lined up the symbols just right, you enter a bonus round that includes a spinning wheel and a short clip from the show that lasts maybe 10 seconds. "For your $20, you should at least get to see a little of Jeannie," Kaminkow says with a wink.

Over the years, Kaminkow has handed down a long list of edicts that I.G.T. designers call "Joe's rules." Early on, for example, the sidekick he brought with him from Sega overheard an older man complain to his companion that he had left his reading glasses in the room and couldn't see well enough to play. Kaminkow declared that henceforth the lettering on all I.G.T. machines would be large enough so that pretty much everyone but the legally blind could play. Sometimes he would reach the bonus round in a game but win no money, so that became another of Joe's rules: no zonks; players who experience the fanfare of a bonus round receive at the very least a consolation payout. He also dictated that whenever a bonus round offered players a choice, the machine would reveal the values of the options not selected. "You want the player to have the feeling, 'I almost picked that one; I'll get it next time,'" says Randy Mead, a game designer at I.G.T. The games also include periodic free spins and other gimmicks designed, as Mead puts it, "to give players time for a small break—to light a cigarette, order a drink, to stand and stretch."

"Joe brought this way of thinking, Look, we've got to wow them," says Dave Forshey, a graphic designer who arrived at I.G.T. shortly before Kaminkow. "It's not just push the red button and watch the wheels spin. Make people want to sit there. Use sight and sound and everything at our disposal to get people's juices going." Before Kaminkow's arrival, I.G.T.'s games weren't quiet—hardly—but they didn't take full advantage of the power of special effects like "smart sounds"—bright bursts of music. So Kaminkow decreed that every action, every spin of the wheel, every outcome, would have its own unique sound. The typical slot machine featured maybe 15 "sound events" when Kaminkow first arrived at I.G.T.; now that average is closer to 400. And the deeper a player gets into a game, the quicker and usually louder the music.

"I'm not sure players even notice," says Bill Hecht, I.G.T.'s top sound designer, "but the effect is to get them more excited." Every time the reels spin on "Jeannie," a player hears a few seconds of the show's theme song, and Hecht even orchestrated a bossa nova rendition heard only when someone reaches the bonus round. "Something for the regular players to look forward to," he says. "We want to get your heart rate going a little."

It wasn't Kaminkow who devised what are called multiline games—multi-coin games that allow you to win on 1, 15 or 25 lines, assuming you wager enough coins. (Picture an enlarged tic tac toe board that lets you win in any number of crazy zigzag ways.) But under his stewardship, I.G.T. has taken full advantage of whatever design changes have allowed penny and nickel games to earn like dollar machines. "It used to be that the goal of casinos was to move their nickel players to quarters, the quarter players to dollars, the dollar players to five dollars," Baerlocher says. "Now they don't bother, because we've figured out how to get nickel and even penny machines to play like dollar machines." How? By offering jackpots in the hundreds of thousands, if not millions, of dollars. A penny machine like I.G.T.'s "Beverly Hillbillies" can be played for a penny a spin, but in most jurisdictions you're eligible for the big prize, which starts at $200,000, only if you wager the maximum bet per spin of $2.50. The odds of winning that big jackpot may be in the tens of millions to one, but there's a 100 percent chance you'll be kicking yourself for eternity if you see five Beverly Hillbillies line up on the machine's reels after you bet less than the maximum needed to win. "The truth is, nowadays you can lose more money faster on a nickel slot machine than at a $10 blackjack table," says Nigel Turner, a scientist at the Center for Addiction and Mental Health in Toronto. The true brilliance of the industry's emphasis on nickel and penny machines is perhaps best seen by comparing how much of "the handle," or the total amount wagered, they pay out compared with dollar machines. The average nickel machine pays back to winners somewhere between 88 and 92 percent of the money wagered, Baerlocher says, compared with the roughly 95 percent that dollar machines pay out.

Early on, Kaminkow's secretary, Pam Foster, told him, "The way you spend money, you'd better be good." Apparently all the millions he spent have paid off. By the time I first visited I.G.T., in 2002, the company had a 70 percent share of the domestic slot market, and Kaminkow no longer saw himself as competing against Bally, WMS Gaming and the Australian-based Aristocrat so much as competing for the attention of the tens of millions of Americans who had yet to discover the magic of his slot machines. Although the number of men who are playing the slots is increasing, they tend to be on the far side of 60, and women in their late 50's still represent the slot machine's most trustworthy devotees. So Kaminkow is devoting a sizable portion of his time to what he benignly calls "expanding his market." To appeal to a younger, male cohort, he signed licensing deals with the people behind "South Park" and "Austin Powers" (with mixed results) and then negotiated the even bigger deals with Drew Carey and George Lucas for "Star Wars." At the same time, he has been pursuing the potential of the Latino market by designing a line of games that lets gamblers play in Spanish with the push of a button. "I want my competitors to cry when they see my new games," he says. "I want them unable to get out of bed because they realize, Damn, they've done what we didn't even think possible."

The makers of slot machines may rely on the lure of life-changing jack- *25*
pots to attract customers, but the machines' ability to hook so deeply into a player's cerebral cortex derives from one of the more powerful human feedback mechanisms, a phenomenon behavioral scientists call infrequent random reinforcement, or "intermittent reward." Children whose parents consistently shower them with love and attention tend to take that devotion for granted.

Those who know they'll never be rewarded by their parents stop trying after a while. But those who are rewarded only intermittently—in the fashion of a slot machine—will often pursue positive outcomes with a persistent tenacity. "That hard-wiring that nature gave us didn't anticipate electronic gaming devices," says Howard Shaffer, director of the division on addictions at Harvard Medical School and perhaps the country's foremost authority on gambling disorders.

"The slot machine is brilliantly designed from a behavioral psychology perspective," says Nancy Petry, a professor of psychiatry at the University of Connecticut School of Medicine. "The people who are making these machines are using all the behavioral techniques to increase the probability that the behavior of gambling will reoccur." She refers to intermittent reward and "second-order conditioning"—the lights and sounds that go off when a player wins, for example, or the two cherries in a row that convinces people they're getting closer.

"No other form of gambling manipulates the human mind as beautifully as these machines," concludes Petry, who has studied gambling treatments since 1998. "I think that's why that's the most popular form of gambling with which people get into trouble."

Anti-gambling activists refer to slots as "the crack cocaine of gambling." Though gambling's loudest critics tend to be alarmists, the crack analogy may be apt. Just as crack addicts have frequently seemed to self-destruct much faster than those abusing powdered cocaine, there is abundant, albeit still largely anecdotal, evidence suggesting that the same is true of today's computer-driven slot machines—video-based slots especially. Where social workers once found that the woes of a typical problem gambler tended to mount gradually—with a period of 20 or more years commonly passing between a first wager and a bottoming-out event like bankruptcy, divorce or even suicide—addiction cycles of a few years are, if not typical, commonplace among slots players.

"Treatment folks are definitely identifying people who are experiencing what we call 'telescoping'—a shortening of the period of time that it takes for someone to get into trouble," says Rachel Volberg, president of the National Council on Problem Gambling and the author of "When the Chips Are Down: Problem Gambling in America." Volberg, who runs Gemini Research, an organization that specializes in gambling-related investigations, says it remains to be seen whether the problem lies in "something special about these machines or in the people who prefer playing them." Female slots players in particular, Petry says, "tend to experience this telescoping phenomenon—and we know from research that women are quicker to seek treatment."

Gambling counselors regularly encounter people like Ricky Brumfield, a _30_ working-class Phoenix woman who won $3,700 the first time she ever touched a slot machine—a day that turned out to be the unluckiest of her life. That was in 1997, when Brumfield, then 43, traveled to Las Vegas to help a friend celebrate the Fourth of July. Within nine months, she had hocked her jewelry and gone through $100,000 in cash and credit-card debt. She only stopped, she confesses, because the Sheriff's Department arrested her on child-abuse charges for leaving her two young kids locked in a car in a casino parking lot while she played the slots inside. "I knew it was really wrong to do that, but the urge to go into the casino was stronger than my instincts as a mother," Brumfield says. She had only recently had back surgery, but she found that when she played, she never felt pain. "I think the dopamine and serotonin levels, when they kicked in—that blocked off the pain," says Brumfield, who now works for the Arizona Council on Compulsive Gambling. "You feel hypnotized by the machine. You don't think of anything else." Near the end, the hold the machines had over her, she says, was akin to that of an unfaithful lover. She would fall into a jealous rage when a favorite machine paid a jackpot to another, less devoted player.

"Slot machines have a different impact on the brain than other forms of gambling," Howard Shaffer says. Unlike table games, which are played in groups, slots are played in isolation, and therefore they lack the same safeguards social situations provide. "And because the video form is faster than the mechanical form, they hold the potential to behave in the fashion of psychostimulants, like cocaine or amphetamines. They energize and de-energize the brain in more rapid cycles. The faster on, faster off, the greater the risk." Colleagues of Shaffer have compared the brain scans of people high on cocaine with those of people while gambling: similar neurocircuitry is lighted up in both sets of images.

Shaffer predicts that in time electronic games will "protect players." Just as the car industry implemented basic technologies like seat belts to save lives, he expects the gambling industry (which finances many of his studies) to eventually employ strategies to interrupt people when they play too fast. As Bill Eadington, the University of Nevada, Reno, professor and a consultant to Indian tribes, governments and casinos around the world, puts it, "I worry that we're burning out players too fast."

The typical slots player initiates a new game every six seconds. That works out to 10 games per minute, 600 per hour. If the average player bets $2 a spin, that player is wagering roughly $1,200 every hour. Slot designers have experimented with machines that play even faster, but the industry standard remains a six-second cycle. "It wouldn't be much fun if we took your money any faster than that," Kaminkow told me with a slight shrug of his shoulder, suggesting that just how fast people play is entirely up to him.

I asked Kaminkow if he ever worried that the potent mix of TV, technology and the prodigious talents of his creative people will produce machines that are too powerful. "What kind of question is that?" he replied. In his natural state, Kaminkow is a breezy and sarcastic jokester who revels in politically incorrect jokes. But he suddenly sounded as if he were addressing a Rotary Club. "I take responsible gaming very seriously," he said. "We're not an alcohol, we're not a drug." He is in the entertainment business, he added, a "maker of small little movies" that bring a touch of joy and laughter to the lives of the elderly and others.

"I'm not looking for people who say, 'I spent my milk money,'" he said. *35* "I think people need to be very responsible in their gaming habits. I know I am." . . .

Most of the people I met inside I.G.T. told me they never played slot machines on their own time. Anthony Baerlocher turned out to be the exception rather than the rule. Kaminkow's wife, Kim, says she plays only "when Joe hands me $20 and tells me I'm supposed to play some new machine." Even one corporate P.R. staff member couldn't resist shaking her head in disbelief as she described scenes of people lining up to play a new machine. "It was unfathomable to me," she told me. When I asked one I.G.T. artist if he ever plays, he acted as if I had insulted him. "Slots are for losers," he spat, and then, coming to his senses, begged me to consider that an off-the-record comment. "Big Balls of Cash" was designed to hold roughly 10 cents for every dollar played, but saying the obvious inside I.G.T—that the very math of the slot machine makes it a loser's game—would not be a very good career move.

Every so often during my time inside I.G.T. someone let me into a locked showroom just off the building's main lobby. Inside, I would find myriad machines clamoring for my attention. They were in what slot designers describe as "attract mode." A "Dick Clark's New Year's Rockin' Eve" kept announcing, "It's a cold one in Times Square tonight." A voice that sounded vaguely like Yosemite Sam asked: "Do you want to be rich? Oil rich?" A familiar voice from my TV past cried out, "Come on down!" Applause emanated from a machine in the corner, and I heard Frank Sinatra's voice: "Thank you, ladies and gentlemen."

On my first visit to the showroom, I jumped from game to game, but on my second visit I stuck with a single game, "The Price Is Right," which Baerlocher designed expressly for the uninitiated. The showroom machine had 8,000 credits on it—$400. It wasn't my money, so I played the maximum of $2.25 per spin. The machine constantly emitted noises: clapping sounds, little bright chimes, the occasional yodel. The show's theme song never stopped, driving me batty, until finally I hit a bonus—suddenly that theme song turned sweet. Slot designers call it a "rolling sound": the more credits you win, the longer the song plays. At first I seemed to be winning, gathering credits on every second or third spin. But after about 15 minutes, I was down nearly 7,000 credits. I was winning the virtual equivalent of 15 or 20 nickels every time I scored—but I was spending more than twice that with every spin. After 45 minutes, I was down below 5,000 credits. If I were playing for real money, I would have lost more than $150.

Playing free credits is nothing like playing with your own money, of course, so at 2 A.M. one sleepless night I slipped a 20-dollar bill into a "Jeannie" machine in the Sands casino in Reno. That bought me a full 25 minutes on the machine and one brief bonus glimpse of Jeannie. I'm pretty much the age of those Kaminkow is targeting with his newer machines—and in fact I grew up dreaming of Jeannie—but it's hard to imagine being seduced by any celebrity he might trot out, even Neil Young or Lou Reed.

My brief crack at slots left me feeling somewhere between stupid and glum. At that hour there were no cheery tourists in brightly-patterned shirts amid the chirping of the slots, no sunny smiles on the faces of elderly women happy for a few hours out on the town. Several machines down from me an older man sat slumped in his chair. His T-shirt was riding up his overabundant belly, but he didn't seem to care. He stared at the video screen in front of him in a toddler-staring-at-television kind of way. Other players around me were dressed in sweatsuits and slippers, and there was even a woman in curlers. The hairstyles were generally what you would expect if a fire alarm forced people out of bed in the middle of the night. It wasn't pleasure I saw on their faces so much as determination.

The scene called to mind an evening one year earlier when I spent time with several undercover cops who work for Colorado's division of gambling. Walking the casinos of Black Hawk and Central City, a pair of side-by-side mountain towns with dozens of casinos, we came across a woman who had just won $5,000 playing a dollar slot machine. The people at the Isle of Capri Casino had trotted out a photographer and an oversize poster-board check, but the woman wasn't smiling. In fact, she looked sad. "I'll tell you," said Michael Lask, one of the undercover officers, "she probably lost $10,000 to win that $5,000. And she knows that next week she'll be giving that $5,000 right back." For the most part, the only smiling faces I saw while delving into the realm of slot machines were on the faces of I.G.T.'s designers, unless you count the players posing on the oversize pictures that hang in the atrium of the company's entrance.

QUESTIONS FOR DISCUSSION

1. What does Rivlin achieve by introducing readers to a casino through Anthony Baerlocher's point of view?
2. Rivlin refers to clothing at several points in this article—mentioning, for example, "green polyester pants" and a "sparkly pink sweatsuit ensemble." What do these details suggest to you?
3. How does Rivlin establish that his subject is worth writing about?
4. What accounts for the rising popularity of slot machines? What are the users of these machines not likely to understand about how they are designed?
5. Why do you think slot machines are primarily designed for women over 55?
6. What is your impression of Joe Kaminkow based on how he is presented in this article?
7. Many of the machines described in this piece are associated with old television shows. Why do you think television images could be useful for the gambling industry?

8. How effective is the conclusion to this article? How well does it relate to what Rivlin has conveyed about the gambling industry?

SUGGESTIONS FOR WRITING

1. Rivlin quotes a source describing casinos as providing "day care for the elderly." Research how the gambling industry reaches out to senior citizens, and write an essay explaining why older Americans have been drawn to casino life.
2. Discover what the gambling laws are in your state and explain what they are meant to accomplish.
3. Gambling can become an addiction. Write an essay on how addiction can be overcome.

LINKS

■ Within the Book

In "Please, Please, You're Driving Me Wild" (pages 313–326), Jean Kilbourne discusses what inspires another form of addictive behavior.

■ Elsewhere in Print

Eades, John. *Gambling Addiction: the Problem, the Pain, and the Path to Recovery.* Ventura: Vine, 2003.

Kilby, Jim, Jim Fox, and Anthony Lucas. *Casino Operations Management.* New York: Wiley, 2004.

Ladouceur, Robert, et al. *Understanding and Treating the Pathological Gambler.* New York: Wiley, 2002.

Rivlin, Gary. *Drive-By.* New York: Holt, 1995.

———. *Fire on the Prairie: Chicago's Harold Washington and the Politics of Race.* New York: Holt, 1992.

———. *The Godfather of Silicon Valley: Ron Conway and the Fall of the Dot-coms.* New York: AtRandom, 2001.

———. *The Plot to Get Bill Gates.* New York: Random, 1999.

■ Online

www.mhhe.com/motives

Click on "More Resources" then "Writing to Explain Information."

WOMEN'S BRAINS

Stephen Jay Gould

Stephen Jay Gould (1941–2002) was the Alexander Agassiz Professor of Zoology at Harvard University, where he was also a professor of geology and Curator of Invertebrate Paleontology in the Harvard Museum of Comparative Zoology. He also served as the Vincent Astor Visiting Research Professor of Biology at New York University. During the late twentieth century, he wrote almost 300 articles about science for his monthly column in Natural History. *When asked by an interviewer, "What ultimate effect would you like your work to have?" he responded: "I hope it will be one further step in the kind of humility that would benefit humans enormously with regard to our powers and possibilities on this planet. I think we want to be around for a while. We'd better understand that we weren't meant to be, and we don't have dominion over everything, and we're not always as smart as we think."*

In the following essay, first published in 1980, Gould reports information about a French scientist named Paul Broca who falsely concluded that women are less intelligent than men. As you read this essay, consider Gould's purpose in reporting the story of Broca's research. Consider also what this essay reveals about the importance of explaining information.

In the prelude to *Middlemarch,* George Eliot° lamented the unfulfilled lives of talented women:

> Some have felt that these blundering lives are due to the inconvenient indefiniteness with which the Supreme Power has fashioned the natures of women: if there were one level of feminine incompetence as strict as the ability to count three and no more, the social lot of women might be treated with scientific certitude.

Eliot goes on to discount the idea of innate limitation, but while she wrote in 1872, the leaders of European anthropometry were trying to measure "with scientific certitude" the inferiority of women. Anthropometry, or measurement of the human body, is not so fashionable a field these days, but it dominated the human sciences for much of the nineteenth century and remained popular until intelligence testing replaced skull measurement as a favored device for making invidious comparisons among races, classes, and sexes. Craniometry, or measurement of the skull, commanded the most attention and respect. Its unquestioned leader, Paul Broca (1824–80), professor of

---

°*George Eliot:* The pen name of English novelist Mary Ann Evans (1819–1880).

clinical surgery at the Faculty of Medicine in Paris, gathered a school of disciples and imitators around himself. Their work, so meticulous and apparently irrefutable, exerted great influence and won high esteem as a jewel of nineteenth-century science.

Broca's work seemed particularly invulnerable to refutation. Had he not measured with the most scrupulous care and accuracy? (Indeed, he had. I have the greatest respect for Broca's meticulous procedure. His numbers are sound. But science is an inferential exercise, not a catalog of facts. Numbers, by themselves, specify nothing. All depends upon what you do with them.) Broca depicted himself as an apostle of objectivity, a man who bowed before facts and cast aside superstition and sentimentality. He declared that "there is no faith, however respectable, no interest, however legitimate, which must not accommodate itself to the progress of human knowledge and bend before truth." Women, like it or not, had smaller brains than men and, therefore, could not equal them in intelligence. This fact, Broca argued, may reinforce a common prejudice in male society, but it is also a scientific truth. L. Manouvrier, a black sheep in Broca's fold, rejected the inferiority of women and wrote with feeling about the burden imposed upon them by Broca's numbers:

> Women displayed their talents and their diplomas. They also invoked philosophical authorities. But they were opposed by *numbers* unknown to Condorcet or to John Stuart Mill. These numbers fell upon poor women like a sledge hammer, and they were accompanied by commentaries and sarcasms more ferocious than the most misogynist imprecations of certain church fathers. The theologians had asked if women had a soul. Several centuries later, some scientists were ready to refuse them a human intelligence.

Broca's argument rested upon two sets of data: the larger brains of men in modern societies, and a supposed increase in male superiority through time. His most extensive data came from autopsies performed personally in four Parisian hospitals. For 292 male brains, he calculated an average weight of 1,325 grams; 140 female brains averaged 1,144 grams for a difference of 181 grams, or 14 percent of the male weight. Broca understood, of course, that part of this difference could be attributed to the greater height of males. Yet he made no attempt to measure the effect of size alone and actually stated that it cannot account for the entire difference because we know, a priori, that women are not as intelligent as men (a premise that the data were supposed to test, not rest upon):

> We might ask if the small size of the female brain depends exclusively upon the small size of her body. Tiedemann has proposed this explanation. But we must not forget that women are, on the average, a little less intelligent than men, a difference which we should not exaggerate but which is, nonetheless, real. We are therefore permitted to

suppose that the relatively small size of the female brain depends in part upon her physical inferiority and in part upon her intellectual inferiority.

In 1873, the year after Eliot published *Middlemarch,* Broca measured the cranial capacities of prehistoric skulls from L'Homme Mort cave. Here he found a difference of only 99.5 cubic centimeters between males and females, while modern populations range from 129.5 to 220.7. Topinard, Broca's chief disciple, explained the increasing discrepancy through time as a result of differing evolutionary pressures upon dominant men and passive women:

> The man who fights for two or more in the struggle for existence, who has all the responsibility and the cares of tomorrow, who is constantly active in combating the environment and human rivals, needs more brain than the woman whom he must protect and nourish, the sedentary woman, lacking any interior occupations, whose role is to raise children, love, and be passive.

In 1879, Gustave Le Bon, chief misogynist of Broca's school, used these data to publish what must be the most vicious attack upon women in modern scientific literature (no one can top Aristotle). I do not claim his views were representative of Broca's school, but they were published in France's most respected anthropological journal. Le Bon concluded:

> In the most intelligent races, as among the Parisians, there are a large number of women whose brains are closer in size to those of gorillas than to the most developed male brains. This inferiority is so obvious that no one can contest it for a moment; only its degree is worth discussion. All psychologists who have studied the intelligence of women, as well as poets and novelists, recognize today that they represent the most inferior forms of human evolution and that they are closer to children and savages than to an adult, civilized man. They excel in fickleness, inconstancy, absence of thought and logic, and incapacity to reason. Without doubt there exist some distinguished women, very superior to the average man, but they are as exceptional as the birth of any monstrosity, as, for example, of a gorilla with two heads; consequently, we may neglect them entirely.

Nor did Le Bon shrink from the social implications of his views. He was horrified by the proposal of some American reformers to grant women higher education on the same basis as men:

> A desire to give them the same education, and, as a consequence, to propose the same goals for them, is a dangerous chimera. . . . The day when, misunderstanding the inferior occupations which nature has given her, women leave the home and take part in our battles: on this

day a social revolution will begin, and everything that maintains the sacred ties of the family will disappear.

Sound familiar?*

I have reexamined Broca's data, the basis for all this derivative pronouncement, and I find his numbers sound but his interpretation ill-founded, to say the least. The data supporting his claim for increased difference through time can be easily dismissed. Broca based his contention on the samples from L'Homme Mort alone—only seven male and six female skulls in all. Never have so little data yielded such far-ranging conclusions.

In 1888, Topinard published Broca's more extensive data on the Parisian hospitals. Since Broca recorded height and age as well as brain size, we may use modern statistics to remove their effect. Brain weight decreases with age, and Broca's women were, on average, considerably older than his men. Brain weight increases with height, and his average man was almost half a foot taller than his average woman. I used multiple regression, a technique that allowed me to assess simultaneously the influence of height and age upon brain size. In an analysis of the data for women, I found that, at average male height and age, a woman's brain would weigh 1,212 grams. Correction for height and age reduces Broca's measured difference of 181 grams by more than a third, to 113 grams.

I don't know what to make of this remaining difference because I cannot   *10* assess other factors known to influence brain size in a major way. Cause of death has an important effect: Degenerative disease often entails a substantial diminution of brain size. (This effect is separate from the decrease attributed to age alone.) Eugene Schreider, also working with Broca's data, found that men killed in accidents had brains weighing, on average, 60 grams more than men dying of infectious diseases. The best modern data I can find (from American hospitals) records a full 100-gram difference between death by degenerative arteriosclerosis and by violence or accident. Since so many of Broca's subjects were elderly women, we may assume that lengthy degenerative disease was more common among them than among the men.

More importantly, modern students of brain size still have not agreed on a proper measure for eliminating the powerful effect of body size. Height is partly adequate, but men and women of the same height do not share the same body build. Weight is even worse than height, because most of its variation reflects nutrition rather than intrinsic size—fat versus skinny exerts little influence upon the brain. Manouvrier took up this subject in the 1880s and argued that muscular mass and force should be used. He tried to measure this elusive

---

*When I wrote this essay, I assumed that Le Bon was a marginal, if colorful, figure. I have since learned that he was a leading scientist, one of the founders of social psychology, and best known for a seminal study on crowd behavior, still cited today (*La psychologie des foules,* 1895), and for his work on unconscious motivation.

property in various ways and found a marked difference in favor of men, even in men and women of the same height. When he corrected for what he called "sexual mass," women actually came out slightly ahead in brain size.

Thus, the corrected 113-gram difference is surely too large; the true figure is probably close to zero and may as well favor women as men. And 113 grams, by the way, is exactly the average difference between a 5 foot 4 inch and a 6 foot 4 inch male in Broca's data. We would not (especially us short folks) want to ascribe greater intelligence to tall men. In short, who knows what to do with Broca's data? They certainly don't permit any confident claim that men have bigger brains than women.

To appreciate the social role of Broca and his school, we must recognize that his statements about the brains of women do not reflect an isolated prejudice toward a single disadvantaged group. They must be weighed in the context of a general theory that supported contemporary social distinctions as biologically ordained. Women, blacks, and poor people suffered the same disparagement, but women bore the brunt of Broca's argument because he had easier access to data on women's brains. Women were singularly denigrated, but they also stood as surrogates for other disenfranchised groups. As one of Broca's disciples wrote in 1881: "Men of the black races have a brain scarcely heavier than that of white woman." This juxtaposition extended into many other realms of anthropological argument, particularly to claims that, anatomically and emotionally, both women and blacks were like white children— and that white children, by the theory of recapitulation, represented an ancestral (primitive) adult stage of human evolution. I do not regard as empty rhetoric the claim that women's battles are for all of us.

Maria Montessori did not confine her activities to educational reform for young children. She lectured on anthropology for several years at the University of Rome, and wrote an influential book entitled *Pedagogical Anthropology* (English edition, 1913). Montessori was no egalitarian. She supported most of Broca's work and the theory of innate criminality proposed by her compatriot Cesare Lombroso. She measured the circumferences of children's heads in her schools and inferred that the best prospects had bigger brains. But she had no use for Broca's conclusions about women. She discussed Manouvrier's work at length and made much of his tentative claim that women, after proper correction of the data, had slightly larger brains than men. Women, she concluded, were intellectually superior, but men had prevailed heretofore by dint of physical force. Since technology has abolished force as an instrument of power, the era of women may soon be upon us: "In such an epoch there will really be superior human beings, there will really be men strong in morality and in sentiment. Perhaps in this way the reign of women is approaching, when the enigma of her anthropological superiority will be deciphered. Woman was always the custodian of human sentiment, morality and honor."

This represents one possible antidote to "scientific" claims for the constitutional inferiority of certain groups. One may affirm the validity of biological distinctions but argue that the data have been misinterpreted by prejudiced

15

men with a stake in the outcome, and that disadvantaged groups are truly superior. In recent years, Elaine Morgan has followed this strategy in her *Descent of Woman,* a speculative reconstruction of human prehistory from the woman's point of view—and as farcical as more famous tall tales by and for men.

I prefer another strategy. Montessori and Morgan followed Broca's philosophy to reach a more congenial conclusion. I would rather label the whole enterprise of setting a biological value upon groups for what it is: irrelevant and highly injurious. George Eliot well appreciated the special tragedy that biological labeling imposed upon members of disadvantaged groups. She expressed it for people like herself—women of extraordinary talent. I would apply it more widely—not only to those whose dreams are flouted but also to those who never realize that they may dream—but I cannot match her prose. In conclusion, then, the rest of Eliot's prelude to *Middlemarch:*

> The limits of variation are really much wider than anyone would imagine from the sameness of women's coiffure and the favorite love stories in prose and verse. Here and there a cygnet is reared uneasily among the ducklings in the brown pond, and never finds the living stream in fellowship with its own oary-footed kind. Here and there is born a Saint Theresa, foundress of nothing, whose loving heartbeats and sobs after an unattained goodness tremble off and are dispersed among hindrances instead of centering in some long-recognizable deed.

QUESTIONS FOR DISCUSSION

1. Research what is now known about the differences between the female and the male brain, and explain how scientists have reached those determinations.
2. When reporting the accomplishments of the French scientist Paul Broca, Gould declares that information was carefully collected and that the numbers are reliable. But he then observes, "Numbers, by themselves, specify nothing. All depends upon what you do with them." How was Broca misled by his numbers? What did he fail to take into account?
3. What does Gould mean when he supports the claim that "women's battles are for all of us"?
4. What is the significance of Gould's note on the bottom of page 217?
5. This article includes several long quotations. Are they all necessary? Which affected you the most?

SUGGESTIONS FOR WRITING

1. Do research on either George Eliot or Paul Broca, and explain why she or he became respected. Be sure to reveal your sources, and try to consult at least one work written by the person you are investigating.

2. In paragraph 14, Gould refers to the work of Maria Montessori. Research how Montessori schools operate in the United States, and write an essay explaining what makes them distinctive.

LINKS

■ Within the Book

In "Same-Sex Sexuality" (pages 221–238), Joan Roughgarden shows how contemporary scientists are still struggling to explain differences that can easily be misunderstood.

■ Elsewhere in Print

Baaron-Cohen, Susan. *The Truth about the Male and Female Brain.* New York: Perseus, 2003.

Belenky, Mary Field, Blythe Clinchy, Nancy Goldberger, and Jill Tarule. *Women's Ways of Knowing: The Development of Self, Voice, and Mind.* New York: Basic, 1986.

Eliot, George. *Middlemarch.* 1872. Ed. Gordon S. Haight. Boston: Houghton, 1956.

Gould, Stephen Jay. *Dinosaur in a Haystack: Reflections on Natural History.* New York: Harmony, 1995.

———. *Ever Since Darwin: Reflections in Natural History.* New York: Norton, 1977.

———. *The Flamingo's Smile: Reflections in Natural History.* New York: Norton, 1985.

Jolly, Allison. *Lucy's Legacy: Sex and Intelligence in Human Evolution.* Cambridge: Harvard UP, 1999.

Morgan, Elaine. *The Descent of Woman.* New York: Stein, 1972.

■ Online

www.mhhe.com/motives

Click on "More Resources" then "Writing to Explain Information."

■ ■ ■

SAME-SEX SEXUALITY

Joan Roughgarden

Critics of homosexuality often condemn it as "unnatural." But how "unnatural" is same-sex sexuality in animals other than in humans? This is one of the questions that Joan Roughgarden set out to answer through research that led to the 2004 publication of her book Evolution's Rainbow—*from which the following selection is excerpted.*

Born as a male in 1946, Jonathan Roughgarden earned his Ph.D. from Harvard and has taught at Stanford University since 1972. The winner of a Guggenheim Fellowship among other awards, Roughgarden founded and directed the Earth Systems Programs at Stanford. He is the author of many specific articles and is an internationally respected authority on lizards. In 1998, Jonathan Roughgarden became Joan Roughgarden. She addresses this change in a short interview that you will find on page 235. (For the information included in Roughgarden's notes, visit www.mhhe.com/motives and click on "More Resources" then "Writing to Explain Information."

By 1984 male homosexual behavior had been reported in sixty-three mammalian species.[1] A 1999 review featured detailed descriptions of male and female homosexual behavior in over one hundred mammalian species.[2] From the many examples now available, I've selected sheep to begin with because both behavior and physiology have been studied in the field and in the lab.

Bighorn sheep are card-carrying members of the charismatic mega-fauna high on people's conservation priority list. Living on rugged slopes of the Rocky Mountains, bighorn sheep inspire visitors to the Banff and Kootenay National Parks in Canada, and the National Bison Range in Montana. The males (rams), with large thick horns and curl back from above the eye to behind the ear, weigh up to 300 pounds. Their macho appearance has become a symbol for many male athletic teams. The females (ewes) live separately from the males. The sexes associate only during breeding season, called the rutting season, which extends from mid fall to early winter. A female is receptive for about three days, and will not allow herself to be mounted outside of those three days.[3]

The males have been described as "homosexual societies." Almost all males participate in homosexual courting and copulation. Male-male courtship begins with a stylized approach, followed by genital licking and nuzzling, and often leads to anal intercourse in which one male, usually the larger, rears up on his hind legs and mounts the other. The mounted male arches his back, a posture known as lordosis, which is identical to how a female arches her back during heterosexual mating. The mounting male has an erect penis, makes anal penetration, and performs pelvic thrusts leading to ejaculation.

Bighorn sheep.

The few males who do not participate in homosexual activity have been labeled "effeminate" males. These males are identical in appearance to other males but behave quite differently.[4] They differ from "normal" males by living with the ewes rather than joining all-male groups. These males do not dominate females, are less aggressive overall, and adopt a crouched, female urination posture. These males refuse mounting by other males. These nonhomosexual males are considered "aberrant," with speculation that some hormone deficiency must underlie the effeminate behavior. Even though in physical appearance, including body size and horn development, these males are indistinguishable from other males, scientists urge further study of their "endocrinological profile."

This case turns the meanings of normal and aberrant upside down. The "normal" macho bighorn has full-fledged anal sex with other males. The "aberrant" ram is the one who is straight—lack of interest in homosexuality is considered pathological. Now, why would being straight be a pathology, requiring a hormone checkup? According to the researchers, what's aberrant is that a macho-looking bighorn ram acts feminine! He pees like a female—even worse than being gay!

This Alice-in-Wonderland mixing of what's normal and what's pathological continues in laboratory studies of homosexuality in domesticated sheep. These studies, funded by the U.S. Department of Agriculture, were carried out at the government's U.S. Sheep Experimental Center in Dubois, Idaho.

The project escaped the congressional knife because it was camouflaged with the goal of improving the economic success of sheep farmers.[5]

Homosexual behavior in male domesticated sheep has been documented since the 1970s.[6] Two investigators write, "It is commonly accepted that male-male mounting of prepubertal animals in important in their development of normal rear orientation in mount interactions," and they cite a study on homosexual cattle.[7] This argument has been a familiar escape over the years from dealing with the reality of gay animals—gayness in youth is necessary for straight life later on. Really, though, let's be honest. Homosexual sheep and cattle are actually gay, not playing make-believe.

Investigators coined the term "dud stud" for a ram attracted only to other rams. Preference, not ability, is the issue: "No matter how many bullets there are in the clip, nothing happens when firing commences."[8] Now, consider that rams cost from $350 up to $4,000. A sheep farmer has a ratio of one ram to 30 to 50 ewes, and a "high-performance" stud can service 100 to 125 ewes. Having a dud-stud, then, deprives a sheep farmer of profit because more studs must be purchased for each lamb produced. The investigators developed tests to determine whether a ram had bullets in his clip ("servicing test") and whether he knows where to aim them ("preference test"). The long-term goal was to determine the biological and genetic basis of homosexual behavior, so that duds could be weeded out of the domestic sheep, enhancing the economics of sheep raising.[9]

To separate gay sheep from straight sheep, rams were exposed to receptive ewes for various periods. If the rams didn't mount the females, they were candidates to be considered homosexual. Next a candidate gay ram was strapped into a stanchion, a big crate with holes on each side to keep sheep in a fixed position. By arranging sheep of both sexes around the stanchion, the candidate gay ram was allowed to respond to a variety of females and males. The candidate gay male could indicate his preference for a female, or another male, within the stanchion.

A candidate wasn't offered just any male. He was specifically provided with males previously identified as "receivers" based on their willingness to be mounted by other males in the pen where they lived. If a candidate male chose a receiver rather than a female for courtship, he was classified as homosexual. If a candidate failed the gay preference test, he was given a second chance. If he wouldn't mount some other male in the home pen, he was then provided with that special other male. Eight out of ninety-four males representing Rambouillet, Targhee, Columbia, Polypay, and Finnish Landrace breeds tested as gay. Interestingly, six of these males would mount receiver males. Two, though, would only mount each other and none else, suggesting that they were somehow pair-bonded.

After all of this preparation, the hormonal response of the gay males was determined. The investigators hypothesized that gay rams would respond hormonally to receiver males in the same way straight males respond to receptive females. They were wrong. Gay males don't think another male is a female, and don't respond as if they did.

Gayness is expected in domesticated sheep because wild sheep are gay. The social structure in which being gay makes sense in nature is undoubtedly also present to some degree in the pens where the animals live. The removal of gayness from rams to increase sheep-farming profits would also produce a change in their social system. I bet any economic gain from breeding out duds will be offset by lower survival rates among the remaining studs in an increasingly dysfunctional domestic social system.

Many other creatures with hair have been documented as engaging in same-sex mating.[10] White-tailed deer, black-tailed deer, red deer (also called elk), reindeer, moose, giraffes, pronghorns, kobs, waterbucks, blackbucks, Thomson's gazelles, Grant's gazelles, musk oxen, mountain goats, American bison, mountain zebras, plains zebras, warthogs, collared peccaries, vicuñas (a llama), African elephants, and Asiatic elephants have all been documented in scientific reports as engaging in some degree of same-sex mating.[11] In some species, same-sex mating is sporadic; in others, very common, comprising over half of all copulations. In some, males engage in most of the same-sex matings; in others, mostly females do it; and in still others, both sexes participate. Same-sex mating is common among female red deer, male giraffes, female kobs, male blackbucks, male and female mountain goats, male American bison, and male African and Asiatic elephants.

To continue, lions, cheetahs, red foxes, wolves, grizzly bears, black bears, and spotted hyenas have been documented as engaging in same-sex mating. Again, the frequency varies from sporadic to common, with either or both sexes involved, depending on the species.[12] The gray kangaroo, red-necked wallaby, whiptail wallaby, rat kangaroo, Doria's kangaroo, Matschie's kangaroo, koala, dunnart, and quoll all enjoy same-sex mating too, although at relatively low frequency.[13]

The red squirrel, gray squirrel, least chipmunk, Olympic marmot, hoary marmot, dwarf cavy, yellow-toothed cavy, wild cavy, long-eared hedgehog, gray-headed flying fox, Livingstone's fruit bat, and vampire bat show various degrees of same-sex mating.[14] For example, female red squirrels occasionally form a bond, with sexual and affectionate activities leading to joint parenting. The female squirrels take turns mounting each other, and raise a single litter of young. Although only one member of the pair is the mother, both nurse the young. Only females form such pair-bonds; male and female red squirrels don't form pair-bonds. Among male red squirrels, 18 percent of the mounts are homosexual. Concerning vampire bats, recall that females form special long-lasting friendships with affectionate gestures, including grooming and kissing [. . .]. No genital-genital contact has been reported among female vampire bats, but male vampire bats hang belly to belly licking one another, both with an erect penis.

The bottlenose dolphin, spinner dolphin, Amazon river dolphin, killer whale, gray whale, bowhead whale, right whale, gray seal, elephant seal, harbor seal, Australian sea lion, new Zealand sea lion, northern fur seal, walrus, and West Indian manatee are exceedingly active in same-sex genital behavior.[15] Nearly everyone has marveled at the playful personality of dolphins, often featured in children's movies—lots of makin' whoopee going on in all directions. Male bottlenose dolphins are especially well studied. A male places its erect penis into another male's genital slit, nasal aperture, or anus. They nuzzle each other's genital slit with their beak, and they can interact sexually in threesomes and foursomes. In mixed-sex groups, homosexual activity occurs as much or more than heterosexual activity. The same-sex courtship is part of forming and maintaining lifelong pair-bonds between male dolphins of the same age. They bond as adolescents, becoming constant companions and often traveling widely. Paired males may take turns watching out while their partner rests, and they protect one another against sharks and predators. On the death of a partner, the widower must search for a new companion, usually failing unless he encounters another widower.

Sometimes one finds lifelong bonds among a trio of dolphins rather than a pair. And to complete this picture of facile sexuality, male same-sex matings occur *between* species too! Male bottlenose dolphins mate with male Atlantic dolphins *(Stenella frontalis)* and may band together for interspecies cooperation. All is not sweetness and light, though. These pair-bonds are part of a system of "nested alliances." Teams composed of pairs and trios of the Indian Ocean bottlenose dolphins *(Tursiops aduncus)* fight other such teams in contests over females.[16] Thus, a huge story remains to be told about same-sex matings among mammals under the sea.

OUR CLOSEST RELATIVES

We come at last to our closest relatives in the animal world—the primates. By now you might expect that primates, like other mammals, would show a good deal of same-sex courtship and mating. You won't be disappointed.

Japanese macaques *(Macaca fuscata)* are one of the best-known of the old world monkeys and the northernmost of all primates other than humans. Both sexes have gray-brown fur, a noticeably red face, often red genitals as well, and a small tail. Their maximum height as about 2 feet, and they can weigh up to 40 pounds. Japanese macaques are mostly vegetarian, eating fruits, seeds, leaves, and bark, with some snails, crayfish, and bird eggs thrown in. Japanese macaques become adults at about five years and can live up to thirty years. A free-living group (the Arashimaya West troop) was introduced to Texas in 1972 and has thrived there, even inventing a special alarm call for rattlesnakes.

Their social structure consists of mixed groups of around fifty to two *20* hundred females and males in an area of 100 to 500 hectares. The females stay put, and a group consists of several matrilines, or female descendants of an elder female. The ratio of females to males in a group is typically around four females to one male. The males migrate between groups every two to four years. The social system revolves primarily around females and the interactions among them.

The females are described as having a rigid dominance hierarchy, and all the females can be ordered along a line from top to bottom. Here's how the hierarchy works. Suppose the three elder females are ranked A, B, and C from top to bottom. All female offspring inherit the rank of their mother. So, if the daughter of A is A1, the daughter of B is B1, and the daughter of C is C1, then the overall dominance hierarchy goes A, A1, B, B1, C, C1. And if A1 has a daughter too, say A11, and similarly for B11, C11, and so on, the overall dominance hierarchy spanning three generations would be A, A1, A11, B, B1, B11, C, C1, C11. However, matters are a bit more fluid than this picture suggests. This hierarchy is produced because elders come to the defense of their daughters and granddaughters. At birth, A11 is subordinate to the C matriline, but after interventions on her behalf by A1 and A, the status of A11 is raised to that of A matriline. Dominance testing goes on continually. No one just accepts her place unquestioningly.

Against this backdrop, same-sex courtship and copulation are also going on. Same-sex relationships happen *not* between close kin but between distantly related individuals. These same-sex copulations produce bonds that go beyond the straight-line lineage-based dominance hierarchy, building crosscutting links and suggesting a network structure in the social system. Same-sex courtship and copulation take place in what are called female-female consorts. These are short-term relationships (STRs) that last for less than an hour up to four days. During this time, the two females mount each other frequently, engaging in genital-genital contact. When not having sex together, they huddle, sleep, and forage together, groom each other, and defend each other from challenges. For the duration of their STR, a pair is monogamous. After a few days, though, they form new STRs. During the STR the mountings are bidirectional and mutually pleasurable, and there is no sign of dominance or submissiveness within the relationship.[17] Indeed, the presence of any aggressiveness in the relationship destroys the "mood," and forecasts the dissolution of the STR.

The males have a hard time while all this lesbian love is going on. When a guy approaches to mate with a female, her partner usually shoos him away.[18] Females back each other up while in an STR. The lower-ranking member of an STR increases in rank temporarily because of her partner's support.[19] This temporary increase in rank ends when the STR dissolves. Although the lower-ranking member of a consort temporarily rises in rank, a low-ranking female shows no tendency to pair up preferentially with a high-ranking female, as would be expected if she were interested in finding a more powerful ally. Instead, the higher-ranking female is responsible for starting the relationship. Neither is forming a consort a means for two females to share parental care. The consort partners do not help raise each other's young. A partner does not support the other's young in conflicts, nor does she groom the other's young. If anything, partners tend to be aggressive toward each other's young.

Japanese macaques.

A subgroup in which females outnumbered males by eleven to one was formed experimentally to see if the females would show increased competition for the male's favor, or if they would instead increase the number of same-sex relationships. Instead of competing more intensely for the one male, they formed more female-female relationships. Nonetheless, the majority of females who rejected a sexual solicitation from the one lucky guy in favor of a same-sex partner did later form a heterosexual consortship with him, showing him to be an acceptable mate.[20]

As these studies show, research on homosexuality in primates has advanced beyond the "Gee, do they really do it?" stage of other vertebrate groups. Homosexuality is so conspicuous among primates, so in-your-face, that it cannot be ignored, resulting in a relatively extensive literature going back to the 1970s.[21] Yet, if the fact of extensive same-sex sexuality in primates is well established, the reasons for this homosexuality are open to debate. The macaques don't participate in homosexual relationships because heterosexual partners aren't available, or as an expression of dominance and submission, or to form alliances, or to acquire help in raising their young. So why do female macaques spend so much of their time in same-sex courtship and copulation?

With no ready explanation for female homosexuality in Japanese macaques, investigators have wondered "whether our line of questioning is not faulty."[22] Does homosexuality really have to further overall lifetime reproduction, albeit in some indirect way? An alternative view—what I call the neutralist

25

position—is that homosexuality is a neutral byproduct of the evolution of other traits.[23] Homosexuality, it is argued, doesn't disappear during evolution because homosexuality is harmless. Female macaques have lots of offspring, and they participate in heterosexual matings whenever they need some sperm. Homosexuality doesn't interfere with their reproduction, so why would natural selection remove this harmless behavior? By chance, it is suggested, over the course of evolution homosexuality has drifted into prominence in some species, while remaining nearly absent in others. Or maybe in some species chance has genetically linked homosexuality to important genes, and homosexuality has "hitchhiked" into prominence on the coattails of these genes. Either way, it is contended, this behavior serves no evolutionary purpose.

Since lots of traits are neutral, does some causal mechanism determine which of these traits actually evolves? One suggestion is pleasure. Why do macaques participate in same-sex copulation instead of, say, the monkey equivalent of reading Kant in their spare time? Neither increases reproductive success, we may suppose. Yet sexual stimulation is pleasurable, and reading Kant isn't. Therefore sexual activity, and not reading Kant, evolves to take place when not carrying out reproductively important activities. Although "sexual pleasure was selected for because it motivates individuals to engage in fertile sex, . . . sexual pleasure is not specific to reproductive sex but can be satisfied by many non-reproductive sexual outlets as well."[24] In this view, evolutionary theory is incomplete because it applies only to traits that affect reproduction and survival. This pleasure principle extends evolutionary theory to explain which among the set of selectively neutral traits evolve and which don't. Homosexuality is viewed as existing under the radar screen of natural selection, subject only to the winds of passion.

I don't buy this neutralist position, at least not yet. I'm from the other school, the adaptationist school, which holds that nearly all behaviors and traits benefit organisms, and our task is to figure out how. Here's where I'm coming from. In my experience, animals don't have lots of free time for hanging out. The lizards I work with are busy all day. When not actively eating, mating, or displaying to one another, lizards are looking around intently for food or keeping tabs on neighbors. Sure, lizards sleep now and then, and they stay in bed on a cold day, when they're too slow to catch prey anyway. Still, lizards use their time wisely and don't waste it. We're always underestimating animals. Long ago we thought lizards were mindless little robots. We find now that throughout the day they make complex decisions of the sort that top business executives pay expensive consultants to solve.[25] From this fieldwork, one becomes wary of claims that a trait is useless.

What about the macaques? Is every day another day in paradise, an endless party filled with evolutionary meaningless play? Why should macaques be so lucky, while the rest of us poor sods have to work for a living? To my mind, homosexual interaction occupies far too much time in the lives of female macaques to be evolutionarily incidental.

My hunch is that the social system has been oversimplified. Traditionally   *30*
if A attacks B, and B backs down, then A is said to be dominant over B. A is
assumed to get whatever is wanted as long as A remains dominant. However,
this assumption isn't always true. I've sat on a rock in the woods watching a
juvenile lizard, about 1 inch long, take territorial space from the male lizard
five times as big. Here's how. The juvenile goes to the edge of the big lizard's
territory. The big lizard sees this and rushes over. The juvenile scurries away—
he's lost. So the big lizard goes back to his perch, and the juvenile lizard tip-
toes back. The big lizard then runs over again and chases the juvenile away.
The juvenile loses again. And so on. After five of these chases, the big lizard
has had enough and doesn't bother to chase the juvenile anymore. The sliver
of land the juvenile wants isn't worth the fuss from the big lizard's standpoint.[26] Overall, the juvenile lost every single pairwise interaction but still
won a slice of the dominant male's territory. He lost every battle but won the
war. Thus saying the big lizard is dominant over the juvenile just because the
juvenile always backs down in pairwise contests doesn't capture the true
power relationship. Furthermore, even pairwise interactions don't take place
in a vacuum. A lizard lives on every tree. All these lizards are watching, and
they remember what they see. So the meaning of the interaction extends beyond the two lizards in the pair to all the lizards who were watching. A social
system isn't the sum of isolated pairwise disputes.

For macaques, the ranking scheme is assembled from records of many
pairwise interactions, and may miss much of the true social organization. The
question comes down to whether female macaques are participating in sex
for fun only, or whether they're networking for future profit. If the homosexuality is only for fun, why are STRs not between close kin, but only between
matrilines? In heterosexual mating, an "incest taboo" prevents inbreeding. In
homosexual matings, no offspring are conceived, so there is no reason for
STRs to be avoided between relatives. I suggest that STRs between close kin
have no strategic value because close kin already share a bond, the kinship
bond itself. STRs are needed to build bonds beyond kinship. Furthermore, if
the homosexuality is only for fun, why should high-ranking females be more
responsible for maintaining the STRs than low-ranking ones; shouldn't rank
be immaterial and the STRs be formed solely on the basis of who is the most
enjoyable sexual partner?

Let's look at it another way. Calling this social structure a dominance hierarchy may exaggerate the power of a high-ranking female. Is the alpha female given her status by the consent of the governed? Does she have to solicit
their support, ask for their votes, continue as their alpha? Perhaps high-ranking
females need support from low-ranking females, and forming STRs secures
their friendship. If the social system is based on a network of power rather
than a dominance hierarchy, then female choice of homosexual partners may
be adaptive not for climbing a dominance ladder but for navigating a political
network.

So a horse race is shaping up. Neutralists have often squared off against adaptationists in evolutionary biology. The dispute may be over quickly, though. Evolutionary theory includes an acid test for neutralist and adaptationist theories.[27] For homosexuality to be evolutionarily neutral, females, who do, and don't, participate in short-term homosexual relationships need to have nearly identical average reproduction over a lifetime.

I doubt that homosexuality is selectively neutral in Japanese macaques. I suspect that the fate is bleak for a female who doesn't participate in homosexual STRs, as she is likely kicked out of the group and left to die. Being kicked out of the group would greatly reduce her average lifelong reproduction because she wouldn't live long enough to reproduce, and any offspring she did have would not have access to group resources or protection. If participating in STRs is necessary for inclusion in female social groups, then female same-sex sexuality in this species is what I call a social-inclusionary trait. . . . Not to participate in the STRs bound together wth same-sex sexuality would be lethal.

Consider now another primate with extensively documented same-sex sexuality. The bonobo *(Pan paniscus)* is not just any primate. Bonobos, or pygmy chimpanzees, are our closest relatives, along with the common chimpanzee *(Pan troglodytes)*. *Pan* and human lineages split apart about eight million years ago. The *Pan* line went on to divide into pygmy and common chimpanzees, while the *Homo* line divided into various forms of early humans. Because *Homo sapiens* is the only remaining species from the human lineage, our closest living relatives are these chimpanzee species. Chimpanzees* have become well known for their male-male power games, whereas bonobos illustrate female-female relationships and the social uses of sexuality. Bonobos are less well-known but just as relevant, if not more so, to the way people actually live.

Bonobos, which live in the tropical lowland rainforests of Zaire, in central Africa, grow to about 2 to 3 feet in height, weigh about 70 to 85 pounds, and have black hair. They live about forty years, beginning to breed after thirteen years or more. Bonobos eat fruit, insects, and small mammals, and are more nearly vegetarian than chimpanzees. Chimpanzees actually hunt monkeys for food, whereas bonobos don't. In captive situations bonobos use tools skillfully, but in the wild they show less tool use than chimpanzees. Bonobos are as intelligent as chimpanzees, and more sensitive. During World War II bombing in Germany, bonobos in a zoo near Hellabrun died of fright from the noise, while the chimpanzees were unaffected.

Bonobos live in mixed-sex, mixed-age groups of about sixty individuals. In bonobo females, a pink swelling around the genitals signals readiness to

*The word "chimpanzee" will hereafter refer to the common chimpanzee unless otherwise qualified, and "bonobo" to the pygmy chimpanzee.

mate. Bonobo females are receptive almost continuously, whereas female chimpanzees are receptive for only a few days during their cycle. In bonobo between-sex matings, one-third take place face to face, the remaining two-thirds taking place front to back, with the male mounting the female. By contrast, all chimpanzee between-sex matings are front to back, with the male mounting.

In bonobo female same-sex encounters, the two females face each other. One clings with arms and legs to her partner, who lifts her off the ground. The females rub their genital swellings side to side, then grin and squeal during orgasm, a form of mating called genito-genital rubbing (GG-rubbing). In bonobo male same-sex encounters, the two males rub humps: standing back to back, one male rubs his scrotum against the buttocks of the other. Another position, penis-fencing, involves two males hanging face to face from a branch while rubbing their erect penises together. Bonobos don't have anal intercourse, but they do have sporadic oral sex, hand massages of the genitals, and lots of intense French kissing. With all these choices of sexual activity, bonobos have even developed a set of hand signals to tell each other what they'd like. These signals are used in both between-sex and same-sex sexual encounters.

Bonobo life isn't a continuous orgy, as the extensive menu of sexual activity might suggest. Daily life consists of numerous brief episodes scattered throughout the day. Each female participates in GG-rubbing once every two hours or so. A sexual encounter lasts about ten to fifteen seconds, so in total, sex doesn't take a lot of time. At least six situations lead to sex:

1. Sex facilitates sharing. When a zoo caretaker approaches bonobos with food, male bonobos develop erections. Before the food is tossed in, males invite females, females invite males, and females invite each other for sex. After sex, the meal begins. In the field, at the Lomako Forest in Zaire, bonobos engage in sex after they enter trees loaded with figs, or after one has captured a prey animal. When five or ten minutes of sexual contact have passed, they all settle down to dine together. Sex facilitates sharing not only food but anything in demand. When a cardboard box used as a toy is given to bonobos in a zoo, they mount each other before beginning to play with the box. Most primate species would squabble and fight over it instead.

2. Sex is used for reconciliation after a dispute, such as arguing over who had the right of way when walking along a branch.

3. Sex helps integrate a new arrival into the group. When females migrate to a new group, the new arrivals establish relationships with the established matriarchs through frequent GG-rubbing and grooming.

4. Sex helps form coalitions. Female bonobos bond through GG-rubbing to form coalitions against males who would otherwise be

dominant. When food is given to chimpanzees, the males eat their fill before the females are allowed their turn, whereas in bonobos, the females eat when they want, regardless of male presence. Females together chase off harassing males.

5. Sex is candy. In return for sex, a female may take a bundle of branches and leaves, or sugarcane, from a male.

6. Oh, I almost forgot—sex is used for reproduction.[28]

Why has homosexuality evolved between female bonobos? Females maintain strong friendships with unrelated females, females control access to food, females share food with one another more often than with males, and females form alliances in which they cooperatively attack and even injure males. Their increased control over food and the lessened threat from males allows bonobo females to reproduce starting at an earlier age compared to chimpanzee females, who don't form such friendships. An earlier age of first reproduction in turn leads to higher lifetime reproductive success.[29] A female who doesn't participate in this social system, including its same-sex sexuality, will not share in these group benefits. For a female bonobo, not being lesbian is hazardous to your fitness.

For these reasons, female same-sex sexuality in bonobos is what I call a social-inclusionary trait. . . . The evolution of female homosexuality is driven by the need to be included in the social group that controls resources, and not belonging is near-lethal. The selection in favor of participating in same-sex sexuality, given that this mode of bonding is already in place, is exceedingly strong.

Bonobos and common chimpanzees offer an interesting contrast in social organization. Physically, they are much the same, the main difference being that common chimpanzees have grayish hair under their chins and bonobos don't. Yet chimpanzees have a male-dominated society and bonobos a female-centered society, and as we've seen, bonobos have a love life that chimpanzees can only envy.

In case you're wondering about other primates, here are some in which same-sex courtship and mating are documented. Lemurs, such as Verreaux's sifaka *(Propithecus verreauxi)* from Madagascar, have limited same-sex mating between males—up to 14 percent of all matings in one study.[30] New world monkeys, like the wild squirrel monkey *(Saimiri sciureus)* and the white-faced capuchin *(Cebus capucinus)* from South America, have same-sex genital interactions.[31] Female squirrel monkeys form short-term sexual relationships, and also have close female "friends" with whom they travel and rest and occasionally coparent. Males too have same-sex genital displays. Mounts between females occurred once every forty minutes during a week out of each month, and 40 percent of all genital displays were same-sex, one-quarter between females. In white-faced capuchins, more than half of the mountings were same-sex and included specialized courtship gestures and vocalizations.[32]

40

Old world monkeys have an extensive record of same-sex sexual encounters. In addition to the Japanese macaque *(Macaca fuscata)* already discussed, the rhesus macaque *(Macaca mulatta)* and stumptail macaque *(Macaca arctoides)* engage in same-sex sexuality as a regular part of life. In rhesus macaques, about a third of all mountings are same-sex, 80 percent of which are between males. Females form short- to medium-term relationships, as do male/female pairs.[33] Male-male genital contact in stumptail macaques includes anal intercourse, with penetration and ejaculation, and mutual oral sex. Homosexual activity accounts for 25–40 percent of all sexual encounters.[34]

The savanna baboon *(Papio cynocephalus),* hamadryas baboon *(Papio hamadryas),* and gelada baboon *(Theropithecus gelada)* from Africa have extensive same-sex relationships. Savanna baboon males have numerous same-sex genital contacts, including "diddling," in which males fondle each other's genitals, called "greeting" behaviors. Some males form long-lasting coalitions with mutual exchange of sexual favors. Savanna baboons protect and help one another, and their associations can last for many years, constituting long-term relationships (LTRs). Approximately 20 percent of the mountings are between males, and 9 percent between females.

Baboon life is marked by violence. Male savanna baboons coerce matings with females, often seriously injuring them. When an outside male takes over a troop, he may attack mothers and infants, injuring females, causing miscarriages, and killing infants. Males often "kidnap" infants, and the youngsters may be injured. In this social system, same-sex courtship is used specifically for coalition-building. For baboons, coalitions are threatening to those who exercise power and dominance.[35] Attempts by powerful males to break up threatening coalitions among subordinates emerge as a form of homophobia.

Hanuman langurs *(Presbytis entellus)* are medium-sized monkeys from India know for their exceptional violence toward infants and juveniles.[36] Attacks by adult males may account for half of all infant deaths. The stress of this violence causes females to abort fetuses spontaneously. Females may also induce abortion by pressing their bellies on the ground or allowing other females to jump on them. Females are not necessarily award-winning mothers, either. Maternal mistreatment includes abandonment; dangling, dropping, and dragging the baby; shoving it against the ground; biting or kicking it; and throwing the infant out of trees. Females from one group may kidnap a baby from a neighboring group, keeping it for three days before allowing the mother to retrieve it. The presence of this behavior was controversial when first reported.[37]

The same-sex sexual activity of langurs is rather ordinary. All females mount each other. Interestingly, females do mount close relatives (27 percent of all lesbian mountings are between half-sisters) and show no homosexual incest taboo, whereas an incest taboo does govern heterosexual mountings. Males also mount each other. The mountee initiates the mounting with a special head-shaking display. Males sometimes form duos, a pair-bond lasting for about a month. Males who have bonded through homosexual mounting may cooperate in launching attacks against males in neighboring groups.

The white-handed gibbon *(Hylobates lar)* of Thailand and the siamang *(Hylobates syndactylus)* of the Malay peninsula and Sumatra, in welcome contrast to langurs and baboons, are primarily monogamous, although some divorce happens. In a study over six years of eleven male/female gibbon pairs, five split up and six remained intact. Females breed for four or five months every two to three years, and between-sex sexual behavior is largely limited to breeding periods. Nonabusive intrafamily same-sex behavior is common. A male parent and offspring have sexual contact—primarily penis-fencing leading to orgasm and ejaculation—about as often as between-sex mating occurs during the breeding period. Although gibbons are monogamous, about 10 percent of the heterosexual matings are extra-pair. The whole system seems quite similar to avian monogamy, with the addition of the same-sex father/offspring sexual activity.[38]

Gorillas *(Gorilla gorilla)* live in groups of one male with three to six adult   50
females plus their offspring, as well as in all-male groups. Same-sex genital contact occurs in females and males. Females have favorite female partners in the mixed-sex groups. Most of the male-male homosexual behavior takes place in the all-male groups. Males have preferred partners too; some interact with only one partner, others with up to five partners. Male also commit infanticide, causing more than 40 percent of the infant deaths in one study.[39]

All in all, lots of same-sex courtship and mating takes place among primates. A look at the family tree of primates suggests a pattern. From its base near the ground, the tree trunk splits first into the prosimians on one side and the anthropoids on the other. The prosimian branch, including bush babies, lemurs, and tarsiers, appears to have only incidental same-sex mounting while in heat and no evidence of a major social role for same-sex courtship. The anthropoid branch splits into two sub-branches: the new world primates and the old world primates. The new world primates, including marmosets, tamarins, and monkeys with prehensile tails, such as spider monkeys, show some homosexual behavior. It is in the old world primates that homosexual courtship becomes prominent. The old world primates, including macaques, baboons, gibbons, orangutans, gorillas, chimpanzees, bonobos, and humans, contain the most sophisticated of the primate societies. In these societies, individuals form complex relationships, relationships clearly fostered through both same-sex and between-sex sexuality.[40] This pattern of occurrence across the primate family tree suggests that homosexuality in primates is an evolutionary innovation originating around fifty million years ago, when the major prosimian and anthropoid lineages began their divergence.

OBJECTIVITY AND HOMOSEXUALITY

My coverage of homosexuality in animals will be seen by some as a litmus test of objectivity. Am I simply going to assert that because homosexuality is common in animals, it is legitimate in people? I want to be clear about where

COMPANION TEXT   *An Interview with Joan Roughgarden*

A reporter from the New York Times, *Solomon interviewed the author of this work upon publication of the book from which it is excerpted. Here is part of the interview, first published in 2004.*

You launch a vigorous attack on Darwin in your new book, "Evolution's Rainbow: Diversity, Gender and Sexuality in Nature and People." The party line according to Darwin and most sociobiologists is that females are looking for males with great genes. The proposition is clearly nonsense.

You're a professor of biology at Stanford who believes many animals look for same-sex partners. There are 300 vertebrate species in which homosexual relationships are a regular part of the natural social system.

But isn't that just a tiny fraction of the total number of vertebrate species, which numbers around 50,000? And how can you discredit Darwin's widely accepted ideas on natural selection? The issue is whether scientists are really telling the truth, or whether they are playing to the market, which is what they are doing in the case of homosexuality. I know for a fact that some biologists are embarrassed if their animals turn out to be gay.

How often does that happen? Basically, if you ask any biologist, they can verify for you that they have either seen homosexuality in animals, or they know someone who has seen it, and never reported it.

What about gay biologists? Wouldn't they be more sympathetic? Within the sciences, gays and lesbians are highly underrepresented, which I think has to do with the atmosphere of the laboratory. It is a difficult environment for women and gays because of the sexually explicit humor.

You make the lab sound like a locker room. Yes. In the sciences, the dynamic is toward being a team player. Scientists talk about the desire to test hypotheses, but there's enormous peer pressure for confirming existing dogma. . . .

Your name used to be Jonathan, and you were a male professor until about six years ago. When you first come out as a transgendered person, you spend your first year in absolute euphoria. Then reality sets in, and you have to make a life and deal with the stigma. . . .

Why didn't you elaborate on your transgendered status in your book, since it could certainly help explain your distrust of Darwin? Oh, every woman has some story, and I don't think mine is so different.

Deborah Solomon

I stand on the issues of how widespread animal homosexuality is and what relevance such information has for affirming human homosexuality.

I believe the moral assessment of human behavior is independent of what animals do, as I've mentioned before. Infanticide by males is common in animals, and female animals choose mates in part to manage this danger. The naturalness of male infanticide in animals is clearly no justification for infanticide in humans—human infanticide is wrong, period. By contrast, I believe that affirming homosexual expression is right for people, not because animals are often homosexual but because endorsing homosexual expression makes for a just and productive society. . . .

Prior to researching this [project], I took for granted that homosexuality was rare. Personally, I still have never seen a mating between lizards that I am certain is homosexual, even after thirty years of working with them. I can sympathize with those who think homosexuality is rare—this has been my experience too. Yet I now know this experience is misleading. Previously, I was aware of one published reference to a homosexual copulation in non-parthenogenic lizards, but I felt the situation was unusual enough to be an isolated instance. As a result, I never checked. Every few days during field-work I see lizards mating. Sometimes I'm sure of the sexes involved. Usually, though, I would assume the bigger lizard was male and the smaller female. If both were about the same size, I would still assume one was male and the other female. To find out, I would have had to catch them while they were in the act of mating, separate them, and inspect their sex by physically palpating them and examining their cloacal opening. This action would be intrusive, would be disturbing and possibly injurious to the animals, and would take time away from a research project that had other goals. For this reason, I don't know how much homosexual mating occurs even in the species I have worked with for many years. I'm sure that many other scientists are in the same situation—we have never really looked.

I was stunned to discover how many reports of homosexuality there are in the primary literature. The seven cases I've reviewed above—whiptail lizards, pukekos and oystercatchers, bighorn and domesticated sheep, Japanese macaques and bonobos—are well documented over many years by multiple investigators. In these, no doubt whatsoever exists of homosexuality. Of the, say, 293 others, for a total of approximately 300 species, some will fall by the wayside and others will be reconfirmed. Today, it's very hard to know how common homosexuality is in natural social systems. The data aren't collected, or the sexes aren't checked, and when data are available, they often aren't reported. My overall conclusion is now that the more complex and sophisticated a social system is, the more likely it is to have homosexuality intermixed with heterosexuality. Any animal in a complex society has to manage both within- and between-sex relationships. Both types of relationships are mediated through physical contact, including embracing, grooming, and genital contact, as well as through vocalizations, bodily symbolism, and behaviors like food-sharing and warning calls.

55

IS SAME-SEX SEXUALITY PROBLEMATIC?

Let us suppose, on the basis of the available evidence, that same-sex sexuality is now known to be natural and common. Would this discovery be a problem? Here are the questions I'm usually asked.

What's the function of homosexuality? Same-sex sexuality promotes friendship. Genitals have sensory neurons that provide pleasure. Activating one another's genital neurons sends a friendly message and builds relationships. The friendship's purpose depends on context. The purpose of friendship might be innocent or threatening. Friendly bats huddling together through the cold nights are innocent. Friendly baboons building coalitions to overturn an alpha male are threatening; the alpha male will try to prevent this friendship, which would be seen as homophobia.

Does a gay gene exist? The question doesn't really ask about DNA. The question asks whether homosexuality is inherited. Homosexuality in animals is obviously inherited in some way, but no single gay gene exists. Homosexuality is a complex social behavior. Complex traits are not caused by single genes. Reports of a gay gene in humans are erroneous. . . .

Doesn't homosexuality contradict evolution? This question usually confuses same-sex sexuality with nonbreeding. Nonbreeding *is* an evolutionary problem; same-sex sexuality isn't. The two aren't necessarily connected. Nonbreeders always exist, heterosexual and homosexual. In most species, only some members breed, while the rest don't, reflecting the population's reproductive skew. Some nonbreeding homosexual animals are expected to exist simply because of the population's reproductive skew, and this can be explained by whatever causes that skew. Indeed, the main evolutionary issue is to explain where the reproductive skew comes from, not whether same-sex genital contact occurs.

Although some homosexual animals don't breed, most do. Homosexuals who breed can have either a lower or higher fertility than heterosexuals who breed, depending on circumstances. Breeding homosexual animals could have a lower fertility than breeding heterosexuals because of a tradeoff between fertility and survival. Natural selection favors traits that increase average total offspring production throughout life, which depends on both fertility *and* survival. A homosexual strategy could increase same-sex matings to obtain higher survival through friendships. This homosexual strategy might result in decreased fecundity because of fewer between-sex matings. However, the homosexual strategy might yield more offspring averaged over a life span than an exclusively heterosexual strategy because of the increased survival.

Alternatively, breeding homosexual animals might have an even higher fertility rate than breeding heterosexual animals because homosexually bonded friendships might access more resources than those available to exclusively heterosexual animals, yielding a fertility advantage. Homosexuality can be a social-inclusionary trait. In this situation, homosexuality might increase both fertility and survival, and be favored by natural selection even without taking into account a possible tradeoff between fertility and survival. Thus same-sex sexuality doesn't necessarily go against evolution, either in general or in particular.

Although homosexuality doesn't contradict evolution, widespread homosexuality among animals does open new perspectives on how we think about bodies and social relationships.

QUESTIONS FOR DISCUSSION

1. Why do you think Roughgarden chose to open her discussion by focusing on bighorn sheep?
2. What does Roughgarden achieve by establishing that studies she cites were conducted by the U.S. Department of Agriculture? She implies that these studies could have been passed over for federal funding. Why might Congress hesitate to fund research on the sexual orientation of animals?
3. After focusing eleven paragraphs on sheep, Roughgarden then introduces many other species in paragraphs 13–16. What is the rhetorical impact of listing so many species in a row?
4. In your opinion, how appropriate is language such as "straight" and "gay" when discussing animals?
5. When discussing sexuality as a biologist, Roughgarden must refer to body parts and how they are used. How successfully does she do so? Is she more graphic than she needs to be?
6. In paragraphs 30 and 34, Roughgarden uses "hunch," "doubt," and "suspect." Do words such as these enhance or diminish her authority as a writer?
7. Why do you think Roughgarden structures her discussion so that she focuses on primates only after discussing other mammals?
8. What does Roughgarden achieve by including a numbered list in paragraph 39?
9. To what extent does Roughgarden's work challenge standard assumptions about evolution?
10. In your opinion, does Roughgarden's status as a transgendered person have any relevance to her research?

SUGGESTIONS FOR WRITING

1. Research on one of the species that Roughgarden discusses, and then write an essay that confirms or challenges Roughgarden's explanation of same-sex sexuality.
2. Toward the end of this selection, Roughgarden refers to the debate about whether homosexuality is an inherited trait. Research work on "gay genes," and explain what you discover.
3. Write an explanation of "evolution" that establishes how scientists view this concept and why it is sometimes questioned on religious grounds.

LINKS

■ Within the Book

In "Women's Brains," (pages 214–219) Stephen Jay Gould uses science to explain an erroneous belief in the nineteenth century.

■ Elsewhere in Print

Darwin, Charles. *The Origin of Species.* 1859. New York: Gramercy, 1995.

Dixon, Alan. *Primate Sexuality: Comparative Studies in the Prosimians, Monkeys, Apes, and Humans.* New York: Oxford UP, 1999.

Larson, Edward. *Evolution: The Remarkable History of a Scientific Theory.* New York: Modern, 2004.

Hamer, Dean. *Science and Desire: The Gay Gene and the Biology of Behavior.* New York: Touchstone, 1995.

Marks, Jonathan. *What it Means to be 98% Chimpanzee: Apes, People, and Their Genes.* Berkeley: U of California P, 2003.

Stein, Edward. *The Science, Theory, and Ethics of Sexual Orientation.* New York: Oxford UP, 2001.

Zuk, Marlene. *Sexual Statistics: What We Can and Can't Learn about Sex from Animals.* Berkeley: U of California P, 2003.

■ Online

www.mhhe.com/motives

Click on "More Resources" then "Writing to Explain Information."

■ ■ ■

4

Writing to Evaluate Something

When you are trying to decide whether you want to buy a wool sweater or a cotton one, when you bet your brother that your team will win the big game this weekend, when you decide which dictionary to buy or which candidate to vote for—when you do any of these things, you are *evaluating*. Evaluating means thinking critically so that you can make intelligent choices—and, when you make your evaluation public, influence others to accept your judgments.

Evaluation requires that you determine the nature or the quality of what you are judging. For instance, if you decide to consume less caffeine, that decision is probably based on a judgment that caffeine can be bad for you. Your purchase of a name-brand lawn mower rather than a store brand rests on your evaluation of the quality of the two brands to assure yourself that you will have a reliable, well-made machine; in this situation, your concern is with quality. Evaluation also means determining importance, benefit, or worth. For example, importance will be the issue if you are trying to determine which in a long list of tasks you absolutely have to get done before the weekend. You are concerned with benefit if you decide that a course in art history will be more useful to you as an architecture major than will a course in music history. When you buy a house or a car, you will most likely ask yourself if it is worth what you have to pay for it.

In the preceding examples, you are trying to convince yourself of something. But there will be plenty of times when your evaluation must convince someone else: Which supplier should you recommend to your employer? What should you say when asked to write a letter of recommendation? Whose opinion should prevail when a couple disagree about which of two apartments to rent? Addressing situations like these means you have to define your assumptions, anticipate opposition, and draw conclusions.

When writing an evaluation, you also need to assure your readers that you have the credentials to make judgments about the subject you're addressing. Demonstrating that you know what you're talking about is essential if you want your readers to take your evaluation seriously. The more your readers think you know about your subject, the more likely they are to follow your advice. But no matter how knowledgeable you may be, try not to sound as if you have a monopoly on good advice. People can take perverse pleasure in not following the advice of a critic who seems arrogant.

CONSIDERING AUDIENCE

An audience for an evaluation usually has two concerns. If unfamiliar with the material, readers will expect to learn if they could benefit from it or safely forget about it. If familiar with the material, readers will assess whether they agree with what they are reading. When drafting, focus on the first of these concerns; when revising, consider the second. Most of the people who read evaluations are looking to obtain a reliable assessment of a person, product, or service about which they lack adequate information. But since there are also readers who are drawn to evaluations of what is already familiar to them—as in the case of the person who reads a review of a movie she has already seen—considering this second part of your potential audience can help you during revision by prompting you to make sure that you have written accurately.

When writing to evaluate, it is especially important to consider the relationship between your topic and your audience. When pursuing another motive for writing, you can engage the attention of readers simply by writing well. For example, some readers will be drawn to a piece of informative or explanatory writing on a topic that would not normally interest them simply because the writing is so good that the material becomes compelling. This can also happen when writing to evaluate. Someone who is not interested in, say, architecture might end up enjoying the evaluation of a new building merely because the piece is written so well. In other words, a writer can reach an extended audience by using language (and possibly illustrations) to attract readers who are not part of the primary audience—the audience that already has an interest in the topic.

Keep your primary audience in mind when writing. If you end up attracting a secondary audience because you write so well, then that is a bonus. But when you begin by making sure that you have chosen a topic that is well suited for your target audience, you can be confident that your writing will be read by the people most likely to benefit from it. Common sense will help you choose a topic for which there is already an audience or an audience for a topic that you already have in mind. For instance, people who like to dine out will probably be interested in a restaurant review, and people who want to lose weight will probably be interested in a review of a new diet book or fitness center.

You can begin with either the topic or the audience, depending on the context. If you are free to write for an audience of your own choice, then you can begin by choosing a topic that you will enjoy addressing and then write about that topic while envisioning the group of readers most likely to share your interest in that topic. But if you need to write for a specific audience, then you must make sure that your topic is suitable for that audience. For example, if you are writing for an audience of college freshmen, you will be wiser to address a topic like inexpensive restaurants than luxury hotels. Sometimes, however, a specific audience assigns you a topic and indicates what your assessment should provide. At work, for example, you might be required to write a self-assessment that indicates what you have accomplished and what you still hope to achieve—and you understand that this evaluation will be a factor in determining whether you receive a raise or a promotion.

Keep in mind that any audience for an evaluation will expect you to have clear evaluation criteria, to give a reliable assessment of whatever you are evaluating, and to provide enough evidence so that anyone acting upon your advice— whether it be by purchasing a product or undertaking a new experience—will do so with a clear understanding of what is in store. You may enjoy writing an evaluation—as both YiLing Chen-Josephson and Dara Moskowitz seem to do in this chapter—but whatever pleasure you have in praising or damning should be subordinate to satisfying the needs of your audience. Assume that your readers will take your evaluation seriously and be capable of letting you know if they feel that you have misled them.

PLANNING YOUR ESSAY

When you are ready to choose a subject for evaluation, consider what you have some experience in and knowledge of, as well as what you are interested in. If you are knowledgeable about a subject, you will usually have a good idea of what criteria people use when evaluating it. This knowledge will help you focus on how to make your evaluation satisfy your readers' needs. For example, if you recently bought a stationary exercise bicycle for home use and think that your written evaluation of the available models will help others decide which one to buy, make sure you don't base your evaluation only on which bicycle is cheapest. Readers also need to know what they are getting for their money. Report what you know about features such as mileage counters and tension adjustment; then discuss how well different bikes perform and how likely they are to hold up under use. Otherwise, a reader may wind up with a bicycle that cost less because it lacked important features or because it was difficult to use.

If you have the time to do research, writing an evaluation can be an excellent way to prepare for a decision you need to make. Thus, if you are planning to buy exercise equipment but cannot decide between a stationary bicycle and a stair stepper, you can use evaluation as a way to decide. Careful shoppers go through this process routinely. They may visit a number of stores, question salespeople and friends who have experience with the product, and—if the purchase is large—search for information on the World Wide Web or go to the library and consult one or more of the magazines available for consumers. Writing an evaluation of a product you expect to purchase is a way of discovering and reporting the results of this process.

In this chapter, an evaluation by YiLing Chen-Josephson offers a clear example of how to rate competing products for the same markets—in this case, the kind of gossip magazines that you can find when standing in line at a grocery store. Similarly, a review by Dara Moskowitz shows how an evaluation can help diners decide whether to try a specific restaurant and, if they go, what to order. But, as the article by Jonathan Rowe demonstrates, the evaluation of a product does not have to focus on the cost and features of the product itself. In "Reach Out and Annoy Someone," Rowe evaluates cell phones by discussing the consequences of using them in public. He finds that cell phones have harmful effects regardless of which brand is being used—a very different approach from evaluating specific models to determine which to buy. You could write an evaluation along these lines by deciding to discuss the effects of such products as coffee, computer games, or sport utility vehicles.

Writing to evaluate can also help readers understand the merits of a particular activity or the product that results from that activity. In "She: Portrait of the Essay as a Warm Body," Cynthia Ozick discusses why she likes to read and write essays. She is not trying to convince readers that one essayist is better than another or that writing essays is better than writing fiction. Instead, she focuses on why essays are worth reading and writing by offering a positive evaluation of what can be accomplished through this kind of nonfiction. If you are interested in writing an evaluation along these lines, you might consider subjects such as the merits of a particular type of music or the benefits of studying chemistry. You could also address subjects such as these when writing to understand experience (as in Chapter 1). But in that case, the emphasis would be on experience involving the subject rather than the subject itself. In "Levi's" (pages 55–58), for example, Marilyn Schiel focuses on what a pair of jeans meant to her as a child—which is different from evaluating the quality of Levi's or evaluating the impact of jeans on American culture. When writing to evaluate, you need to focus on the subject itself—as you would when writing to report information or to explain information (see Chapters 2 and 3, repectively). Your experience with that subject may be part of the evaluation you compose, but you should emphasize the subject rather than yourself (unless you are the subject, as in a self-assessment required by a teacher or employer).

Writers like Moskowitz, Rowe, and Ozick all use a kind of *cause-and-effect analysis* (see pages 178–179) when evaluating their subjects. Other situations require other strategies. But whatever your subject, you should examine what kind of information you have about it and assess whether you have to do research. Information is essential, because you must support your evaluation with specific evidence. For example, when evaluating the career of Johnny Cash, Francis Davis notes that Cash won a Grammy, received several awards from the Country Music Association, and composed a song that "reached No. 1 on the country charts"—in addition to mentioning various tributes that were offered upon Cash's death. Evidence such as this supports Davis's own favorable assessment of Cash as a major force in American music. Moreover, anyone reading this evaluation is likely to recognize that Davis has spent many hours listening to Cash's recordings. Similarly, Susanna Kaysen needed to obtain copies of her medical records and consult a medical handbook to evaluate the accuracy of the diagnosis she received when hospitalized for mental illness. Whatever strategy you need to employ when preparing to write an evaluation, be sure to present readers with enough information so they can decide whether your judgment is worth taking seriously.

A good way to begin an evaluation is to think about your subject analytically. Here is a basic process for using analysis to plan an evaluation:

- Divide your subject by identifying its major components. For example, if you are evaluating a movie, you might address plot, acting, and special effects. Or if you are evaluating a book, you can judge it according to content, style, and organization.

- Consider what information you have (or can obtain) to discuss the divisions you have identified.

- Ask yourself which of these divisions are most likely to be important to readers, and consider whether you have overlooked any important part of your subject that your readers would probably want information about. Unless you are writing for your own benefit, eliminate any division that seems to be a personal interest unlikely to concern other readers.

- Decide whether to discuss all the important divisions you have identified or to focus on only one if you have enough information about it and feel sure that you would be focusing on something important. An evaluation of a restaurant, for example, can be limited to a discussion of its food (although you would probably end up subdividing that subject somehow—according to appetizers, entrées, and desserts or according to selection, presentation, and taste).

When planning an evaluation, you should also consider how strongly you feel about your subject. Some people believe that you should always write about something you have a real investment in, because your enthusiasm will make your writing lively. Others think that this approach leads to one-sided evaluation. If you've just bought a new car and really love it, you may lack the objectivity to evaluate it fairly. But if you've driven the car for a year and still love it, you probably have enough distance from your purchase to offer a balanced judgment. One of the strengths of Dara Moskowitz's "The Sad Comedy of Really Bad Food" is that she looks for things to praise even though she's disappointed by the restaurant she's reviewing. When you read her evaluation, you will find that she made several visits to the restaurant in question to make sure that her evaluation was fair.

DEFINING YOUR CRITERIA

Effective, accurate evaluations are not the result of whim; they are based on standards that most people agree with, that the authority of the writer bolsters, or that can be independently verified. Evaluation requires you to make the criteria you use for judging absolutely clear. In "Sweet and Lowdown," Yiling Chen-Josephson establishes her criteria within a separate section before moving on to apply these criteria to various tabloids and magazines. Moreover, she uses boldface to identify key words: "reliability," "exclusives," "subject matter," "story quality," "value," and "fun"—after each of which she explains what she has in mind.

In many cases, a writer's criteria are implied by the evaluation without being specifically stated. When reviewing a restaurant in Minneapolis, Dara Moskowitz complains about the service, the atmosphere, and the quality of most of the food she sampled—while praising the wine list and several desserts. From this, we can infer that she appreciates being offered a nice selection of wine and desserts but places greater emphasis on service, atmosphere, and the quality of the menu as a whole—hence her negative review of the restaurant. In other words, her implicit criteria are that a restaurant should offer good food and good service in a pleasant setting. Another writer with different criteria (such as how big the servings are or whether the restaurant draws a fashionable crowd) could come to a different assessment of the same place. As a general rule, *subjective* criteria, which are based on someone's values, are easier to challenge than *objective* criteria, which can be confirmed through empirical testing. But an evaluation based on subjective criteria can be persuasive if the evaluator seems well informed and fair-minded. (For additional information on persuasion, see pages 451–465.)

Whether subjective or objective, criteria should be appropriate for your audience. Suppose that your criterion for evaluating a magazine for entrepreneurs is that each issue should include an article on how to dress in the workplace. This criterion is inappropriate because entrepreneurs are more likely to be interested in how to acquire capital, attract clients, and generate profits. Similarly, if you base your judgment of stocks on which ones will double your money the fastest, your standard is inappropriate for advising retirees whose primary interest in stocks involves securing a safe income. Or to take another example, if you are evaluating local housing for an audience of college students who want to party, you will not want to rate housing higher because playgrounds and day care facilities are available, whereas that information could be vital for married couples or single parents. You should set criteria you think your readers will agree with—or at least will not reject.

Examine your criteria and ask yourself if they justify the evaluation you plan to make. You may be furious at one of the local apartment complexes for charging you two months' rent as a deposit because you have a pet, but your sense of having been victimized is not necessarily a legitimate criterion for giving that complex a negative rating in your guide to local housing. It would be much better simply to state the policy; perhaps other prospective tenants would not object to such a high deposit—or might even approve of it. Base your evaluation of the apartment complex on more objective criteria. For example, what is the rent per square foot? Are the apartments furnished? What appliances are included? Is there a fireplace? What kind of storage is available? Is there access to a swimming pool and party facility? Have there been complaints about how the complex is maintained? What about late-payment policies?

You also need to consider the kind of evidence that will persuade your audience to accept your evaluation. If you want the single students on campus to accept your negative evaluation of the apartment complex with the high deposit for pets, you might consider investigating what the management's policies about parties are, whether guests can use the pool, and how management handles summer sublets. If these policies are strict, single students should be informed. They may choose to rent elsewhere even though there is a great party room, every unit has a fireplace, and the rent is reasonable. You should offer evidence according to what you think your readers expect to find out and how knowledgeable they are. Rarely will any subject elicit the kind of universal agreement that will permit you to use the same criteria and information for all audiences.

Readers expect to find enough information to reconstruct the reasoning you used to arrive at your evaluation. Be sure to provide adequate information for readers unfamiliar with the subject you are evaluating. When readers are unfamiliar with a subject, a thorough evaluation can take many pages. But whatever the level of expertise your audience possesses, you are responsible for making sure they understand the information you give them—and the criteria you are using to interpret that information—so the judgment you reach will be both clear and credible.

ORGANIZING YOUR ESSAY

However you choose to proceed, you should state your judgment clearly and place it prominently. It is your main point and, depending on other decisions you make, may appear near the beginning or the end of your piece. Generally, it is useful to put it in both places. By placing it near the beginning, you prepare readers for the conclusion you will draw; by placing it near the end, you demonstrate how specific evidence has led to that conclusion. It is also usually wise to show your readers that you have considered both the strengths and the weaknesses of your subject. To do so, you may wish to adapt the following classical pattern for evaluations:

- Present your subject. (This discussion includes background information, description, and acknowledgment of weaknesses.)
- State your criteria. (If your criteria are controversial, be sure to justify them.)
- Make your judgment. (State it as clearly and emphatically as possible.)
- Give your reasons. (Be sure to present evidence for each one.)
- Refute opposing evaluations. (Let your reader know you have given thoughtful consideration to opposing views, when they exist.)
- State your conclusion. (Restate your judgment, and make recommendations for improvement if your evaluation is negative.)

Notice that the refutation comes near the end, after the judgment is well established. An alternative strategy is to refute opposing evaluations early in the essay; this strategy can be especially effective when opposing views are already widely held and you intend to advance a new point of view. In this case, recognizing views that your audience may already hold can clear the way for a fresh evaluation.

When deciding how to present your evaluation, you should also consider the possibility of developing your position through the use of *comparison or contrast*. Comparative judgments focus on similarities, and contrasting judgments focus on differences, but the two can be combined. In any comparison or contrast, you must find a point of significant similarity between what you are evaluating and another item. In this chapter, YiLing Chen-Josephson compares and contrasts different gossip magazines, and Cynthia Ozick contrasts the nature of an essay with the nature of fiction. In an essay of your own, you might incorporate comparison or contrast into almost any plan that you choose for organizing your ideas.

In some cases, however, you may find it helpful to organize an entire essay in terms of a comparison or contrast. Doing so is especially useful when the purpose of your evaluation is to help you—and your audience—choose between different products or options, as in deciding which of two cars to buy or which of two schools to attend. This strategy can also be useful when evaluating the abilities of different people, as in deciding which of two teachers to recommend or determining which of two senators is doing the better job of representing your state. If you choose comparison or contrast as the primary means for organizing your evaluation, you might use one of two common patterns to organize your evaluation: subject by subject or point by point.

When two subjects are evaluated in a *subject-by-subject pattern,* the first subject is discussed thoroughly before the second is discussed at all. In a *point-by-point pattern,* both subjects are discussed throughout the essay, with the discussion organized around different aspects (or points) of evaluation. If you want to evaluate the pizza served at two local restaurants, for example, you might use a subject-by-subject approach and complete your discussion of the first restaurant before beginning your discussion of the second. But if you are comparing two subjects with many components, then you might do a point-by-point comparison. A comparison of two similar cars made by different manufacturers might be organized along the following lines: standard features of both vehicles, available options for both vehicles, performance of both vehicles, and reliability of both vehicles. This kind of organization has the advantage of not requiring readers to keep the whole subject in mind, but the frequent switches between the subjects compared can sometimes seem choppy. Only one switch is necessary in subject-by-subject comparison, but readers must keep a whole subject in mind. For a long or complicated comparison, this can become difficult.

Comparison and contrast are by no means limited to evaluations; elsewhere in this book, you will find writers using these strategies for other purposes. But comparison and contrast are especially useful for evaluation, because placing two subjects alongside each other can lead to a better understanding of both—and can often help you decide whether one is superior. If offered two different jobs, both of which seem attractive, for example, you can probably clarify which is preferable by comparing them carefully.

It would be a mistake, however, to assume that evaluation must always lead to a rating of some sort. Although criticism usually leads to a judgment on quality or worth, it is also concerned with improving knowledge of what is being evaluated. In this chapter, "God's Lonely Man" by Francis Davis provides the clearest example of how evaluation can be informative. Although he focuses on the work of Johnny Cash and offers many details about that work, Davis—a nationally respected music critic—also locates Cash within the history of twentieth-century music. Thus, he provides a context in which Cash's achievement can be more easily understood and introduces the names of other performers whom readers may decide to investigate. A critic reviewing a book or movie in a newspaper is expected to give the work an overall rating, because that is what newspaper readers most want to know: Is this work worth my time and money? But evaluation isn't always a matter of getting people to do (or not do) something. Sometimes it's simply devoted to getting people to see something that they might otherwise miss, as in Cynthia Ozick's tribute to the essay. Understanding that there is more to something than we had realized can lead us to reappraise our valuation of it, even if we do not need to make a choice or decide on a specific action (as, for example, by reading more essays or buying gossip magazines).

As we have seen, motives for writing can overlap. You will usually need to report and explain information to show readers how you reached a particular judgment—and if you want your evaluation to be persuasive, you may need to draw on some of the strategies discussed in the introduction to Chapter 7. The selections that follow in this chapter will give you a sense of different types of evaluation. As you read them, try to evaluate the extent to which each succeeds in accomplishing what it sets out to do.

TIPS FOR READING AND WRITING EVALUATIONS

When Reading

- ▨ Consider whether the writer has clearly defined evaluation criteria and applied them appropriately.
- ▨ Decide whether these evaluation criteria are sufficient for providing you with an assessment suited for your own needs. If the criteria seem irrelevant to your own standards, consider how you differ from the audience for which the evaluation was originally written and whether you could benefit from modifying the way you make judgments of your own.
- ▨ Decide whether the writer is qualified to be evaluating the material in question.
- ▨ Determine if the writer has provided sufficient evidence to support any claims made in the evaluation.
- ▨ Consider whether the evaluation would motivate you to undertake any action.

When Writing

- ▨ Choose a topic that will interest the audience you have in mind.
- ▨ Select evaluation criteria that are appropriate for both the topic and the audience. For example, there is no need to evaluate the wine lists at fancy restaurants if you are writing for an audience that is interested in fast food.
- ▨ If evaluating more than one product or service, apply your evaluation criteria consistently.
- ▨ Be sure to give adequate and fair attention to whatever you choose to evaluate.
- ▨ Organize your ideas so that readers can easily locate your judgment and see where you support that judgment. For example, readers may expect to find your overall assessment in the first or last paragraph—or established visually with stars or numbers, as in a movie review.

REACH OUT AND ANNOY SOMEONE

Jonathan Rowe

Cell phones seem almost everywhere these days—in schools, offices, airports, restaurants, cars, and buses, and on the street. How do all these cell phones affect the quality of public life? Jonathan Rowe believes that increasing reliance on cell phones has had negative effects on both the users of these phones and the people who are near them. If you enjoy the use of your own cell phone, you may think his evaluation is too one-sided. But as you prepare to read, understand that Rowe chose to focus on the social consequences of cell phone use—not the convenience of such phones for the individuals who use them.

Rowe is a contributing editor of The Washington Monthly, *which published "Reach Out and Annoy Someone" in 2000. He has also written for the* Christian Science Monitor *and* The Atlantic. *Currently, he is a senior fellow at Redefining Progress, which describes itself as "a public policy organization that seeks to ensure a more sustainable and socially equitable world for our children and our children's children."*

In the latter 1990s, in the midst of the high-tech boom, I spent a lot of time in a coffee shop in the theater district in San Francisco. It was near Union Square, the tourist hub, and I observed a scene play out there time and time again. Mom is nursing her mocha. The kids are picking at their muffins, feet dangling from their chairs. And there's Dad, pulled back slightly from the table, talking into his cell phone.

I would watch the kids' faces, vacant and a little forlorn, and wonder what happens to kids whose parents aren't there even when they are. How can we expect kids to pay attention if we are too busy to pay attention to them? Peter Breggin, the psychiatrist, says much "attention deficit disorder" is really "dad deficit disorder." Maybe he's right.

As I sat there, I would think, too, about the disconnect between the way we talk about the economy in the U.S. and the way we actually experience it. The media were enthusing daily about the nation's record "expansion," and here were these kids staring off into space. It was supposed to be a "communications revolution," and yet here, in the technological epicenter, the members of this family were avoiding one another's eyes.

With technology in particular, we can't seem to acknowledge the actual content of our economic experience; and we discuss the implications only within a narrow bandwidth of human concern. Is there a health risk? Might the thing cause cancer? That's about it with cell phones, computers, genetic engineering, and a host of other new developments. As a result, we must await the verdict of the doctors to find out whether we are permitted to have qualms or reservations. Jacob Needleman, the contemporary philosopher, says that we Americans are "metaphysically repressed," and the inability to discuss the implications of technology—except in bodily or stock market terms—is a case in point.

I don't discount the significance of cancer. But there is something missing   5
from a discussion that can't get beyond the most literal and utilitarian concerns. Actually, some of the problems with cell phones aren't at all squishy or abstract. If you've been clipped by a car tooling around the corner while the driver sits gabbing, cell phone in hand, then you are aware of this. The big problem, of course, is the noise. For sheer intrusiveness, cell phones rank with mega-amp car stereos and political commercials, and they are harder to escape.

We all know the drill. First the endearing beep, which is like an alarm clock going off at 5:30 A.M. Then people shout into the things, as though they are talking across the Cross Bronx Expressway. It's become a regular feature at movies and ball games, restaurants and parks. I've heard the things going off in men's room stalls. They represent more than mere annoyances. Cell phones affect life in ways that are, I suspect, beyond the capacity of the empirical mind to grasp.

Travel is an example. Thomas Carlyle once advised Anthony Trollope° to use travel as a time to "sit still and label his thoughts." For centuries, travel played this quiet role. I have a hunch that the eloquence and depth of this nation's founders had partly to do with their mode of travel. Madison, Jefferson, and the others had that long ride to Philadelphia in which to sort out their thoughts and work over their sentences in their minds. There was time in which thought could expand; we can hear the echoes today in the spaciousness and considered quality of such documents as the *Federalist Papers*—a quality that political argument today rarely achieves.

In more recent times, trains have served as a link to that kind of travel. I used to look forward to Amtrak rides almost as a sanctuary. They provided precious hours in which to work or read or simply muse without the interruptions of the telephone and office. But now, cell phones have caught up with me. They have turned Amtrak into a horizontal telephone booth; on a recent trip to New York my wife and I were besieged by cell phones and their cousins, high-powered Walkmen, literally on all sides. The trip, which used to be a pleasure, has become one long headache.

I wrote the president of Amtrak to tell him this. I tried to be constructive. There is a real opportunity here for Amtrak to get ahead of the curve, I said. Why not provide "Quiet Cars" the way they provided No Smoking cars when smoking first became an issue? Amtrak could give riders a choice, which is what America is supposed to be about—and which Amtrak's main competitors, the airlines, cannot do. This seemed like a no-lose proposition.

°*Thomas Carlyle:* Scottish historian and social critic (1795–1881) who influenced many important thinkers in the nineteenth century. *Anthony Trollope:* British novelist (1815–1882) best known for *Barchester Towers* and *The Warden.*

The yakkers could yak, others could enjoy the quiet, and Amtrak could have a PR coup. (In a just world, the cell phoners would have to sit together in Noise Cars, but I was trying to be accommodating.)

The argument seemed pretty convincing. As the weeks passed, I imagined my letter circulating at the highest levels. Perhaps I'd even be called in as a consultant. Now that I have the reply, I'm not holding my breath. But the reasons that Amtrak offered for inaction are worth a few moments, since they suggest how quickly a technology invokes its own system of rationalization.

For example, the letter said that Amtrak does not want to inconvenience the "responsible" users of cell phones. That's typical; try to isolate a few aberrant users and so legitimate the rest. But cell phones are like cigarettes in this respect—they are intrusive when used normally, as intended. They beep like a seat belt warning or play a tinny melody like a musical toilet seat. People usually shout into them. They produce secondhand noise, just as cigarettes produce secondhand smoke; and from the standpoint of the forced consumer of this noise, the only responsible use is non-use.

Then the letter turned the issue upside down. "We hesitate to restrict responsible users of cell phones," it said, "especially since many customers find train travel to be an ideal way to get work done." But that is exactly why cell phones should be restricted—because many travelers are trying to get work done. For one thing, the notion that people are busily working on cell phones is New Economy hype. I have been a coerced eavesdropper on more conversations than I could count. I have listened to executives gab about their shopping hauls and weekend conquests. I once had to endure, between Philadelphia and New York, an extended brag from an associate sports agent regarding the important people he was meeting. It is not often that I hear anyone actually discussing work.

But more importantly, consider the assumption here. We have two people who arguably are trying to get some work done. There's the cell phone user, who wants to make noise. And there's myself (and probably numerous others), who would appreciate a little quiet. Why does the noise automatically take precedence over the quiet? Why does the polluter get first dibs on the air?

This is where the trail starts to get warm, I think. There is something about technology that enables it to take front seat in any situation it enters; which is to say, there is something in ourselves that seeks to give it this seat. A Maine essayist by the name of John Gould once noted this about the ordinary telephone. He was up on his roof one day when his wife called to him about something. "Later," he said, "Can't you see I'm working?" Later came, and this time the phone rang. Gould scrambled down the ladder in a frantic attempt to get to that phone.

Afterwards he reflected upon what had happened. His wife could wait, he thought, but the phone rang with the authority of Mussolini in a bad mood. Most of us probably have had this experience. We've been making a purchase when the phone rang and the clerk dropped us cold and got into a long conversation on the phone. Or perhaps we had a visitor in our own

COMPANION TEXT *Saved, and Enslaved, by the Cell*

Concerns about the cell phone continue to surface. The following report appeared in the New York Times *in October 2004.*

First in phone-company marketing, and now in popular culture, the cellular phone has taken on the aura of an amulet of safety, an indispensable lifeline: wherever you are, you can always reach help. . . .

There is no question that instant access to a phone can save lives. People report fires and robberies, heart attacks and car crashes; parents keep tabs on children; grown children stay in touch with elderly parents. Knowing that you can always call for help in an emergency makes people feel safer.

But they also tether people more closely and constantly to others, and in recent months a growing number of experts have identified and begun to study a distinct downside in that: cellphone use may be making us less autonomous and less capable of solving problems on our own, even when the answers are right in front of us.

According to Christine Rosen, a senior editor at the journal New Atlantis and the author of "Our Cellphones, Ourselves," a recent article exploring the social effects of the mobile phone, the ease of obtaining instant advice encourages cellphone users to respond to any uncertainty, crucial or trivial, by dialing instead of deciding. The green sweater or the blue, pizza or Chinese, the bridge or the tunnel—why take responsibility for making up your own mind when you can convene a meeting in a minute?

"Cellphones foster a curious dependency," Ms. Rosen said. "The cellphone erodes something that is being obliterated in American society: self-reliance."

She offered an example. "I was taught how to change a tire so I can get a spare on and get to a garage," she said. "But who changes a tire now? You just call AAA."

Oddly, being able to keep constant track of friends and family can introduce a whole new kind of insecurity. For a parent, a call to a cellphone-carrying child may bring reassurance, but when the child doesn't answer the phone, the parent starts thinking the worst. . . .

"We are less self-reliant than ever, not because we are less independent, but because we are so much more connected," said Mark Federman, chief strategist at the McLuhan Program in Culture and Technology at the University of Toronto.

That cellphones help "reverse independence into dependence" is neither good nor bad, Mr. Federman said, just a natural outgrowth of technological innovation. Reflection, introspection, thinking for yourself—these tools of the mind, he said, exist separately from any technology.

There are also those who argue that cellphones ultimately empower rather than debilitate. We can make more intelligent choices and avoid more mistakes, they say, when we can quickly gather information and consult others.

"If you are left to your own, what would you think about?" said Kenneth J. Gergen, a professor of psychology at Swathmore College, . . ."You have to have other voices, reports and news. The best decisions are made in a whole set of dialogues."

Ken Belson

office and interrupted the conversation to pick up the phone. Whatever is happening, the telephone comes first. Call waiting ratchets up the authority structure like a dictatorship that adds minions at the top. Now there are intrusions upon the intrusions; how many of us hear that click and think, "Oh, just let it ring."

What is it about these things that makes us so obedient, and so oblivious to that which lies outside them—such as actual people? I once asked a man who was bellowing into a cell phone in the coffee shop in San Francisco why he was talking so loudly. A bad connection, he said. It had not crossed his mind that anything else mattered at that moment. Like computers and television, cell phones pull people into their own psychological polar field, and the pull is strong. I've watched people complete a conversation, start to put the thing away, and then freeze. They sit staring at it, as though trying to think of someone else to call. The phone is there. It demands to be used, almost the way a cigarette demands to be smoked. Does the person own the cell phone, or is it the other way around?

And what does that suggest about where this "communications revolution" is taking us? When I was in Hong Kong a year and a half ago, it was becoming a cell-phone hell. The official statistics said there was one phone for every two people, but it often felt like two for one. They were everywhere; the table scenes in the splendid food courts in the high-rise malls were San Francisco to the second or third power. At a table with four people, two or three might be talking on the phone. You'd see a couple on a date, and one was talking on the phone.

In a way, I could understand the fixation. Hong Kong is crowded almost beyond belief. It makes parts of Manhattan feel like Kansas, and I suspect that a cell phone offers an escape, a kind of crack in space. It is an entrance to a realm in which you are the center of attention, the star. Access becomes a status symbol in itself. A lawyer friend of mine there described the new ritual at the start of business meetings. Everyone puts their cell phone on the conference table, next to their legal pad, almost like a gun. My power call against yours, *gweilo* (Chinese for foreigner; literally "ghost"). The smallest ones are the most expensive and therefore have the most status.

In places like Hong Kong, moreover, most people live in cramped quarters, which means consumption must take less space-consuming forms. That's all understandable. To a lesser degree, such considerations apply in places such as Washington and New York.

There is something lonely about a wired world. The more plugged in *20* everyone else is, the more we feel we have to be there too. But then effect becomes cause. The very thing that pulls us away from live public spaces begins to make those spaces uninhabitable. It is the pollution of the aural commons, the enclosure of public space by giant telecommunications firms, and the result is to push us all towards private space—if we can afford it.

This is technological Reaganism, a world in which personal desires are all that matters and to hell with everything else. So everything else starts to go to hell. The libertarian dogmatics of the computer crowd thus become self-fulfilling prophecies. But there's this, too. Not only are they saying, "Get out of my face." They are also saying, "I can't stop myself. I'm hooked." It is a communications revolution all right, but one that requires psychologists and anthropologists to understand. Economists just don't get it. They couch these events in the language of Locke and Smith—of rational people seeking a rational self-interest. But in reality it's the old dark stuff: the vagrant passions and attachments of the human heart.

But forgive me. I forgot. This is the longest economic expansion on record we are talking about here, so we aren't supposed to get too deep. So I'll just close with a prediction. Secondhand noise is going to become a bigger issue in the next decade than secondhand smoke was in the last. It will be part of the big second wave of environmentalism—the fight against cognitive pollution, the despoiling of the aural and visual commons, whether by cell phones and Walkmen or by advertising everywhere.

It's going to be a wrenching battle, but I predict at least one early victory. Quiet cars on Amtrak within five years. Meanwhile, I have my eye on a company in Israel, called NetLine Technologies, that makes small portable devices to block cell phones. Technically, they are illegal, and I doubt that more technology ultimately is the answer. But they do raise a useful question. If some people can use technology to pollute the air we share, why can't other people use technology to clean it up again?

QUESTIONS FOR DISCUSSION

1. Rowe claims that Americans rarely discuss the implications of technology. Do you agree?
2. Why does Rowe believe that cell phones "represent more than mere annoyances"? Why is the public use of cell phones problematic?
3. In paragraph 15, Rowe notes that salespeople sometimes take phone calls even when they are already working with someone in the store—giving the caller priority over the shopper. Has this ever happened to you? Why might salespeople work this way?
4. How would you respond if someone you were dating took a call when you were having dinner together in a restaurant?
5. Why can technology become addictive?
6. How fair is Rowe's assessment of cell phones? Do you think he should have discussed how cell phones can make a positive contribution to society? Or was he wise to focus on the negative aspects of these phones?

SUGGESTIONS FOR WRITING

1. In paragraphs 7 and 8, Rowe comments on how noisy travel has become. Consider your own travel experience, especially trips made by bus, train, or plane. Then write an evaluation of a specific journey.

2. Imagine that you are writing for an audience interested in purchasing a cell phone. Compare three cell phones that are widely used today, evaluating their quality and value.
3. Think about how the public use of the Walkman and other portable CD players affects social life. Write an evaluation in which you appraise both the positive and negative aspects of this form of technology.

LINKS

■ Within the Book

For a humorous essay on technology, see Patricia Volk's "Technology Makes Me Mad" (pages 577–578).

■ Elsewhere in Print

Carlo, George L., and Martin Schram. *Cell Phones: Invisible Hazards in the Wireless Age.* New York: Carroll, 2001.

Carter, Stephen. *Civility: Manners, Morals, and the Etiquette of Democracy.* New York: Basic, 1998.

Dresser, Norine. *Multicultural Manners: New Rules of Etiquette for a Changing Society.* New York: Wiley, 1996.

Forni, P. M. *Choosing Civility: The Twenty-Five Rules of Considerate Conduct.* New York: St. Martin's, 2003.

Pachter, Barbara, and Susan Magee. *The Jerk with the Cell Phone: A Survival Guide for the Rest of Us.* New York: Marlowe, 2004.

Post, Peggy. *Emily Post's Etiquette,* 16th ed. New York: Harper, 1997.

Post, Peter. *Essential Manners for Men; What to Do, When to Do It, and Why.* New York: Harper, 2003.

■ Online

www.mhhe.com/motives

Click on "More Resources" then "Writing to Evaluate Something."

■ ■ ■

SWEET AND LOWDOWN

YiLing Chen-Josephson

Even if you have never checked out the cover of a gossip magazine while standing in line at the supermarket, or leafed through an issue of People *while waiting in a doctor's office, you may enjoy the following evaluation of magazines and tabloids that focus on the weird and the celebrated. First published in* Slate, *an online magazine, in 2004, "Sweet and Lowdown" is organized so that it can be easily read on the screen as well as on the page. As you read it, note how the author provides clear evaluation criteria and then applies those criteria to the publications she reviews.*

A graduate of Harvard University, where she won the Thomas Hoopes Prize for the best undergraduate thesis and the Joan Gray Untermyer Prize for poetry, YiLing Chen-Josephson worked on the editorial staff of the New York Review of Books *before becoming a full-time writer. About her writing she states: "I like that writing makes me slow down. I sometimes feel that I can read something or experience something and not really have taken it in; when I'm writing, though, I can't afford to skim. For me writing is not so much about inventing a scenario out of whole cloth as it is about looking so closely—or slowly—at the things that are actually in front of me that they become transformed; my writing is more like a process of alchemy than imagination. I especially like writing about things that surround me but that don't normally receive my attention. This slowness is a bit of a double-edged sword; ideas come to me slowly and, once I have one, the writing itself is slow-going. I need to spend quite a bit of time with a topic before I feel I have enough of a foothold to write about it."*

Superficiality, envy, cattiness, schadenfreude, mockery, and melodrama: I normally try hard to deplore them all—except when I'm buying a celebrity gossip magazine, in which case they are just the ticket. Between tabloids and glossies, there are seven weekly gossip magazines from which to choose my opiate. Tabloids (the *National Enquirer,* the *Globe,* the *National Examiner*) are printed on newsprint and run only sensationalistic stories about celebrities (the majority of whom reached the apex of their fame decades ago), but also pieces on the particularly bad, bizarre, or heartwarming behavior of "real people." They are padded with health tips, crosswords, and photos of readers' babies and, unlike the more legitimate magazines, will pay sources for gossip about the stars. Glossies (*Us Weekly, In Touch, People,* and, after a recent extreme makeover, *Star*) are printed on shinier, thicker paper stock. With the exception of *People,* they focus extensively on celebrities—primarily youthful ones—and their tone is more upbeat, irreverent, and less credulous than their tabloid counterparts.

In the last few years, two developments have changed the landscape of these magazines. The first is that the tabloids (the *Star* included) have all come under the ownership of a single company, American Media Inc. The second is that, while for decades respectful *People* and the lurid tabloids were the only games in town, cheeky *Us Weekly* and its Johnny-come-lately clone, *In Touch*, have begun crowding in on the market share and making the other magazines rethink their strategies. Bonnie Fuller, the editor responsible for the *Us Weekly* approach—an interest not so much in the dark secrets of the stars as in how banal their lives can be, how they're "just like us"—was even wooed away to the American Media empire and charged with remaking *Star* in *Us'* image. But, although all the weeklies are converging on younger, hipper celebrity coverage, there remain important differences in prose styles, perspectives, scopes, and degrees of turpitude.

I spent the last four months reading all of these magazines every week in an attempt to pick the one (OK, two) worth buying regularly. A welcome by-product of the testing was that I finally exhausted my seemingly limitless ability to wring enjoyment, diversion, and procrastination from the lives of the stars and am looking forward to reading something without pictures and exclamation points, preferably a dry philosophical treatise.

MY CRITERIA

Reliability (10 points): This category was, admittedly, somewhat hard to score. Are Demi and Ashton planning a June wedding? Is Sandra Dee drinking herself to death? I have no idea. The best I could do was dock points when a magazine published something that, in the course of the last few months, was subsequently proven false. (Kate Hudson gave birth to a *boy*, not a girl, *In Touch*!) I also frowned on particularly misleading cover questions—the answers to *Star's* "Justin: Cheating on Cameron?" and "Nude *Apprentices*? Will they pose for *Playboy*?" are both revealed inside to be, simply, no—and, worse, misleading cover *statements*. (The *Globe's* cover story on John Kerry's "Sex Disease Scandal—It could keep him out of the White House" turns out to refer only to the fact that he may have had an STD while he was serving in Vietnam.)

Exclusives (10 points: 5 for scoops, 5 for access): Will a magazine be the first to bring you the latest happenings or, at least, the latest news on old happenings (e.g., the *Enquirer's* recent piece—"The Passion of Mel!"—about a woman with whom Mel Gibson allegedly had cheated on his wife—in 1988)? Separately, will celebrities actually grant it interviews?

Subject matter (10 points): Magazines get points for breadth of focus—*Star* covers *The O.C.* starlets *and* Tina Louise of *Gilligan's Island*—and percentage of things covered that are inherently (i.e., to me) interesting: couplings, feuds, scandals, reality TV, "where are they now?" features = interesting; losing weight, having babies, makeovers, whether J. Lo is going to return Ben's ring = not.

Story quality (10 points): Even if I haven't heard about or don't care about the subject of the story, is the prose sensationalistic, wide-eyed, or saucy enough to keep me reading? (For the record, this is not the prose I seek in a non-celebrity magazine.) And is the piece a well-reported exposé I can sink my teeth into, as opposed to something I could skim in a checkout line?

Value (10 points): All of these magazines have flashy headlines designed to pull the reader in, but will it reward more than a casual flip-through? I factored in the presence and interest level of regular features—from fashion coverage and reviews to advice columns and contests.

Fun (10 points): Is the magazine juicy, playful, and irreverent, but still gripping?

Here are the results, from worst to best: *10*

Globe $2.35

Any celebrity magazine is, of course, a guilty pleasure. Usually this guilt is manageably mild and stems from both the opportunity cost (oh insidious concept!) of time spent reading it as well as from supporting a culture of vapid celebrity worship (oh well). Buying the *Globe,* however, ups the guilt quotient a thousandfold. I feel awful paying money for a publication that repeatedly prints the name and full photos of Kobe Bryant's accuser, brandishing pictures of her partying as proof that Kobe must be innocent; that loves to do all it can to tarnish the reputations of politicians, as long as they're Democrats; that is rabid on the scent of any behavior that might be GAY, a word which is never mentioned without being in all caps; and that is just plain mean—it seems one thing to point out that a celebrity has had cosmetic surgery but another altogether to run a photo of Mary Tyler Moore with commentary from a doctor about why she needs *more* work done. So don't give them your money. Now that I've made that clear, I can bemoan the baby I'm throwing out with the bath water: the dish from people who've had sex with stars; the "Globe Trotter" section, in which readers send in pictures of themselves with celebrities ("He smiled his famous smile when I asked if he was indeed THE Donald Rumsfeld"); features like "10 Bloopers and Blunders from *The Passion of the Christ*" ("No. 4: While Mary is holding Jesus after he dies, you can see him blink a few times"); and Ivana Trump—the *Globe's* unlikely advice columnist—gamely fielding questions such as, "My son takes great delight in chopping up frogs, lizards, and anything else that moves . . . Do you think he could have a problem?"

Reliability: 3; Exclusives: 5.5 (scoops: 4.5/access: 1); Subject matter: 6.5; Story quality: 8; Value: 10; Fun: 6; Special REPREHENSIBILITY category: –10.
Total: 29.

National Examiner $2.19

The *Examiner*'s celebrity coverage is mostly limited to people over age 70. ("Janet Leigh's Sad Last Days," "Tony Randall's Brave Last Days," "Jerry Lewis Cheats Death," etc.) A younger star has the best chance of making it in if he or she exhibits behavior that wouldn't have passed muster in the 1940s (a headline trumpeting Gwyneth Paltrow's "baby scandal" turns out to be about how "Old-time Hollywood wouldn't have forgiven an out of wedlock pregnancy") or if he or she is dead (Princess Di, John Ritter). The *Examiner* also has the highest percentage of stories about non-celebrities, most of whom, like the "97 year old [who] has cleaned buses for 70 years and only missed one day of work" are of the vintage of their Hollywood peers. But while even the freshest issue off the press reeks of mothballs, there's good reading material to peruse as a consolation. You might find a story about the unlucky senior who was nearly put to sleep by his vet ("We were just going to euthanize our little Yorkie . . .") or empathize with the problems of readers who write in to "America's Top Psychic Healer." ("Dear Tony: I was a flower child of the '60s, full of love and hope. It's been downhill ever since.") One of my favorite things about the *Examiner,* as well as about the *Globe* and the *Enquirer,* is its ads—from full-page color spreads of Tractor Sounds Wall Clocks to classifieds where you can find everything from a new identity to a service offering "personalized, heartfelt" love letters. ("Send yours and sweetheart's nicknames, reason for letter.")
Reliability: 6.5; Exclusives: 2 (1/1); Subject matter: 2.5; Story quality: 8; Value: 8; Fun: 3.
Total: 30.

People $3.29

People is the only magazine that seems to actually *like* people, celebrity or not. It isn't giddy when announcing breakups (c.f. *Us* and *Star*) or impending deaths (*Globe,* the *Enquirer,* and the *Examiner*). It likes people most when they have just lost weight (in the issues I read in the last few months, covers celebrated the shed pounds—whether by surgery or more old-fashioned methods—of everyone from Drew Barrymore to Randy Jackson), but it will applaud them, sympathize with them, and, above all, profile them for whatever they do. *People* gets the most access to celebrities out of all these magazines, but this is a double-edged sword. It's nice, of course, to read exclusives (even the president sits for an annual interview), and hearing things straight from the horses' mouths makes *People* seem more trustworthy. Celebrities talk to *People,* however, because they know they'll be handled with kid gloves. Exclusive interviews are rarely more than puff pieces—Bush was asked about his "favorite family traditions" and what he puts in his girls' Christmas stockings ("lip gloss, gum, socks, books"). But my main complaint is that its range of coverage can make for a not nearly mindless enough read. Sure, you'll find pages of celebrities and tales of hero pets, but your update on the winner of *Average Joe* is as likely to be followed by a story on John Edwards, or the Madrid bombings, or a teen who died after taking an antidepressant, as by a spotlight on Matt LeBlanc's new baby. The real world impinges too jarringly on the fun.

Reliability: 9.5; Exclusives: 6 (1/5); Subject matter: 4.5; Story quality: 7; Value: 5; Fun: 4.
Total: 36.

In Touch $1.99

In Touch is a poor man's *Us* (see below), literally—$1.99 to *Us'* $3.29—and idiomatically. It covers the same stars and much of the same gossip but in a slightly nicer, slightly blander, and slightly more cringe-worthy manner: Among "secrets" revealed about Christina Aguilera's boyfriend, for example, No. 2 is that "his favorite color is blue," and a regular page has a C-list celebrity talking about which A-list celebrity his or her pet most resembles. ("He's like Ben Affleck," an actress who has had small parts in some recent hit movies says of her Dalmation. "He's killer handsome.") Sometimes, though, *In Touch* gets the balance between earnestness and irreverence so right that a shiver runs down my spine: Each photo in a feature on stars breaking down during TV interviews came accompanied by commentary from a body language expert. "This is really profound crying," the expert decreed about Britney Spears, shown sobbing in a freeze frame from a *Prime Time Live* interview in which she discussed her split from Justin Timberlake. Meanwhile, Jennifer Aniston, who shed tears on *Oprah* over the imminent end of *Friends,* "feels vulnerable but doesn't want to mess up her makeup."

Reliability: 7.5; Exclusives: 5.5 (3/2.5); Subject matter: 7; Story quality: 4; Value: 6; Fun: 7.
Total: 37.

Us Weekly $3.29

Although Bonnie Fuller has left the building, the breezy formula she pioneered remains: *Us* opens by showing celebrities looking glamorous and enviable on the red carpet, points out with fond amusement a few pages later ways in which celebrities are not like us ("they have people who hold umbrellas for them!"), goes on to print paparazzi photos of them getting parking tickets or sneezing into a napkin or buying coffee in the now-widely copied "Stars—They're Just Like Us!" feature, then ends with the "Fashion Police" gleefully weighing in on sartorial missteps. For a star to make it into the lustrous pages of *Us* in the first place, he or she should be 1) young and pretty; 2) an actor, singer, or reality-TV personality; 3) and, ideally, Jessica Simpson, Jennifer Aniston, or Jennifer Lopez, one of whom has been on the cover of

almost every issue I've bought during the past four months. No one in *Us* is ever dying—it helps matters that no one is ever old—and the only bad things that happen are fashion missteps and breakups, the latter of which are conveyed by a perky headline ("It's over!") and a picture of the couple in happier times with a Photoshopped rip down the middle. *Us* is like a sugar rush—enjoyable while it lasts and over quickly. There's not much there there, as Gertrude Stein would have said, but *Us* is a consistent source of entertaining photos, snappy captions ("Faux Lo" is *Us'* term for Ben Affleck's assistant, who has been caught dressing like Ben's ex-fiancee), the latest gossip (*"Apprentice*'s Bill is dating *Bachelor*'s Jen!"), and fun features (a piece on "Fur Lovers vs. Fur Loathers" includes a sidebar of "Fur Flip-Floppers" like Naomi Campbell, who once posed for a PETA ad but has since modeled fur).
Reliability: 8.5; Exclusives: 8 (4.5/3.5); Subject matter: 8.5; Story quality: 3; Value: 6; Fun: 10.
Total: 44.

Star $3.29

Star's transformation from tabloid duckling to magazine swan has not been without its glitches: In the four months since I started reading it, it has tried out four "regular" back pages—from the lame "Public Displays of Consumption," which spotlighted products purchased by celebrities (and was little more than advertisements for said products) to the more hard-hitting "Style Stalkers," in which a star's outfit might get described as "1 part Oompa Loompa + 1 part Michael Jackson" to the current "Hey! Remember Me?" featuring the likes of Susan "Cindy Brady" Olsen and the members of Abba. Its new incarnation swings somewhat vertiginously between the fawning interview of *People* and the starlet-centric frivolity of *Us*. When it attempts the latter, it does so with its dark tabloid roots showing through: Where *Us* did a cover on a slow news week touting the "20 Best Makeovers" (Jennifer Aniston is No. 1, Jessica Simpson is No. 2, Jennifer Lopez No. 4), *Star* entered the fray with "Scariest Hollywood Makeovers!" featuring Farrah ("What has she done?") Fawcett. And while every publication ran a bit about Courtney Love's recent meltdown, *Star* was the only one to print a picture of the random man in Wendy's actually sucking at her breast. *Star* also get points for its breadth and for its often surprising choice of cover stories: Kirstie Alley's weight gain, Cindy Crawford's cheating husband, and a riveting piece on the South-African relatives Charlize Theron is snubbing (including a "dying granny" and a 9-year-old cousin who waits fruitlessly for an autograph as Charlize's limo zips by). If *Star* can work out its kinks, it'll serve as a nice bridge between the vapid world of the glossies and the tawdry world of the tabloids.
Reliability: 7; Exclusives: 7 (4.5/2.5); Subject matter: 9.5; Story quality: 4; Value: 7.5; Fun: 10.
Total: 45.

National Enquirer $2.65

There is something comforting about having your celebrity news delivered to you with no waffling, no wondering, just blithe certainty. And no other magazine cover comes close to the *Enquirer's* exclamation-point-to-question-mark ratio of 31 to 2. (At the other end of the spectrum, *People's* ratio is 18 to 15.) In order to produce the news with such assurance, the *Enquirer's* virtuosic reporters hunt down old yearbooks, find ex-husbands, investigate murders, and demonstrate conclusively that Suzanne Somers has lost weight by comparing two photos of her in the same belt worn on different notches. And I love how the *Enquirer* writes about the furthest fringes of celebrity: those who were once mildly famous ("*Hazel* child star: 'Mold may kill me!'"), those who are famous in the narrowest of arenas ("It took 5 years, a civil suit and a court ruling to say what I've known all along—that I'll always be Mrs. Pennsylvania 1998"), those who are intimate with someone famous ("Zsa Zsa's Hubby hits back at driver in crash"), and those whose work in Hollywood has brought them into contact with many of the famous ("Kenny Rogers ordered fresh salmon for himself, and chicken parmesan for the rest of his crew. But he didn't touch the salmon," dishes a caterer). And I love the *Enquirer's* subscription page, which lures readers with the offer of savings *and* a lucky blue dot, almost exactly like the "simulated" one depicted, only "specially energized and numbered for your good fortune." (Subscribers credit their blue dots with helping them to catch fish, survive car accidents, and, above all, win big at casinos.) If you're looking for more mainstream celebrity news, you're better off with *Us* or *Star,* but you can't beat the *Enquirer* for counterprogramming.
Reliability: 6; Exclusives: 7 (4.5/2.5); Subject matter: 7; Story quality: 9; Value: 10; Fun: 7.5.
Total: 46.5.

QUESTIONS FOR DISCUSSION

1. What is the difference between a tabloid and a glossy? Which would you be most likely to read as "a guilty pleasure"?
2. How clear are Chen-Josephson's evaluation criteria? How effective is her strategy of locating them within separate paragraphs near the beginning of her evaluation?
3. Why do you think Chen-Josephson makes a point of establishing that her reading is not limited to gossip magazines?
4. In her discussion of *Globe,* Chen-Josephson refers to "a culture of vapid celebrity worship." What does she mean by this? Can you provide additional evidence that such a culture exists?
5. As a reader, do you see a difference between *GAY* and *gay?*
6. What kind of questions would be most likely to occur in a "fawning interview"? Why do some reporters confine themselves to questions of this sort, and why are people willing to read the answers?

7. Chen-Josephson organizes her evaluation so that it moves from the magazine with the lowest score, according to her criteria, to the one with the highest. What is the advantage of this strategy? Is there any risk to it?

SUGGESTIONS FOR WRITING

1. Read recent issues of at least three of the magazines discussed in this article, and then write an evaluation focused on how accurate you think Chen-Josephson's assessment is.
2. In her evaluation of *People,* Chen-Josephson notes that it includes news stories unrelated to the lives of celebrities. Examine the last six months of *People,* and then write an assessment of its news coverage.
3. Write an evaluation of another kind of mass-market product that provides "guilty pleasure" within the United States.

LINKS

▪ Within the Book

In "She: Portrait of the Essay as a Warm Body" (pages 295–301), Cynthia Ozick focuses on the pleasures of another kind of reading.

▪ Elsewhere in Print

De la Cruz, Melissa, and Karen Rabinowitz. *How to Become Famous in Two Weeks or Less.* New York: Ballantine, 2003.

Gamson, Joshua. *Claims to Fame.* Berkeley: U of California P, 1994.

Johnson, Sammye, and Patricia Prijatel. *The Magazine from Cover to Cover.* New York: McGraw, 1999.

Marshall, P. David. *Celebrity and Power.* Minneapolis: U of Minnesota P, 1997.

Orth, Maureen. *The Importance of Being Famous.* New York: Holt, 2004.

▪ Online

www.mhhe.com/motives

Click on "More Resources" then "Writing to Evaluate Something."

▪ ▪ ▪

THE SAD COMEDY OF REALLY BAD FOOD

Dara Moskowitz

No matter how many people enjoy eating out, some restaurants never succeed in attracting business. Others become so popular that customers will wait in line for a table. Food critics play a significant role in determining where people choose to go when they're looking for a good meal. Responsible critics visit a restaurant anonymously at least twice before reporting on it to make sure that their experience is representative of what other people can expect. If you have ever been disappointed by bad service or bad food, you may have wished to make your views known to others. Dara Moskowitz does just that in the following review of a fashionable restaurant in Minnesota.

A graduate of Carlton College, Dara Moskowitz is a weekly columnist for the City Pages, *an alternative newspaper published in Minneapolis. Her restaurant reviews have earned her a James Beard Award, as well as multiple awards from the Association of Food Journalists. About her work, she writes: "My philosophy of writing is that readers are bored, stressed, or ignored by the world around them, and I try to give them some-thing when they come to my page—laughs, insights into their world, understanding and solace, or information about a good place to eat. My thinking is this: People don't even have twenty minutes some weeks for their nearests-and-dearests, and if they're going to be generous enough to give you their twenty minutes, you better make it worth their while. . . . Too many writers treat writing like a college term paper—like there's someone being paid to read what you write. Not so, bucky! Nobody cares about you unless you give them a reason to, so get out there and sing, sing, sing."*

Mpls. Cafe
1110 Hennepin Ave., Mpls.; 672-9100

When people find out what I do for a living, they invariably ask whether restaurateurs know when I'm coming. The answer is that, no, they never do, because I want to get the same treatment that any Josie Blow coming in off the street would get. This policy presents several major benefits: First, it makes me feel ethically smug; second, it means I can write off my many wig and prosthetic-nose purchases; and third, it makes me laugh. Or at least it makes me laugh through what would ordinarily be a merely painful meal. For exam-ple, consider the terrible times I've endured recently at the Mpls. Cafe.

There I was, withered to my bones with dehydration. Tumbleweeds rat-tled around in the bone-dry mesa of my water glass. My waiter had appar-ently given up the profession and lit out for a better life. The floor manager was busy giving free drinks to another, louder table, to apologize to them for all the things they wanted that they couldn't have—like food, and for them wine, since no one thought to entrust the floor manager with the key to the tantalizing wine cellar. It had been a long hour since I placed an appetizer order, and I might as well have been waiting for a bus for all the fine dining I was doing. . . . Had I not been a food critic—and in this case, incredibly, dining with *another* local food critic—I would have wept.

Yet instead, when our waiter, apparently having met disappointment on the coasts, returned at one hour 10 minutes (sans H_2O), and asked, incredibly, whether we needed more *bread*—well, that was merely the beginning of the hilarity. I laughed. When I said no, we had plenty of bread, the waiter, not trusting me—and why should he, with me sneaking into his section and marring a life of vagabond adventure—unwrapped the focaccia in its napkin-nest, peeked in at it, rewrapped it, and strode off again to his lair. I laughed so hard I thought I'd rupture something. Actually, I'm still laughing about it. Because it's not just me getting the worst service in the world: It's me getting the worst service in the world while taking notes. I'm Allen Funt in my own private *Candid Camera*. (By the way, focaccia here isn't mere bread, it's "farm-fresh focaccia," freshly hoed up from the focaccia fields.)

When the food eventually arrived, one of the dishes, the Turkey Mediter-ranean Tulips (turkey wings baked and finished on the grill with a jerk sauce, $6.75) was the best thing I had at the Mpls. Cafe. They were smoky, tender, spicy. The Potato Cakes with Balsamic Syrup ($6.25) were dull as paint—simply giant patties of underseasoned mashed potatoes served in a watery balsamic-vinegar sauce that eventually soaked into the potatoes, leaving them soggy and brownish. It seemed like ill-conceived leftovers.

After so many hours the entrées, of course, arrived just on the heels of   5 the appetizers, and things went downhill from there. The bouillabaisse-style Soupe Canoise ($5.95/$9.95) tasted burnt and had a little black hot-pepper-looking thing lolling suspiciously to one side. I asked my bus-friend, the only person who ever attended the table, what it was, and, as he didn't know, he set out in pursuit of our waiter, who it took another 15 minutes to track down. Flyboy had never seen it either; it's been my experience that, if you ask any member of the wait staff at Mpls. Cafe what anything on the menu is, they become startled and disappear for maddening amounts of time in search of answers—so he went looking for a manager.

When the young, key-free manager arrived and he identified the little stem-on vegetable as a Japanese eggplant, I couldn't stop giggling. Then I tasted it, and I stopped laughing. It was bitter, charred, and awful—it made me want to spit. (If you ever wondered why people salt and drain eggplants, take a cute little past-prime Japanese eggplant, char it over an open flame, and pop it into your mouth. You'll salt forevermore.)

Of course, one bad experience does not make a bad restaurant. So I returned. And returned again. Each time the service was comical, and the food, while conceptually interesting, often seemed as though no one had tasted it after the idea was put to paper. The Salmon Tartar ($11.25), minced salmon served in a pool of cayenne-infused olive oil, tasted dusty and inedibly oily; Wood Roasted Quail Provençale ($17.95) was teeth-achingly salty; Casablanca Risotto with Saffron Infused Chicken Kabob ($13.25) was a pair of painfully over-salted kabobs resting on a mountain of gummy risotto; New Zealand Rack of Lamb ($21.50) was virtually ruined, as each small lamb chop was heaped with a spoon of raw, biting sorrel-garlic pesto; Chicken Garlic Basil Rigatoni ($10.75) was dull and undifferentiated; and worst of all was a special of lobster ravioli with fresh blueberries. I imagined puffs of tender lobster meat with a dozen or so blueberries thrown in for color and contrast. I got raviolis enriched with crunchy bits of shell, drowning in a thick, sour, jam-like paste.

On the up side, I liked the Caesar salad ($3.95/$6.95), which was lemony, spare, and honest; the pizzas are very good, wood-roasted, crisp, and simple; and the Planked Cochonnailles—a trio of pâtés served with spicy French gherkins and oil-cured olives—were fine. But I could have, in good con-science, sent back three out of four dishes that arrived from the Mpls. Cafe kitchen. It was hilarious, in its fashion.

It was also really funny when I went to order dessert on another visit and my waitress said, "That's the only good thing here." Then she backpedaled and clarified, saying, "What I mean is, in my opinion, it's my favorite part of the menu." She's right, many of the desserts are spectacular: I loved the crème brûlée ($4.95), which is presented in a glamorous haze of smoke as your server brands the top with a hot iron plate. The Pear Obsession ($5.95), poached pear slices on a layer of flaky, almond-laced pastry drizzled with a cinnamon-caramel sauce, is also truly wonderful. And the Crepe à la Gundel ($5.95), a tender crepe filled with warm fresh berries and dressed with two spectacular sauces, a crème anglaise and a Grand Marnier caramel syrup, is absolutely per-fect; for everything I didn't like about the Mpls. Cafe, I'll be back for this wonder.

Mpls. Cafe also takes the prize for the most artful, ample, and delicious   10
sauce-painting I've ever seen. It also must be said that its wine list is masterful. Champagnes and sparkling wines are nicely represented, and premium bottles can be had at reasonable prices. The rest of the list is global in scope, arranged in an exceedingly user-friendly manner, and considerately showcases many wines in every price range. Mpls. Cafe has only been open for two months, and perhaps the time will come when the food lives up to the strengths of the desserts. Until then it's a fine place for music, late-night gatherings, post-theater, pre-Holidazzle,° and the like—as long as you bring your sense of humor.

But wait—I totally forgot to tell you about how the rice in the Moroc-can rice salad arrives as a large, ice-cold dome surrounded by hot, delicate

---

°*Holidazzle:* A nightly parade in downtown Minneapolis during the Christmas shopping season.

seafood that (predictably) turns icy in a matter of moments. And how there are four televisions showing sports in a place with $175 bottles of champagne on the menu. Oh, and get this: One time, at a neighboring table, a customer spilled a glass of water, and it splashed all over the floor, and no one ever came to wipe it up, leaving patrons to pick their purses up off the floor to avoid the streaming rivulets; and then this one bus-guy actually told a waitress to watch out for the spilled water, because she might slip on it, and so they both avoided the spot for the rest of the night but never wiped it up. Man, was that funny. Oh, and the time I went by the open kitchen and a chef had this magazine spread out over his cutting board, and this other time . . .

Oh well. I guess it was just one of those things where you had to be there. But it was really funny.

QUESTIONS FOR DISCUSSION

1. Moskowitz opens her review by discussing her life as a restaurant critic. What is her purpose in doing so?
2. The service at this restaurant is clearly a disappointment to Moskowitz. What does it take to be a good server? In your experience, why does service sometimes break down?
3. According to Moskowitz, she could have "in good conscience, sent back three out of four dishes that arrived from the Mpls. Cafe kitchen." If she's disappointed in the food, why doesn't she send it back to the kitchen? Under what circumstances would you ask a server to return your meal?
4. Although this is an unusually negative review, Moskowitz does find some things to praise. What does she achieve by reporting that the restaurant in question had a good wine list and good desserts?
5. How would you describe the tone of this review? Does it seem appropriate under the circumstances?

SUGGESTIONS FOR WRITING

1. Visit a new restaurant in your area with two or three other people with whom you can share impressions. Then write a review in which you let readers know what they can expect if they decide to go there for a meal.
2. Choose a kind of food—like burgers or pizza—that is available at several restaurants in your area. Within no more than a week, sample this item at several sites. Then write a review in which you describe where you went and rank what you ate.
3. Write an evaluation of the food served on your campus that would help visitors learn where to go and what to order.

LINKS

■ Within the Book

In "Breakfast at the FDA Café" (pages 580–582), John R. Alden envisions a restaurant where the service is too attentive.

■ Elsewhere in Print

Allen, Gary. *The Resource Guide for Food Writers.* New York: Routledge, 1999.
Fisher, M. F. K. *The Gastronomical Me.* 1943. San Francisco: North Point, 1989.
———. *How to Cook a Wolf.* 1942. San Francisco: North Point, 1988.
Hughes, Holly, ed. *Best Food Writing 2004.* New York: Marlowe, 2004.
Trillin, Calvin. *Travels with Alice.* New York: Ticknor, 1989.
———. *The Tummy Trilogy: American Fried/Alice, Let's Eat/Third Helpings.* New York: Farrar, 1994.
Warde, Alan, and Lydia Martens. *Eating Out: Social Differentiation, Consumption and Pleasure.* New York: Cambridge UP, 2000.

■ Online

www.mhhe.com/motives

Click on "More Resources" then "Writing to Evaluate Something."

■ ■ ■

GOD'S LONELY MAN

Francis Davis

Although an evaluation of music often focuses on a specific performance or album, critics sometimes appraise a musician's work as a whole—especially when an artist has a proven record of attracting listeners, and an event such as death calls for retrospection. The following assessment of Johnny Cash was first published in 2004, shortly after the singer's death. It originally appeared in The Atlantic, *where Francis Davis has been a contributing editor since 1992. When you read it, you will find that Davis is interested in the social significance of the music he discusses.*

In an interview, Davis emphasized the importance of three beliefs: "that art criticism is implicitly social criticism, that criticism is a kind of literature, that opinions and impressions and ideas are of real value." His work has earned him fellowships from the Guggenheim and Pew Foundations as well as a Grammy nomination, but success did not come easily. When discussing his career as a freelance writer, he laughed and quoted another writer who said, "You have to be prepared to live like a graduate student well into your 30s and 40s." Conceding that he is "not the world's fastest writer," Davis notes, "if I'm writing about something, I'm more critical about it, but I also enjoy it more. If I'm taking notes, I'm much sharper; I have more involvement with it somehow."

In 1956, when he recorded "I Walk the Line" for Sun Records, Johnny Cash became an overnight sensation. But it was his many years of singing as if he knew from personal experience all of humankind's strengths and failings— as if he had both committed murder and been accepted into God's light— that made him a favorite of liberals and conservatives, MTV and the Grand Ole Opry, Gary Gilmore and Billy Graham. A tall piece of timber, Cash was often likened to John Wayne, to whom he otherwise bore only the slightest resemblance. The biggest difference was that Wayne never really lived up to (and probably only dimly comprehended) the democratic ideals he personified on screen—which were more likely the ideals of the directors he worked with anyway. Cash took on a greater variety of roles as a singer than Wayne did as an actor, and both he and the characters he gave voice to admitted their weaknesses. From song to song he was a cowboy or a white outcast who rode with Indians, a family man or a drifter, a believer in eternal life or a condemned murderer with no tomorrows anywhere. His credibility as all of these owed as much to the moral effort involved in endlessly putting himself in others' shoes as it did to his professional savvy in putting a song across.

Waking to the radio last September 12 and hearing that Cash had died in the middle of the night, I remembered thinking about Cash just days after the attacks two years earlier, while watching a nationally televised prayer service attended by the President and the First Lady and featuring a performance by the mezzo-soprano Denyce Graves. It should have been moving—but as I listened to a mannered black diva render an old spiritual as if it were a European art song, it was impossible not to think that the occasion called for a more homegrown performance style. If the point was to rally Americans to draw on their inner resources, it would have been a comfort to hear from Johnny Cash, who stood for what Christopher Wren, his first biographer, called "the dignity of the commonplace and the redeeming grace of hard knocks."

I thought of Cash frequently in the weeks and months that followed 9/11, as music written in response to the attacks began to be released. With few exceptions, rock's singer-songwriters lapsed into their habitual pattern of dissent, and country singers beat the drums for retaliation. All of it reminded me of that period in the late 1960s, before public opinion solidified against the Vietnam War, when we heard "The Ballad of the Green Berets" and "I Ain't Marchin' Anymore"—neither side giving any ground—and when Cash became a voice of reason. The lyrics to "I Walk the Line" pledge sexual fidelity regardless of temptation; but whenever Cash performed this song in the early 1970s (as he surely must have at every show), he might just as well have been describing his principled balancing act in opposing our military policy in Southeast Asia while continuing to voice support for our troops. "Singing in Vietnam Talking Blues," "What Is Truth?," and "The Man in Black"—Cash's antiwar songs—weren't among his best numbers, and they didn't really say anything that countless rockers and folkies hadn't said already. They were powerful by virtue of who sang them: not a hippie leading a chant at Woodstock but a country-music icon who was risking the sort of ire unleashed last year against Natalie Maines, of the Dixie Chicks, when she told a British audience she was embarrassed that George W. Bush was a fellow Texan.

In 1969 *The New York Times* ran a Sunday magazine article on Cash titled "First Angry Man of Country Singers"—a reference not just to Cash's activism in behalf of prisoners and Indians but also to his having generally made life miserable for those closest to him, a few years earlier, when he was taking huge daily doses of amphetamines and barbiturates. If suicidal habits and self-destructive behavior are the primary definition of "angry," Hank Williams (for one) was years ahead of Cash. But unless you count Woody Guthrie—which the Nashville establishment does not, even though it should—Cash *was* country music's first protest singer. "Singing in Vietnam Talking Blues" was released as a single in May of 1971, and it isn't much of an exaggeration to say that his performance of the song on television early that year marked a turning point: If Johnny Cash wasn't buying this war, why should anybody?

That performance was on Cash's own TV show, which aired on ABC from 1969 to 1971. According to his own accounts, Cash fought only two battles with his network bosses, who eventually gave in to him on both. One disagreement arose from his desire to introduce a hymn by declaring his own faith in Jesus. The other was over an appearance by Pete Seeger, whom Cash

5

defended as "a good American as I've ever met." One can imagine the same thing being said of Cash.

In 1975, when an interviewer for *Penthouse* asked him if he was a political radical, he replied, "I'm just tryin' to be a good Christian"—a good Christian, but not a professional one, despite his many songs about Jesus and his tours as a member of his friend Billy Graham's Crusades. He was a Christian who didn't cast stones, a patriot who didn't play the flag card.

Cash's image evolved in tandem with his musical style. The albums that he recorded on the fly at Folsom and San Quentin in the late 1960s made do with a bare-bones instrumentation that recalled his early singles for Sun, and their crossover into pop may have been what convinced him that he was better off without the background choirs and instrumental "sweetening" featured on most of that day's country recordings, including too many of his own. He dispensed with other frills as well. In the late 1950s and early 1960s, around the same time that Frank Sinatra was popularizing the "concept" album, Cash brought the idea to country music. His album jackets often showed him costumed in keeping with a musical theme: he was a farmhand on *Now, There Was a Song!*, for example, and a gunfighter on both *Ride This Train* and *Johnny Cash Sings the Ballads of the True West*. By 1969, however, he had settled on one style of dress. In his frock coat and morning pants, he was "the man in black"—a look and a nickname, but also a singular persona. Though he said in the 1971 song of that name that he wore black to remind himself and his audiences of society's injustices, he must have known that it was flattering to him—and made him stand out from that era's rhinestone cowboys.

He was in his late thirties and already had plenty of mileage on him when he was discovered by television; longer hair and the shadows and dents of middle age brought out the character in his face, making him almost handsome. He appeared in a couple of movies around this time, but gave what I think of as his finest performance in John Frankenheimer's *I Walk the Line* (1970), for which he merely supplied the score. His songs do such a good job of letting us know what's going on in the mind of the character played by Gregory Peck (a small-town Tennessee sheriff in the grip of a midlife crisis) that it's as if he and Peck were sharing the role. The movie was a flop at the box office, but "Flesh and Blood"—perhaps the single most beautiful song Cash ever wrote, and one whose lyrics could stand alone as inspired nature poetry—reached No. 1 on the country charts.

With maturity Cash grew into his voice. To read his obituaries, one might think that his credibility as a singer depended entirely on his credibility as a man. True, he never developed his upper range to the point where he could trust it, and the clear emphasis he gave every single word would have precluded gliding from note to note even if he had been able to. Among the singers of his own generation he lacked the bravura and the sheer lung power of such country Carusos as Elvis Presley, Conway Twitty, Roy Orbison, Ferlin

Husky, and the young Waylon Jennings. We tend not to value deep voices as much as we do high, soaring ones, perhaps because the effort involved in producing a low note is less apparent. Something about hearing a singer go low strikes most ears as a trick, a human special effect. The bass singer does the grunt work in doo-wop and rhythm and blues, sometimes literally. There is a style of country music, however, in which a male singer's descent to a virile low note at the end of a phrase, or for the closing chorus, supplies the same payoff as a soul singer's falsetto—one conveys masculine certainty and the other uncontrollable passion, but each signifies a moment of truth. No country singer was better at this than Cash, and few singers in any field of music have been as expressive or as instantly recognizable.

Cash wasn't usually thought of as a folk singer, but in terms of updating   10
traditional material and writing new songs in the same vein, he was the closest thing to an authentic troubadour to emerge since the end of World War II "Don't Take Your Guns to Town" (1958), about a headstrong young man who comes to a violent end after ignoring his mother's advice, was based on an Irish ballad that found its way to the American South. "Five Feet High and Rising" (1959), about the devastation caused by a 1937 flood of the Mississippi, was entirely his own creation. Anyone listening to these two songs and unfamiliar with their sources would be hard put to guess which was traditional and which original. Possibly at the instigation of Seeger and Bob Dylan, Cash performed at the Newport Folk Festival in 1964. It was Freedom Summer, and the festival was a recruiting ground for the voter-registration movement and for leftist causes in general. The presence of a country-music star must have raised a few eyebrows. But the organizers must have recognized that Cash virtually defined folk music in his relationship to his primary audience—a country-music audience that embraced him because his music reflected their experience, even if his political beliefs occasionally differed from theirs.

Cash was one of the original Sun rockabillies, along with Presley, Carl Perkins, Jerry Lee Lewis, and the forgotten Warren Smith and Billy Lee Riley—like him, southerners who had grown up aspiring to country stardom before anyone had ever heard of rock-and-roll. Yet Bono, Bruce Springsteen, and Tom Petty smiled on Cash as one of their own: they heard something close to rock-and-roll in his music, and recognized it for sure in his independent stance. After country radio turned its back on his generation in the 1990s, in favor of young beefcake cowpokes like Toby Keith and Tim McGraw, Cash attracted the attention of MTV by recording his own versions of songs by groups such as Soundgarden, Depeche Mode, and Nine Inch Nails for Rick Rubin, a producer identified with rap and heavy metal.

For all that, whenever Cash made the Top 40 (as he did with some regularity for twenty years, beginning in 1956 with "I Walk the Line"), it was always with what sounded like a country song, not one that conformed to current pop trends. Country-music record buyers didn't extend him the same loyalty, nor did the Nashville power brokers. Cash was a posthumous winner

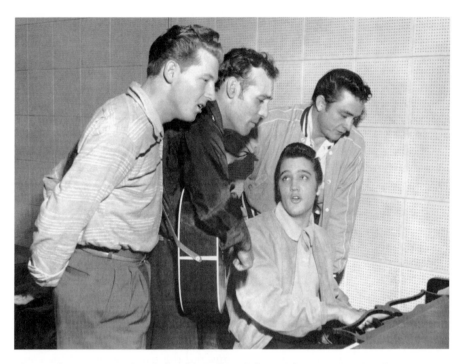

Elvis at the piano, standing behind him from left to right, Jerry Lee Lewis, Carl Perkins, and Johnny Cash.

in three categories at last year's Country Music Association Awards. *American IV: The Man Comes Around,* his fourth album for Rubin and the last to be released before his death, was named Album of the Year, and his version of "Hurt"—a song written by Trent Reznor, of Nine Inch Nails—won for Single of the Year and Music Video of the Year. But there was an air of atonement to these awards, which were given out in November, less than two months after Cash's death. Not counting his election to the association's Hall of Fame, in 1980 (the equivalent of being kicked upstairs), he hadn't received a CMA award since 1969. The association had completely ignored *American Recordings,* his first album for Rubin and arguably his greatest work, even though it won a Grammy as the best contemporary folk recording of 1994. Cash was in any case never part of the country-music establishment, and at the height of his celebrity, in the early 1970s, he towered above it.

Cash wasn't an outlaw—just an outsider, in a way that had nothing to do with stage image. He even seemed a little out of place in the Highwaymen, the country-music supergroup he started recording with in the 1980s, which also featured the shaggy Nashville "outlaws" Waylon Jennings, Willie Nelson, and Kris Kristofferson. His singing and the way he carried himself did influence a number of country singers of his generation and slightly younger, most notably Merle Haggard and Kristofferson. But among today's younger country performers, the only ones who sound like they've listened much to Cash are somehow related to him: his daughter Rosanne Cash, his stepdaughter Carlene Carter, and his former sons-in-law Marty Stuart and Rodney Crowell. Where his influence is still widespread is in the work of performers ignored by country stations but likely to be on the playlists of classic-rock stations and public radio's *World Café*—such younger singer-songwriters as Steve Earle and Billy Bragg, along with Bob Dylan and Bruce Springsteen.

In the movie *Taxi Driver*, Cybill Shepherd tells Robert De Niro that he reminds her of Kris Kristofferson's song "The Pilgrim": "He's a walking contradiction/Partly truth and partly fiction." That song was actually Kristofferson's homage to Cash; but the line from the movie that best describes him is "God's lonely man," De Niro's reference to himself. Cash seemed a man alone even when surrounded by his family on stage, and there was a brooding quality to even his songs about doing right by his fellow man and finding redemption through Jesus.

"Cheating" songs are a dime a dozen in country, but the one of Cash's that most readily comes to mind may be unique: his adaptation of the traditional ballad "The Long Black Veil," whose narrator chooses to hang for a murder he didn't commit rather than reveal that he was in bed with his best friend's wife on the night in question. His songs about the wild life usually end with someone either serving time or bleeding to death on a barroom floor. 15

Cash identified with society's victims, but the true measure of his compassion was his realization that some of us become victims of our own dark impulses. The inmates we hear cheering for him on the albums he recorded at Folsom and San Quentin sensed his empathy for them, even though they may have misinterpreted it. According to legend, many of these men believed that Cash was one of them—that he had served hard time himself. In truth his jail time was limited to what he often humorously described as "seven one-night stands" in the 1950s and early 1960s, all after busts for drunkenness or possession when he was popping pills. On both albums the loudest cheers—the most frightening ones—come during "Folsom Prison Blues," when Cash delivers his famous line about killing a man in Reno "just to watch him die." The prisoners we hear whooping at that line took it to be a boast; but Cash once wrote that he had written it after asking himself what was the most unforgivable reason he could imagine for taking another person's life. He was the favorite singer of Gary Gilmore, who was especially fond of "Don't Take Your Guns to Town." It's too bad Gilmore didn't live to hear "Delia's Gone," the opening number on *American Recordings*. No other song I know has ever probed so chillingly the mind of a murderer—particularly the ability of a psychopath to dissociate himself from his own deeds.

For the most part, *American Recordings* presented Cash alone, accompanying himself on guitar. The album's beauty was in its starkness and simplicity, with Rubin producing Cash in much the same way that country blues performers were recorded in the 1930s: just sit the man down and roll the tapes while he sings whatever he wants to—his own songs along with others he knows and likes. In their own way, Cash's interpretations of Leonard Cohen's "Bird on a Wire" and Nick Lowe's "The Beast in Me" (a song actually written for him by another of his former sons-in-law) were just as compelling as "Delia's Gone." Three of the album's new songs rank among the most touching Cash ever wrote: "Oh, Bury Me Not," a variation on an old cowboy lament with a half-spoken introduction in which Cash tells us he senses God's hand in nature more than he does in churches; "Drive On," in which he sings from the point of view of a Vietnam veteran who's leading a normal life though still haunted by his wartime experiences; and "Like a Soldier," a love song presumably addressed either to Jesus or to June Carter Cash, and so gorgeous it hardly matters which.

American Recordings represented an apotheosis, but the albums that followed it were overproduced and unextraordinary; the musicians who accompanied Cash on them somehow managed to sound at once sympathetic and superfluous. Cash was no longer in good voice, and the newer songs that Rubin chose for him (death figured in quite a few) wallowed in a kind of adolescent self-pity that made them all wrong for a performer who, whatever else he was, was always an adult. It turns out that some of the best performances Cash recorded for Rubin were passed over for release until after his death, and finally surfaced on the unfortunately titled *Cash Unearthed,* a five-CD boxed set that arrived in stores in November. My favorite of these is Cash's version of Billy Joe Shaver's "If I Give My Soul," in which a man bargains with the Lord in much the same way that Robert Johnson is said to have bargained with the devil at a Mississippi crossroads—except that instead of prowess on the guitar, this man's asking price is sobriety and winning back the love of his estranged wife and son. It's a song full of adult sorrow that leaves "Hurt" in the dust.

Whatever his actual relationship to rock-and-roll, Cash was the only surviving performer from its first wave who was still in the thick of things at the beginning of the new century (Chuck Berry, Jerry Lee Lewis, and Little Richard having long ago accepted their fate as oldies acts). Rock-and-roll has been with us for almost fifty years now—an eternity by the standards of popular music, but well short of the average human life-span. Until very recently the only dead rock-and-rollers were the ones who died young—casualties of their own bad habits, of car wrecks and plane crashes, of wronged women and obsessed fans with guns. For all their shortcomings, Cash's last few CDs exerted considerable power by presenting us with something we hadn't really heard before in pop music: a man long past middle age confronting his own mortality, and implicitly asking us to contemplate ours.

Cash made the cover of *Time* following his death, and inside was an eloquent meditation on his career by Richard Corliss. But what really caught my eye was an op-ed piece in the *Philadelphia Daily News,* headlined "WHY THIS LESBIAN LOVED THE MAN IN BLACK." The writer, Debbie Woodell, lovingly recalled how she and her brother used to sing along as children to their

20

grandparents' Lefty Frizzell and Eddy Arnold records. "But not Johnny. With Johnny, we listened." There was a tribute to Cash at the Country Music Awards in November, with Willie Nelson, Kris Kristofferson, Travis Tritt, Sheryl Crow, Hank Williams Jr., and the Nitty Gritty Dirt Band all singing his songs and wearing black in his honor. Yet to me, a more meaningful tribute was the Johnny Cash album covers I saw in the windows of a few New York used-record stores well into the fall. Many of these shops didn't even carry country music; the owners or employees had brought in albums from their own collections. It reminded me of a scene in the movie *High Fidelity*, when John Cusack, playing the owner of a store called Championship Vinyl, faces us and says, deadpan, "My all-time favorite book is Johnny Cash's autobiography *Cash,* by Johnny Cash." Nothing if not ironic, he's aware of the humor in his repetition, but you can tell he sincerely loves saying the name. There are some of us for whom music is a form of religion as well as an addiction, filling the same need in our lives that our President says Scripture fills in his. If the point of having Cash record songs by Depeche Mode and Nine Inch Nails was to make it hip to like him again, Rubin needn't have bothered. For us, it's always been hip to like Johnny Cash. You could even say it's one of the definitions.

QUESTIONS FOR DISCUSSION

1. How does Davis account for the broad appeal Cash enjoyed throughout his long career? Why is it useful for him to establish this?
2. What do you think Christopher Wren meant when he wrote of "the dignity of the commonplace and the redeeming grace of hard knocks"?
3. Where does Davis incorporate evidence in this evaluation that Cash was less than perfect? What does this admission achieve?
4. Davis describes Cash as "a Christian who didn't cast stones; a patriot who didn't play the flag card." What does this mean to you, and what does it imply?
5. Why do you think Davis compares Cash with other musicians—ranging from Elvis Presley to Bruce Springsteen?
6. Why do you think the country-music industry tended to ignore Cash after 1969?
7. The title for this article comes from paragraph 14, where Davis establishes that it is a phrase originally used by Robert DeNiro as a movie character. Does Davis convince you that it is an appropriate description for Cash?

SUGGESTIONS FOR WRITING

1. Listen to the albums, mentioned in paragraph 16, in which the voices of prisoners can be heard responding to Cash when he performed for them. Then write an evaluation of one of these albums focused on what the prisoners respond to and what their voices add to the recording.

2. According to Davis, "'Cheating' songs are a dime a dozen in country . . ." Listen to a series of "cheating" songs, and then write an evaluation contrasting one you consider successful to one you do not.
3. Survey the career of your own favorite musician, and then write an evaluation that establishes that performer's highs and lows.

LINKS

▪ Within the Book

In "Et in Arcadia Ego" (pages 617–625), John Berger pays tribute to the life and achievement of another kind of artist—a painter who was also a close friend.

▪ Elsewhere in Print

Cash, Johnny. *Cash*. San Francisco: Harper, 1998.
Davis, Francis. *Bebop and Nothingness*. Boston: Schirmer, 1996.
———. *In the Moment: Jazz in the 1980s*. New York: Oxford UP, 1986.
———. *Outcats*. New York: Oxford UP, 1990.
———. *The History of the Blues*. New York: Hyperion, 1995.
Kingsbury, Paul, et al. *The Encyclopedia of Country Music*. New York: Oxford UP, 1998.
Urbanski, Dave. *The Man Comes Around*. Relevant, 2003.
Zwonitzer, Mark, and Charles Hirschberg. *Will You Miss Me When I'm Gone?* New York: Simon, 2002.

▪ Online

www.mhhe.com/motives

Click on "More Resources" then "Writing to Evaluate Something."

■ ■ ■

MY DIAGNOSIS

Susanna Kaysen

A common form of assessment is a personal evaluation. An evaluation of this sort could take the form of a letter of recommendation, an annual job review, or notes written in the record of a hospital patient. "My Diagnosis" is an excerpt from Girl, Interrupted (1993), Susanna Kaysen's memoir of what it was like to be hospitalized for mental illness when she was eighteen—an experience that was by then more than twenty years in her past. After studying the notes written in her chart, as well as the definition of her diagnosis published by the American Psychiatric Association, Kaysen writes a self-evaluation that is, among other things, an evaluation of her evaluation.

In an interview about Girl, Interrupted, Kaysen told Publisher's Weekly that she decided to incorporate hospital records in her memoir "because the contrast between their language and my language was interesting" and "provided a viewpoint on the experience that I couldn't provide." Although Girl, Interrupted is her best-known work and became a movie starring Winona Ryder and Angelina Jolie, Kaysen is also the author of two novels: Asa: As I Knew Him (1987) and Far Afield (1990).

Page _____   F-90

McLEAN HOSPITAL

№. 22 201   **Name**   KAYSEN, Susanna

1968
9-4

DISCHARGE ON VISIT SUMMARY:

G.   Formal Diagnosis:
Schizophrenic reaction, paranoid type (borderline)--
currently in remission. Patient is functioning on
a passive-aggressive personality, passive-dependent
type.

12

KAYSEN, Susanna N.
Hospital No. 22201

CASE REPORT--CONT'D

B. Prognosis: The resolution of the depressive effect
and suicidal drive should be expected as a result of the
hospitalization. The degree of personality integration and ego
function which may be achieved for the long term is hard to
predict. We may say that with a good intensive working relationship in therapy and a successful relationship to
the hospital the patient may be able to achieve a more
satisfactory means of adapting. Nevertheless because of
the chronicity of the illness and the basic deficiencies
involved in personality structuring, a more complete
recovery is not to be expected at this time. However, the
patient may learn to make more wise choices for herself within
the boundaries of her personality so that she is
able to achieve a satisfactory dependent relationship if necessary which will sustain her for a long period of time.

So these were the charges against me. I didn't read them until twenty-five years later. "A character disorder" is what they'd told me then.

I had to find a lawyer to help me get my records from the hospital; I had to read line 32a of form A1 of the Case Record, and entry G on the Discharge on Visit Summary, and entry B of Part IV of the Case Report; then I had to locate a copy of the *Diagnostic and Statistical Manual of Mental Disorders* and look up Borderline Personality to see what they really thought about me.

It's a fairly accurate picture of me at eighteen, minus a few quirks like reckless driving and eating binges. It's accurate but it isn't profound. Of course, it doesn't aim to be profound. It's not even a case study. It's a set of guidelines, a generalization.

I'm tempted to try refuting it, but then I would be open to the further charges of "defensiveness" and "resistance."

All I can do is give the particulars: an annotated diagnosis.   5

"[U]ncertainty about several life issues, such as self-image, sexual orientation, long-term goals or career choice, types of friends or lovers to have ..." I relish that last phrase. Its awkwardness (the "to have" seems superfluous) gives it substance and heft. I still have that uncertainty. Is this the type of friend or lover I want to have? I ask myself every time I meet someone new. Charming but shallow; good-hearted but a bit conventional; too handsome for his own good; fascinating but probably unreliable; and so forth. I guess I've had my share of unreliables. More than my share? How many would constitute more than my share?

Fewer than for somebody else—somebody who'd never been called a borderline personality?

That's the nub of my problem here.

If my diagnosis had been bipolar illness, for instance, the reaction to me and to this story would be slightly different. That's a chemical problem, you'd say to yourself, manic-depression, Lithium, all that. I would be blameless, somehow. And what about schizophrenia—that would send a chill up your spine. After all, that's real insanity. People don't "recover" from schizophrenia. You'd have to wonder how much of what I'm telling you is true and how much imagined.

I'm simplifying, I know. But these words taint everything. The fact that I   10
was locked up taints everything.

What does *borderline personality* mean, anyhow?

It appears to be a way station between neurosis and psychosis: a fractured but not disassembled psyche. Though to quote my post-Melvin° psychiatrist: "It's what they call people whose lifestyles bother them."

He can say it because he's a doctor. If I said it, nobody would believe me.

An analyst I've known for years said, "Freud and his circle thought most people were hysterics, then in the fifties it was psychoneurotics, and lately, everyone's a borderline personality."

°*Melvin:* Kaysen's psychiatrist when she was a patient at McLean Hospital.

Here is an excerpt from the third edition of the Diagnostic and Statistical Manual of Mental Disorders *(1987), one of the sources Kaysen consulted when evaluating the way she was perceived as an adolescent.*

An essential feature of this disorder is a pervasive pattern of instability of self image, interpersonal relationships, and mood, beginning in early adulthood and present in a variety of contexts.

A marked and persistent identity disturbance is almost invariably present. This is often pervasive, and is manifested by uncertainty about several life issues, such as self-image, sexual orientation, long-term goals or career choice, types of friends or lovers to have, and which values to adopt. The person often experiences this instability of self-image as chronic feelings of emptiness and boredom.

Interpersonal relationships are usually unstable and intense, and may be characterized by alternation of the extremes of overidealization and devaluation. These people have difficulty tolerating being alone, and will make frantic efforts to avoid real or imagined abandonment.

Affective instability is common. This may be evidenced by marked mood shifts from baseline mood to depression, irritability, or anxiety, usually lasting a few hours or, only rarely, more than a few days. In addition, these people often have inappropriately intense anger with frequent displays of temper or recurrent physical fights. They tend to be impulsive, particularly in activities that are potentially self-damaging, such as shopping sprees, psychoactive substance abuse, reckless driving, casual sex, shoplifting, and binge eating.

Recurrent suicidal threats, gestures, or behavior and other self-mutilating behavior (e.g., wrist-scratching) are common in the more severe forms of the disorder. This behavior may serve to manipulate others, may be a result of intense anger, or may counteract feelings of "numbness" and depersonalization that arise during periods of extreme stress. . . .

Associated Features. Frequently this disorder is accompanied by many features of other Personality Disorders, such as Schizotypal, Histrionic, Narcissistic, and Antisocial Personality Disorders. In many cases more than one diagnosis is warranted. Quite often social contrariness and a generally pessimistic outlook are observed. Alternation between dependency and self-assertion is common. During periods of extreme stress, transient psychotic symptoms may occur, but they are generally of insufficient severity or duration to warrant an additional diagnosis.

Impairment. Often there is considerable interference with social or occupational functioning.

Complications. Possible complications include Dysthymia [depressive neurosis], Major Depression, Psychoactive Substance Abuse, and psychotic disorders such as Brief Reactive Psychosis. Premature death may result from suicide.

Sex Ratio. The disorder is more commonly diagnosed in women.

Prevalence. Borderline Personality Disorder is apparently common.

Predisposing and Familial Pattern. No information. . . .

APA

When I went to the corner bookstore to look up my diagnosis in the *Manual,* it occurred to me that I might not find it in there anymore. They do get rid of things—homosexuality, for instance. Until recently, quite a few of my friends would have found themselves documented in that book along with me. Well, they got out of the book and I didn't. Maybe in another twenty-five years I won't be in there either.   15

"[I]nstability of self-image, interpersonal relationships, and mood . . . uncertainty about . . . long-term goals or career choice . . ." Isn't this a good description of adolescence? Moody, fickle, faddish, insecure: in short, impossible.

"[S]elf-mutilating behavior (e.g., wrist-scratching) . . ." I've skipped forward a bit. This is the one that caught me by surprise as I sat on the floor of the bookstore reading my diagnosis. Wrist-scratching! I thought I'd invented it. Wrist-banging, to be precise.

This is where people stop being able to follow me. This is the sort of stuff you get locked up for. Nobody knew I was doing it, though. I never told anyone, until now.

I had a butterfly chair. In the sixties, everyone in Cambridge had a butterfly chair. The metal edge of its upturned seat was perfectly placed for wrist-banging. I had tried breaking ashtrays and walking on the shards, but I didn't have the nerve to tread firmly. Wrist-banging—slow, steady, mindless—was a better solution. It was cumulative injury, so each bang was tolerable.

A solution to what? I quote from the *Manual:* "This behavior may . . . counteract feelings of 'numbness' and depersonalization that arise during periods of extreme stress."   20

I spent hours in my butterfly chair banging my wrist. I did it in the evenings, like homework. I'd do some homework, then I'd spend half an hour wrist-banging, then finish my homework, then back in the chair for some more banging before brushing my teeth and going to bed. I banged the inside, where the veins converge. It swelled and turned a bit blue, but considering how hard and how much I banged it, the visible damage was slight. That was yet one more recommendation of it to me.

I'd had an earlier period of face-scratching. If my fingernails hadn't been quite short, I couldn't have gotten away with it. As it was, I definitely looked puffy and peculiar the next day. I used to scratch my cheeks and then rub soap on them. Maybe the soap prevented me from looking worse. But I looked bad enough that people asked, "Is something wrong with your face?" So I switched to wrist-banging.

I was like an anchorite with a hair shirt. Part of the point was that nobody knew about my suffering. If people knew and admired—or abominated—me, something important would be lost.

I was trying to explain my situation to myself. My situation was that I was in pain and nobody knew it; even I had trouble knowing it. So I told myself, over and over, You are in pain. It was the only way I could get through to myself ("counteract feelings of 'numbness'"). I was demonstrating, externally and irrefutably, an inward condition.

"Quite often social contrariness and a generally pessimistic outlook are   *25*
observed." What do you suppose they mean by "social contrariness"? Putting
my elbows on the table? Refusing to get a job as a dental technician? Disappointing my parents' hope that I would go to a first-rate university?

They don't define "social contrariness," and I can't define it, so I think it
ought to be excluded from the list. I'll admit to the generally pessimistic outlook. Freud had one too.

I can honestly say that my misery has been transformed into common
unhappiness, so by Freud's definition I have achieved mental health. And my
discharge sheet, at line 41, Outcome with Regard to Mental Disorder, reads
"Recovered."

Recovered. Had my personality crossed over that border, whatever and
wherever it was, to resume life within the confines of the normal? Had I
stopped arguing with my personality and learned to straddle the line between
sane and insane? Perhaps I'd actually had an identity disorder. "In Identity
Disorder there is a similar clinical picture, but Borderline Personality . . . preempts the diagnosis . . . if the disturbance is sufficiently pervasive and . . . it is
unlikely that it will be limited to a developmental stage." Maybe I was a victim of improper preemption?

I'm not finished with this diagnosis.

"The person often experiences this instability of self-image as chronic   *30*
feelings of emptiness or boredom." My chronic feelings of emptiness and boredom came from the fact that I was living a life based on my incapacities, which
were numerous. A partial list follows. I could not and did not want to: ski,
play tennis, or go to gym class; attend to any subject in school other than English and biology; write papers on any assigned topics (I wrote poems instead
of papers for English; I got F's); plan to go or apply to college; give any reasonable explanation for these refusals.

My self-image was not unstable. I saw myself, quite correctly, as unfit for
the educational and social systems.

But my parents and teachers did not share my self-image. Their image of
me was unstable, since it was out of kilter with reality and based on their
needs and wishes. They did not put much value on my capacities, which were
admittedly few, but genuine. I read everything, I wrote constantly, and I had
boyfriends by the barrelful.

"Why don't you do the assigned reading?" they'd ask. "Why don't you
write your papers instead of whatever you're writing—what is that, a short
story?" "Why don't you expend as much energy on your schoolwork as you
do on your boyfriends?"

By my senior year I didn't even bother with excuses, let alone explanations.

"Where is your term paper?" asked my history teacher.   *35*

"I didn't write it. I have nothing to say on that topic."

"You could have picked another topic."

"I have nothing to say on any historical topic."

One of my teachers told me I was a nihilist. He meant it as an insult but I
took it as a compliment.

Boyfriends and literature: How can you make a life out of those two   *40*
things? As it turns out, I did; more literature than boyfriends lately, but I guess
you can't have everything ("a generally pessimistic outlook [is] observed").

Back then I didn't know that I—or anyone—could make a life out of
boyfriends and literature. As far as I could see, life demanded skills I didn't
have. The result was chronic emptiness and boredom. There were more per-
nicious results as well: self-loathing, alternating with "inappropriately intense
anger with frequent displays of temper. . . ."

What would have been an appropriate level of intensity for my anger at
feeling shut out of life? My classmates were spinning their fantasies for the future: lawyer, ethnobotanist, Buddhist monk (it was a very progressive high
school). Even the dumb, uninteresting ones who were there to provide "balance" looked forward to their marriages and their children. I knew I wasn't
going to have any of this because I knew I didn't want it. But did that mean I
would have nothing?

I was the first person in the history of the school not to go to college. Of
course, at least a third of my classmates never finished college. By 1968, people
were dropping out daily.

Quite often now, people say to me, when I tell them I didn't go to college, "Oh, how marvelous!" They wouldn't have thought it was so marvelous
back then. They didn't; my classmates were just the sorts of people who now
tell me how marvelous I am. In 1966, I was a pariah.

What was I going to do? a few of my classmates asked.   *45*

"I'm going to join the WACs,°" I told one guy.

"Oh, yeah? That will be an interesting career."

"Just kidding," I said.

"Oh, uh, you mean you're not, really?"

I was stunned. Who did they think I was?   *50*

I'm sure they didn't think about me much. I was that one who wore black
and—really, I've heard it from several people—slept with the English teacher.
They were all seventeen and miserable, just like me. They didn't have time to
wonder why I was a little more miserable than most.

Emptiness and boredom: what an understatement. What I felt was complete desolation. Desolation, despair, and depression.

Isn't there some other way to look at this? After all, angst of these dimensions is a luxury item. You need to be well fed, clothed, and housed to have
time for this much self-pity. And the college business: My parents wanted me
to go, I didn't want to go, and I didn't go. I got what I wanted. Those who
don't go to college have to get jobs. I agreed with all this. I told myself all this
over and over. I even got a job—my job° breaking au gratin dishes.

But the fact that I couldn't hold my job was worrisome. I was probably
crazy. I'd been skirting the idea of craziness for a year or two; now I was closing in on it.

°*WACs:* Women's Army Corps.
°*my job:* A position in a cookware store, where Kaysen accidentally dropped things.

Pull yourself together! I told myself. Stop indulging yourself. There's   *55*
nothing wrong with you. You're just wayward.

One of the great pleasures of mental health (whatever that is) is how
much less time I have to spend thinking about myself.

I have a few more annotations to my diagnosis.

"The disorder is more commonly diagnosed in women."

Note the construction of that sentence. They did not write, "The disorder is more common in women." It would still be suspect, but they didn't
even bother trying to cover their tracks.

Many disorders, judging by the hospital population, were more com-   *60*
monly diagnosed in women. Take, for example, "compulsive promiscuity."

How many girls do you think a seventeen-year-old boy would have to
screw to earn the label "compulsively promiscuous"? Three? No, not enough.
Six? Doubtful. Ten? That sounds more likely. Probably in the fifteen-to-twenty
range, would be my guess—if they ever put that label on boys, which I don't
recall their doing.

And for seventeen-year-old girls, how many boys?

In the list of six "potentially self-damaging" activities favored by the borderline personality, three are commonly associated with women (shopping
sprees, shoplifting, and eating binges) and one with men (reckless driving).
One is not "gender-specific," as they say these days (psychoactive substance
abuse). And the definition of the other (casual sex) is in the eye of the beholder.

Then there is the question of "premature death" from suicide. Luckily, I
avoided it, but I thought about suicide a lot. I'd think about it and make myself sad over my premature death, and then I'd feel better. The idea of suicide
worked on me like a purgative or a cathartic. For some people it's different—
Daisy,° for instance. But was her death really "premature"? Ought she to have
sat in her eat-in kitchen with her chicken and her anger for another fifty
years? I'm assuming she wasn't going to change, and I may be wrong. She
certainly made that assumption, and she may also have been wrong. And if
she'd sat there for only thirty years, and killed herself at forty-nine instead of
at nineteen, would her death still be "premature"?

I got better and Daisy didn't and I can't explain why. Maybe I was just   *65*
flirting with madness the way I flirted with my teachers and my classmates. I
wasn't convinced I was crazy, though I feared I was. Some people say that
having any conscious opinion on the matter is a mark of sanity, but I'm not
sure that's true. I still think about it. I'll always have to think about it.

I often ask myself if I'm crazy. I ask other people too.

"Is this a crazy thing to say?" I'll ask before saying something that probably isn't crazy.

I start a lot of sentences with "Maybe I'm totally nuts," or "Maybe I've
gone 'round the bend."

°*Daisy:* Another patient on the ward who gorged on chicken and eventually committed suicide.

If I do something out of the ordinary—take two baths in one day, for example—I say to myself: Are you crazy?

It's a common phrase, I know. But it means something particular to me: ₇₀ the tunnels, the security screens, the plastic forks, the shimmering, ever-shifting borderline that like all boundaries beckons and asks to be crossed. I do not want to cross it again.

QUESTIONS FOR DISCUSSION

1. According to the chart reprinted on page 280, Kaysen was said to be in "remission" when she was discharged from the hospital. What are the implications of this? If you thought you had recovered from a mental illness, how would it feel to be told you were in remission?
2. What are the characteristics of Borderline Personality Disorder? Why does Kaysen believe that the description of this disorder contains gender bias?
3. In your experience, to what extent do the characteristics of Borderline Personality Disorder seem to apply to the typical American teenager?
4. Why does Kaysen mention that homosexuality is no longer listed as an illness in the *Diagnostic and Statistical Manual of Mental Disorders*? What is she implying?
5. Recalling her adolescence, Kaysen writes, "My self-image was not unstable. I saw myself, quite correctly, as unfit for the educational and social systems." How would you describe Kaysen's self-image now that she is middle-aged?
6. What do you think would motivate someone to research how she was seen in the past? What is Kaysen trying to accomplish?

SUGGESTIONS FOR WRITING

1. Imagine that you are someone who had authority over you at some point in your past. Write an evaluation of yourself at that age based on how you imagine that person saw you.
2. Evaluate the quality of medical treatment you have received in recent years.
3. Write a self-assessment of your academic performance this year.

LINKS

▪ Within the Book

Judy Ruiz reconsiders her mental health when she was younger in "Oranges and Sweet Sister Boy" (pages 656–663).

▪ Elsewhere in Print

Beam, Alex. *Gracefully Insane: The Rise and Fall of America's Premier Mental Hospital.* New York: Public, 2001.

Kaysen, Susanna. *Far Afield.* New York: Vintage, 1990.

——. *Girl, Interrupted.* New York: Turtle Bay, 1993.

——. *The Camera My Mother Gave Me.* New York: Knopf, 2001.

Moskovitz, Richard A. *Lost in the Mirror: An Inside Look at Borderline Personality Disorder.* Dallas: Taylor, 1996.

Plath, Sylvia. *The Bell Jar.* 1963. New York: Harper, 2000.

Santoro, Joseph, with Ronald Cohen. *The Angry Heart: Overcoming Borderline and Addictive Disorders: An Interactive Self-Help Guide.* Oakland: New Harbinger, 1997.

▪ Online

www.mhhe.com/motives

Click on "More Resources" then "Writing to Evaluate Something."

▪ ▪ ▪

HIGH-TECH BIBLIOPHILIA

Paul Goldberger

"High-Tech Bibliophilia" was originally published in The New Yorker *in 2004. It is an evaluation of what was then the brand-new library in downtown Seattle. If you have never thought seriously about architecture or wondered why good architecture matters, this article might help you to understand how a well-designed building can lift spirits and become an emblem of civic pride.*

A graduate of Yale University, Paul Goldberger is the architecture critic for The New Yorker. *He was also architecture critic for the* New York Times *for twenty-five years, and his work at the* Times *earned him a Pulitzer Prize in 1984. Goldberger's other awards include the Medal of the American Institute of Architects, The Medal of Honor of the New York Landmarks Preservation Foundation, and the Roger Starr Journalism Award. About his work as an architecture critic, Goldberger has spoken of his "sense of wonder at this extraordinary subject, at once an art and a practical pursuit, a subject that really touches how we live and that goes in continually new directions. I feel lucky to be writing about what I love, and I am always learning from it."*

If you wanted to build a new library downtown somewhere, Rem Koolhaas is probably the last architect you would think to hire. For years, Koolhaas has been ranting about how traditional cities don't matter anymore, and how the rise of new technologies has made public space obsolete, and how when people leave their houses the only thing they want to do is shop. His firm, the Office for Metropolitan Architecture, which is based in Rotterdam, wasn't on the original list of architects being considered for a new library in Seattle, but one day in 1999 Koolhaas's partner Joshua Ramus, who comes from Seattle, got a phone call from his mother saying she had read in the local newspaper that any architect who wanted to be considered should show up the next day for a briefing. Ramus rushed to the airport, flew to Seattle, and eventually the firm got the job.

The result is the most important new library to be built in a generation, and the most exhilarating. Koolhaas has always been a better architect than social critic, and the building conveys a sense of the possibility, even the urgency, of public space in the center of a city. The design is not so much a rejection of traditional monumentality as a reinterpretation of it, and it celebrates the culture of the book as passionately, in its way, as does the New York Public Library on Fifth Avenue. The Seattle building is thrilling from top to bottom. Koolhaas and Ramus started out by investigating how libraries actually work, and how they are likely to change. They went with Deborah Jacobs, Seattle's chief librarian, and several trustees and staff members to look at libraries around the country, and then they held a series of seminars about the future of the book with scholars and representatives of Microsoft, Amazon, M.I.T.'s Media Lab, and other organizations. They concluded, not surprisingly, that people are not ready to give up on books and that they are not ready to give up on libraries, but that they find most libraries stuffy, confusing, and uninviting. Patrons wanted a more user-friendly institution, and librarians wanted one that was more flexible, and would not require constant rearrangement as collections expanded.

The architects saw that in most older libraries, where books are stored on rows of shelves on separate floors, collections are arbitrarily broken apart, depending on the amount of space available on each floor. But since the Dewey Decimal System is a continuous series of numbers, they reasoned, why couldn't books be stored on a continuous series of shelves? And what if the shelves wound up and up, in a spiral? They saw that it was possible to design stacks in the manner of a parking garage, with slanted floors joined in a series of zigzagging ramps. The stacks, which the architects named the Spiral, take up the equivalent of four floors in the middle of the eleven-story building. They are open, which means that you can browse. You get to the Spiral via a chartreuse-colored escalator and stairway that slices through the middle of the ramped floors. (All vertical circulation in the building, including the elevator cabs, is chartreuse.)

Above the stacks area, on the tenth floor, is a spectacular reading room, with slanted glass walls. The room has an unusual perspective on the Seattle skyline, since the library building is surrounded by skyscrapers, and the waters of Elliott Bay are visible only between the towers. The soaring glass shed is as spectacular, in its way, as the Rose Main Reading Room in the Fifth Avenue library. Just below the stacks is a room full of computers. Koolhaas calls it the Mixing Chamber, which sounds more high-tech and radical than it really is. The Mixing Chamber is simply a reinterpretation of the traditional library reference room. People who visit it are directed to the books they need. Koolhaas's verbiage is always a little annoying. He calls an expansive, atrium-style lobby the Living Room. The Living Room is a splendid vestibule that anoints the act of reading with grandeur and civic pride, and Seattle is lucky to have it. But what Koolhaas has done here is not so different, in its way, from what Carrère & Hastings were trying to achieve when they put Astor Hall at the entrance to the New York Public Library.

I thought of the Carrère & Hastings building often as I walked through   5
the Seattle library. Two buildings could not possibly look less alike, but both were born of a marriage of earnestness and opulence. When the library on Fifth Avenue was finished, in 1911, a grand library that was free to the public was still a fresh, almost radical notion, and the architecture was intended to give it gravitas. In the same way that McKim, Mead & White designed the original Pennsylvania Station to confer a kind of nobility on the act of entering and leaving the city, Carrère & Hastings expected the public library not only to house books but to dignify the act of seeking them out.

The Seattle Central Library (completed in 2004).

Koolhaas and Ramus did not pretend that the world is unchanged since 1911—a view that held sway in Chicago a few years ago when a huge new central library designed by the architect Thomas Beeby went up. It looks vaguely like a nineteenth-century train station and is overbearing and bombastic. The complex polygonal form of the Seattle library, which is sheathed almost entirely in glass set in a diamond-shaped grid, has a dazzling energy; it's the most alluring architectural object to arrive in this city's downtown since the Space Needle. The building manages the neat trick of seeming exotic but not bizarre. Once you have walked around the block a couple of times, it seems almost conventional. In a few years, the great glass tent will connote the appeal of reading as much as New York's marble lions do. It's significant that the building was put up in the land of Microsoft (and with some of the company's money), since it is such a powerful testament to architecture as a container for the delivery of information. We don't need big library buildings the way we once did, but if you surf the Internet at home you are just a click away from a video game. When you do it here, you feel that you are engaged in a serious pursuit. A building like this emphasizes the value a culture places on literacy. (It cost a hundred and sixty-five million dollars, most of which was paid by voter-approved city bonds.)

The library, for which the Seattle firm of LMN Architects served as associate designer, is clearly organized and will be easy to use. When Koolhaas and Ramus designed the building, they did what architects often do—they made a diagram. It was, essentially, five boxes: the book stacks were one box,

The New York Public Library (completed in 1911).

the administrative offices were another, and there were boxes for staff work areas, meeting rooms, and below-ground parking. Then they did something remarkable. For all intents and purposes, they built the diagram. They sketched the boxes floating in space and placed the large public areas—the Living Room, the Mixing Chamber, and the Reading Room—above and below them, surrounded by glass. Turning a diagram into an actual architectural form seems like something of a parlor trick, not to mention being crudely indifferent to aesthetics. In fact, it was neither of these things. The building has a logic to it: functional sections are the starting point, but they are placed so that the spaces between them are large enough and spectacular enough to produce powerful architectural effects. The glass skin is thrown over the entire structure, like a blanket. The diamond pattern in the skin is actually seismic bracing, engineered to protect the building in the event of an earthquake or strong winds.

Deborah Jacobs seems to have been about as close to an ideal client as could be imagined, and she protected the architects from some of their worst instincts. She rejected the green-colored, unfinished Sheetrock that they had used in other projects, including the Prada store in New York, on the ground that it was trite and cheap-looking. "I thought it was important that you have a sense of awe when you come into a public building, especially a library," she said. But she had no interest in a traditional building: "This is the first library of the twenty-first century." Jacobs analyzed every aspect of the library's operations, and insisted that there be no compromise in accommodating them. When the library's trustees saw Koolhaas and Ramus's first design, they were relieved to find that the building fulfilled all the practical demands that had been set. The architects presented the building as a reinvention of the idea of the public library, which in many ways it is. Their greatest achievement, though, is not reinventing the library but in reaffirming it.

QUESTIONS FOR DISCUSSION

1. Goldberger opens his review with an anecdote about how the architect responsible for the new library in Seattle learned about the project. What does this information contribute to the evaluation as a whole?
2. According to Goldberger, technology companies such as Microsoft and Amazon contributed to the discussions that led to planning the new library. How might representatives from such companies offer a perspective different from that of scholars and librarians?
3. What does Goldberger achieve by comparing Seattle's new library with the New York Public Library on Fifth Avenue? What do these two buildings share, as different as they may be to the eye?
4. Goldberger writes that the architects "greatest achievement . . . is not in reinventing the library but in reaffirming it." What does he mean by this?
5. What evaluation criteria are implicit in this review?
6. This evaluation gives high praise to Seattle's new library, describing it "as the most important new library to be built in a generation, and the most exhilarating." (Imagine how you might feel if something like that were said about an essay you had written or a job you had completed.) Does Goldberger offer sufficient evidence to support this praise?

SUGGESTIONS FOR WRITING

1. Write an essay evaluating the design of a library on your campus or in your community. Consider how easy the building is to use and what the design of the building says about the significance of reading.
2. Research the Office for Metropolitan Architecture, and then write an evaluation of another building designed by Rem Koolhaas.
3. Study images of the library in Chicago designed by Thomas Beeby. Goldberger complains that it "is overbearing and bombastic." Write an essay in response, being sure to consider images of both the interior and the exterior.

▌ **LINKS**

▪ **Within the Book**

In "The Re-rebranding of Berlin" (pages 354–357), Annie Bourneuf offers a perspective on architecture in another great city.

■ **Elsewhere in Print**

Brown, Carol. *Interior Design for Libraries.* Chicago: American Library Assn.,
    2002.

DeLaubier, Guillame, et al. *The Most Beautiful Libraries in the World.* New York:
    Abrams, 2003.

Goldberger, Paul. *Architecture and Design in a Postmodern Age.* New York:
    Times, 1983.

———. *The City Observed, New York: A Guide to the Architecture of Manhattan.*
    New York: Random, 1979.

———. *The Skyscraper.* New York: New York: Knopf, 1981.

———. *The World Trade Center Remembered.* New York: Abbeville, 2001.

Rush, Leland. *American Architecture.* New York: Perseus, 2003.

Scully, Vincent. *American Architecture and Urbanism.* New York: Holt, 1988.

■ **Online**

www.mhhe.com/motives

Click on "More Resources" then "Writing to Evaluate Something."

■ ■ ■

SHE: PORTRAIT OF THE ESSAY AS A WARM BODY

Cynthia Ozick

One of the most widely admired American essayists writing today, Cynthia Ozick is also the author of finely crafted short stories. A frequent contributor to the New York Review of Books, *among other periodicals, she published the following essay in a 1998 issue of* The Atlantic. *Instead of evaluating the work of a specific writer, she chose to evaluate the merit of a specific genre: the essay. As you read, be alert for how Ozick distinguishes an "essay" from other genres such as a "tract" and a "novel." Bearing her distinctions in mind could help you to determine which of the selections in this book are essays and which are articles—as well as understand how fiction differs from nonfiction.*

When discussing writing in an interview with Katie Bolick for Atlantic Unbound, *the online version of* The Atlantic, *Ozick stated, "I don't agree with the sentiment 'write what you know.' That recommends circumspection. I think one should write what one doesn't know. The world is bigger and wider and more complex than our small subjective selves. One should prod, goad the imagination. That's what it's there for." Consider what goads your own imagination as you read the following essay.*

An essay is a thing of the imagination. If there is information in an essay, it is by-the-by, and if there is an opinion, one need not trust it for the long run. A genuine essay rarely has an educational, polemical, or sociopolitical use; it is the movement of a free mind at play. Though it is written in prose, it is closer in kind to poetry than to any other form. Like a poem, a genuine essay is made of language and character and mood and temperament and pluck and chance.

I speak of a "genuine" essay because fakes abound. Here the old-fashioned term *poetaster* may apply, if only obliquely. As the poetaster is to the poet—a lesser aspirant—so the average article is to the essay: a look-alike knockoff guaranteed not to wear well. An article is often gossip. An essay is reflection and insight. An article often has the temporary advantage of social heat—what's hot out there right now. An essay's heat is interior. An article can be timely, topical, engaged in the issues and personalities of the moment; it is likely to be stale within the month. In five years it may have acquired the quaint aura of a rotary phone. An article is usually Siamese-twinned to its date of birth. An essay defies its date of birth—and ours, too. (A necessary caveat: Some genuine essays are popularly called "articles"—but this is no more than an idle, though persistent, habit of speech. What's in a name? The ephemeral is the ephemeral. The enduring is the enduring.)

A small historical experiment. Who are the classic essayists who come at once to mind? Montaigne, obviously. Among the nineteenth-century English masters, the long row of Hazlitt, Lamb, De Quincey, Stevenson, Carlyle,

Ruskin, Newman, Martineau, Arnold. Of the Americans, Emerson. Nowadays, admittedly, these are read only by specialists and literature majors, and by the latter only under compulsion. However accurate this observation, it is irrelevant to the experiment, which has to do with beginnings and their disclosures. Here, then, are some introductory passages:

> One of the pleasantest things in the world is going a journey; but I like to go by myself. I can enjoy society in a room; but out of doors, nature is company enough for me. I am then never less alone than when alone.
>
> > —William Hazlitt, "On Going a Journey"

> To go into solitude, a man needs to retire as much from his chamber as from society. I am not solitary whilst I read and write, though nobody is with me. But if a man would be alone, let him look at the stars.
>
> > —Ralph Waldo Emerson, "Nature"

> . . . I have often been asked, how I first came to be a regular opium-eater; and have suffered, very unjustly, in the opinion of my acquaintance, from being reputed to have brought upon myself all the sufferings which I shall have to record, by a long course of indulgence in this practice purely for the sake of creating an artificial state of pleasurable excitement. This, however, is a misrepresentation of my case.
>
> > —Thomas De Quincey,
> > "Confessions of an English Opium-Eater"

> The human species, according to the best theory I can form of it, is composed of two distinct races, *the men who borrow, and the men who lend.*
>
> > —Charles Lamb, "The Two Races of Men"

> I saw two hareems in the East; and it would be wrong to pass them over in an account of my travels; though the subject is as little agreeable as any I can have to treat. I cannot now think of the two mornings thus employed without a heaviness of heart greater than I have ever brought away from Deaf and Dumb Schools, Lunatic Asylums, or even Prisons.
>
> > —Harriet Martineau, "The Hareem"

> The future of poetry is immense, because in poetry, where it is worthy of its high destinies, our race, as time goes on, will find an ever surer and surer stay. There is not a creed which is not shaken, not an accredited dogma which is not shown to be questionable, not a received tradition which does not threaten to dissolve. . . . But for poetry the idea is everything; the rest is a world of illusion, of divine illusion.
>
> > —Matthew Arnold, "The Study of Poetry"

The changes wrought by death are in themselves so sharp and final, and so terrible and melancholy in their consequences, that the thing stands alone in man's experience, and has no parallel upon earth. It outdoes all other accidents because it is the last of them. Sometimes it leaps suddenly upon its victims, like a Thug; sometimes it lays a regular siege and creeps upon their citadel during a score of years. And when the business is done, there is sore havoc made in other people's lives, and a pin knocked out by which many subsidiary friendships hung together.

—Robert Louis Stevenson, "*Aes Triplex*"

It is recorded of some people, as of Alexander the Great, that their sweat, in consequence of some rare and extraordinary constitution, emitted a sweet odour, the cause of which Plutarch and others investigated. But the nature of most bodies is the opposite, and at their best they are free from smell. Even the purest breath has nothing more excellent than to be without offensive odour, like that of very healthy children.

—Michel de Montaigne, "Of Smells"

What might such a little anthology of beginnings reveal? First, that language differs from one era to the next: archaism intrudes, if only in punctuation and cadence. Second, that splendid minds may contradict each other (outdoors, Hazlitt never feels alone; Emerson urges others to go outdoors in order to feel alone). Third, that the theme of an essay can be anything under the sun, however trivial (the smell of sweat) or crushing (the thought that we must die). Fourth, that the essay is a consistently recognizable and venerable—or call it ancient—form. In English, Addison and Steele in the eighteenth century, Bacon and Browne in the seventeenth, Lyly in the sixteenth, Bede in the eighth. And what of the biblical Koheleth (Ecclesiastes), who may be the oldest essayist reflecting on one of the oldest subjects—world-weariness?

So the essay is ancient and various; but this is a commonplace. Something   *5* else, more striking yet, catches our attention—the essay's power. By "power" I mean precisely the capacity to do what force always does: coerce assent. Never mind that the shape and inclination of any essay is against coercion or suasion, or that the essay neither proposes nor purposes to get us to think like its author—at least not overtly. If an essay has a "motive," it is linked more to happenstance and opportunity than to the driven will. A genuine essay is not a doctrinaire tract or a propaganda effort or a broadside. Thomas Paine's "Common Sense" and Emile Zola's "*J'Accuse . . . !*" are heroic landmark writings; but to call them essays, though they may resemble the form, is to misunderstand. The essay is not meant for the barricades; it is a stroll through someone's mazy mind. This is not to say that no essayist has ever been intent on making a moral argument, however obliquely—George Orwell is a case in point. At the end of the day the essay turns out to be a force for agreement. It co-opts agreement; it courts agreement; it seduces agreement. For the brief hour we give to it, we are sure to fall into surrender and conviction. And this will occur even if we are intrinsically roused to resistance.

To illustrate: I may not be persuaded by Emersonianism as an ideology, but Emerson—his voice, his language, his music—persuades me. When we look for words of praise, not for nothing do we speak of "commanding" or "compelling" prose. If I am a skeptical rationalist or an advanced biochemist, I may regard (or discard) the idea of the soul as no better than a puff of warm vapor. But here is Emerson on the soul: "When it breathes through [man's] intellect, it is genius; when it breathes through his will, it is virtue; when it flows through his affection, it is love." And then—well, I am in thrall; I am possessed; I believe.

The novel has its own claims on surrender. It suspends our participation in the society we ordinarily live in, so that for the time we are reading, we forget it utterly. But the essay does not allow us to forget our usual sensations and opinions. It does something even more potent: it makes us deny them. The authority of a masterly essayist—the authority of sublime language and intimate observation—is absolute. When I am with Hazlitt, I know no greater companion than nature. When I am with Emerson, I know no greater solitude than nature.

And what is oddest about the essay's power to lure us into its lair is how it goes about this work. We feel it when a political journalist comes after us with a point of view—we feel it the way the cat is wary of the dog. A polemic is a herald complete with feathered hat and trumpet. A tract can be a trap. Certain magazine articles have the scent of so much per word. What is indisputable is that all of these are more or less in the position of a lepidopterist with his net: They mean to catch and skewer. They are focused on prey—us. The genuine essay, in contrast, never thinks of us; the genuine essay may be the most self-centered (the politer word would be subjective) arena for human thought ever devised.

Or else, though still not having us in mind (unless as an embodiment of common folly), it is not self-centered at all. When I was a child, I discovered in the public library a book that enchanted me then, and the idea of which has enchanted me for life. I have no recollection of either the title or the writer—and anyhow, very young readers rarely take note of authors; stories are simply and magically *there*. The characters include, as I remember them, three or four children and a delightful relation who is a storyteller, and the scheme is this: each child calls out a story element, most often an object, and the storyteller gathers up whatever is supplied (blue boots, a river, a fairy, a pencil box) and makes out of these random, unlikely and disparate offerings a tale both logical and surprising. An essay, it seems to me, may be similarly constructed—if so deliberate a term applies. The essayist, let us say, unexpectedly stumbles over a pair of old blue boots in a corner of the garage, and this reminds her of when she last wore them—twenty years ago, on a trip to Paris, where on the bank of the Seine she stopped to watch an old fellow sketching, with a box of colored pencils at his side. The pencil wiggling over his sheet is a grayish pink, which reflects the threads of sunset pulling westward in the sky, like the reins of a fairy cart . . . and so on. The mind meanders, slipping from one impression to another, from reality to memory to dreamscape and back again.

In the same way Montaigne, when contemplating the unpleasantness of   *10*
sweat, ends with the pure breath of children. Stevenson, starting out with mortality, speaks first of ambush, then of war, and finally of a displaced pin. No one is freer than the essayist—free to leap out in any direction, to hop from thought to thought, to begin with the finish and finish with the middle, or to eschew beginning and end and keep only a middle. The marvel is that out of this apparent causelessness, out of this scattering of idiosyncratic seeing and telling, a coherent world is made. It is coherent because, after all, an essayist must be an artist, and every artist, whatever the means, arrives at a sound and singular imaginative frame—call it, on a minor scale, a cosmogony.

Into this frame, this work of art, we tumble like tar babies, and are held fast. What holds us there? The authority of a voice, yes; the pleasure—sometimes the anxiety—of a new idea, an untried angle, a snatch of reminiscence, bliss displayed or shock conveyed. An essay can be the product of intellect or memory, lightheartedness or gloom, well-being or disgruntlement. But always we sense a certain quietude, on occasion a kind of detachment. Rage and revenge, I think, belong to fiction. The essay is cooler than that. Because it so often engages in acts of memory, and despite its gladder or more antic incarnations, the essay is by and large a serene or melancholic form. It mimics that low electric hum, which sometimes rises to resemble actual speech, that all human beings carry inside their heads—a vibration, garrulous if somewhat indistinct, that never leaves us while we are awake. It is the hum of perpetual noticing: the configuration of someone's eyelid or tooth, the veins on a hand, a wisp of string caught on a twig; some words your fourth-grade teacher said, so long ago, about the rain; the look of an awning, a sidewalk, a bit of cheese left on a plate. All day long this inescapable hum drums on, recalling one thing and another, and pointing out this and this and this. Legend has it that Titus, Emperor of Rome, went mad because of the buzzing of a gnat that made her home in his ear; and presumably the gnat, flying out into the great world and then returning to her nest, whispered what she had seen and felt and learned there. But an essayist is more resourceful than an Emperor, and can be relieved of this interior noise, if only for the time required to record its murmurings. To seize the hum and set it down for others to hear is the essayist's genius.

It is a genius bound to leisure, and even to luxury, if luxury is measured in hours. The essay's limits can be found in its own reflective nature. Poems have been wrested from the inferno of catastrophe or war, and battlefield letters, too; these are the spontaneous bursts and burnings that danger excites. But the meditative temperateness of an essay requires a desk and a chair, a musing and a mooning, a connection to a civilized surround; even when the subject itself is a wilderness of lions and tigers, mulling is the way of it. An essay is a fireside thing, not a conflagration or a safari.

This may be why, when we ask who the essayists are, we discover that though novelists may now and then write essays, true essayists rarely write novels. Essayists are a species of metaphysician: They are inquisitive, and analytic, about the least grain of being. Novelists go about the strenuous business of marrying and burying their people, or else they send them to sea, or to Africa, or at the least out of town. Essayists in their stillness ponder love and death. It is probably an illusion that men are essayists more often than women, especially since women's essays have in the past frequently assumed the form of unpublished correspondence. (Here I should, I suppose, add a note about maleness and femaleness as a literary issue—what is popularly termed "gender," as if men and women were French or German tables and sofas. I *should* add such a note—it is the fashion, or, rather, the current expectation or obligation—but nothing useful can be said about any of it.) Essays are written by men. Essays are written by women. That is the long and the short of it. John Updike, in a genially confident discourse on maleness ("The Disposable Rocket"), takes the view—though he admits to admixture—that the "male sense of space must differ from that of the female, who has such interesting, active, and significant inner space. The space that interests men is outer." Except, let it be observed, when men write essays, since it is only inner space—interesting, active, significant—that can conceive and nourish the contemplative essay. The "ideal female body," Updike adds, "curves around centers of repose," and no phrase could better describe the shape of the ideal essay—yet women are no fitter as essayists than men. In promoting the felt salience of sex, Updike nevertheless drives home an essayist's point. Essays, unlike novels, emerge from the sensations of the self. Fiction creeps into foreign bodies: The novelist can inhabit not only a sex not his own but also beetles and noses and hunger artists and nomads and beasts. The essay is, as we say, personal.

And here is an irony. Though I have been intent on distinguishing the marrow of the essay from the marrow of fiction, I confess that I have been trying all along, in a subliminal way, to speak of the essay as if it—or she— were a character in a novel or a play: moody, fickle, given to changing her clothes, or the subject, on a whim; sometimes obstinate, with a mind of her own, or hazy and light; never predictable. I mean for her to be dressed—and addressed—as we would Becky Sharp, or Ophelia, or Elizabeth Bennet, or Mrs. Ramsay, or Mrs. Wilcox, or even Hester Prynne. Put it that it is pointless to say (as I have done repeatedly, disliking it every time) "the essay," or "an essay." The essay—an essay—is not an abstraction; she may have recognizable contours, but she is highly colored and individuated; she is not a type. She is too fluid, too elusive, to be a category. She may be bold, she may be diffident, she may rely on beauty or cleverness, on eros or exotica. Whatever her story, she is the protagonist, the secret self's personification. When we knock on her door, she opens to us; she is a presence in the doorway; she leads us from room to room. Then why should we not call her "she"? She may be privately indifferent to us, but she is anything but unwelcoming. Above all, she is not a hidden principle or a thesis or a construct: She is *there,* a living voice. She takes us in.

QUESTIONS FOR DISCUSSION

1. According to Ozick, what is the difference between an "essay" and an "article"? Why does Ozick prefer the essay?
2. How do essays differ from fiction?
3. What is your personal response to the introductory passages quoted by Ozick in paragraph 3? Based on these quotations, which essay would most interest you? Which would interest you the least?
4. In paragraph 8, Ozick writes, "A tract can be a trap." What do you think she means by this?
5. Why does Ozick believe that "No one is freer than the essayist"?
6. What do you think of Ozick's use of gender in characterizing the essay? If the essay is a "she," what assumptions are being made about what it means to be a woman?

SUGGESTIONS FOR WRITING

1. Write an essay defining the criteria with which you evaluate either essays or articles.
2. Read one of the essays quoted in paragraph 3, and write an evaluation of it.
3. Evaluate a literary genre or other art form that strikes you as a "he" rather than a "she."

LINKS

■ Within the Book

For examples of essays that have the qualities Ozick admires, see Annie Dillard's "Living Like Weasels" (pages 82–85), André Aciman's "Lavender" (pages 87–94), and John Berger's "Et in Arcadia Ego" (pages 617–625).

■ Elsewhere in Print

Anderson, Chris, ed. *Literary Nonfiction: Theory, Criticism, Pedagogy.* Carbondale, Southern Illinois UP, 1989.
Gutkind, Lee, ed. *In Fact: The Best of Creative Nonfiction.* New York: Norton, 2004.

■ Elsewhere in Print (continued)

Ozick, Cynthia. *The Cannibal Galaxy.* New York: Knopf, 1983.
———. *Fame and Folly.* New York: Knopf, 1996.
———. *Heir to a Glimmering World.* Boston: Houghton, 2004.
———. *Metaphor and Memory.* New York: Knopf, 1989.
———. *Quarrel and Quandary: Essays.* New York: Knopf, 2000.

■ Online

www.mhhe.com/motives

Click on "More Resources" then "Writing to Evaluate Something."

■ ■ ■

5

Writing to Analyze Images

Because you learn through what you see, as well as by what you read or write, the ability to analyze images can help you to determine why some images are memorable while others go unnoticed, how some facilitate learning while others foster misconceptions. Instead of a passive recipient subconsciously influenced by the images your eye takes in, you become a critic who can understand how images are composed and what can be learned from these compositions. In other words, you understand their design and purpose, analyzing images as texts that can be "read" and interpreted. As you proceed, you will discover that different viewers have different responses to images. This is because individuals notice different aspects of images and respond with different degrees of thoughtfulness.

Images are visual representations of people, animals, objects, and concepts. An image can be a painting, drawing, sculpture, map, logo, or photograph (in which there is no written text to accompany the image) or an advertisement, cartoon, or Web page (in which pictures are combined with text). Of course, variations on these possibilities exist: A map may have place names inscribed upon it; a newspaper photograph may have a caption; and even a logo or painting may have words or phrases embedded within it. When you write to analyze an image that includes written as well as visual text, take both into account. Within this chapter, the selections by Jean Kilbourne and Susan Bordo provide the clearest examples of how to analyze works in which visual and written texts are combined.

Both Kilbourne and Bordo focus on the images conveyed through advertising. As one of the principal means by which Americans are exposed to images, advertisements shape markets and even identity in some cases (as, for example, when the use of unusually thin models makes some people believe that self-worth is tied to body weight). Kilbourne and Bordo address issues such as these by focusing on how gender is used to sell products ranging from ice cream to underwear. Kilbourne discusses the use of the female body in advertising, Bordo the use of the male. As with many ads, most of those featured in their analyses use photographs, one of the most important ways images are conveyed to viewers.

Photographs, of course, are not limited to advertising. In addition to the images you keep on your desk or in your album, photographs appear in newspapers, magazines, and books as well as in galleries and museums. When deciding which photographic images to publish or display, editors and curators usually sort through many possibilities before making their selections. In her book *Remembering to Forget: Holocaust Memory through the Camera's Eye,* Barbie Zelizer discusses how photographers tried to communicate the horror of Nazi concentration camps to American and British audiences and how newspaper editors decided what kind of images could be printed. She also discusses how the captions for these images helped shape the way the images were perceived upon publication. In the excerpt from that book reprinted in this chapter, "Conveying Atrocity in Image," Zelizer provides a model analysis that you can use to discuss a series of closely related photographs. Zelizer's work may also help you to understand the selection that follows it in this chapter: "The Pentagon's Secret Stash," by Matt Welch. Like Zelizer, Welch also discusses a series of disturbing photographs—in this case, images showing Iraqi prisoners being abused by American soldiers who seem to be having fun when posing for the camera.

In "The Re-rebranding of Berlin," in contrast, Annie Bourneuf focuses on a single photograph. When doing so, however, she considers what existed before the photograph was taken and what was about to happen afterwards. Her essay can help you to see how a writer can find cultural significance in an image that looks ordinary rather than disturbing.

UNDERSTANDING THE PURPOSE OF ANALYSIS

Like writing to evaluate, writing to analyze images requires the ability to discern the difference between the effective and the ineffective and to explain why you have made this judgment. Moreover, analysis is almost always instructive to some extent. As in writing to explain information, as well as in writing to evaluate something, writing an analysis helps readers to increase their understanding of the subject you have chosen. Moreover, in writing an analysis you will probably increase your own understanding of your subject.

As the article by Jean Kilbourne shows, the use of images often serves a business interest. Similarly, producing an appealing and easily identifiable logo can help make a business or institution seem attractive and memorable. At the same time, understanding how companies and institutions use images can also help make investors, customers, clients, and service users understand that a handsome image does not necessarily prove that a reliable product is behind that image.

Advertising provides an especially clear example of how images are tied to dollars and cents. In a competitive marketplace, companies that can afford it will invest great sums to foster the creation of advertisements and the wide circulation of these images. Good choices can make a company profitable. Consider, for example, how the entrepreneurs behind Abercrombie & Fitch captured a large part of the clothing market for young Americans. Founded in 1892, Abercrombie & Fitch specialized in high-quality outdoor gear. In 1988, the store's parent company was acquired by the owners of The Limited, a chain of casual clothing stores. The new owners then used the distinguished-sounding name of "Abercrombie & Fitch" to launch another chain of casual clothing stores. Although the clothing sold in these stores is unremarkable, it has been successfully tied to images of clean-cut, handsome, and muscular young men who are often partially undressed—with a woman occasionally included in a group scene to suggest that the men in question are heterosexual. Sensible people should understand that wearing clothes from this store will not make them look like the images linked to the brand. But the ads continue to appear, and the clothes continue to sell because effective advertisements often appeal to desire rather than to intelligence.

The need to analyze images is often independent of the marketplace, however. A psychologist, for example, may need to analyze drawings by a young child to help that child therapeutically. An astronomer may need to analyze photographs sent back to Earth from a spacecraft thousands of miles away. A radiologist may need to analyze an X ray when giving a presentation at a professional conference or teaching younger physicians. And a cartographer, anthropologist, or historian may need to analyze ancient maps to determine how another culture understood the rest of the world.

Moreover, writing to analyze images plays an important role in the humanities and fine arts, most notably art history. When you write about a painting, sculpture, or photograph, your purpose may be to show your instructor that you have made a careful study of a specific work of art. But if you do so successfully, you will be achieving a higher purpose: understanding what makes a work of art a thing of beauty or horror, why it haunts the imagination or soothes the spirit. Similarly, a theater major trying to understand why a specific production of a play was successful may need to study photographs of its sets or of the actors at work. An English major may need to analyze the illustrations included in the original edition of a novel, especially if the images in question were made or selected by the novelist.

The full range of how writers in various disciplines analyze images is beyond the reach of this chapter. What matters is that you understand that such writers always have a purpose for analysis, and that purpose is usually educational. A thoughtful analysis of a compelling advertisement may help others become wiser consumers. An accurate analysis of scientific images can help save lives. And a scholarly analysis of art can help readers understand the nature of aesthetics as well as gain knowledge of diverse cultures. As you plan your own essay, remember that you will be assuming the role of a teacher, and decide what you most want your audience to learn from your work.

ESTABLISHING A FRAMEWORK FOR ANALYSIS

To analyze is to separate something into parts and to determine how these parts function together or how one part contributes to the whole. (See page 245.) Accordingly, you must identify the components of the image you wish to analyze, and arrange them in a coherent, easy-to-follow order. The selections in this chapter will help you understand how other writers have met this challenge.

Barbie Zelizer discusses Holocaust photographs in terms of where evidence of atrocity is *placed* within a photograph, the *number* of people in each shot, and the *gaze* of the people portrayed, having established through her research that "near identical images arrived over the wires within hours and days of each other, differing only slightly in focus, distance, exposure, and perspective." This being the case, she decided to analyze these images in terms of what elements they had in common, and these elements provide the structure for her analysis: After discussing *placement,* she discusses *number,* and after number she discusses *gaze.*

As in Zelizer's analysis, photographs and other images can be analyzed in terms of placement, number, and gaze. But other factors are also relevant. Consider the following questions:

- *Subject:* Who or what is in the image? If more than one person, animal, or object appear, what is their relationship to one another?
- *Number:* How many figures or objects appear in the image?
- *Placement:* How are these figures or objects arranged? What appears in the foreground? What appears in the background? What is most prominent in the image? What is of secondary or tertiary importance?
- *Pose:* Do figures appear naturally, or do they seem posed? If posed, what does the pose suggest about the purpose of the image?
- *Gaze:* If there are people or animals in the picture, where are they looking? If they are looking toward the viewer, what does the expression in their eyes convey to you? If they are looking at someone or something else, what does this reveal?
- *Mouth:* Are figures smiling or unsmiling? If smiling, do the smiles seem genuine or forced? Does the smiling mouth correspond to the gaze? Why are these figures smiling? If unsmiling, do the figures seem serious, thoughtful, or unhappy?
- *Clothing:* How are the people in the image dressed? What does their clothing indicate about them? If a person appears partially undressed

or nude, what does this indicate? Does the lack of clothing make this figure seem natural, artistic, silly, or seductive?

- *Color:* If the image is in color, what does the color communicate? Do some colors seem warm or cold—and others neutral? Does color emphasize any specific parts of the image? If the image is in black and white, how do these colors—as well as shades of gray—influence what you see? Are some images more effective in color and others more effective in black and white?

- *Light:* How is the image illuminated? Are all parts of the image equally bright, or does lighting draw your eye in a specific direction? Is the light subtle or harsh? Where is it coming from?

- *Size:* How large is the image? If you are analyzing an image reprinted in a book, newspaper, or magazine, are you seeing the image in its original size, or has the image been reduced or enlarged? How does the size you are seeing influence your perception of the image? How would the image change if its size were changed (for example, if a magazine advertisement were used to fill a large billboard)?

- *Context:* Where and when did the image originally appear? How would this context affect the choice of subject and the way the subject is treated? How does the image appear when studied outside its original context?

- *Association:* Does the image seem similar in any way to other images you have seen? If so, do you think the image maker was influenced directly by work done by someone else? Or are you making a comparison on your own that could help readers understand the work in question?

Most of these questions are also appropriate for the analysis of paintings and photographs that do not include human figures. If writing about a landscape, for example, you could analyze that image by discussing *subject, placement, color, light, size, context,* and *association.* These factors are also useful when analyzing abstract contemporary art (or other images such as a map or logo). Although there may be occasions when you can benefit from considering all the factors in the preceding list, do not think that you must always do so. Work with those that seem best suited to the specific image you wish to analyze.

CONSIDERING AUDIENCE

Finding the right audience can be challenging for writers who are drawn to analyzing images. Such audiences exist—as demonstrated by the publication history of the works included in this chapter. The writers include people interested in ethics, history, advertising, and urban planning. But many people are initially resistant to the thoughtful analysis of images. "It's just a picture," they might say, or "I don't know much about art, but I know what I like." The cliché that "a picture is worth a thousand words" reflects the mistaken assumption that images speak for themselves. In fact, no matter how powerful or commonplace an image may seem at first glance, there is almost always a good deal to say about it. So one of your challenges when writing to analyze images is to find an audience that will read your analysis attentively. There may be occasions when that audience is right before you. For example, if you are taking a course in art history, you can reasonably assume that your professor will be prepared to take your work seriously. Similarly, you may find an academic audience ready to read an analysis of images of the female body (in a sociology or women's study course), of a logo or advertisement (in a course on marketing), or of an old photograph (in a history course). And, of course, the instructor who has required this book and assigned this chapter is likely to be an attentive audience for visual analysis.

But if you are interested in reaching a larger audience, you can take heart in recognizing that people who initially resist visual analysis can nevertheless become engaged by your ideas if you choose a suitable topic and say something meaningful about it. Consider, in this respect, what happens when friends or co-workers share snapshots with one another. The photographer almost always provides some commentary on the images, and the viewers often ask questions about what they are seeing. Conversations such as these may be brief (even if the pile of photographs is large), but they remind us that many pictures do not speak for themselves and that people can enjoy the analysis of images if the presenter (or author) establishes a friendly or professional connection with them.

When you are free to envision your own audience, you can imagine that you are writing for a group of art historians, fashion editors, or anyone else you think will already have an interest in your topic. But when you begin with an audience and then must decide what material to analyze for that audience (as could be the case when writing for classmates in a required English course), you need to think about how to generate interest when interest does not already exist. And a good way to proceed is to think about what interests you. If you are interested in the images you decide to analyze, and successfully convey that feeling to others (as opposed, say, to sounding as if you are writing merely to complete an assignment), then there is a good chance you will interest readers in your material as well.

CHOOSING A SUBJECT

Images are broadcast to you throughout the day, and you encounter other images by leading the life you want to live. If you choose to visit a museum, for example, you will see images that differ from those in general-circulation magazines. And if you spend much of your time in cyberspace, you will see images that may never reach someone who does not use a computer. When choosing a subject, consider what kinds of images you have the most familiarity with or what kinds you most want to learn about. Remember also that the nature of an image ultimately matters less than what you have to say about it. While a painting may be worth millions of dollars in terms of market value and a photograph only a dollar or two, a thoughtful analysis of a photograph can be much more educational than a superficial analysis of a great work of art. But be sure to consider the needs and expectations of your audience as well: What kind of image would your readers be most likely to enjoy? What might be new for them and helpful to understand?

Look for images that catch your attention because you find them compelling or disturbing. Choosing as your subject an image that evokes a strong personal response can help get you get started. As you analyze the image, you can then determine what elements provoked your response. You might even include this personal response in the introduction or conclusion of your essay. Remember, however, that you will be analyzing an image, not analyzing yourself. You must be able to focus on the image itself, discussing its different components rather than dwelling on your feelings. In other words, look closely at the image you choose, and write about its design and purpose. Include your feelings about the image only if you can tie these feelings to details in the image, and devote most of your essay to these details.

Several of the writers in this chapter discuss multiple images because they want to show how a pattern emerges—a pattern that can help readers to analyze similar images that they discover on their own. Undertaking work of this kind requires extensive research and limits the extent to which any single image can be analyzed. When planning a short essay of your own, you will usually benefit from focusing on a single image or on two images that can become more easily understood when compared.

Experienced though you may be in seeing images, writing about images may be new to you. If so, you may benefit from choosing an image that has some complexity. For example, an image of two or three people who seem to have some kind of relationship to each other may give you more to write about than an image of a single person. On the other hand, the image of a single person may generate lots of ideas if this person's appearance or setting is noteworthy. Similarly, a painting done in many colors may give you more to say than a painting done in two. A Web page with interesting colors and other design elements may be easier to discuss than a page that consists entirely of text laid out in an unremarkable pattern. As you gain experience in analyzing images, you will find that you are able to see complexity in images that seem simple at first glance, because you are learning to read visual texts as closely as you read written texts. But if you begin with a simple image (such as a conventional head-and-shoulders photograph in a high school yearbook), you may be undertaking too great a challenge at first. Give yourself the opportunity to develop an essay on a subject about which much can be said.

ORGANIZING YOUR ESSAY

Considering the elements listed on pages 306–307 can help you decide how to organize your essay. The first step is to determine which elements will help you analyze the image you have chosen; the second is to decide on the order in which to arrange the discussion of these elements. There is no single pattern that is appropriate for every analysis. The sequence in which you arrange your ideas should be determined by what you want to say and what pattern will help you to move easily from one part of your analysis to another.

The following guidelines may be useful, however:

- *Introduction:* Because your readers will need some kind of orientation before they can appreciate your analysis, you can help them by introducing your *subject*. This is the time to define the subject and to identify who created it (if the artist or designer is known to you). The introduction is also a good place to explain where you found the image and why you have chosen to work with it. Moreover, if you plan to provide information about *context,* the introduction may be the best place to do so because details about the work's history can give readers useful background. Finally, information about *size* is also helpful when placed early in an analysis.

- *Body:* Discussion of *number* should usually proceed discussion of *placement* because it is easier to discuss how figures, objects, and space are arranged after you have established how many components exist in the image. In other words, number provides information that can help you to introduce placement. When discussing number, do not settle for identifying the number in question. Name each of the figures, objects, or other elements in the image you are analyzing, and arrange this list in the order you will follow when discussing placement. If your image includes human figures, keep your discussion of elements such as pose, gaze, mouth, and clothing together rather than discussing pose and then color, and then moving back to gaze. Similarly, color and lighting are closely related, so if you are planning to discuss both of these, it probably is best to locate them next to each other.

- *Conclusion:* Although *association* can form the body of an essay when your purpose is to compare or contrast two works, it can contribute to the conclusion of an essay about a single image. People often learn new ideas when these ideas are linked to something they already know. Considering the nature and expectations of your audience, you might decide that it will be helpful to conclude your essay with a paragraph linking the image you have been discussing with other images that may be more familiar to your readers. Of course, the conclusion also provides a good opportunity to summarize your main points or to indicate why you think readers can benefit from your analysis. If you have not done so in your introduction (and perhaps even if you have), the conclusion also provides an opportunity to emphasize the most important point you want your audience to understand about the image or images in question.

ADDITIONAL CONSIDERATIONS

As you draft your analysis, remember that you are writing about an image, not about the reality that may have inspired the image. If you are analyzing a painting of Niagara Falls, you are writing about the painting—not the actual waterfall. Similarly, if you are writing about an advertisement for an automobile, you are writing about the ad—not the car. Information about the reality behind the image is relevant only if it helps readers better understand the image—for example, "In order to emphasize the grandeur of the falls, the artist has made them appear larger than they actually are," or "Photographed from this angle, the car seems to have a larger interior than it actually has." In most cases, however, you must stay focused on the image. If you are writing about an image of a person or place you care about, or perhaps an advertisement for some product you long to acquire, you could easily drift away from the image to your own memories and dreams. If you accidentally do so when drafting, eliminate these passages when you revise, unless a brief discussion along these lines helps you to introduce or conclude your essay. The body of the essay must address the elements you identify in the image.

Because writers often benefit from narrowing their focus, you may decide to address only one or two elements in a short essay. For example, you could write an essay focused exclusively on an artist's use of color in a specific painting or on a photographer's use of placement. When narrowing your focus, however, think twice before eliminating any element that is closely related to your focus. If you are discussing the foreground of a photograph, for example, your readers may expect you to balance this discussion with analysis of the background. If you are analyzing a painting of a woman and child seated in a garden, you might decide to focus on the human figures rather than on the setting. But if you write about the woman, your audience will probably expect you to write about the child as well.

When you have drafted and revised your essay, be sure to attach a copy of the image or images you are analyzing. You can attach photocopies of the work in question at the end of your essay as a kind of appendix, including an image of the work as a whole and, if useful, an enlargement of parts of the work you want your audience to see clearly. If you have the necessary software and skills, you can communicate better with your audience by locating the image (and various parts of the image) within the text of your essay. If the work you are analyzing appeared in color, and you are discussing the use of color in your analysis, use a color printer or photocopier, and check the accuracy of the color reproduction you have achieved. If there is any variation of the color in the image you originally encountered and the image copy you are including in your essay, be sure to alert your audience to this difference.

TIPS FOR READING AND WRITING ANALYSES OF IMAGES

When Reading

■ Consider why the writer has chosen to analyze the image or images in question. What benefit can be derived from understanding the nature of these images?

■ Determine what the writer has detected in the image or images under analysis, and think about whether you can see what the writer saw.

■ If the writer has analyzed more than one image, consider how closely they are related and how well they are arranged.

■ Ask yourself if you see anything in the image or images that the writer has failed to detect.

When Writing

■ Choose images that offer grounds for analysis; avoid those to which you want to attach a story that is not evoked by specific visual components.

■ Assume that any good image is worth more than a thousand words.

■ Confine yourself to one or two images unless you are able to write at length.

■ Use the questions on pages 306–307 to generate ideas.

■ Organize your analysis so that your audience can tell why you are discussing the various components of the image or images in a certain sequence.

■ Make sure that both your introduction and your conclusion establish why the image or images you have analyzed have significance for your audience.

PLEASE, PLEASE, YOU'RE DRIVING ME WILD

Jean Kilbourne

Named by the New York Times *as one of the three most popular speakers on campuses across the country, Jean Kilbourne has done groundbreaking work on the effects of using images of women in advertisements for tobacco, alcohol, and food. Drawing upon her research, Kilbourne has produced three award-winning documentaries:* Killing Us Softly, Slim Hopes, *and* Pack of Lies. *Currently a visiting scholar at Wellesley College, she has also served as an advisor to the U.S. Surgeon General.*

The following selection is a chapter in her book Deadly Persuasion: Why Women and Girls Must Fight the Addictive Power of Advertising *(1999). As you read it, note how Kilbourne is careful to give credit to the creativity of the advertising industry even though she is deeply concerned about the addictive behaviors she believes are encouraged by advertisements for food and diets. (For information about Kilbourne's sources, visit www.mhhe.com/motives and click on "More Resources" then "Writing to Analyze Images.")*

While men are encouraged to fall in love with their cars, women are more often invited to have a romance, indeed an erotic, experience with something even closer to home, something that truly does pump the valves of our hearts—the food we eat. And the consequences become even more severe as we enter into the territory of compulsivity and addiction.

Women have always been closely linked with food—with its gathering, preparation, and serving. We're called peaches, tomatoes, pieces of meat, dishes . . . honey, sugar, sweetie. Beautiful women, especially those who accompany playboys and older men, are "arm candy." And increasingly, as with ads for cars and other products, the thing becomes the lover, as in the ad in a Thai publication featuring two scoops of ice cream as a woman's breasts.

Food is intertwined with love throughout our culture. We give chocolates on Valentine's Day. We say that we are "starved for affection." We think of certain foods, such as custard, ice cream, and macaroni and cheese, as "comfort foods." In infancy and early childhood, food was a major way we were connected to someone else, the most important way that we were nurtured. Many of us had caregivers who used food as a reward or a punishment. Others suffered terrible trauma in childhood and learned to use food for solace and escape. No wonder feeding ourselves can sometimes be an attempt to re-create some sense of wholeness and connection. No wonder it is so easy to confuse food and love.

Food has long been advertised as a way for women both to demonstrate our love and to ensure its requital. Countless television commercials feature a woman trying to get her husband and children to love her or just to pay

Hiding behind a door while eating ice cream out of its container.

attention to her via the cakes and breakfast cereals and muffins she serves them. "Bake a Comstock pie," one ad says, "they'll love you for it." Instant oatmeal "warms your heart and soul," a print ad tells us, "like a hug that lasts all day." "Awesome Mom" is the tagline for an ad featuring a little boy smiling widely, obviously delighted to find prepackaged junk food in his lunchbox. "Skip the Zip on my little girl's sandwich and give up one of her bear hugs? Not in her lifetime," says a mother hugging her daughter in a mayonnaise ad. The implication, of course, is that the child won't hug her mother unless she gets the right kind of mayonnaise on her sandwich. As always, the heartfelt connection, the warm relationship is simply a device to sell something—and even our children's love for us is contingent upon our buying the right product.

Very few ads feature women being given food by men or even by other women. More often, when a woman is being fed, she is feeding herself. A television commercial for candy features a series of vignettes in which what a woman does for others (such as making a costume for her daughter) is ignored and unappreciated. At the end of each vignette, the woman pops a piece of candy in her mouth and says, "I thank me very much with Andy's Candies." Another commercial featuring a woman feeding herself candy has the tagline "From you to you."

In many of these commercials, the woman is not only rewarding herself, she also is coping with her disappointment at being unappreciated. Advertisers often offer food as a way to repress anger, resentment, and hurt feelings. "What to do for dinner after a long day of eating your words and swallowing your pride" says an ad for frozen chicken. "Got a big mouth?" asks an ad for caramel candies, "Put a soft chewy in it." "Not satisfied with your payday?" asks an ad for Payday candy bars. "Try ours." And an ice cream ad featuring a young woman walking her dog says, "He never called. So Ben and I went out for a pint of Frusen Glädjé. Ben's better looking anyway." Another ad features the empty foil wrappings of twelve pieces of candy with statements beneath them, from "I didn't sleep late" to "I didn't call him" to "I didn't buy it," "I didn't put off the laundry," "I didn't get upset" to "I didn't skip gym," ending with "He called."

It is interesting that the ad includes so many ways that people escape from difficulties with relationships (shopping, sleeping, watching television) and yet encourages one of the most common escape routes of all, overeating. I am especially struck by "I didn't get upset." Sometimes getting upset is the healthiest and most appropriate response. Certainly it is better to get upset than to numb one's feelings with an overdose of chocolate. Better for us, that is—not better for candy manufacturers. No wonder they run ads like the one that says, "Whatever mood you're in, you're always in the mood for chocolate."

A 1995 Häagen-Dazs ad features a large spoon dipping into a pint of ice cream and the copy, "Your fiance agreed to have a big wedding. *Have a Häagen-Dazs.* He wants to have it in a Sports Bar. *Have some more.*" Again the message to women is clear. When your man upsets you, don't make trouble, don't argue, just eat something—or have a drink or a tranquilizer or a cigarette. "At least one thing in your day will go smoothly," says an ad for a candy bar. Sadly, many women do eat compulsively in an attempt to assuage loneliness and disappointment within relationships (from the past as well as in the present). Family therapist Jill Harkaway says, "When you are lonely, you can't count on people, but you can count on your refrigerator or the nearby 7-Eleven not to let you down." Of course, this fails to address the real problems, thus ensuring continued feelings of isolation and alienation, while breeding eating disorders.

Advertisers spend a lot of money on psychological research. They know that many people, especially women, use food to help us deal with loneliness and disappointment and also as a way to connect. The ads play on this. "You know that empty feeling you have when you're watching what you eat?" asks a four-page ad featuring an empty dessert bowl on the first page. "Start filling up," the ad continues on the next two pages, which picture a variety of sugar-free puddings. A 1999 Burger King commercial features flashes of food and the Burger King logo while Leslie Gore's old hit "It's My Party" plays in the background—"It's my party and I'll cry if I want to." The final caption reads "Stop crying and start eating," and the burger disappears in three large bites.

Advertisers especially offer food as a way to relate romantically and sexu-   *10*
ally. A television commercial for a pasta sauce features a couple eating and
gazing intensely at each other while "I don't know why I love you like I do"
plays in the background. "In the mood for something really intense?" asks the
sexy female voiceover. The couple feed each other while the words "Unexpected . . . Intense . . . Bold" appear onscreen. In the last shot, the woman is
suggestively licking the man's finger while the voiceover says, "You're gonna
love it." And an ad for a frozen mousse dessert features Dr. Ruth Westheimer,
America's sexual guru, digging in and advising the reader, "Achieving mutual
satisfaction is easy. Just share some Mousse du Jour."

One of my favorite ads of all time ran in the early 1980s in many women's
magazines. It showed a closeup of a woman's face. She was smiling very seductively, and the copy said, "Whatever you're giving him tonight, he'll enjoy it
more with rice." As I said to my audiences at the time, "I don't think I'm particularly naive, but I haven't figured out what the hell you do with rice." "Maybe
it's wild rice," someone suggested. Another woman called out, "Let's just hope it
isn't Minute Rice." The 1990s version of using sex to sell rice is much more
explicit, of course: an ad for Uncle Ben's rice shows a woman feeding a man a
forkful of rice by candlelight. The copy says, "Passion Lesson #13. From now
on every night would be different . . . filled with endless variety."

One of the most erotic commercials I have ever seen is a British one (no
doubt too racy for America) that features a man and a woman making love
while feeding each other something. Because the commercial is shot with in-
frared film, we see only their shapes and intense patterns of red and yellow
and blue. "Make Yourself Comfortable" is playing on the record player. They
lick some substance off each other's bodies, while an elderly man below bangs
on the ceiling with a broomstick, shouting "Mr. Rogers" (thus playing on the
British slang "to roger," meaning to have intercourse, and also implying that
the man is single and that this is a tryst, not a marriage). At the very end of
the commercial we see that the couple's erotic toy is a pint of Häagen-Dazs
ice cream. "Dedicated to pleasure" is the slogan.

This campaign ran in print too, with erotic black and white photographs
by French photographer Jeanloup Sieff. In just a few months after the campaign broke in upscale magazines such as *Tatler* and *Vogue,* sales of Häagen-
Dazs in Great Britain rose 400 percent. This spectacular success indicates that
advertisers do indeed sometimes know what they are doing.

Of course, we are not stupid. We don't for a minute believe that we're actually going to improve our relationships with ice cream or pasta sauce. But
these ads do contribute to a cultural climate in which relationships are constantly trivialized and we are encouraged to connect via consumption. An obsession with food interferes with real relationships just as any other obsession
does, yet food advertising often normalizes and glamorizes such an obsession.

We are not only offered connection via the product, we are offered con-   *15*
nection *with* the product. Food becomes the lover. "Rich, impeccable taste
and *not an ounce of fat*. Wow, if only I could find a guy like that," says a woman

holding a candy bar. "Looking for a light cheesy relationship?" asks an ad for macaroni and cheese, which concludes with a shot of the package and the copy, "Oh, baby, where have you been all my life?" And another ad features an extreme closeup of potatoes with the headline, "Potatoes that get more oohs and aahs than a supermodel." This ad ran in women's magazines and clearly targets women, so the promise is that the woman can distract her husband's attention from supermodels by cooking the right food.

Men are sometimes also targeted, however, with the message that food is love. In a commercial broadcast on Valentine's Day, romantic music plays as we see a couple coming out of the Tunnel of Love at an amusement park, embracing passionately. A voiceover says, "Can you put a price on love?" As the next boat comes out of the tunnel, carrying a man alone, eating a large hamburger, the voiceover continues, "You betcha—if the object of your affection is a McDonald's Big Mac!" The man seems delirious with happiness as he eats his burger, and the voiceover gives some details about the price and says, "Taste that makes you swoon. Or, if you're a two-timer, get cozy with two Big Mac sandwiches. But hurry—your love may be eternal but these prices aren't." The commercial ends with the old man who is running the ride looking with envy at the man with the burger while saying to his helper, "Where does one find such love?"

However, women and girls are targeted far more often. A television commercial broadcast during *Sabrina, the Teenage Witch,* a show popular with teenage girls, features a woman reading a book by a window. "You are my destiny, you share my reverie, you're more than life can be" plays in the background. The woman takes a bite of a cookie and fantasizes a handsome man on a white horse coming to her, riding his horse into her house. "Ah," a female voiceover says, "the new moister-than-ever devil's food cookie from SnackWell." The man reaches for the cookie and the woman turns him into a frog. "Passion, desire, devotion?" says the voiceover while the words appear on screen. "Nah, it goes way beyond that." This is funny, of course, but it also normalizes an obsession with food that takes precedence over human connection.

Another television commercial goes even further. It begins with an extreme closeup of the peaks and swirls of frosting on a cake. A woman's voice passionately says, "Oh, my love." A man's voice says, "Huh?" and the woman replies, "Not you—the frosting!" With increasing excitement, she continues, "It's calling my name!" and the man replies, "Janet?" The woman cries out, "I'm yours!" as a male voiceover says, "Give in to the rich and creamy temptation of Betty Crocker frosting." As one of the peaks of the frosting peaks, so to speak, and then droops, the woman says, in a voice rich with satisfaction, "That was great." As is often the case, this ad is very funny and seemingly harmless. But also, as is often the case, it is frightful upon reflection. A human relationship is trivialized and ignored ("Not you—the frosting!") while someone connects passionately with a product. Imagine if this were an ad for alcohol ("Not you—the bourbon!"). Perhaps we'd understand how sad and alienating it is.

"I had a dream about salad dressing. Is that weird?" asks a woman lifting a lettuce leaf to her mouth. Of course it's weird! A Cool Whip ad shows a manicured hand plunging a strawberry into whipped cream and the caption, "Go skinny dippin'." And an ad for frozen yogurt features a closeup of a woman's face in what looks like sexual ecstasy and the copy, "Vanilla so pure it sends chills down your spine and back up again." Another version of the ad shows the same ecstatic face and the copy, "Your tastebuds cry out yes yes. Oh, yes." Shades of Molly Bloom!°

Certainly food can be an important part of loving ourselves and others. It [20] can be comforting as well as nourishing, and indeed it can be sexy. When a friend of mine told her husband on the phone that she had just eaten a persimmon, he said, "You had sex without me!" Who can forget the erotic feasting scene in the film *Tom Jones,* the characters looking hungrily at each other, grease glistening on their lips, while ripping meat from bones? This scene, which shocked many people back in 1963, would be tame compared to many food advertisements today.

Often food is shot in extreme closeup and is very sensually inviting. "Bet this little lite will turn you on," says an ad that features a very suggestive closeup of the inside of a candy bar. Another ad featuring a Fudgsicle oozing its chocolate filling is headlined, "Introducing our deep, dark secret," and an ad for a cereal bar says, "Trapped inside this wholesome rolled oats crust is a sultry little French pastry struggling to get out."

A hilarious ad for sour cream features a baked potato begging for the sour cream's touch, "Please . . . please . . . you're driving me wild." Another baked potato is brought to ecstasy by a bottle of tabasco sauce (named "The Exciter"). Indeed there were a series of ads featuring tabasco sauce as a stud. At the end of what must have been a wild night in the kitchen, the bottle is on its side, empty, and the copy says, "A good time was had by all." These ads are powerful examples of the wit, humor, and sheer cleverness one sometimes finds in advertising. There is no harm and indeed much delight in them individually, but their cumulative impact is another story.

Just what is this cumulative impact? What's the problem? For one thing, when food is sex, eating becomes a moral issue—and thinness becomes the equivalent of virginity. The "good girl" today is the thin girl, the one who keeps her appetite for food (and power, sex, and equality) under control. "I'm a girl who just can't say no. I insist on dessert," proclaims a thin woman in an ad for a sugar-free gelatin. It used to be that women who couldn't say no were talking about something other than food. Women were supposed to control their sexual appetites. Now we're supposed to control our appetite for food. If a woman comes back from a weekend and says she was "bad," we assume she broke her diet, not that she did something interesting sexually. The *ménage à trois* we are made to feel ashamed of is with Ben and Jerry.

°*Molly Bloom:* Character in *Ulysses* by James Joyce who speaks the final words in the novel, words that signify her willingness to have sex: "yes I said yes I will Yes."

"Pizza without guilt," declares an ad featuring a heavyset woman tied up to keep her from eating regular pizza. Weight Watchers ads feature extreme closeups of rich foods and the slogan, "Total indulgence. Zero guilt." As if women should feel guilty about eating!

In the old days, bad girls got pregnant. These days they get fat—and are 25 more scorned, shamed, and despised than ever before. Prejudice against fat people, especially against fat women, is one of the few remaining prejudices that is socially acceptable. This strikes fear into the hearts of most women, who are terrified of inspiring revulsion and ridicule. And this contributes mightily, of course, to the obsession with thinness that has gripped our culture for many years, with devastating consequences for many women and girls.

A television commercial for ice cream features actor Bernadette Peters in slinky pajamas in her kitchen at night. "I love being naughty," she says in her little-girl voice, "especially when I can get away with it. Like with Breyer's light ice cream. It has less fat so I can indulge in sinful fudge . . . real vanilla." Her voice is rising as she becomes more excited and builds to an orgasmic crescendo—"Mmmm, pure true taste!" Almost out of breath, she slides down the refrigerator door, saying, "I feel like I'm cheating, but I'm not . . . what a shame."

This moral tone shows up again and again, often with religious connotations. A rich chocolate sundae is labeled "Temptation" on one side of a page. On the other is the "Salvation," a low-calorie shake. "40% Sin 60% Forgiveness," proclaims an ad featuring a priest eating a blend of butter and margarine. And an ad for pork, touting its leanness, says, "We lead you to temptation but deliver you from evil."

However, unlike traditional religious morality in which one has to suffer, to do penance in order to be saved, we are offered products that will allow us to sin without consequence. Just as advertising constantly offers us sex without the burdens and responsibilities of a relationship, it offers us the pleasure of consuming rich foods without having to "pay the price." Now that we have birth control, to eliminate the "sin" of pregnancy but not the joy of sex, all we need is girth control, to eliminate the "sin" of obesity but not the joy of overeating. It doesn't matter if we are "guilty" as long as we don't look it. If we can remain thin by taking laxatives or diet pills or chugging artificially sweetened colas and eating low-fat ice cream rather than exercising moderately and eating healthfully or joining a recovery program, so much the better. In fact, bulimia is the ultimate solution.

Another problematic aspect of the cumulative impact of food advertising is that many ads normalize and glamorize harmful and often dangerous attitudes toward food and eating. And we suffer drastically as a culture from the negative consequences of these attitudes. About eighty million Americans are clinically obese, and nearly three out of four are overweight. Indeed, in a culture seemingly obsessed with thinness and fitness, Americans are fatter than ever and fatter than people in most other cultures. Eight million Americans suffer from an eating disorder and as many as 10 percent of all college-age women are bulimic. Eating disorders are the third most common chronic illness among females. In fact, they are so common it really is misleading to refer to them as "disorders." More accurately, they are a common way that women cope with the difficulties in their lives and with the cultural contra-dictions involving food and eating. Few of us aren't touched by some kind of problem with food (not to mention the thirty million at risk for hunger and malnutrition).

There are many reasons for these problems, ranging from the decrease in   30 physical education in our schools to our use of the automobile to the devel-opment of the TV remote control to fear of crime, which keeps people in-doors, often in front of the television set with its blaring litany of commercials for junk food and diet products. American children see over ten thousand commercials for food on television each year. Ninety-five percent are for four food groups: soft drinks, candy, fast food, and sugar-coated cereal. There's a lot of money at stake: Americans spend an estimated $14 billion a year on snack foods, $15 billion on chocolate, and $86 billion on fast food restaurants.

The commercials are only one part of the problem, but they are a signifi-cant part. Just as alcohol ads teach us that drinking leads inevitably to good times, great sex, athletic prowess, and success, without any risks or negative consequences whatsoever, so do the food ads associate eating and overeating with only good things. The negative consequences are obliterated. Indeed, in order to maximize their profits, the junk food and the diet industries need to normalize and glamorize disordered and destructive attitudes toward food and eating.

One of the clearest examples of this is the advertising campaigns for Häagen-Dazs ice cream over a period of several years. In 1990 "Enter the state of Häagen-Dazs" was the slogan for this popular ice cream. The ads fea-tured blissful men and women eating Häagen-Dazs. Sometimes the container was empty, but the people seemed calm and happy, somewhat smug, maybe even slightly stoned. The focus was on the smiling person in the ad, not the product, and the ad was in full color.

In 1991 a new Häagen-Dazs campaign featured ghostly black-and-white photographs of people with copy inscribed over their faces. In one a man is say-ing, "Maybe I'm a bit of a perfectionist. My CD's are in alphabetical order. . . . Yet everytime I have Häagen-Dazs I seem to lose control. . . . Each creamy spoonful was a moment suspended in time. I would have stopped before I finished the whole pint. Only problem was, I couldn't find the lid."

In another, a woman says, "I pride myself on my level-headed approach to life. . . . But all it takes is one smooth taste of Häagen-Dazs Strawberry ice cream and I find myself letting go. . . . I must do something about this Häagen-Dazs passion. Maybe I could organize it, structure it or control it . . . tomor-row." The campaign slogan is "Täaste the Passion." What an invitation to binge this is! People who feel too controlled in their lives, with too few avenues to real passion, often turn to food or other potentially addictive products as a way to loosen up, to relax. This campaign normalizes and legitimizes this process.

By 1992 there were no longer people in the ads at all, simply a large pho-   35 tograph of the pint of ice cream, with copy beginning in small letters and gradually growing larger and larger. "Wow have you seen it? Another outrageous Exträs ice cream from Häagen-Dazs. . . . Oh my gosh! Luscious fudge chunks too. Give me the entire pint of Cookie Dough Dynamo!"

These few years of Häagen-Dazs advertising perfectly illustrate the progression of addiction. The first ad features a woman nibbling on an ice cream bar, somewhat spaced-out but still in control. In the second, a man talks about losing control and unintentionally finishing a pint. In the third, someone is shouting "I need it" and "Give me the entire pint." Granted, this is not heroin we're talking about. But compulsive overeaters will certainly say that their addiction rules and ruins their lives as completely as any other.

Although addiction to food is often trivialized, it is in fact a major problem for many women and men. People who binge on food and overeat compulsively say this has the same effect on their minds and lives as does addiction to alcohol and other drugs. They experience the terror of loss of control, diminished self-esteem, damaged relationships, and even such consequences as hangovers and blackouts. In *Make the Connection,* her best-selling book about overcoming a lifelong eating problem, Oprah Winfrey writes about a binge she had when all she could find in her kitchen was salt, Tabasco sauce, starch, maple syrup, and frozen hot dog buns. "Quickly I turned the oven on broil, threw the buns in to thaw out, and even before they could, I grabbed the syrup and smeared it over the partly burnt, partly frozen buns. Looking back, I see no difference between myself and a junkie, scrambling for a needle and whatever dope might be around. Food was my drug."

There are those who question whether food can be truly addictive. They believe that compulsive overeaters simply lack willpower. Some people still feel this way about alcoholics, although there is much more evidence these days that alcoholism is a disease. Scientists increasingly are discovering physiological and biochemical bases for eating disorders just as for alcoholism. A 1999 study, published in the American Medical Association's *Archives of General Psychiatry,* found that bulimia springs at least in part from a chemical malfunction in the brain resulting in low levels of serotonin, a mood-and-appetite-regulating chemical.

These days many people are cross-addicted. In fact, it is rare to find someone with a single addiction. Most alcoholics are addicted to other drugs too, especially nicotine. Women often wash their tranquilizers down with alcohol or become addicted to amphetamines in an attempt to control their obsession with food. The frequency of eating disorders is significantly higher in alcoholic women than in the general population. Many women with eating disorders come from alcoholic homes. Current research indicates that alcoholism and eating disorders often occur together but are transmitted independently in families. Whatever the origins, it is clear that neither alcoholism nor eating disorders are linked with any character weaknesses.

Advertisers are clearly aware of the psychology of food addiction and compulsive overeating. Since food addicts spend a lot of money on food, it is to the advertisers' advantage to make their obsessive and addictive attitudes seem normal and appropriate. An ad featuring a suggestive closeup of a candy

40

bar says, "What you do in the dark is nobody else's business." Compulsive eaters almost always binge alone and feel terribly ashamed. This ad is clearly meant both to tempt and to assuage guilt feelings, to help the eater rationalize his or her behavior, to create the climate of denial so essential for addictions to flourish.

A 1998 SnackWell's campaign cuts right to the heart of the matter by openly declaring that eating cookies will boost a woman's self-esteem. The commercials show scenes of women in warm family embraces, while a voiceover says that eating SnackWell's isn't about feeding yourself but "feeding your self-esteem," "treating yourself well," and "fulfilling yourself." Even Bob Garfield of *Advertising Age* responded to this campaign with "Women of America, feel better about yourselves: Pig out on crap!" He continues, "Feeling a bit down on yourself? Have a cookie. Career stagnating and love life not working out? Have 28 cookies. Suicidal depression? Get the caramel-filled one, melt it in a spoon and inject it directly into your vein." Eating to feel better about oneself is not a healthy idea—it is a symptom of a problem.

A recent candy commercial further illustrates this normalization of problematic attitudes. The commercial begins with a middle-aged man seated in an armchair, holding a piece of candy in his hand. He says, "What a combination—crunchy Werther's toffee and delicious milk chocolate . . . mmm." The scene switches to a beautiful young blond woman standing beside her car. She is holding a bag of the candy and says, "I keep one bag in the car, one in my desk, one in the living room, and one next to my bed." Hoarding the supply is one of the signs of addiction. Although alcoholics are best known for this (hiding bottles in toilet tanks and linen closets), most addicts do it. Surely a woman who can't be far from her stash of candy has got a problem.

The next scene in the commercial features a man in a suit holding up one piece of candy, almost as if it were a cigar, and saying, "Now that's where there's quality." Next we see a middle-aged woman pouring the candy into a dish in her kitchen. She says, "Nothing but the best for my guests." Next, a woman in a slinky black dress is seated in an armchair beside a blazing fire. A bag of chocolates is cuddled up against her. She slowly unwraps one piece and pops it in her mouth, saying suggestively, "It's going to be a *nice* evening." At this point, we see a closeup of a bowl of candy, and a male voiceover touts its virtues. The commercial ends with another attractive young blond woman, sitting barefoot on a bench outdoors and holding a bag of the candy. Pulling one from the bag, she says, giggling, "I start on them right after breakfast."

This commercial normalizes some potentially dangerous attitudes toward food in some rather subtle ways. The women in trouble—the two young blondes and the woman by the fireplace—are sandwiched between people with more healthful attitudes. These three women are holding the entire bag of candy, whereas the men are holding only one piece and the middle-aged woman is pouring the candy into a bowl to serve to others. The first troubled woman is hoarding her supply, the second is seemingly preparing for a binge, and the third is rationalizing eating the candy all day long, beginning in the morning.

Thus, women with disordered attitudes toward food, women who seem   45
to be compulsive eaters, are presented as normal, desirable, and even especially
attractive. Why would the candy manufacturers want to do this? Because the
compulsive eaters, obviously, are going to spend a great deal more on the
candy than are the people who eat it infrequently, a piece or two at a time.
No matter what a company is selling, the heavy user is their best customer.
Thus, it is always in their best interest to normalize and encourage heavy use,
even if that might have destructive or even deadly consequences.

Obsession with food is also presented as normal and even as attractive in
an ad for sugar-free pudding that features a pretty young woman with a spoonful of pudding in her mouth and the headline, "Dessert? It's always on the tip
of my tongue." The copy continues, "Really. I mean, if I'm not eating dessert,
I'm talking about it. If I'm not talking about it, I'm eating it. And I'm always
thinking about it. . . . It's just always on my mind." Like the women who obsess
about candy, this young woman has a problem.

And, as is always the case in the world of advertising, the solution to her
problem is a product, in this case a diet product. The ad promises her, as almost
all the diet ads do, that she can have her pudding and eat it too. How odd this
is, when we think about it. Here we are surrounded by all these tempting,
luscious ads for food. We are told, on the one hand, give in, reward yourself,
indulge. But, on the other hand, we (especially women) are told that we must
be thin, indeed that there is no greater sin than being fat.

It might seem strange that there are so many ads for diet products inter-
spersed with ads for rich foods. It might seem stranger still that it is often so
difficult to tell the difference between the junk food ads and the diet ads.
However, this is not strange at all. The tempting food ads do not contradict
the message of the diet culture. They are an integral part of it. The junk food
industry and the diet industry depend on each other.

In order to be profitable, both these industries require that people be
hooked on unhealthy and mostly unsatisfying food, high in fat and sugar. In
addition, the diet industry depends upon a rigid cultural mandate for women
to be thin. If we ate and took pleasure in basically healthy food and were
physically active, if we recognized that bodies come in many different sizes
and shapes, and we did not consider it necessary for women to be bone-thin
to be attractive—the junk food industry would lose a great deal of money,
and there would be no diet industry.

The success of the diet industry primarily depends on women being dis-   50
satisfied with their bodies. Many people say that advertising simply reflects
the society. But certainly the body images of women that advertising reflects
today are as distorted as the reflections in a funhouse mirror. Since advertising
cashes in on women's body-hatred and distorted self-images, it sometimes
deliberately promotes such distortion. A yogurt ad says, "How to go from seeing yourself like this . . . to seeing yourself like this," and portrays the "before"
image with a pear. In fact, it is perfectly normal for a woman to be pear-
shaped. Many more women have pear-shaped bodies than have the V-shaped

bodies of the models, but we don't see them in the media. Instead, we get the message that this shape is unacceptable.

The use of body doubles in films and commercials makes it even less likely that we'll see real women's bodies. A photograph of Julia Roberts and Richard Gere that was widely used to advertise the hit film *Pretty Woman* featured Julia Roberts's head but not her body. Apparently, even *her* body wasn't good enough or thin enough to be in the ad. A body double was also used for Roberts when she was nude or partially nude in the film. This is common practice in the industry. Not surprisingly, at least 85 percent of body doubles have breast implants.

Unfortunately, the obsession with thinness is becoming a problem throughout the developed world. "Le diete S.O.S.," the title of an article featured on the cover of an Italian magazine, is understood in many languages. Italy used to be a country where voluptuous women could still feel desirable, but the model on the cover shown measuring her waist is extremely thin by any standards.

The dieter, even more than the addict, is the ideal consumer. She (most dieters are women) will spend a lot on food and then spend even more to lose weight—and the cycle never stops. Sales of low-fat frozen yogurt soar, but so do sales of high-fat premium ice cream. The diet industry, which includes diet drugs and other products, diet workshops and books, health spas, and more, has tripled in recent years, increasing from a $10 billion to a $36 billion-a-year industry. No one loses, especially the dieter (although she doesn't win either).

Some research indicates that thin people do live longer than overweight people. Some people have latched on to this as proof that we needn't worry about people dieting—in fact, we should worry more if they don't diet. The truth, however, is that fatness is related to the obsession with thinness. Chronic dieting is part of the generally bad eating and exercise habits that make so many Americans overweight and unhealthy. Although being thin is good for one's heart, dieting is bad for everyone.

The fat-free products we consume in great quantities are often bad for us. We eat them instead of eating healthy foods, drinking Coke and Pepsi instead of water, lunching on low-fat cold cuts instead of grains and vegetables and snacking on cholesterol-free cookies instead of fruit. We welcome artificial sweeteners and fake fats, even if they have unpleasant or unhealthy side effects. Olestra, the latest fake fat, not only removes some fat-soluble vitamins from the body, it also sometimes causes bloating, diarrhea, and cramping, as well as what is referred to as "rectal leakage."

55

Sometimes the ads themselves acknowledge the dangers of dieting. As is typical of advertising, however, the solution is not to stop the dangerous practice: The solution is another product. One ad for yogurt features a very young, very thin woman, and the headline "A body like this could be missing out on a lot." The ad acknowledges that the dieting required to keep this teenager so thin is robbing her body of necessary minerals and vitamins. Similarly, another ad reminds us that dieting damages skin tone. The solution, as always, is the product, a skin cream. Neither ad questions the practice of dieting.

An ad featuring a beautiful blonde says, "Christina is a 5′10″, 125 lb. fashion model of Scandinavian heritage. Everyone thinks she has the most marvelous bone structure. She doesn't. She is on her way to osteoporosis." The copy continues, "Her cheekbones are to die for, but not her vertebrae. Too many diets and too little calcium have left her bone density below average. If she doesn't do something, she'll shrink. Her spine will compact. Her clothes won't fit. Looking up at the sky will be impossible." The solution to this impending catastrophe? Certainly not for Christina to stop dieting. Rather, she simply should take calcium supplements. Maybe she should just buy a periscope so she can continue to see the sky.

Christina is five feet ten inches tall and weighs 125 pounds! She is a genetic freak. It's hard not to be a dieter when this is the ideal body type reflected throughout the media and the consequences for not having it are so extreme. Ninety-five percent of all women are excluded from this ideal, which is virtually unattainable by most women, yet it is *they* who feel abnormal and deviant. As an ad for the Body Shop, featuring a voluptuous Barbie-type doll, says, "There are 3 billion women who don't look like supermodels and only 8 who do." As a result, more than half the adult women in the United States are currently dieting, and over three-fourths of normal-weight American women think they are "too fat."

Certainly this delusion comes at least in part from the media images that surround us. Yesterday's sex symbols by today's standards would be considered fat: Betty Grable, Jane Russell, Marilyn Monroe—or just the pretty young woman on the beach featured on a cover of *Life* magazine in 1970. To be sure, there are some large women today, such as Rosie O'Donnell, the plus-size model Emme, and Delta Burke, who are very successful. However, it has been estimated that twenty years ago the average model weighed 8 percent less than the average woman; today she weighs 23 percent less.

Ironically, what is considered sexy today is a look that almost totally suppresses female secondary sexual characteristics, such as large breasts and hips. Thinness is related to decreased fertility and sexuality in women. Indeed, many of the ultrathin models have ceased to menstruate. Chronic dieting is damaging to one's health and upsets the body's natural metabolism. In 1997 the drug combination of fenfluramine and phentermine, known as fen/phen, was pulled off the market by the FDA because of a high incidence of heart problems among patients who take it. Not surprisingly, research has also found that dieters often experience a temporary drop in mental abilities and thus have less energy to focus on tasks other than controlling their food. 60

Although the dangers of dieting are sometimes mentioned in women's magazines, the warning is certainly diminished, if not entirely negated, by the ads surrounding the articles. The May 1997 issue of *Vogue* contained an article about the dangers of diet pills called "Dying to Lose Weight." However, on the opposite page is an ad for Special K, a low-calorie cereal, featuring a tiny bikini and the tagline, "It's not doing you any good tucked away in your bottom drawer." To Kellogg's credit, it completely revamped the Special K campaign in 1998 and ran ads and commercials that explicitly challenged the emphasis on thinness and uniformity. The funniest was a commercial featuring several men sitting around talking about their bodies in the way that women often do—"Do these jeans make my butt look big?" and "I have to face it—I have my mother's thighs." The commercial made it obvious how absurd this kind of conversation is and how different are the cultural expectations for women and men. Unfortunately, commercials like this are very few and far between.

In addition to all the psychic and physical damage the diet products do, they don't even fulfill their purpose, at least not for long. Ninety-five percent of dieters are even fatter after five years of dieting than before they began. This information, if widely disseminated throughout the mass media, could be as damaging to corporate profits as is the information that cigarette smoking causes lung cancer. It is no surprise that, in both cases, there is widespread distortion and suppression of such information. Indeed, the only thing that could destroy the diet industry faster than the truth about the failure rates of diets would be a diet that did work.

A Weight Watchers ad features a Boston cream pie, oozing its creamy filling, and the caption, "Feel free to act on impulse." Why would Weight Watchers, of all companies, use such tempting images? Because it is, after all, in Weight Watchers' best interest for its customers to fail, to relapse, to have to return again and again. If people really lost weight and kept it off, Weight Watchers and other such programs would quickly go out of business.

Food ads are often funny, clever, highly entertaining. But food that is heavily advertised is seldom nourishing and rarely deeply satisfying. Often it is sold in a way that exploits and trivializes our very basic human need for love and connection. It is wonderful to celebrate food, to delight in it. Food can nourish us and bring us joy . . . but it cannot love us, it cannot fill us up emotionally. If we turn to food as a substitute for human connection, we turn away from that which could fill up the emptiness we sometimes feel inside— authentic, mutual, satisfying relationships with other human beings. And when people use food as a way to numb painful feelings, to cope with a sense of inner emptiness, and as a substitute for human relationships, for living fully, many of them end up with eating problems that can destroy them and that certainly, ironically, destroy any pleasure they might get from food.

QUESTIONS FOR DISCUSSION

1. In paragraph 3, Kilbourne notes that "it is so easy to confuse food and love." In your experience, what circumstances are likely to generate this confusion?
2. What cultural factors, aside from advertising, encourage women to use food to cope with anxiety or disappointment?
3. Are ads wrong to suggest that food plays a role in romance?

4. Where does Kilbourne recognize that there is a positive dimension to the ads she discusses? Why is it useful for her to recognize this?
5. Consider Kilbourne's claim in paragraph 25: "Prejudice against fat people, especially against fat women, is one of the few remaining prejudices that is socially acceptable." Do you agree?
6. What is the relationship between ads that promote junk food such as ice cream and candy and those that promote diet products?
7. The companies responsible for the advertisements discussed refused permission to reprint them. (You can, however, find them in Kilbourne's book.) Why do you think they refused?

SUGGESTIONS FOR WRITING

1. Go through recent issues of a magazine directed toward an audience of women, and examine advertisements for food and diet products. Select an image that illustrates the concerns Kilbourne raised. Then write a detailed analysis of that advertisement.
2. Analyze how images are used to persuade women to purchase a product unrelated to food.
3. In her opening sentence, Kilbourne claims that advertising encourages men "to fall in love with their cars." Review car ads in magazines directed to an audience of men, and analyze one of the images.

LINKS

■ Within the Book

In "Beauty (Re)discovers the Male Body" (pages 329–346), Susan Bordo considers how advertisements use images of men—as well as what those images signify about gender expectations and sex appeal.

■ Elsewhere in Print

Barletta, Martha. *Marketing to Women: How to Understand, Reach, and Increase Your Share of the Largest Market Segment.* New York: Dearborn, 2002.
Cortese, Anthony J. *Provocateur: Images of Women and Minorities in Advertising.* Lanham: Rowman, 1999.
Johnson, Lisa, and Andrea Learned. *Don't Think Pink: What Really Makes Women Buy—and How to Increase Your Share of This Crucial Market.* New York: American Management Assn., 2004.
Kilbourne, Jean. *Can't Buy Me Love: How Advertising Changes the Way We Think and Feel.* Fwd. Mary Pipher. New York: Touchstone, 2000.
———. *Deadly Persuasion: Why Women and Girls Must Fight the Addictive Power of Advertising.* New York: Free, 1999.

■ **Elsewhere in Print (continued)**

Pipher, Mary. *Reviving Ophelia: Saving the Souls of Adolescent Girls.* New York: Putnam, 1994.

Quinlan, Mary Lou. *Just Ask a Woman: Cracking the Code of What Women Want and How They Buy.* Hoboken: Wiley, 2003.

Schutzman, Mady. *The Real Thing: Performance, Hysteria, and Advertising.* Hanover: UP of New England, 1999.

■ **Online**

www.mhhe.com/motives

Click on "More Resources" then "Writing to Analyze Images."

■ ■ ■

BEAUTY (RE)DISCOVERS THE MALE BODY

Susan Bordo

A professor of English and women's studies, Susan Bordo holds the Otis A. Singletary Chair in the Humanities at the University of Kentucky. A feminist philosopher who is especially interested in the nature of gender, she has been credited with having created an interdisciplinary interest in "body studies." Bordo also lectures widely on the relationship between popular culture and people's perceptions of their bodies, addressing such issues as eating disorders and cosmetic surgery. Her books include Unbearable Weight: Feminism, Western Culture, and the Body; Twilight Zones: The Hidden Life of Cultural Images from Plato to O.J.; *and* The Male Body *(1999), in which the following selection (illustrated with additional advertisements) appears as a chapter.*

Reviewers across the country praised The Male Body *upon its initial publication, using words such as "provocative," "unexpected," "funny," and "compelling." Excerpts appeared in* Mademoiselle, Elle, Vanity Fair, *and* The New York Times Magazine. *As you read the following excerpt, be prepared for some frank language as well as erotically charged images. But be alert for how Bordo provides thoughtful analysis of what these images reveal about the use of eroticism in marketing. (A list of her sources can be found online at www.mhhe.com/motives and click on "More Resources" then "Writing to Analyze Images."*

Putting classical art to the side for the moment, the naked and near-naked female body became an object of mainstream consumption first in *Playboy* and its imitators, then in movies, and only then in fashion photographs. With the male body, the trajectory has been different. Fashion has taken the lead, the movies have followed. Hollywood may have been a chest-fest in the fifties, but it was male clothing designers who went south and violated the really powerful taboos—not just against the explicit depiction of penises and male bottoms but against the admission of all sorts of forbidden "feminine" qualities into mainstream conceptions of manliness.

It was the spring of 1995, and I was sipping my first cup of morning coffee, not yet fully awake, flipping through *The New York Times Magazine,* when I had my first real taste of what it's like to inhabit this visual culture as a man. It was both thrilling and disconcerting. It was the first time in my experience that I had encountered a commercial representation of a male body that seemed to deliberately invite me to linger over it. Let me make that stronger—that seemed to reach out to me, interrupting my mundane but peaceful Sunday morning, and provoke me into erotic consciousness, whether or not I wanted it. Women—both straight and gay—have always gazed covertly, of course, squeezing our illicit little titillations out of representations designed for—or pretending to—other purposes than to turn us on. *This* ad made no such pretense. It caused me to knock over my coffee cup, ruining the more cerebral pleasures of the *Book Review.* Later, when I had regained my equilibrium, I made a screen-saver out of him, so I could gaze at my leisure.

I'm sure that many gay men were as taken as I was, and perhaps some gay women too. The erotic charge of various sexual styles is not neatly mapped onto sexual orientation (let alone biological sex). Brad Pitt's baby-butch looks are a turn-on to many lesbians, while I—regarded by most of my gay friends as a pretty hard-core heterosexual—have always found Anne Heche irresistible (even before Ellen did). . . . Despite such complications, until recently only heterosexual men have continually been inundated by popular cultural images *designed* with their sexual responses (or, at least, what those sexual responses are imagined to be) in mind. It's not entirely a gift. On the minus side is having one's composure continually challenged by what Timothy Beneke has aptly described as a culture of "intrusive images," eliciting fantasies, emotions, and erections at times and in places where they might not be appropriate. On the plus side is the cultural permission to be a voyeur.

Some psychologists say that the circuit from eyes to brain to genitals is a quicker trip for men than for women. "There's some strong evidence," popular science writer Deborah Blum reports, citing studies of men's responses to pictures of naked women, "that testosterone is wired for visual response." Maybe. But who is the electrician here? God? Mother Nature? Or Hugh Hefner? Practice makes perfect. And women have had little practice. The Calvin Klein ad made me feel like an adolescent again, brought me back to that day when I saw Barry Resnick on the basketball court of Weequahic High and realized that men's legs could make me weak in the knees. Men's legs? I knew that *women's* legs were supposed to be sexy. I had learned that from all those hose-straightening scenes in the movies. But men's legs? Who had ever seen a woman gaga over some guy's legs in the movies? Or even read about it in a book? Yet the muscular grace of Barry's legs took my breath away. Maybe something was wrong with me. Maybe my sex drive was too strong, too much like a man's. By the time I came across that Calvin Klein ad, several decades of feminism and life experience had left me a little less worried about my sex drive. Still, the sight of that model's body made me feel that my sexual education was still far from complete.

I brought the ad to classes and lectures, asking women what they thought of him. Most began to sweat the moment I unfolded the picture, then got their bearings and tried to explore the bewitching stew of sexual elements the picture has to offer. The model—a young Jackson Browne look-alike— stands there in his form-fitting and rip-speckled Calvin Klein briefs, head lowered, dark hair loosely falling over his eyes. His body projects strength, solidity; he's no male waif. But his finely muscled chest is not so overdeveloped as to suggest a sexuality immobilized by the thick matter of the body. Gay theorist Ron Long, describing contemporary gay sexual aesthetics—lean, taut, sinuous muscles rather than Schwarzenegger bulk—points to a "dynamic tension" that the incredible hulks lack. Stiff, engorged Schwarzenegger bod-

An invitation to linger: a body with "dynamic tension."

ies, he says, seem to *be* surrogate penises—with nowhere to go and nothing to do but stand there looking massive—whereas muscles like this young man's seem designed for movement, for sex. His body isn't a stand-in phallus; rather, he *has* a penis—the real thing, not a symbol, and a fairly breathtaking one, clearly outlined through the soft jersey fabric of the briefs. It seems slightly erect, or perhaps that's his nonerect size; either way, there's a substantial presence there that's palpable (it looks so touchable, you want to cup your hand over it) and very, very male.

At the same time, however, my gaze is invited by something "feminine" about the young man. His underwear may be ripped, but ever so slightly, subtly; unlike the original ripped-underwear poster boy Kowalski°, he's hardly a thug. He doesn't stare at the viewer challengingly, belligerently, as do so many models in other ads for male underwear, facing off like a street tough passing a member of the rival gang on the street. ("Yeah, this is an underwear ad and I'm half naked. But I'm still the one in charge here. Who's gonna look away first?") No, this model's languid body posture, his averted look are classic signals, both in the "natural" and the "cultural" world, of willing subordination. He offers himself nonaggressively to the gaze of another. Hip cocked in the snaky S-curve usually reserved for depictions of women's bodies, eyes downcast but not closed, he gives off a sultry, moody, subtle but undeniably seductive

---

°*Kowalski:* Stanley Kowalski, lead character in *A Streetcar Named Desire* by Tennessee Williams—a role first played by Marlon Brando. (See photograph on page 347.)

consciousness of his erotic allure. Feast on me, I'm here to be looked at, my body is for your eyes. Oh my.

Such an attitude of male sexual supplication, although it has (as we'll see) classical antecedents, is very new to contemporary mainstream representations. Homophobia is at work in this taboo, but so are attitudes about gender that cut across sexual orientation. For many men, both gay and straight, to be so passively dependent on the gaze of another person for one's sense of self-worth is incompatible with being a real man. As we'll see, such notions about manliness are embedded in Greek culture, in contemporary visual representation, and even (in disguised form) in existentialist philosophy. "For the woman," as philosopher Simone de Beauvoir° writes, ". . . the absence of her lover is always torture; he is an eye, a judge . . . away from him, she is dispossessed, at once of herself and of the world." For Beauvoir's sometime lover and lifelong soul mate Jean-Paul Sartre°, on the other hand, the gaze (or the Look, as he called it) of another person—including the gaze of one's lover—is the "hell" that other people represent. If we were alone in the world, he argues, we would be utterly free—within physical constraints—to be whomever we wanted to be, to be the creatures of our own self-fantasies, to define our behavior however we like. Other people intrude on this solipsism, and have the audacity to see us from their own perspective rather than ours. The result is what Sartre calls primordial Shame under the eyes of the Other, and a fierce desire to reassert one's freedom. The other person has stolen "the secret" of who I am. I must fight back, resist their attempts to define me.

I understand, of course, what Sartre is talking about here. We've all, male and female alike, felt the shame that another pair of eyes can bring. Sartre's own classic example is of being caught peeking through a keyhole by another person. It isn't until those other eyes are upon you that you truly feel not just the "wrongness" of what you are doing, but—Sartre would argue—the very fact that you are doing it. Until the eyes of another are upon us, "catching us" in the act, we can deceive ourselves, pretend. Getting caught in moments of fantasy or vanity may be especially shameful. When I was an adolescent, I loved to pretend I was a radio personality, and talking into an empty coffee can created just the right sound. One day, my mother caught me speaking in the smooth and slightly sultry tones that radio personalities had even in those days. The way I felt is what Sartre means when he describes the Look of another person as the fulcrum of shame-making. My face got hot, and suddenly I saw how ridiculous I must have seemed, my head in the Chock Full O' Nuts, my narcissistic fantasies on full display. I was caught, I wanted to run.

The disjunction between self-conception and external judgment can be especially harsh when the external definitions carry racial and gender stereotypes with them. Sartre doesn't present such examples—he's interested in cap-

---

°*Simone de Beauvoir:* French writer (1908–1986) best known for *The Second Sex.*
°*Jean-Paul Sartre:* French philosopher (1905–1980) who is widely associated with existentialism.

turing the contours of an existential situation shared by all rather than in analyzing the cultural differences that affect that situation—but they are surely relevant to understanding the meaning of the Look of the Other. A black man jogs down the street in sweat clothes, thinking of the class he is going to teach later that day; a white woman passes him, clutches her handbag more tightly, quickens her step; in her eyes, the teacher is a potentially dangerous animal. A Latin American student arrives early the first day of college; an administrator, seeing him in the still-deserted hall, asks him if he is the new janitor. The aspiring student has had his emerging identity erased, a stereotype put in its place by another pair of eyes. When women are transformed from professionals to "pussies" by the comments of men on the street, it's humiliating, not so much because we're puritans as because we sense the hostility in the hoots, the desire to bring an uppity woman down to size by reminding her that she's just "the sex" (as Beauvoir put it).

We may all have felt shame, but—as the different attitudes of Beauvoir 10 and Sartre suggest—men and women are socially sanctioned to deal with the gaze of the Other in different ways. Women learn to anticipate, even play to the sexualizing gaze, trying to become what will please, captivate, turn shame into pride. (In the process, we also learn how sexy being gazed at can feel— perhaps precisely because it walks the fine edge of shame.) Many of us, truth be told, get somewhat addicted to the experience. I'm renting a video, feeling a bit low, a bit tired. The young man at the counter, unsolicited, tells me I'm "looking good." It alters everything, I feel fine, alive; it seems to go right down to my cells. I leave the store feeling younger, stronger, more awake. When women sense that they are not being assessed sexually—for example, as we age, or if we are disabled—it may feel like we no longer exist.

Women may dread being surveyed harshly—being seen as too old, too fat, too flat-chested—but men are not supposed to enjoy being surveyed *period*. It's feminine to be on display. Men are thus taught—as my uncle Leon used to say—to be a moving target. Get out of range of those eyes, don't let them catch you—even as the object of their fantasies (or, as Sartre would put it, don't let them "possess," "steal" your freedom). This phobia has even distorted scientific research. . . . Evolutionary theorists have long acknowledged display as an important feature of courting behavior among primates—except when it comes to *our* closest ancestors. With descriptions of hominid behavior, male display behavior "suddenly drops out of the primate evolutionary picture" (Sheets-Johnstone) and is replaced by the concept of year-round female sexual receptivity. It seems that it has been intolerable, unthinkable for male evolutionary theorists to imagine the bodies of their male ancestors being on display, sized up, dependent on selection (or rejection) by female hominids.

Scientists and "ordinary guys" are totally in synch here, as is humorously illustrated in Peter Cattaneo's popular 1997 British film *The Full Monty*. In the film, a group of unemployed metalworkers in Sheffield, England, watch a Chippendale's show and hatch the money-making scheme of presenting their own male strip show in which they will go right down to the "full Monty." At the start of the film, the heroes are hardly pillars of successful manliness (Gaz, their leader, refers to them as "scrap"). Yet even they have been sheltered by their guyhood, as they learn while putting the show together. One gets a penis pump. Another borrows his wife's face cream. They run, they wrap their bellies in plastic, they do jumping jacks, they get artificial tans. The most overweight one among them (temporarily) pulls out of the show. Before, these guys hadn't lived their lives under physical scrutiny but in male action mode, in which men are judged by their accomplishments. Now, anticipating being on display to a roomful of spectators, they suddenly realize how it feels to be judged as women routinely are, sized up by another pair of eyes. "I pray that they'll be a bit more understanding about us" than they've been with women, David (the fat one) murmurs.

They get past their discomfort, in the end, and their show is greeted with wild enthusiasm by the audience. The movie leaves us with this feel-good ending, not raising the question obvious to every woman watching the film: Would a troupe of out-of-shape women be received as warmly, as affectionately? The climactic moment when the men throw off their little pouches is demurely shot from the rear, moreover, so we—the audience—don't get "the full Monty." Nonetheless, the film gently and humorously makes an important point: For a heterosexual man to offer himself up to a sexually evaluating gaze is for him to make a large, scary leap—and not just because of the anxieties about size . . . (the guy who drops out of the show, remember, is embarrassed by his fat, not his penis). The "full Monty"—the naked penis—is not merely a body part in the movie (hence it doesn't really matter that the film doesn't show it). It's a symbol for male exposure, vulnerability to an evaluation and judgment that women—clothed or naked—experience all the time.

I had to laugh out loud at a 1997 *New York Times Magazine* "Style" column, entitled "Overexposure," which complained of the "contagion" of nudity spreading through celebrity culture. "Stars no longer have private parts," the author observed, and fretted that civilians would soon also be measured by the beauty of their buns. I share this author's concern about our body-obsessed culture. But, pardon me, he's just noticing this now??? Actresses have been baring their breasts, their butts, even their bushes, for some time, and ordinary women have been tromping off to the gym in pursuit of comparably perfect bodies. What's got the author suddenly crying "overkill," it turns out, is Sly Stallone's "surreally fat-free" appearance on the cover of *Vanity Fair,* and Rupert Everett's "dimpled behind" in a Karl Lagerfeld fashion spread. Now that *men* are taking off their clothes, the culture is suddenly going too far. Could it be that the author doesn't even "read" all those naked female bodies as "overexposed"? Does he protest a bit too much when he declares in the first sentence of the piece that he found it "a yawn" when Dirk Diggler unsheathed his "prosthetic shillelagh" ("penis" is still a word to be avoided whenever possible) at the end of *Boogie Nights?* A yawn? My friend's palms were sweating profusely, and I was not about to drop off to sleep either.

As for dimpled behinds, my second choice for male pinup of the decade   *15*
is the Gucci series of two ads in which a beautiful young man, shot from the
rear, puts on a pair of briefs. In the first ad, he's holding them in his hands,
contemplating them. Is he checking out the correct washing-machine temp?
It's odd, surely, to stand there looking at your underwear, but never mind. The
point is: His underwear is in his hands, not on his butt. *It*—his bottom, that
is—is gorgeously, completely naked—a motif so new to mainstream advertising (but since then catching on rapidly) that several of my friends, knowing I
was writing about the male body, e-mailed me immediately when they saw
the ad. In the second ad, he's put the underwear on and is adjusting it to fit.
Luckily for us, he hasn't succeeded yet, so his buns are peeking out the bottom
of the underwear, looking biteable. For the *Times* writer, those buns may be
an indecent exposure of parts that should be kept private (or they're a boring
yawn, I'm afraid he can't have it both ways), but for me—and for thousands of
gay men across the country—this was a moment of political magnitude, and a
delicious one. The body parts that *we* love to squeeze (those plastic breasts,
they're the real yawn for me) had come out of the closet and into mainstream
culture, where *we* can enjoy them without a trip to a specialty store.

But all this is very new. Women aren't used to seeing naked men frankly
portrayed as "objects" of a sexual gaze (and neither are heterosexual men, as
that *Times* writer makes clear). So pardon me if I'm skeptical when I read
arguments about men's greater "biological" responsiveness to visual stimuli.
These "findings," besides being ethnocentric (no one thinks to poll Trobriand
Islanders), display little awareness of the impact of changes in cultural representations on our capacities for sexual response. Popular science writer Deborah Blum, for example, cites a study from the Kinsey Institute which showed
a group of men and women a series of photos and drawings of nudes, both
male and female:

> Fifty-four percent of the men were erotically aroused versus 12 per-
> cent of the women—in other words, more than four times as many
> men. The same gap exists, on a much larger scale, in the business of
> pornography, a $500-million-plus industry in the U.S. which caters
> almost exclusively to men. In the first flush of 1970s feminism, two
> magazines—*Playgirl* and *Viva*—began publishing male centerfolds.
> *Viva* dropped the nude photos after surveys showed their readers
> didn't care for them; the editor herself admitted to finding them
> slightly disgusting.

Blum presents these findings as suggestive of a hard-wired difference between men and women. I'd be cautious about accepting that conclusion. First
of all, there's the question of which physiological responses count as "erotic
arousal" and whether they couldn't be evidence of other states. Clearly, too,
we can *learn* to have certain physiological responses—and to suppress them—
so nothing biologically definitive is proved by the presence or absence of
physical arousal.

Studies that rely on viewers' *own* reports need to be carefully interpreted too. I know, from talking to women students, that they sometimes aren't all that clear about *what* they feel in the presence of erotic stimuli, and even when they are, they may not be all that comfortable admitting what they feel. Hell, not just my students! Once, a lover asked me, as we were about to part for the evening, if there was anything that we hadn't done that I'd really like to do. I knew immediately what that was: I wanted him to undress, very slowly, while I sat on the floor and just watched. But I couldn't tell him. I was too embarrassed. Later, alone in my compartment on the train, I sorely regretted my cowardice. The fact is that I love to watch a man getting undressed, and I especially like it if he is conscious of being looked at. But there is a long legacy of shame to be overcome here, for both sexes, and the cultural models are only now just emerging which might help us move beyond it.

Perhaps, then, we should wait a bit longer, do a few more studies, before we come to any biological conclusions about women's failure to get aroused by naked pictures. A newer (1994) University of Chicago study found that 30 percent of women ages eighteen to forty-four and 19 percent of women ages forty-five to fifty-nine said they found "watching a partner undress" to be "very appealing." ("Not a bad percentage," Nancy Friday° comments, "given that Nice Girls didn't look.") There's still a gender gap—the respective figures for men of the same age groups were 50 percent and 40 percent. We're just learning, after all, to be voyeuses. Perhaps, too, heterosexual men could learn to be less uncomfortable offering themselves as "sexual objects" if they realized the pleasure women get from it. Getting what you have been most deprived of is the best gift, the most healing gift, the most potentially transforming gift— because it has the capacity to make one more whole. Women have been deprived not so much of the *sight* of beautiful male bodies as the experience of having the male body *offered* to us, handed to us on a silver platter, the way female bodies—in the ads, in the movies—are handed to men. Getting this from her partner is the erotic equivalent of a woman's coming home from work to find a meal prepared and ready for her. Delicious—even if it's just franks and beans.

THANKS, CALVIN!

Despite their bisexual appeal, the cultural genealogy of the ads I've been discussing and others like them is to be traced largely through gay male aesthetics, rather than a sudden blossoming of appreciation for the fact that women might enjoy looking at sexy, well-hung young men who don't appear to be about to rape them. Feminists might like to imagine that Madison Avenue heard our pleas for sexual equality and finally gave us "men as sex objects."   20

°*Nancy Friday:* Feminist writer best known for *My Secret Garden.*

But what's really happened is that women have been the beneficiaries of what might be described as a triumph of pure consumerism—and with it, a burgeoning male fitness and beauty culture—over homophobia and the taboos against male vanity, male "femininity," and erotic display of the male body that have gone along with it.

Throughout this century, gay photographers have created a rich, sensuous, and dramatic tradition which is unabashed in eroticizing the male body, male sensuousness, and male potency, including penises. But until recently, such representations have been kept largely in the closet. Mainstream responses to several important exhibits which opened in the seventies—featuring the groundbreaking early work of Wilhelm von Gloeden, George Dureau, and George Platt Lynes as well as then-contemporary artists such as Robert Mapplethorpe, Peter Hujar, and Arthur Tress—would today probably embarrass the critics who wrote about them when they opened. John Ashbery, in *New York* magazine, dismissed the entire genre of male nude photography with the same sexist tautology that covertly underlies that *Times* piece on cultural "overexposure": "Nude women seem to be in their natural state; men, for some reason, merely look undressed . . . When is a nude not a nude? When it is male." (Substitute "blacks" and "whites" for "women" and "men" and you'll see how offensive the statement is.)

For other reviewers, the naked male, far from seeming "merely undressed," was unnervingly sexual. *New York Times* critic Gene Thompson wrote that "there is something disconcerting about the sight of a man's naked body being presented as a sexual object"; he went on to describe the world of homoerotic photography as one "closed to most of us, fortunately." Vicki Goldberg, writing for the *Saturday Review,* was more appreciative of the "beauty and dignity" of the nude male body, but concluded that so long as its depiction was erotic in emphasis, it will "remain half-private, slightly awkward, an art form cast from its traditions and in search of some niche to call its home."

Goldberg needed a course in art history. It's true that in classical art, the naked human body was often presented as a messenger of spiritual themes, and received as such. But the male bodies sculpted by the Greeks and Michelangelo were not exactly nonerotic. It might be more accurate to say that in modernity, with the spiritual interpretation of the nude body no longer a convention, the contemporary homophobic psyche is not screened from the sexual charge of the nude male body. Goldberg was dead wrong about something else too. Whatever its historical lineage, the frankly sexual representation of the male body was to find, in the next twenty years, a far from private "niche to call its home": Consumer culture discovered its commercial potency.

Calvin Klein had his epiphany, according to one biography, one night in 1974 in New York's gay Flamingo bar:

> As Calvin wandered through the crowd at the Flamingo, the body
> heat rushed through him like a revelation; this was the cutting edge. . . .
> [The] men! The men at the Flamingo had less to do about sex for him

than the notion of portraying men as gods. He realized that what he was watching was the freedom of a new generation, unashamed, in-the-flesh embodiments of Calvin's ideals: straight-looking, masculine men, with chiseled bodies, young Greek gods come to life. The vision of shirtless young men with hardened torsos, all in blue jeans, top button opened, a whisper of hair from the belly button disappearing into the denim pants, would inspire and inform the next ten years of Calvin Klein's print and television advertisements.

Klein's genius was that of a cultural Geiger counter; his own bisexuality   25 enabled him to see that the phallic body, as much as any female figure, is an enduring sex object within Western culture. In America in 1974, however, that ideal was still largely closeted. Only gay culture unashamedly sexualized the lean, fit body that virtually everyone, gay and straight, now aspires to. Sex, as Calvin Klein knew, sells. He also knew that gay sex wouldn't sell to straight men. But the rock-hard, athletic gay male bodies that Klein admired at the Flamingo did not advertise their sexual preference through the feminine codes—limp wrists, raised pinkie finger, swishy walk—which the straight world then identified with homosexuality. Rather, they embodied a highly masculine aesthetic that—although definitely exciting for gay men—would scream "heterosexual" to (clueless) straights. Klein knew just the kind of clothing to show that body off in too. As Steven Gaines and Sharon Churcher tell it:

> He had watched enough attractive young people with good bodies in tight jeans dancing at the Flamingo and Studio 54 to know that the "basket" and the behind was what gave jeans sex appeal. Calvin sent his assistants out for several pairs of jeans, including the classic five-button Levi's, and cut them apart to see how they were made. Then he cut the "rise," or area from the waistband to under the groin, much shorter to accentuate the crotch and pull the seam up between the buttocks, giving the behind more shape and prominence. The result was instant sex appeal—and a look that somehow Calvin just *knew* was going to sell.

So we come to the mainstream commercialization of the aesthetic legacy of Stanley Kowalski and those inspired innovations of Brando's costumer in *A Streetcar Named Desire*. When I was growing up, jeans were "dungarees"— suitable for little kids, hayseeds, and juvenile delinquents, but not for anyone to wear on a date. Klein transformed jeans from utilitarian garments to erotic second skins. Next, Klein went for underwear. He wasn't the first, but he was the most daring. In 1981, Jockey International had broken ground by photographing Baltimore Oriole pitcher Jim Palmer in a pair of briefs (airbrushed) in one of its ads—selling $100 million worth of underwear by year's end. Inspired by Jockey's success, in 1983 Calvin Klein put a forty-by-fifty-foot Bruce Weber photograph of Olympic pole vaulter Tom Hintinauss in Times Square, Hintinauss's large penis clearly discernible through his briefs. The

Bronzed and beautiful Tom Hintinauss: a breakthrough ad for Calvin Klein—and the beginning of a new era for the unabashed erotic display of the male body.

Hintinauss ad, unlike the Palmer ad, did not employ any of the usual fictional rationales for a man's being in his underwear—for example, the pretense that the man is in the process of getting dressed—but blatantly put Hintinauss's body on display, sunbathing on a rooftop, his skin glistening. The line of shorts "flew off the shelves" at Bloomingdale's, and when Klein papered bus shelters in Manhattan with poster versions of the ad, they were all stolen overnight.

Images of masculinity that will do double (or triple or quadruple) duty with a variety of consumers, straight and gay, male and female, are not difficult to create in a culture like ours, in which the muscular male body has a long and glorious aesthetic history. That's precisely what Calvin Klein was the first to recognize and exploit—the possibility and profitability of what is known in the trade as a "dual marketing" approach. Since then, many advertisers have taken advantage of Klein's insight. A recent Abercrombie & Fitch ad, for example, depicts a locker room full of young, half-clothed football players getting a postmortem from their coach after a game. Beautiful, undressed male bodies doing what real men are "supposed to do." Dirty uniforms and smudged faces, wounded players, helmets. What could be more straight? But as iconography depicting a culture of exclusively male bodies, young, gorgeous, and well-hung, what could be more "gay"?

It required a Calvin Klein to give the new vision cultural form. But the fact is that if we've entered a brave, new world of male bodies it is largely because of a more "material" kind of epiphany—a dawning recognition among advertisers of the buying power of gay men. For a long time prejudice had triumphed over the profit motive, blinding marketers to just how sizable— and well-heeled—a consumer group gay men represent. (This has been the case with other "minorities" too. Hollywood producers, never bothering to do any demographics on middle-class and professional African-American women—or the issues that they share with women of other races and classes in this culture—were shocked at the tremendous box office success of *Waiting to Exhale.* They won't make that particular mistake again.) It took a survey conducted by *The Advocate* to jolt corporate America awake about gay consumers. The survey, done between 1977 and 1980, showed that 70 percent of its readers aged twenty to forty earned incomes well above the national median. Soon, articles were appearing on the business pages of newspapers, like one in 1982 in *The New York Times Magazine,* which described advertisers as newly interested in "wooing . . . the white, single, well-educated, well-paid man who happens to be homosexual."

"Happens to be homosexual": the phrasing—suggesting that sexual identity is peripheral, even accidental—is telling. Because of homophobia, dual marketing used to require a delicate balancing act, as advertisers tried to speak to gays "in a way that the straight consumer will not notice." Often, that's been accomplished through the use of play and parody, as in Versace's droll portraits of men being groomed and tended by male servants, and Diesel's overtly narcissistic gay posers. "Thanks, Diesel, for making us so very beautiful," they gush. Or take the ad . . . with its gorgeous, mechanically inept model admitting that he's "known more for my superb bone construction and soft, supple hair than my keen intellect." The playful tone reassures heterosexual consumers that the vanity (and mechanical incompetence) of the man selling the product is "just a joke." For gay consumers, on the other hand, this reassurance is *itself* the "joke"; they read the humor in the ad as an insider wink, which says, "This is for *you,* guys." The joke is further layered by the fact that they know the model in the ad is very likely to be gay.

Contrast this ad to the ostentatious heterosexual protest of a Perry Ellis ad   *30* which appeared in the early 1990s (and no, it's not a parody):

> I hate this job. I'm not just an empty suit who stands in front of a camera, collects the money and flies off to St. Maarten for the weekend.
>
> I may model for a living, but I hate being treated like a piece of meat. I once had a loud-mouthed art director say "Stand there and pretend you're a human." I wanted to punch him, but I needed the job.
>
> What am I all about? Well, I know I'm very good-looking, and there are days when that is enough. Some nights, when I'm alone, it's not.

I like women—all kinds.

I like music—all kinds.

I like myself so I don't do drugs.

Oh yeah, about this fragrance. It's good. Very good.

When I posed for this picture, the art director insisted that I wear it while the pictures were being taken. I thought it was silly, but I said "What the hell? It's their money."

After a while, I realized I like this fragrance a lot. When the photo shoot was over, I walked right over, picked up the bottle, put it in my pocket and said "If you don't mind, I'd like to take this as a souvenir." Then I smiled my best f— you smile and walked out.

Next time, I'll pay for it.

It's that good.

Today, good-looking straight guys are flocking to the modeling agencies, much less concerned about any homosexual taint that will cleave to them. It's no longer necessary for an ad to plant its tongue firmly in cheek when lavishing erotic attention on the male body—or to pepper the ad with proofs of heterosexuality. It used to be, if an advertisement aimed at straight men dared to show a man fussing over his looks with seemingly romantic plans in mind, there had better be a woman in the picture, making it clear just *whom* the boy was getting pretty for. To sell a muscle-building product to heterosexuals, of course, you had to link it to virility and the ability to attract women on the beach. Today, muscles are openly sold for their looks; Chroma Lean nutritional supplement unabashedly compares the well-sculpted male body to a work of art (and a gay male icon, to boot)—Michelangelo's "David." Many ads display the naked male body without shame or plot excuse, and often exploit rather than resolve the sexual ambiguity that is generated.

Today, too, the athletic, muscular male body that Calvin plastered all over buildings, magazines, and subway stops has become an aesthetic norm, for straights as well as gays. "No pecs, no sex," is how the trendy David Barton gym sells itself: "My motto is not 'Be healthy'; it's 'Look better naked,'" Barton says. The notion has even made its way into that most determinedly heterosexual of contexts, a Rob Reiner film. In *Sleepless in Seattle,* Tom Hanks's character, who hasn't been on a date in fifteen years, asks his friend (played by Rob) what women are looking for nowadays. "Pecs and a cute butt," his friend replied without hesitation. "You can't even turn on the news nowadays without hearing about how some babe thought some guy's butt was cute. Who the first woman to say this was I don't know, but somehow it caught on." Should we tell Rob that it wasn't a woman who started the craze for men's butts?

ROCKS AND LEANERS

We "nouvelles voyeuses" thus owe a big measure of thanks to gay male designers and consumers, and to the aesthetic and erotic overlap—not uniform or total, but significant—in what makes our hearts go thump. But although

I've been using the term for convenience, I don't think it's correct to say that these ads depict men as "sex objects." Actually, I find that whole notion misleading, whether applied to men or women, because it seems to suggest that what these representations offer is a body that is inert, depersonalized, flat, a mere thing. In fact, advertisers put a huge amount of time, money, and creativity into figuring out how to create images of beautiful bodies that are heavy on attitude, style, associations with pleasure, success, happiness. The most compelling images are suffused with "subjectivity"—they *speak* to us, they seduce us. Unlike other kinds of "objects" (chairs and tables, for example), they don't let us use them in any way we like. In fact, they exert considerable power over us—over our psyches, our desires, our self-image.

How do male bodies in the ads speak to us nowadays? In a variety of ways. Sometimes the message is challenging, aggressive. Many models stare coldly at the viewer, defying the observer to view them in any way other than how they have chosen to present themselves: as powerful, armored, emotionally impenetrable. "I am a rock," their bodies (and sometimes their genitals) seem to proclaim. Often, as in the Jackson Browne look-alike ad, the penis is prominent, but *unlike* the penis in that ad, its presence is martial rather than sensual. Overall, these ads depict what I would describe as "face-off masculinity," in which victory goes to the dominant contestant in a game of will against will. Who can stare the other man down? Who will avert his eyes first? Whose gaze will be triumphant? Such moments—"facing up," "facing off," "staring down"—as anthropologist David Gilmore has documented, are a test of macho in many cultures, including our own. "Don't eyeball me!" barks the sergeant to his cadets in training in *An Officer and a Gentleman;* the authority of the stare is a prize to be won only with full manhood. Before then, it is a mark of insolence—or stupidity, failure to understand the codes of masculine rank. In *Get Shorty,* an unsuspecting film director challenges a mob boss to look him in the eye; in return, he is hurled across the room and has his fingers broken.

"Face-off" ads, except for their innovations in the amount of skin exposed, are pretty traditional—one might even say primal—in their conception of masculinity. Many other species use staring to establish dominance, and not only our close primate relatives. It's how my Jack Russell terrier intimidates my male collie, who weighs over four times as much as the little guy but cowers under the authority of the terrier's macho stare. In the doggie world, size doesn't matter; it's the power of the gaze—which indicates the power to stand one's ground—that counts. My little terrier's dominance, in other words, is based on a convincing acting job—and it's one that is very similar, according to William Pollack, to the kind of performance that young boys in our culture must learn to master. Pollack's studies of boys suggest that a set of rules—which he calls "The Boy Code"—govern their behavior with each other. The first imperative of the code—"Be a sturdy oak"—represents the emotional equivalent of "face-off masculinity": Never reveal weakness. Pretend to be confident even though you may be scared. Act like a rock even when you feel shaky. Dare others to challenge your position.

"Face-off masculinity."

The face-off is not the only available posture for male bodies in ads today. Another possibility is what I call "the lean"—because these bodies are almost always reclining, leaning against, or propped up against something in the fashion typical of women's bodies. James Dean was probably our first pop-culture "leaner"; he made it stylish for teenagers to slouch. Dean, however, never posed as languidly or was as openly seductive as some of the high-fashion leaners are today. A recent Calvin Klein "Escape" ad depicts a young, sensuous-looking man leaning against a wall, arm raised, dark underarm hair exposed. His eyes seek out the imagined viewer, soberly but flirtatiously. "*Take Me,*" the copy reads.

Languid leaners have actually been around for a long time. Statues of sleeping fauns, their bodies draped languorously, exist in classical art alongside more heroic models of male beauty. I find it interesting, though, that Klein has chosen Mr. Take Me to advertise a perfume called "Escape." Klein's "Eternity" ads usually depict happy, heterosexual couples, often with a child. "Obsession" has always been cutting-edge, sexually ambiguous erotica. This ad, featuring a man offering himself up seductively, invitingly to the observer,

A "languid leaner."

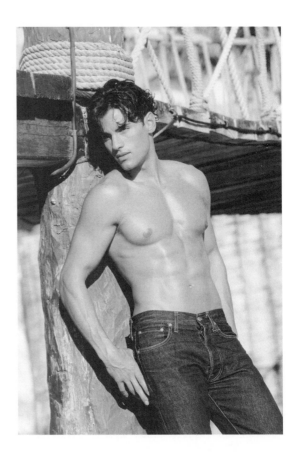

promises "escape." From what? *To* what? Men have complained, justly, about the burden of always having to be the sexual initiator, the pursuer, the one of whom sexual "performance" is expected. Perhaps the escape is from these burdens, and toward the freedom to indulge in some of the more receptive pleasures traditionally reserved for women. The pleasures, not of staring some-one down but of feeling one's body caressed by another's eyes, of being the one who receives the awaited call rather than the one who must build up the nerve to make the call, the one who doesn't have to hump and pump, but is permitted to lie quietly, engrossed in reverie and sensation.

Some people describe these receptive pleasures as "passive"—which gives them a bad press with men, and is just plain inaccurate too. "Passive" hardly describes what's going on when one person offers himself or herself to another. Inviting, receiving, responding—these are active behaviors too, and rather thrilling ones. It's a macho bias to view the only *real* activity as that which takes, invades, aggresses. It's a bias, however, that's been with us for a long time, in both straight and gay cultures. In many Latin cultures, it's not a disgrace to sleep with other men, so long as one is *activo* (or *machista*)—the penetrator rather than the penetratee. To be a *pasivo*, on the other hand, is to be socially stigmatized. It's that way in prison cultures too—a good indication of the power hierarchies involved. These hierarchies date back to the ancient Greeks, who believed that passivity, receptivity, penetrability were marks of inferior feminine being. The qualities were inherent in women; it was our nature to be passively controlled by our sexual needs. (Unlike us, the Greeks viewed women—not men—as the animalistic ones.) Real Men, who unlike women had the necessary rationality and will, were expected to be judicious in the exercise of their desires. But being judicious and being "active"—deciding when to pursue, whom to pursue, making advances, pleading one's case—went hand in hand.

Allowing oneself to be pursued, flirting, accepting the advances of another, offering one's body—these behaviors were permitted also (but only on a temporary basis) to still-developing, younger men. These young men—not little boys, as is sometimes incorrectly believed—were the true "sex objects" of elite Greek culture. Full-fledged male citizens, on the other hand, were expected to be "active," initiators, the penetrators not the penetratees, masters of their own desires rather than the objects of another's. Plato's *Symposium* is full of speeches on the different sexual behaviors appropriate to adult men with full beards and established professions and glamorous young men still revered more for their beauty than their minds. But even youth could not make it okay for a man to behave *too much* like a woman. The admirable youth was the one who—unlike a woman—was able to remain sexually "cool" and remote, to keep his wits about him. "Letting go" was not seemly.

Where does our culture stand today with respect to these ideas about   *40*
men's sexuality? Well, to begin with, consider how rarely male actors are shown—on their faces, in their utterances, and not merely in the movements of their bodies—having orgasms. In sex scenes, the moanings and writhings of the female partner have become the conventional cinematic code for heterosexual ecstasy and climax. The male's participation is largely represented by caressing hands, humping buttocks, and—on rare occasions—a facial expression of intense concentration. She's transported to another world; he's the pilot of the ship that takes her there. When men are shown being transported themselves, it's usually been played for comedy (as in Al Pacino's shrieks in *Frankie and Johnny,* Eddie Murphy's moanings in *Boomerang,* Kevin Kline's contortions in *A Fish Called Wanda*), or it's coded to suggest that something is not quite normal about the man—he's sexually enslaved, for example (as with Jeremy Irons in *Damage*). Mostly, men's bodies are presented like action-hero toys—wind them up and watch them perform.

Hollywood—still an overwhelmingly straight-male-dominated industry—is clearly not yet ready to show us a man "passively" giving himself over to another, at least not when the actors in question are our cultural icons. Too feminine. Too suggestive, metaphorically speaking, of penetration by another. But perhaps fashion ads are less uptight? I decided to perform an experiment.

I grouped ads that I had collected over recent years into a pile of "rocks" and a pile of "leaners" and found, not surprisingly, that both race and age played a role. African-American models, whether in *Esquire* or *Vibe,* are almost always posed facing-off. And leaners tend to be younger than rocks. Both in gay publications and straight ones, the more languid, come-hither poses in advertisements are of boys and very young men. Once a certain maturity line is crossed, the challenging stares, the "face-off" postures are the norm. What does one learn from these ads? Well, I wouldn't want to claim too much. It used to be that one could tell a lot about gender and race from looking at ads. Racial stereotypes were transparent, the established formulas for representing men and women were pretty clear (sociologist Erving Goffman even called ads "gender advertisements"), and when the conventions were defied it was usually because advertisers sensed (or discovered in their polls) that social shifts had made consumers ready to receive new images. In this "postmodern" age, it's more of a free-for-all, and images are often more reactive to each other than to social change. It's the viewers' jaded eye, not their social prejudices, that is the prime consideration of every ad campaign, and advertisers are quick to tap into taboos, to defy expectations, simply in order to produce new and arresting images. So it wouldn't surprise me if we soon find languid black men and hairy-chested leaners in the pages of *Gentlemen's Quarterly.*

But I haven't seen any yet. At the very least, the current scene suggests that even in this era of postmodern pastiche racial clichés and gender taboos persist; among them, we don't want grown men to appear too much the "passive" objects of another's sexual gaze, another's desires. We appear, still, to have somewhat different rules for boys and men. As in ancient Greece, boys are permitted to be seductive, playful, to flirt with being "taken." *Men* must still be in command. Leonardo Di Caprio, watch out. Your days may be numbered.

QUESTIONS FOR DISCUSSION

1. What makes certain images "intrusive"? Can you identify any that have intruded upon your own consciousness?
2. What role have "gay male aesthetics" played in the development of ads that are directed, at least in part, to heterosexuals?
3. Consider the discussion of Jean-Paul Sartre in paragraph 7. What does this discussion of looking (and being seen) have to do with the advertisements discussed by Bordo?
4. What does Bordo disclose about herself in this piece, and how do these disclosures influence your response to her work?
5. How is the response to naked bodies determined by gender? To what extent do other factors determine how men and women respond to images of the naked male body?
6. Why does Bordo believe that the images she analyzes do not treat men as "objects"?

Marlon Brando as Stanley Kowalski.   *Gordon Hanson, 1954,* by George Platt Lynes.

SUGGESTIONS FOR WRITING

1. Study images of the female body in magazine advertisements, and analyze how these images are designed to inspire consumption of specific products.
2. Consider how either men or women most frequently dress on your campus, and analyze what this clothing conveys about the people in question.
3. Write an analysis of one of the male images reprinted on this page.

LINKS

■ Within the Book

For another article on advertising, see the selection by Jean Kilbourne (pages 313–326) on how advertisements are designed to appeal to women.

■ Elsewhere in Print

Bordo, Susan. *The Male Body: A New Look at Men in Public and Private.* New York: Farrar, 1999.
———. *Unbearable Weight: Feminism, Western Culture, and the Body.* Berkeley: U of California P, 1995.
Boyreau, Jacques. *The Male Mystique: Men's Magazine Ads in the 1960s and '70s.* San Francisco: Chronicle, 2004.

■ **Elsewhere in Print (continued)**

Faludi, Susan. *Stiffed: The Betrayal of the American Man*. New York: Morrow, 1999.

Kassen, John F. *Houdini, Tarzan, and the Perfect Man: The White Male Body and the Challenge of Modernity in America*. New York: Hill, 2002.

Kimmel, Michael. *Manhood in America,* New York: Free, 1996.

Luciano, Lynne. *Looking Good: Male Body Image in Modern America*. New York: Hill, 2002.

Pope, Harrison G., Katharine A. Phillips, and Roberto Olivardia. *The Adonis Complex*. New York: Free, 2000.

Tuana, Nancy, et al. *Revealing Male Bodies*. Bloomington: Indiana UP, 2001.

■ **Online**

www.mhhe.com/motives

Click on "More Resources" then "Writing to Analyze Images."

■ ■ ■

NeXT: UNDERSTANDING A CORPORATE LOGO

Steven Heller and Karen Pomeroy

A senior art director at the New York Times, *Steven Heller is the author of more than sixty books on graphic design. He is also editor of* AIGA Journal of Graphic Design *as well as a contributing editor to* Print, ID, *and* Eye *magazines. Based in Los Angeles, Karen Pomeroy is a writer and graphic designer who is the co-author of* Designing with Illustration. *The following article is from* Design Literacy: Understanding Graphic Design, *which Heller and Pomeroy published in 1997. If the subject of the design of a corporate logo seems remote from your daily concerns, bear in mind that how corporations present themselves through design plays a role in how they are perceived by the public. Given the power that many corporations enjoy and the importance of presentation in business life, good design can affect a company's income and status.*

It is difficult enough to invent a meaningful corporate logo, sign, or mark to express conventional business issues without having to depict the future as well. However, that is what was demanded of Paul Rand (1914–1996) when in 1988 he was commissioned to design a logo for NeXT, an educational computer company headed by Steven Jobs, the founder of Apple Computer Company. Although NeXT's new product was cast in secrecy, the corporate name alluded to its futuristic positioning—not simply a *new* computer, but the *next* wave of information processing for the educational market. With only a few clues, Rand was given a month to devise a logo that would embody as much symbolic power as the memory of a silicon chip.

Rand had made identity systems out of whole cloth many times before. He created time-honored marks for IBM, UPS, and ABC. In each he found the most identifiable graphic forms: stripes for IBM, a gift box atop a shield for UPS, the repetition of circles for the lowercase letters *abc.* Designing such charged—and lasting—logos is not magic, but it does take an acute understanding of the nature of perception and the ability to translate that into a visual form. "Logos are *aides de mémoire* that give you something to hook onto when you see it, and especially when you don't see it," explained Rand. And the problem with the word NeXT was that it was not depictable. "What are you going to show? A barber shop with somebody pointing, 'You're next'? It's simply not describable in typographic terms."

Graphic devices that represent the future, such as the arrow, were made meaningless by overuse, but the NeXT computer was contained in a black cube, which gave Rand the idea he needed. He decided to frame the word in a cube to evoke the product itself. However, at the time the logo was introduced to the public, the computer's shape and form were completely secret.

349

"It was understandable only as a cube, nothing else," he explained. "But without that reference point, I would have had to devise something out of the blue." In fact, for Rand it was not so much a question of having a reference point as using that reference point. "The client mentioned the cube to me when I was given the problem, and I'm sure the other designers who worked on the logo must also have heard about it," Rand presumed.

The NeXT logo was successful in part because the cube was symbolically related to the product itself, but Rand insisted that the shape was only important in sparking the idea. "Some reference was made to it being like a child's block," he continued. "I really think that is one of its virtues and part of its charm. However, the logo is not designed to be charming, it is designed to identify."

Before the logo could do the job, however, Rand had to sell the mark to   5
Jobs. For this he had a pronged strategy. The first was to present only one logo. This underscored his own confidence in the solution and deflected indecision on the part of the client. The second was to "speak" only through a presentation booklet that concisely explained the rationale and showed the applications of the logo. Jobs had seen all the timeworn futuristic clichés—arrows, clouds, lightning bolts—in the book. However, he was unprepared for Rand's twenty-page book entitled "The Sign of the Next Generation of Computers *for Education*. . . ."

From the beginning of this limited (fifty copies), Platonic document, Rand announced his premise: "What should a logo for NeXT look like?" he asked in text set in Caslon, which led into a concise narrative that condensed decades of communications history into ten minutes of reading time.

First he introduced the concept of type itself: "Choosing a typeface as the basis for the design of a logo is a convenient starting point. Here are two examples: Caslon and Bifur. Caslon is an alphabet designed as far back as 1725 by William Caslon. It appears to be a good choice because it is both elegant and bookish, qualities well suited for educational purposes. . . ." He described the nature of his faces, their quirks and virtues, and concluded by admitting, "Attributing certain magical qualities to particular typefaces is, however, largely a subjective matter."

Next he defused the client's need to sample a variety of typefaces: "One reason for looking at a number of possible typefaces is to satisfy one's curiosity. Another, and perhaps more meaningful one, is to study the relationship of different letter combinations, to look for visual analogies, and to try to elicit ideas that the design of a letter or group of letters might inspire." He offered some examples that were intended to pique the reader's interest, and offered this warning: "Personal preferences, prejudices, and stereotypes often dictate what a logo looks like, but it is *needs,* not wants, *ideas,* not type styles, which determine what its form should be. . . ."

Then Rand took a representative typeface and set it in caps to explain why this particular iteration was unsuccessful: "Set in all capitals, the word NEXT is sometimes confused with EXIT, possibly because the EXT grouping is so dominant. A combination of capitals and lowercase letters alleviates this problem." And after winning the argument, he provided a textbook example of a more successful application: "Here are some possibilities which explore the use of lowercase letters. The *e* is differentiated so as to provide a focal point and visual contrast among the capital letters which, otherwise, consist only of straight lines. Happily the *e* also could stand for: education, excellence, expertise, exceptional, excitement, $e = mc^2$, etc."

This brief lesson in typographic style segued into an explanation of how a mark should function: "Ideally, a logo should explain or suggest the business it symbolizes, but this is rarely possible or even necessary. There is nothing about the IBM symbol, for example, that suggests computers, except what the viewer reads into it. Stripes are now associated with computers because the initials of a great computer company happen to be striped. . . ." And then he introduced the idea underlying his version of NeXT: "A logo takes on meaning, only if over a period of time it is linked to some product or service of a particular organization. What is essential is finding a meaningful device, some idea—preferably product-related—that reinforces the company name. The cube, in which the computer will be housed, can be such a device because it has visual impact and is easy to remember. Unlike the word *Next,* it is depictable, possesses the *promise of meaning* and the *pleasure of recognition.*" 10

Understanding that questions would arise concerning the application of the cube, Rand talked about versatility: "This idea in no way restricts its application to any one product or concept. The three-dimensional effect functions as an underscore to attract the viewer's attention." Once established that the cube was the appropriate form, Rand addressed the basic structure of the logo: "Splitting the logo into two lines accomplishes several things: It startles the viewer and gives the word a new look, thus making it easier to separate from common usage. And even more importantly, it increases the letter size twofold, within the framework of the cube. For small space use, a one-line logo would have been too small to fit within this same framework." Rand showed that readability was not affected because the word was too simple to be misread. "Moreover, people have become accustomed to this format with such familiar four-letter word combinations as LOVE."

He concluded his primer with a down-to-earth analysis: "The adaptation of this device to miniaturization—tie tacks, charm bracelets, paperweights, stickers, and other promotional items—is endless. It lends itself as well to large-scale interpretation—signs, exhibits in the shape of cubes, in which the actual exhibit is housed, as well as exhibit stands. For printed matter, its infinite adaptability and attention-compelling power is self-evident."

Upon presentation, Rand did not utter a word, he just sat silently watching as Jobs read. "The book itself was a big surprise." Jobs recalled, "I was convinced that each typographic example on the first few pages was the final logo. I was not quite sure what Paul was doing until I reached the end. And at that moment I knew we had the solution. . . . Rand gave us a jewel, which in retrospect seems so obvious." Moreover, as it turned out, Rand's user-friendly teaching aid underscored Jobs' own commitment to the process of education.

QUESTIONS FOR DISCUSSION

1. What does this article reveal about the principles that determined the way Paul Rand approached assignments for designing corporate logos?
2. What were the challenges that faced Rand in designing a logo for NeXT?
3. What does Heller mean when he describes the booklet Rand prepared as a "Platonic document"?
4. What specific arguments did Rand advance on behalf of his design?
5. Heller quotes Steven Jobs as saying, "Rand gave us a jewel, which in retrospect seems obvious." Is this a compliment? In what sense is the NeXT logo "obvious"?

SUGGESTIONS FOR WRITING

1. Write an analysis of the logo that appears on the stationery of your college or university.
2. Choose a commercial emblem (such as the Morton Salt girl or the image of Betty Crocker), and research how it has evolved since first published. Then analyze the significance of the changes you discover.
3. Heller notes that Paul Rand also designed the logos for IBM and UPS. Choose one of these logos, analyze its components, and explain what the image communicates.

LINKS

▪ Within the Book

For another view of American business, see Eric Schlosser's "The American Flavor Industry" (pages 125–134).

▪ Elsewhere in Print

Bierut, Michael, William Drenttel, Steven Heller, and D. K. Holland, eds. *Looking Closer: Critical Writings on Graphic Design.* New York: Allworth, 1994.

Haig, William L., and Laurel Harper. *The Power of Logos: How to Create Effective Company Logos.* Hoboken: Wiley, 1997.

Heller, Steven, and Marie Finamore, eds. *Design Culture: An Anthology of Writing from the AIGA Journal of Graphic Design.* New York: Allworth, 1997.

Millen, Anistasia, and James M. Brown. *What Logos Do: And How They Do It.* Gloucester: Rockport, 2000.

Sparkman, Don. *Selling Graphic Design,* 2nd ed. New York: Allworth, 1999.

Votolato, Gregory. *American Design in the Twentieth Century: Personality and Performance.* New York: Manchester UP, 1998.

▪ Online

www.mhhe.com/motives

Click on "More Resources" then "Writing to Analyze Images."

▪ ▪ ▪

THE RE-REBRANDING OF BERLIN

Annie Bourneuf

Unless they are dated or contain objects such as cars or people wearing clothing that dates from a specific era, images of a place can easily seem timeless to the inexperienced eye—as if the place always was and always will be as shown in a photograph or painting. But just as readers can benefit from considering what may be missing from a written text (see pages 387–389), so can writers who analyze a visual text benefit from considering what preceeded the image and what may have happened after the image was constructed. The image of a place may carry within it reminders of what the place used to be as well as signs indicating the kind of place it is likely to become. This is especially true in cities, where an entire block can be demolished for a new office building, or in suburbs where new shopping malls and access roads consume what had been farmland.

In "The Re-rebranding of Berlin," Annie Bourneuf addresses this kind of cultural change by analyzing a 2004 image of a large European plaza where a palace once stood. A graduate of Harvard who is an Andrew Mellon Fellow at Princeton, Bourneuf is an art historian who focuses on photography. Her analysis originally appeared in Harper's. *About her work, she notes, "It may be harder to break into a photograph, to investigate its insides and its workings, than a written text. The surface of a photograph can seem impermeable to analysis. . . . But a writer can break this seeming impermeability and draw the photograph into conversations which catch the photograph, so to speak, off guard. In this case, my job was made easier by the brokenness and contradictions of the Schlossplatz itself; such contradictions break the seal of the photograph from the outset, and ease the writer's way in."*

This is the Schlossplatz in the center of Berlin. In the former capitals of old Central European statelets there are dozens of *Schloss plätze,* each a central plaza *(Platz)* laid out neatly before the former castle *(Schloss)* of the local prince. In Berlin, however, Schlossplatz designates the space left behind by the imperial home of the Hohenzollern,° dynamited and cleared away by the East German government in 1950—the space that, per a 2002 Bundestag decision, will be filled with a replica of the old Schloss and therefore disappear. This is a *Platz* not in the sense of "plaza," but in the sense of vacated position, as in *Machen Sie Platz*—"make room," "get out of the way." In fact, the effort to "rebuild" the Schloss bears many similarities to the effort to destroy it. It

---

°*Hohenzollern:* The ruling family of Germany from 1871–1918, the period known as the Second Reich (or empire). For an image of the old palace, go to www.mhhe.com/motives and click on "More Resources" then "Writing to Analyze Images."

The Schlossplatz in Berlin (with the Palace of the Republic at left).

will be not so much a restoration of the past as a potentially lucrative remodeling of it, in line with the fashion of the day.

(A) In 1950, when the 1,210-room stone Schloss was demolished and cleared, the year-old East German state had already begun to organize itself as a Stalinist dictatorship; the Stasi° was created that February. Eventually, in the 1970s, the government filled part of the cleared ground with this, the Palace of the Republic—a socialist mall fitted out with shops, bars, a disco, a bowling alley, and a video arcade. This was an act of grave and conscious symbolism: here, on the former seat of monarchy, the worker could enjoy pleasures (Harry Belafonte concerts, banana splits) beyond the imagination of kaisers. When nostalgic Germans had protested the Schloss's demolition, the government had avoided discussion of ideological taste altogether. The mayor of East Berlin announced that "expert opinion has determined" that the castle had been destroyed already by Allied bombing, despite appearances to the contrary. "If the castle were still undestroyed," he said, "no one would have seriously considered tearing it down."

(B) Today, Berlin is $47 billion in debt, and its unemployment rate is nearly 20 percent. Socialist modernist blocks such as these, many as tenantless

---

°*Stasi:* The East German secret police.

as the Palace, are the déclassé signs of reunification's failure to redecorate quickly, and they are torn down whenever possible. In the city's hopeful *Stadtmarketing*—its brochures aimed at tourists and investors—pictures of restored prewar buildings and the placeless architecture of the market, specifically of the nineties construction boom, dominate. To the "Ostalgic" East Germans who remember the Palace's pleasures fondly, the politicians have advanced, as in 1950, a seemingly unassailable practical argument: in this case, asbestos contamination. Avoiding questions of politics entirely, Chancellor Gerhard Schröder, a strong advocate of the new Schloss, declared that if the Palace "weren't so ugly and full of asbestos, it could stay, as far as I'm concerned." Now the decontamination work is finished and the Palace asbestos-free, but it remains, of course, condemned.

(C) For all its ideological bluster, the Communist government did not present itself as entirely ahistorical, as a revolutionary blank slate. It manufactured its own claim to Germanness by cobbling together bits of pre-1933 history that it felt it could use. Even as it destroyed the old Schloss, it kept this section, which includes the balcony Karl Liebknecht stood on when he proclaimed the German socialist republic in 1918, and lodged it into the center of the State Council building. Even the futuristic Palace was designed to mirror the old Schloss in its interior layout, and photographs of the castle's facade ornamented the Palace's beer bar. For the East German government, which justified its existence in large part on the claim that West Germany was not "antifascist" enough, such homages implied that East Germany was in fact the true heir to the Second Reich, not as a continuation or a negation but as a sort of dialectical synthesis.

(D) These panels, installed by supporters of the new Schloss, are covered with photographs of the castle from before the kaiser's abdication. Since reunification, the official template for the city's remodeling has been the Berlin of the Second Reich, images of which are everywhere: on posters and postcards, in subways, in picture books available at newsstands and railway stations. One mayor during the 1990s presented his entire plan for the economic and cultural revitalization of the city as returning to it "the character and charm of . . . old black-and-white photographs." Rebuilding the Schloss—a project expected to cost nearly $800 million—will advance precisely this rebranding, an Epcot-style appropriation of the nationalist Second Reich in the service of *Stadtmarketing.* Far from attempting to situate itself within German history, a rebuilt Schloss will destroy its own context.

(E) Behind these trees, excavated foundations of the Schloss are already visible. Although the date of the resurrection is still unspecified, the Bundestag voted in November to destroy the Palace without delay, no doubt because its divisiveness—as an eyesore for West Germans, a shrine for East Germans—shows just how incomplete reunification remains. The great publicity coup for the rebuilt Schloss came in 1993, when its advocates covered the *Platz* with a life-sized model, made of painted cloth hung over a scaffold. It looked as if the city of the photographs had magically returned. Here was an unbroken historical surface, a smooth gliding progression from the Second Reich to the present. The new Schloss itself will be of little more substance. In lending Berlin the pleasant "historicalness" the tourism industry demands, the castle will irrevocably remodel (*sanieren,* which also means "to sanitize" and "to restore to profitability") the site's actual history. As such, a rebuilt Schloss will serve as a fitting monument not to the Hohenzollern but to the ruling ideology of today.

QUESTIONS FOR DISCUSSION

1. According to Bourneuf, rebuilding a major palace in Berlin would be similar to destroying it. What is the connection?
2. Paragraphs 2 and 3 include examples of how men in authority rationalized decisions to demolish buildings. What does Chancellor Schröder have in common with the mayor of East Berlin who authorized the destruction of the Hohenzollern palace in 1950?
3. Consider how part of a historic building is incorporated in the State Council Building erected by the East German government. In your opinion, how successful is this combination?
4. Paragraphs 4 and 5 refer to the Second Reich, a period of German history that ranged from 1871 to 1918, when Germany became a republic (as opposed to the Third Reich, or empire, in which Hitler ruled Germany from 1933 to 1945). Why would Germans with different values want to emphasize a connection to the nineteenth century?
5. Is there a difference between honoring the past and seeking to re-create it?

SUGGESTIONS FOR WRITING

1. Bourneuf draws attention to how the city of Berlin uses images to attract tourists and investors. How are images used by your school to attract students or donors? Focus your analysis on an admissions brochure, a magazine mailed to alumni, or your school's Web site.
2. Photgraph an urban or suburban place that might look unremarkable to someone simply passing by. Then write an analysis in which you focus on determining what makes the site distinctive and located at a specific moment in time.
3. Bourneuf refers to "Epcot-style appropriation" of the past. Download an image from Epcot or Disney World that presents a sanitized version of the past. Then analyze this image, pointing to what has been emphasized and what has been left out.

LINKS

■ Within the Book

For an evaluation of a work of contemporary architecture, see Paul Goldberger's "High-Tech Bibliophilia" (pages 289–293).

■ Elsewhere in Print

Brendgens, Guido, et al. *Berlin Architecture.* New York: Jovis, 2002.

Jacobs, Jane. *The Death and Life of Great American Cities.* New York: Vintage, 1992.

Kierren, Martin. *New Architecture in Berlin 1990–2000.* New York: Jovis, 1998.

Marling, Karel Ann, et al. *Designing Disney's Theme Parks.* New York: Flammarion, 1998.

Mumford, Lewis. *The City in History,* New York: Harvest, 1968.

Silver, Nathan. *Lost New York.* New York: Mariner, 2000.

Simpson, William. *The Second Reich.* New York: Cambridge UP, 1995.

Wise, Michael. *Capital Dilemma.* Princeton: Princeton Architectural P, 1998.

■ Online

www.mhhe.com/motives

Click on "More Resources" then "Writing to Analyze Images."

■ ■ ■

CONVEYING ATROCITY IN IMAGE

Barbie Zelizer

A former columnist for The Nation, *Barbie Zelizer teaches at the highly respected Annenberg School of Communication at the University of Pennsylvania. She has also taught at Columbia University, Princeton University, and the Hebrew University in Jerusalem. Her books include* Covering the Body: The Kennedy Assassination, the Media, and the Shaping of Collective Memory. *She is also the co-author of* Almost Midnight: Reforming the Late-Night News.

The following selection is an abridgement of one of her chapters in Remembering to Forget: Holocaust Memory through the Camera's Eyes, *published by the University of Chicago Press in 1998. As you prepare to read this piece, it might be useful to bear in mind that more than six million Jews were killed during the Nazi regime (1933–1945), most of them in concentration camps during the Second World War. Millions of other victims perished as well. The images in the following selection may disturb you, but if you find them distressing, you might consider the huge difference between viewing images of the Holocaust and being one of its direct victims.*

When discussing her interest in analyzing photographs, Zelizer cautions that "visual memory is deceptive" and that photos seen out of context can "undermine our ability to understand the contingent details of Holocaust atrocity" as well as "our capacity to respond to atrocities today in Rwanda, Bosnia, Cambodia, and elsewhere." As you read this example of her work, be alert for how images become more meaningful through analysis. (Zelizer's notes, as well as an extensive bibliography, can be found online at www.mhhe.com/motives and click on "More Resources" then "Writing to Analyze Images.")

Using images to bear witness to atrocity required a different type of representation than did words. Images helped record the horror in memory after its concrete signs had disappeared, and they did so in a way that told a larger story of Nazi atrocity. As the U.S. trade journal *Editor and Publisher* proclaimed, "the peoples of Europe, long subjected to floods of propaganda, no longer believe the written word. Only factual photographs will be accepted."[1]

While words produced a concrete and grounded chronicle of the camps' liberation, photographs were so instrumental to the broader aim of enlightening the world about Nazi actions that when Eisenhower proclaimed, "Let the world see," he implicitly called upon photography's aura of realism to help accomplish that aim. Through its dual function as carrier of truth–value and symbol, photography thus helped the world bear witness by providing a context for events at the same time as it displayed them.

ATROCITY PHOTOS AS TOOLS
OF DOCUMENTATION

The photographs that became available on the liberation of the western camps were too numerous and varied to be published together by any one U.S. or British publication. This was because scores of photographers in different capacities—professional, semiprofessional, and amateur photographers as well as soldiers bearing cameras—accompanied the liberating forces into the camps, and most were placed immediately under the aegis of the U.S. Signal Corps, the British Army Film and Photographic Unit, and other military units. Making available numerous atrocity photos already in the first days after the camps' liberation, these photographers displayed horror so wide-ranging and incomprehensible that it enhanced the need to bear witness, forcing an assumption of public responsibility for the brutality being depicted.

How did photographers record the scenes of barbarism that they encountered? Like reporters, photographers accompanying the liberating forces received few instructions concerning which camps they were entering or what they should do once they arrived; they were given even fewer guidelines about which shots to take or how to take them. This meant that for many the so-called professional response to the event was simply one of "making do," an improvisory reaction to often faulty equipment, bad weather, and uneven training and experience. As one photographer with the British Army Film and Photographic Unit said simply, "we did what [we] saw at the time."[2]

The atrocity photos played a complex role in recording the atrocities. [5] Like words, the images were of limited representativeness, providing only a partial picture of the consequences of years of forced torture, harassment, and eventual death—not the Holocaust per se but a partial depiction of its final phase. As British M.P. Mavis Tate commented, "you can photograph results of suffering but never suffering itself." But photography also offered graphic representations of atrocity that were more difficult to deny than with words. Photographers, one reporter claimed, sent pictures bearing such "irrefutable evidence of Nazi degradation and brutality" that were "so horrible that no newspaper normally would use them, but they were less horrible than the reality." Photographs thus pushed the authenticity of unbelievable camp scenes by pitching depictions closely to the events being described at the same time as they signaled a broader story of Nazi atrocity. It is no surprise, then, that photographs flourished for the press as an effective mode of documenting what was happening.[3] . . .

Practices of Composition:
Placement, Number, and Gaze

Though numerous and wide-ranging in their depictions of horror, the atrocity photos were somewhat unusual due to the repetitive scenes reproduced by different photographers, regardless of their degree of professional training.

While varying the depiction—by changing the camera position, camera angle, focal length of the lens, light, and length of exposure—might have lent an individualized signature to the photos, this was generally not characteristic of these photos. Instead, near identical images arrived over the wires within hours and days of each other, differing only slightly in focus, distance, exposure, and perspective.

Placement The decision of where to place evidence of atrocity in a photo created a layering between the atrocity photos' foreground and background, for the two often communicated different levels of specificity about what was being depicted. Witnesses and bodies were depicted in many of the images, and one was used as context for the other.

Evidence of atrocity usually meant pictures of corpses, and it often alternated with witnesses in either the shot's foreground or background. One widely circulated image portrayed General Eisenhower and other ranking generals at Ohrdruf viewing corpses strewn across the camp's forecourt [Figure 1]. Eisenhower and company faced the camera from the back of the shot

FIGURE 1. General Eisenhower and other officers examine corpses at Ohrdruf, April 12, 1945, by NARA.°

°*NARA:* National Archives and Records Administration.

while they overlooked the dead bodies in its foreground that spilled into the camera. Taken by an unidentified photographer, the photograph appeared in the *Washington Post* on April 16 and resurfaced frequently over the next two weeks. It played in the *Illustrated London News* as a full front-page photo whose legend told readers that "the usually genial General Eisenhower shows by his grim aspect his horror of German brutality." The photo not only heightened the role of the American GI as witness to atrocity but juxtaposed the reader with the GI across the space of the bodies. It was impossible to contemplate the GI's act of witnessing without first contemplating the corpses.[4]

Elsewhere the foreground and background were switched, with the corpses positioned in the back of the shot. The British *News Chronicle* ran a front-page picture of Belsen that showed women cooking and peeling potatoes in the foreground and heaps of dead bodies in the background. Another frequently circulated triangular shot of the Buchenwald courtyard depicted a visual confrontation juxtaposing U.S. soldiers, a stack of dead bodies on a wagon, and the backs of German civilians [Figure 2]. The bodies occupied the back right-hand corner of the shot, soldiers the back left-hand corner, and civilians the foreground. In viewing the shot, the reader had to look over

FIGURE 2. German civilians view corpses at Buchenwald, April 16, 1945, by NARA.

the shoulders of the German civilians in order to see the bodies, creating a layering between the shot's foreground (where the Germans were standing) and the background (where the victims and liberators stood). The effect was magnified by the middle of the shot, where a seemingly impassable white space kept the groups at a distance from each other. That aesthetic was reproduced in other atrocity photos.[5]

Number   A second practice of composition had to do with the numbers of people who were depicted in atrocity photos. The photos oscillated between pictures of the many and pictures of the few. Pictures of the many portrayed mass graves, where bodies had been thrown together so indiscriminately that it was difficult, if not impossible, to discern which appendage belonged to which body; pictures of the few portrayed single individual bodies frozen in particularly horrific poses—a starved man stretched out in rigor mortis on the grounds of one of the camps. Taken together, the images portrayed both individual agony and the far-reaching nature of mass atrocity, suggesting that the depiction of each individual instance of horror represented thousands more who had met the same fate. The photos functioned not only referentially but as symbolic markers of atrocity in its broadest form.[6]

On the whole, the press presented collective images of atrocity more frequently than it did those of individuals. Perhaps because the group shots suggested a collective status that helped offset public disbelief, group shots appeared frequently regardless of the type of collective represented—groups of victims, survivors, or witnesses. Group images tended to be less graphic than those of individuals, partly because the rarely visible eyes and faces worked against the possibility of identifying the victims being depicted. Foremost here was a famous shot by Margaret Bourke-White, captioned simply "Victims of the Buchenwald Concentration Camp." Unaccredited at the time it originally appeared, the photo portrayed piles of human feet and heads angled away from the camera; the pile gave viewers the impression that it was about to spill over onto the photographer, and that it was barred from doing so only by a length of chain at the bottom of the picture [Figure 3]. Other photographs, less renowned than Bourke-White's, showed the same pile of bodies from a long shot, a perspective that revealed them to be stacked atop a wagon in the camp's courtyard. That same wagon, portrayed from an even further distance, was featured in the aforementioned triangular shot of the Buchenwald courtyard [Figure 2].[7]

Images of other kinds of groups—survivors, German civilians, German perpetrators, and official witnesses—also proliferated, each displayed with repeated visual characteristics. Groups of witnesses were nearly always portrayed at one side of the frame, looking sideways at corpses that were either inside or outside the field of the camera. Groups of German perpetrators, for instance, were almost always portrayed at harsh angles to the camera and in rigid and upright postures [Figure 4]. These individuals looked angry and cruel, almost maniacal. That perception was upheld in the captions that accompanied

FIGURE 3. Corpses of civilians killed at Buchenwald, April–May 1945, by NARA.

images of this type, as when the *Illustrated London News* labeled a group of perpetrators "The Female Fiends."[8]

Often the shots depicted confrontations between groups—German civilians and victims or news editors and survivors. One image—which circulated under the caption "Slave Laborer Points Finger of Guilt"—depicted a survivor of an unidentified camp pointing at a German guard [Figure 5]. The guard stood at the right-hand corner of the image, his contorted face twisting away from both the camera lens and the accusing, outstretched finger of the former prisoner. Although the prisoner was portrayed sideways to the camera, the photographer's empathy with him was clear.[9] Behind the two figures stood other officials, one of whom was witnessing the confrontation.

Thus, in each case framing the depiction as an act of collective, not individual, contemplation reflected a need to collectively address and understand the atrocities. While the emphasis on collective representation may have worked against a recognition of the individual tragedies that lay underneath each photo, the emphasis on groups fit more effectively than did an individual focus on Eisenhower's aim to use the photos as persuasive tools for the war effort. Groups, more than individuals, lent the war effort urgency. Under-

FIGURE 4. Women SS guards at Bergen–Belsen, April 17, 1945, courtesy of The Imperial War Museum, London.

FIGURE 5. Russian survivor identifies former camp guard at Buchenwald, April 14, 1945, by NARA.

FIGURE 6. Former prisoners of Buchenwald, April 16, 1945, by NARA.

standing the scope and magnitude of atrocity, in this sense, was equally important to recognizing its individual cases.

Gaze   Yet a third compositional practice had to do with the gaze of those   15
being depicted. The gaze of emaciated, near-dead survivors, whose eyes
seemed not to comprehend the target of vision, tended to be frontal and appeared to signify frankness—though, as one British Army Film and Photographic Unit photographer of Belsen recalled, many of the same people were
"incapable of coherent thought.... It was a very quiet, silent business. They
sat about, very little movement. Some of them were too far gone to move."
The survivors were almost always represented in frontal gazes that stared
directly at the camera or at a short distance behind the photographer [see
Figure 6].[10] In a sense, atrocity survivors appeared to see without seeing. One
such photo, which appeared in *PM,* depicted two young adult women in a
close shot that echoed their hollowed cheekbones and vacant eyes [Figure 7].
"Here's How Nazis Treat Their Captives . . . ," read the caption to the photo,
as it implored readers to look at the "faces of these women."[11] . . .

German perpetrators generally were depicted in side views or three-
quarter gazes, their eyes averted and narrowed [Figure 8]. Often they were
depicted looking sideways at a survivor or soldier, who nearly always stared
either directly at them or toward the camera. One such widely circulated

FIGURE 7. Two survivors in Bergen-Belsen, April 30, 1945, courtesy of
The Imperial War Museum, London.

image was that of Belsen commander Josef Kramer. It portrayed him walking
in Belsen, his mouth pursed and features tight, under a guard's watchful eye,
who stared at him intently from the right-hand corner of the photograph.
The same figures were portrayed from a greater distance in the *Daily Mail,*
where Kramer was shown to be accompanied on his stroll not only by a soldier at his side but by another soldier prodding a rifle into his back.[12]

CONCLUSION

In composition, then, the published photos depicted a level of horror that
went beyond one specific instance of brutality so as to present it as a representative incident. The combination of corpses and witnesses in the photos
facilitated both the display of a particular act of barbarism and its more general context of atrocity; the number of individuals depicted in atrocity photos
facilitated an emphasis on the collectives involved in atrocity—either as victims,
survivors, perpetrators, or witnesses; and the gaze of those associated with
atrocity opened the photographic document to the act of bearing witness in

FIGURE 8. Former women guards at Bergen–Belsen, April 1945, courtesy of The Imperial War Museum, London.

different configurations for victims, survivors, and perpetrators. In each case, on the level of composition photographs offered more than just the referential depiction of one specific event, action, or camp. Compositional practices suggested a broader level of the story that went beyond the concrete target of photographic depiction. . . .

All of this suggests that by capitalizing on the symbolic dimensions of images, the press set in place a broader interpretive scheme for comprehending and explaining the atrocities. Playing to the symbolic dimensions of these images had an important effect on publics, not only because they may have been the most effective and least uncomfortable way to comprehend the tragedies of Nazi Europe, but also because they framed events in such a way that all who saw the photos could bear witness to the atrocities. Within that frame, the exact details of the atrocities mattered less than the response of bearing witness. For those inundated with a guilt that came from not having responded earlier, this was no small aim.

QUESTIONS FOR DISCUSSION

1. Why did photographs play such an important role in conveying the nature of the Holocaust? Why might people in the 1940s and later have doubted the reality of the Holocaust?
2. Why did newspapers and magazines publish "images of witnessing"? Why were these images significant? What kind of context had to be established before such images could be understood?
3. How did photographers decide to frame images of victims? What role did "placement" have in influencing how viewers responded to these images?
4. Why were "collective images of atrocity" published more frequently than images of individuals?
5. How are the images included in this selection "symbolic"? To what extent are historical details—such as the names of individuals or the precise sites where the pictures were taken—important?
6. Zelizer notes that newspapers used captions for atrocity pictures, such as "The Female Fiends," which differ from those used in this text. If a newspaper editor asked you to write new captions for the images reproduced here, what words would you write?
7. If you were given the responsibility of sorting through thousands of photographs of an atrocity and deciding which images to select for publication, how would you proceed?

SUGGESTIONS FOR WRITING

1. The photographs reprinted within this reading as Figures 2 and 3 were taken at the same site. Consider how they differ. Supplement Zelizer's analysis by writing your own.
2. Write an analysis of Figure 6 in which you discuss number, placement, and gaze.
3. Analyze the composition of one of the photographs on pages 370–371.

LINKS

▪ Within the Book

For another analysis of atrocity images, see Matt Welch's "The Pentagon's Secret Stash" (pages 372–377).

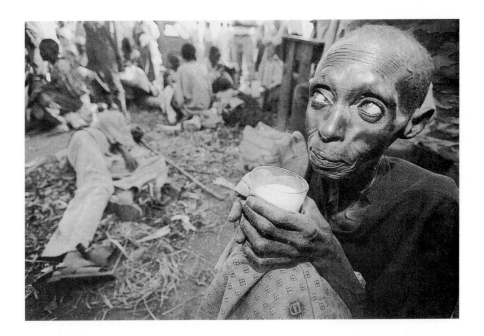

▪ Elsewhere in Print

Amishai-Maisels, Ziva. *Depiction and Interpretation: The Influence of the Holocaust on the Visual Arts.* New York: Pergamon, 1993.

Caiger-Smith, Martin, ed. *The Face of the Enemy: British Photographers in Germany, 1944–1952.* London: Nishen, 1988.

Connerton, Paul. *How Societies Remember.* New York: Cambridge UP, 1989.

Friedländer, Saul. *Memory, History, and the Extermination of the Jews of Europe.* Bloomington: Indiana UP, 1993.

Lipstadt, Deborah. *Beyond Belief: The American Press and the Coming of the Holocaust, 1944–1945.* New York: Free, 1986.

Tagg, John. *The Burden of Representation: Essays on Photographies and Histories.* Amherst: U of Massachusetts P, 1988.

Zelizer, Barbie. *Remembering to Forget: Holocaust Memory through the Camera's Eyes.* Chicago: U of Chicago P, 1998.

———. *Taking Journalism Seriously: News and the Academy.* Thousand Oaks: Sage, 2004.

▪ Online

www.mhhe.com/motives

Click on "More Resources" then "Writing to Analyze Images."

▪ ▪ ▪

THE PENTAGON'S SECRET STASH

Matt Welch

> *In April 2004, photographs of prisoner abuse at Abu Ghraib prison in Iraq became the focus of international attention. Some of the images showed American soldiers happily posing with prisoners who were stripped naked and placed in humiliating positions. Other pictures showed prisoners who seemed to be undergoing torture. Foreign commentators critical of the American presence in Iraq pointed to these pictures as evidence that the United States did not have the moral authority to be waging a preemptive war. Many Americans were horrified as well—not just by the images of what the soldiers were doing, but by the sense that military discipline had broken down—and the soldiers themselves were victims of poor leadership. A handful of these images appeared in newspapers and on television; others appeared online.*
>
> *A year after these photographs became public, Matt Welch decided to honor that anniversary by reminding readers of what had been shown and what had never been disclosed. Currently based in Los Angeles, Welch has written for a wide range of publications. His special interests include writing about the media, international affairs, and events following from the terrorist attacks of September 11, 2001. He is currently U.S. correspondent for the* National Post of Canada *and an associate editor of* Reasononline—*which published the following piece as part of its mission to "making a principled case for liberty and individual choice in all areas of human activity."*

The images, Defense Secretary Donald Rumsfeld told Congress, depict "acts that can only be described as blatantly sadistic, cruel, and inhuman." After Sen. Saxby Chambliss (R–Ga.) viewed some of them in a classified briefing, he testified that his "stomach gave out." NBC News reported that they show "American soldiers beating one prisoner almost to death, apparently raping a female prisoner, acting inappropriately with a dead body, and taping Iraqi guards raping young boys." Everyone who saw the photographs and videos seemed to shudder openly when contemplating what the reaction would be when they eventually were made public.

But they never were. After the first batch of Abu Ghraib images shocked the world on April 28, 2004, becoming instantly iconic—a hooded prisoner standing atop a box with electrodes attatched to his hands, Pfc. Lynndie England dragging a naked prisoner by a leash, England and Spc. Charles Graner giving a grinning thumbs–up behind a stack of human meat—no substantial second round ever came, either from Abu Ghraib or any of the other locations in Iraq, Afghanistan, and Guantanamo Bay where abuses have been alleged. ABC News broadcast two new photos from the notorious Iraq prison

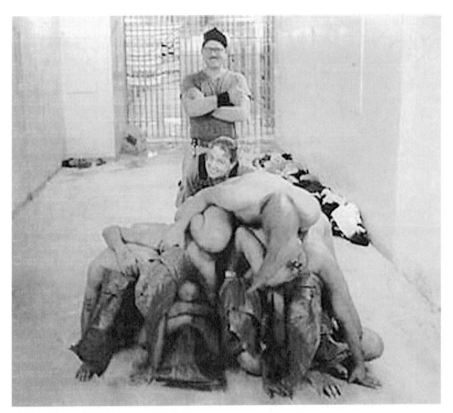

Naked and hooded prisoners piled in a heap.

on May 19, *The Washington Post* printed a half-dozen on May 20 and three more on June 10, and that was it.

"It refutes the glib claim that everything leaks sooner or later," says the Federation of American Scientists' Steven Aftergood, who makes his living finding and publishing little-known government information and fighting against state secrecy. "While there may be classified information in the papers almost every day, there's a lot more classified information that never makes it into the public domain."

It's not for lack of trying, at least from outside the government. Aftergood, for example, sent a Freedom of Information Act request to the Defense Department on May 12, asking generally for "photographic and video images of abuses committed against Iraqi prisoners" and specifically for the material contained on three compact discs mentioned by Rumsfeld in his testimony. The Defense Department told him to ask the U.S. Central Command, which sent him back to Defense, which said on second thought try the Army's Freedom of Information Department, which forwarded him to the Army's Crime

Records Center, which hasn't yet responded. "It's not as if this is somehow an obscure matter that no one's quite ever heard of," Aftergood notes.

Officials have given two legal reasons for suppressing images of prisoner   5
abuse: "unwarranted invasion of privacy" and the potential impact on law enforcement. The Freedom of Information Act's exemptions 6 and 7 (as these justifications are known, respectively) have been used repeatedly to rebuff the American Civil Liberties Union (ACLU), which since October 2003 has unearthed more than 600 torture-related government documents but zero images.

The privacy objection is easily answered: Why not just obscure any identifying features? The law enforcement question, which has a firmer legal footing, is whether distribution of the images could "deprive a person of a fair trial or an impartial adjudication." Yet even there, the globally publicized photographs of Charles Graner, for instance, were ruled by a military judge to be insufficient grounds to declare his trial unfair. And Graner, sentenced to 10 years for his crimes, is the only one of the eight charged Abu Ghraib soldiers to contest his case in court.

"We've seen virtually no criminal investigations or criminal prosecutions," says ACLU staff attorney Jameel Jaffer, who plans to challenge the nondisclosure in court. "The vast majority of those photographs and videotapes *don't* relate to ongoing criminal investigations; on the contrary they depict things that the government approved of at the time and maybe approves of now."

Legalities are one thing, but the real motivation for choking off access is obvious: Torture photos undermine support for the Iraq war. In the words of Donald Rumsfeld, "If these are released to the public, obviously it's going to make matters worse."

The Abu Ghraib photos did more to kneecap right-wing support for the Iraq war, and put a dent in George Bush's approval ratings, than any other single event in 2004. Conservative *New York Times* columnist David Brooks wrote two glum pieces about "the failure to understand the consequences of American power"; *The Washington Post*'s George Will called for Rumsfeld's head; blogger Andrew Sullivan turned decisively against the president he once championed; and Sen. John McCain (R–Ariz.) warned: "We risk losing public support for this conflict. As Americans turned away from the Vietnam War, they may turn away from this one."

News analyses about the war coalition's crackup competed for front-page   10
space with the Abu Ghraib reports for nearly two weeks, until a videotape emerged showing American civilian Nick Berg getting his head sawed off in Iraq. Suddenly, editorialists were urging us to "keep perspective" about "who we're fighting against."

By that time, the executive and legislative branches had learned their lesson: Don't release images. The day after the Berg video, members of Congress were allowed to see a slide show of 1,800 Abu Ghraib photographs. The overwhelming response, besides revulsion, was, in the words of Senate Armed Services Committee Chairman John Warner (R–Va.), that the pictures "should

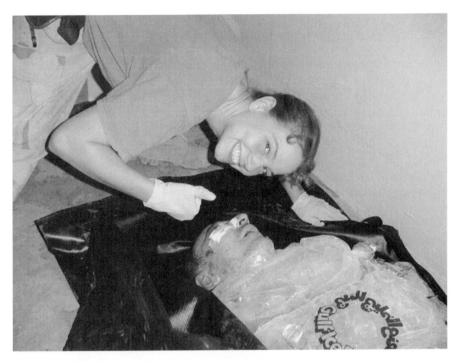

Smiling for the camera by the corpse of a prisoner.

not be made public." "I feel," Warner said, "that it could possibly endanger the men and women of the armed forces as they are serving and at great risk."

Just before former White House counsel Alberto Gonzales, author of two memos relating to interrogation methods and the Geneva Conventions, faced confirmation hearings to become attorney general, there were press whispers that the ranking Democrat on the Senate Armed Services Committee, Carl Levin (D-Mich.), might choose the occasion to force more disclosure of torture photos. It didn't happen. "He and Senator Warner," says Levin spokeswoman Tara Andringa, "are on the same page."

As is, no doubt, a good percentage of the U.S. population. Public opinion of journalism has long since plummeted below confidence levels in government. Prisoner abuse wasn't remotely an issue in the 2004 presidential campaign, let alone an electoral millstone for the governing party. The mid-January discovery of photographs showing British soldiers abusing Iraqis barely caused a ripple in the States. Neither did the Associated Press' December publication of several new photos of Navy SEALs vamping next to injured and possibly tortured prisoners (prompting the *New York Post* to demand an apology from . . . the Associated Press).

As *The Wall Street Journal's* James Taranto put it, with great cynicism and possibly great accuracy, "if the Democrats really think that belaboring complaints

The following article, first published on June 13, 2004, in the New York Times, *focuses on how one of the images from Abu Ghraib came to symbolize the abuses that occurred in that prison.*

Icons live their own lives. Of all the photographs of American soldiers tormenting Iraqi prisoners in the Abu Ghraib prison, one alone has become the icon of the abuse.

A crude echo of the Statue of Liberty.

The image appears in mock advertisements in New York, in paintings in San Francisco, on murals in Tehran and on mannequins in Baghdad. It shows no dogs, no dead, no leash, no face, no nakedness, no pileup, no thumbs-up. It is a picture of a hooded prisoner standing on a box, electrodes attached to his outstretched arms.

Why this image above all the rest? It is far from the most violent, but easily the most graphic. You need less than a second's glance to know exactly what it is. The triangle of the hood silhouettes sharply against the hot pink or chartreuse background of a fake iPod ad. Andy Warhol himself could not have done better. It holds its own on murals meant to be read from far away. It plays well against the Statue of Liberty. It suggests Christ on the Cross. And, best yet, the hooded figure in the photograph is on a pedestal. It is already an icon.

> As a symbolic shape, the hood is almost as strong as a cross. The difference is that the hood has generally been the sign of the persecutor, not of the victim. It is the uniform of the executioner, the sheet of the Klansman, the mask of Death. Until now. In these images, you can see the hood's meaning begin to change and take root.
>
> Maybe it's because the hood resembles a veil. [There is a] photograph of two people in Tehran walking by murals based on the Abu Ghraib photographs: the hooded figure on the box—echoing the robed and veiled Muslim woman passing in front of it—becomes every Muslim. The photo is an ad for martyrdom, made in America.
>
> Sarah Boxer

about harsh treatment of the enemy is the way to 'score points with the public,' they're more out of touch than we thought."

Looking ahead to the next four years, there is little doubt that the adminis- 15 tration, its supporters, and Congress will use whatever legal means are available to prevent Abu Ghraib—the public relations problem, not the prisoner abuse— from happening again. The Defense Department has commissioned numerous studies about America's problem with "public diplomacy" since the September 11 massacre; all those compiled since last May hold up the iconic torture images as the perfect example of what not to let happen again.

"The Pentagon realizes that it's images that sell the story," Aftergood says. "The reason that there is a torture scandal is because of those photographs. There can be *narratives* of things that are much worse, but if they aren't accompanied by photos, they somehow don't register. . . . The Abu Ghraib photos are sort of the military equivalent of the Rodney King case.° . . . And I hate to attribute motives to people I don't know, but it is easy to imagine that the officials who are withholding these images have that fact in mind."

QUESTIONS FOR DISCUSSION

1. What does Welch achieve by opening with quotations from Defense Secretary Donald Rumsfeld and a Republican Senator?
2. Instead of analyzing images that had circulated a year earlier, Welch refers to some of these images in paragraph 2 and then moves on to focus on images that were kept from circulation. Would his case be stronger if he offered an analysis of one of photographs to which he refers, or would doing so weaken his focus?

°*Rodney King:* An African American beaten by white police officers in Los Angeles; the focus of national concern in 1991 because an amateur photographer videotaped the beating.

3. In paragraph 8, Welch quotes Donald Rumsfeld arguing against the release of additional photographs by stating, "If these are released to the public, obviously it's going to make matters worse." For whom or what would these images "make matters worse"? Could they conceivably make anything better?

4. Welch claims, in paragraph 16, that photos can have more impact than narratives. Do you agree? Would that be true of any photograph? In your opinion what kinds of pictures does it take to make bad news really register with people? Would the same be true for good news?

5. Under what circumstances do you think government has the right or responsibility to classify documents or images so that citizens cannot gain access to them?

6. To whom do you think digital images belong after they have been circulated online?

SUGGESTIONS FOR WRITING

1. Write an analysis of one of the images included in this piece—or another image from Abu Ghraib that you have been able to find on the Internet.

2. Find an image that shows the impact of terrorist attacks in Iraq, reflect upon your response, and then analyze why you find the image compelling.

3. Find an image that conveys a positive image of the U.S. military, and analyze how the image is composed and why it projects ideals that can be respected.

■ LINKS

■ Within the Book

For another analysis of war-related photographs, see Barbie Zelizer's "Conveying Atrocity in Image" (pages 359–369).

■ Elsewhere in Print

Danner, Mark. *Torture and Truth: America, Abu Ghraib, and the War on Terror.* New York: New York Review, 2004.

Hersch, Seymour. *The Road from 9/11 to Abu Ghraib.* New York: Harper, 2004.

Jinks, Derek. *The Rules of War: The Geneva Conventions in the Age of Terror.* New York: Oxford UP, 2005.

Roberts, Adam and Richard Guelff, eds. *Documents on the Laws of War.* 3rd ed. New York: Oxford UP, 2000.

Sontag, Susan. "Regarding the Torture of Others." *The New York Times Magazine.* 23 May 2004: 25+.

Strasser, Steven, ed. *The Abu Ghraib Investigation: The Official Independent Panel and Pentagon Reports on the Shocking Prisoner Abuse in Iraq.* New York: PublicAffairs, 2004.

Tripp, Charles. *A History of Iraq.* New York: Cambridge UP, 2002.

Wright, Evan. *Generation Kill: Devil Dogs, Icemen, Captain America, and the New Face of American War.* New York: Putman, 2004.

▪ Online

www.mhhe.com/motives

Click on "More Resources" then "Writing to Analyze Images."

▪ ▪ ▪

6

Writing to Analyze Texts

Texts rarely speak for themselves. Four hundred years after Shakespeare composed *MacBeth,* scholars continue to discover new ways of understanding this play. Theologians still work at analyzing religious texts such as the Bible, thousands of years after these texts were first written down. And when hearing a case, judges must be prepared to listen not only to the arguments that are made to them but also to what laws say (and do not say). The readings in this chapter provide examples of how texts are analyzed within these three disciplines: English, theology, and the law. But examples can be found in almost any discipline.

One reason important texts continue to generate more than one interpretation is that words do not exist in a vacuum. No matter how carefully a writer composes a text, those words simply sit on the page (or on the screen) until a reader engages with them. A text comes alive through the interaction of a reader with it. Without an active reader, one who is responding to the text and analyzing it, words are no more than a sequence of letters stored in a file or sitting on a shelf.

There is no single "correct" way of analyzing a text. Different writers generate different kinds of analyses, and not every analysis deserves the same degree of respect. Some are written in haste by writers who do not seem to have paid close attention to the text. But even people who take the trouble to read attentively and write carefully can reach significantly different conclusions of equal merit. However different their conclusions may be, these writers demonstrate that they have paid close attention to a text and advanced a thesis supported by it.

To help you see how different writers can reach different conclusions when analyzing the same text, the readings in this chapter are paired: Two writers offer different analyses of the same short story, the same passage in Genesis, and the same amendment to the U.S. Constitution. To facilitate your understanding of these analyses, this book includes the texts being analyzed.

The two articles by literary scholars are parallel to the two articles by theologians: In both cases, attention is focused primarily on a single text. In the two Supreme Court opinions, there is close attention to the text as well as to the facts of a case that required the justices to take another look at a sentence they probably knew by heart—the Fourth Amendment to the U.S. Constitution: "The right of the people to be secure in their persons, houses, papers, and effects, against unreasonable searches and seizures, shall not be violated, and no warrants shall issue, but upon probable cause, supported by oath or affirmation, and particularly describing the place to be searched, and the persons or things to be seized." The case of *Groh v. Ramirez* reached the Supreme Court because the lower courts were unable to resolve whether a specific search (and the warrant for that search) was constitutional. To make their ruling, the justices needed to consider both the wording of the Fourth Amendment and relevant rulings by other courts. You may find these two selections, one representing the majority opinion and one a dissenting opinion, challenging, but understanding how judges analyze a text can help prepare you for Chapter 7, "Writing to Persuade Others."

UNDERSTANDING WHY READERS REACH DIFFERENT CONCLUSIONS ABOUT TEXTS

Readers usually have values that help shape their understanding of what they read. These values usually arise from their cultural background, which is determined by factors like these:

- Age
- Geography
- Gender
- Religion
- Ethnicity
- Racial identity
- Social class
- Sexual orientation

Although it is important not to stereotype or prejudge individuals or groups, you will often find that someone who is seventy years old has different values than someone who is twenty. Someone raised in Mississippi may differ from someone raised in Montana. A Baptist will differ from a Buddhist, and a man from a woman. Readers with differences such as these may well discover that they have common ground, but their initial responses to ideas, including those they encounter through reading, may be far apart.

Cultural background is also shaped by factors that are harder to determine than age or place of birth. Many people are uncomfortable discussing social class or simply assume that everyone they know is "middle class"—a category that is now so broad that it embraces people with very different incomes. A highly successful trial lawyer may claim to be "middle class" despite having a seven-figure annual income because of the wish to bond with clients or juries. A single mother struggling to make ends meet while earning minimum wage without benefits may need to perceive herself as "middle class" even if achieving that status is currently beyond her means. One of her co-workers, however, may fully understand that he is a member of the country's economic underclass.

Class, of course, cannot be determined by wages alone. It is also shaped by upbringing and education—so someone earning $20,000 may have more "class" than someone earning $200,000. In short, social class shapes how people respond to the world around them, but assessing someone's social class (even your own) is more challenging than determining her or his religion or gender.

Similarly, racial identity is complex. Although various forms continue to ask North Americans to check a box that defines their race, many scholars believe that race is a social construct, by which they mean that race is not fixed but is determined by specific people at a specific time. These scholars note that in many slave-holding states prior to the Civil War, a person could be legally defined as "Negro" and thus sold as property even if only one-eighth African American. As late as 1900, many Americans did not consider either Jews or Italians to be "white," but "whiteness" now includes both groups (while Hispanics continue to be considered as other-than-white). So how will racial lines be drawn twenty years from now, especially as the number of Americans with diverse racial backgrounds continues to grow? With this question in mind, it can be more helpful to consider what race a person identifies with than to label what race you perceive that person to be.

Like social class and racial identity, sexual orientation can be difficult to determine. The words we have to define something as complex as human sexuality may be inadequate. We speak of people being "heterosexual," "homosexual," or "bisexual" as if these were three tidy categories. But rather than thinking in terms of labeling others, it might be more useful to consider how sexuality—or exposure to diverse expressions of sexuality—affects how readers perceive meaning, regardless of what they themselves may be doing in the privacy of their own homes or encountering in relationships they value. For example, a "straight" man with a "gay" brother or neighbor may be more sensitive to homophobic comments than someone who is under the illusion that he does not know any gay people just because no one has ever come out to him.

Cultural differences such as those outlined here have provided the foundation for different ways of analyzing texts, because they apply not only to readers but also to writers. Some scholars focus on gender when analyzing texts by asking, "What does this text say about how the author understood what it means to be a man or woman?" Scholars interested in social class often focus on what a text reveals about how economic conditions privilege some characters and put others at a disadvantage. And someone interested in racial identity may be especially sensitive to the assumptions about race that appear within a text they are analyzing.

Moreover, it is important to consider when texts were composed and what cultural circumstances prevailed at that time (see page 6)—circumstances that may be very different from those of the present. Doing so can enrich your understanding of a document by helping you to determine what it probably meant when first composed and how it is likely to be read today. The difference can be telling. Consider, for example, the following quotation from the Declaration of Independence—the full text of which appears on pages 481–484:

> We hold these truths to be self-evident, that all men are created equal, that they are endowed by their Creator with certain unalienable Rights, that among these are Life, Liberty, and the pursuit of Happiness.

While not part of American law, this declaration of principle has had a powerful impact on how Americans see themselves and their country. But the careful reader might ask several questions: What does "truths" mean in this context, and why are the truths in question "self-evident"? Does "men" mean "adult males" or all of humankind? If the right to life and liberty is "unalienable," how can people be executed or kept imprisoned? What does "Happiness" mean, and how does "the pursuit of Happiness" differ from "Happiness"?

When published in 1776, the Declaration of Independence was signed by fifty-six white men, many of them southerners. Collectively, they are called "the Founding Fathers," and it may be culturally significant that we never hear about "the Founding Mothers." Since the delegates who signed the document were all of the same gender, and considered themselves members of the same race and social class, were they writing about what could be expected for people like them—or were they making an imaginative leap and envisioning rights for people who were significantly different from them? While it is difficult to say for certain, the former is more likely than the latter. African Americans would be denied the right to vote until after the Civil War (and, in practice, often for more than a hundred years after that war). And women would not get the vote until the early twentieth century. Moreover, we know from other texts by the Founding Fathers that black men were not considered equal to white men. Once it was determined that the federal government would include a House of Representatives and that population levels would determine how many congressmen (as they were then called) would be apportioned to each state, members of the Constitutional Convention (who were, like the signers of the Declaration of Independence, male and apparently white) had to decide how to conduct a census. Since slaves were part of a slave-holding state's population, it was decided that they should be counted in the official census, but since slaves were not the equal of free men, they were not to be counted as whole human beings. For the purpose of determining how many congressional representatives would come from each state, the following formula was used: Five slaves would count as three "persons," confirming that the federal government considered slaves to be less than fully human. (To do the math another way, a slave was counted as three-fifths of a "person.") It follows then that "unalienable Rights" proclaimed in the Declaration of Independence were initially intended for some men, not all people.

But ideas are powerful, especially those that stir the imagination, touch the heart, or shape a nation. Once the words of the Declaration of Independence had become deeply embedded in the American consciousness, it was only a question of time before disenfranchised Americans would ask, in effect, "What about us?" Belief in the importance of equality in the United States eventually paved the way for the emancipation of slaves, the extension of the right to vote, and various initiatives designed to help make sure that all Americans, whatever their race or gender, could have access to a good public education and entry into all aspects of the nation's workforce. And debates informed by this eighteenth-century text continue to take place. For example, if we as a nation now agree that all men are equal, that "men" means "men and women," and that we all have the "unalienable" right to pursue "happiness," why should the right to marry be limited to couples presumed to be heterosexual? Why shouldn't it be extended to couples of the same gender who also wish to enter into a long-term relationship recognized by the law? Or, to choose another example, if men and women have an equal right to pursue happiness, what happens when their versions of happiness conflict—as when a woman wants an abortion but her partner wants to become a father?

Being attentive to cultural differences does not mean that you must change your own core values in order to write thoughtfully about the texts you read. Recognizing that cultural differences exist, however, can help you understand why other equally thoughtful writers may compose an analysis significantly different from your own. And there is, of course, a big difference between a value and a prejudice. The former empowers while the latter restricts.

Human nature being what it is, we can sometimes be drawn to texts that confirm what we are already inclined to believe and to reject texts that seem to challenge our understanding of the world in which we live. Whatever your own cultural background, you can often benefit from asking yourself why your initial response is either positive or negative:

- Do I like this text because it tells me what I want to hear?
- Do I dislike this text because it is making me consider something I don't want to think about?

These questions can help you to engage more deeply with the text as you prepare to analyze it because they prompt you to consider your own role in establishing meaning. Moreover, you can expand your capacity for understanding how other people think and feel by imagining how someone with a different cultural background would respond to a text you initially like or dislike. Doing so can help you to generate ideas for writing and empathy for diverse points of view without turning yourself into a person you do not want to be.

READING THE LINES

As noted previously, two of the selections in this chapter focus on the Fourth Amendment to the U.S. Constitution, an amendment that reads:

> The right of the people to be secure in their persons, houses, papers, and effects, against unreasonable searches and seizures, shall not be violated, and no warrant shall issue, but upon probable cause, supported by oath or affirmation, and particularly describing the place to be searched, and the person or things to be seized.

If you want to understand that amendment, you need to examine every word within it (such as what is meant by "unreasonable" or "affirmation"), as well as how the two clauses interrelate. For example, does this amendment establish two independent rights, one of which protects Americans from "unreasonable searches and seizures" and the second of which defines the circumstances under which a warrant can be issued? Or does the amendment establish only a single right—in which case the issuing of warrants is limited by the right to security established by the first clause? The decisions by two Supreme Court justices (see pages 434–441) may help you to complete your own analysis.

In the meantime, however, consider the Second Amendment—one of the most famous of all amendments because it defines the circumstances under which Americans can have guns. These circumstances are often debated by people who believe that the Constitution protects their right to own guns and by others who believe that the Constitution allows for some forms of gun control. The Second Amendment reads:

> A well regulated militia being necessary to the security of a free state, the right of the people to keep and bear arms, shall not be infringed upon.

A thoughtful analysis of this short text would need to consider why the right to bear arms is linked to a militia—and not just any militia but a "well regulated militia." Moreover, what is the significance of "bear"? Does it mean firearms that can be carried by a person, such as a rifle or a handgun, but not weapons that would need to be hauled on a truck? Although the framers of the Constitution tried to write clearly, the precise meaning of their words— and, by extension, the meaning of laws that have been passed since the Constitution was adopted—remains the subject of scholarly discussion. And if such discussion seems far removed from your own life, imagine how you would feel if arrested for carrying a gun or forced to stand by as the police went through your desk and bureau drawers.

Now that you have considered how a single sentence calls for careful analysis, you can better understand the challenge of analyzing a long text. Because writers usually need to confine themselves to a limited number of pages, they often benefit from analyzing relatively short texts or a specific excerpt from a longer text. In this chapter, Angelyn Mitchell and Lawrence Berkove demonstrate how to analyze a short story. The story in question, "The Story of an Hour," is one of the shortest in American literature. Both articles are longer than the story itself, and this is not unusual in literary studies. If a story is complex, there will be a great deal to say about it—just as you could write many pages devoted to an analysis of the Second Amendment. Similarly, a great poem may fill only half a page but generate many pages of analysis as a writer seeks to determine the significance of each of the words and the way they are arranged.

When you are drawn to a longer text, you usually need to read the complete text but then focus your analysis on one of its components. In the case of literary scholarship, that often means focusing on a specific character or scene. You cannot hope to analyze a thousand pages of *War and Peace* in a ten-page paper, but you can set yourself the goal of analyzing what happens in a scene set in a ballroom or on a battlefield. Similarly, it would be difficult to undertake a project such as analyzing what the Bible says about the nature of God and the meaning of faith. Even if you decided to focus on a specific subject, such as what the Bible says about women, you would still be addressing an issue that might be more appropriate for a book than for a paper. For a paper, it would be more appropriate to analyze a specific passage. In this chapter, two theologians discuss the passage in Genesis in which Noah places a curse on some of his descendants, a text once used to justify slavery in the United States. You could undertake a comparable analysis of almost any other passage in the Bible, Koran, or Bhagavad Gita among other religious and philosophic texts. But whatever text you choose to analyze, be sure to consider it word by word and line by line.

READING BETWEEN THE LINES

People frequently use the expression "reading between the lines" to describe what a careful reader or writer is doing when paying close attention to the words in every line. Strictly speaking, the only thing "between the lines" is empty space (with the notable exception of a draft that has been marked for revision). This empty space is worth considering, however. In addition to noting what a text seems to be saying, textual analysis considers what it does not say. Omissions, or gaps, are often significant.

To take a relatively simple example, you may be asked to sign a lease or some other legally binding agreement. In this case, you would be wise to make sure you understand every word and sentence within this document. But you would also be wise to reflect upon what the document does not say.

Does it omit an important safeguard that you may need or a clause that would clarify whether you can sublet?

When you study the Bible and other ancient texts, you are likely to find many gaps, because the texts we have in writing began as stories passed orally from one generation to another, and many different writers undertook the challenge of recording this oral tradition. The Old Testament was composed over a period of 350 years, and by writers who were not always familiar with what other writers had composed. The four gospels of the New Testament were composed during a much shorter time—approximately 40 years. But by the time the last of these gospels was written, the author of the first gospel had died. Many scholars have studied how these four documents vary.

Accordingly, analysis of the Bible reveals points that seem to contradict each other or to suggest that an important part of the story has been left out. To recognize this is not to diminish the importance of the Bible, but it does mean that theologians, clergy, and laypeople of faith, after careful analysis, must try to reconstruct whatever seems missing. Within this chapter, Gene Rice analyzes a passage in Genesis that has puzzled many scholars, one in which Noah curses Canaan in response to an act committed by Canaan's father, Ham. The puzzle, in this case, is why "a righteous man, blameless among the people of his time" (Gen. 6:9) would curse his grandson instead of the son who had offended him.

In legal documents such as a lease or a court ruling, texts should be without gaps in their composition. Ideally, these texts are so well crafted that they are absolutely clear, enabling judges to make just decisions. Nevertheless, attorneys often discover gaps—called "loopholes" in this case—within laws and use these discoveries to challenge the law or to make a case for a client who might otherwise be found guilty. Bearing this in mind, you can see why the analysis of written texts is so important. Absolute clarity is almost impossible to achieve in a document because there is always something "between the lines" that did not make it into the document itself. Analysis can discover where those gaps are and then fill them in.

Gaps are especially likely to appear in good fiction and other literary works. Rather than explain exactly what is going on in the stories they are telling (which would be to pursue a different motive for writing, the motive discussed in Chapter 3), writers of fiction usually want their stories to speak for themselves, and they want readers to think about what they have just read. A good story or novel, like a good poem or play, leaves readers puzzled to some extent; they come away asking, "What was going on in that story?" or "What do I wish I could ask the author?" Texts of this sort are not carelessly written. Whatever is not explained away occurs because the author is conveying some aspect of human experience that cannot be given a tidy explanation or because the author wants readers to work out solutions on their own.

Willa Cather, an important novelist and critic, was interested in how fiction as an art could transcend "the teeming, gleaming, stream of the present" in which countless details distract our attention. She argued on behalf of a form she called the "novel démeublé" or "unfurnished novel"—a novel from which all unnecessary detail is removed. In her essay "The Novel Démeublé," she discussed how a literary text consists of more than the words on the page: "Whatever is felt upon the page without being specifically named there— that, one might say, is created. It is the overtone divined by the ear but not heard by it, the verbal mood, the emotional aura of the fact or the thing or the deed, that gives high quality to the novel or the drama, as well as to po- etry itself." She was, in other words, distinguishing between listing and creat- ing. It is one thing to describe a room, listing every detail about it. But the writer of fiction, she argued, must somehow convey a sense of what cannot be seen in the room but can nevertheless be felt there. She was calling, in short, for a kind of writing that calls for reading between the lines.

Cather was no fan of Kate Chopin—a story by whom is included in this chapter. When reviewing *The Awakening,* Chopin's most famous novel, Cather claimed that the central character demanded "more romance out of life than God put into it" and that women like her "expect the passion of love to fill and gratify every need of life, whereas nature only intended that it should meet one of many demands." The woman in question, Edna Pontellier, com- mits suicide by swimming out to sea after a passionate love affair has come to an end. From Cather's point of view, women were capable of doing much more than that. There is no record, however, of how Cather responded to "The Story of an Hour"—the Chopin story on pages 394–396. When you read it, you will find that a woman is once again the central character and that this woman dies. But why she dies is not nearly as clear as why Edna Pontel- lier dies—hence the very different analyses written by Angelyn Mitchell and Lawrence Berkove.

In short, as you read between the lines, you need to understand that some gaps are deliberate and others are accidental. Ambiguity can be a characteris- tic of great art, but it can also be a sign of carelessness. Look for both kinds in the texts you analyze, and be careful to avoid accidental gaps in the papers you write.

CONSIDERING AUDIENCE

When writing to analyze a text, you need to consider whether your audience is already familiar with the text. If you have reason to believe that your audi- ence has not read (or has not recently read) the text, it can be helpful to sum- marize it. A summary is not necessary, however, for an audience that is already familiar with the text in question. For example, if you have just spent a week discussing *The Great Gatsby* in a college English course, you would not need to summarize the plot if writing for your instructor or classmates. If you did so, your audience might wonder, "Why am I being asked to read this summary? Doesn't the writer remember that I just read the same text?" In a case such as this, you should avoid an unnecessary summary and move directly into analysis.

Summarizing a text can be a useful exercise, however. When you are unsure what you think and are having a hard time getting started with your analysis, drafting a summary can sometimes help you generate ideas about the text. You can then delete the summary from your draft when writing for an audience familiar with the text. On the other hand, drafting a clear summary of a text is a useful prelude to analysis if your audience is unfamiliar with the text. This might be the case, for example, if you are planning to submit your paper for review by peers who have not read the text in question. If you know that your instructor is familiar with that text, you can then delete the summary after it has helped you to get a useful response from other students.

When writing for a specific instructor, you can also benefit from considering what you have learned about the instructor through previous assignments or through interaction in class. Will your instructor be pleased or disappointed to read an analysis that does nothing more than repeat points already made in class discussion? Although most instructors welcome signs of originality, some may be uncomfortable with an analysis that challenges their own view of the text. Even if all teachers theoretically agree that "there is no right way to read a text," some have problems with views radically different from their own. On the other hand, many instructors are disheartened by papers that offer nothing more than a regurgitation of their own views. Teachers such as these might respond to a preliminary draft by noting that you have done a good job of conveying what *they* think but that they now wish to know what *you* think.

In either case, your audience for textual analysis will expect you to cite evidence that supports your thesis. That evidence can take the form of words, phrases, or sentences, or direct quotations (which must be properly cited). But it can also be simply a reference to a scene with which your audience will be familiar or a paraphrase of a passage that is not important enough to quote. When you do quote, you can benefit from the following guideline: The longer the quote, the more you need to say about it. Quotations should not be expected to speak for themselves. It is your responsibility as a writer to demonstrate why each quotation is significant. In a quotation of more than one sentence, you may not need to discuss every word. But you should direct the attention of your readers to the words or phrases that you consider especially significant and explain that significance.

Attention to audience will help you to decide how formal you should sound and what kind of vocabulary choices you should make. In this chapter, the articles by Angelyn Mitchell and Lawrence Berkove were originally written for an audience of college English teachers. If these writers had chosen to write for a different kind of audience (such as potential English majors interested in learning what kind of scholarship professors are engaged in), a number of adjustments would have been necessary. With this in mind, be fair to writers by considering the audience for which they originally wrote. If they were not writing with you in mind, it is not especially useful to complain that they had other readers in mind—although noting the difference between you and these other readers might help you to make insightful comments about the text itself.

Finally, considering the cultural differences discussed earlier can help you to connect with readers who have backgrounds different from your own and to avoid alienating them. When reviewing a draft, ask yourself if you have said anything that could offend someone who differs from you in age, location, gender, religion, ethnicity, social class, racial identity, or sexual orientation. Doing so does not mean that your final paper will become bland, but it could lead you to rephrase a specific sentence or to generate a new paragraph that clarifies your thinking.

ORGANIZING YOUR PAPER

The easiest way to organize a paper in which your motive is to analyze a text is to begin with your thesis and then work sequentially through the text you are analyzing, citing appropriate evidence as it occurs. If you discover a piece of evidence that conflicts with your thesis, you can devote a paragraph to that exception, explaining why it has not caused you to abandon your thesis. Following this strategy shows your audience that you are reading carefully and making an effort to be fair-minded. When you find that you do need to devote a paragraph or two responding to evidence that apparently contradicts your thesis, placing that discussion toward the beginning of your paper is often more helpful than placing it toward the end. In doing so, you can use the rest of your paper to advance your own position instead of seeming to wander away from it just before you conclude.

An alternative plan, especially in a long paper, is to divide your analysis into a series of problems that need to be resolved and then address each of these problems within separate sections. In this chapter, Gene Rice uses this strategy. His article consists of four sections: the first of which sets forth the various aspects of the biblical text he finds problematic, two of which (sections 2 and 4) advance his analysis, and one of which (section 3) recognizes the views of other scholars, most notably a work with which Rice disagrees. In his majority decision for the Supreme Court, Justice John Paul Stevens also divides his work into numbered sections. In his opening paragraph, he establishes the sequence of issues that will provide the structure for his analysis.

When you are writing about a long work, you almost always need to focus on one aspect of that work. But when you are analyzing a short work such as a poem, you can organize your work into sections devoted to different aspects of it—such as imagery, symbols, and sound effects. The sequence with which you discuss these aspects will vary from one work to another. A plan that often serves writers well is to move from the least important idea to the most important, so that the paper grows more interesting, not less, as it develops. But you also need to consider how the various aspects you discuss relate to one another. If imagery is closely related to symbols, it might be better to discuss one after the other than to insert a section on sound effects (such as alliteration and assonance) between the two. Reviewing what you draft provides you with a good opportunity to rearrange paragraphs that seem out of sequence for some reason. But when you move paragraphs, which is easy to do with word-processing software, remember that you will often need to compose new transitions to facilitate the flow from one paragraph to the next.

DOCUMENTING YOUR SOURCES

Writing to analyze a text requires that you quote the text under consideration and possibly other texts as well (if you have researched how other readers have analyzed the text you are working upon). Your instructor will probably specify the documentation style appropriate for your work. If not, honor the guidelines set forth by one of the following:

- *The ACS Style Guide,* for work in chemistry
- *AIP Style Manual,* for work in physics
- *The Chicago Manual of Style* (CMS), for work in history and any discipline that does not have its own documentation style
- *A Manual for Authors of Mathematical Papers,* for work in mathematics
- *MLA Handbook for Writers of Research Papers,* for work in literary studies
- *Publication Manual of the American Psychological Association* (APA), for work in psychology
- *Scientific Style and Format: The CBE Manual for Authors, Editors, and Publishers,* for work in biology
- *A Uniform System of Citation,* for work in the law

Detailed information about these styles can be found online and through print volumes available for easy reference by writers who frequently need to use documentation. When you commit yourself to work within a specific discipline, you can benefit from purchasing the handbook published by the principal organization for that disciple.

In this chapter, the articles by Angelyn Mitchell and Lawrence Berkove illustrate MLA style. Additional information about MLA style, as well as APA style, can be found on pages 667–676. The following Web sites may also be useful, as professional organizations sometimes update their requirements before a new print volume can be published:

- APA: www.apastyle.org
- CMS: www.press.uchicago.edu/Misc/Chicago/cmosfaq.html
- CBE: www.cbe.org
- MLA: www.mla.org

TIPS FOR READING AND WRITING TEXTUAL ANALYSIS

When Reading

■ Consider how closely the author has worked with the text being analyzed.

■ Check to see if the author is quoting the text accurately.

■ Determine the extent to which the author's analysis is influenced by cultural factors or an ideological agenda.

■ Appraise how respectfully the author has considered analyses of the text published by others.

When Writing

■ Choose a text that you would like to understand better.

■ Read the text you select at least twice.

■ Annotate the text as you read so that you can note key passages and puzzling components.

■ Discover the meaning of any term that you do not understand.

■ Consider the text's organization and how that organization influences your response to it.

■ Look for contradictions or inconsistencies within the text.

■ Look for gaps in the reasoning or explanations and determine the significance of these gaps.

■ Identify or explain the points your audience is least likely to already understand.

Core Text

THE STORY OF AN HOUR

Kate Chopin (1850–1904) began writing fiction after the 1882 death of her hus-band—a cotton merchant in New Orleans whose business had failed. His death caused her to assume financial responsibility for her children, and she moved with them back to St. Louis, the city of her birth. Chopin's fiction was thus composed dur-ing a relatively short period, and readers sometimes speculate about what she would have achieved had she lived longer or begun to write sooner. One of Chopin's best known works, the following story was first published in 1894.

Knowing that Mrs. Mallard was afflicted with a heart trouble, great care was taken to break to her as gently as possible the news of her husband's death.

It was her sister Josephine who told her, in broken sentences; veiled hints that revealed in half concealing. Her husband's friend Richards was there, too, near her. It was he who had been in the newspaper office when intelligence of the railroad disaster was received, with Brently Mallard's name leading the list of "killed." He had only taken the time to assure himself of its truth by a second telegram, and had hastened to forestall any less careful, less tender friend in bearing the sad message.

She did not hear the story as many women have heard the same, with a paralyzed inability to accept its significance. She wept at once, with sudden, wild abandonment, in her sister's arms. When the storm of grief had spent itself she went away to her room alone. She would have no one follow her.

There stood, facing the open window, a comfortable, roomy arm-chair. Into this she sank, pressed down by a physical exhaustion that haunted her body and seemed to reach into her soul.

She could see in the open square before her house the tops of trees that were all aquiver with new spring life. The delicious breath of rain was in the air. In the street below a peddler was crying his wares. The notes of a distant song which some one was singing reached her faintly, and countless sparrows were twittering in the eaves.

There were patches of blue sky showing here and there through the clouds that had met and piled one above the other in the west fac-ing her window.

She sat with her head thrown back upon the cushion of the chair, quite motionless, except when a sob came up into her throat and shook her, as a child who has cried itself to sleep continues to sob in its dreams.

She was young, with a fair, calm face, whose lines bespoke repression and even a certain strength. But now there was a dull stare in her eyes, whose gaze was fixed away off yonder on one of those patches of blue sky. It was not a glance of reflection, but rather indicated a suspension of intelligent thought.

There was something coming to her and she was waiting for it, fearfully. What was it? She did not know; it was too subtle and elusive to name. But she felt it, creeping out of the sky, reaching toward her through the sounds, the scents, the color that filled the air.

Now her bosom rose and fell tumultuously. She was beginning to recognize this thing that was approaching to possess her, and she was striving to beat it back with her will—as powerless as her two white slender hands would have been.

When she abandoned herself a little whispered word escaped her slightly parted lips. She said it over and over under the breath: "free, free, free!" The vacant stare and look of terror that had followed it went from her eyes. They stayed keen and bright. Her pulses beat fast, and the coursing blood warmed and relaxed every inch of her body.

She did not stop to ask if it were or were not a monstrous joy that held her. A clear and exalted perception enabled her to dismiss the suggestion as trivial. She knew that she would weep again when she saw the kind, tender hands folded in death; the face that had never looked save with love upon her, fixed and gray and dead. But she saw beyond that bitter moment a long procession of years to come that would belong to her absolutely. And she opened and spread her arms out to them in welcome.

There would be no one to live for during those coming years; she would live for herself. There would be no powerful will bending hers in that blind persistence with which men and women believe they have a right to impose a private will upon a fellow-creature. A kind intention or a cruel intention made the act seem no less a crime as she looked upon it in that brief moment of illumination.

And yet she had loved him—sometimes. Often she had not. What did it matter! What could love, the unsolved mystery, count for in the face of this possession of self-assertion which she suddenly recognized as the strongest impulse of her being!

"Free! Body and soul free!" she kept whispering.

Josephine was kneeling before the closed door with her lips to the keyhold, imploring for admission. "Louise, open the door! I beg; open the door—you will make yourself ill. What are you doing, Louise? For heaven's sake open the door."

"Go away. I am not making myself ill." No; she was drinking in a very elixir of life through that open window.

Her fancy was running riot along those days ahead of her. Spring days, and summer days, and all sorts of days that would be her own.

She breathed a quick prayer that life might be long. It was only yester-day she had thought with a shudder that life might be long.

She arose at length and opened the door to her sister's importuni-ties. There was a feverish triumph in her eyes, and she carried herself unwittingly like a goddess of Victory. She clasped her sister's waist, and together they descended the stairs. Richards stood waiting for them at the bottom.

Some one was opening the front door with a latchkey. It was Brently Mallard who entered, a little travel-stained, composedly carry-ing his grip-sack and umbrella. He had been far from the scene of the accident, and did not even know there had been one. He stood amazed at Josephine's piercing cry; at Richards' quick motion to screen him from the view of his wife.

When the doctors came they said she had died of heart disease—of the joy that kills.

Kate Chopin

FEMININE DOUBLE CONSCIOUSNESS IN KATE CHOPIN'S "THE STORY OF AN HOUR"

Angelyn Mitchell

One of the principle approaches to contemporary literary analysis has been provided by feminist scholars. In feminist analysis, which can be used by men as well as women, the emphasis is on understanding what a literary text reveals about the treatment or perception of women and how that perspective leads to new interpretations of the work as a whole. Because she frequently wrote about women in problematic situations, Kate Chopin has drawn attention from many feminist scholars. The following article by Angelyn Mitchell provides an example of a feminist approach.

Mitchell teaches English at Georgetown University, where she is director of the African American Studies Program. She also directs the Minority Mentoring Program at Georgetown. When discussing her writing life, Mitchell observes, "I believe analytic writing is just as muse-driven and process-driven as creative writing. My writing is never finished; I only stop to meet the deadline. For me, writing is a way of making sense of the world as I join in conversation with the writers whose works I engage. Interpreting literature fuels my imagination in unexpected ways; it helps me to see the world anew. My hope is that my writing will help others to do the same." Her article on Chopin first appeared in CEA Magazine, an academic journal read primarily by college English teachers, in 1993.

In an illuminating moment of self-reflection, Janie, the protagonist of Zora Neale Hurston's *Their Eyes Were Watching God* (1937) achieves a remarkable insight into the divided psychological state of women in the thralls of patriarchal hegemonies. After her second husband, Joe Starks, strikes her for verbally expressing her individuality, an action that does not concur with his construct of feminine conduct, Janie searches her unconscious self and realizes that she must not conflate her outer self, i.e., her public self, with her inner self, i.e., her private desires, if she is to have a semblance of happiness in her marriage and in her life. Janie, Hurston writes,

> found that she had a host of thoughts she never expressed to him, and
> numerous emotions she had never let Jody know about. Things
> packed up and put away in parts of her heart where he could never
> find them. . . . She had an inside and an outside now and suddenly she
> knew how not to mix them. (112–13)

In this instance, Janie realizes that she cannot afford to reveal her inner desires in a society dependent on the subjugation of women; thus, she suppresses her private desires to adapt to her hostile environment. Janie does achieve a short-lived emancipation after her husband's death; however, she remarries and suffers suppression of a different sort in a relationship which also ends tragically.

While the search for feminine wholeness and unified selfhood motivates the action of Hurston's novel, Hurston, an African American, was not the first female to examine what I term a feminine double consciousness—a divided state of the female psyche engendered by the cultural constructs of gender and by the biological determinants of sex.[1] While Hurston did provide perhaps the best twentieth-century depiction of this phenomenon of feminine dualism, the divided psychological state of women preoccupies nineteenth-century as well as twentieth-century American women writers. Some years earlier, Kate Chopin, an Anglo-American writer of the late nineteenth century, perceptively illuminated and interrogated this theme of feminine double consciousness, particularly in her then controversial novel *The Awakening* (1899) and in many of her short stories. Of particular interest is Chopin's "The Story of an Hour" (1894), in which the protagonist, Mrs. Louise Mallard, becomes aware, like Janie, of her duality as a result of a traumatic experience; begins the painful process of unifying her "inside" with her "outside" in order to achieve wholeness; and subsequently pays dearly for her chance of a unified selfhood in a society which conspires against self-empowerment. The problem of bridging the duality caused by gender constructs creates a state of enslavement and highlights Chopin's constant preoccupation with the problem of freedom. In "The Story of an Hour," the quest for freedom is complicated by three important factors: biological determination, patriarchal social conditioning, and the patriarchal institution of marriage.

As a prelude to understanding the complications of freedom involved in "The Story of an Hour," a brief look at Chopin's first short story, "Emancipation: A Life Fable" (1869 or 1870), should prove illuminating. In this story, a bird born in captivity, a situation certainly analogous to the condition of the nineteenth-century woman, accidentally escapes his confinement. Although the bird has received adequate care and sustenance, he chooses freedom in spite of his dread of "the unaccustomed" (177). "So does he live," Chopin reports, "seeking, finding, joying, and suffering. The door which accident had opened is open still, but the cage remains forever empty!" (178). In Chopin's view, all creatures innately desire and seek freedom, a freedom always attained with great difficulties.

Biological determinism permeates the opening of "The Story of an Hour" as Mrs. Mallard's heart condition is revealed. Because of this condition, which is biologically fated, Richards, a friend of her husband, rushes to relate the sad news of his death before someone "less careful, less tender" (213) can do so. Mrs. Mallard, a young woman "with a fair calm face" (214), receives the news, given with "great care" (213) by her sister, a female whose biological formation and familial bond dictate her role as the appointed conveyor of Richards' news. Mrs. Mallard's sister, Josephine, also exhibits a belief in biological determinism as she refuses to honor Mrs. Mallard's wish to be left alone in her room. Spying through the keyhole, Josephine pleads, "Louise, open the door! I beg; open the door—you will make yourself ill. What are you doing, Louise? For heaven's sake, open the door" (215). From these examples one immediately discerns Chopin's employment of determinism to reveal the ways in which women are fated in a society which constructs gender-specific behaviors and responses.

Patriarchy's social conditioning creates codes of feminine behavior to ensure   5
the suppression of feminine desires. Most striking is Mrs. Mallard's initial and atypical response to the tragic news. Chopin foreshadows Mrs. Mallard's awakening in her resistance to traditional modes of behavior. Mrs. Mallard, Chopin writes,

> did not hear the story as many women have heard the same, with a paralyzed inability to accept its significance. She wept at once, with sudden, wild abandonment, in her sister's arms. When the storm of grief had spent itself she went away to her room alone. She would have no one follow her. (213)

Mrs. Mallard retreats to "a room of [her] own" in order to examine the plethora of emotions she feels. Before an open window, "her open boat," on a significantly beautiful spring day, Mrs. Mallard sits "in a suspension of intelligent thought" (214). She escapes the established codes of feminine behavior by contemplating the implications of her nascent freedom. This escape is an excellent example of Nietzsche's concept, in *Thus Spoke Zarathustra,* of self-overcoming, in which a creature must first become capable of commanding itself in order to escape the subjection of others. Simply wishing or willing alone cannot and does not liberate Mrs. Mallard. Like the bird, she too dreads the unaccustomed—the unknown; consequently, freedom ravishes her. In a passage loaded with sexual imagery, Chopin writes,

> There was something coming to her and she was waiting for it, fearfully. What was it? She did not know; it was too subtle and elusive to name. But she felt it, creeping out of the sky, reaching toward her through the sounds, the scents, the color that filled the air.
>
> Now her bosom rose and fell tumultuously. She was beginning to recognize this thing that was approaching to possess her, and she was striving to beat it back with her will—as powerless as her two white slender hands would have been.
>
> When she abandoned herself, a little whispered word escaped her slightly parted lips. She said it over and over under her breath, "free, free, free!" (214)

While freedom is an innate desire for all creatures, patriarchal society conditions women to suppress and to repress their desire for freedom, so much so that the possibility of freedom, when available, is frightening. After Mrs. Mallard overcomes her fear, "the vacant stare and the look of terror that had followed it" go from her eyes, and she looks forward to "a long procession of years to come that would *belong to her absolutely. And she opened and spread her arms out to them in welcome*" (214; emphasis added).

The patriarchal institution of marriage, an institution grounded in the ownership of women, is the culprit; this institution, not Brently Mallard, has enslaved Mrs. Mallard. Tragically, she can escape only if her husband, whose face "had never looked save with love upon her" (214), dies. In a scathing attack on marriage, Chopin writes of Mrs. Mallard,

> There would be no one to live for her during those coming years; she would live for herself. There would be no powerful will bending hers in that blind persistence with which men and women believe they have a right to impose a private will upon a fellow-creature. A kind intention or a cruel intention made the act seem no less a crime as she looked upon it in that brief moment of illumination. (214–15)

Chopin vehemently disagrees with an institution that benevolently or malevolently suggests the suppression and repression of individual desires.

Furthermore, Chopin deconstructs the pillar of marriage, the notion of romantic love, by allowing Mrs. Mallard to discover that self-assertion or self-reclamation is "the strongest impulse of her being" (215). Love, purported to be the elixir of life, causes Mrs. Mallard to dread the thought of longevity before her emancipation. After examining her inner desires and accepting her freedom, Mrs. Mallard prays "that life might be long" (215). This prayer reflects Mrs. Mallard's femininity: women are biologically created with the capacity to sustain the creation of life and, subsequently, are concerned with preserving life.

After mediating her "outside" with her "inside" as Janie later does, Mrs. Mallard exits from her room like the phoenix rising from its ashes. She is able to resume the expected feminine code of behavior, now fortified with her self-possession. Fate, however, intercedes. Mr. Mallard has not been killed, and because she is not the phoenix, Mrs. Mallard cannot be reborn. Mrs. Mallard dies of the fated heart condition, "of joy that kills" (215). While the ending could intimate that the joy of her husband's return kills Mrs. Mallard, Chopin, however, employs irony to suggest that the "monstrous joy" of denied self-assertion causes Mrs. Mallard's demise.

In the story's bitterly ironic ending, the reader infers that the complications involved in unifying the feminine double consciousness—a consciousness of societal expectations warring with a consciousness of private desires—are insurmountable. Perhaps Chopin further suggests, as indicated in the story's title, that the task of self-empowerment, and consequently the mediation of the feminine double consciousness, takes far longer than an hour, particularly if one considers the recent works of Toni Morrison, Gloria Naylor, Alice Walker, Maxine Hong Kingston, Joyce Carol Oates, or Anne Tyler in which they address the same feminist concerns almost one hundred years later.

10

NOTE

1. In *The Souls of Black Folk* (1903; New York: Signer, 1969), Dr. W.E.B. DuBois articulated a theory of racial double consciousness in which "the Negro is a sort of seventh son, born with a veil, and gifted with second-sight in this American world,—a world that yields him no true self-consciousness, but only lets him see himself through the revelation of the other world" (45).

WORKS CITED

Chopin, Kate. *The Awakening and Selected Stories.* Intro. Sandra M. Gilbert. New York: Viking, Penguin, 1986.

Hurston, Zora Neale. *Their Eyes Were Watching God.* 1937; Urbana: U of Illinios P, 1978.

QUESTIONS FOR DISCUSSION

1. What does Mitchell achieve by opening her discussion of Chopin with a discussion of a work by Zora Neal Hurston? Was this a good writing decision?
2. After describing Hurston as "African American," Mitchell describes Chopin as "Anglo-American." What does it mean to be "Anglo-American"? What are the advantages or risks of describing people this way?
3. How successfully does Mitchell link her discussion of "The Story of an Hour" to Chopin's "Emancipation: A Life Fable"?
4. What does Mitchell mean by "biological determinism"?
5. Consider how Mitchell uses brackets to insert "her" into a short quotation at the beginning of paragraph 6. Can you identify the literary allusion she achieves by this editorial change?
6. Consider how Mitchell uses italics to emphasize part of a quotation included in paragraph 6. In doing so, she is correctly following the MLA's rule for how to add emphasis to words within a quotation, and you may want to use this practice in a paper of your own. But what does Mitchell achieve by emphasizing the words in question?

SUGGESTIONS FOR WRITING

1. Study "Emancipation: A Life Fable," and then write an analysis of that story in which you incorporate Mitchell's view of it.
2. Choose another short story that includes a married couple, and then write an analysis in which you determine whether the story presents marriage as "patriarchal" or "an institution that benevolently or malevolently suggests the suppression and repression of individual desires."
3. Write a paper in which you explain what it means to analyze literature from a "feminist" perspective.

LINKS

■ Within the Book

Mitchell is one of the sources used by Lawrence Berkove in "Fatal Self-Assertion in Kate Chopin's 'The Story of an Hour'" (pages 403–409).

■ Elsewhere in Print

Gilbert, Sandra M., ed. *Kate Chopin: Complete Novels and Short Stories.* New York: Lib. of America, 2002.

Gilbert, Sandra M, and Susan Guar. *The Madwoman in the Attic: The Woman Writer in the Nineteenth-Century Literary Imagination.* 2nd ed. New Haven: Yale UP, 2000.

Hurston, Zora Neal. *Their Eyes Were Watching God.* 1937. New York: Harper, 1998.

Mitchell, Angelyn. *The Freedom to Remember: Narrative, Slavery, and Gender in Contemporary Women's Fiction.* New Brunswick: Rutgers UP, 2002.

———. *Within the Circle: An Anthology of African-American Literary Criticsim from the Harlem Renaissance to the Present.* Durham: Duke UP, 1994.

Morrison, Toni. *Beloved.* 1987. New York: Plume, 1998.

Showalter, Elaine. *The New Feminist Criticism: Essays on Women, Literature, Criticism, and Theory.* New York: Pantheon, 1985.

■ Online

www.mhhe.com/motives

Click on "More Resources" then "Writing to Analyze Texts."

■ ■ ■

FATAL SELF-ASSERTION IN KATE CHOPIN'S "THE STORY OF AN HOUR"

Lawrence I. Berkove

Although feminist perspectives have been influential in literary studies during the last quarter century, scholars applying other perspectives have challenged feminist analyses and offered significantly different interpretations. The following article is a response to feminist scholars who have argued that "The Story of an Hour" is about an oppressed woman. Written, perhaps coincidentally, by a man, it argues that the woman in question is "an immature egoist and a victim of her own self-assertion."

Professor Emeritus at the University of Michigan–Dearborn, Lawrence I. Berkove is a nationally respected expert on nineteenth-century American writers such as Ambrose Bierce and Mark Twain. He has served on the board of the College English Association and presented his ideas at many scholarly conferences. His article "Fatal Self-assertion in Kate Chopin's 'The Story of an Hour'" was first published in the winter of 2000 in *American Literary Realism, a scholarly journal published by the University of Illinois. When asked about his life as a scholar, he responded: "I was first attracted to literary studies by what they revealed about the unique ethical vitality and imagination of authors and the periods in which they wrote. As I came to realize that the unexpected and intricate ways in which authors selected and applied principles to new situations were inextricably connected to literary artistry, I learned the necessity of close analytical reading—and of always assuming that the author was deeper and more skillful than the reader. The task, therefore, of studying how authors both disclosed and yet hid their personal values became an exciting challenge. . . . As I further learned the importance of honesty and precision in representing an author's positions . . . revising my essays repeatedly—even, sometimes, to the point of revising my original conclusions—became a necessary part of my method, my conception of what a student of literature must do in order to represent and evaluate one's subject accurately."*

Kate Chopin's thousand-word short story, "The Story of an Hour," has understandably become a favorite selection for collections of short stories as well as for anthologies of American literature. Few other stories say so much in so few words. There has been, moreover, virtual critical agreement on what the story says: its heroine dies, ironically and tragically, just as she has been freed from a constricting marriage and has realized self-assertion as the deepest element of her being. Confidence in this interpretation, however, may be misplaced, for using the standard proposed for the story by Toth and Seyersted— "every detail contributes to the emotional impact"[1]—there is evidence of a deeper level of irony in the story which does not regard Louise Mallard as a heroine but as an immature egoist and a victim of her own extreme self-assertion. This self-assertion is achieved not by reflection but, on the contrary, by "a suspension of intelligent thought" masked as "illumination." As a result, a pattern of basic contradictions and abnormal attitudes emerges which gives structure to the story and forecasts its conclusion. The key to recognizing this deeper, ironic level is to carefully distinguish between the story's narrator, author, and unreliable protagonist.

Seyersted's early biography of Chopin describes the story neutrally as "an extreme example of the theme of self-assertion."[2] More recent interpretation has largely followed a strong, and at times an extreme, feminist bent. Representative of this in both approach and language is Emily Toth's well-known characterization of the story as one of Chopin's "most radical . . . an attack on marriage, on one person's dominance over another."[3] Toth further elaborates this position in a later article in which she comments that "[a]lthough Louise's death is an occasion for deep irony directed at patriarchal blindness about women's thoughts, Louise dies in the world of her family where she has always sacrificed for others."[4] Ewell similarly sees in the story's "surfaces" Louise's struggles for selfhood against "society's decree" for female "selflessness, being for others."[5]

But in the text of this very short story there is no hard evidence whatsoever of patriarchal blindness or suppression, constant or selfless sacrifice by Louise, or an ongoing struggle for selfhood. These positions are all read into the story from non-textual assumptions.[6] The simple truth is that this story is not about society or marriage, but about Louise Mallard. The single possible reference in the text to difficulties in her life is a sentence, which says that the lines of her face "bespoke repression and a certain strength."[7] It is not at all clear, however, what the cause of that "repression" was; whether, for instance, it might have been external, in society or in her marriage, or whether it was internal, a recognition that it takes strength to control one's feelings or whims. Such few hints as the story supplies incline toward the latter position. While the text enables us to make certain inferences about Louise, it does not supply us with any information about the truth of her life except her perceptions, and these, as I intend to show, are unreliable and, insofar as they are taken as the statements of the story's omniscient narrator, misleading and contradicted by other textual evidence.

Support for this position is spread throughout the story but the most dramatic elements appear in the following three paragraphs:

> There would be no one to live for her during those coming years; she would live for herself. There would be no powerful will bending her in that blind persistence with which men and women believe they have a right to impose a private will upon a fellow-creature. A kind intention or a cruel intention made the act seem no less a crime as she looked upon it in that brief moment of illumination.
>
> And yet she had loved him—sometimes. Often she had not. What did it matter! What could love, the unsolved mystery, count for in the

face of this possession of self-assertion which she suddenly recognized as the strongest impulse of her being!

"Free! Body and soul free!" she kept whispering.

In these paragraphs, the story's omniscient narrator takes us into Louise's mind. However, while the attitudes expressed are definitely Louise's there is no textual justification for also ascribing them to the narrator. Further, it would be a mistake to project them onto Chopin, for that would confuse narrator with author, a move that denies Chopin the full range of literary technique, and that would reduce this brilliant and subtle work of fiction to behind-the-scenes sermonizing.

It is significant, in the quotation's first line, that Louise wishes to "live for herself." This has been generally understood to imply that she had hitherto sacrificed herself for her husband; however, there is no evidence for this in the text. Nor is there any evidence that her husband had done her living "for her," whatever that might mean. It is an ipse dixit comment,° arbitrary, without support, one of several she makes.

In the quotation's second paragraph, Louise discounts love as secondary to self-assertion. While this is undoubtedly her position, there is no textual reason to assume it is also Chopin's. Louise also recognizes self-assertion as "the strongest impulse of her being." This is a peculiar value for a married person and is indeed incompatible with marriage, where an emphasis upon shared goals and mutual commitment is the opposite of self-assertion. The unreasoning self-centeredness of Louise partly explains the first two sentences of the quotation's second paragraph, and they tell us more about her than about her husband. Of course, even married people who sincerely love each other have occasional disagreements and may not feel much love for the other at particular times. For most lovers this is not so much a contradiction as a paradox; the moments of hate occur within the larger context of love. But the warmest sentiment that Louise can express after being married to a man whose benevolence the previous paragraph explicitly affirms with its description of his "kind, tender hands" and his face "that had never looked save with love upon her" is the niggardly concession that she had loved him "sometimes."

It is obvious that there is quite a discrepancy between the way Louise and Brently Mallard feel about each other, but all the mystery of the difference is on Louise's side.

Whatever her original reason had been for marrying Brently, it is clear now that feeling the way she does about him she would be better off not being married. Her love for herself—"she would live only for herself"—does not leave room for anyone else. How, then, would she live?

Her justification for preferring to live for herself, the second and third sentences of the quotation's first paragraph, are extravagant, unrealistic statements,

---

°*ipsedixit comment:* An assertion made on authority but not proved.

each segment of which is controversial. She views her husband's constant love as a "powerful will bending hers in [a] blind persistence." Blind? Why is it blind? Inasmuch as Louise has apparently repressed her true feelings about her husband and marriage, if his love for her is blind it is because she has blinded him. In the absence of open communication about her feelings, how would he know what she wants, or what to do or say? In that circumstance, his persistence, which clearly annoys her, may only be a natural attempt on his part to please her and to convince her of his love. The failure of Brently's persistence is due at least in part to Louise's strange view of love—and the wording of the second sentence includes her as well as her husband—as a "crime," a powerful will that "bends" the other person. This is a distorted view of love, which typically delights in pleasing and giving to the other. Believing love a "crime" cannot be considered a normal attitude, much less an emotionally healthy one.

But even if we grant this point of view, where can we go where the presence of other people does not "impose" some conditions upon us that limit our freedom? There are only two places on earth that meet this specification: an uninhabited spot or the grave. If we have friends, it is assumed that we hold values that are in concord with theirs, and that we do not act in such a way as to violate friends or their principles. Even if we do not have friends but just live in society, there are laws and mores which, out of mere civility, we follow as a condition of being acceptable members of society. And this works equally in reverse. Does Louise not expect that friends will somehow fulfill and continue to meet her personal standards and thereby be more desirable for a closer relationship with her than would strangers? Is this "imposition"? Is she not by her contentions denying herself both friends and society, unless she has no expectations that fellow creatures will observe certain basic laws and mores? If this is true for friends and fellow members of society, how much more is this so for people in love, and especially those who are married! How can the extreme sort of freedom that Louise contemplates, in which there are no expectations or obligations upon anyone, co-exist with living with other human beings?

Marriage of course restricts freedom. Whoever marries, or even loves, gives up large areas of freedom—usually willingly. It is aberrant, therefore, to reduce love merely to an "imposition" of a "private will upon a fellow creature." Inasmuch as Brently loves her "tenderly," her attitude about imposition reveals that she is only irritated by a display of affection and equates it with a loss of freedom. One paragraph later, Louise first characterizes love as "an unsolved mystery," and then immediately dismisses what she admittedly does not understand in preference for the "impulse" of self-assertion, which she, ironically, also appears not to understand either in its form of self-love or in its consequence of radical loneliness.

Even more astonishingly, why is no distinction to be made between a kind and a cruel intention? Here is yet another product of her "suspension of intelligent thought," another arbitrary and whimsical dictum that would incriminate both friend and spouse. But the proposition is contradicted by actions in the story. At the beginning of the story, for example, her husband's

10

friend Richards hastens to tell Louise himself the news of her husband's death, "to forestall any less careful, less tender friend in bearing the sad message." At any end, Richards attempts vainly to screen Brently from the view of his wife. Are these loving acts of kind intentions crimes? Even more to the point, Louise's whims imperiously put her husband into a no-win situation where *anything* he does is not only wrong, but also a crime against her absolute freedom. These conceits go beyond being merely strange and impossible views for any social relations, let alone a marriage. What Louise regards as "illumination" are dark and twisted fantasies that reflect a confused and unhealthy mind.

In truth, Louise is sick, emotionally as well as physically. The story's first line tells us that "Mrs. Mallard was afflicted with a heart trouble." The phraseology is vague; however, the rest of the story gradually makes clear the nature of the heart trouble. Alone in her room, when she "abandoned" herself, a whispered word "escaped" her lips: "Free!" The conjunction first of abandonment and then of something escaping her is significant. What was then in her heart is made clear by the two lines of the next paragraph: "She did not stop to ask if it were or were not a monstrous joy that held her. A clear and exalted perception enabled her to dismiss the suggestion as trivial." Again, Chopin's omniscient narrator makes a subtle but very significant shift from reporting "objectively" in the first line what Louise is thinking to letting us, in the second line, know Louise's opinion about her thinking process. First, she believes that she is enjoying a "clear and exalted perception." Two paragraphs later she exalts this self-congratulatory perception to an "illumination" when she concludes that love is a crime. Here again, while these extravagant value judgments are certainly Louise's, they cannot be confidently ascribed to either the narrator or Chopin.

Next, Louise, dismisses as "trivial" the suggestion of doubt as to whether or not her joy was "monstrous." But the question most certainly is not trivial. It is a natural question, an important and a healthy one, an intelligent check on unreflected impulse, and the fact that Louise does not address it is ominous. She does not give the question a chance; she does not even face it; she dismisses it out of hand. What Chopin is doing, very subtly, is depicting Louise in the early stages of the delusion that is perturbing her precariously unstable health by aggravating her pathological heart condition. The "monstrous" surge of joy she experiences is both the cause and first sign of a fatal overload to her feeble heart.

In the next paragraph Louise contemplates "a long procession of years . . . that would belong to her absolutely." "Absolutely" is a loaded word, further evidence of her extreme and unrealistic egotism in preferring her own company exclusively. In light of Aristotle's statement that "whatsoever is delighted in solitude, is either a wild beast or a god,"[8] the joy that Louise takes in the thought of absolute possession of future years may indeed qualify as "monstrous." And for someone afflicted with heart trouble, the anticipation that those future years will be a long procession is also presumptuous. Louise is not thinking clearly. Insofar as her anticipation reflects growing mental confusion and raises unrealistic hopes, it is also perilous.

After she puts off her sister Josephine, who "implores" admission to the room out of fear that Louise will make herself ill (another case of a "crime" of a powerful will attempting to bend her by imposing a kind intention?), we are told in the next paragraph that "[h]er fancy was running riot." "Fancy," with its connotations of fantastic and capricious imaginings, is another signal that Louise is not thinking clearly, and the narrator's observation that it is "running riot" is an additional indication that she is well on the way to losing control of her mind.

This prospect is enhanced by a sentence in the next paragraph: "There was a feverish triumph in her eyes, and she carried herself unwittingly like a goddess of Victory." Here Chopin's displays her remarkable ability to compress layers of complexity and irony into a single line. "Feverish" is the key word that diagnoses Louise's pathological condition, and the phrase in which it occurs ironically suggests that the fever has already progressed to the point where it is fatally triumphant over her. The rest of the short sentence rapidly but elegantly elaborates on the situation. "Unwittingly," with its connotation of the absence of reason, reinforces the idea that Louise's fever has triumphed, and her assumption of the posture of the "goddess of Victory" is a double delusion: she is no goddess and she has achieved no victory.

Her husband's unexpected reappearance ends the delusion based on "a monstrous joy." It has long been recognized that the story's last line is ironic, but it is even more ironic than has previously been surmised. The doctors were technically correct: she did die "of joy that kills." Louise was indeed doubly afflicted with heart trouble. Physically, her heart was weak, and emotionally, it had no room for anyone else.

We can infer from both the way the description of Louise unfolds and from the absurd nature of Louise's ideal that Kate Chopin was not a romantic. On the one hand, Chopin did not regard marriage as a state of pure and unbroken bliss, but on the other, she could not intelligently believe that it was desirable, healthy, or even possible for anyone to live as Louise, in the grip of her feverish delusion, wishes: to be *absolutely* free and to live totally and solely for oneself. Absolute freedom is possible only for a divinity, and Louise demonstrates by her death as well as her life that she is not divine. Although earthly love is not ideally perfect, it may at least be the closest thing to the ideal that we can know. Louise's "self-assertion," really in her case a manifestation of an extreme of self-love, is exposed in this story as an emotional affliction of her heart that has physical consequences. What she wants is, literally, not obtainable in this life. It is a fantasy, a dream, and "A Story of an Hour" was indeed first published in *Vogue* magazine in 1894 under the more revealing title of "The Dream of an Hour."[9]

Given her dissatisfaction with the best that life has to offer her and her unrealistic expectations of absolute freedom, therefore, there is no other option for Louise except death. The conclusion of the story follows logically upon Louise's specifications of her deepest wishes. Chopin's exposé of the fanciful dream of Louise is richly subtle, and is an exquisite example of her remarkable ability to present an untenable view in a seemingly sympathetic way.[10]

In "The Story of an Hour" Chopin projects with delicately incisive irony what would happen if an immature and shallow egotist were to face the earthly consequence of an impossible dream of her afflicted heart.

NOTES*

1. Emily Toth and Per Seyersted, eds., *Kate Chopin's Private Papers* (Bloomington: Indiana UP, 1998), p. 245.
2. Per Seyersted, *Kate Chopin: A Critical Biography* (Baton Rouge: Louisiana State UP, 1969), p. 58.
3. Emily Toth, *Kate Chopin* (New York: Morrow, 1990) 252–53. Similarly, the story's emphasis upon a woman was equated in a subsequent article by another critic with an attack on the institution of marriage, which is treated as the "culprit" of the story because by its means "[p]atriarchy's social conditioning creates codes of social behavior to ensure the suppression of feminine desires." Angelyn Mitchell, "Feminine Double Consciousness in Kate Chopin," *CEA Magazine,* 3 (Fall 1993) 59–64.
4. Emily Toth, "Kate Chopin Thinks Back Through Her Mothers: Three Stories by Kate Chopin," *Kate Chopin Reconsidered,* ed. Lynda S. Boren and Sara deSaussure Davis (Baton Rouge: Louisiana State UP, 1992) 24.
5. Barbara C. Ewell, "Chopin and the Dream of Female Selfhood," *Kate Chopin Reconsidered* 160, 162.
6. The film, "Five Stories of an Hour" (Films for the Humanities, Inc., 1991), widely available and used in educational settings, is a testimony as to how the sparseness of the text invites explanations which require additional text and details. Although the skits which comprise this film complement the story's fictile possibilities by means of creative reader responses, in modifying and going beyond the text those skits do not and cannot explain the text itself.
7. Kate Chopin, *The Complete Works of Kate Chopin,* ed. Per Seyersted (Baton Rouge: Louisiana State UP, 1969) 52–54. The entire story occupies only three pages, so page numbers are not used.
8. Aristotle, *Politics* I, qtd. in Francis Bacon, "Of Friendship."
9. Toth, "Kate Chopin Thinks Back," 22–23.
10. For an example of how this phenomenon appears in other of her stories, see my article, "'Acting Like Fools': The Ill-Fated Romances of 'At the 'Cadian Ball' and 'The Storm,'" *Critical Essays on Kate Chopin,* ed. Alice Hall Petry (New York: Hall, 1996), pp 184–96.

QUESTIONS FOR DISCUSSION

1. What is Berkove's thesis, and where does he introduce it?
2. In paragraph 3, Berkove refers to ideas that he believes have been "read into the story." At what point, in your opinion, does literary analysis reach the point of making unjustifiable claims about a work?

---

*For a discussion of the note style used here, see pages 667–673.

3. Consider the long quotation that Berkove includes in paragraph 4. Did he need to quote so much? How well does he make use of the quotation?
4. In paragraphs 8–10, Berkove raises a series of questions. What does he achieve by asking so many questions? Does he answer the questions he raises? Is it necessary for writers to answer any question they raise?
5. How would you describe the tone of this analysis?
6. Are you convinced by Berkove's case? Why or why not?

SUGGESTIONS FOR WRITING

1. Read at least three of the sources cited by Berkove, and then write a paper in which you determine how fairly he has used them.
2. Write an analysis in which you focus on the shortcomings of a character from another short story or novel who is usually treated sympathetically.
3. It there any reason to believe that men read differently than women? Write an essay, based on research, in which you focus on the role of gender in learning.

LINKS

■ Within the Book

Angelyn Mitchell argues on Mrs. Mallard's behalf in "Feminine Double Consciousness in Kate Chopin's 'Story of an Hour'" (pages 397–400).

■ Elsewhere in Print

Belenky, Mary Field, et al. *Women's Ways of Knowing: The Development of Self, Voice, and Mind.* New York: Basic, 1986.

Berkove, Lawrence I. *A Prescription for Adversity.* Columbus: Ohio State UP, 2002.

———, ed. *The Best Short Stories of Mark Twain.* New York: Modern, 2004.

Evans, Robert. *Kate Chopin's Short Fiction: A Critical Companion.* West Cornwall: 2001.

Toth, Emily, *Unveiling Kate Chopin,* Oxford: U of Mississippi P, 1999.

Walker, Nancy A. *Kate Chopin: A Literary Life,* New York: Palgrave, 2001.

■ Online

www.mhhe.com/motives

Click on "More Resources" then "Writing to Analyze Texts."

■ ■ ■

Core Text

BOOK OF GENESIS, CHAPTER 9

The first book of the Bible, Genesis includes such famous stories as the account of how God created the world, how Adam and Eve were expelled from the Garden of Eden, how Cain killed his brother Abel, and how Noah built the ark on which life survived during a terrible flood. Chapter 9 focuses on Noah's life after the flood. Although the authors of the scholarship included in this textbook focus on verses 18–27 of Chapter 9, the full chapter is reprinted here so that you can see these verses in context.

Scholars disagree about who wrote the Book of Genesis, but it is traditionally attributed to Moses—with the understanding that Moses was working from earlier texts that are now lost. Many translations of the Bible exist. The text that follows is from the New Revised Standard translation published in 1989.

God blessed Noah and his sons, and said to them, "Be fruitful and multiply, and fill the earth. [2]The fear and dread of you shall rest on every animal of the earth, and on every bird of the air, on everything that creeps on the ground, and on all the fish of the sea; into your hand they are delivered. [3]Every moving thing that lives shall be food for you; and just as I gave you the green plants, I give you everything. [4]Only, you shall not eat flesh with its life, that is, its blood. [5]For your own lifeblood I will surely require a reckoning: from every animal I will require it and from human beings, each one for the blood of another, I will require reckoning for human life. [6]Whoever sheds the blood of a human, by a human shall that person's blood be shed; for in his own image God made humankind. [7]And you, be fruitful and multiply, abound on the earth and multiply in it."

[8]Then God said to Noah and to his sons with him, [9]"As for me, I am establishing my covenant with you and your descendants after you, [10]and with every living creature that is with you, the birds, the domestic animals, and every animal of the earth with you, as many as came out of the ark. [11]I establish my covenant with you, that never again shall all flesh be cut off by the waters of a flood, and never again shall there be a flood to destroy the earth."

[12]God said, "This is the sign of the covenant that I make between me and you and every living creature that is with you, for all future generations: [13]I have set my bow in the clouds, and it shall be a sign of the covenant between me and the earth. [14]When I bring clouds over the earth and the bow is seen in the clouds, [15]I will remember my covenant that is between me and you and every living creature of all flesh; and the waters shall never again become a flood to destroy all

flesh. [16]When the bow is in the clouds, I will see it and remember the everlasting covenant between God and every living creature of all flesh that is on the earth." [17]God said to Noah, "This is the sign of the covenant that I have established between me and all flesh that is on the earth."

[18]The sons of Noah who went out of the ark were Shem, Ham, and Japheth. Ham was the father of Canaan. [19]These three were the sons of Noah; and from these the whole earth was peopled. [20]Noah, a man of the soil, was the first to plant a vineyard. [21]He drank some of the wine and became drunk, and he lay uncovered in his tent. [22]And Ham, the father of Canaan, saw the nakedness of his father, and told his two brothers outside. [23]Then Shem and Japheth took a garment, laid it on both their shoulders, and walked backward and covered the nakedness of their father; their faces were turned away, and they did not see their father's nakedness.

[24]When Noah awoke from his wine and knew what his youngest son had done to him, [25]he said, "Cursed be Canaan; lowest of slaves shall he be to his brothers." [26]He also said, "Blessed be the LORD my God be Shem; and let Canaan be his slave. [27]May God make space for Japheth, and let him live in the tents of Shem; and let Canaan be his slave."

[28]After the flood Noah lived three hundred fifty years. [29]All the days of Noah were nine hundred fifty years; and he died.

NOAH'S NAKEDNESS AND THE CURSE
OF CANAAN: A CASE OF INCEST?

Frederick W. Bassett

Although many people believe that the Bible means exactly what it says, theologians usually work from the assumption that the Bible as we know it today needs to be read analytically. These theologians point to evidence suggesting that the stories included in the Bible were originally part of an oral tradition and that this tradition could have undergone many changes before being written down. The following article attempts to explain one section of the Old Testament: the story in Genesis in which Noah places an extraordinary curse upon his grandson Canaan for a sin apparently committed by Canaan's father, Ham. The sin itself has also been puzzling, for standard editions of the Bible indicate only that Ham had seen his father naked when he walked into his father's tent. What, you may wonder, was so bad about that?

Executive director of the Hilton Head College Center, Frederick W. Bassett taught theology for many years at Limestone College in South Carolina. It was while he was at Limestone that he published the following article, which first appeared in Vetus Testamentum *in 1972.* Vetus Testamentum *(Latin for "Old Testament") is a scholarly journal read primarily by theologians. In addition to his work in theology, Bassett is a poet—and he has drawn upon his interest in poetry to edit some of the poetry in the Bible so that it is accessible to contemporary readers.*

The Old Testament story of the curse of Canaan (Gen. 9:20–27) is perhaps best understood as an ethnological° tradition which grew out of the Israelite conquest of Canaan. The story seems clearly designed to discredit the Canaanites and justify the Israelite and Philistine hegemony over them.[1] This interpretation has been well argued by a number of critical interpreters and need not be discussed further here.

The extant text of the tradition, however, is laden with exegetical° problems, some of which have perhaps not yet been adequately explained. Two such problems are: 1) the nature of the offense which led Noah to curse Canaan, and 2) the identity of the offender. Critical exegetes generally agree that the tradition has suffered significantly in transmission at these points and have attempted to reconstruct the original details of the story. The following discussion is devoted anew to these two problems.

°*ethnological:* Pertaining to the origin and development of culture or race.
°*exegetical:* Textual in the sense of the words on the page as opposed to what could be surmised about gaps in a text.

As it now stands, the text pictures the offense as nothing more than an accidental case of Ham's viewing his naked father. While drunken Noah lies uncovered in his tent, Ham sees him thus reposed and tells his two brothers (v. 22). This understanding of the offense is now clearly demanded by verse 23 which describes how Shem and Japheth walk backward into Noah's tent with a garment over their shoulders and cover their naked father. They avoid Ham's offense by keeping their faces turned away from Noah. Ham's action, however, hardly seems sufficient grounds to justify the curse of Canaan which follows. Thus, both Jewish tradition and modern interpretation understandably indicate that more than this was involved in the original story.

A number of midrashim° say that the offense involved the castration of Noah.[2] Some say that Ham himself did the castrating. Others say that Ham's little son Canaan unmanned Noah by mischievously looping a cord about his genitals and drawing it tight. Ham's guilt in these accounts lies in the fact that he entered the tent, saw what had happened, and smilingly told his brothers. A sense of justice has obviously influenced the direction some of these midrashim have taken. Whether they all are only attempts to justify the curse or whether they preserve information about the castration of Noah which goes back in an oral form to the original story is not clear. They do support from a different direction the interpretation of the offense offered below in this study.

Apart from these traditions, critical interpreters have frequently noted   5
that the Old Testament text itself points to an offense involving more than just seeing. Noah's reaction to the offense is based on his awareness of "what his youngest son *had done* (ʿāśāh) to him" (v. 24). It has been suggested, therefore, that the original story probably contained an account of an indecent attack by Canaan on his father which has been omitted from motives of delicacy.[3]

That the original offense was part sexual gains additional support from the Old Testament usage of the expression "to see the nakedness of someone" (rā'āh ʿerwat). In the laws prohibiting certain sexual relations in Lev. 18 and 20, this expression clearly has an idiomatic force, meaning to have sexual intercourse. Although the idiom typically used in these laws is "to uncover the nakedness of someone" (gālāh ʿerwaṭ), both idioms are used in parallelism in Lev. 20:17. This verse reads, "And if a man takes his sister, either his father's daughter or his mother's daughter, and sees (rā'āh) her nakedness, it is a shameful thing, and they shall be cut off in the sight of the children of their people; he has uncovered (gillāh) his sister's nakedness; he shall bear his iniquity." It would appear, therefore, that the redactor, or perhaps a later editor, has missed the idiomatic meaning of the tradition that Noah's son saw his father's nakedness and has added the reference to the brothers' covering their father's nakedness with a garment.

°*midrashim:* Early Jewish commentary on the Bible.

While the offense undoubtedly involved sexual intercourse, the identity of the offender and his sex partner calls for additional study. According to the existing text, Ham is the offender. Noah reacts to the offense, however, by cursing Canaan. Since Canaan is clearly intended to bear the curse, it has been widely assumed by modern critics that the story belongs to a stratum of tradition which identified the sons of Noah as Shem, Japheth, and Canaan.[4] Canaan is cursed, it is asserted, because he was the original offender. It is thus believed that the original text was altered by making Ham the offender so that the story would harmonize with the standard Biblical genealogy of Noah's descendants.

It has also been argued that the Biblical phrases which refer to the offender as Noah's "youngest son" (v. 24) and to Canaan's subjugation by "his brothers" (v. 25) point likewise to an older trilogy of Shem, Japheth, and Canaan. J. Hoftijzer has correctly shown, however, that these phrases do not in themselves point to a new genealogy but can be reconciled with the Biblical genealogy which knows Canaan to be Noah's grandson by Ham.[5] In fact, the suggested genealogy appears improbable since it is contradicted by both priestly and Yahwistic° genealogies in the Old Testament.[6]

It is possible, moreover, to interpret the story without theorizing that there has been a shift in the identity of the offender. The key to such an interpretation lies in the meaning of the statement, "And Ham, the father of Canaan, saw the nakedness of his father" (v. 22a). As already noted, the phrase "to see someone's nakedness" is an idiom, referring to sexual intercourse. But what is even more significant for the problem under discussion, the idiom is used to describe not homosexual but heterosexual intercourse, even when it speaks of a man seeing another man's nakedness. "To see a man's nakedness" means to have sexual relations with his wife. The following parallelisms from Lev. 18 make this abundantly clear. "The nakedness of your father" is explained as "the nakedness of your mother" (v. 7). "The nakedness of your father's wife" is described as "the nakedness of your father" (v. 8). "The nakedness of your father's brother," is further clarified as "his wife" and "your aunt" (v. 14). "The nakedness of your brother's wife" parallels "your brother's nakedness" (v. 16). While these verses in themselves clearly establish the idiomatic meaning of a man's nakedness, there are three references in Lev. 20 which specifically say that if one lies with or takes someone's wife, he has uncovered that man's nakedness. These references read as follows: "If a man lies with his father's wife, he has uncovered his father's nakedness" (v. 11). "If a man lies with his uncle's wife, he has uncovered his uncle's nakedness . . ." (v. 20). "If a man takes his brother's wife—it is impurity—he has uncovered his brother's nakedness . . ." (v. 21).

°*Yahwistic:* Characteristic of those parts of the Old Testament, especially the first six books, in which God is referred to as Yahweh or Jehovah.

On the basis of the above references which establish the idiomatic mean- *10*
ing of the expression under discussion, it is possible that the statement that
Ham saw the nakedness of his father originally meant that he had sexual intercourse with his father's wife. If so, this would explain the seriousness of the
offense which led to the curse. It would also explain why Noah cursed only
one of Ham's several sons, if it is further assumed that Canaan was the fruit of
such a case of incest.

The problem of the nature of the offense and the identity of the offender
may never be settled conclusively. There are, however, several reasons for preferring the above solution based on the idiomatic interpretation of Noah's
nakedness.

In the first place, it illuminates, without altering the well-established genealogy of Noah's sons, the seemingly unjust Biblical story in which Noah
curses Canaan for something Ham did. Idiomatically understood, Canaan
bears Noah's curse of slavery, because he is the fruit of Ham's incest.

In the second place, the idiomatic interpretation has parallel support from
at least one other Old Testament tradition with a similar etiological° interest
in explaining the low estate of a people. Reuben's incestuous affair with Bilhah,
his father's concubine, is explicitly cited as the reason why he and his descendants lose their natural right of pre-eminence in Israel as the first born (Gen.
49:3–4; 35:22). It is also possible that the story of Lot's sons by his daughters
(Gen. 19:30–38) has a similar etiological purpose of disparaging the Moabites
and Ammonites. This interpretation, however, has been rejected by a number
of scholars following Gunkel's argument that the tradition originated among
these people to proclaim the heroism of their ancestral mothers and the purity
of their blood.[7]

Whether Gunkel's interpretation is correct or not, it is clear that an act of
incest between father and daughter is not on a par with that between mother
and son in the Old Testament. There are no sex laws in the Old Testament
which prohibit sexual relations between father and daughter.[8] Apparently, the
father's only loss in such a case would be the marriage price of a virgin. But
a son who has sexual relations with his mother or step-mother commits a
rebellious sin against his father, since the possession of a man's wife is seen
also as an effort to supplant the man himself. This meaning of the act is especially clear in cases in which a rival is trying to supplant a royal figure. Thus,
for example, Absalom lies publicly with his father's concubines in his effort to
supplant him and take over the kingdom (2 Sam. 16:20–23).

In this light, the idiomatic interpretation is strengthened by the midrashic *15*
stories of Noah's castration. Castration is also a well documented motif in
ancient stories of the usurpation of royal power. Robert Graves and Raphael
Patai have, in fact, already pointed out the relation of these midrashic stories
to Greek and Hittite myths in which a son castrates his father and takes over

---

°*etiological:* Inquiring into causes.

the throne.[9] In Greek tradition, for example, Cronus castrates and supplants his father Uranus only to suffer the same fate at the hands of his son Zeus. According to Ulf Oldenburg, both motifs are present in the myths of Hadad's rise to power. Hadad both castrates El and takes over his wife Asherah in his effort to establish his right to the throne.[10] The midrashic stories thus correlate nicely with the idiomatic interpretation and add their weight to it.

Finally, the idiomatic interpretation is so firmly established in Leviticus that it should be accepted as the normal one unless some other meaning is demanded by the context. The reverse, however, is true here. Rather than creating additional problems, the idiomatic interpretation explains the difficulties of the tradition. One has only to view v. 23, which tells how Shem and Japheth covered their father's nakedness, as a later addition by someone who did not understand the idiom.

NOTES

1. Differently, J. Hoftijzer has argued that the tradition was intended not only to explain Israel's subjugation of Canaan but her own subsequent domination by a foreign people as well. He sees a reference to Israel's own loss of independence in the statement, "let him (Japheth) dwell in the tents of Shem" (v. 27). This reference can allude, in his opinion, to the Philistine, the Assyrian, or (more probably) the Babylonian victory over Israel ("Some Remarks to the Tale of Noah's Drunkenness," in B. Gemser et al., *Studies on the Book of Genesis,* Oudtestamentische Studien, XII, Leiden 1958, pp. 25–26). While the Old Testament usage of the expression "to dwell in someone's tent" seems in itself to support Hoftijzer's interpretation, the last half of v. 27 seems to call for a different conclusion. The imprecation, "let Canaan be his slave," appears to indicate that Canaan rather than Israel is to bear the brunt of Japheth's dwelling in the tents of Shem. This imprecation thus seems to support the interpretation of a joint possession of Canaan by descendants of Shem and Japheth.

2. For summaries with references, see Robert Graves and Raphael Patai, *Hebrew Myths: The Book of Genesis* (Garden City, 1964), pp. 120 ff.

3. So, for example, Cuthbert A. Simpson, "The Book of Genesis, Introduction and Exegesis," in *The Interpreter's Bible,* Vol. I, p. 556.

4. See Gerhard von Rad, *Genesis, A Commentary,* trans. John H. Marks (Philadelphia, 1961), pp. 131–132.

5. Hoftijzer, *op. cit.,* pp. 22–25.

6. The priestly genealogy consistently lists Noah's sons as Shem, Ham, and Japheth (Gen. 7:13; 9:18; 10:1), Canaan being his grandson by Ham (Gen 10:6). Although Noah's sons are not now listed in the fragmented Yahwistic genealogy in Gen. 10, it is equally clear that Canaan is not one of Noah's sons. According to the Yahwistic manner of recording the generations, the brothers Shem and Japheth are representatives of the oldest generation cited. The editor has not preserved any Yahwistic reference to a third brother. While their relationship is not given in the Yahwistic references that now supplement the P genealogy, Cush, Egypt, Canaan, and Arpachshad are, nevertheless, all members of a younger generation than Shem and Japheth.

7. Hermann Gunkel, *Genesis,* 5th ed.(Göttingen: HKAT, 1922), pp. 196 ff.

8. Salomo Luria, "Tochterschändung in der Bibel," *Archiv Orientalni,* 33 (1965), pp. 207–208.

9. Graves and Patai, *op. cit.,* p. 122.

10. Ulf Oldenburg, *The Conflict Between El and Ba'al in Canaanite Religion* (Leiden, 1969).

QUESTIONS FOR DISCUSSION

1. Is it possible that the story of the curse of Canaan is incomplete? If so, why might the Bible as we know it be either missing important details or including details that are of questionable authenticity?
2. Why is it important for biblical scholars to know ancient languages such as Hebrew and Greek?
3. How crucial is the book of Leviticus to Bassett's analysis of Genesis 9: 20–27? What would happen to his case if he were required to keep his focus exclusively on Genesis?
4. Why do you think an ancient people would use a phrase like "to see someone's nakedness" as a way of indicating sexual intercourse? Are there ways in contemporary English of indicating sexual intercourse euphemistically?
5. Do you agree with Bassett's claim that "the nature of the offense and the identity of the offender may never be conclusively known"? Why or why not?
6. What are the implications of the reference Bassett makes in paragraph 13 to "the low estate of a people"? Can the Bible be used to justify why some people have lower status than others?

SUGGESTIONS FOR WRITING

1. Research what contemporary scholars say about Genesis 9:20–27, and, drawing on what you learn, offer an analysis of these verses that differs from Bassett's.
2. Choose another section of verses from either Genesis or Leviticus, and analyze those verses by paying close attention to the precise language with which they are told in two different editions of the Bible.
3. Write an analysis focused on what one or more books of the Old Testament say about the relationship between fathers and sons or fathers and daughters.

LINKS

■ Within the Book

Gene Rice draws on Bassett in his analysis of Genesis in "The Curse That Never Was" (pages 420–429).

▣ Elsewhere in Print

Bassett, Frederick W. *Awake My Heart: Psalms for Life.* Orleans: Paraclete, 1998.

Hamilton, Victor P. *The Book of Genesis.* Grand Rapids: Eerdemans, 1990.

Kitchen, K. A. *On the Reliability of the Old Testament.* Grand Rapids: Eerdemans, 2003.

Milgrom, Jacob. *Leviticus, 1–16.* New York: Anchor Bible, 1998.

———. *Leviticus, 17–23.* New York: Doubleday, 2000.

———. *Leviticus, 23–27.* New York: Anchor Bible, 2001.

Waltke, Bruce K. *Genesis.* Grand Rapids: Zondervan, 2001.

▣ Online

www.mhhe.com/motives

Click on "More Resources" then "Writing to Analyze Texts."

▪ ▪ ▪

THE CURSE THAT NEVER WAS

Gene Rice

During much of American history, the story of Noah's curse on Canaan was used to support the argument that slavery was a legitimate institution and that African Americans were inferior to Americans of European descent. According to this argument, evidence of which can be found in nineteenth-century sermons and other texts, Africans were the descendants of Canaan while Europeans descended from his older brothers, Shem and Japheth. The key lines in this analysis are words attributed to Noah: "Cursed be Canaan; / a slave shall he be to his brothers. . . . / Blessed by the Lord my God shall be Shem; / and let Canaan be his slave. / God enlarge Japheth, / and let him dwell in the tents of Shem; / and let Canaan be his slave."

Gene Rice teaches theology at Howard University, an institution founded in 1867 to give African Americans access to higher education when most universities were reluctant to accept students of color. Located in Washington, DC, Howard is widely respected for its history and mission. It publishes the Journal of Religious Thought, *in which the following article first appeared in 1972, only a few years after the assassination of Martin Luther King and during an ongoing struggle for the extension of civil rights to African Americans. To conserve space, the 108 notes that support Rice's analysis have been moved online. To retrieve them, visit www.mhhe.com/motives and click on "Writing to Analyze Texts."*

Of all the passages in the Bible none is more infamous than Genesis 9:18–27. Many a person has used this text to justify to himself and others his prejudice against people of African descent. Indeed, it has been widely used to claim divine sanction for slavery and segregation. Often the location of the passage is unknown and one is not familiar with the details, but with the certainty of unexamined truth it is asserted that the Bible speaks of a curse on Black people. And this notion has exercised so powerful an influence precisely because its adherents by and large have been "good Church people." While the hey-day of this understanding of Gen. 9:18–27 was during the last and early part of this century, it persists to this day. Whether wittingly or unwittingly, a recent article by F. W. Bassett of Limestone College, Gaffney, South Carolina, lends aid and comfort and helps to perpetuate it.[1] It is time that the misunderstanding and abuse of this passage come to an end.

I would like to express appreciation to Kingsley Dalpadado, Samuel L. Gandy, Jack H. Goodwin, and Frank M. Snowden, Jr., without whose generous help this article in its present form would not have been possible.

I.

Rarely have such clear and unambiguous claims been made of so obscure and difficult a passage. Its complexity is apparent from the outset. It begins by naming the sons of Noah who went forth from the ark, namely, Shem, Ham, and Japheth, but goes on to add in a statement that takes one completely by surprise:"Ham was the father of Canaan." And this information is repeated in v. 22. By its position immediately following the account of the flood, it is implied that the episode of 9:18–27 took place shortly thereafter. Moreover, the account gives the impression that Noah's sons have not yet set up separate households but are still unmarried and living with their father in the family tent. This impression is strengthened by the fact that one of the sons is designated as "the youngest" (v. 24). Also the offense against Noah is the kind one might expect from a teen-ager but hardly from a mature, married man. Yet the two references to Ham as the father of Canaan pre-suppose that Noah's sons have left their father's tent, set up separate households, and that a number of years have passed in the course of which Canaan, who is Ham's fourth son (Gen. 10:6), was born and has become either a teen-ager or a young adult.

While the reference to Ham as the father of Canaan is awkward in every respect, one can infer from the context that it was introduced because later on Canaan is cursed for the misdeed of Ham. But instead of clarifying matters this only creates another problem. Why should Canaan be cursed for the wrong of his father? The biblical text provides no answer to this question.

The attentive reader of Gen 9:18–27 is confronted, in the third place, by two different conceptions of the extent of Noah's family. Genesis 9:19a states that from Shem, Ham, and Japheth "the whole world was peopled." But according to 9:25–27 the sons of Noah all live in the land of Palestine.

In the fourth place, there is the perplexing fact that the sons of Noah are listed in the order Shem, Ham and Japheth in 9:18 and on the basis of Gen. 5:32 this is most naturally understood as the order of their birth. In 9:24, however, the offender against Noah is expressly identified as Noah's "youngest'" son. From the order Shem, Ham, and Japheth, the youngest son is Japheth. But Japheth is not cursed.

This brings us to the fifth and most enigmatic of all the difficulties of Gen. 9:18–27. In 9:24–25 Noah identifies the offender against him both as his youngest son and as Canaan:"When Noah awoke from his wine and knew what his youngest son had done to him, he said, 'Cursed be Canaan; a slave of slaves shall he be to his brothers.'" Then in vs. 26–27 Noah names the two brothers to whom Canaan is to be slave: "Noah also said: 'Blessed be the LORD, the God of Shem; and let Canaan be his slave. God enlarge Japheth, and let him dwell in the tents of Shem; and let Canaan be his slave.'" Thus whereas the sons of Noah are Shem, Ham and Japheth in 9:18, they are Shem, Japheth, and Canaan in 9:24–27.

II.

All the tensions of Gen. 9:18–27 are resolved when it is recognized that this passage contains two parallel but different traditions of Noah's family. In one tradition Noah's family consists of Shem, Ham, and Japheth and these three are the ancestors of all the peoples known to ancient Israel. This tradition is universal, catholic in scope. It is found in Gen. 9:18–19a (and elsewhere in 5:32; 6:10; 7:13; 10:1; I Chron. 1:4). In the other tradition Noah's family consists of Shem, Japheth, and Canaan and they all live in Palestine. This tradition is limited, parochial in scope. It is found in 9:20–27 (and seems to be presupposed in 10:21 where Shem is referred to as the elder brother of Japheth).

The understanding of Gen. 9:18–27 is so confused because the text in its present form represents an effort to minimize the discrepancy between these two traditions by equating Ham in the one with Canaan in the other. This was done by the notation in 9:18b, "Ham was the father of Canaan," and by adding in 9:22a, "Ham the father of" before Canaan. When these two harmonizing notes are recognized as such the two different traditions of Noah's family stand out sharply: vs. 18–19a reflect one tradition, vs. 20–27 embody the other. Instead of trying to harmonize them, each should be considered in its own right. When this is done it becomes clear that Noah's discovery of wine and his cursing and blessing of his sons is an independent, coherent narrative in which the offender against his father as well as the one cursed in Canaan. This becomes graphically clear if the harmonizing notes are placed in brackets or removed as in the following citation of the text:

> [20]Noah was the first tiller of the soil. He planted a vineyard; [21]and he drank of the wine, and became drunk, and uncovered himself in his tent. [22]And . . . Canaan saw the nakedness of his father, and told his two brothers outside. [23]Then Shem and Japheth took a garment, laid it upon both their shoulders, and walked backward and covered the nakedness of their father; their faces were turned away, and they did not see their father's nakedness. [24]When Noah awoke from his wine and knew what his youngest son had done to him, [25]he said,
>
> "Cursed be Canaan;
>   a slave of slaves shall he be to his brothers."
> [26]He also said,
>
> "Blessed be the LORD, the GOD of Shem;
>   and let Canaan be his slave.
> [27]God enlarge Japheth,
>   and let him dwell in the tents of Shem;
>   and let Canaan be his slave."[2]

This is a not a new interpretation. It was first proposed by J. Wellhausen in 1876.[3] Among those who have subsequently adopted and defended it are: K. Budde (who devotes ninety pages to Gen 9:18–27!),[4] A. Kuenen,[5] A. Westphal,[6] W. R. Harper,[7] B. Stade,[8] H. Holzinger,[9] B. W. Bacon,[10] C. H Cornill,[11]

W. E. Addis,[12] E. Kautsch,[13] D. S. Margoliouth,[14] J. E. Carpenter and C. Hartford-Battersby (with reserve),[15] H. Gunkel,[16] S. R. Driver (with reserve),[17] W. H. Bennett,[18] E. Meyer,[19] A. R. Gordon,[20] C. F. Kent,[21] J. Skinner,[22] F. Böhl,[23] R. Smend,[24] C. Steuernagel,[25] O. Procksch,[26] H. E. Ryle,[27] W. Eichrodt,[28] J. R. Dummelow,[29] W. M. Patton,[30] E. S. Brightman,[31] A. S. Peake,[32] O. Eissfeldt,[33] S. Mowinckel,[34] R. H. Pfeiffer,[35] W. Zimmerli,[36] E. G. Kraeling,[37] C. A. Simpson,[38] G. von Rad,[39] A. Lods,[40] E. B. Redlich,[41] J. Chaine (with reserve),[42] A. Clamer,[43] C. T. Fritsch,[44] J. Heemrood,[45] A. Halder,[46] L. Hicks,[47] J. H. Marks,[48] A. H. McNeile and T. W. Thacker,[49] R. Graves and R. Patai,[50] G. Fohrer,[51] E. H. Maly,[52] and T. E. Fretheim.[53] A variation of this interpretation is represented by A. Dillman,[54] J. Hermann,[55] and L. Rost[56] who maintain that originally the passage had to do only with Canaan (Dillman) or with Canaan and Shem (Herrmann, Rost) and that the reference to the other brother(s) has been added later.[57]

The above roster of scholars is sufficient to indicate that after its introduction in the 1870's the interpretation presented above quickly won the assent of the majority of authorities and has maintained that position to the present. And it would be difficult to draw up a more distinguished company of scholars. Nevertheless this interpretation has not lacked for opposition nor have there been wanting vigorous defenders of an alternative point of view.

III.

Among those who assume the unity of Gen. 9:18–27 and therefore regard Ham as the offender are: A. Köhler,[58] C. A. Briggs,[59] Franz Delitzsch,[60] W. H. Green,[61] H. L. Strack,[62] J. Halevy,[63] C. J. Ball,[64] T. K. Cheyne,[65] M. Dods,[66] A. Ehrlich,[67] W. Möller,[68] L. Murillo,[69] E. König,[70] P. Heinisch,[71] B. Jacob,[72] H. C. Leupold,[73] U. Cassuto,[74] H. Junker,[75] H. Frey,[76] A. Richardson,[77] W. M. Logan,[78] R. H. Elliott,[79] J. de Fraine,[80] and F. W. Bassett.[81] To these may be added a small group of scholars who take the position that there is only one tradition of the sons of Noah, namely, Shem, Ham, and Japheth, but that part or all of the cursing of Canaan and the blessing of Shem and Japheth is later than the story about Noah's discovery of wine. Among these are: B. D. Eerdmans,[82] J. Hoftijzer,[83] H. W. Wolff,[84] and D. Neiman.[85]

Perhaps the most serious obstacle to those who defend the unity of 9:18–27 is the fact that Ham is regularly named as Noah's second son whereas the offender is specifically designated as Noah's youngest son (v. 24). One of the oldest and simplest expedients to avoid this difficulty is to accept the order Shem, Ham, and Japheth as the proper one chronologically but to construe the adjective, young, not as a superlative but as a comparative. That is, in relation to Shem, Ham is Noah's "younger" son.[86] Not two but three sons are compared, however, and when this is the case the proper construction is the superlative.

There is an old and well represented tradition, on the other hand, that the order Shem, Ham, and Japheth is not chronological and that Ham actually was Noah's youngest son.[87] This understanding is arrived at by construing Gen. 10:21 to read, "Shem, the brother of Japheth, the eldest" and by taking "youngest son" in 19:24 to refer to Ham. But almost all authorities are agreed that the proper construction of Gen. 10:21 is "Shem . . . the elder brother of Japheth." And if the "youngest son" in 9:24 is Ham the cursing of Canaan is completely unmotivated and without meaning.

Still others would solve this problem by contending that "youngest" in 9:24 should not be understood chronologically but morally in the sense of "the least, the contemptible."[88] But there are a number of words in the Hebrew language better suited to express moral condemnation and it is difficult to see why so ambiguous a term would have been chosen in this context.

Accepting that "youngest son" is to be understood chronologically and that the reference is to Canaan, some have sought a way out of the dilemma by calling attention to the fact that son is sometimes used in the sense of grandson.[89] Such usage is attested but never in conjunction with son used in the literal sense as in the present passage.

A few scholars assert that the original text consistently referred to Ham as the offender and as the one cursed and that Canaan is a later addition to the text.[90] But this is pure speculation for which there is no firm support in the ancient texts and versions. This position is rendered completely untenable, moreover, by the statements, "Ham was the father of Canaan," and "Ham the father of." If Ham was the consistent reading of the original text these statements are superfluous and unintelligible. And if someone added Canaan to the text why did he not remove all references to Ham?

Various explanations are offered to account for Canaan being cursed for the offense of Ham. Some find here the working of a principle of retribution: as Noah suffered at the hands of his youngest son, Ham, so Ham is afflicted in the person of his youngest son, Canaan. But nowhere is such a principle enunciated in the Bible nor is an example to be found where the guilty father is passed over and his son punished in his stead.

Others account for the cursing of Canaan on the grounds that one whom God had blessed (Ham in Gen. 9:1) could not be cursed. Equally valid is the principle that the innocent should not be cursed for the misdeed of the guilty.

Still others would account for the presence of Canaan in the curse because Canaan was the nearest and best known of Hamitic peoples to the Israelites. Rather, that only Canaan is mentioned in the curse most naturally suggests that all other Hamitic peoples are excluded from it. And if Ham is the guilty party, the text provides no answer as to why only Canaan and not all Hamitic peoples should be cursed.

Finally, it has been maintained that both Ham and Canaan are guilty, that Canaan first saw Noah's nakedness and Ham told his brothers. There are also traditions that either Ham or Canaan (or a lion) rendered Noah impotent (or attacked him homosexually) and that this was what "his youngest son had done to him" (v. 24). But the context indicates that the disrespectful seeing it-

15

20

self was the offense done to Noah.[91] And if both father and son are guilty, why is the father treated as less responsible than the son?

A completely different tack is taken by Bassett. On the basis of the usage attested in Lev. 18 and 20 that to see a man's nakedness may have the idiomatic meaning of having sexual intercourse with his wife, Bassett interprets the passage to mean that Ham committed incest with his mother and that Canaan was cursed because he was the fruit of this illicit union. Bassett thinks that the case of the Reubenites who lost their preeminence among the tribes of Israel because of Reuben's affair with his father's concubine, Bilhah, and the midrashic traditions that Ham's offense against Noah was one of castration (which also has to do with displacing one's father) support his understanding of the passage. In order to maintain this interpretation, however, Bassett has to delete 9:23 as the later addition of a redactor or editor who "missed the idiomatic meaning"[92] of the seeing of Noah's nakedness.

Bassett overstates the case for the sexual implications of nakedness. E. A. Speiser points out on the basis of Gen. 42:9, 12 that nakedness in the first instance "relates to exposure" and "does not necessarily imply sexual offenses" (cf. Gen. 2:25; Ex. 20:26; II Sam. 6:20).[93] In a passage that may have been formulated under the influence of Gen. 9:18–27, Hab. 2:15,[94] drunkenness and nudity are associated with each other without any sexual overtones (cf. also Lam. 4:21).

Furthermore, the proper idiomatic expression for intercourse is to uncover the nakedness of another. Except for one instance, "uncover" is consistently the verb of the idiom for intercourse in Lev. 18 and 20. In Lev. 20:17 "uncover" and "see" are used in parallelism to each other, but this usage of "see" is clearly exceptional for the parallelism with "uncover" has to be made explicit. Bassett cites no other passages where to see the nakedness of another means to have sexual intercourse. Nor do the standard lexicons give this as a meaning for r'h. Still more damaging to Bassett's argument is the fact that "uncover" and "see" are used in adjoining sentences in Gen. 9:18–27 (vs. 21, 22) but there is no effort to relate them to each other and here they clearly are not synonymous. Canaan does not uncover Noah; Noah uncovers himself.[95] In short, Bassett has not established a case for the general usage of the expression to see the nakedness of another as meaning sexual intercourse. Nor does the context in Gen. 9:18–27 support such a usage. Quite simply the text states that Noah uncovered himself and Canaan witnessed him in this state.

Not only does Bassett overstate the case but he is inconsistent. He asserts on the one hand that "the idiomatic interpretation is so firmly established in Leviticus that it should be accepted as the normal one unless some other meaning is demanded by the context" yet maintains that Gen. 9:23 was added "by someone who did not understand the idiom"![96] On the one hand, Bassett commits himself to the limited, parochial tradition of Noah's family in that he takes 9:20–27 to be an ethnological tradition "designed to discredit the Canaanites and justify the Israelite and Philistine hegemony over them."

The major burden of the paper, on the other hand, is to defend the catholic tradition of Noah's family according to which the sons are Shem, Ham, and Japheth (pp. 234ff.).

Critical to Bassett's position is his assertion that 9:23 is secondary. There is no evidence in the ancient texts and versions to support this claim. No other scholar has found reason to regard only this verse as alien to its context. Rather, the blessing of Shem and Japheth is unintelligible apart from some such meritorious act on their part as reported in v. 23. And if v. 23 is integral to its context it is fatal to Bassett's theory. For, as Cassuto observes, "if the covering was an adequate remedy, it follows that the misdemeanour was confined to seeing."[97] For that matter, v. 22 stands in great tension with Bassett's position. If Ham committed incest with his mother, it is likely that he would come outside and tell his brothers?

There are other flaws in Bassett's interpretation. If Ham's offense was incest it is difficult to see how Noah could curse by name the issue of this union at the time of conception and completely ignore the perpetrators of the deed. There is a persistent and often bitter polemic against the Canaanites in the Old Testament. Had Canaan's origin been an incestuous one it almost certainly would have been exploited (cf. Gen. 19:30–38) but nowhere is there any reference to it. Finally, Bassett's position leaves unsolved the questions that arise in connection with "youngest son" in v. 24.

Almost three hundred years ago a position essentially identical with that of Bassett was put forward by Hermann von der Hardt.[98] It received prompt rebuttal[99] and has since enjoyed the oblivion it deserves.

Unsatisfactory also is the attempt to master the difficulties of Gen. 9:18–27 by separating the curse and blessing from the preceding narrative. The following structure is transparent in the text:

> ### Introduction: Noah's vineyard and drunkenness
> I. The behavior of Noah's sons
>   A. Canaan's disrespect and shamelessness
>   B. The respect and piety of Shem and Japheth
> II. Noah's response to his son's behavior
>   A. Curse on Canaan
>   B. Blessing on Shem and Japheth.[100]

The two parts of the passage correspond symmetrically and necessarily to each other. And this correspondence is unmarred by literary seams, formal dislocations, or other incongruities.

Those scholars then who defend the unity of Gen. 9:18–27 or who maintain that there was only one tradition of Noah's sons have not presented an interpretation that does justice to the text. They are at odds with each other and cannot agree on a common understanding. None of them has taken seriously the conflict between the catholic and parochial conceptions of Noah's family standing in juxtaposition to each other. In short, no satisfactory explanation of Gen. 9:18–27 has been given on the assumption that it is organic literary unity speaking with a single voice, nor, on this assumption, is one possible.

IV.

The earliest evidence of a racist interpretation of Gen. 9:18–27 is found in Bereshith Rabbah, an expository commentary on Genesis utilizing the work of rabbis from the second to the fourth centuries and probably completed in the early fifth century.[101] Alluding to a tradition that Ham castrated Noah, Rabbi Joseph has Noah say to Ham: "You have prevented me from doing something in the dark (cohabitation), therefore your seed will be ugly and dark skinned."[102] "The descendants of Ham through Canaan therefore have red eyes, because Ham looked upon the nakedness of his father; they have misshapen lips, because Ham spoke with his lips to his brothers about the unseemly condition of his father; they have twisted curly hair, because Ham turned and twisted his head round to see the nakedness of his father; and they go about naked, because Ham did not cover the nakedness of his father."[103] And according to Pesahim, 113b of the Babylonian Talmud, "Five things did Canaan charge his sons: Love one another, love robbery, love lewdness, hate your masters and do not speak the truth."

    This view gained no prominence in the ancient world, however, which by and large was free of color prejudice.[104] Moreover, in the Middle Ages when the wise men came to be regarded as three it was apparently with conscious reference to the three sons of Noah, and one of them, Melchoir or Balthasar, was depicted as black.[105] Nevertheless, the racist interpretation of Gen. 9:18–27 remained alive[106] and gained new life with the colonial expansion of Europe and the development of slavery in America. Emphasis was now placed on all Black people as being descended from Ham and/or Canaan and by that fact condemned to perpetual servitude because of Noah's curse. While this understanding only became a popular notion in the nineteenth century, it was intellectuals, often within the Church, who "sold" it to an age that found it expedient to exploit it.[107]

    The proper clarification of Gen. 9:18–27 was not possible until the composite character of the Hexateuch° was established and this was not until the time of Wellhausen in the 1870's. Even so, the interpreter has never been without ample resources for arriving at a non-racist interpretation of the passage. From the fact that the biblical text explicitly identifies Canaan—and only Canaan—as the one cursed one may reasonably infer that the other sons of Ham, Cush (Ethiopia), Egypt, and Put (Libya), who are African peoples properly speaking, were not cursed.

°*Hexateuch:* The first six books of the Old Testament.

30

Secondly, the immediate context forbids a racist understanding of Gen. 9:18–27. Genesis 10 has to do with all the peoples of the world known to ancient Israel and since this chapter immediately follows the episode of Noah's cursing and blessing it would have been most appropriate to express here any prejudicial feelings toward African peoples. Not only are such feelings absent, but all peoples are consciously and deliberately related to each other as brothers. No one, not even Israel, is elevated above anyone else and no disparaging remark is made about any people, not even the enemies of Israel. Indeed, the point of Gen. 10 is that the great diversity and multiplicity of peoples is the fulfillment of God's command to Noah and his sons: "Be fruitful and multiply, and fill the earth" (Gen. 9:1). As God inspected his creative work in Gen. 1 and found it good, so in Gen. 10 he approves and rejoices in mankind in all its manifestations.

Had the ancient Israelites been conscious of some taint upon African peoples one would expect Abraham to have alluded to it when he went down to Egypt because of a famine in Canaan. Nor do Abraham and Sarah have any qualms about Hagar because of her Egyptian origin. They are glad to use her to get an heir and so secure through their own efforts God's promise of a great posterity (Gen. 16). While Miriam and Aaron spoke out against Moses because of his Cushite wife, the context clearly shows that what they are really protesting is Moses' authority (Nu. 12:1ff.).

The prophet Isaiah is very critical of Egypt, which, incidentally, was ruled over by an Ethiopian dynasty during the latter part of his ministry, because he wants to dissuade Israel from relying on Egypt in its bid for independence from Assyria. But nowhere does he appeal to some ancient curse. He does make a few disparaging remarks about Egypt's help (cf., e.g., Is. 19:11ff.; 30:5, 7; ct. 18:1ff.), but his point to Judah is: "The Egyptians are men, and not God; and their horses are flesh, and not spirit" (31:3).   *35*

It is surely not without significance that Aaron's grandson, who is regarded as the ancestor of the Zadokite priesthood (Ex. 6:25; Nu. 25:6ff.; Josh. 22:30; 24:33; I Chron. 6:4, 50; Ezr. 8:2; Ps. 106:30), and one of the sons of Eli (I Sam. 1:3; 2:34; 4:11, 17; 4:3) were given the Egyptian name, Phinehas, which means literally, the Nubian. Nor is it without important implications for the understanding of Gen. 9:18–27 that the introduction to the prophecies of Zephaniah tells us that his great, great grandfather was (King) Hezekiah and that his father was Cushi, that is, the Ethiopian.

Psalm 87 contains a vision of Zion as the spiritual mother of all men and among these African peoples are explicitly mentioned. Is. 19:24–25 anticipates the time when "Israel will be the third with Egypt and Assyria, a blessing in the midst of the earth, whom the LORD of hosts has blessed, saying, 'Blessed be Egypt my people, and Assyria the work of my hands, and Israel my heritage.'"

Simon from the North African city of Cyrene (Lk. 23:26) was not regarded as unworthy to bear Jesus' cross. Nor did Philip feel it incumbent upon himself to discuss Gen. 9:18–27 with the Ethiopian minister of Candace (Acts

8:26ff.). In short, nowhere in the Bible is there any support for the idea that people of African descent are under a curse. On the contrary, there is much evidence that they were regarded without prejudice and on an equal basis with other people.[108]

While Gen. 9:18–27 may well be the most misunderstood and abused passage of the Bible this is not a reflection on the Bible itself. Rather this misuse and abuse attest to what perversity the human spirit and intellect can sink and with what pains and ingenuity man finds ways to justify to himself and to others his sin.

COMPANION TEXT *Psalm 87*

Hymns used to praise God, offer thanksgiving, express grief, or convey wisdom, psalms were collected and organized into what is now called the Old Testament approximately five hundred years before the birth of Christ. The following text is from the New Revised Standard version of the Bible.

[1]On the holy mount stands the city he founded;
  [2]the LORD loves the gates of Zion more than all the dwellings of Jacob.
  [3]Glorious things are spoken of you, O city of God. *Selah*
  [4]Among those who know me I mention Rahab and Babylon; Philistia too, and Tyre, with Ethiopia—"This one was born there," they say.
  [5]And of Zion it shall be said, "This one and that one were born in it"; for the Most High himself will establish it.
  [6]The LORD records, as he registers the peoples, "This one was born there." *Selah*
  [7]Singers and dancers alike say, "All my springs are in you."

QUESTIONS FOR DISCUSSION

1. Why does Rice devote so much attention to disputing the argument made by Frederick Bassett (the text of which can be found on pages 413–417)? What is it about Bassett's argument that he finds disturbing?
2. How effective is Rice's response to Bassett? What would Rice's argument be like if references to Bassett were deleted?
3. How clearly does Rice establish the nature of Noah's family and explain why people have disagreed about Canaan's identity?
4. What does Bassett mean when he refers, in paragraph 7, to traditions that are "catholic in scope" and "parochial in scope"?
5. Consider paragraph 9, which consists mostly of a long list of names. How do you respond to this paragraph as a reader? What do you think Rice sought to achieve with this paragraph?

6. Why would it be unjust for a son to be punished for a sin committed by his father? To what extent should our understanding of ancient cultures be influenced by contemporary understandings of justice?
7. How helpful is the outline provided in paragraph 28?
8. It is only in section IV that Bassett turns his attention to racist interpretations of Genesis 9:18–27, a topic introduced in paragraph 1. Is this part of his argument sufficiently developed? How closely is it related to the sections that precede it?

SUGGESTIONS FOR WRITING

1. Research how Genesis 9:18–27 was used to justify slavery, focusing on arguments made in the United States during the nineteenth century, and then analyze one of the texts you discover.
2. Compare the analyses of Bassett and Rice, and determine to what extent they share common ground.
3. Write a paper focused on determining what the Old Testament says about drunkenness.

LINKS

■ **Within the Book**

"Noah's Nakedness and the Curse of Canaan: A Case of Incest?"—one of the principal sources for Rice's analysis—can be found on pages 413–417.

■ **Elsewhere in Print**

Goldenberg, David M. *The Curse of Ham: Race and Slavery in Early Judaism, Christianity, and Islam.* Princeton: Princeton UP, 2003.

Hayes, Stephen R. *Noah's Curse: The Biblical Justification of American Slavery.* New York: Oxford UP, 2002.

Isaac, Benjamin. *The Invention of Racism in Classical Antiquity.* Princeton: Princeton UP, 2004.

Rice, Gene. *Nations under God: A Commentary on the Book of Kings.* Grand Rapids: Eerdmans, 1990.

Wimbush, Vincent. *African Americans and the Bible.* New York: Continuum, 2001.

■ **Online**

www.mhhe.com/motives

Click on "More Resources" then "Writing to Analyze Texts."

■ ■ ■

Core Text

THE BILL OF RIGHTS

When the U.S. Constitution was signed in 1787, many citizens were concerned that the newly created federal government did not guarantee sufficient civil rights for individuals and argued that the concept of civil liberty had been at the heart of the American Revolution. Accordingly, the First Congress passed twelve amendments to the Constitution guaranteeing specific protections from the federal government—of which ten were subsequently ratified by the states. Collectively, these ten amendments are called "the Bill of Rights." Although the Supreme Court decisions included in this chapter concern the interpretation of the Fourth Amendment, the full Bill of Rights is reprinted here so that you can see the Fourth Amendment in its context.

In addition to considering the Fourth Amendment, the justices needed to review the details of a specific case that had reached them: Groh v. Ramirez. *Here is a summary of that case: In 1997, Jeff Groh was a special agent working for the Bureau of Alcohol, Tobacco, and Firearms; Joseph Ramirez and his family lived on a large ranch in Montana. Having been informed by a concerned citizen that a large stockpile of weapons, including a rocket launcher, was being stored on the Ramirez ranch, Groh prepared and signed an application for a warrant to search it. A magistrate subsequently signed a search warrant that was less precise than Groh's application and included an error. The law enforcement officers who searched the Ramirez ranch the day after the warrant was signed did not discover any illegal weapons or explosives, and no charges were filed against the Ramirezes—who subsequently sued on the grounds that their Fourth Amendment rights had been violated. This case reached the Supreme Court after a lower court sided with Groh but noted that the warrant used for the search was invalid.*

AMENDMENT I

Congress shall make no law respecting an establishment of religion, or prohibiting the free exercise thereof; or abridging the freedom of speech, or of the press; or of the right of the people peaceably to assemble, and to petition the government for a redress of grievances.

AMENDMENT II

A well regulated militia, being necessary to the security of a free state, the right of the people to keep and bear arms, shall not be infringed.

AMENDMENT III

No soldier shall, in time of peace be quartered in any house, without the consent of the owner, nor in time of war, but in a manner to be prescribed by law.

AMENDMENT IV

The right of the people to be secure in their persons, houses, papers, and effects, against unreasonable searches and seizures, shall not be violated, and no warrants shall issue, but upon probable cause, supported by oath or affirmation, and particularly describing the place to be searched, and the persons or things to be seized.

AMENDMENT V

No person shall be held to answer for a capital, or otherwise infamous crime, unless on a presentment or indictment of a grand jury, except in cases arising in the land or naval forces, or in the militia, when in actual service in time of war or public danger; nor shall any person be subject for the same offense to be twice put in jeopardy of life or limb; nor shall be compelled in any criminal case to be a witness against himself, nor be deprived of life, liberty, or property, without due process of law; nor shall private property be taken for public use, without just compensation.

AMENDMENT VI

In all criminal prosecutions, the accused shall enjoy the right to a speedy and public trial, by an impartial jury of the state and district wherein the crime shall have been committed, which district shall have been previously ascertained by law, and to be informed of the nature and cause of the accusation; to be confronted with the witnesses against him; to have compulsory process for obtaining witnesses in his favor, and to have the assistance of counsel for his defense.

AMENDMENT VII

In suits at common law, where the value in controversy shall exceed twenty dollars, the right of trial by jury shall be preserved, and no fact tried by a jury, shall be otherwise reexamined in any court of the United States, than according to the rules of the common law.

AMENDMENT VIII

Excessive bail shall not be required, nor excessive fines imposed, nor cruel and unusual punishments inflicted.

AMENDMENT IX

The enumeration in the Constitution, of certain rights, shall not be construed to deny or disparage others retained by the people.

AMENDMENT X

The powers not delegated to the United States by the Constitution, nor prohibited by it to the states, are reserved to the states respectively, or to the people.

GROH V. RAMIREZ: A MAJORITY DECISION

John Paul Stevens

> *Appointed to the Supreme Court by President Gerald Ford in 1975, John Paul*
> *Stevens is a Republican who has established a reputation for being fair-minded and for*
> *writing carefully reasoned decisions. He is now the senior-most justice on the Court, sec-*
> *ond only to Chief Justice William Rehnquist in tenure. In the case of Groh v. Ramirez, he*
> *composed the Court's majority opinion—the decision, in other words, that not only deter-*
> *mines the outcome of a specific case but also has the greatest influence in shaping sub-*
> *sequent policy and interpretation of the law.*
>
> *The following decision has been lightly edited in order to make it more accessible,*
> *and Stevens's notes have been moved online (visit www.mhhe.com/motives, click on*
> *"More Resources" then "Writing to Analyze Texts"). Nevertheless, you may still find it a*
> *challenging reading assignment. If you are uncertain about whether it is worth the effort,*
> *note that this decision protects some of your rights, and recognize that being able to*
> *understand a court decision could empower you at a time in your life that you may not*
> *yet anticipate. You might also note that the following decision was first published in*
> *2004, well after the federal government obtained additional police powers in the after-*
> *math of the attacks our nation sustained on September 11, 2001.*
>
> *The "petitioner" in this case is the law enforcement officer who conducted a search*
> *at the Ramirez home and sought to have this act vindicated; the "respondents" are*
> *Mr. And Mrs. Ramirez, who sought the Court's protection.*

Petitioner conducted a search of respondents' homes pursuant to a warrant that failed to describe the "persons or things to be seized." U.S. Const., Amdt. 4. The questions presented are (1) whether the search violated the Fourth Amendment, and (2) if so, whether petitioner nevertheless is entitled to qualified immunity, given that a Magistrate Judge (Magistrate), relying on an affidavit that particularly described the items in question, found probable cause to conduct the search.

I

Respondents, Joseph Ramirez and members of his family, live on a large ranch in Butte-Silver Bow County, Montana. Petitioner, Jeff Groh, has been a Special Agent for the Bureau of Alcohol, Tobacco and Firearms (ATF) since 1989. In February 1997, a concerned citizen informed petitioner that on a number of visits to respondents' ranch the visitor had seen a large stock of weaponry, including an automatic rifle, grenades, a grenade launcher, and a rocket launcher.[1] Based on that information, petitioner prepared and signed an application for a warrant to search the ranch. The application stated that the search was for "any automatic firearms or parts to automatic weapons, destructive devices to include but not limited to grenades, grenade launchers, rocket launchers, and any and all receipts pertaining to the purchase or manufacture of automatic weapons or explosive devices or launchers." App. to Pet. for Cert. 28a° Petitioner supported the application with a detailed affidavit, which he also prepared and executed, that set forth the basis for his belief that the listed items were concealed on the ranch. Petitioner then presented these documents to a Magistrate, along with a warrant form that petitioner also had completed. The Magistrate signed the warrant form.

Although the application particularly described the place to be searched and the contraband petitioner expected to find, the warrant itself was less specific; it failed to identify any of the items that petitioner intended to seize. In the portion of the form that called for a description of the "person or property" to be seized, petitioner typed a description of respondents' two-story blue house rather than the alleged stockpile of firearms.[2] The warrant did not incorporate by reference the itemized list contained in the application. It did, however, recite that the Magistrate was satisfied the affidavit established probable cause to believe that contraband was concealed on the premises, and that sufficient grounds existed for the warrant's issuance.[3]

The day after the Magistrate issued the warrant, petitioner led a team of law enforcement officers, including both federal agents and members of the local sheriff's department, in the search of respondents' premises. Although respondent Joseph Ramirez was not home, his wife and children were. Petitioner states that he orally described the objects of the search to Mrs. Ramirez in person and to Mr. Ramirez by telephone. According to Mrs. Ramirez, however, petitioner explained only that he was searching for "'an explosive device in a box.'" *Ramirez v. Butte-Silver Bow County,* 298 F.3d 1022, 1026 (CA9 2002). At any rate, the officers' search uncovered no illegal weapons or explosives. When the officers left, petitioner gave Mrs. Ramirez a copy of the search warrant, but not a copy of the application, which had been sealed. The following day, in response to a request from respondents' attorney, petitioner faxed the attorney a copy of the page of the application that listed the items to be seized. No charges were filed against the Ramirezes.

Respondents sued petitioner and the other officers under *Bivens v. Six Unknown Fed. Narcotics Agents,* 403 U.S. 388, 29 L. Ed. 2d 619, 91 S. Ct. 1999 (1971), and Rev Stat § 1979, 42 USC § 1983 [42 USCS § 1983], raising eight claims, including violation of the Fourth Amendment. App. 17–27. The District Court entered summary judgment for all defendants. The court found no Fourth Amendment violation, because it considered the case comparable to one in which the warrant contained an inaccurate address, and in such a case,

5

°*App. to Pet. for Cert 28a:* A legal citation to one of the documents submitted in the case—an application to petition in this instance.

the court reasoned, the warrant is sufficiently detailed if the executing officers can locate the correct house. App. To Pet. For Cert 20a–22a. The court added that even if a constitutional violation occurred, the defendants were entitled to qualified immunity because the failure of the warrant to describe the objects of the search amounted to a mere "typographical error." *Id., at* 22a–24a.

The Court of Appeals affirmed the judgment with respect to all defendants and all claims, with the exception of respondents' Fourth Amendment claim against petitioner. 298 F. 3d at 1029–1030. On that claim, the court held that the warrant was invalid because it did not "describe with particularity the place to be searched and the items to be seized," and that oral statements by petitioner during or after the search could not cure the omission. *Id., at* 1025–1026. The court observed that the warrant's facial defect "increased the likelihood and degree of confrontation between the Ramirezes and the police" and deprived respondents of the means "to challenge officers who might have exceeded the limits imposed by the magistrate." *Id., at* 1027. The court also expressed concern that "permitting officers to expand the scope of the warrant by oral statements would broaden the area of dispute between the parties in subsequent litigation." *Ibid.* The court nevertheless concluded that all of the officers except petitioner were protected by qualified immunity. With respect to petitioner, the court read our opinion in *United States v. Leon*, 468 U.S. 897, 82 L. Ed. 2d 677, 104 S. Ct. 3405 (1984), as precluding qualified immunity for the leader of a search who fails to "read the warrant and satisfy [himself] that [he] understand[s] its scope and limitations, and that it is not defective in some obvious way." 298 F. 3d at 1027. The court added that "[t]he leaders of the search team must also make sure that a copy of the warrant is available to give to the person whose property is being searched at the commencement of the search, and that such copy has no missing pages or other obvious defects." *Ibid* (footnote omitted). We granted certiorari. 537 U.S. 1231, 155 L. Ed. 2d 195, 123 S. Ct. 1354 (2003).

II

The warrant was plainly invalid. The Fourth Amendment states unambiguously that "no Warrants shall issue, but upon probable cause, supported by Oath or affirmation, and *particularly describing* the place to be searched, and *the persons or things to be seized.*" (Emphasis added.) The warrant in this case complied with the first three of these requirements: It was based on probable cause and supported by a sworn affidavit, and it described particularly the place of the search. On the fourth requirement, however, the warrant failed altogether. Indeed, petitioner concedes that "the warrant . . . was deficient in particularity because it provided no description of the type of evidence sought." Brief for Petitioner 10.

The fact that the *application* adequately described the "things to be seized" does not save the *warrant* from its facial invalidity. The Fourth Amendment by its terms requires particularity in the warrant, not in the supporting documents. See *Massachusetts v. Sheppard,* 468 U.S. 981, 988, n. 5, 82 L. Ed. 2d 737, 104 S. Ct. 3424 (1984) ("[A] warrant that failures to conform to the particularity requirement of the Fourth Amendment is unconstitutional"); see also *United States v. Stefonek,* 179 F. 3d 1030, 1033 (CA7 1999) ("The Fourth Amendment requires that the warrant particularly describe the things to be seized, not the papers presented to the judicial officer . . . asked to issue the warrant"). And for good reason: "The presence of a search warrant serves a high function," *McDonald v. United States,* 335 U.S. 451, 455, 93 L. Ed. 153, 69 S. Ct. 191 (1948), and that high function is not necessarily vindicated when some other document, somewhere, says something about the objects of the search, but the contents of that document are neither known to the person whose home is being searched nor available for her inspection. We do not say that the Fourth Amendment forbids a warrant from cross-referencing other documents. Indeed, most Courts of Appeals have held that a court may construe a warrant with reference to a supporting application or affidavit if the warrant uses appropriate words of incorporation, and if the supporting document accompanies the warrant. See, *e.g., United States v. McGrew,* 122 F. 3d 847, 849–850 (CA9 1997); *United States v. Williamson,* 1 F. 3d 1134, 1136, n. 1 (CA10 1993); *United States v. Blakeney,* 942 F.2d 1001, 1025–1026 (CA6 1991); *United States v. Maxwell,* 287 U.S. App. D.C. 234, 920 F.2d 1028, 1031 (CADC 1990); *United States v. Curry,* 911 F.2d 72, 76–77 (CA8 1990); *United States v. Roche,* 614 F.2d 6, 8 (CA1 1980). But in this case the warrant did not incorporate other documents by reference, nor did either the affidavit or the application (which had been placed under seal) accompany the warrant. Hence, we need not further explore the matter of incorporation.

Petitioner argues that even though the warrant was invalid, the search nevertheless was "reasonable" within the meaning of the Fourth Amendment. He notes that a Magistrate authorized the search on the basis of adequate evidence of probable cause, that petitioner orally described to respondents the items to be seized, and that the search did not exceed the limits intended by the Magistrate and described by petitioner. Thus, petitioner maintains, his search of respondents' ranch was functionally equivalent to a search authorized by a valid warrant.

We disagree. This warrant did not simply omit a few items from a list of 10 many to be seized, or misdescribe a few of several items. Nor did it make what fairly could be characterized as a mere technical mistake or typographical error. Rather, in the space set aside for a description of the items to be seized, the warrant stated that the items consisted of a "single dwelling residence . . . blue in color." In other words, the warrant did not describe the items to be seized *at all.* In this respect the warrant was so obviously deficient that we must regard the search as "warrantless" within the meaning of our case law. See *Leon,* 468 U.S., at 923, 82 L. Ed. 2d 677, 104 S. Ct. 3405; cf. *Maryland v. Garrison,* 480 U.S. 79, 85, 94 L. Ed. 2d 72, 107 S. Ct. 1013 (1987); *Steele v. United States,* 267 U.S. 498, 503–504, 69 L. Ed. 757, 45 S. Ct. 414 (1925).

"We are not dealing with formalities." *McDonald,* 335 U.S., at 445, 93 L. Ed. 153, 69 S. Ct. 191. Because "'the right of a man to retreat into his own home and there be free from unreasonable governmental intrusion'" stands "'[a]t the very core' of the Fourth Amendment," *Kyllo v. United States,* 533 U.S. 27, 31, 150 L. Ed. 2d 94, 121 S. Ct. 2038 (2001) (quoting *Silverman v. United States,* 365 U.S. 505, 511, 5 L. Ed. 2d 734, 81 S. Ct. 679 (1961)). Our cases have firmly established the "'basic principle of Fourth Amendment law' that searches and seizures inside a home without a warrant are presumptively unreasonable," *Payton v. New York,* 445 U.S. 573, 586, 63 L. Ed. 2d 639, 100 S. Ct. 1371 (1980) (footnote omitted). Thus, "absent exigent circumstances, a warrantless entry to search for weapons or contraband is unconstitutional even when a felony has been committed and there is probable cause to believe that incriminating evidence will be found within." *Id.,* 445 U.S. at 587–588, 63 L. Ed. 2d 639, 1010 S. Ct. 1371 (footnote omitted). See *Kyllo,* 533 U.S., at 29, 150 L. Ed. 2d 94, 121 S. Ct. 2038; *Illinois v. Rodriguez,* 497 U.S. 177, 181, 111 L. Ed. 2d 148, 110 S. Ct. 2793 (1990); *Chimel v. California,* 395 U.S. 752, 761–763, 23 L. Ed. 2d 685, 89 S. Ct. 2034 (1969); *McDonald,* 335 U.S., at 454, 93 L. Ed. 153, 69 S. Ct. 191; *Johnson v. United States,* 333 U.S. 10, 92 L. Ed. 436, 68 S. Ct. 367 (1948).

We have clearly stated that the presumptive rule against warrantless searches applies with equal force to searches whose only defect is a lack of particularity in the warrant. In *Sheppard,* for instance, the petitioner argued that even though the warrant was invalid for lack of particularity, "the search was constitutional because it was reasonable within the meaning of the Fourth Amendment." 468 U.S., at 988, n. 5, 82 L. Ed. 2d 737, 104 S. Ct. 3424. In squarely rejecting that position, we explained:

> "The uniformly applied rule is that a search conducted pursuant to a warrant that fails to conform to the particularity requirement of the Fourth Amendment is unconstitutional. *Stanford v. Texas,* 379 U.S. 476 [13 L. Ed. 2d 431, 85 S. Ct. 506] (1965); *United States v. Cardwell,* 680 F. 2d 75, 77–78 (CA9 1982); *United States v. Crozier,* 674 F.2d 1293, 1299 (CA9 1982); *United States v. Klein,* 565 F. 2d 183, 185 (CA1 1977); *United States v. Gardner,* 537 F.2d 861, 862 (CA6 1976); *United States v. Marti,* 421 F.2d 1263, 1268–1269 (CA2 1970). That rule is in keeping with the well-established principle that 'except in certain carefully defined classes of cases, a search of private property without proper consent is "unreasonable" unless it has been authorized by a valid search warrant.' *Camara v. Municipal Court,* 387 U.S. 523, 528–529 [18 L. Ed. 2d 930, 87 S. Ct. 1727] (1967). See *Steagald v. United States,* 451 U.S. 204, 211–212 [68 L. Ed. 2d 38, 101 S. Ct. 1642] (1981); *Jones v. United States,* 357 U.S. 493, 499 [2 L. Ed. 2d 1514, 78 S. Ct. 1253] (1958)." *Ibid.*

Petitioner asks us to hold that a search conducted pursuant to a warrant lacking particularity should be exempt from the presumption of unreasonableness if the goals served by the particularity requirements are otherwise satisfied. He maintains that the search in this case satisfied those goals—which he says are "to prevent general searches, to prevent the seizure of one thing under a warrant describing another, and to prevent warrants from being issued on vague or dubious information," Brief for Petitioner 16—because the scope of the search did not exceed the limits set forth in the application. But unless the particular items described in the affidavit are also set forth in the warrant itself (or at least incorporated by reference, and the affidavit present at the search), there can be no written assurance that the Magistrate actually found probable cause to search for, and to seize, every item mentioned in the affidavit. See *McDonald,* 355 U.S., at 455, 93 L. Ed. 153, 69 S. Ct. 191 ("Absent some grave emergency, the Fourth Amendment has interposed a magistrate between the citizen and the police. This was done . . . so that an objective mind might weigh the need to invade [the citizen's] privacy in order to enforce the law"). In this case, for example, it is at least theoretically possible that the Magistrate was satisfied that the search for weapons and explosives was justified by the showing in the affidavit, but not convinced that any evidentiary basis existed for rummaging through respondents' files and papers for receipts pertaining to the purchase or manufacture of such items. Cf. *Stanford v. Texas,* 379 U.S. 476, 485–486, 13 L. Ed. 2d 431, 85 S. Ct. 506 (1965). Or, conceivably, the Magistrate might have believed that some of the weapons mentioned in the affidavit could have been lawfully possessed and therefore should not be seized. See 26 USC § 5861 [26 USCS § 5861] (requiring registration, but not banning possession of, certain firearms). The mere fact that the Magistrate issued a warrant does not necessarily establish that he agreed that the scope of the search should be as broad as the affiant's request. Even though petitioner acted with restraint in conducting the search, "the inescapable fact is that this restraint was imposed by the agents themselves, not by a judicial officer." *Katz v. United States,* 389 U.S. 347, 356, 19 L. Ed. 2d 576, 88 S. Ct. 507 (1967).[4]

We have long held, moreover, that the purpose of the particularity requirement is not limited to the prevention of general searches. See *Garrison,* 480 U.S., at 84, 94 L. Ed. 2d 72, 107 S. Ct. 1013. A particular warrant also "assures the individual whose property is searched or seized of the lawful authority of the executing officer, his need to search, and the limits of his power to search." *United States v. Chadwick,* 433 U.S. 1, 9. 53 L. Ed. 2d 538, 97 S. Ct. 2476 (1977) (citing *Camara v. Municipal Court of City and County of San Francisco,* 387 U.S. 523, 532, 18 L. Ed. 2d 930, 87 S. Ct. 1727 (1967)), abrogated on other grounds, *California v. Acevedo,* 500 U.S. 565, 114 L. Ed. 2d 619, 111 S. Ct. 1982 (1991). See also *Illinois v. Gates,* 462 U.S. 213, 236, 76 L. Ed. 2d 527, 103 S. Ct. 2317 (1983) ("[P]ossession of a warrant by officers conducting an arrest or search greatly reduces the perception of unlawful or intrusive police conduct").[5]

Petitioner argues that even if the goals of the particularity requirement are broader than he acknowledges, those goals nevertheless were served because he orally described to respondents the items for which he was searching. Thus, he submits, respondents had all of the notice that a proper warrant would have accorded. But this case presents no occasion even to reach this argument, since respondents, as noted above, dispute petitioner's account. According to Mrs. Ramirez, petitioner stated only that he was looking for an "'explosive device in a box.'" 298 F.3d at 1026. Because this dispute is before us on petitioner's motion for summary judgment, App. to Pet. For Cert. 13a, "[t]he evidence of the nonmovant is to be believed, and all justifiable inferences are to be drawn in [her]favor," *Anderson v. Liberty Lobby, Inc.,* 477 U.S. 242, 255, 91 L. Ed. 2d 202, 106 S. Ct. 2505 (1986) (citation omitted). The posture of the case therefore obliges us to credit Mrs. Ramirez's account, and we find that petitioner's description of "'an explosive device in a box'" was little better than no guidance at all. See *Stefonek,* 179 F. 3d at 1032-1033 (holding that a search warrant for "'evidence of crime'" was "[s]o open-ended" in its description that it could "only be described as a general warrant").

It is incumbent on the officer executing a search warrant to ensure the search is lawfully authorized and lawfully conducted.[6] Because petitioner did not have in his possession a warrant particularly describing the things he intended to seize, proceeding with the search was clearly "unreasonable" under the Fourth Amendment. The Court of Appeals correctly held the search was unconstitutional. *15*

III

Having concluded that a constitutional violation occurred, we turn to the question whether petitioner is entitled to qualified immunity despite that violation. See *Wilson v. Layne,* 526 U.S. 603, 609, 143 L Ed. 2d 818, 119 S. Ct. 1692 (1999). The answer depends on whether the right that was transgressed was "'clearly established'"—that is, "whether it would be clear to a reasonable officer that his conduct was unlawful in the situation he confronted." *Saucier v. Katz,* 533 U.S. 194, 202, 150 L. Ed. 2d 272, 121 S. Ct. 2151 (2001).

Given that the particularity requirement is set forth in the text of the Constitution, no reasonable officer could believe that a warrant that plainly did not comply with that requirement was valid. See *Harlow v. Fitzgerald,* 457 U.S. 800, 818–819, 73 L. Ed. 2d 396, 102 S. Ct. 2727 (1982) ("If the law was clearly established, the immunity defense ordinarily should fail, since a reasonably competent public official should know the law governing his conduct"). Moreover, because petitioner himself prepared the invalid warrant, he may not argue that he reasonably relied on the Magistrate's assurance that the warrant contained an adequate description of the things to be seized and was therefore valid. Cf. *Sheppard,* 468 U.S., at 989–990, 82 L. Ed. 2d 737, 104 S. Ct. 3424. In fact, the guidelines of petitioner's own department placed him on notice that he might be liable for executing a manifestly invalid warrant. An ATF° directive in force at the time of this search warned: "Special agents are liable if they exceed their authority while executing a search warrant and must be sure that a search warrant is sufficient on its face even when issued

---

°*ATF:* Bureau of Alcohol, Tobacco, Firearms, and Explosives—a branch of the federal government.

by a magistrate." Searches and Examinations, ATF Order O 3220.1(7)(d) (Feb. 13, 1997). See also *id.,* at 3220.1(23)(b) ("If any error or deficiency is discovered and there is a reasonable probability that it will invalidate the warrant, such warrant shall not be executed. The search shall be postponed until a satisfactory warrant has been obtained").[7] And even a cursory reading of the warrant in this case—perhaps just a simple glance—would have revealed a glaring deficiency that any reasonable police officer would have known was constitutionally fatal.

No reasonable officer could claim to be unaware of the basic rule, well established by our cases, that, absent consent or exigency, a warrantless search of the home is presumptively unconstitutional. See *Payton,* 445 U.S., at 586–588, 63 L. Ed. 2d 639, 100 S. Ct. 1371. Indeed, as we noted nearly 20 years ago in *Sheppard:* "The uniformly applied rule is that a search conducted pursuant to a warrant that fails to conform to the particularity requirement of the Fourth Amendment is unconstitutional." 468 U.S., at 988, n. 5, 82 L. Ed. 2d 737, 104 S. Ct. 3424.[8] Because not a word in any of our cases would suggest to a reasonable officer that this case fits within any exception to that fundamental tenet, petitioner is asking us, in effect, to craft a new exception. Absent any support for such an exception in our cases, he cannot reasonably have relied on an expectation that we would do so.

Petitioner contends that the search in this case was the product, at worst, of a lack of due care, and that our case law requires more than negligent behavior before depriving an official of qualified immunity. See *Malley v. Briggs,* 475 U.S. 335, 341, 89 L. Ed. 2d 271, 106 S. Ct. 1092 (1986). But as we observed in the companion case to *Sheppard,* "a warrant may be so facially deficient—*i.e.,* in failing to particularize the place to be searched or the things to be seized—that the executing officers cannot reasonably presume it to be valid." *Leon,* 468 U.S., at 923, 82 L. Ed. 2d 677, 104 S. Ct. 3405. This is such a case.[9] . . .

Accordingly, the judgment of the Court of Appeals is affirmed.   20

QUESTIONS FOR DISCUSSION

1. In his opening paragraph, Stevens establishes that his ruling will address two issues. How are these issues related, and why does he organize his work to address the first issue before the second?
2. What was wrong with the warrant presented by law enforcement officials at the Ramirez home before they began to search it? Why does Stevens conclude that there is no reason to excuse the error in the warrant?
3. Why did a lower court support the law enforcement officers in question? Why did this case reach the Supreme Court?
4. Is it significant that no charges were filed against the Ramirezes? Would they be entitled to constitutional protection even if charges had been filed against them?
5. When Stevens uses the first-person plural ("we"), as he does at the beginning of paragraph 10, how inclusive is that pronoun?

6. In paragraph 16, Stevens reveals that law enforcement officers searched through files and papers while in the Ramirez home. If officers came to search your house for weapons, would you expect them to search through your paper or electronic files?
7. Where does Stevens quote the Fourth Amendment, and why is it useful to have the words of this text within his ruling?
8. Why did Stevens conclude that the officer who served the invalid warrant is not entitled to legal immunity?
9. Writing a ruling that would be studied closely by attorneys and judges, Stevens cites numerous legal cases throughout his decision. In doing so, he is following a necessary convention for the kind of writing he has undertaken. But how do these references affect you as a reader?

SUGGESTIONS FOR WRITING

1. Write an essay in which you explain the meaning of the Fourth Amendment to an audience of intelligent adults who are unfamiliar with the Constitution. Analyze the amendment word by word.
2. Choose another of the first ten amendments to the Constitution, and analyze what it means, doing research if necessary.
3. Locate one of the previous cases cited by Stevens, and analyze the meaning of that text.

▌ LINKS

■ Within the Book

The analysis offered by Stevens in this decision is disputed by Justice Clarence Thomas in his dissenting opinion (pages 434–441).

■ Elsewhere in Print

Greenholgh, William W. *A Chronological Survey of Supreme Court Decisions.* Washington, DC: American Bar Assn., 2002.

Hall, Kermit. *The Oxford Guide to United States Supreme Court Decisions.* New York: Oxford UP, 2001.

Irons, Peter. *A People's History of the Supreme Court.* New York: Penguin, 2000.

Manaster, Kenneth A. *Illinois Justice: The Scandal of 1969 and the Rise of John Paul Stevens.* Chicago: U of Chicago P, 2001.

Sickels, Robert Judd. *John Paul Stevens and the Court: The Search for Balance.* State College: Penn State UP, 1988.

■ Online

www.mhhe.com/motives

Click on "More Resources" then "Writing to Analyze Texts."

■ ■ ■

■ ■ ■

GROH V. RAMIREZ: A DISSENTING OPINION

Clarence Thomas

A Republican and one of the youngest members of the Supreme Court, Clarence Thomas attended Yale University, before focusing on tax law as a corporate lawyer and as an aide to Senator John Danforth of Missouri. It was through Danforth that Thomas came to the attention of President Ronald Reagan, who appointed him to head the Equal Employment Opportunity Commission. In this post, Thomas worked to reverse earlier efforts to enforce civil rights in the workplace, and he had no judicial experience when President George H. Bush nominated him to the Supreme Court in 1991. The nomination was controversial because of Thomas's relative lack of experience and the fact that he was being nominated to replace Justice Thurgood Marshall—one of the most distinguished members of the Court and the first African American to serve on it. In the midst of this controversy, an attorney named Anita Hill came forward with claims that Thomas had sexually harassed her when she was under his supervision. From October 10 to 13, 1991, Americans watched Hill submit to hostile questioning during the nationally televised hearings. The nomination was eventually confirmed by a 52–48 Senate vote, and Thomas joined the Court on October 23 of that year.

Since joining the Court, Thomas has emerged as one of its two most conservative members, often siding with Justice Antonin Scalia. Because he rarely speaks during Court hearings, his written opinions have become the best way for determining his legal reasoning. In filing a dissenting opinion in Groh v. Ramirez, *he was following a standard practice of the Court. Justices who disagree with the majority ruling frequently file opinions that explain their votes, and these dissents become grounds upon which subsequent arguments can be built.*

The Fourth Amendment provides: "The right of the people to be secure in their persons, houses, papers, and effects, against unreasonable searches and seizures, shall not be violated, and no Warrants shall issue, but upon probable cause, supported by Oath or affirmation, and particularly describing the place to be searched, and the persons or things to be seized." The precise relationship between the Amendment's Warrant Clause and Unreasonable Clause is unclear. But neither Clause explicitly requires a warrant. While "it is of course textually possible to consider [a warrant requirement] implicit within the requirement of reasonableness," *California v. Acevedo,* 500 U.S. 565, 582, 114 L. Ed. 2d 619, 111 S. Ct. 1982 (1991) (Scalia, J., concurring in judgment), the text of the Fourth Amendment certainly does not mandate this result. Nor does the Amendment's history, which is clear as to the Amendment's principal target (general warrants), but not as clear with respect to when warrants were required, if ever. Indeed, because of the very different nature and scope of federal authority and ability to conduct searches and arrests at the founding, it is possible that neither the history of the Fourth Amendment nor the common law provides much guidance.

As a result, the Court has vacillated between imposing a categorical warrant requirement and applying a general reasonableness standard. Compare *Thompson v. Louisiana,* 469 U.S. 17, 20, 83 L. Ed. 2d 246, 105 S. C. 409 (1984) *(per curiam),* with *United States v. Rabinowitz,* 339 U.S. 56, 65, 94 L. Ed. 653, 70 S. Ct. 430 (1950). The Court has most frequently held that warrantless searches are presumptively unreasonable, see, *e.g., Katz v. United States,* 389 U.S. 347, 357, 19 L. Ed. 2d 576, 88 S. Ct. 507 (1967); *Payton v. New York,* 445 U.S. 573, 583, 63 L. Ed. 2d 639, 100 S. Ct. 1371 (1980), but has also found a plethora of exceptions to presumptive unreasonableness, see, *e.g., Chimel v. California,* 395 U.S. 752, 762–763, 23 L. Ed. 2d 685, 89 S. Ct. 2034 (1969) (searches incident to arrest); *United States v. Ross,* 456 U.S. 798, 800, 72 L. Ed. 2d 572, 102 S. Ct. 2157 (1982) (automobile searches); *United States v. Biswell,* 406 U.S. 311, 315–317, 32 L. Ed. 2d 87, 92 S. Ct. 1593 (1972) (searches of "pervasively regulated" businesses); *Camara v. Municipal Court of City and County of San Francisco,* 387 U.S. 523, 534–539, 18 L. Ed. 2d 930, 87 S. Ct. 1727 (1967) (administrative searches); *Warden, Md. Penitentiary v. Hayden,* 387 U.S. 294, 298, 18 L. Ed. 2d 782, 87 S. Ct. 1642 (1967) (exigent circumstances); *California v. Carney,* 471 U.S. 386, 390–394, 85 L. Ed. 2d 406, 105 S. Ct. 2066 (1985) (mobile home searches); *Illinois v. Lafayette,* 462 U.S. 640, 648, 77 L. Ed. 2d 65, 103 S. Ct. 2605 (1983) (inventory searches); *Almeida-Sanchez v. United States,* 413 U.S. 266, 272, 37 L. Ed. 2d 596, 93 S. Ct. 2535 (1973) (border searches). That is, our cases stand for the illuminating proposition that warrantless searches are *per se* unreasonable, except, of course, when they are not.

Today the Court holds that the warrant in this case was "so obviously deficient" that the ensuing search must be regarded as a warrantless search and thus presumptively unreasonable. . . . However, the text of the Fourth Amendment, its history, and the sheer number of exceptions to the Court's categorical warrant requirement seriously undermine the bases upon which the Court today rests its holding. Instead of adding to this confusing jurisprudence, as the Court has done, I would turn to first principles in order to determine the relationship between the Warrant Clause and the Unreasonableness Clause. But even within the Court's current framework, a search conducted pursuant to a defective warrant is constitutionally different from a "warrantless search." Consequently, despite the defective warrant, I would still ask whether this search was unreasonable and would conclude that it was not. Furthermore, even if the Court were correct that this search violated the Constitution (and in particular, respondents' Fourth Amendment rights), given the confused state of our Fourth Amendment jurisprudence and the reasonableness of petitioner's actions, I cannot agree with the Court's conclusion that petitioner is not entitled to qualified immunity. For these reasons, I respectfully dissent.

I

"[A]ny Fourth Amendment case may present two separate questions: whether the search was conducted pursuant to a warrant issued in accordance with the second Clause, and, if not, whether it was nevertheless 'reasonable' within the meaning of the first." *United States v. Leon,* 468 U.S. 897,961, 82 L. Ed. 2d 677, 104 S. Ct. 3405 (1984) (Stevens J., dissenting). By categorizing the search here to be a "warrantless" one, the Court declines to perform a reasonableness inquiry and ignores the fact that this search is quite different from searches that the Court has considered to be "warrantless" in the past. Our cases involving "warrantless" searches do not generally involve situations in which an officer has obtained a warrant that is later determined to be facially defective, but rather involve situations in which the officers neither sought nor obtained a warrant. See, *e.g., Anderson v. Creighton,* 483 U.S.635, 97 L. Ed. 2d 523, 107 S. Ct. 3034 (1987) (officer entitled to qualified immunity despite conducting a warrantless search of respondents' home in the mistaken belief that a robbery suspect was hiding there); *Payton v. New York, supra,* (striking down a New York statute authorizing the warrantless entry into a private residence to make a routine felony arrest). By simply treating this case as if no warrant had even been sought or issued, the Court glosses over what should be the key inquiry: whether it is always appropriate to treat a search made pursuant to a warrant that fails to describe particularly the things to be seized as presumptively unreasonable.

The court bases its holding that a defect in the particularity of the warrant by itself renders a search "warrantless" on a citation of a single footnote in *Massachusetts v. Sheppard,* 468 U.S. 981, 82 L. Ed. 2d 737, 104 S. Ct. 3424 (1984). In *Sheppard,* the Court, after noting that "the sole issue . . . in th[e] case is whether the officers reasonably believed that the search they conducted was authorized by a valid warrant," *id.,* 468 U.S. at 988, 82 L. Ed. 2d 737, 104 S. Ct. 3424, rejected the petitioner's argument that despite the invalid warrant, the otherwise reasonable search was constitutional, *id.,* 468 U.S. at 988, n. 5, 82 L. Ed. 2d 737, 104 S. Ct. 3424. The Court recognized that under its case law a reasonableness inquiry would be appropriate if one of the exceptions to the warrant requirement applied. But the Court declined to consider whether such an exception applied and whether the search actually violated the Fourth Amendment because that question presented merely a "fact-bound issue of little importance." *Ibid.* Because the Court in *Sheppard* did not conduct any sort of inquiry into whether a Fourth Amendment violation actually occurred, it is clear that the Court assumed a violation for the purposes of its analysis. Rather than rely on dicta buried in a footnote in *Sheppard,* the Court should actually analyze the arguably dispositive issue in this case.

The Court also rejects the argument that the details of the warrant application and affidavit save the warrant, because "'[t]he presence of a search warrant serves a high function.'" . . . (quoting *McDonald v. United States,* 335 U.S.

451, 445, 93 L. Ed. 153, 69 S. Ct. 191 (1948)). But it is not only the physical existence of the warrant and its typewritten contents that serve this high function. The Warrant Clause's principal protection lies in the fact that the "Fourth Amendment has interposed a magistrate between the citizen and the police . . . so that an objective mind might weigh the need to invade [the searchee's] privacy in order to enforce the law." *Ibid.* The Court has further explained,

> "The point of the Fourth Amendment . . . is not that it denies law
> enforcement the support of the usual inferences which reasonable men
> draw from evidence. Its protection consists in requiring that those
> inferences be drawn by a neutral and detached magistrate instead of
> being judged by the officer engaged in the often competitive enter-
> prise of ferreting out crime. Any assumption that evidence sufficient
> to support a magistrate's disinterested determination to issue a search
> warrant will justify the officers in making a search without a warrant
> would reduce the Amendment to a nullity and leave the people's
> homes secure only in the discretion of police officers. . . . When the
> right of privacy must reasonably yield to the right of search is, as a
> rule, to be decided by a judicial officer, not by a policeman or govern-
> ment enforcement agent." *Johnson v. United States,* 333 U.S. 10, 13–14,
> 92 L. Ed. 436, 68 S. Ct. 367 (1948) (footnotes omitted).

But the actual contents of the warrant are simply manifestations of this protection. Hence, in contrast to the case of a truly warrantless search, a warrant (due to a mistake) does not specify on its face the particular items to be seized but the warrant application passed on by the magistrate judge contains such details, a searchee still has the benefit of a determination by a neutral magistrate that there is a probable cause to search a particular place and to seize particular items. In such a circumstance, the principal justification for applying a rule of presumptive unreasonableness falls away.

In the instant case, the items to be seized were clearly specified in the warrant application and set forth in the affidavit, both of which were given to the Judge (Magistrate). The Magistrate reviewed all of the documents and signed the warrant application and made no adjustment or correction to this application. It is clear that respondents here received the protection of the Warrant Clause, as described in *Johnson* and *McDonald.* Under these circumstances, I would not hold any ensuing search constitutes a presumptively unreasonable warrantless search. Instead, I would determine whether, despite the invalid warrant, the resulting search was reasonable and hence constitutional.

II

Because the search was not unreasonable, I would conclude that it was constitutional. Prior to execution of the warrant, petitioner briefed the search team and provided a copy of the search warrant application, the supporting affidavit, and the warrant for the officers to review. Petitioner orally reviewed the terms of the warrant with the officers, including the specific terms for which the officers were authorized to search. Petitioner and his search team then conducted the search entirely within the scope of the warrant application and warrant; that is, within the scope of what the Magistrate had authorized. Finding no illegal weapons or explosives, the search team seized nothing. *Ramirez v. Butte-Silver Bow County,* 298 F.3d 1022, 1025 (CA9 2002). When petitioner left, he gave respondents a copy of the search warrant. Upon request the next day, petitioner faxed respondent a copy of the more detailed warrant application. Indeed, putting aside the technical defect in the warrant, it is hard to imagine how the actual search could have been carried out any more reasonably.

The court argues that this eminently reasonable search is nonetheless unreasonable because "there can be no written assurance that the Magistrate actually found probable cause to search for, and to seize, every item mentioned in the affidavit" "unless the particular items described in the affidavit are also set forth in the warrant itself." [. . .] The Court argues that it was at least possible that the Magistrate intended to authorize a much more limited search than the one petitioner requested. *Ibid.* As a theoretical matter, this may be true. But the more reasonable inference is that the Magistrate intended to authorize everything in the warrant application, as he signed the application and did not make any written adjustments to the application or the warrant itself.

The Court also attempts to bolster its focus on the faulty warrant by arguing that the purpose of the particularity requirement is not only to prevent general searches, but also to assure the searchee of the lawful authority for the search. . . . But as the Court recognizes, neither the Fourth Amendment nor Federal Rule of Criminal Procedure 41 requires an officer to serve the warrant on the searchee before the search. . . . Thus, a search should not be considered *per se* unreasonable for failing to apprise the searchee of the lawful authority prior to the search, especially where, as here, the officer promptly provides the requisite information when the defect in the papers is detected. Additionally, unless the Court adopts the Court of Appeals' view that the Constitution protects a searchee's ability to "be on the lookout and to challenge the officers," while the officers are actually carrying out the search, 298 F.3d at 1027, petitioner's provision of the requisite information the following day is sufficient to satisfy this interest.

III

Even assuming a constitutional violation, I would find that petitioner is entitled to qualified immunity. The qualified immunity inquiry rests on "the 'objective legal reasonableness' of the action, *Harlow [v. Fitzgerald,* 457 U.S. 800, 819, 73 L. Ed. 2d 396, 102 S. Ct. 2727 (1982)], assessed in light of the legal rules that were 'clearly established' at the time it was taken." *Anderson v. Creighton,* 483 U.S., at 639, 97 L. Ed. 2d 523, 107 S. Ct. 3034. The outcome of this inquiry "depends substantially upon the level of generality at which the relevant 'legal rule' is . . . identified. For example, the right to due process of law is quite clearly established by the Due Process Clause, and thus there is a sense in which any action that violates that Clause . . . violates a clearly established right." *Ibid*. To apply the standard at such a high level of generality would allow plaintiffs "to convert the rule of qualified immunity . . . into a rule of virtually unqualified liability simply by alleging violation of extremely abstract rights." *Ibid*. The Court in *Anderson* criticized the Court of Appeals for considering the qualified immunity question only in terms of the petitioner's "right to be free from warrantless searches of one's home unless the searching officers have probable cause and there are exigent circumstances." *Id.*, 483 U.S. at 640, 97 L. Ed. 2d 523, 107 S. Ct. 3034. The Court of Appeals should have instead considered "the objective (albeit fact-specific) question whether a reasonable officer could have believed Anderson's warrantless search to be lawful, in light of clearly established law and the information the searching officers possessed." *Id.*, 483 U.S. at 641, 97 L. Ed. 2d 523, 107 S. Ct. 3034.

The Court errs not only by defining the question at too high a level of generality but also by assessing the question without regard to the relevant circumstances. Even if it were true that no reasonable officer could believe that a search of a home pursuant to a warrant that fails the particularity requirement is lawful absent exigent circumstances—a proposition apparently established by dicta buried in a footnote in *Sheppard*—petitioner did not know when he carried out the search that the search warrant was invalid—let alone legally nonexistent. Petitioner's entitlement to qualified immunity, then, turns on whether his belief that the search warrant was valid was objectively reasonable. Petitioner's belief surely was reasonable.

The Court has stated that "depending on the circumstances of the particular case, a warrant may be so facially deficient . . . that the executing officers cannot reasonably presume it to be valid." *United States v. Leon,* 468 U.S., at 923, 82 L. Ed. 2d 677, 104 S Ct. 3405. This language makes clear that this exception to *Leon*'s good-faith exception does not apply in every circumstance. And the Court does not explain why it should apply here. As an initial matter, the Court does not even argue that the fact that petitioner made a mistake in preparing the warrant was objectively unreasonable, nor could it. Given the sheer number of warrants prepared and executed by officers each year, combined with the fact that these same officers also prepare detailed and sometimes somewhat comprehensive documents supporting the warrant applications, it is inevitable that officers acting reasonably and entirely in good faith will occasionally make such errors.

The only remaining question is whether petitioner's failure to notice the defect was objectively unreasonable. The Court today points to no cases directing an officer to proofread a warrant after it has been passed on by a neutral magistrate, where the officer is already fully aware of the scope of the intended search and the magistrate gives no reason to believe that he has authorized anything other than the requested search. Nor does the Court point to any case suggesting that where the same officer both prepares and executes the invalid warrant, he can never rely on the magistrate's assurance that the warrant is proper. Indeed, in *Massachusetts v. Sheppard,* 468 U.S. 981, 82 L. Ed. 2d 737, 104 S. Ct. 3424 (1984), the Court suggested that although an officer who is not involved in the warrant application process would normally read the issued warrant to determine the object of the search, an executing officer who is also the affiant might not need to do so. *Id.,* 468 U.S. at 989, n. 6, 82 L. Ed. 2d 737, 104 S. Ct. 3424.

Although the Court contends that it does not impose a proofreading re-   15 quirement upon officers executing warrants . . . , I see no other way to read its decision, particularly where, as here, petitioner could have done nothing more to ensure the reasonableness of his actions than to proofread the warrant. After receiving several allegations that respondents possessed illegal firearms and explosives, petitioner prepared an application for a warrant to search respondents' ranch, along with a supporting affidavit detailing the history of allegations that respondents, petitioner's investigation into these allegations, and petitioner's verification of the sources of the allegations. Petitioner properly filled out the warrant application, which described both the place to be searched and the things to be seized, and obtained the Magistrate's signature on both the warrant application and the warrant itself. Prior to execution of the warrant, petitioner briefed the search team to ensure that each officer understood the limits of the search. Petitioner and his search team then executed the warrant within those limits. And when the error in the search warrant was discovered, petitioner promptly faxed the missing information to respondents. In my view, petitioner's actions were objectively reasonable, and thus should be entitled to qualified immunity.

For the foregoing reasons, I respectfully dissent.

QUESTIONS FOR DISCUSSION

1. What does Thomas achieve by opening his dissent by quoting the Fourth Amendment?
2. Consider the use of "vacillated" at the beginning of paragraph 2. What does it imply about the Court? How would you characterize the tone of the last sentence in this paragraph?
3. Thomas says the Court "glosses over what should be the key inquiry." Do you agree?
4. How useful is the block quotation included in paragraph 6?
5. On what grounds does Thomas believe that the search in *Groh v. Ramirez* was "not unreasonable"?
6. Consider the argument made by Thomas in paragraph 13 that officers are bound to make mistakes because of "the sheer number of warrants prepared and executed each year." Do you think the volume with which an activity is undertaken justifies making mistakes within that activity?
7. Thomas claims that the Court has imposed a "proofreading requirement" about law enforcement officers. What does "proofreading" mean to you? Do you agree or disagree with Thomas on this point?

SUGGESTIONS FOR WRITING

1. Write an essay in which you define the difference between "reasonable" and "unreasonable" behavior in terms of law enforcement.
2. Research and analyze another dissenting opinion by Clarence Thomas.
3. Obtain the transcript of Anita Hill's testimony during the confirmation hearings for Thomas, and then write an analysis focused on how she was addressed by the senators who questioned her.

LINKS

■ Within the Book

The majority decision by the Court, from which Thomas is dissenting, appears on pages 434–441.

■ Elsewhere in Print

Carter, Scott Douglas. *First Principles: The Jurisprudence of Clarence Thomas.* New York: New York UP, 2002.

Foskett, Ken. *Judging Thomas: The Life and Times of Clarence Thomas.* New York: Morrow, 2004.

Hill, Anita. *Speaking Truth to Power.* New York: Anchor, 1998.

Leone, Richard C., and Greg Anig, Jr. *The War on Freedom: Civil Liberties in the Age of Terrorism.* New York: PublicAffairs, 2003.

Morrison, Toni, ed. *Race-ing Justice, En-Gendering Power: Essays on Anita Hill, Clarence Thomas and the Construction of Social Reality.* New York: Pantheon, 1992.

Smitherman, Geneva. *African American Women Speak Out on Anita Hill and Clarence Thomas.* Detroit: Wayne State UP, 1995.

■ Online

www.mhhe.com/motives

Click on "More Resources" then "Writing to Analyze Texts."

■ ■ ■

7

Writing to Persuade Others

Persuasion ranges from advertising to scholarly arguments. Between these extremes lie dozens of situations in which persuasion is fundamental to everyday life. When you apply for a job, propose marriage, try to borrow money, or ask your landlord to fix the plumbing, you are using persuasion in an attempt to get someone to do something you want for yourself. Other times you use persuasion to achieve benefits for others—as when trying to raise money for the victims of a famine or trying to persuade the government to protect an endangered species. And on occasion you use persuasion when there is no question of benefits but there is a problem that needs to be resolved— as in trying to improve the functioning of a committee on which you serve when it cannot accomplish anything because of personal conflicts. What all of these examples have in common is that they assume as a given the need to change someone's mind. We need to persuade others only when differences of opinion exist. Persuasion is unnecessary when there is already consensus, and it is inappropriate when questions allow for only one correct answer.

Classical rhetoric recognized that persuasion was accomplished through three means: the credibility of the writer/speaker (*ethos*), the logic of the argument (*logos*), and the skill with which appropriate feelings are inspired (*pathos*). This threefold approach to persuasion has prevailed in the West for almost two thousand years, but its practitioners vary in what strategies they emphasize. Aristotle, for example, believed that ethos is the most important aspect of persuasion and that we make ourselves believable by how we present ourselves in what we say and write. But Aristotle defined ethos as something created within the work (from which it would follow that a bad person could seem to be credible because of his skill in arguing). Other rhetoricians have argued that ethos cannot be created artificially and that only good people (or people who are actively trying to be good) can write truly persuasive arguments. Still others have emphasized the role of pathos. Cicero, one of the greatest speakers of the ancient world, argued that nothing is more important than being able to move an audience: "For men decide far more problems by hate, or love, or lust, or rage, or sorrow, or joy, or hope, or fear, or illusion, or some other inward emotion, than by reality, or authority, or any legal standard, or judicial precedent, or statute."

In short, there has been—and there still is—no universal agreement about how to persuade others. Different opinions prevailed in the classical world, and the debate is still going on. But you can be guided by two basic principles:

- Your strategy may vary depending on the topic and your audience, but you should always consider the extent to which you have employed ethos, logos, and pathos. As a general rule, an argument depending on only one of these methods probably won't be as persuasive as an argument using more than one.

- Although people sometimes make decisions on impulse, and some forms of persuasion (like television commercials) are designed to inspire unreasoned decisions, the most persuasive arguments are those that still make sense after you have thought about them for a while. It follows that persuasion should appeal to the mind as well as the heart.

USING LOGIC

Appealing to the mind requires at least some familiarity with *logic*. Classical rhetoric teaches two types of logic: inductive and deductive reasoning. Modern rhetoric has explored alternative forms of logic such as substantive reasoning designed to complement traditional approaches. Whatever type of logic you decide best suits your needs in a specific argument, you should realize that writers are usually free to use one or more of the following options.

Inductive Reasoning

To *reason inductively* means to use examples to discover what seems to be true. In an inductive argument, a writer presents a series of examples (or pieces of evidence) and draws a conclusion from their significance. Reaching this conclusion means going beyond the accumulated evidence and making a reasonable guess, the *inductive leap*. Induction is persuasive when the evidence is sufficient to justify the conclusion. Writers who make an inductive leap based on insufficient evidence are said to be jumping to conclusions, a failure in reasoning so common that it has become a cliché.

When you use induction carefully, you reach a conclusion that is probably true. But you should recognize that your conclusion is probable rather than absolute. It is always possible that other evidence, which you haven't considered, could point to a different conclusion. For example, suppose it is the first week of classes and you are taking a math course from a professor with whom you have never worked before. For each of the first three classes, the professor arrives late and lectures in a disorganized manner that is difficult to understand. Tomorrow is the last day you can drop the class and add a new one in its place. Concluding that you are dealing with a bad math teacher, you decide to drop his course and substitute another. Within the constraints of daily life, which often require us to make decisions quickly, you have used induction to make a decision that seems reasonable under the circumstances. However, it is possible that the professor had a bad week because he was staying up all night with a sick child and that his performance will improve dramatically in the following weeks.

As a rule, your conclusions will be the strongest when they rest on a foundation built of many separate pieces of evidence. When a serious conclusion is arrived at inductively, it will almost certainly have extensive information behind it. The scientific method illustrates induction at its best. Researchers conduct hundreds and sometimes thousands of experiments before arguing for a new type of medical treatment, and after results are published, other researchers seek to verify them independently. But however solid these conclusions seem to be, they are often challenged by new studies that take a different approach. So, no matter how many examples support an inductively derived conclusion, you can never be certain that you have managed to discover an absolute truth.

Deductive Reasoning

To *reason deductively* means to identify assumptions that are already believed to be true and to discover an additional truth that follows from these widely accepted beliefs. A deductive argument reflects the logic of a *syllogism* in which a major and a minor premise lead to a conclusion that is necessarily true:

Major premise:	All men have hearts.
Minor premise:	Bill is a man.
Conclusion:	Bill has a heart.

In this case, the reasoning is both valid and true. It is *valid* because it follows the conventions of logic: If we accept the major and minor premises, then we must recognize that the conclusion follows logically from them. Occasionally, however, you will find syllogisms that are valid but untrue.

Major premise:	All chemistry professors are boring.
Minor premise:	Veronica is a chemistry professor.
Conclusion:	Veronica is boring.

Although this syllogism follows the same pattern as the previous one and is valid, it is untrue because it rests on a highly questionable major premise. For a syllogism to be *true* as well as valid, both the major and minor premises must be universally accepted.

Unfortunately, there are relatively few propositions that everyone accepts as true—or "self-evident," as Thomas Jefferson declares at the beginning of the Declaration of Independence. And the number seems to be decreasing. Consider what happens if we modify our first example:

Major premise: All men have functioning kidneys.
Minor premise: Bill is a man.
Conclusion: Bill has functioning kidneys.

A hundred years ago, this syllogism would have been both valid and true; today, it is valid but untrue, since dialysis machines allow people to live without functioning kidneys. Conceivably, the day may come when people can function without hearts. (We have already seen several attempts to support life with artificial hearts.)

Consider, also, that different readers have different responses to language and that the same reader can respond differently to the same words in different contexts. To put it simply, words can (and do) change meaning. The major premise of our first example ("All men have hearts") is already more questionable than it would have been fifty years ago. A writer beginning with this statement could face such questions as "What do you mean by *men*? Does that include women?" and "What about *hearts*? Do you mean a body organ or a capacity for feeling emotion?"

But writing an essay is not the same as writing a syllogism: You have more than three sentences to make your case. If you want to organize an essay deductively because your position derives from a fundamental principle that you are confident your audience will share, you should pace yourself according to the needs of the situation. On some topics, for some audiences, you may need to spend several paragraphs establishing your premise. At other times, you may be able to take your premise for granted and offer what is called an *enthymeme*— a two-part deductive argument from which the major premise has been omitted. Abbreviating an argument in this way does not necessarily mean that it will be shorter; it simply means that you have omitted one step in order to emphasize other aspects of your case.

Substantive Reasoning

Over the years, philosophers have favored deductive reasoning because it seemed to be the type of logic most likely to lead to truth. But many writers find it ill-suited for argumentation, and philosophers increasingly acknowledge other forms of reasoning. After spending many years analyzing arguments in fields such as politics and law, Chaim Perelman concluded that formal logic is seldom appropriate, because argument is more concerned with gaining the adherence of an audience than with demonstrating the truth of abstract propositions:

What are we to think of this reduction to two forms of reasoning of all the wide variety of arguments that men use in their discussions and in pleading a cause or in justifying an action? Yet, since the time of Aristotle, logic has confined its study to deductive and inductive reasoning. . . . As a result, an argument that cannot be reduced to canonical form is regarded as logically valueless. (*The New Rhetoric and the Humanities* [Dordrecht: Reidel, 1979], p. 26)

Perelman showed that, when we actually examine arguments that we find persuasive, we realize that many of them seem reasonable even though they do not conform strictly to the conventions of induction or deduction.

At about the same time that Perelman was conducting his research in Belgium, the British philosopher Stephen Toulmin was reaching a conclusion similar to Perelman's. Analyzing arguments made within various fields, Toulmin discovered that they had certain features in common. This discovery led him to offer a new model of argument that is easy for writers to use. *Substantive logic* was the term he preferred for his system, a working logic suitable for the needs of the diverse range of arguments identified by Perelman and other theorists.

According to Toulmin, every argument includes a *claim*, which is the assertion or conclusion the argument is trying to prove. The claim is supported by *data*, which describe the various types of evidence (such as facts, personal experience, or appeals to authority) that lead an audience to decide that the claim is reasonable. Both the claim and the data are stated explicitly in the argument. Underlying them, however, and not necessarily made explicit (although they can be) are what Toulmin called *warrants*. He described warrants as "bridges [that] authorize the sort of step to which our argument commits us." Warrants may be directly stated, but very often (especially when they are obvious) they are not.

Here is one of the examples that Toulmin used to illustrate his model:

Claim: Harry is a British subject.
Data: Harry was born in Bermuda.
Warrant: A man born in Bermuda will be a British subject.

As you can see from this example, the claim is based directly on its data. The warrant is simply explanatory; its function is to show why the claim follows from the data. A good way to understand the warrant, especially when it has not been explicitly stated, is to imagine a statement beginning with either *since* or *because*. In the example just cited, the data support the claim, since people born in Bermuda are British subjects. If you were making this argument in Bermuda or in England, you could probably assume that your audience would understand the warrant even if you did not state it. On the other hand, if you were making this argument in Tibet, you would probably need to make sure that the warrant was clearly understood.

Behind any warrant is what Toulmin called *backing*. The backing, or grounds, for a warrant will vary from argument to argument and from field to field. In the Bermuda example, the backing consists of the specific pieces of legislation that determine British citizenship. Like the warrant, backing may be either explicit or implicit in an argument. But unlike the warrant, which is a generalization, backing consists of facts. If you use Toulmin's model for writing persuasive essays, you should always ask yourself if you could come up with backing for your warrant if someone were to question its legitimacy.

For writers, one of the advantages of Toulmin's model is that it does not require a fixed pattern of organization. You can arrange your ideas in whatever sequence seems best suited for your work, as long as you provide data for any claim you make and are able to explain why the data support the claim when the link between them is not immediately clear. Another advantage of Toulmin's model is that it easily incorporates *qualifiers,* such as *probably* or *unless,* that protect the overall integrity of your arguments from exceptions that could be used to challenge them. When arguing about Harry's citizenship, for example, you could point out that the data support the claim unless Harry's parents were aliens in Bermuda or unless he has become a naturalized citizen of another country.

The Toulmin model for reasoning provides a useful means of analyzing the arguments you write and read. However an argument is organized, and whatever rhetorical strategies are used within it, the work should include a clear assertion or proposition (the claim), evidence to support that claim (or data), and a principle or assumption that gives further support to the claim (the warrant). The warrant should be easy to identify even if it is not explicitly stated, and there should be additional support (or backing) that could be introduced if the warrant is challenged. Consider, for example, the argument in this chapter on racial profiling by Stuart Taylor, Jr. His claim is that "racial profiling involves real discrimination." He backs this claim with data from states such as New Jersey, Maryland, Florida, and Louisiana. Although he does not explicitly state his warrant, it can be inferred from the argument: American citizens of any race should enjoy equal protection under the law. Even if this warrant is not always honored, backing for it can be found in the U.S. Constitution, Supreme Court decisions, laws passed by Congress, and the laws of many states.

RECOGNIZING LOGICAL FALLACIES

Whatever type of reasoning you use, you should be alert for certain errors that can undermine your case. The detailed study of logic reveals many different ways arguments can break down. Dwelling on these *logical fallacies,* as they are called, can sometimes make writers feel that writing to persuade is more difficult than it really is. Nevertheless, having some familiarity with a few of the most common fallacies can help you evaluate the arguments you read and revise those you write.

Ad Hominem Argument

Latin for "to the man," *ad hominem* refers to an argument that involves a personal attack on someone whose view differs from that of the arguer. Writers who make *ad hominem* arguments undermine their credibility in at least two ways. First, to attack an opponent, rather than what an opponent has argued, is to ignore the real issues under consideration. Second, personal attacks appear to be mean-spirited and can alienate an impartial audience. For example, when a writer arguing for gun control attacks members of the National Rifle Association as "macho men who don't understand the definition of a civilized society," she is offending the people she most needs to persuade and probably is making unbiased readers sympathize with the opponents she has attacked.

In some situations, it can be legitimate to question the personal integrity of an opponent. In a political campaign, for example, voters might decide that a candidate who has cheated on his taxes cannot be trusted to govern, no matter how appealing his positions on various issues are. But even in politics, where personal attacks can sometimes be justified, people quickly tire of campaigns that seem to consist of nothing but *ad hominem* arguments. As a general rule, it is more honorable to focus argument on ideas than on personalities.

Appeal to False Authority

A good way to support an argument is to cite testimony from authorities in the field you are writing about. If you are writing about child care, for instance, you may wish to incorporate the views of a respected pediatrician. But knowledge in one field does not make someone expert in another. Citing the pediatrician in an argument about the space program is an appeal to a false authority. Advertising offers many examples of this fallacy by attempting to persuade us to buy products that have been endorsed by well-known actors or athletes who probably know no more about the product than we do.

But *appeals to false authority* also appear in written arguments—in part because well-known people sometimes enjoy making public statements on anything that happens to interest them. Quote a novelist on writing novels, and you will have appealed to a legitimate authority. Quote that same novelist on American foreign policy, and, unless the novelist happens to be an expert on international affairs as well, you will have appealed to a false authority.

Begging the Question

Writers *beg the question* when they begin an argument by assuming what they actually need to prove. At its most obvious, begging the question takes the form of a statement that leads nowhere because it goes around in a circle. Consider this argument: "College is too expensive because it costs more than it is worth." This statement simply makes the same assertion two ways. An argument could be written to show that college is too expensive, but it would need to be supported with evidence rather than repetition. Begging the question can also take more subtle forms, such as introducing a word (like *unfair*) that expresses an unsupported value judgment.

Hasty Generalization

This fallacy, sometimes called *jumping to conclusions,* occurs when writers draw conclusions based on insufficient evidence. Consider, for example, a personnel director who decides, "I don't think we should hire any other graduates of that school; we hired Randy, and he couldn't do anything right." To judge all the graduates of a school by one person is to jump to a conclusion. People often jump to conclusions in daily life, especially when decisions are influenced by feeling: "I know you two are going out together. I saw you talking after class today!"

Writers sometimes make hasty generalizations because they lack evidence or because they are anxious to complete an assignment. Rather than jumping to a conclusion your argument has not supported, you should either search for additional evidence or modify your claim in such a way that your evidence does support it.

Post Hoc, Ergo Propter Hoc

From the Latin for "after this, therefore because of this," *post hoc* arguments, as they are called for short, confuse cause with coincidence. Examples of *post hoc* reasoning are often found in discussions of large social questions: "Since MTV began broadcasting, the number of teenage pregnancies has risen sharply." This statement assumes that MTV is causing teenagers to get pregnant. Although the lyrics of rock music and the sensual imagery of rock videos may contribute to an atmosphere that encourages sexual activity, there are almost certainly many causes for the rise of teenage pregnancy during the same period that MTV happened to be broadcasting.

Superstitions can embody a type of *post hoc* reasoning: "I failed the quiz because I walked under a ladder yesterday." It is important to realize that every event is preceded by many unrelated events: The sun may come up shortly after the rooster crows, but that doesn't prove that the rooster is making the sun rise.

Slippery Slope

Although it is reasonable to consider the probable effects of any change that is being argued for, it is fallacious to base opposition to that change entirely on the prediction of some future result that is, at best, a guess. Writers who use *slippery slope arguments* are using what is almost always a type of fear tactic: "Give them an inch, and they'll take a mile." An argument like this shifts attention away from the issue at hand. Because the future is hard to predict, and one change does not necessarily lead to another, it is wiser to consider the immediate effects of what is being debated than to draw frightening pictures of what could happen someday.

ORGANIZING YOUR ESSAY

By using logical reasoning, you can determine the organization of your essay. When you use inductive reasoning, you could present several pieces of evidence and then draw a conclusion from them. In this chapter, Stuart Taylor, Jr., uses inductive reasoning when arguing for the collection of data on how race determines the frequency with which police stop motorists—a practice known as *racial profiling*. When you use deductive reasoning, you could begin by establishing a principle that you expect your readers to agree with and then show how this principle leads to a certain conclusion. This is the approach used by Thomas Jefferson in "The Declaration of Independence," an argument based on a principle, or premise, familiar to most Americans: "We hold these truths to be self-evident, that all men are created equal, that they are endowed by their Creator with certain unalienable rights, that among these rights are life, liberty, and the pursuit of happiness." And when using substantive reasoning, you can make your claim at the beginning or at the end of your essay, as long as you provide sufficient evidence to support it and establish a reasonable warrant. This kind of flexibility allows Adolph L. Reed, Jr., to include both his warrant and his claim in his opening paragraph.

But while your writing can benefit from an understanding of logic, you need not confine yourself to a single method of reasoning or follow the pattern of organization called for by that method. Many writers choose to combine inductive and deductive reasoning within a single essay, and we have already seen how substantive reasoning does not require a specific pattern of organization. Here, then, is additional advice for organizing a persuasive essay.

You may adapt a type of organization used in debates and sometimes called *presenting the stock issues*. This method calls for showing that there is a problem and then proposing a solution. In the first part of your essay, you would establish a need for change by demonstrating how the status quo is unacceptable. In the second part, you would propose a solution to the problem and demonstrate that your solution would work. Within the essays in this chapter, the clearest example of this approach is provided by Aaron Belkin and Melissa Embser-Herbert in their argument for including gays and lesbians in the U.S. military. They provide evidence that the current system is not working and then offer five recommendations that address the problem they have identified.

Unfortunately, writers do not always have solutions for problems; sometimes they can offer a useful service simply by persuading others that a problem exists. But when you have a specific proposal in mind, you can follow the time-honored pattern recommended by classical rhetoric:

- *Introduction:* Identify your issue and capture the attention of your audience by opening with a vivid example, dramatic anecdote, memorable quotation, or emotional appeal to common values.

- *Statement of background facts:* Report the information you think your audience needs to know to understand your position.

- *Exposition:* Interpret the information you have reported, and define key terms.

- *Proposition:* Introduce the specific proposal you want to advance.

- *Proof:* Provide evidence to support your thesis. These paragraphs will be the heart of your essay, for you cannot be persuasive unless you prove that your position is sound.

- *Refutation of opposing arguments:* Show why you are not convinced by the arguments of people who disagree with you.

- *Conclusion:* Summarize your key points, stimulate emotions appropriate for the context, and make your audience personally well disposed toward you.

However you choose to proceed, *refutation* is an important part of persuasive writing. Unfortunately, many writers are so firmly committed to their own positions that they fail to demonstrate that they have considered the views of others. Even if they are credible sources advancing sound positions, their ethos suffers because they seem one-sided. Your own writing will benefit if you respond thoughtfully to opposition, and you do not need to wait until the end of your essay to do so. When you are taking an unpopular position, you may need to respond to prevailing views before you can gain a fair hearing for your own. The standard arrangement associated with classical rhetoric can be modified in order to allow you to address prevailing views immediately. (See page 6.)

CONSIDERING AUDIENCE

When writing to persuade, writers usually begin with a clear idea of what they think. Unfortunately, some writers are content to write what they think without considering their audience or the purpose of argumentation. If you read the op-ed page of your local newspaper, you will probably find columns that focus exclusively on conveying a single point of view and using language that could alienate anyone who does not already share that point of view. The results may satisfy the writers, and it may also please readers who already share that position. But it is unlikely to be persuasive.

Persuasion involves changing the way people think about something and perhaps getting them to undertake an action they would not otherwise have. When you write a persuasive argument, you will probably begin by choosing as a topic something that you believe and want others to believe as well. The challenge then is to define for yourself what those "others" are like, to consider what concerns they are likely to have, and to treat these concerns with respect. Ask yourself, "Who is most likely to disagree with me?" Ask also,

"What kind of readers probably have not yet made up their minds on my topic?" These are the kinds of readers you should envision when writing to persuade. If you settle for writing for people who already think as you do, you may inspire them (see Chapter 8), but you will not persuade them: they are already on your side. Your goal, in writing persuasively, is to reconcile differences and bring others to your side.

One of the best ways to consider audience when preparing to write persuasively is to listen respectfully to diverse points of view and to read articles expressing opinions that you do not already hold. That may seem like common sense. But there is reason to believe that political passion frequently obscures common sense. Nowadays, too many people read or listen to only those commentators who reinforce their own political and social views—shutting out information that might require them to adjust their thinking. The Internet has contributed to this polarization as well, for it is possible to customize the way news is conveyed on a personal computer and to dwell exclusively in chat rooms or discussion groups with the like-minded.

Polarization occurs for another reason as well: In recent years, both television and radio broadcasts have broadcast an increasing number of "debates" that feature opinioned people talking *at* rather than *to* each other. If you watch a channel such as Fox News, you will find commentators ridiculing each other's opinions and relentlessly advancing predetermined views instead of honestly searching for common ground. Shows such as these have contributed to a decline in the quality of civic discourse. One of your goals when writing to persuade can be to raise the level of that discourse. Instead of ridiculing what others think, take their ideas seriously. An audience that has been treated respectfully is more likely to be persuaded to value what you think than an audience that has been treated scornfully.

When you have a predetermined audience—such as the students in your writing class—pay close attention to the interests and differences that surface in that audience. In this case, you should give extra consideration to your audience before choosing your topic. Ask yourself if there are any topics that would be problematic because audience members hold entrenched views— or would simply have difficulty paying attention because their own concerns are so different. Look at what you have in common with this audience. You may, for example, all be working in jobs that are less than fully satisfying, or you may all have had a bad experience with public education. Looking for similarities in background and experience can help you to find a good topic when you know your audience before you begin to write for it.

RESPONDING TO OPPOSITION

Because persuasion assumes the existence of an audience with views different from yours, it is essential to recognize these differences and respond to them fairly. One-sided arguments are almost never convincing. To be persuasive, writers must show that they have considered views that differ from their own. After anticipating the arguments most likely to be advanced by opponents, you can respond by either refuting these arguments or conceding that they have merit.

Of these two strategies, rhetoric has traditionally emphasized refutation. By introducing an opposition argument into your own essay, and then showing why that argument is faulty, you demonstrate good credibility or ethos. You also improve the logos of your case by resolving concerns that readers may have. Many writers find that the easiest way to introduce opposition arguments without obscuring their own position is to begin a paragraph with an argument offered by opponents and then devote the rest of the paragraph to providing a counterargument. By following this method, they get the chance to have the last word.

When you consider opposing arguments, you may find one (or more) that you cannot refute. Controversy usually exists because there is at least one good argument that can be made on different sides. If you want to be persuasive, you should be prepared to concede any point you cannot refute. By admitting that you see merit in one of the arguments made by your opponents, you show that you are fair-minded and make it easier for opponents to recognize merit in your own case. Saying "I am completely right, and you are completely wrong" is more likely to annoy people than persuade them. But when you say, in effect, "I admit that you have a good point there," you create a bridge over which people can cross to your side.

Martin Luther King's "Letter from Birmingham Jail" provides examples of both refutation and concession. King responds to specific charges that had been brought against him and demonstrates why these charges were unfair. Writing at a time when the nation was badly divided over the cause he represented, King also anticipates a number of other arguments that could be raised against him and answers them eloquently. At other points, however, he reaches out to establish common ground with his opponents. In the very first paragraph, for example, he states that his critics are "men of genuine good will" who have expressed their views sincerely; later, he tells them, "You express a great deal of anxiety over our willingness to break laws. This is certainly a legitimate concern."

Strategies like these demonstrate that the purpose of "Letter from Birmingham Jail" is very different from the purpose of "I Have a Dream" (which is reprinted in Chapter 8). In "I Have a Dream," King speaks to his supporters and inspires them to hold fast to their beliefs; in "Letter from Birmingham Jail," he addresses people who disagree with him and seeks to change their minds. Comparing these two pieces can help you understand the difference between writing designed primarily to inspire others and writing designed primarily to persuade others. Like other motives for writing, these two may overlap—hence, the role of pathos within persuasion. But if you choose to inspire feelings as a strategy for persuading people to change their minds about something, remember that persuasion requires other strategies as well—such as reasoning logically, presenting evidence to support claims, and responding thoughtfully to opposing views.

By attempting to overcome the differences that exist between you and your opponents, you are using what Kenneth Burke called *identification*. According to Burke, identification is the necessary corrective to the divisions that exist between people. Even though individuals are distinct and may disagree strongly about a particular issue, they can be united by some shared principle. Persuasion is achieved by identifying your cause with the interests of your audience. Responding to the clergy of Birmingham, King emphasizes that he too is a clergyman and makes numerous theological references. But the principle of identification goes far beyond such overt statements. Once you begin to think about what you have in common with others, including your opponents, you can often detect ties that you had not previously recognized—an important discovery if you are genuinely interested in solving problems and not simply in chalking up points in a debate.

USING ROGERIAN ARGUMENT

An emphasis on identification and problem solving shapes a kind of persuasion known as *Rogerian argument,* which incorporates the principles put forth by Carl Rogers, a psychotherapist who believed in the importance of "listening with understanding." Rogers developed his model as a kind of dialogue that could operate between individuals who are in conflict. Imagine, for example, that you are having a serious disagreement with a close friend, a disagreement that could easily escalate into a quarrel if you either attack your friend's position or seem to ignore it as you forge ahead with your own ideas. At a moment like this, Rogers would have recommended calming down and restating—*as clearly and fairly as possible*—what you heard your friend say to you. By demonstrating that you actually heard what your friend said (as opposed to missing half of it as you focused on what you wanted to say next), you help defuse tension. If your friend agrees that you represented her position fairly, she might then restate your position—or ask you to state it and then restate, when you are finished, what she heard you say. When restating another person's position in this way, it is essential to avoid judging it. After both parties in a disagreement agree that their views have been restated fairly, each can move on to noting what he or she can agree with and what the other needs to agree to in order to resolve the conflict.

Because it operates as a dialogue rather than a monologue, Rogerian argument is especially effective when you can engage in oral, face-to-face problem solving. But it can also be adapted for written arguments. To write an argument organized along Rogerian lines, you can follow this plan:*

---

*Adapted from Richard Coe, *Form and Substance* (New York: Wiley, 1981).

- State the nature of the problem.
- Summarize what opponents have argued.
- Recognize those elements of the opposition's argument that have merit.
- Summarize your own position.
- Demonstrate why your position has merit.
- Conclude with a proposal that can appeal to the self-interest of both sides in the conflict.

In other words, a Rogerian argument emphasizes the importance of concession rather than refutation and places these concessions in a relatively early position. Ideally, it leads to a win-win situation rather than a win-lose situation. Instead of making your view prevail in a way that could leave people who held different views feeling as if they lost a debate, you help conflicting parties to feel that differences have been valued and some reconciliation has been achieved.

However you choose to structure your own arguments, it is important to treat your opponents with respect and to use persuasion as a means of overcoming division and drawing people together. At its crudest levels, persuasion may draw people together superficially through manipulative rather than honorable means: A successful advertising campaign can convince thousands of people to buy a product they really don't need. (For discussion of advertising, see pages 313–326 and 329–346.) But when you write about ideas and treat your opponents respectfully, you open the way for long-lasting agreements built on shared beliefs.

Persuasion should thus be conducted honorably. You should never overlook important evidence that operates against your conclusion, and you should never exaggerate or misrepresent views that differ from yours. You will find that some writers follow these principles and others lose sight of them, but try not to be influenced by the bad habits of others. Whenever you attempt to write persuasively, show that you are fair-minded, and be sure that your own position is clear, sincerely held, and well supported.

TIPS FOR READING ARGUMENTS AND WRITING PERSUASIVELY

When Reading

- Consider the purpose of the argument. Is it to establish that a problem exists, to advocate a specific proposal, to reconcile differences, or to attack people who disagree with the writer?
- Has the writer supported all claims with adequate evidence?
- Have opposing views been recognized and treated respectfully?

■ Does the writer seem ethical and well informed?
■ Does the argument play on the feelings of the audience?
■ Does the writer reason effectively?
■ Are there any contradictions or gaps in the argument?

When Writing

■ Have a clear goal in mind.
■ Make sure that your position is clearly stated and well supported.
■ Reflect on any assumptions underlying your position and determine if these are premises your audience is likely to share.
■ Consider views different from your own, and respond to them thoughtfully.
■ Organize your argument in a pattern best suited for your audience and purpose.
■ Avoid logical fallacies.

MAJORING IN DEBT

Adolph L. Reed, Jr.

If you are concerned about the cost of a college education, you are not alone. These costs have been climbing, and as a result, increasing numbers of students must work while going to school, and many potential applicants have decided that college is now beyond their reach. What can be done about this problem? The following argument claims that the federal government should pay for all tuition and other academic fees. It was first published in a 2004 issue of The Progressive, *a monthly magazine that advocates liberal causes.*

National co-chair of the campaign for Free Higher Education, Adolph L. Reed, Jr. teaches political science at the University of Pennsylvania. Educated at the University of North Carolina at Chapel Hill and Atlanta University, he has also taught at Yale, the University of Illinois in Chicago, and the New School in New York. His most recent book is Posing as Politics and Other Thoughts on the American Scene.

Higher education is a basic social good. As such, it should be available to all, without cost, who meet admission standards. The federal government, as the guarantor of social rights, should bear primary responsibility for providing free college for all.

This proposal isn't prohibitively costly; the total bill for all students currently enrolled in public institutions is under $27 billion, less than one-third of what George W. Bush is spending on Iraq this year. Closing recently opened corporate tax loopholes would also more than meet the program's cost, even if enrollments doubled as a result of eliminating tuition as a constraint.

Moreover, this program isn't pie in the sky. It has a clear precedent in living memory. The GI Bill paid full tuition and fees, as well as a living wage stipend, for nearly eight million returning World War II veterans. We've done it before, we can do it again, and this time for everyone.

The crisis in public education is intensifying. As almost every state reels from the effects of recession and tax cuts, legislatures slash funding for higher education, the largest discretionary item in most state budgets. Colleges respond with hefty tuition increases, reduced financial assistance, and new fees. These measures put an extra burden on the average family, whose net worth has declined over the last two years for the first time in half a century.

Increased tuition, coupled with dwindling financial aid, is a significant problem for millions of families. According to the College Board, over the last decade, average tuition and fees at public four-year colleges increased 40 percent, and last year alone it increased by 14 percent. Community colleges increased tuition by a similar percentage last year. 5

Financial aid is not picking up the slack. Three decades ago, the financial aid system, with Pell grants as the backbone, guaranteed access to public colleges for primarily low- and moderate-income students. Millions of Americans earned college degrees as a result. In 1975, the maximum Pell grant covered 84 percent of costs at a four-year public college. Now, the grant covers only 42 percent of costs at four-year public colleges and only 16 percent of costs at four-year private colleges.

Meanwhile, colleges are shifting away from grants and toward loans. A decade ago, 50 percent of student aid was in the form of grants and 47 percent was in the form of loans. Today, grants are down to 39 percent of all aid; loans have increased to 54 percent.

What's worse, many of these loans are irrespective of need. In 1992, Washington decided to further help out the wealthier by making unsubsidized loans available to all students, changing the definition of need, and increasing the limits for subsidized loans. Now unsubsidized loans, although the most expensive, account for more than half of all federal loan monies.

In a bureaucratic maneuver, the Bush Administration recently changed the federal needs formula that determines how much of a family's income is really discretionary—and therefore fair game for covering college costs. A report by the Congressional Research Service states that the new financial formula will reduce Pell grants by $270 million, disqualify 84,000 students from receiving any Pell grants, and reduce the amount of Pell grants for hundreds of thousands more students.

Skyrocketing tuition and reliance on interest-carrying loans force some students to forgo college altogether, while others drop out or delay graduation.   10

By reducing tuition subsidies, public colleges violate their mandates to individuals and to society to provide a quality education to all who qualify. Many universities are retreating from their commitments to provide low-cost education for state residents, as they shift the balance of admissions more toward out-of-state applicants who pay substantially higher tuition. State schools have traditionally been the ladders to good jobs for students from working families. Soon, only the wealthiest will be able to afford the best public colleges and universities.

In fact, the Congressional Advisory Committee on Student Financial Assistance reports that by the end of this decade as many as 4.4 million college-qualified high school graduates will be unable to enroll in a four-year college, and two million will not go to college at all because they can't afford it.

Many students who do go to college have to work long hours, which adversely affects their education. A whopping 53 percent of low income freshmen who work more than thirty-five hours per week drop out and do not receive a degree. Contrast this with low income freshmen who work fewer hours: Of those who work one-to-fourteen hours per week, only 20 percent do not receive a degree, according to the Congressional Advisory Committee on Student Financial Assistance.

Those who graduate carry an enormous debt. The majority of students (64 percent) graduate with an average debt of almost $17,000, up significantly from $8,200 in 1989. Faced with repaying huge loans, students often reconsider their career plans. Our society suffers if students abandon lower paying occupations in teaching, social services, and health care in order to seek courses of study that lead to higher income jobs that speed loan repayment.

Budget cuts and tuition increases ripple throughout the academic community. They result in more hiring freezes and early retirements among full time faculty. Poorly paid and overworked contingent instructors replace them, classrooms become more crowded, and students have fewer courses to choose from. 15

Another widespread effect of budget cuts is to make public institutions more private, as they seek to supplement their loss of public monies with private gifts. This fits right in with the Bush Administration's agenda to privatize public services. And it will only make the promise of education for all more remote.

These days, many young people see the military as their only way to get an education. But Uncle Sam uses a bait and switch. The offer "Join the Army and earn up to $50,000 for college" does not often pan out. Almost 66 percent of recruits never get any college funding from the military (although they have paid into the college fund), and many who do qualify end up getting far less than $50,000.

To receive any education benefit from the Montgomery GI Bill and the Army College Fund or Navy Fund, enlistees must contribute $100 per month for the first twelve months of their tour. Even if recruits change their minds about attending college, the military will not cancel the monthly payment or refund the accumulated $1,200. The military bestows benefits only on those who receive a fully honorable discharge; "general" discharges and those "under honorable conditions" mean no college benefits.

To be eligible for the $50,000 benefit, enlistees must qualify (and only one in twenty enlistees do) for the Army or Navy College Fund by scoring in the top half of the military entry tests and enlisting in specific military occupations, typically unpopular jobs that have no transferable skills in the civilian job market. To receive the maximum amount, the military requires graduation with a four-year degree, achieved only by 15 percent of those who qualify. However, the majority of enlistees attend two-year schools and therefore can receive only a maximum of $7,788.

It's time for us now to demand that the federal government guarantee access to higher education, just as it does for K–12. This is the norm in nearly all other industrialized countries and even much of the impoverished Third World. Today, the intensifying crisis of affordability provides a perfect opportunity to insist on the principle of higher education as a basic right. . . . 20

Universities themselves are responding. The University of North Carolina at Chapel Hill recently announced a plan to cover the full costs of education for poor students without forcing them to take on loans. Students will have to work in state and federal work-study programs at a manageable ten-to-twelve hours per week.

However, it is a mistake to imagine that states can shoulder this burden on their own. Because of the budget crisis, Georgia, for instance, may discontinue it's decade-old scholarship program for all students who maintain a B average.

The Debs-Jones-Douglass Institute, a non-profit educational organization associated with the Labor Party, is building a national campaign to make higher education a right, available to everyone meeting admission standards and without regard to cost and ability to pay. The campaign calls for the federal government to pay all tuition and fees for all students attending two-year and four-year public colleges and universities. Period.

Early response to the campaign has underscored how great a concern the cost of higher education is with students and their families. The campaign for Free Higher Education already has been adopted by dozens of union bodies and other organizations, including large faculty and staff unions in Massachusetts, New Jersey, New York, and California, as well as the state federations of labor in Oregon and South Carolina.

We can generate a vibrant, exciting national movement around it on campuses, at workplaces, and in communities around the country.   25

This is an issue that can be won.

QUESTIONS FOR DISCUSSION

1. Consider the first sentence in this argument. To what extent does Reed's argument depend on his audience agreeing with this statement? Do you agree with it?
2. Reed claims that the cost of higher education is increasing while grant money is decreasing. Is this true in your state?
3. Consider the statistics in paragraph 13. What are their implications for you? If you are working while going to school, how many hours are you working, and how does your work schedule affect your academic performance?
4. Many people join the military with the expectation of receiving benefits for higher education. What do you think of the system described in paragraphs 18–19?
5. How effective is Reed's conclusion? What is the effect of ending with a single-sentence paragraph?

SUGGESTIONS FOR WRITING

1. Reed claims that the United States compares poorly, in terms of funding higher education, with "nearly all other industrialized nations." Research the kinds of funding available to students in one industrialized nation (such

as Japan, China, France, or Germany), and write an argument for funding reform that draws on the information you discover.

2. Research how tuition increases have affected enrollments at a state university in your area, and write an argument calling for additional grants or a temporary freeze on tuition increases.

3. If you do not believe that everyone has the right to a higher education, write an argument establishing who deserves this kind of education and who does not.

LINKS

■ Within the Book

In "Unchartered Territory" (pages 136–145), Elizabeth Kolbert reports on an education reform that has had mixed results.

■ Elsewhere in Print

Anderson, Trent, Seepy Bisili, and Morton Schapiro. *The Student Aid Game.* Princeton: Kaplan P, 2003.

Ehrenberg, Ronald G. *Tuition Rising: Why College Costs So Much.* Cambridge: Harvard UP, 2002.

Laurenzo, Peter. *College Financial Aid: How to Get Your Fair Share.* 6th ed. New York: Hudson, 2002.

Reed, Adolph L. *The Jesse Jackson Phenomenon: The Crisis of Purpose in Afro-American Politics.* New Haven: Yale UP, 1986.

———. *Stirrings in the Jug: Black Power in the Post-Segregation Era.* Minneapolis: U of Minnesota P, 1999.

———, ed. *Without Justice for All: The New Liberalism and Our Retreat from Racial Equality.* New York: Perseus, 1999.

■ Online

www.mhhe.com/motives

Click on "More Resources" then "Writing to Persuade Others."

■ ■ ■

FLUNKING THE NCAA

Sally Jenkins

College sports at Division I schools have become the equivalent of big businesses, as the result of pressure from alumni to produce winning teams as well as from the owners of professional sports teams who expect the NCAA to produce players. Lucrative deals with television networks to broadcast Division I games encourage university administrators and coaches not only to offer attractive terms to promising athletes but also to view them as potential sources of revenue. Lots of pressure combined with lot of money generates scandals that lead to periodic calls for reform. You may be interested by the following argument, which directs attention to the responsibility of college presidents in initiating reform, even if sports are conducted honorably on your own campus. It was first published in the spring of 2004 in the Washington Post, *the most important newspaper published in the nation's capital.*

A former writer for Sports Illustrated, *Sally Jenkins is the author of several books on sports and currently writes a regular column about sports for the* Washington Post. *When discussing motives for writing, she notes, "The best motivation for writing is honesty. To me it's all about perfuming a page with candor, because that quality will rise up and grasp readers and hold them. It seems to me that it's the first thing readers notice subconsciously. They read the first sentence and one of two things happen; either the tuning fork goes off, and rings true, or it doesn't, and they throw your work down and look for something else more interesting to read."*

The day a college president has the spine to stand up and say, "I will defend the athletic scholarship with my last breath and moreover sports have intellectual content and are consistent with education even when athletes don't graduate," is the day I will trust him or her. Until then, count me as a cynic who regards most NCAA officials and college administrators as phony pipe suckers and glad-handers who have only occasional moral spasms. Furthermore, put me down as a stone skeptic when it comes to this latest piece of cover-their-butts policy.

The NCAA college presidents are playing to the public again, hoping to assuage my cynicism and yours, probably for the sake of TV ratings, with a new "package of academic reforms." Starting in 2006, schools will have to stay above a still-undetermined "cut line" of graduation rates and other academic criteria, or risk losing scholarships and postseason money. NCAA President Myles Brand calls this a "sea change." My question is why does the NCAA need a "sea change" to ensure satisfactory academic progress, something that college presidents should have been seeing to all along on the campuses right in front of them, their own?

They don't need national legislation to know if a kid is making decent academic progress. So what do they need legislation for? To look good.

For every new rule, there is an unintended consequence. One potential consequence of this showy new "reform" package, other than the increased temptation for academic fraud, is this: Rather than actually educating students that most need it, the more honest schools will simply stop recruiting and admitting athletes who they consider too "at risk" academically. And that's too bad because we may lose some of the most gratifying success stories in sports.

The best and most meaningful byproduct of the athletic scholarship is that it's an opportunity for students who wouldn't otherwise get one. "I've got guys on Wall Street," says former Georgetown coach John Thompson. NCAA presidents, in their pose of stern reform-mindedness, may have just undermined their truest mission, out of sheer self-consciousness and buried guilt.

What college athletics need is not more "reform" but rather some realism and redefinition. Athletics and academics cohabitate uneasily on the modern Division I-A campuses, thanks to billion-dollar TV deals, and the complicating presence of the pro leagues waiting just offshore for the most talented undergrads. But it's wrong—and unhelpful—to insist that professionalism is tainting campuses, and that academic fraudulence is rampant, and to pin it all solely on athletic departments.

Sixty-two percent of all Division I student-athletes graduated in 2002, three percentage points better than the overall student body. The graduation rate in Division I men's basketball is at 44 percent; in football, it's 54 percent. While these numbers aren't fabulous, they aren't horrendous, and contained within them are legions of people who got degrees they might not have without an athletic scholarship. And that's not counting the scores of guys in the pros who didn't graduate but got something out of campus life, and gave something back, too.

When a coach with a history of fraudulent behavior such as Jim Harrick is employed by the University of Georgia, it's because a university president hired him. And when a coach's contract includes massive financial incentives for reaching a Final Four but not a penny in incentive for graduating players, it's because a university president wrote it that way. So let's put the emphasis and the spotlight where it belongs.

These so-called "reform" movements in college athletics usually blame the wrong people, provide cover for the real culprits, and obscure the real problems.

"It's legislation predicated on thievery and dishonesty," says Thompson, who turned out his share of college graduates and articulate men, regardless of what you may think of him and his occasional failures. "It's, 'You steal, and I steal, and we both know it.' They act on public perception, not the best interest of the kids."

When a university's grad rate is woeful, who gets blamed? Usually the coach, and the recruit from the blighted high school who is labeled a mercenary and an academic fraud because he uses college as a steppingstone to the pros. The president gets off scot-free and goes on preaching the evil of professionalism while he sells his school to ABC for a rights fee. So let me ask you something: Of the three, who is the biggest cynic?

Graduation rates don't tell the whole story, either. They only tell a very small part of it, and they are notoriously deceptive. They reflect absolutes. They don't reflect when a kid left a program because he was homesick, or if he was kicked out of a program for stealing in the dorm, or if he needed remedial work but blossomed into a real learner before he left. The more important questions is, what are college athletics really for? The NCAA continues to wrestle with this, and it's not easy to answer, but what's certain is that they have a place on campuses and they aren't going away, nor should they. Play is an important, maybe even critical, way to develop certain kinds of intelligence. According to the human intelligence theory, athleticism itself may even be a brand of intelligence.

Howard Gardner, the Harvard professor and author of "Frames of Mind: Theories of Multiple Intelligences," believes intelligence can't be measured by one strict standard, because people have disproportionate strengths and weakness, and intelligence may be related to all sorts of factors, even ecology. Gardner posits there are seven or maybe eight types of intelligence, including verbal, musical, spatial, logical, and kinesthetic (physical). Is kinesthetic intelligence less worthy or valuable? Certainly not. According to Gardner, the seven intelligences almost never work alone.

And then there is the theory of Henry Luce, the founder of Sports Illustrated, who said: "Sport has aspects, too, of creativity. Man is an animal that works, plays and prays. . . . No important aspect of life should be devalued. And if play does correspond to some important elements of spiritual man, then it is a bad thing for it to be devalued. And sport has been devalued. It has become a lowbrow proposition. It does not get serious attention." He wanted, he said, "to put it in proper place as one of the great modes of expression."

Oddly enough, many NCAA college presidents seem to devalue athletics. They either don't really like them, or they like them way too much and for the wrong reasons, and in either case they fail to define their proper role in education and treat them as potential evils.   15

"They're afraid of what they'll be thought of," Thompson says. "If they would just look at it and see the good, I always felt they'd be more concerned, and more conscientious. Thousands and millions of kids have profited from the system. Academic people at some point have to be comfortable enough with what they're doing right. When presidents of colleges can look at their own institutions, and don't need to follow a group mentality, that's when this thing will be solved."

QUESTIONS FOR DISCUSSION

1. Consider how Jenkins uses phrases such as "phony pipe suckers" and "cover-their-butts policy." How appropriate is language such as this for an argument by a sports columnist?

2. Why should college presidents accept responsibility for how sports are conducted at their schools?
3. How could higher academic standards for college athletes lead to academic fraud?
4. A former basketball coach for Georgetown uses "kids" to describe college athletes. Are college students "kids"? What are the consequences of thinking that they are?
5. When he founded *Sports Illustrated* in 1954, Henry Luce (who also founded *Time* magazine) claimed that sports "does not get serious attention." Is this still true? Do you think it ever was?
6. Do you think college athletes should be held to the same standards as other students?

SUGGESTIONS FOR WRITING

1. Research the recruitment procedures used at a Division I school, and then write an argument either defending the current practice or pushing for a specific reform.
2. Research the background of Jim Harrick, who was hired to coach at the University of Georgia. Imagining that you are writing for an audience consisting of the trustees for that school, write an argument for or against Harrick's appointment.
3. Write an argument on behalf of a reform that would increase the graduation rate of college athletes at your school.

LINKS

■ Within the Book

In "Majoring in Debt" (pages 466–469), Adolph L. Reed, Jr. focuses on a problem affecting college students at all levels, not just Division I schools.

■ Elsewhere in Print

Bowen, William, and Sarah Levin. *Reclaiming the Game: College Sports and Educational Values.* Princeton: Princeton UP, 2003.

Jenkins, Sally. *Funny Cide: How a Horse, a Trainer, a Jockey, and a Bunch of High School Buddies Took on the Sheiks and Bluebloods . . . and Won.* New York: Berkeley, 2005.

———. *Men Will Be Boys: A Modern Woman Explains Football and Other Amusing Male Rituals.* New York: Bantam, 1996.

Sack, Allan, and Ellen Staurowsky. *College Athletes for Hire: The Evolution and Legacy of the NCAA's Amateur Myth.* Westport: Praeger, 1998.

■ **Elsewhere in Print (continued)**

Sperber, Murray. *Beer and Circus: How Big-Time College Sports Is Crippling Undergraduate Education.* 2nd ed. New York: Owl, 2001.

Zimblist, Andrew. *Unpaid Professionals: Commercialism and Conflict in College Sports.* Princeton: Princeton UP, 2001.

■ **Online**

www.mhhe.com/motives

Click on "More Resources" then "Writing to Persuade Others."

■ ■ ■

RACIAL PROFILING: THE LIBERALS ARE RIGHT

Stuart Taylor, Jr.

"Racial Profiling" describes a controversial law-enforcement procedure in which police target people of color as potential criminals. In it's most common practice, racial profiling leads police officers to stop and search black and Hispanic American drivers much more frequently than white drivers. In recent years, liberals have taken the lead in questioning the justice of this practice. With this in mind, Stuart Taylor, Jr., seeks to persuade moderates and conservatives that liberals may be right on this point. His argument was originally published in a 1999 issue of National Journal, *a periodical read primarily by conservatives—hence its provocative title. As you read, look for ways in which Taylor seeks to identify with a conservative audience as part of a strategy designed to persuade them to support a position that would strike them as liberal.*

A graduate of Princeton University and Harvard Law School, Stuart Taylor, Jr., was a Supreme Court reporter for the New York Times *before becoming a contributing editor at* Newsweek. *He has also written feature articles and essays for* The American Lawyer. *In addition, he frequently provides legal commentary on National Public Radio as well as on television networks such as ABC, CBS, NBC, and CNN.*

While fueled by demagogic rhetoric and political opportunism, the current uproar over allegedly racist police practices in New York City and elsewhere has spotlighted one clearly abusive practice that moderates, conservatives, and, indeed, police chiefs should join liberals in assailing: racial profiling. That is the apparently widespread police habit of using skin color or ethnicity as a factor in deciding whom to stop and search for evidence of a crime.

Just this week, New Jersey Gov. Christine Todd Whitman° admitted that a 111-page internal review had confirmed a 1996 judicial ruling that some state police officers had engaged in racial profiling in deciding which cars to search during traffic stops on the turnpike.

Around the country, thousands of minority-group members have been humiliated by police stops and searches, often for conduct no more suspicious than "driving while black" or walking the streets of their communities. This, in turn, has helped to breed a deeply corrosive mistrust of law enforcement.

The full extent and the perniciousness of racial profiling are difficult to grasp for those of us who have not been targeted. The practice is virtually invisible to whites, except in the minority of cases in which police find illegal

---

°*Christine Todd Whitman:* A Republican who subsequently became administrator of the Environmental Protection Agency from January 31, 2001, to June 27, 2003.

drugs or guns and make arrests. Almost all police organizations deny that they condone racial profiling. It is easily camouflaged by nonracial pretexts for searching cars and pedestrians; and it is sometimes confused with proper police work.

All this, plus the assumption that falling crime rates mean that the police   5 must be doing something right, helps explain why moderate and conservative leaders have so far expressed relatively little concern about racial profiling. But the result has been to leave a void to be filled by race-card-carrying police-bashers such as Al Sharpton (sponsor of the Tawana Brawley hoax)° and Jesse Jackson (who recently accused police in New York City of declaring "open season on blacks").

This issue is too important to be left to opportunists such as these. More law enforcement officials and politicians alike should recognize that whatever short-term benefits racial profiling may produce in catching a few criminals are far outweighed by the long-term cost. The biggest cost is the poisoning of police relations with minority-group communities, and thus with potential witnesses and jurors in the communities most in need of effective law enforcement.

While there have been few systematic studies of racial profiling, the scattered data collected so far are striking.

In New Jersey, the report released on April 20 showed that 77 percent of motorists searched on the turnpike were black or Hispanic, even though 60 percent of those stopped were white.

In Maryland, according to statistics compiled by state police as part of a 1995 court settlement, 70 percent of the drivers searched on a stretch of Interstate 95 from January 1995 through September 1996 were black—even though blacks made up only 17 percent of all drivers (and of all speeders) on that road, according to a related study by the American Civil Liberties Union.

Thus, an innocent black driver was four times as likely to be searched as   10 an innocent white driver. And this was after the state police had (in the court settlement) issued a written policy barring race-based stops.

Studies of car stops in places ranging from Volusia County, Fla., to Eagle County, Colo., also reflect dramatic racial disparities. And in Louisiana, a state police training film a few years ago told officers to use traffic stops to do drug searches of "males of foreign nationalities, mainly Cubans, Columbians, Puerto Ricans, or other swarthy outlanders."

The most telling evidence of the extent and offensiveness of race-based stops and searches may be the personal accounts of the many black and Hispanic people who see such stops as emblematic of a discriminatory criminal justice system.

°*Al Sharpton:* New York clergyman and political activist who draws media attention to racial conflict. *Tawana Brawley:* Teenager who, in 1987, falsely claimed she had been abducted and raped by six police officers.

"You cannot talk to an African-American who has not either had this experience or had a relative go through it," says David A. Harris, a law professor at the University of Toledo, whose research on car stops and searches has included interviews with large numbers of middle-class blacks. "It's a humiliating and angering experience," Harris reports. "One man said it's like someone pulling your pants down around your ankles.... And any African-American who has teenage kids, especially male kids, ... they've had 'the talk' with them, about what to do when—not if, when—they are stopped. This is in the nature of instructions for survival."

Is there any justification for racial profiling? Defenders of the practice point out that certain crimes are disproportionately committed by young black and Hispanic men—or by members of particular ethnic groups, such as Jamaicans or Colombians—and that police logically look for evidence where the criminals live, in the inner cities.

Such rationales reflect the tendency of practitioners and critics alike to confuse racial profiling with a different phenomenon: the policies of police in places like New York City to patrol (and stop, and search) most aggressively in high-crime neighborhoods. When done with respect and sensitivity, this can produce safer communities and better community relations. When it veers into wholesale intimidation, and indiscriminate frisking of young men on the street, it can become indistinguishable from racial profiling.   15

Even critics acknowledge that racial profiling is not entirely irrational in treating young black inner-city men as presumptively more worthy of attention than, say, grandmothers. Jesse Jackson himself implied this when he said in 1993: "There is nothing more painful to me at this stage in my life than to walk down the street and hear footsteps and start thinking about robbery—then look around and see somebody white and feel relieved."

A citizen such as Jackson might be justified in keeping a prudent distance from a group of black youths in certain settings. But a police officer would not be justified (absent some particularized basis for suspicion) in picking up a black youth, standing him against a wall, and frisking him.

While "it is rational to be more suspicious of a young black man than an elderly white woman," in the words of a trenchant new book by David Cole, *No Equal Justice: Race and Class in the American Criminal Justice System,* that "does not make it right. First, the correlation of race and crime remains a stereotype, and most blacks will not conform to the stereotype.... A police officer who relies on race in stopping and questioning individuals is therefore likely to stop many more innocent than guilty individuals. Second, our nation's historical reliance on race for invidious discrimination renders suspect such consideration of race today, even if it might be 'rational' in some sense."

And outside of the inner cities, it's unclear that such practices as race-based traffic stops on major highways—in which police are usually looking not for murderers, rapists, or robbers but for drugs—produce any significant law enforcement benefit at all.

Meanwhile, the costs mount, as innocent people who are searched come *20* away feeling mistreated. This takes an incalculable toll on the willingness of many black and Hispanic citizens to cooperate with police, to provide leads, to testify as witnesses, and, when they serve as jurors, to convict guilty people.

What can be done about racial profiling? The practice is too deeply ingrained in police culture, and too easily camouflaged, to be eradicated by legislation or lawsuits. The best remedy may be for police chiefs to train their officers to shun such profiling, and to recruit more black and Hispanic officers.

In the short run, we need more studies to expose the extent of racial profiling. San Diego and San Jose, Calif., are both doing studies of their own police forces. Political pressure, lawsuits, and enlightened self-interest should spur other cities and states to do the same.

Meanwhile, Congress should give careful consideration to a proposal by Rep. John Conyers Jr., D-Mich., to require the Justice Department to collect and study racial and ethnic data about the drivers stopped and searched by state and local police.

Racial statistics can, of course, be manipulated to draw misleading inferences of discrimination, such as the wrong-headed notion that elite colleges discriminate against minorities by giving weight to Scholastic Aptitude Test scores in admissions. But unlike the case of SAT scores, racial profiling involves real discrimination. And on this issue, sunlight may be the best disinfectant.

QUESTIONS FOR DISCUSSION

1. At what points in this argument is it clear that Taylor is writing for an audience of moderates and conservatives?
2. Consider Taylor's characterization in paragraph 5 of Al Sharpton and Jesse Jackson. Is this an *ad homimem* argument or a justifiable attempt to identify with his audience?
3. How do you respond to the statistics quoted in paragraphs 8 and 9?
4. Where does Taylor recognize and respond to views different from his own?
5. At the conclusion of his argument, Taylor offers a series of propositions. Was it a good writing decision to hold these propositions back until the conclusion? Is it effective to offer more than one solution to the problem of racial profiling?
6. If Taylor had shared a draft of this argument with you before publishing it, what would you have told him about his final paragraph?

SUGGESTIONS FOR WRITING

1. Write an argument for or against a widely used police procedure.
2. Focusing on the war on terrorism, write an argument for or against using racial profiling at airports.
3. Write an argument designed to establish whether race should or should not be considered when making decisions about people in areas that do not involve law enforcement.

LINKS

■ Within the Book

For an argument for racial justice made from an African-American point of view, see "Letter from Birmingham Jail" by Martin Luther King, Jr. (pages 488–501).

■ Elsewhere in Print

Cole, David. *No Equal Justice: Race and Class in the American Criminal Justice System*. New York: New, 1999.

Markowitz, Michael W., and Delores D. Jones-Brown, eds. *The System in Black and White: Exploring the Connections between Race, Crime, and Justice*. Westport: Praeger, 2000.

Meeks, Kenneth. *Driving While Black: What to Do If You Are the Victim of Racial Profiling*. New York: Broadway, 2000.

Pallone, Nathaniel J., ed. *Race, Ethnicity, Sexual Orientation, Violent Crime: The Realities and the Myths*. New York: Haworth, 2000.

Russell, Katheryn K. *The Color of Crime: Racial Hoaxes, White Fear, Black Protectionism, Police Harassment, and Other Macroaggressions*. New York: New York UP, 1998.

■ Online

www.mhhe.com/motives

Click on "More Resources" then "Writing to Persuade Others."

■ ■ ■

THE DECLARATION OF INDEPENDENCE

Thomas Jefferson

In addition to serving two terms as president of the United States, Thomas Jefferson (1743–1826) was also vice president of the United States, secretary of state, minister to France, and governor of Virginia. A man of many interests and deep learning, he was also president of the American Philosophical Society and founder of the University of Virginia. But when surveying his long and distinguished career toward the end of his life, he was especially proud of his work on the Declaration of Independence.

As you read it, look closely at the principles with which Jefferson begins, think about what they mean, and consider how they contribute to the argument that follows. Pay close attention as well to Jefferson's language throughout this argument. Although the Declaration of Independence has become part of our national heritage, it began as a writing assignment that went through a number of different drafts. Before approving this document on July 4, 1776, Congress made twenty-four changes and deleted more than three hundred words. As you read the final draft, ask yourself how you would respond if given the chance to edit Jefferson. Would you vote to adopt the Declaration of Independence exactly as it stands, or would you recommend any changes?

When in the course of human events, it becomes necessary for one people to dissolve the political bands which have connected them with another, and to assume among the powers of the earth, the separate and equal station to which the Laws of Nature and of Nature's God entitle them, a decent respect to the opinions of mankind requires that they should declare the causes which impel them to the separation.

We hold these truths to be self-evident, that all men are created equal, that they are endowed by their Creator with certain unalienable rights, that among these are life, liberty and the pursuit of happiness. That to secure these rights, governments are instituted among men, deriving their just powers from the consent of the governed. That whenever any form of government becomes destructive of these ends, it is the right of the people to alter or to abolish it, and to institute new government, laying its foundation on such principles and organizing its powers in such form, as to them shall seem most likely to effect their safety and happiness. Prudence, indeed, will dictate that governments long established should not be changed for light and transient causes; and accordingly all experience hath shown, that mankind are more disposed to suffer, while evils are sufferable, than to right themselves by abolishing the forms to which they are accustomed. But when a long train of abuses and usurpations, pursuing invariably the same object, evinces a design to reduce them under absolute despotism, it is their right, it is their duty, to throw off such government, and to provide new guards for their future security. Such has been the patient sufferance of these Colonies; and such is now the necessity which constrains them to alter their former systems of government. This history of the present King of Great Britain° is a history of repeated injuries and usurpations, all having in direct object the establishment of an absolute tyranny over these States. To prove this, let facts be submitted to a candid world.

He has refused his assent to laws, the most wholesome and necessary for the public good.

He has forbidden his Governors to pass laws of immediate and pressing importance, unless suspended in their operation till his assent should be obtained; and when so suspended, he has utterly neglected to attend to them.

He has refused to pass other laws for the accommodation of large districts   5
of people, unless those people would relinquish the right of representation in the legislature, a right inestimable to them and formidable to tyrants only.

He has called together legislative bodies at places unusual, uncomfortable, and distant from the depository of their public records, for the sole purpose of fatiguing them into compliance with his measures.

He has dissolved representative houses repeatedly, for opposing with manly firmness his invasions on the rights of the people.

He has refused for a long time, after such dissolutions, to cause others to be elected; whereby the legislative powers, incapable of annihilation, have returned to the people at large for their exercise; the State remaining in the meantime exposed to all the dangers of invasion from without and convulsions within.

He has endeavoured to prevent the population of these states; for that purpose obstructing the laws for naturalization of foreigners; refusing to pass others to encourage their migration hither, and raising the conditions of new appropriations of lands.

He has obstructed the administration of justice, by refusing his assent to   10
laws for establishing judiciary powers.

He has made judges dependent on his will alone, for the tenure of their offices, and the amount and payment of their salaries.

He has erected a multitude of new offices, and sent hither swarms of officers to harass our people, and eat out their substance.

He has kept among us, in times of peace, standing armies without the consent of our legislatures.

He has affected to render the military independent of and superior to the civil power.

He has combined with others to subject us to a jurisdiction foreign to   15
our constitution, and unacknowledged by our laws; giving his assent to their acts of pretended legislation:

For quartering large bodies of armed troops among us:
For protecting them, by a mock trial, from punishment for any murders which they should commit on the inhabitants of these States:

°*the present King of Great Britain:* George III, who ruled from 1760 to 1820.

For cutting off our trade with all parts of the world:

For imposing taxes on us without our consent:

For depriving us in many cases of the benefits of trial by jury:

For transporting us beyond seas to be tried for pretended offences:

For abolishing the free system of English laws in a neighbouring Province, establishing therein an arbitrary government, and enlarging its boundaries so as to render it at once an example and fit instrument for introducing the same absolute rule into these Colonies:

For taking away our Charters, abolishing our most valuable laws, and altering fundamentally the forms of our governments:

For suspending our own legislatures, and declaring themselves invested with power to legislate for us in all cases whatsoever.

He has abdicated government here, by declaring us out of his protection and waging war against us.

He has plundered our seas, ravaged our coasts, burnt our towns, and destroyed the lives of our people.

He is at this time transporting large armies of foreign mercenaries to complete the works of death, desolation and tyranny, already begun with circumstances of cruelty and perfidy scarcely paralleled in the most barbarous ages, and totally unworthy the head of a civilized nation.

He has constrained our fellow citizens taken captive on the high seas to bear arms against their country, to become the executioners of their friends and brethren, or to fall themselves by their hands.

He has excited domestic insurrections amongst us, and has endeavoured   20
to bring on the inhabitants of our frontiers, the merciless Indian savages, whose known rule of welfare, is an undistinguished destruction of all ages, sexes, and conditions.

In every stage of these oppressions we have petitioned for redress in the most humble terms: our repeated petitions have been answered only by repeated injury. A prince whose character is thus marked by every act which may define a tyrant is unfit to be the ruler of a free people.

Nor have we been wanting in attention to our British brethren. We have warned them from time to time of attempts by their legislature to extend an unwarrantable jurisdiction over us. We have reminded them of the circumstances of our emigration and settlement here. We have appealed to their native justice and magnanimity, and we have conjured them by the ties of our common kindred to disavow these usurpations, which would inevitably interrupt our connections and correspondence. They too have been deaf to the voice of justice and consanguinity. We must, therefore, acquiesce in the necessity, which denounces our separation, and hold them, as we hold the rest of mankind, enemies in war, in peace friends.

We, therefore, the Representatives of the United States of America, in General Congress assembled, appealing to the Supreme Judge of the world for the rectitude of our intentions, do, in the name, and by authority of the good people of these Colonies, solemnly publish and declare, That these

United Colonies are, and of right ought to be, Free and Independent States; that they are absolved from all allegiance to the British Crown, and that all political connection between them and the state of Great Britain, is and ought to be totally dissolved; and that as Free and Independent States, they have full power to levy war, conclude peace, contract alliances, establish commerce, and to do all other acts and things which Independent States may of right do. And for the support of this declaration, with a firm reliance on the protection of Divine Providence, we mutually pledge to each other our lives, our fortunes, and our sacred honor.

QUESTIONS FOR DISCUSSION

1. What do you think Jefferson meant by "men" in paragraph 2? What does it mean to have "unalienable rights"? And what do you think "the pursuit of happiness" means?
2. Jefferson begins his argument with truths that he declares to be "self-evident." Do any of the statements in paragraph 2 strike you as open to dispute?
3. Of the various charges Jefferson makes against King George III, which do you think are the most serious?
4. How fairly has Jefferson treated Native Americans in this document?
5. Has Jefferson taken any steps to protect his fellow colonists from the charge that they were acting rashly in declaring independence?
6. Modern conventions governing capitalization differ from those that were observed in the eighteenth century. When first published, paragraph 23 began with a reference to the "Representatives of the united States of America." Is there a difference between "united states of America" and "United States of America"?

SUGGESTIONS FOR WRITING

1. Slavery was legal in this country for almost a hundred years after the Declaration of Independence, and women were not allowed to vote in national elections until 1920. Do you think there are people living in this country today who still do not enjoy the right to "life, liberty, and the pursuit of happiness"? If so, write a "declaration of independence" supporting their rights.
2. According to Jefferson, George III was a tyrant guilty of "cruelty and perfidy scarcely paralleled in the most barbarous ages." Do research on George III, and then write an argument on his behalf.
3. Canada remained part of the British Empire when the United States became independent, and Canada continues to be part of the British Commonwealth. Research the British Commonwealth, and write an argument for or against this kind of international organization.

LINKS

▪ Within the Book

After reading the Declaration of Independence, consider how it provides support for Martin Luther King, Jr.'s "Letters from Birmingham Jail" (pages 488–501).

▪ Elsewhere in Print

Becker, Carl Lotus. *The Declaration of Independence: A Study in the History of Political Ideas.* 1922. New York: Random, 1958.

Boyd, Julian, P. *The Declaration of Independence: The Evolution of the Text.* Ed. Gerard W. Gawalt. Rev. ed. Charlottesville: Intl. Center for Jefferson Studies, 1999.

Eicholz, Hans. *Harmonizing Sentiments: The Declaration of Independence and the Jeffersonian Ideal of Self-Government.* New York: Lang, 2001.

Maier, Pauline. *American Scripture: Making the Declaration of Independence.* New York: Knopf, 1997.

▪ Online

www.mhhe.com/motives

Click on "More Resources" then "Writing to Persuade Others."

▪ ▪ ▪

| COMPANION TEXT | *A Letter from the Clergy* |

In response to civil rights work that Martin Luther King was doing in Birmingham, Alabama, in the spring of 1963, eight prominent clergymen published a letter criticizing him and commending the local authorities. It was this letter, reprinted below, that inspired King to write "Letter from Birmingham Jail," which begins on page 488.

April 12, 1963

We the undersigned clergymen are among those who, in January, issued "An Appeal for Law and Order and Common Sense," in dealing with racial problems in Alabama. We expressed understanding that honest convictions in racial matters could properly be pursued in the courts, but urged that decisions of those courts should in the meantime be peacefully obeyed.

Since that time there had been some evidence of increased forbearance and a willingness to face facts. Responsible citizens have undertaken to work on various problems which cause racial friction and unrest. In Birmingham, recent public events have given indication that we all have opportunity for a new constructive and realistic approach to racial problems.

However, we are now confronted by a series of demonstrations by some of our Negro citizens, directed and led in part by outsiders. We recognize the natural impatience of people who feel that their hopes are slow in being realized. But we are convinced that these demonstrations are unwise and untimely.

We agree rather with certain local Negro leadership which has called for honest and open negotiation of racial issues in our area. And we believe this kind of facing of issues can best be accomplished by citizens of our own metropolitan area, white and Negro, meeting with their knowledge and experience of the local situation. All of us need to face that responsibility and find proper channels for its accomplishment.

Just as we formerly pointed out that "hatred and violence have no sanction in our religious and political traditions," we also point out that such actions as incite to hatred and violence, however technically peaceful those actions may be, have not contributed to the resolution of our local problems. We do not believe that these days of new hope are days when extreme measures are justified in Birmingham.

We commend the community as a whole, and the local news media and law enforcement officials in particular, on the calm manner in which these demonstrations have been handled. We urge the public to continue to show restraint should the demonstrations continue, and the law enforcement officials to remain calm and continue to protect our city from violence.

We further strongly urge our own Negro community to withdraw support from these demonstrations, and to unite locally in working peacefully for a better Birmingham. When rights are consistently denied, a cause should be pressed in the courts and in negotiations among local leaders, and not in the streets. We appeal to both our white and Negro citizenry to observe the principles of law and order and common sense.

Signed by:

C. C. J. Carpenter, D.D., LL.D., *Bishop of Alabama*

Joseph A. Durick, D.D., *Auxiliary Bishop, Diocese of Mobile, Birmingham*

Rabbi Milton L. Grafman, *Temple Emanu-El, Birmingham, Alabama*

Bishop Paul Hardin, *Bishop of the Alabama–West Florida Conference of the Methodist Church*

Bishop Nolan B. Harmon, *Bishop of the North Alabama Conference of the Methodist Church*

George M. Murray, D.D., LL.D., *Bishop Coadjutor, Episcopal Diocese of Alabama*

Edward V. Ramage, *Moderator, Synod of the Alabama Presbyterian Church in the United States*

Earl Stallings, *Pastor, First Baptist Church, Birmingham, Alabama*

LETTER FROM BIRMINGHAM JAIL IN RESPONSE TO PUBLIC STATEMENT BY EIGHT ALABAMA CLERGYMEN

Martin Luther King, Jr.

By 1963, the movement for civil rights for African Americans had become a national issue, and the United States was bitterly divided between people who perceived this movement as a threat to social order and those who recognized that social justice required serious changes in our country. In that year, Martin Luther King, Jr. (1929–1968) led a nonviolent campaign to end segregation in Birmingham, Alabama. As a result, he was jailed for eight days—one of fourteen times he was imprisoned because of his work for civil rights. While in jail, he read a published statement by eight prominent clergymen who condemned his work and supported the police (see pages 492–493). King began his response by writing in the margins of the newspaper in which he had been denounced, continued it on scraps of paper supplied by a prison trustee, and concluded on a pad that his attorneys were eventually allowed to give him.

April 16, 1963

My Dear Fellow Clergymen:

While confined here in the Birmingham city jail, I came across your recent statement calling my present activities "unwise and untimely." Seldom do I pause to answer criticism of my work and ideas. If I sought to answer all the criticisms that cross my desk, my secretaries would have little time for anything other than such correspondence in the course of the day, and I would have no time for constructive work. But since I feel that you are men of genuine good will and that your criticisms are sincerely set forth, I want to try to answer your statement in what I hope will be patient and reasonable terms.

I think I should indicate why I am here in Birmingham, since you have been influenced by the view which argues against "outsiders coming in." I have the honor of serving as president of the Southern Christian Leadership Conference, an organization operating in every southern state, with headquarters in Atlanta, Georgia. We have some eighty-five affiliated organizations across the South, and one of them is the Alabama Christian Movement for Human Rights. Frequently we share staff, educational and financial resources with our affiliates. Several months ago the affiliate here in Birmingham asked us to be on call to engage in a nonviolent direct-action program if such were deemed necessary. We readily consented, and when the hour came we lived up to our promise. So I, along with several members of my staff, am here because I was invited here. I am here because I have organizational ties here.

But more basically, I am in Birmingham because injustice is here. Just as the prophets of the eighth century B.C. left their villages and carried their "thus saith the Lord" far beyond the boundaries of their home towns, and just as the Apostle Paul left his village of Tarsus and carried the gospel of Jesus Christ to the far corners of the Greco-Roman world, so am I compelled to carry the gospel of freedom beyond my own home town. Like Paul, I must constantly respond to the Macedonian call for aid.

Moreover, I am cognizant of the interrelatedness of all communities and states. I cannot sit idly by in Atlanta and not be concerned about what happens in Birmingham. Injustice anywhere is a threat to justice everywhere. We are caught in an inescapable network of mutuality, tied in a single garment of destiny. Whatever affects one directly, affects all indirectly. Never again can we afford to live with the narrow, provincial "outside agitator" idea. Anyone who lives inside the United States can never be considered an outsider anywhere within its bounds.

You deplore the demonstrations taking place in Birmingham. But your   5
statement, I am sorry to say, fails to express a similar concern for the conditions that brought about the demonstrations. I am sure that none of you would want to rest content with the superficial kind of social analysis that deals merely with effects and does not grapple with underlying causes. It is unfortunate that demonstrations are taking place in Birmingham, but it is even more unfortunate that the city's white power structure left the Negro community with no alternative.

In any nonviolent campaign there are four basic steps: collection of the facts to determine whether injustices exist; negotiation; self-purification; and direct action. We have gone through all these steps in Birmingham. There can be no gainsaying the fact that racial injustice engulfs this community. Birmingham is probably the most thoroughly segregated city in the United States. Its ugly record of brutality is widely known. Negroes have experienced grossly unjust treatment in the courts. There have been more unsolved bombings of Negro homes and churches in Birmingham than in any other city in the nation. These are the hard, brutal facts of the case. On the basis of these conditions, Negro leaders sought to negotiate with the city fathers. But the latter consistently refused to engage in good-faith negotiation.

Then, last September, came the opportunity to talk with leaders of Birmingham's economic community. In the course of the negotiations, certain promises were made by the merchants—for example, to remove the stores' humiliating racial signs. On the basis of these promises, the Reverend Fred Shuttlesworth and the leaders of the Alabama Christian Movement for Human Rights agreed to a moratorium on all demonstrations. As the weeks and months went by, we realized that we were the victims of a broken promise. A few signs, briefly removed, returned; the others remained.

As in so many past experiences, our hopes had been blasted, and the shadow of deep disappointment settled upon us. We had no alternative except to prepare for direct action, whereby we would present our very bodies as a means of laying our case before the conscience of the local and the national community. Mindful of the difficulties involved, we decided to undertake a process of self-purification. We began a series of workshops on nonviolence, and we repeatedly asked ourselves: "Are you able to accept blows without retaliating?" "Are you able to endure the ordeal of jail?" We decided to schedule our direct-action program for the Easter season, realizing that except for Christmas, this is the main shopping period of the year. Knowing that a strong economic-withdrawal program would be the by-product of direct action, we felt that this would be the best time to bring pressure to bear on the merchants for the needed change.

Then it occurred to us that Birmingham's mayoral election was coming up in March, and we speedily decided to postpone action until after election day. When we discovered that the Commissioner of Public Safety, Eugene "Bull" Connor,° had piled up enough votes to be in the run-off, we decided again to postpone action until the day after the run-off so that the demonstrations could not be used to cloud the issues. Like many others, we waited to see Mr. Connor defeated, and to this end we endured postponement after postponement. Having aided in this community need, we felt that our direct-action program could be delayed no longer.

You may well ask: "Why direct action? Why sit-ins, marches and so forth? Isn't negotiation a better path?" You are quite right in calling for negotiation. Indeed, this is the very purpose of direct action. Nonviolent direct action seeks to create such a crisis and foster such a tension that a community which has constantly refused to negotiate is forced to confront the issue. It seeks so to dramatize the issue that it can no longer be ignored. My citing the creation of tension as part of the work of the nonviolent resister may sound rather shocking. But I must confess that I am not afraid of the word "tension." I have earnestly opposed violent tension, but there is a type of constructive, nonviolent tension which is necessary for growth. Just as Socrates felt that it was necessary to create a tension in the mind so that individuals could rise from the bondage of myths and half-truths to the unfettered realm of creative analysis and objective appraisal, so must we see the need for nonviolent gadflies to create the kind of tension in society that will help men rise from the dark depths of prejudice and racism to the majestic heights of understanding and brotherhood.

The purpose of our direct-action program is to create a situation so crisis-packed that it will inevitably open the door to negotiation. I therefore concur with you in your call for negotiation. Too long has our beloved Southland been bogged down in a tragic effort to live in monologue rather than dialogue.

10

°*Eugene "Bull" Connor:* Commissioner of Public Safety in Birmingham, 1937–1953 and 1957–1963. One of three commissioners responsible for governing Birmingham, and the commissioner with the most seniority, Connor (1897–1973) was a powerful opponent of integration who used the police to make war on civil rights demonstrators.

One of the basic points in your statement is that the action that I and my associates have taken in Birmingham is untimely. Some have asked: "Why didn't you give the new city administration time to act?" The only answer that I can give to this query is that the new Birmingham administration must be prodded about as much as the outgoing one, before it will act. We are sadly mistaken if we feel that the election of Albert Boutwell as mayor will bring the millennium to Birmingham. While Mr. Boutwell is a much more gentle person than Mr. Connor, they are both segregationists, dedicated to maintenance of the status quo. I have hope that Mr. Boutwell will be reasonable enough to see the futility of massive resistance to desegregation. But he will not see this without pressure from devotees of civil rights. My friends, I must say to you that we have not made a single gain in civil rights without determined legal and nonviolent pressure. Lamentably, it is an historical fact that privileged groups seldom give up their privileges voluntarily. Individuals may see the moral light and voluntarily give up their unjust posture; but, as Reinhold Niebuhr has reminded us, groups tend to be more immoral than individuals.

We know through painful experience that freedom is never voluntarily given by the oppressor; it must be demanded by the oppressed. Frankly, I have yet to engage in a direct-action campaign that was "well timed" in the view of those who have not suffered unduly from the disease of segregation. For years now I have heard the word "Wait!" It rings in the ear of every Negro with piercing familiarity. This "Wait" has almost always meant "Never." We must come to see, with one of our distinguished jurists, that "justice too long delayed is justice denied."

We have waited for more than 340 years for our constitutional God-given rights. The nations of Asia and Africa are moving with jetlike speed toward gaining political independence, but we still creep at horse-and-buggy pace toward gaining a cup of coffee at a lunch counter. Perhaps it is easy for those who have never felt the stinging darts of segregation to say, "Wait." But when you have seen vicious mobs lynch your mothers and fathers at will and drown your sisters and brothers at whim; when you have seen hate-filled policemen curse, kick, and even kill your black brothers and sisters; when you see the vast majority of your twenty million Negro brothers smothering in an airtight cage of poverty in the midst of an affluent society; when you suddenly find your tongue twisted and your speech stammering as you seek to explain to your six-year-old daughter why she can't go to the public amusement park that has just been advertised on television, and see tears welling up in her eyes when she is told that Funtown is closed to colored children, and see ominous clouds of inferiority beginning to form in her little mental sky, and see her beginning to distort her personality by developing an unconscious bitterness toward white people; when you have to concoct an answer for a five-year-old son who is asking: "Daddy, why do white people treat colored people so mean?"; when you take a cross-country drive and find it necessary to sleep night after night in the uncomfortable corners of your automobile because no motel will accept you; when you are humiliated day in and day out by nagging signs reading "white" and "colored"; when your first name becomes "nigger," your middle name becomes "boy" (however old you are) and your last name becomes "John," and your wife and mother are never given the respected title "Mrs."; when you are harried by day and haunted by night by the fact that you are a Negro, living constantly at tiptoe stance, never quite knowing what to expect next, and are plagued with inner fears and outer resentments; when you are forever fighting a degenerating sense of "nobodiness"—then you will understand why we find it difficult to wait. There comes a time when a cup of endurance runs over, and men are no longer willing to be plunged into the abyss of despair. I hope, sirs, you can understand our legitimate and unavoidable impatience.

You express a great deal of anxiety over our willingness to break laws. 15 This is certainly a legitimate concern. Since we so diligently urge people to obey the Supreme Court's decision of 1954 outlawing segregation in the public schools, at first glance it may seem rather paradoxical for us consciously to break laws. One may well ask: "How can you advocate breaking some laws and obeying others?" The answer lies in the fact that there are two types of laws: just and unjust. I would be the first to advocate obeying just laws. One has not only a legal but a moral responsibility to obey just laws. Conversely, one has a moral responsibility to disobey unjust laws. I would agree with St. Augustine that "an unjust law is no law at all."

Now, what is the difference between the two? How does one determine whether a law is just or unjust? A just law is a man-made code that squares with the moral law or the law of God. An unjust law is a code that is out of harmony with the moral law. To put it in the terms of St. Thomas Aquinas: An unjust law is a human law that is not rooted in eternal law and natural law. Any law that uplifts human personality is just. Any law that degrades human personality is unjust. All segregation statutes are unjust because segregation distorts the soul and damages the personality. It gives the segregator a false sense of superiority and the segregated a false sense of inferiority. Segregation, to use the terminology of the Jewish philosopher Martin Buber, substitutes an "I–it" relationship for an "I–thou" relationship and ends up relegating persons to the status of things. Hence, segregation is not only politically, economically and sociologically unsound, it is morally wrong and sinful. Paul Tillich has said that sin is separation. Is not segregation an existential expression of man's tragic separation, his awful estrangement, his terrible sinfulness? Thus it is that I can urge men to obey the 1954 decision of the Supreme Court, for it is morally right; and I can urge them to disobey segregation ordinances, for they are morally wrong.

Let us consider a more concrete example of just and unjust laws. An unjust law is a code that a numerical or power majority group compels a minority group to obey but does not make binding on itself. This is *difference* made legal. By the same token, a just law is a code that a majority compels a minority to follow and that it is willing to follow itself. This is *sameness* made legal.

Let me give another explanation. A law is unjust if it is inflicted on a minority that, as a result of being denied the right to vote, had no part in enacting or devising the law. Who can say that the legislature of Alabama which set up that state's segregation laws was democratically elected? Throughout Alabama all sorts of devious methods are used to prevent Negroes from becoming registered voters, and there are some counties in which, even though Negroes constitute a majority of the population, not a single Negro is registered. Can any law enacted under such circumstances be considered democratically structured?

Sometimes a law is just on its face and unjust in its application. For instance, I have been arrested on a charge of parading without a permit. Now, there is nothing wrong in having an ordinance which requires a permit for a parade. But such an ordinance becomes unjust when it is used to maintain segregation and to deny citizens the First-Amendment privilege of peaceful assembly and protest.

I hope you are able to see the distinction I am trying to point out. In no   20
sense do I advocate evading or defying the law, as would the rabid segregationist. That would lead to anarchy. One who breaks an unjust law must do so openly, lovingly, and with a willingness to accept the penalty. I submit that an individual who breaks a law that conscience tells him is unjust, and who willingly accepts the penalty of imprisonment in order to arouse the conscience of the community over its injustice, is in reality expressing the highest respect for law.

Of course, there is nothing new about this kind of civil disobedience. It was evidenced sublimely in the refusal of Shadrach, Meshach and Abednego to obey the laws of Nebuchadnezzar, on the ground that a higher moral law was at stake. It was practiced superbly by the early Christians, who were willing to face hungry lions and the excruciating pain of chopping blocks rather than submit to certain unjust laws of the Roman Empire. To a degree, academic freedom is a reality today because Socrates practiced civil disobedience. In our own nation, the Boston Tea Party represented a massive act of civil disobedience.

We should never forget that everything Adolf Hitler did in Germany was "legal" and everything the Hungarian freedom fighters° did in Hungary was "illegal." It was "illegal" to aid and comfort a Jew in Hitler's Germany. Even so, I am sure that, had I lived in Germany at the time, I would have aided and comforted my Jewish brothers. If today I lived in a Communist country where certain principles dear to the Christian faith are suppressed, I would openly advocate disobeying that country's antireligious laws.

I must make two honest confessions to you, my Christian and Jewish brothers. First, I must confess that over the past few years I have been gravely disappointed with the white moderate. I have almost reached the regrettable

---

°*Hungarian freedom fighters:* In 1956 Hungarian citizens rose up against the Communist dictatorship in their country. Their revolt was suppressed when the Soviet Union responded by sending tanks into Budapest.

conclusion that the Negro's great stumbling block in his stride toward freedom is not the White Citizen's Counciler or the Ku Klux Klanner, but the white moderate, who is more devoted to "order" than to justice; who prefers a negative peace which is the presence of tension to a positive peace which is the presence of justice; who constantly says: "I agree with you in the goal you seek, but I cannot agree with your methods of direct action"; who paternalistically believes he can set the timetable for another man's freedom; who lives by a mythical concept of time and who constantly advises the Negro to wait for a "more convenient season." Shallow understanding from people of good will is more frustrating than absolute misunderstanding from people of ill will. Lukewarm acceptance is much more bewildering than outright rejection.

I had hoped that the white moderate would understand that law and order exist for the purpose of establishing justice and that when they fail in this purpose they become the dangerously structured dams that block the flow of social progress. I had hoped that the white moderate would understand that the present tension in the South is a necessary phase of the transition from an obnoxious negative peace, in which the Negro passively accepted his unjust plight, to a substantive and positive peace, in which all men will respect the dignity and worth of human personality. Actually, we who engage in nonviolent direct action are not the creators of tension. We merely bring to the surface the hidden tension that is already alive. We bring it out in the open, where it can be seen and dealt with. Like a boil that can never be cured so long as it is covered up but must be opened with all its ugliness to the natural medicines of air and light, injustice must be exposed, with all the tension its exposure creates, to the light of human conscience and the air of national opinion before it can be cured.

In your statement you assert that our actions, even though peaceful, must be condemned because they precipitate violence. But is this a logical assertion? Isn't this like condemning a robbed man because his possession of money precipitated the evil act of robbery? Isn't this like condemning Socrates because his unswerving commitment to truth and his philosophical inquiries precipitated the act by the misguided populace in which they made him drink hemlock? Isn't this like condemning Jesus because his unique God-consciousness and never-ceasing devotion to God's will precipitated the evil act of crucifixion? We must come to see that, as the federal courts have consistently affirmed, it is wrong to urge an individual to cease his efforts to gain his basic constitutional rights because the quest may precipitate violence. Society must protect the robbed and punish the robber.

I had also hoped that the white moderate would reject the myth concerning time in relation to the struggle for freedom. I have just received a letter from a white brother in Texas. He writes: "All Christians know that the colored people will receive equal rights eventually, but it is possible that you are in too great a religious hurry. It has taken Christianity almost two thousand years to accomplish what it has. The teachings of Christ take time to come to earth." Such an attitude stems from a tragic misconception of time,

25

from the strangely irrational notion that there is something in the very flow of time that will inevitably cure all ills. Actually, time itself is neutral; it can be used either destructively or constructively. More and more I feel that the people of ill will have used time much more effectively than have the people of good will. We will have to repent in this generation not merely for the hateful words and actions of the bad people but for the appalling silence of the good people. Human progress never rolls in on wheels of inevitability; it comes through the tireless efforts of men willing to be co-workers with God, and without this hard work, time itself becomes an ally of the forces of social stagnation. We must use time creatively, in the knowledge that the time is always ripe to do right. Now is the time to make real the promise of democracy and transform our pending national elegy into a creative psalm of brotherhood. Now is the time to lift our national policy from the quicksand of racial injustice to the solid rock of human dignity.

You speak of our activity in Birmingham as extreme. At first I was rather disappointed that fellow clergymen would see my nonviolent efforts as those of an extremist. I began thinking about the fact that I stand in the middle of two opposing forces in the Negro community. One is a force of complacency, made up in part of Negroes who, as a result of long years of oppression, are so drained of self-respect and a sense of "somebodiness" that they have adjusted to segregation; and in part of a few middle-class Negroes who, because of a degree of academic and economic security and because in some ways they profit by segregation, have become insensitive to the problems of the masses. The other force is one of bitterness and hatred, and it comes perilously close to advocating violence. It is expressed in the various black nationalist groups that are springing up across the nation, the largest and best-known being Elijah Muhammad's Muslim movement. Nourished by the Negro's frustration over the continued existence of racial discrimination, this movement is made up of people who have lost faith in America, who have absolutely repudiated Christianity, and who have concluded that the white man is an incorrigible "devil."

I have tried to stand between these two forces, saying that we need emulate neither the "do-nothingism" of the complacent nor the hatred and despair of the black nationalist. For there is the more excellent way of love and nonviolent protest. I am grateful to God that, through the influence of the Negro church, the way of nonviolence became an integral part of our struggle.

If this philosophy had not emerged, by now many streets of the South would, I am convinced, be flowing with blood. And I am further convinced that if our white brothers dismiss as "rabble-rousers" and "outside agitators" those of us who employ nonviolent direct action, and if they refuse to support our nonviolent efforts, millions of the Negroes will, out of frustration and despair, seek solace and security in black-nationalist ideologies—a development that would inevitably lead to a frightening racial nightmare.

Oppressed people cannot remain oppressed forever. The yearning for freedom eventually manifests itself, and that is what has happened to the American Negro. Something within has reminded him of his birthright of freedom,   *30* and something without has reminded him that it can be gained. Consciously or unconsciously, he has been caught up by the *Zeitgeist,*° and with his black brothers of Africa and his brown and yellow brothers of Asia, South America and the Caribbean, the United States Negro is moving with a sense of great urgency toward the promised land of racial justice. If one recognizes this vital urge that has engulfed the Negro community, one should readily understand why public demonstrations are taking place. The Negro has many pent-up resentments and latent frustrations, and he must release them. So let him march; let him make prayer pilgrimages to the city hall; let him go on freedom rides—and try to understand why he must do so. If his repressed emotions are not released in nonviolent ways, they will seek expression through violence; this is not a threat but a fact of history. So I have not said to my people: "Get rid of your discontent." Rather, I have tried to say that this normal and healthy discontent can be channeled into the creative outlet of nonviolent direct action. And now this approach is being termed extremist.

But though I was initially disappointed at being categorized as an extremist, as I continued to think about the matter I gradually gained a measure of satisfaction from the label. Was not Jesus an extremist for love: "Love your enemies, bless them that curse you, do good to them that hate you, and pray for them which despitefully use you, and persecute you." Was not Amos an extremist for justice: "Let justice roll down like waters and righteousness like an ever-flowing stream." Was not Paul an extremist for the Christian gospel: "I bear in my body the marks of the Lord Jesus." Was not Martin Luther an extremist: "Here I stand; I cannot do otherwise, so help me God." And John Bunyan: "I will stay in jail to the end of my days before I make a butchery of my conscience." And Abraham Lincoln: "This nation cannot survive half slave and half free." And Thomas Jefferson: "We hold these truths to be self-evident, that all men are created equal. . . ." So the question is not whether we will be extremists, but what kind of extremists we will be. Will we be extremists for hate or for love? Will we be extremists for the preservation of injustice or for the extension of justice? In that dramatic scene on Calvary's hill three men were crucified. We must never forget that all three were crucified for the same crime—the crime of extremism. Two were extremists for immorality, and thus fell below their environment. The other, Jesus Christ, was an extremist for love, truth and goodness, and thereby rose above his environment. Perhaps the South, the nation and the world are in dire need of creative extremists.

I had hoped that the white moderate would see this need. Perhaps I was too optimistic; perhaps I expected too much. I suppose I should have realized that few members of the oppressor race can understand the deep groans and passionate yearnings of the oppressed race, and still fewer have the vision to see that injustice must be rooted out by strong, persistent and determined

---

°*Zeitgeist:* German for "spirit of the times."

action. I am thankful, however, that some of our white brothers in the South have grasped the meaning of this social revolution and committed themselves to it. They are still all too few in quantity, but they are big in quality. Some—such as Ralph McGill, Lillian Smith, Harry Golden, James McBride Dabbs, Ann Braden and Sarah Patton Boyle—have written about our struggle in eloquent and prophetic terms. Others have marched with us down nameless streets of the South. They have languished in filthy, roach-infested jails, suffering the abuse and brutality of policemen who view them as "dirty niggerlovers." Unlike so many of their moderate brothers and sisters, they have recognized the urgency of the moment and sensed the need for powerful "action" antidotes to combat the disease of segregation.

Let me take note of my other major disappointment. I have been so greatly disappointed with the white church and its leadership. Of course, there are some notable exceptions. I am not unmindful of the fact that each of you has taken some significant stands on this issue. I commend you, Reverend Stallings, for your Christian stand on this past Sunday, in welcoming Negroes to your worship service on a nonsegregated basis. I commend the Catholic leaders of this state for integrating Spring Hill College several years ago.

But despite these notable exceptions, I must honestly reiterate that I have been disappointed with the church. I do not say this as one of those negative critics who can always find something wrong with the church. I say this as a minister of the gospel, who loves the church; who was nurtured in its bosom; who has been sustained by its spiritual blessings and who will remain true to it as long as the cord of life shall lengthen.

When I was suddenly catapulted into the leadership of the bus protest in Montgomery, Alabama, a few years ago, I felt we would be supported by the white church. I felt that the white ministers, priests and rabbis of the South would be among our strongest allies. Instead, some have been outright opponents, refusing to understand the freedom movement and misrepresenting its leaders; all too many others have been more cautious than courageous and have remained silent behind the anesthetizing security of stained-glass windows.

In spite of my shattered dreams, I came to Birmingham with the hope that the white religious leadership of this community would see the justice of our cause and, with deep moral concern, would serve as the channel through which our just grievances could reach the power structure. I had hoped that each of you would understand. But again I have been disappointed.

I have heard numerous southern religious leaders admonish their worshipers to comply with a desegregation decision because it is the law, but I have longed to hear white ministers declare: "Follow this decree because integration is morally right and because the Negro is your brother." In the midst of blatant injustices inflicted upon the Negro, I have watched white churchmen stand on the sideline and mouth pious irrelevancies and sanctimonious trivialities. In the midst of a mighty struggle to rid our nation of racial and economic injustice, I have heard many ministers say: "Those are social issues, with which the gospel has no real concern." And I have watched many churches commit themselves to a completely otherworldly religion which makes a strange, un–Biblical distinction between body and soul, between the sacred and the secular.

I have traveled the length and breadth of Alabama, Mississippi and all the other southern states. On sweltering summer days and crisp autumn mornings I have looked at the South's beautiful churches with their lofty spires pointing heavenward. I have beheld the impressive outlines of her massive religious-education buildings. Over and over I have found myself asking: "What kind of people worship here? Who is their God? Where were their voices when the lips of Governor Barnett dripped with words of interposition and nullification? Where were they when Governor Wallace gave a clarion call for defiance and hatred? Where were their voices of support when bruised and weary Negro men and women decided to rise from the dark dungeons of complacency to the bright hills of creative protest?"

Yes, these questions are still in my mind. In deep disappointment I have wept over the laxity of the church. But be assured that my tears have been tears of love. There can be no deep disappointment where there is not deep love. Yes, I love the church. How could I do otherwise? I am in the rather unique position of being the son, the grandson, and the great-grandson of preachers. Yes, I see the church as the body of Christ. But, oh! How we have blemished and scarred that body through social neglect and through fear of being nonconformists.

There was a time when the church was very powerful—in the time when   *40* the early Christians rejoiced at being deemed worthy to suffer for what they believed. In those days the church was not merely a thermometer that recorded the ideas and principles of popular opinion; it was a thermostat that transformed the mores of society. Whenever the early Christians entered a town, the people in power became disturbed and immediately sought to convict the Christians for being "disturbers of the peace" and "outside agitators." But the Christians pressed on, in the conviction that they were "a colony of heaven," called to obey God rather than man. Small in number, they were big in commitment. They were too God-intoxicated to be "astronomically intimidated." By their effort and example they brought an end to such ancient evils as infanticide and gladiatorial contests.

Things are different now. So often the contemporary church is a weak, ineffectual voice with an uncertain sound. So often it is an archdefender of the status quo. Far from being disturbed by the presence of the church, the power structure of the average community is consoled by the church's silent—and often even vocal—sanction of things as they are.

But the judgment of God is upon the church as never before. If today's church does not recapture the sacrificial spirit of the early church, it will lose its authenticity, forfeit the loyalty of millions, and be dismissed as an irrelevant social club with no meaning for the twentieth century. Every day I meet young people whose disappointment with the church has turned into outright disgust.

Perhaps I have once again been too optimistic. Is organized religion too inextricably bound to the status quo to save our nation and the world? Perhaps I must turn my faith to the inner spiritual church, the church within the church, as the true *ekklesia*° and the hope of the world. But again I am thankful to God that some noble souls from the ranks of organized religion have broken loose from the paralyzing chains of conformity and joined us as active partners in the struggle for freedom. They have left their secure congregations and walked the streets of Albany, Georgia, with us. They have gone down the highways of the South on tortuous rides for freedom. Yes, they have gone to jail with us. Some have been dismissed from their churches, have lost the support of their bishops and fellow ministers. But they have acted in the faith that right defeated is stronger than evil triumphant. Their witness has been the spiritual salt that has preserved the true meaning of the gospel in these troubled times. They have carved a tunnel of hope through the dark mountain of disappointment.

I hope the church as a whole will meet the challenge of this decisive hour. But even if the church does not come to the aid of justice, I have no despair about the future. I have no fear about the outcome of our struggle in Birmingham, even if our motives are at present misunderstood. We will reach the goal of freedom in Birmingham and all over the nation, because the goal of America is freedom. Abused and scorned though we may be, our destiny is tied up with America's destiny. Before the pilgrims landed at Plymouth, we were here. Before the pen of Jefferson etched the majestic words of the Declaration of Independence across the pages of history, we were here. For more than two centuries our forebears labored in this country without wages; they made cotton king; they built the homes of their masters while suffering gross injustice and shameful humiliation—and yet out of a bottomless vitality they continued to thrive and develop. If the inexpressible cruelties of slavery could not stop us, the opposition we now face will surely fail. We will win our freedom because the sacred heritage of our nation and the eternal will of God are embodied in our echoing demands.

Before closing I feel impelled to mention one other point in your statement that has troubled me profoundly. You warmly commended the Birmingham police force for keeping "order" and "preventing violence." I doubt that you would have so warmly commended the police force if you had seen its dogs sinking their teeth into unarmed, nonviolent Negroes. I doubt that you would so quickly commend the policemen if you were to observe their ugly and inhumane treatment of Negroes here in the city jail; if you were to watch them push and curse old Negro women and young Negro girls; if you were to see them slap and kick old Negro men and young boys; if you were to observe them, as they did on two occasions, refuse to give us food because 45

°*ekklesia:* Greek for "assembly" or "congregation."

we wanted to sing our grace together. I cannot join you in your praise of the Birmingham police department.

It is true that police have exercised a degree of discipline in handling the demonstrators. In this sense they have conducted themselves rather "nonviolently" in public. But for what purpose? To preserve the evil system of segregation. Over the past few years I have consistently preached that nonviolence demands that the means we use must be as pure as the ends we seek. I have tried to make clear that it is wrong to use immoral means to attain moral ends. But now I must affirm that it is just as wrong, or perhaps even more so, to use moral means to preserve immoral ends. Perhaps Mr. Connor and his policemen have been rather nonviolent in public, as was Chief Pritchett in Albany, Georgia, but they have used the moral means of nonviolence to maintain the immoral end of racial injustice. As T. S. Eliot has said: "The last temptation is the greatest treason: To do the right deed for the wrong reason."

I wish you had commended the Negro sit-inners and demonstrators of Birmingham for their sublime courage, their willingness to suffer and their amazing discipline in the midst of great provocation. One day the South will recognize its real heroes. They will be the James Merediths, with the noble sense of purpose that enables them to face jeering and hostile mobs, and with the agonizing loneliness that characterizes the life of the pioneer. They will be old, oppressed, battered Negro women, symbolized in a seventy-two-year-old woman in Montgomery, Alabama, who rose up with a sense of dignity and with her people decided not to ride segregated buses, and who responded with ungrammatical profundity to one who inquired about her weariness: "My feets is tired, but my soul is at rest." They will be the young high school and college students, the young ministers of the gospel and a host of their elders, courageously and nonviolently sitting in at lunch counters and willingly going to jail for conscience' sake. One day the South will know that when these disinherited children of God sat down at lunch counters, they were in reality standing up for what is best in the American dream and for the most sacred values in our Judaeo-Christian heritage, thereby bringing our nation back to those great wells of democracy which were dug deep by the founding fathers in their formulation of the Constitution and the Declaration of Independence.

Never before have I written so long a letter. I'm afraid it is much too long to take your precious time. I can assure you that it would have been much shorter if I had been writing from a comfortable desk, but what else can one do when he is alone in a narrow jail cell, other than write long letters, think long thoughts and pray long prayers?

If I have said anything in this letter that overstates the truth and indicates an unreasonable impatience, I beg you to forgive me. If I have said anything that understates the truth and indicates my having a patience that allows me to settle for anything less than brotherhood, I beg God to forgive me.

I hope this letter finds you strong in faith. I also hope that circumstances will soon make it possible for me to meet each of you, not as an integrationist or a civil-rights leader but as a fellow clergyman and a Christian brother. Let us all hope that the dark clouds of racial prejudice will soon pass away and the deep fog of misunderstanding will be lifted from our fear-drenched communities, and in some not too distant tomorrow the radiant stars of love and brotherhood will shine over our great nation with all their scintillating beauty.

Yours for the cause of Peace and Brotherhood
Martin Luther King, Jr.

QUESTIONS FOR DISCUSSION

1. How does King present himself in this letter? Is his own character a factor in the argument he makes?
2. How does King respond to the specific charges that were made against him in the letter reprinted on pages 486–487?
3. Why do you think King's letter is so much longer than the letter to which he is responding?
4. Where does King make concessions that would appeal to people who held views different from his own? How does he seek to assure such readers that he understands their concern and recognizes signs of good faith?
5. Most of paragraph 14 consists of a single sentence. How is this sentence structured, and what is its effect? If you were to divide this sentence, where would you do so? What would be the effect of breaking this long sentence down into several shorter ones?
6. According to King, how can we tell the difference between laws that we should obey and laws that we should break? Under what circumstances is it acceptable to break a law?
7. Where does King show that he is writing for an audience of clergymen? Is there any evidence suggesting that he may also have had a larger audience in mind as he wrote?
8. How does King see the church? How does he think Christianity has changed? What does he believe the church should be like?
9. What does King's letter reveal about African-American history?

SUGGESTIONS FOR WRITING

1. What elements of this letter make it persuasive? Write an essay explaining how King has structured his argument and identifying the rhetorical strategies that make it effective.
2. Are you concerned about social justice? Identify a social problem in the world today, and write a letter that would persuade your classmates to do something about it.
3. King was awarded the Nobel Peace Prize, a prize given since 1901. The world, however, is rarely at peace. Write a letter to the United Nations, the World Trade Organization, the government of a specific country, or an organized group operating outside the law in which you argue for a change that would make the world more peaceful.

LINKS

■ **Within the Book**

Itabari Njeri (pages 71–75) and Gloria Naylor (pages 66–69) also discuss prejudice against African Americans. For another example of King's work, see "I Have a Dream" (pages 535–538).

■ **Elsewhere in Print**

Bass, S., Jonathan. *Blessed Are the Peacemakers: Martin Luther King, Jr., Eight White Religious Leaders, and the "Letter from Birmingham Jail."* Baton Rouge: Louisiana State UP, 2001.

Buber, Martin. *Good and Evil: Two Interpretations.* Trans. Ronald G. Smith and Michael Bullock. 1953. Upper Saddle River: Prentice, 1990.

Calloway-Thomas, Carolyn, and John Louis Lucaites, eds. *Martin Luther King, Jr., and the Sermonic Power of Public Discourse.* Tuscaloosa: U of Alabama P, 1993.

King, Martin Luther. *The Papers of Martin Luther King, Jr.: On the Threshold of a New Decade, January 1959–December 1960.* Berkeley: U of California P, 2005.

Lesher, Stephan. *George Wallace: American Populist.* Reading: Addison, 1994.

McWhorter, Diane. *Carry Me Home: Birmingham, Alabama: The Climactic Battle of the Civil Rights Revolution.* New York: Simon, 2001.

Tillich, Paul. *The Courage to Be.* 1952. New Haven: Yale UP, 2000.

Ward, Brian, and Tony Badger, eds. *The Making of Martin Luther King and the Civil Rights Movement.* New York: New York UP, 1996.

■ **Online**

www.mhhe.com/motives

Click on "More Resources" then "Writing to Persuade Others."

PRIVACY AND THE U.S. MILITARY

Aaron Belkin and Melissa S. Embser-Herbert

The role of gays and lesbians in the U.S. military emerged as a national issue in 1992 when Bill Clinton promised to integrate the armed services if elected president. Facing opposition from senior military officials and powerful members of Congress, he subsequently initiated a policy known as "Don't ask; don't tell." This policy prohibited military recruiters and officers from asking about sexual orientation, but it also prohibited gays and lesbians from disclosing the nature of their sexuality. Disclosure—which could take many forms—became grounds for discharge. As a result, the number of gay and lesbian soldiers dismissed from military service increased dramatically during the decade that followed even as demands upon the U.S. military increased. The authors of the following argument, which was first published in the fall of 2002 by the Center for Strategic and International Studies at the Massachusetts Institute of Technology, wrote with these developments in mind.

Both Aaron Belkin and Melissa Embser-Herbert have written extensively about social justice. Belkin, who earned his Ph.D. at the University of California–Berkeley, teaches political science at the University of California–Santa Barbara. Embser-Herbert earned her doctorate at the University of Arizona—and her J.D. at Hamline University in St. Paul, Minnesota, where she teaches sociology. In discussing her writing process, she says, "I think the most challenging thing, in terms of process is getting to the point where I can say, 'Enough, more editing, toying, etc. won't help.' I had a professor . . . who, in our first semester, talked about diminishing returns and I've always tried to remember that!" (For information about Belkin and Embser-Herbert's sources, visit www.mhhe.com/motives and click on "More Resources" then "Writing to Persuade Others.")

Efforts to promote racial, ethic, religious, and gender diversity in the U.S. armed forces have often provoked controversy between civil rights advocates and those who fear that integration could undermine organizational effectiveness. Recent debates over sexual orientation have been no less divisive.[1] When President Bill Clinton attempted to overturn Department of Defense regulations that prohibited gays and lesbians from serving in the military, congressional opponents formulated a new policy on homosexuality that became part of the 1994 National Defense Authorization Act, the first congressional statute to include a gay ban.[2] The Defense Department then drafted regulations known as "Don't Ask, Don't Tell, Don't Pursue, Don't Harass" that exclude open homosexuals from the services.[3] According to these regulations, military recruiters are no longer supposed to ask enlistees if they are homosexual, but service members who disclose that they are homosexual are subject to dismissal.

Although the issue of gays and lesbians in the military has received less attention since the terrorist attacks in the United States on September 11, 2001, it remains a hot-button topic that reemerges frequently as the focus of highly charged partisan debates. Democratic presidential candidates Bill Bradley and Al Gore promised to lift the ban during the 2000 primary, but opponents forced Gore to retreat immediately when he proposed that appointees to the Joint Chiefs of Staff would be required to adopt his position. Despite Gore's reversal, future contenders for the Democratic nomination will likely be obliged to oppose the ban as they seek to attract gay and lesbian voters during primary campaigns. Conversely, although President George W. Bush and his administration support the current policy, influential members of the Republican Party advocate tightening the law by returning to the previous system in which military recruiters asked enlistees if they were homosexual.[4]

The official justification for the gay ban is the unit cohesion rationale, which holds that combat performance would decline if open gays and lesbians were permitted to join the military.[5] According to this perspective, heterosexual service members dislike gays and lesbians and cannot trust them with their lives.[6] As a result, lifting the gay ban would complicate units' ability to function by allowing gays and lesbians to reveal their sexual orientation to their peers.[7] Despite the intuitive plausibility of this argument, a growing body of scholarly evidence has undermined the validity of the unit cohesion rationale. None of the twenty-three foreign militaries that allow gays and lesbians to acknowledge their sexual orientation has reported a deterioration in unit cohesion. Moreover, hundreds of studies now show that whether a unit's members like each other has no impact on its performance.[8]

In response to the diminishing plausibility of the unit cohesion rationale, proponents of the ban on gays and lesbians in the U.S. military have turned increasingly to an emphasis on privacy to justify their position.[9] They claim that the ban is necessary for preserving the privacy rights of heterosexual service members who would be exposed in showers and living quarters if gays and lesbians were allowed to serve openly in the armed forces.[10] As one proponent explained, "I should not be forced to shower with a woman. I shouldn't be forced to shower with an open gay. . . . I would not want to fight for a country in which privacy issues are so trampled upon."[11]

This article is among the first studies to question the plausibility of this increasingly popular justification for the ban on gays and lesbians from the armed forces.[12] We argue that the ban on gays and lesbians does not protect the privacy rights of heterosexual service members and that lifting the ban would not undermine heterosexual privacy. Because the ban itself compromises heterosexual privacy, we contend that its elimination would actually enhance the privacy of heterosexual service members. We begin by defining the privacy rationale and explaining its importance as a justification for the ban on gays and lesbians in the U.S. military. We then examine the relationship between privacy, morale, and military effectiveness. Next we identify five logical flaws in the privacy rationale and conclude with recommendations for policymakers.

5

THE PRIVACY RATIONALE
AND ITS SIGNIFICANCE

The privacy rationale depends on two premises. One is that service members should have at least partial control over the exposure of their bodies and intimate bodily functions. Service in the military entails numerous personal sacrifices and responsibilities that restrict speech, appearance, and behavior. Although members of the armed forces are not entitled to many prerogatives of civilian life, at least they deserve a degree of control over who sees their naked bodies. Second, the privacy rationale assumes that observation of same-sex nudity arouses sexual desire when the observer is homosexual, and only when the observer is homosexual. According to Melissa Wells-Petry of the Family Research Council, the exposure of bodies and intimate bodily functions does not violate privacy rights when heterosexual service members are segregated in all-male or all-female settings. When homosexuals observe naked bodies or intimate bodily functions, however, they violate the privacy as well as the civil rights of heterosexuals. Wells-Petry argues the homosexual gaze expresses sexual yearning and that heterosexuals do not want to be the objects of homosexuals' sexual desire.[13] She concludes that soldiers should not be "stripped unwittingly of their right to choose to whom they reveal themselves in a sexual context. Once this happens, the harm is done. As a matter of law, the privacy violation does not depend on any acting out of sexual attraction toward others. It is complete the moment privacy is breached."[14] In other words, the injury takes place the moment that an open homosexual sees the naked body of a heterosexual peer.

Concerns for heterosexual privacy are widespread. A search of the Lexis/Nexis database reveals that during the debate over President Clinton's proposal to lift the gay ban, 179 newspaper articles and 50 television transcripts addressed the issue of privacy in the military.[15] A 1993 letter to the editor of the *Seattle Times* was typical of the items in our search results: "The exposure of your nude body, in circumstances you have no control over while serving in the military, could occur on a daily basis; people in the armed forces take showers regularly, and private dressing rooms are not provided to most enlistees. . . . [It] is not farfetched to think that a homosexual could be attracted to someone of the same sex who is not homosexual and that that attraction or potential attraction could make a heterosexual feel embarrassed and vulnerable while nude."[16]

In addition to its prominence in popular discourse, the privacy rationale appears frequently in official debates and regulations. In 1991, D.C. Circuit Justice Oliver Gasch invoked the privacy rationale to justify his unwillingness to reinstate a gay sailor, Joseph Steffan, who had been discharged from the military after acknowledging his homosexuality. Gasch said that "with no one present who has a homosexual orientation, men and women alike can undress, sleep, bathe, and use the bathroom without fear or embarrassment that they are being viewed as sexual objects."[17] Indeed, the congressional statute that codifies the ban on gays and lesbians reflects a concern for heterosexual privacy in noting that "members of the armed forces [often must] involuntarily . . . accept living conditions and working conditions that are often spartan, primitive, and characterized by forced intimacy with little or no privacy."[18] Former Chairman of the Joint Chiefs of Staff Colin Powell argued in 1992 that "to introduce a group of individuals who—proud, brave, loyal, good Americans—but who favor a homosexual life-style, and put them in with heterosexuals who would prefer not to have somebody of the same sex find them sexually attractive, put them in close proximity, ask them to share the most private of their facilities together, the bedroom, the barracks, latrines, the showers, I think that's a very difficult problem to give the military."[19] At the time of Powell's remarks, 63 percent of service members who opposed lifting the gay ban explained their position in terms of not wanting to share facilities and living quarters with homosexuals.[20]

Even when not stated explicitly, concerns about heterosexual privacy often seem to lurk beneath the surface of arguments invoked to justify the ban on gays and lesbians, in particular the notion that predatory homosexual service members use seduction or coercion to manipulate or compel heterosexual peers into having sex. Many opponents of gays and lesbians in the military do not believe that predatory homosexuals pose a problem for the armed forces, but others cite this issue as a justification for exclusion. In explaining his opposition to gays and lesbians in the military during testimony before the Senate Committee on the Armed Services, Gen. Norman Schwarzkopf stated: "I am aware of instances where heterosexuals have been solicited to commit homosexual acts, and, even more traumatic emotionally, physically coerced to engage in such acts."[21] During the same hearings, Maj. Kathleen Bergeron of the U.S. Marine Corps told the senators, "I have seen what happens when lesbian recruits and drill instructors prey on more vulnerable recruits, and take advantage of this exposed environment."[22] Such concerns are not new. One World War II veteran, for example, said that his "Navy ship . . . had five 'aggressive homosexuals' who stroked his leg at night and exposed themselves to him. 'All homosexuals aren't rapists,' he wrote. 'But in this closed male society, with its enforced communal living, unchecked homosexual appetites wrought havoc.'"[23] These and other opponents of gays and lesbians in the military do not claim that sexual intimidation is equivalent to the concern for privacy, but they do seem to imply that observation and predatory behavior are separated by a fine line.

Skeptics may question the usefulness of analyzing the privacy rationale given that opponents of homosexuals in the military could invoke another justification for exclusion if the privacy argument is found to be implausible. Indeed, the justification for excluding gay and lesbian service members has changed several times during the past fifty years, as military officials formulated new rationales whenever evidence undermined the plausibility of old justifications.[24] Opponents of homosexuals in the military, however, no longer have unlimited flexibility to articulate new justifications for the ban. To begin,

10

media attention to the issue increased dramatically after President Clinton's attempt to lift the ban, and as mentioned above, the rationale for exclusion now is articulated in congressional law rather than administrative regulation.[25] Officials who altered the rationale for the military's homosexual personnel policy during the Cold War could do so without attracting much media attention, but the same is not true today. In addition, recent polls show for the first time that a majority of the public believes that gays and lesbians should be allowed to serve openly in the military.[26] Because the public no longer supports the gay ban, officials cannot assume that they have complete freedom to substitute new justifications when old ones come to be seen as implausible. To the extent that experts and the public start to believe that the privacy rationale is implausible, Congress may face additional pressure to lift the ban rather than simply replace it with a new reason for exclusion.

Given the widespread use of privacy concerns to justify the exclusion of acknowledged homosexuals from the military, it is useful to consider whether the gay ban preserves heterosexual privacy and whether lifting the ban would erode that privacy. Before addressing this issue, however, we examine the relationship between privacy, morale, and military effectiveness.

| **COMPANION TEXT** | *Guidelines for Fact-Finding Inquiries into Homosexual Conduct* |

The following text is excerpted from policies adopted by the Defense Department in December 2003. It outlines the circumstances under which inquiries about sexual orientation in the U.S. military should be made. It forms the basis of the "Don't ask; don't tell" policy—still in effect as this book went to print.

C. BASES FOR CONDUCTING INQUIRIES

1. A commander will initiate an inquiry only if he or she has credible information that there is a basis for discharge. Credible information exists when the information, considering its source and the surrounding circumstances, supports a reasonable belief that there is a basis for discharge. It requires a determination based on articulable facts, not just a belief or suspicion.

2. A basis for discharge exists if:
   a. The member has engaged in a homosexual act.
   b. The member has said that he or she is a homosexual or bisexual, or made some other statement that indicates a propensity or intent to engage in homosexual acts; or
   c. The member has married or attempted to marry a person of the same sex.

3. Credible information does not exist, for example, when:

a. The individual is suspected of engaging in homosexual conduct, but there is no credible information, as described, to support that suspicion; or

b. The only information is the opinions of others that a member is homosexual; or

c. The inquiry would be based on rumor, suspicion, or capricious claims concerning a member's sexual orientation; or

d. The only information known is an associational activity such as going to a gay bar, possessing or reading homosexual publications, associating with known homosexuals, or marching in a gay rights rally in civilian clothes. Such activity, in and of itself, does not provide evidence of homosexual conduct.

4. Credible information exists, for example, when:

a. A reliable person states that he or she observed or heard a Service member engaging in homosexual acts, or saying that he or she is a homosexual or bisexual or is married to a member of the same sex; or

b. A reliable person states that he or she heard, observed, or discovered a member make a spoken or written statement that a reasonable person would believe was intended to convey the fact that he or she engages in, attempts to engage in, or has a propensity or intent to engage in homosexual acts; or

c. A reliable person states that he or she observed behavior that amounts to a non-verbal statement by a member that he or she is a homosexual or bisexual; i.e., behavior that a reasonable person would believe was intended to convey the statement that the member engages in, attempts to engage in, or has a propensity or intent to engage in homosexual acts.

D. PROCEDURES

1. Informal fact-finding inquiries and administrative separation procedures are the preferred method of addressing homosexual conduct. This does not prevent disciplinary action or trial by courts-martial when appropriate.

2. Commanders shall exercise sound discretion regarding when credible information exists. They shall examine the information and decide whether an inquiry is warranted or whether no action should be taken.

3. Commanders or appointed inquiry officials shall not ask, and members shall not be required to reveal, whether a member is a heterosexual, a homosexual, or a bisexual. However, upon receipt of credible information of homosexual conduct (as described in section C., above) commanders or appointed inquiry officials may ask members if they engaged in such conduct. But the member should first be advised of the DOD policy on homosexual conduct (and rights under Article 31, UCMJ, if applicable). Should the member choose not to discuss the matter further, the commander should consider other available information. Nothing in this provision precludes questioning a member about any information provided by the member in the course of the fact-finding inquiry or any

related proceeding, nor does it provide the member with any basis for challenging the validity of any proceeding or the use of any evidence, including a statement by the member, in any proceeding.

4. At any given point of the inquiry, the commander or appointed inquiry official must be able clearly and specifically to explain which grounds for separation he or she is attempting to verify and how the information being collected relates to those specific separation grounds.

5. A statement by a Service member that he or she is a homosexual or bisexual creates a rebuttable presumption that the Service member engages in, attempts to engage in, has a propensity to engage in, or intends to engage in homosexual acts. The Service member shall be given the opportunity to present evidence demonstrating that he or she does not engage in, attempt to engage in, or have a propensity or intent to engage in homosexual acts.

6. The Service member bears the burden of proving, by a preponderance of the evidence, that he or she is not a person who engages in, attempts to engage in, has a propensity to engage in, or intends to engage in homosexual acts.

U.S. Department of Defense

PRIVACY, MORALE, AND MILITARY EFFECTIVENESS

As described above, most articulations of the privacy rationale emphasize heterosexual service members' civil liberties. Concerns about privacy, however, can also be expressed in terms of military effectiveness. Recently, for example, senior Pentagon officials identified service members' quality of life as "the main factor in retention," and argued that meeting the Defense Department's readiness targets therefore depends on "providing more privacy and amenities."[27] According to this perspective, protecting privacy is necessary for maintaining morale, which in turn drives retention, recruitment, and other elements of military effectiveness. Indeed, a 1992 tri-service survey reported that increasing privacy was the second most frequently mentioned factor when respondents were asked to identify which improvement in the barracks would have the greatest impact on enlisted retention.[28]

When surveys pose specific questions about living conditions, service members often indicate that they would like more privacy. That said, several factors suggest that concerns about privacy are not important determinants of retention and recruitment. To begin, privacy does not have an indirect causal relationship to retention and recruitment through morale. Margaret Harrell and Laura Miller, for example, surveyed personnel throughout the U.S. armed forces with an open-ended question about "why they thought their morale and their units' morales were the way they were." Of the 805 written replies they received, only 6 mentioned living conditions while 17 mentioned quality-of-life and family considerations. [29] Frederick Manning's comprehensive review of the literature on the origins of military morale does not mention privacy. Rather, scholarship on morale stresses physical factors such as "good health, good food, adequate rest and sleep, clean dry clothes, washing facilities and protection from the elements"; psychological factors including confidence and a sense of personal goals and role fulfillment; and group factors such as common experiences, clear group missions, and trust in leadership. [30] An inventory of nineteen causes of military morale does not include privacy. [31] And as far back as the 1950s, a statistical analysis of morale among 11,000 separatees from the U.S. Navy found that submariners (who enjoy little privacy) had the highest morale out of seven different occupational specialties. [32] Because privacy is not a major contributor to morale, it seems unlikely that privacy could have an indirect causal relationship to retention and recruitment through morale.

In addition, even after morale is eliminated as a mediating variable, privacy does not seem to be directly causally related to retention and recruitment. Scholars have identified factors such as pay, promotion timing, education, and civilian unemployment rates as being much more important determinants of successful retention and recruitment than quality-of-life considerations such as housing and privacy. [33] As the General Accounting Office concluded, "There is little evidence to support DOD's assumption that improved barracks will result in improved readiness and higher enlisted retention rates. . . . Further, information collected from members that do not reenlist has shown that factors other than housing, such as pay and promotion opportunities, are usually cited as the reasons members leave the military." [34] Although some studies do argue that the quality and availability of military housing can influence reenlistment decisions, a close look at the data reveals that the desire for privacy does not seem to be a major determinant of dissatisfaction with housing. [35] For example, junior enlisted marines who are married express almost as much dissatisfaction with military housing as those who are single. [36] Given that living quarters for [married] enlisted personnel provide more privacy than bachelor enlisted quarters, it seems unlikely that the desire for privacy is a driving factor behind dissatisfaction with housing.

Finally, even if scholars could demonstrate a theoretical causal relationship   15
between privacy, retention, and recruitment, a new military housing construction program should dispel many of the concerns over the lack of privacy. By the end of the decade, most junior enlisted personnel who live on U.S. Air Force, Army, and Navy bases will be provided with their own bedrooms as well as bathrooms to share with one other individual. [37] As the *Army Times* reported recently, the "Army is spending billions of dollars on a barracks face-lift plan that's giving more and more soldiers their own rooms and making the 'gang latrine' a thing of the past." [38] One soldier remarked that "the privacy is great. [You] have your own personal bathroom you get to share

with one person instead of 60 to 80 people."[39] Service members will have to sacrifice their privacy during basic training and in some field and combat situations, but most enlisted personnel will soon have access to private bedrooms and showers most of the time.

FLAWS IN THE PRIVACY RATIONALE

There are five reasons why the ban on gays and lesbians in the U.S. military does not preserve heterosexual privacy in the showers and the barracks and why lifting the ban would enhance rather than undermine heterosexual privacy.

Heterosexuals Already Shower with Known Homosexuals

The privacy rationale is premised on the assumption that known gays and lesbians do not already serve in the U.S. armed forces. This assumption is an important premise of the privacy rationale because if known homosexuals already serve in the U.S. armed forces, then lifting the ban will not decrease heterosexual privacy (unless numerous gays and lesbians come out of the closet after they are allowed to do so, a possibility that we address below).

Anecdotal and statistical data suggest that known gays and lesbians do serve in the U.S. armed forces. Consider, for example, Melissa Sheridan Embser-Herbert's (hereinafter cited as Herbert) remarks before the Commonwealth Club of California: "One day my drill sergeant called me into his office. And he called me in with another woman in my unit, whom I had been dating on the weekends. He said, "I know what's going on. This is the Army, and you two have got to be more discreet." End of conversation. He was not a bleeding heart liberal, and by all accounts he was heterosexual, as well. But he knew. As did most of the women in Bravo Company, Tenth Battalion. They might not have liked it—that is a different question—but they knew."[40]

Statistical data seem to indicate that this anecdote does not reflect an isolated case. For example, a recent study of 368 officers and enlisted personnel in the U.S. Navy and Marine Corps found that 20.1 percent personally knew a homosexual service member; another 22.3 percent were unsure as to whether they knew a homosexual service member.[41] If these figures are extrapolated to the entire armed forces, then approximately 301,500 service members personally knew a homosexual peer at the time this study was conducted, and approximately 334,500 service members were unsure as to whether they personally knew a homosexual peer. Although this small study may not represent overall trends, it seems to suggest that many service members already bunk and shower with people they know to be gay or lesbian. Indeed, a 1995 study includes an eight-page list of gays and lesbians who served openly in the U.S. military, and a 2001 report offers four case studies of gay and lesbian service members whose sexual orientation was well known by every member of their unit.[42]

In the early 1990s, Herbert collected survey data from 394 female veterans and active-duty service members on their experiences in the U.S. military.[43] She asked participants who identified as heterosexual for any part of their military career to respond to the statement, "I knew military women who were lesbian/bisexual." Seventy-nine percent of the women responded yes. Herbert then asked respondents who identified as lesbian or bisexual during any part of their military career to indicate "definitely not true," "probably not true," "uncertain," "probably true," or "definitely true" to the following statements:

1. Women whom I believe were heterosexual knew that I was lesbian/bisexual.
2. Men whom I believe were heterosexual knew that I was lesbian/bisexual.
3. Some of my supervisors knew that I was lesbian/bisexual.

Of the 111 women who responded, 64 percent indicated that it was "definitely true" or "probably true" that women whom they recognized as heterosexual knew that the respondent was lesbian or bisexual. Fifty-one percent indicated "probably true" or "definitely true" that men they believed to be heterosexual recognized them as lesbian or bisexual. And 56 percent indicated "probably true" or "definitely true" with regard to their supervisors.

Herbert then asked respondents who answered "probably true" or "definitely true" to any of the three items listed above what led them to believe that others thought they were lesbian or bisexual. Of the 86 open-ended responses to this question, slightly more than half were variations of "I told them." Others provided a range of examples of how coworkers and supervisors came to know that they were lesbian or bisexual. For example, one private first-class wrote, "Some just outright asked and I told. Others just had gay-dar I guess." Another wrote, "I told a supervisor who was trying to get me to date him." Some women felt that they had to be honest with supervisors whose help they needed. An enlisted woman in the army wrote, "I told my supervisor because I was breaking up an eight-year relationship with my lover. I needed time off and he supported me a hundred percent." And an army captain offered, "Due to a difficult situation which arose, I informed my commander because I needed his help."

Skeptics might respond that known gays and lesbians do not serve in combat units, and we acknowledge that the survey results presented above do not distinguish between women who served in combat areas and those who did not. That said, statistical evidence from foreign militaries may be relevant to determining whether known gays serve in U.S. combat units. In 2000, Daniel Kaplan and Aaron Belkin asked 194 combat soldiers in the Israel Defense Forces (IDF) if they knew a gay peer in their unit.[44] They found that 21.6 percent of respondents had such knowledge, and an additional 19.6 percent may have known a gay peer in their unit. The claim that no known gays serve in U.S. combat units may not have any more validity than the claim that none serve in Israeli combat units.

Lifting the Ban Will Not Increase Sexual Disclosures

The privacy rationale is based in part on the mistaken premise that numerous gays and lesbians will reveal their sexual orientation after the lifting of the gay ban. If, however, few gays and lesbians reveal their sexual orientation after they are allowed to do so, then the privacy rationale is flawed because little if anything will change in the showers and the barracks once the ban is lifted—even if open homosexuals do undermine heterosexual privacy.

Even though many known gays and lesbians already serve in the U.S. armed forces, the data indicate that few additional homosexuals will reveal their sexual orientation following the lifting of the ban. Four recent studies of gays and lesbians in the Australian, British, Canadian, and Israeli forces found the same pattern: In all four cases, the authors discovered that prior to the lifting of the ban, some gay and lesbian soldiers already were known by their peers to be homosexual, but that few additional homosexual soldiers revealed their sexual orientation once allowed to do so.[45] In Australia, a 1996 report found that three years after the lifting of the ban, only thirty-three homosexual soldiers were willing to identify themselves to the authors of the study.[46] In Canada, the Department of National Defence received only seventeen claims for medical, dental, and relocation benefits for homosexual partners in 1998, six years after the Canadian ban had been lifted. Given the Canadian military's own estimate that 3.5 percent of its personnel are gay or lesbian, the low figure suggests that gay and lesbian service members may hesitate to reveal their sexual orientation by requesting benefits.[47]

In practice, the presence or absence of a ban on gays and lesbians has little to do with disclosure rates.[48] Rather, the culture of the unit is the primary determinant of decisions to reveal sexual orientation: Gay and lesbian service members reveal their sexual orientation only when it is safe to do so. For example, a study of American police departments that allow acknowledged homosexuals to serve identified 7 open gays and lesbians in the Chicago Police Department and approximately 100 in the New York City Police Department.[49] Several factors may account for the variation in disclosure rates, but scholars who have compared police and fire departments believe that much if not most of the variance reflects the fact that personal safety is the primary determinant of Americans' decisions to reveal their sexual orientation. Because individual safety varies from organization to organization depending on whether leaders express clear messages in support of integration, disclosure rates vary as well. Paul Kogel claims that "perhaps one of the most salient factors that influences whether homosexual police officers or firefighters make their sexual orientation known to their departments is their perception of the climate. . . . The more hostile the environment, the less likely it was that people publicly acknowledged their homosexuality."[50] Similar variance can be found in the U.S. military: A recent study found that while 21.2 percent of naval officers knew a gay sailor, only 4.1 percent of U.S. Marine officers knew a gay marine.[51] It seems likely to us that this difference results from the fact that closeted gays believe that it is safer to reveal their homosexuality in the U.S. Navy than in the Marine Corps: Indeed, the same study found attitudes of U.S. Navy personnel to be more tolerant toward homosexuals than those of the marines.[52]

Proponents argue that lifting the ban will increase the number of open gays and lesbians in the U.S. military, and that the presence of open homosexuals will undermine privacy in the shower. The data suggest, however, that few additional homosexuals will reveal their sexual orientation after they are allowed to do so. Thus, even if open homosexuals undermine heterosexual privacy, lifting the gay ban will have little or no impact on conditions in military living quarters.

Few Heterosexuals Are Extremely Uncomfortable around Homosexuals

Proponents of the privacy rationale mistakenly assume that many heterosexual service members are extremely uncomfortable around gays and lesbians and that they will remain so after the lifting of the ban. Although statistical surveys indicate that most U.S. service members oppose showering with homosexuals and lifting the ban, studies indicate that discomfort has diminished considerably and that heterosexual dislike of gays and lesbians is less extreme than advocates of the privacy rationale assume. For example, between 1992 and 1998, the percentage of U.S. Army men who strongly opposed allowing gays and lesbians in the military dropped from 67 percent to 36 percent, while the percentage of army women strongly opposed dropped from 32 percent to 16 percent.[53] Seventy-one percent of naval officers in a recent survey agreed or strongly agreed that "compared with my peers, I consider myself more tolerant on the issue of homosexuals in the military," and 64 percent disagreed or strongly disagreed that they "feel comfortable in the presence of homosexuals and have difficulty interacting normally with them."[54] Armando Estrada, a psychologist at the Naval Postgraduate School, and David Weiss, a professor of psychology at California State University–Los Angeles, measured male marines' attitudes toward homosexuals in a 1999 study and found that on a scale of 0 to 100, the marines' average score was 47.52[55] The specific number is less meaningful than the fact that the average score fell roughly in the middle of the scale, thus indicating mild dislike rather than widespread hatred. Although some people in the military may hate gays and lesbians or be extremely uncomfortable around them, on average one seems to find mild dislike.

Relatedly, the privacy rationale is premised on the assumption that heterosexual service members who are extremely uncomfortable around gays and lesbians will remain so after the lifting of the ban. According to the contact hypothesis, however, this assumption may not be valid. The contact hypothesis, a robust finding that has been confirmed in numerous social scientific experiments, posits that discomfort "can be reduced by personal contact between majority and minority groups in pursuit of common goals."[56] The consensus in the literature is that heterosexual discomfort toward gays and lesbians tends to diminish after personal interaction with homosexual individuals.[57]

Evidence from foreign militaries seems to indicate that heterosexual discomfort does tend to diminish after the lifting of a gay ban. In 1995, for example, the British Ministry of Defence surveyed 13,500 service members and found that 66 percent of the respondents would not have willingly served if the ban were lifted. Despite these findings, only three service members resigned after Britain lifted its gay ban in 2000. An official from the British Ministry of Defence noted that the "media likes scare stories—about showers and what have you. A lot of people were worried that they would have to share body heat in close quarters or see two men being affectionate, and they would feel uncomfortable. But it has proved at first look that it's not an issue."[58]

In Canada, a 1985 survey of 6,580 male service members found that 62 percent would refuse to share showers, undress, or sleep in the same room as a gay soldier. A 1995 survey of 3,202 service members that followed the 1992 lifting of the gay ban found that 67.7 percent of respondents were neutral or satisfied with the policy change.[59] Lessons from foreign forces that lifted their bans seem to cast some doubt on the assumption that the minority of heterosexual U.S. service members who are extremely uncomfortable around gays and lesbians will remain so after the lifting of the ban. *30*

The Analogy to Men and Women in the Shower Is Flawed

Privacy rationale advocates often claim that just as the military does not require men and women to shower together, heterosexuals should not have to shower with open gays and lesbians. According to this perspective, the presumption that every service member in the shower is heterosexual is a useful fiction.

Although men and women use the same facilities in some field environments, the armed forces do maintain separate quarters for them in most settings.[60] In permanent deployments including assignments at sea, for example, men and women typically do not share living quarters or facilities. Moreover, in 1998 Congress required the Defense Department to "provide separate and secure housing for male and female recruits with separate entrances and with sleeping and latrine areas separated by permanent walls."[61]

Despite the military's efforts to maintain separate facilities for the sexes, however, the analogy fails to capture that heterosexuals showering with open gays and lesbians is much less of a departure from the norms of civilian society than men showering with women. If men and women showered together in prisons, gyms, summer camps, university dorms, high school and college locker rooms, as well as professional changing areas in hospitals, courthouses, and fire and police stations, then perhaps it would seem reasonable for men and women to shower together in the military. Men and women do not, however, shower together in any of these civilian settings. Open gays and heterosexuals, by contrast, shower together in all of these settings. In addition, the analogy is premised on the flawed assumption that communal showers typify military practice. As noted above, by the end of the decade most junior enlisted personnel will be housed in private bedrooms with a bathroom to share with just one other individual.[62]

Lifting the Ban Will Enhance Heterosexual Privacy

We have argued throughout this article that the ban on gays and lesbians in the U.S. military does not protect heterosexual privacy and that lifting the ban will not undermine heterosexual privacy. Indeed, because the ban enables a systematic invasion of heterosexual privacy, lifting it would enhance the privacy rights of heterosexual service members. To begin, the ban undermines heterosexual privacy when military investigators inquire into the sexual behavior of spouses, partners, friends, and relatives of service members suspected of being gay. Their questions can be vulgar and intrusive, and a 1995 memorandum from U.S. Air Force headquarters instructs military lawyers to interview parents, siblings, school counselors, educational advisors, school officials, school career development officers, roommates, close friends, and romantic partners of service members who say that they are gay.[63]

In addition, the gay ban can undermine the privacy of heterosexual service members who feel compelled to demonstrate their heterosexuality. For most heterosexual service members, of course, sexual orientation is transparent and no effort is required to avoid being labeled a homosexual. For others, however, particularly men whose gender identity does not reflect traditional notions of masculinity and women who do not conform to stereotypical understandings of femininity, the effort to avoid being labeled as a homosexual can entail a loss of privacy. Twenty-one percent of participants in a study of how military women manage perceptions of gender and sexuality indicated that they consciously employ strategies aimed at ensuring that others do not perceive them to be lesbian or bisexual. Of those 21 percent, more than one-third were heterosexual.[64]

Gender management strategies can entail minor as well as significant privacy compromises for heterosexual service members. Some women in the study mentioned above revealed details of their private lives with peers, including those with whom they might not otherwise share such intimacies. One heterosexual woman mentioned "talk[ing] about guys" to avoid the perception that she was lesbian or bisexual while another described "always having a boyfriend." Of those respondents who acknowledged strategizing to avoid being perceived as lesbian/bisexual, one in five indicated that they dated men to prove their heterosexuality, while one in five acknowledged that this concern was at least part of their motivation for marrying.[65] Marriages of

35

convenience among gays and lesbians are neither surprising nor new, and it is likely that some service members would continue to take such steps to avoid being labeled as homosexual even if the ban were lifted. But, to realize that for some heterosexual women at least part of their motivation to marry is to avoid being perceived as lesbian or bisexual is an indication of the impact of the gay ban on heterosexual privacy.[66]

CONCLUSION

The argument that gays and lesbians must be excluded from the armed forces to preserve the privacy rights of heterosexuals has become an increasingly important basis for the banning of open homosexuals from the U.S. military at the same time that the plausibility of the unit cohesion rationale, the ban's other justification, has greatly diminished. Even if the logic of the privacy rationale were sound, its validity would be undermined by a new housing program that is providing most junior enlisted personnel with their own bedrooms and a bathroom to share with one other person. But the logic of the privacy rationale is not sound. The rationale is premised on the assumptions that heterosexual service members do not already serve with peers they know to be homosexual, that lifting the gay ban will significantly increase the number of open gays and lesbians in the U.S. military, and that the minority of heterosexuals who are extremely uncomfortable around gays and lesbians will remain so after the lifting of the ban. All of these assumptions are required to establish the plausibility of the privacy rationale, yet none of them are valid. Ironically, the gay ban does more to undermine heterosexual privacy than to enhance it when military investigators inquire into the sexual behavior of spouses, partners, friends, and relatives of service members who are suspected of being gay or when some heterosexuals feel compelled to prove their sexual orientation by dating or marrying members of the opposite sex.

Because neither the privacy rationale nor the unit cohesion rationale provides a compelling justification for excluding service members who acknowledge that they are homosexual, congressional leaders should reappraise the necessity of the gay ban. If Congress does decide to lift the ban, five steps would ensure a smooth transition, preserve organizational effectiveness, and minimize cost and disruption. First, Congress should replace Section 571 of the 1994 National Defense Authorization Act with a nondiscrimination pledge concerning sexual orientation and gender identity.[67] Because the gay ban is articulated in law, congressional action is required to eliminate it. Second, the Defense Department should annul implementing regulations associated with the "Don't Ask, Don't Tell, Don't Pursue, Don't Harass" policy and follow Britain's lead by adopting a new code of professional conduct that defines unacceptable behavior without regard to sexual orientation.[68] Third, senior military leaders should declare publicly that they support the integration of open gays and lesbians and that they will discipline individuals who violate the new code of conduct. As studies of organizational diversity have found, successful integration depends on leadership's forceful commitment to inclusion.[69] Fourth, Congress should follow the May 2001 recommendation of the Cox Commission, a panel of experts on military law sponsored by the National Institute of Military Justice, and repeal the prohibition against heterosexual and homosexual sodomy included in Article 125 of the Uniform Code of Military Justice.[70] Finally, the Defense Department should ensure that diversity-training programs explain the new policy thoroughly and that they are consistent across the various branches and commands. Although some in the United States may fear these steps, the experiences of other military and paramilitary organizations that lifted their gay bans show that cohesion, morale, recruitment, retention, and privacy will be preserved or even enhanced by allowing individuals who acknowledge their homosexuality to serve in uniform.[71]

QUESTIONS FOR DISCUSSION

1. What is the function of the first section of this argument (paragraphs 1–5)?
2. In paragraph 5, the authors introduce the first-person plural. How appropriate is the use of "we" given the purpose and tone of the argument as a whole? Later, the authors cite "Embser-Herbert" as one of their sources. Embser-Herbert, however, is one of the co-authors. Is this appropriate given the earlier use of "we"?
3. Consider testimony given in paragraph 9. Do you think that heterosexuals in the military might ever be subject to unwelcome advances from other heterosexuals? Why do you think some people find it more upsetting to be propositioned by a homosexual than by a heterosexual?
4. Why is it significant that the ban on homosexuals in the military became "congressional law rather than administrative regulation," as the authors note in paragraph 10?
5. In paragraph 18, one of the authors reveals her sexual orientation. Was this a good writing decision?
6. Why do you think countries as different as Canada and Israel accept homosexuals into their militaries, but the United States resists doing so?
7. Consider the statistics in paragraph 25. Why do you think that police in Chicago could be so different from police in New York City?
8. The authors conclude with a number of specific proposals. How well does the argument as a whole prepare for these proposals? To what extent do you agree?

SUGGESTIONS FOR WRITING

1. If you are opposed to admitting homosexuals into the military, write an argument based on something other than the privacy and morale issues that were the focus of the piece you just read.

2. Research how another country went about integrating gays and lesbians into its military, and then write an argument focused on what we can learn from this history.
3. Research sexual harassment in the U.S. military, and determine who suffers the most frequently. Then write an argument focused on how sexual harassment should be handled by commanders.

LINKS

■ Within the Book

In "Same-Sex Sexuality" (pages 221–238) Joan Roughgarden reports on scientific research on why animals have sex with other animals of the same gender.

■ Elsewhere in Print

Berube, Allan. *Coming Out under Fire: Gay Men and Women in World War Two.* New York: Penguin, 1990.

Burke, Carol. *Camp All-American, Hanoi Jane, and the High and Tight: Gender, Folklore, and the Changing Military Culture.* New York: Beacon, 2004.

Herek, Gregory, Jared Jobe, and Ralph Carney. *Out in Force: Sexual Orientation and the Military.* Chicago: U of Chicago P, 1996.

National Defense Research Institute. *Sexual Orientation and U.S. Military Policy, Options, and Assessments.* Washington, DC: Rand, 1993.

Shilts, Randy. *Conduct Unbecoming: Gays and Lesbians in the U.S. Military.* New York: St. Martin's, 1993.

Zeeland, Steven. *Barrack Buddies and Soldier Lovers: Dialogues with Gay Young Men in the U.S. Military.* Binghamton: Haworth, 1993.

■ Online

www.mhhe.com/motives

Click on "More Resources" then "Writing to Persuade Others."

■ ■ ■

USING STYLE FOR EMPHASIS

Martin Luther King, Jr.'s "I Have a Dream" speech provides an example of political exhortation at its best. The words on the page and the care with which they are arranged make it a moving piece of prose even without the benefit of our hearing King's voice or being present when this speech was delivered. Visualizing the situation for which this speech was designed, however, can help you understand King's purpose and the techniques he used to arouse his audience's emotions. The occasion was the hundredth anniversary of the Emancipation Proclamation; the scene was the steps of the Lincoln Memorial, from which King faced an audience of more than 200,000 people who had marched to Washington on behalf of civil rights for African Americans. King did not need to persuade that audience that African Americans deserved civil rights. If they didn't already believe this, they would not have come to Washington. What King needed to do was to reinforce the beliefs his audience already shared—to vindicate whatever hardships they had endured and to lift up their hearts.

Although the entire speech deserves close reading, a short excerpt illustrates a number of points essential to our understanding of writing to move. Here are paragraphs 9 and 10 from the eighteen-paragraph-long speech:

> I am not unmindful that some of you have come here out of great trials and tribulations. Some of you have come fresh from narrow jail cells. Some of you have come from areas where your quest for freedom left you battered by the storms of persecution and staggered by the winds of police brutality. You have been the veterans of creative suffering. Continue to work with the faith that unearned suffering is redemptive.
>
> Go back to Mississippi, and go back to Alabama. Go back to South Carolina. Go back to Georgia. Go back to Louisiana. Go back to the slums and ghettos of our Northern cities, knowing that somehow this situation can and will be changed. Let us not wallow in the valley of despair.

When we look closely at these paragraphs, we see that King is not attempting to persuade his audience to undertake a specific action. True, he advises his listeners to go back home and keep on working, but the promise that "somehow this situation can and will be changed" is short on details and unlikely to satisfy someone who has not been moved by the speech as a whole.

A paraphrase focusing only on the content of these two paragraphs might read: "I know you've all had a rough time, but go back home and cheer up. Things are going to get better." Reducing King's prose to this paraphrase is grotesque but illuminating: We have stripped these paragraphs of their beauty and their power to inspire—deprived them of their reason for being. What is it, then, that makes King's prose moving?

In the first place, King was a gifted prose stylist with a fine ear for rhythm; his sentences are so nicely cadenced that they can engage the attention of an audience by the quality of their music. The excerpt (on page 523) uses two techniques that can be found in much of King's work. When he writes "trials and tribulations," he is using a simple form of *parallel construction,* which means putting similar ideas in similar form for the sake of balance. In this case, a plural noun is balanced with a plural noun.

The third sentence in the first paragraph provides another example of parallelism: "battered by the storms of persecution and staggered by the winds of police brutality." "Battered" is balanced against "staggered," "storms" against "winds," and "persecution" against "police brutality"—as can be easily seen when we reformat these lines:

<u>battered</u>   <u>by the storms</u>   <u>of persecution</u>

and

<u>staggered</u>   <u>by the winds</u>   <u>of police brutality</u>

Only "police" keeps this example from being perfectly parallel. It is being used here as an adjective describing "brutality," but there is no equivalent adjective describing "persecution." From this example, we can conclude two things.

- Parallelism does not necessarily require a word-for-word balance—although the more the words are balanced, the stronger the parallel will be.

- A word or phrase that does not fit within a parallel structure will receive increased emphasis because it interferes with the prevailing rhythm. In this case, it is quite possible that King wanted "police" to have this effect. His original audience would have believed that the police were interfering with much more than parallel construction.

Although the second paragraph of the excerpt also features a strong parallel structure in which patterns repeat and harmonize with one another, it also illustrates another rhetorical device—*anaphora,* or deliberate repetition at the beginning of sentences or clauses for the purpose of affecting the reader. King emphasizes "Go back" to such an extent here that the words no longer seem as simple as they would in another context (e.g., "Go back to your room and get a sweater"). As the "Go backs" accumulate, they become a type of song in which the words mean more than they say. Behind these "Go backs" is a meaning that can be felt even though it is unstated. "Go back" becomes "Go back and don't give up; go back and keep on fighting."

The rhetorical use of repetition for emphasis can be thought of as a more sophisticated version of how a cheerleader uses repetition when trying to move a crowd ("*Go* team *go; fight* team *fight*"). Unlike the simple chants you hear at a pep rally, King's prose draws on a variety of techniques and does so for a serious end. Nevertheless, one way of reading "I Have a Dream" is as a type of rallying cry. King's purpose, after all, was to inspire his listeners to continued struggle by reaffirming the importance of their common cause.

Neither parallel construction nor deliberate repetition is limited to exhortation, and you will find examples of both in works that have other motives behind them. But because writing to inspire has strong links to oratory, it is especially likely to draw on strategies like these that make sentences easy to read and remember. When you read "I Have a Dream," you will find that King uses both parallelism and repetition many times. You will also find that he keeps his diction simple. With the possible exception of two words ("tribulations" and "redemptive"), the words of the passage quoted previously could be understood by almost any English-speaking person. King, an experienced speaker, understood that people cannot be moved by what they do not understand. On this occasion, eloquence required simplicity because he was addressing a large and diverse audience.

Style, however, is only one of the factors that explain why King's prose is so much more effective than the paraphrase of it (on page 523). Writing to inspire requires creating a bond between writer and reader. It is one thing to say, "I know you've had a rough time." It is something else to show that you mean it and to leave your audience feeling personally addressed. Many of the people in King's audience would have been touched personally by the sympathetic reference to "narrow jail cells." And almost everyone in that audience would have had some experience with "persecution" and "police brutality." King then makes specific references to five southern states and a more general reference to northern cities. Anyone from Mississippi, Alabama, South Carolina, Georgia, or Louisiana would have felt as if King were addressing him or her as an individual. Furthermore, the list of five is long enough to be understood as representing other states that go unmentioned. And references to different states remind the people in the crowd that they have friends and allies elsewhere because they are part of a nationwide struggle.

As "I Have a Dream" suggests, writing to inspire requires more than eloquent phrasing. It also requires a strong sense of audience, which, in turn, ultimately depends on understanding human nature and the types of experiences that evoke different emotions.

PLANNING AND DEVELOPING YOUR ESSAY

When analyzing "I Have a Dream" and the other readings in this chapter, you can benefit from principles laid down in the eighteenth century by Hugh Blair, a professor at the University of Edinburgh, to determine what makes language inspiring. He offers seven principles that can help you understand the work of other writers and write inspiring essays of your own.*

---

*These principles are adapted from Blair's *Lectures on Rhetoric and Belles Lettres,* first published in 1783. A modern edition edited by Harold E. Harding is available (Carbondale: Southern Illinois UP, 1965).

First, choose a topic that is suitable for writing to move. In the pages that follow, King addresses the subject of social injustice, Ron and Nancy Reagan call for helping the seriously ill, George Orwell raises questions about capital punishment, and Alice Walker reflects on the treatment of an animal. Depending on how a writer proceeds, topics such as these can inspire a number of emotions—including anger, indignation, pity, and grief. There are, of course, many other topics suitable for this type of writing. Larry Carlat, for example, uses writing as a way to help his adopted son understand how much he is loved, and George W. Bush uses rhetoric designed to fortify a nation under attack. However, there are also topics (such as an explanation of how the brain functions) that would be inappropriate for writing to inspire. If you try to inspire an emotion that seems unrelated to the topic, your prose may seem overwrought rather than inspiring.

Second, get right into the topic without warning readers of your intention. If you begin by writing, "I am going to tell you a sad story" (or words to that effect), you are weakening your work in at least two ways. By telling readers how you want them to respond—as opposed to letting the response grow naturally out of the work—you are giving them a ready-made standard for evaluating your work; and you may find someone who responds, "Well, I didn't think that was so sad." Moreover, by putting readers on guard, you lose the strategic advantage of surprise. Readers alerted in advance to "a sad story" could brace themselves against feeling sad or decide to put your work aside to read something more cheerful. When you read "A Hanging," for example, you will find that Orwell never tells us how to feel about the execution he describes.

Third, include details that can evoke the response you intend. Although supporting detail is important in almost all types of writing, it is especially important when writing to inspire. And the details you choose should have emotional appeal. For example, a description of a homeless person sleeping on a sidewalk is likely to be more inspiring than several paragraphs of statistics. Consider, in this regard, how Orwell focuses on a specific prisoner at the hour of his death rather than on providing statistics on capital punishment. Or to choose another example, consider how Garrison Keillor draws attention to his daughter, a co-worker, and a young professor.

Fourth, be moved yourself. Although there are many rhetorical situations in which writers need to keep their feelings to themselves, writing to inspire requires that you yourself feel the emotion that you want others to share. This does not mean that you have to come out and tell readers how you feel; on the contrary, you should focus on your subject rather than on yourself. It happens that all of the writers in this chapter use the first person at some point. But even if you never mention yourself, readers should be able to tell how you feel about your subject. The main thing is to avoid insincerity. If you really don't care about poverty but think it would be proper to sound as if you do, you are unlikely to succeed at inspiring others. Write about what you care about, and don't try to fake emotion.

Fifth, write simply and directly. When you feel something strongly, you are likely to use language that is simple, direct, and bold. Formal diction and long, complicated sentences will seem artful rather than direct and will diminish the sense that you are moved by your subject. Here, for example, is Walker describing her response to eating meat: "I am eating misery, I thought, as I took the first bite. And spit it out." These two sentences may be the result of several drafts, for the words that first occur to writers are not necessarily those that are the simplest and most direct. But the apparent simplicity of these sentences helps convey emotion. The force of "And spit it out" would be lost if, afraid to use a word like *spit,* Walker consulted a thesaurus and tried using, say, *expectorated.* Because of the directness necessary for writing to move, you should find all the selections in this chapter easy to read.

Sixth, be faithful to your purpose. When writing to inspire, you need to avoid any digression that would interrupt the flow of feeling you are trying to inspire. Had King paused in the middle of "I Have a Dream" to offer an analysis of congressional legislation affecting civil rights, he would have weakened the emotional power of his speech. King knew a great deal about his topic, but the context of "I Have a Dream" was one that called for inspiration rather than information. As you revise an essay designed to inspire, be prepared to cut not only digressions but also any sentence that seems too fancy. As Blair put it, "Sacrifice all beauties, however bright and showy, which would divert the mind from the principal object, and which would amuse the imagination, rather than touch the heart."

Seventh, know when to stop. As a general rule, writing designed to inspire needs to be kept fairly short. It is difficult to sustain intensity of feeling at any great length; and if you write too much about your subject, you run the risk of readers deciding that you are making too much of a fuss. Most of the readings in this chapter are only about four pages long, and on an important historic occasion, George W. Bush takes only six. Knowing when to stop cannot be measured by word count alone, however. It is also a matter of understanding where you can afford to linger and where it is best to let a few carefully chosen words convey a sense of things unsaid. When your material is strong, you can often benefit from handling it with restraint, letting readers' imagination fill in the gaps along lines you have merely suggested. Consider, for example, how George Orwell concludes his detailed description of an execution that took place in Burma when that country was part of the British Empire. Francis, the head jailer, remembers cases in which someone had to pull on the legs of a man being hanged to make him die. Here are the last two paragraphs of Orwell's essay:

> I found that I was laughing quite loudly. Everyone was laughing. Even the superintendent grinned in a tolerant way. "You'd better all come out and have a drink," he said quite genially. "I've got a bottle of whiskey in the car. We could do with it."

We went through the big double gates of the prison into the road. "Pulling at his legs!" exclaimed a Burmese magistrate suddenly, and burst into a loud chuckling. We all began laughing again. At that moment Francis' anecdote seemed extraordinarily funny. We all had a drink together, native and European alike, quite amicably. The dead man was a hundred yards away.

When you read "A Hanging," you should be able to understand why these men are laughing immediately after witnessing an execution. And you should also be able to understand why Orwell moves directly from reporting this laughter to the short, simple sentence with which he concludes: "The dead man was a hundred yards away." There is irony in this situation—irony that would almost certainly be less moving if the writer explained it neatly away. Orwell wisely recognized that his material called for a mixture of frankness and restraint.

Of course, writing to inspire cannot be mastered by simply memorizing a few rules. Whatever the reason you may want to inspire people, you should not only practice the techniques outlined here but also watch and listen to other people. You may already know how to touch the hearts of those close to you. By reading the work of other writers and practicing the techniques of writing to inspire, you can ultimately learn to touch people you haven't met. The ability to inspire emotion is one of the most useful achievements of rhetoric. But like any other type of writing, it takes study and practice.

TIPS FOR READING AND WRITING TO INSPIRE

When Reading

- Determine the audience for which the piece was originally composed as well as the values and beliefs the author assumes that audience holds.
- Consider what kind of people seem excluded from the author's audience. Did the author exclude them deliberately or accidentally?
- Be alert for words or examples that evoke the kind of response the author desires.
- Consider if the author has used repetition, parallelism, or other stylistic choices for emphasis or clarity.
- Determine what kind of inspiration the author is trying to evoke. Is she or he drawing attention to positive feelings and examples in order to reinforce the audience's desire to do good? Or is the author drawing attention to problems in the hope of inspiring a change of heart?

When Writing

- Choose an appropriate topic.
- Get right to the topic without warning readers of your intentions.
- Use words and examples that evoke the response you seek.
- Be sincere.
- Write simply and directly, emphasizing key points.
- Stay focused on fulfilling your purpose.
- Keep it short. Other motives for writing may require you to write at length, but if you spend too much time evoking feeling, you may leave your readers bored rather than inspired.

YOU ARE ME

Larry Carlat

How can a father convey to his son the depth of his love, especially in a culture that often discourages men from expressing their feelings? And why might this message be especially important for a child who knows he was adopted? In the following letter, first published in Esquire *in 1998, Larry Carlat tries to make his feelings clear. As you read, imagine that you are the recipient of this letter, and note whether you are moved by it. Based in Woodbury, New York, Carlat is editor of* Toy & Hobby World.

Dear Robbie,

You were born a poet. Let me quote a few of your best lines:

I bet my birth mother is still crying.
I wish God would take the sadness off me.
If she kept me, I never would've known you.
I have a space in my heart that never closes.

As I sit here wrestling with words that invariably elude my grasp, I wish I could write like that. But what do I expect? You are seven, and I am only forty-two.

Before you read any further, you should know that your mom doesn't want me to write this. She doesn't want me to write anything that might one day awaken any doubt in you. So I made a deal with her. I promised that if she feels the same way after I've finished, I'll punt on the whole thing. That's how intensely she feels about you, how fiercely protective she is of you. She doesn't want me to write this letter, because she loves you so much, and I love you so much that I have to write it, even if I don't show it to you until you have kids of your own.

Here are the words your mom fears: *I didn't want to adopt you.*   5

I know that sounds like powerful stuff, but to me those words are as tri-fling as the ants that march across the kitchen floor before you put your thumb to them. They mean nothing because I can't even remember feeling that way. I've searched my heart and can't find any trace of not wanting you. It would be like not wanting air. Still, just as I can't imagine not wanting you now, there was a time when I couldn't imagine *you*. I didn't know that you were going to be you. I knew only that you were not going to be *me*.

Your mom says I was hung up on this crazy little thing called genetics, which should never be mistaken for that crazy little thing called love. It all seems so bizarre, given that my family background includes everything from cancer and heart disease to criminal behavior. Your mom says that I was worried that you wouldn't be perfect, that we would be inheriting somebody else's problem, and that nurture would be revealed as nothing more than nature's cheap consolation prize. Your mom says I can't recollect any of these gory details because sometimes I can be a stubborn bastard.

That must be where you get it from.

Because, Rob, when all is said and done, you are me—only way better looking. You are me if I looked like Brad Pitt and your mom looked like Sharon Stone. You're more like me than Zachary, who inherited torn genes from me and Mom. You and I are both the eldest son, moderately shy, and exceedingly anxious. We love Michael Jordan, movies, scallion pancakes, and the occasional doody joke. We're natural-born outsiders who share the same thin skin.

And there's something else that you and I have in common: I once had a space in my heart that wouldn't close. I still remember the cause. When I was four years old, two very large men wearing very large hats came into our house and hauled my father away. He didn't come back for eight years, and even after he returned, he couldn't repair what had been ripped apart. My dad, like yours, was a sad schmuck, sad in that he never tried to change himself into a dad.

For me, everything changed the moment I saw you.

After four years of infertility and a bout with cancer thrown in for good luck (if I hadn't had it, I never would have known you), I was finally ready to entertain alternatives to producing a mirror image. I tend to arrive at places in my heart long after your mom has moved in and decorated. Your mom always knew that she wanted to be a mom, while I was just beginning to understand what it meant to be a dad. You know the next part from your baby book that you keep under your pillow:

> They met a wonderful young lady who was growing a baby boy in her belly. But she wasn't able to give her baby all the good things the world had to offer, and she wanted that for him very, very much.

Seven months later, I found myself in the hospital, scanning the blue IT'S A BOY! stickers on the bassinets until I saw your birth mother's last name neatly printed in black ink. And at that moment, the space in my heart was filled. It was either magic or God—I've forgotten what I believed in at the time. "You're my son, you're my son," I quietly mouthed to you through the glass again and again, trying to convince myself that you were real. Then I went to your mom, and we hugged and cried while you kept sleeping, our little boy, Robbie James Carlat, unaware of how much joy you could bring to two people.

And the reason I can no longer recall not wanting to adopt you is simple: That feeling completely vanished on the day you were born. "I know, I know. It was love at first sight," you like to say, sounding like a cartoon version of me anytime I bring up the subject of your birth. But it wasn't like that between my dad and me. I don't remember my father ever kissing me or, for

10

that matter, me kissing him. The thought of saying "I love you" to each other, even when he came back from prison or as he lay dying, would have cracked both of us up. In fact, the closest my father ever came to a term of endearment was calling me "kiddo" (which is the full extent of his parental legacy and why I usually answer, "Ditto, kiddo" when you say, "I love you").

There's a black-and-white photograph of my dad holding me up high   15
above his head—I must have been six months old—and it's the only time that I can recall him looking genuinely happy to be with me. I used to think of that picture in the months after you were born, when I danced you to sleep. I never dance, not even with your mom ("They're all going to laugh at you!" from *Carrie* pretty much sums up why), but I loved dancing with you. While you sucked on your bottle, I savored the feeling of your tiny heartbeat against mine. Joni Mitchell's *Night Ride Home* CD was on just loud enough so we wouldn't wake up your mom, and I'd gently sing to you, "All we ever wanted was just to come in from the cold, come in, come in, come in from the cold."

Still, the space you were coming in from was far colder than mine had ever been. It's the original black hole, and all of our kissing and hugging are not enough. All of your incessant *I love yous* and *I love the familys*—words you repeated as if to convince yourself, the same way I did when I first set eyes on you—are not enough. All of the times that you asked me to pick you up and I happily obliged because I knew a day would come when you would stop asking are not enough. Every night when we read your baby book, which desperately tries to explain whose belly you grew in and how you got to us, is not enough.

Nothing is enough, for there's nothing that approaches the clear and direct poetry of "I hate myself because I'm adopted" or "I'm only happy when I'm hugging and kissing you—all the other times I just make-believe." If anything, you get the prize for coming closest to the pin with "Being adopted is hard to understand." And what do you win for saying the darndest things? A profound sadness. And let's not forget its little brother, anger, which you direct at *your* little brother for no apparent reason other than that he serves as a constant reminder that you are the one who is not like the others.

The irony is that Zachy, the prototypical little bro, only wants to be you, while you'd do anything to be him.

I hope that one day God grants your wish and takes the sadness off you, because your mom and I know how truly blessed we are to have two beautiful sons—one chosen by us and one chosen for us. It's like we wrote at the end of your baby book:

> *Mommy and Daddy waited a long time for a baby—a baby boy just like you.*
> *And though it might have been nice to have you grow in Mommy's belly . . .*
> *always remember that you grew in our hearts!*

Perhaps the only thing we neglected to consider at the time was *your*   20
heart. Which reminds me of sand castles. A few summers ago, you and I built a beauty on Uncle Stephen's beach, and you wanted to surround it with a

moat, so we started to dig a hole with your big yellow bucket. We kept digging faster and faster until the hole got so deep that you jumped in. "Daddy, get the water," you said, and I ran into the waves, filled the bucket, dragged it back, and dumped it into the hole. The sand quickly drank it up, so I kept going back and forth, trying to fill the hole with water, but it was like pouring the water down a drain. After a while, we finally said the hell with it and ran into the ocean.

You are the sand, little boy, and I will always be the water.

And that was where I intended to end this letter, until you came padding into the room in your G.I. Joe pajamas. "What are you writing about?" you asked. And when I told you that it was a story about you, you asked, "Is it going to be in a big magazine?"

And I said, "Yeah. How do you feel about that?"

And you said, "Scared."

And I said, "How come?"   25

And you said, "Because I'm going to be in it alone."

And I said, "No you won't. I'll be in it with you."

And you said, "I love you, Daddy."

And that's when I had to stop writing.

QUESTIONS FOR DISCUSSION

1. What do you think Carlat means when he writes, "You are seven, and I am only forty-two"? Why "only"? What is he implying about the relationship between children and adults?
2. Why did Carlat's wife discourage him from writing this letter? What does Carlat achieve by stating the very words she feared he might say: "*I didn't want to adopt you*"?
3. What worried Carlat before meeting his son? Do his anxieties have anything in common with what other parents might experience when expecting the birth of a child?
4. Why does Carlat mention his own father and reveal that he had been sent to prison?
5. Consider the conclusion to this letter. Why does Carlat reach a point where he "had to stop writing"? How well does this point serve as a conclusion?
6. How would you feel if you received a letter like this from a parent or stepparent: embarrassed, indifferent, annoyed, or pleased?

SUGGESTIONS FOR WRITING

1. Write a letter to someone you care about in which you describe your feelings and try to touch his or her heart.
2. Remember what you were like when you were seven, and write a letter to your seven-year-old self in which you convey empathy for the person you used to be.

3. Research conditions in orphanages in a foreign country. Then write an essay that would inspire a married couple in the United States to adopt a child from one of these orphanages.

LINKS

▨ Within the Book

For an essay on the relationship between a father and his daughter, told from the daughter's point of view, see Itabari Njeri's "Life with Father" (pages 71–75).

▨ Elsewhere in Print

Eldridge, Sherrie. *Twenty Life Transforming Choices Adoptees Need to Make.* Colorado Springs: Pinon, 2003.

Klose, Robert. *Adopting Alyosha: A Single Man Finds a Son in Russia.* Jackson: UP of Mississippi, 1999.

Lifton, Betty Jean. *Journey of the Adopted Self: A Quest for Wholeness.* New York: Basic, 1994.

Russell, Marlou. *Adoption Wisdom: A Guide to the Issues and Feelings of Adoption.* Santa Monica: Broken, 1996.

Silber, Kathleen, and Phyllis Speedlin. *Dear Birthmother: Thank You for Our Baby.* San Antonio: Corona, 1983.

Turner, Carole S. *Adoption Journeys: Parents Tell Their Stories.* Ithaca: McBooks, 1999.

▨ Online

www.mhhe.com/motives

Click on "More Resources" then "Writing to Inspire Others."

■ ■ ■

I HAVE A DREAM

Martin Luther King, Jr.

An ordained Baptist minister with a Ph.D. from Boston University, Martin Luther King, Jr. (1929–1968) was arguably the single most important figure in the struggle for civil rights for African Americans during the mid-twentieth century. Founder and president of the Southern Christian Leadership Conference, he was a powerful speaker as well as an effective organizer who inspired many of his contemporaries to see how racial injustice was pervasive throughout the United States. In 1964, he became the youngest man to win the Nobel Peace Prize. He was only thirty-nine years old when he was assassinated in 1968. Although many of the problems King addressed remain unresolved, his memory is honored by a national holiday.

"I Have a Dream" is one of King's most famous speeches, and you may have read it as a document in American history earlier in your education. King gave this speech before a huge audience gathered on the Mall in Washington, DC, as he stood upon the steps of the Lincoln Memorial with the figure of Lincoln behind him. The speech was also recorded and televised. Whether or not you have read it before, read it now as writing designed to inspire strength and hope. As you read, be alert for language that strikes you as especially effective.

I am happy to join with you today in what will go down in history as the greatest demonstration for freedom in the history of our nation.

Five score years ago, a great American, in whose symbolic shadow we stand today, signed the Emancipation Proclamation. This momentous decree came as a great beacon of light of hope to millions of Negro slaves who had been seared in the flames of withering injustice. It came as a joyous daybreak to end the long night of their captivity. But one hundred years later, the Negro still is not free. One hundred years later, the life of the Negro is still sadly crippled by the manacles of segregation and the chains of discrimination. One hundred years later, the Negro lives on a lonely island of poverty in the midst of a vast ocean of material prosperity. One hundred years later, the Negro is still anguished in the corners of American society and finds himself in exile in his own land. And so we have come here today to dramatize a shameful condition.

In a sense we have come to our nation's capital to cash a check. When the architects of our republic wrote the magnificent words of the Constitution and the Declaration of Independence, they were signing a promissory note to which every American was to fall heir. This note was the promise that all men—yes, Black men as well as white men—would be guaranteed the inalienable rights of life, liberty, and the pursuit of happiness.

It is obvious today that America has defaulted on this promissory note insofar as her citizens of color are concerned. Instead of honoring this sacred obligation, America has given the Negro people a bad check, a check which has come back marked "insufficient funds." But we refuse to believe that the bank of justice is bankrupt. We refuse to believe that there are insufficient funds in the great vaults of opportunity of this nation; and so we have come to cash this check, a check that will give us upon demand the riches of freedom and the security of justice.

We have also come to this hallowed spot to remind America of the fierce urgency of *now.* This is no time to engage in the luxury of cooling off or to take the tranquilizing drug of gradualism. *Now* is the time to make real the promises of democracy. *Now* is the time to rise from the dark and desolate valley of segregation to the sunlit path of racial justice. *Now* is the time to lift our nation from the quicksands of racial injustice to the solid rock of brotherhood. *Now* is the time to make justice a reality for all of God's children.

It would be fatal for the nation to overlook the urgency of the moment. This sweltering summer of the Negro's legitimate discontent will not pass until there is an invigorating autumn of freedom and equality. Nineteen sixty-three is not an end, but a beginning. And those who hope that the Negro needed to blow off steam and will now be content will have a rude awakening if the nation returns to business as usual. There will be neither rest nor tranquility in America until the Negro is granted his citizenship rights. The whirlwinds of revolt will continue to shake the foundations of our nation until the bright day of justice emerges.

But there is something that I must say to my people who stand on the warm threshold which leads into the palace of justice. In the process of gaining our rightful place, we must not be guilty of wrongful deeds. Let us not seek to satisfy our thirst for freedom by drinking from the cup of bitterness and hatred. We must forever conduct our struggle on the high plane of dignity and discipline. We must not allow our creative protest to degenerate into physical violence. Again and again we must rise to the majestic heights of meeting physical force with soul force. And the marvelous new militancy which has engulfed the Negro community must not lead us to a distrust of all white people; for many of our white brothers, as evidenced by their presence here today, have come to realize that their destiny is tied up with our destiny, and they have come to realize that their freedom is inextricably bound to our freedom.

We cannot walk alone. And as we walk we must make the pledge that we shall always march ahead. We cannot turn back. There are those who are asking the devotees of civil rights, "When will you be satisfied?" We can never be satisfied as long as the Negro is the victim of the unspeakable horrors of police brutality. We can never be satisfied as long as our bodies, heavy with the fatigue of travel, cannot gain lodging in the motels of the highways and the hotels of the cities. We cannot be satisfied as long as the Negro's basic mobility is from a smaller ghetto to a larger one. We can never be satisfied as long as our children are stripped of their selfhood and robbed of their dignity by signs stating "For Whites Only." We cannot be satisfied as long as the Negro in Mississippi cannot vote and a Negro in New York believes he has nothing for which to vote. No, no, we are not satisfied, and we will not be satisfied until justice rolls down like waters and righteousness like a mighty stream.

I am not unmindful that some of you have come here out of great trials and tribulations. Some of you have come fresh from narrow jail cells. Some of you have come from areas where your quest for freedom left you battered by the storms of persecution and staggered by the winds of police brutality. You have been the veterans of creative suffering. Continue to work with the faith that unearned suffering is redemptive.

Go back to Mississippi, and go back to Alabama. Go back to South Caro-   10
lina. Go back to Georgia. Go back to Louisiana. Go back to the slums and ghettos of our Northern cities, knowing that somehow this situation can and will be changed. Let us not wallow in the valley of despair.

I say to you today, my friends, even though we face the difficulties of today and tomorrow, I still have a dream. It is a dream deeply rooted in the American dream. I have a dream that one day this nation will rise up and live out the true meaning of its creed: "We hold these truths to be self-evident, that all men are created equal." I have a dream that one day, on the red hills of Georgia, sons of former slaves and the sons of former slave owners will be able to sit down together at the table of brotherhood. I have a dream that one day even the state of Mississippi, a state sweltering with the heat of injustice, sweltering with the heat of oppression, will be transformed into an oasis of freedom and justice. I have a dream that my four little children will one day live in a nation where they will not be judged by the color of their skin, but by the content of their character.

I have a dream today. I have a dream that one day down in Alabama—with its vicious racists, with its governor's lips dripping with the words of interposition and nullification—one day right there in Alabama, little Black boys and Black girls will be able to join hands with little white boys and white girls as sisters and brothers.

I have a dream today. I have a dream that one day every valley shall be exalted and every hill and mountain shall be made low, the rough places will be made plain and the crooked places will be made straight, and the glory of the Lord shall be revealed, and all flesh shall see it together.°

This is our hope. This is the faith that I go back to the South with. And with this faith we will be able to hew out of the mountain of despair a stone of hope. With this faith we will be able to transform the jangling discords of our nation into a beautiful symphony of brotherhood. With this faith we will be able to work together, to play together, to struggle together, to go to jail together, to stand up for freedom together, knowing that we will be free one day.

°*every valley shall be . . . see it together:* A quotation from the Old Testament, Isaiah 40:4–5.

And this will be the day—this will be the day when all of God's children   *15*
will be able to sing with new meaning:

> My country, 'tis of thee,
> Sweet land of liberty,
>   Of thee I sing;
> Land where my fathers died,
> Land of the Pilgrims' pride,
> From every mountainside
>   Let freedom ring.

And if America is to be a great nation, this must become true.

And so let freedom ring from the prodigious hilltops of New Hampshire.
Let freedom ring from the mighty mountains of New York. Let freedom ring
from the heightening Alleghenies of Pennsylvania. Let freedom ring from the
snow-capped Rockies of Colorado. Let freedom ring from the curvaceous
slopes of California.

But not only that. Let freedom ring from Stone Mountain of Georgia.
Let freedom ring from Lookout Mountain of Tennessee. Let freedom ring
from every hill and molehill of Mississippi. "From every mountainside let
freedom ring."

And when this happens—when we allow freedom to ring, when we let it
ring from every village and every hamlet, from every state and every city—
we will be able to speed up that day when all of God's children, Black men
and white men, Jews and Gentiles, Protestants and Catholics, will be able to
join hands and sing in the words of the old Negro spiritual: "Free at last! Free
at last! Thank God Almighty. We are free at last!"

QUESTIONS FOR DISCUSSION

1. Why was the Lincoln Memorial an appropriate setting for this speech?
   Can you identify any references in the speech that link it to the setting in
   which it was originally presented?
2. Why does King begin paragraph 2 with "Five score years ago" instead of
   simply saying "one hundred years ago"?
3. *Anaphora,* as noted earlier, is a term that means "the use of repetition at the
   beginning of sentences, clauses, or verses for rhetorical effect." Examples
   are the three sentences beginning "One hundred years later" in paragraph 2.
   Can you identify any other examples?
4. What do you think King meant by "the tranquilizing drug of gradualism"
   in paragraph 5?
5. Paragraph 13 concludes with a quotation from the Bible. Why was it appropriate for King to use the Bible in this speech?
6. What evidence in this work suggests that King recognized that he was
   speaking to an audience already committed to the importance of racial
   equality?

SUGGESTIONS FOR WRITING

1. A *metaphor* is a figure of speech that makes a comparison between two unlike things without using *like* or *as*. When King writes "we have come to our nation's capital to cash a check," he does not mean these words to be taken literally. Instead, he is making an implied comparison between an uncashed check and unfulfilled promises to African Americans. Reread "I Have a Dream" identifying other metaphors King uses. Then paraphrase any five successive paragraphs, eliminating all metaphors and all anaphora.
2. Using both anaphora and metaphors, write a short speech that calls attention to a current social problem that concerns you.
3. Research the struggle for civil rights between 1954, when the Supreme Court ruled against racial segregation in public schools, and 1963, when King composed and delivered "I Have a Dream." Then write an essay in which you provide background information that would help other students understand the rhetorical context of this famous speech.

▌ LINKS

■ Within the Book

To see how inspiring an audience differs from persuading one, compare "I Have a Dream" with King's "Letter from Birmingham Jail" (pages 488–501).

■ Elsewhere in Print

Carson, Clayborne, and Kris Shepard, eds. *A Call to Conscience: The Landmark Speeches of Dr. Martin Luther King, Jr.* New York: Warner, 2001.

Hansen, David D. *The Dream: Martin Luther King, Jr. and the Speech That Inspired a Nation.* New York: Ecco, 2003.

King, Martin Luther, Jr. *Strength to Love.* 1963. Philadelphia: Fortress, 1986.

———. *Why We Can't Wait.* 1964. New York: Signet, 2000.

Miller, Keith D. *Voice of Deliverance: The Language of Martin Luther King, Jr., and Its Sources.* New York: Free, 1992.

Ward, Brian, and Tracy Badger, eds. *The Making of Martin Luther King and the Civil Rights Movements.* New York: New York UP, 1996.

■ Online

www.mhhe.com/motives

Click on "More Resources" then "Writing to Inspire Others."

■ ■ ■

AT THE CAFÉ

Garrison Keillor

Although he began his career in radio while studying at the University of Minnesota, Garrison Keillor's idea for creating his own show was generated by his work on a 1974 article for The New Yorker *on the Grand Ole Opry.* A Prairie Home Companion *had its first broadcast that year, with twelve people in the audience. More than thirty years later, this weekly show, carried by National Public Radio, reaches a national audience drawn by Keillor's wry humor and clearly defined values. In addition to publishing recordings from his show, Keillor is the author of several books. About writing he notes, "Writers are vacuum cleaners who suck up other people's lives and weave them into stories like a sparrow builds a nest from scraps."*

The following selection is an excerpt from a chapter in Keillor's Homegrown Democrat—*a book published in 2004, which was a presidential election year. "At the Café" is the title of the chapter from which the following piece is taken. It opens, "When I am gloomy about politics, I go sit alone in a crowded café in my neighborhood in St. Paul. . . . I sit and inhale the smell of coffee amid the murmur of midwestern voices like water lapping on the shore." Reflections about the values he shares with other people in the café lead up to the following effort to inspire Democrats when Republicans were becoming increasing popular.*

People are united in a civil compact and we know it, even if we don't talk about it. This compact is powerful in the Midwest, and when we midwesterners travel to New York or London or Paris, we wonder: if we were struck by a car and lay bleeding in the gutter, would people stop and help?

One morning three years ago, I heard a shriek from upstairs, a long high-pitched primeval wail, and there was my wife on the landing, holding the stiff body of our little girl. I dashed up and took Maia in my arms and Jenny went to call 911. The child was unconscious, her breathing shallow. She went into convulsions in my arms and her body stiffened, her mouth clamped shut. I thought she was dying. Sheer silent terror on a pleasant spring morning: my four-year-old daughter dying. And in about two minutes the St. Paul fire department paramedics arrived at the door. They came in, four of them, and lifted her out of my arms. They laid her on the floor and tended to her, took her temperature (she was running a fever), put an oxygen mask on her face. One of them began explaining to me about febrile convulsions, how common they are in small children, which Jenny knew about but I didn't, and then I noticed that I was still in my underwear. I pulled on a pair of trousers and we rode off to the hospital and in short order she was okay again.

The rescue squad can get to you anywhere in St. Paul in four minutes or less. That is official policy. These folks came racing up the hill from downtown, about a mile away, but there are EMTs or paramedics at eleven of the sixteen fire stations in the city and they do about eighty runs a day. The EMTs have taken a basic course of 250 class hours, the paramedics a two-year course of more than a thousand, and they know what they're doing. They work alternate 12-hour days for a week—then take four days off, then alternate 12-hour days for another week, then six days off—for an average workweek of 56 hours. They start at $38,000 a year and after three years become journeymen and jump to $50,000. The shift starts at 8 A.M., but most of them come half an hour early to sit around and drink coffee and get ready. When you call and the dispatcher sends the alarm, the paramedics are in the truck and out the door in thirty seconds. The 911 system went into service in the Twin Cities in December 1982, paid for out of the state's general fund. But the paramedics and EMTs are St. Paul city employees. And the four-minute-or-less response represents the nature of our civil compact here in St. Paul: if you urgently need help, someone will be there before panic sets in. In the suburbs, thanks to Republicans and their code of personal responsibility, the coronary victim will have time to read the entire Gospel of St. Mark before help arrives. There is a message here: if lower taxes are your priority over human life, then we know what sort of person you are. The response to a cry for help says a lot about us as human beings. You're at a party late one night and there's a scream from out on the street, and some people stick their heads out to see if there's trouble and other people don't bother. Maybe they'd rather not know.

A Democrat knows that the leaf turns and in the human comedy we are one day spectators and the next day performers. The gains in life come slowly and the losses come on suddenly. You work for years to get your life the way you want it and buy the big house and the time share on Antigua and one afternoon you're run down by a garbage truck and lie in the intersection, dazed, bloodied, your leg unnaturally bent, and suddenly life becomes terribly challenging for six months. In the Prairie Home office, one summer evening a woman walked out the door to go home and was swarmed by wasps and staggered back into the building, bitten so badly that her air passage was swollen half shut. She was almost unconscious, going into shock, and collapsed in the hallway. Luckily, a colleague had stayed late at work and she called 911, and in came the St. Paul paramedics to save Deb's life. Every day at work, I see a bright capable charming woman whose memorial service I might have attended had circumstances been ever so slightly different.

Two blocks from the office lived a brilliant young professor of Middle   5
East studies who had given birth to a little girl with Down syndrome who could not nurse and needed to be fed through a tube stuck down her nasal passage. One morning, the mother, depressed though already on antidepressants, feeling hopeless, broken-hearted at the child's misery, exhausted to the point of derangement, cut the infant's throat with a butcher knife. The mother was arrested and put in Ramsey County Jail where, a few weeks later, she

managed to get a plastic garbage bag, place it over her head, tie it tight around her neck, and suffocate herself. This happened in St. Paul, Minnesota, two blocks from the office where I sit and write silly songs and Guy Noir sketches. In St. Paul, people could not get this tragedy off their minds for a long time. Long after we stopped talking about it—what more could be said—it haunted our consciences, these two souls who had slipped through our fingers and plunged to their deaths. Somehow we could have saved them. What else, dear Lord, should we have done?

The fear of catastrophe could chill the soul but the social compact assures you that if the wasps come after you, if gruesome disease strikes down your child, if you find yourself hopelessly lost, incapable, drowning in despair, running through the rye toward the cliff, then the rest of us will catch you and tend to you and not only your friends but We the People in the form of public servants. This is a basic necessity in a developed society. Men and women make love and have babies in the knowledge that if the baby should be born with cerebral palsy or Down syndrome or a hole in its heart and require heroic care, the people of Minnesota and of St. Paul will stand with you in your dark hour. If you are saddled with trouble too great for a person to bear, you will not be left to perish by the roadside in darkness. Without that assurance, we may as well go live in the woods and take our chances.

This is Democratic bedrock: we don't let people lie in the ditch and drive past and pretend not to see them dying. Here on the frozen tundra of Minnesota, if your neighbor's car won't start, you put on your parka and get the jumper cables out and deliver the Sacred Spark that starts their car. Everybody knows this. The logical extension of this spirit is social welfare and the myriad government programs with long dry names all very uninteresting to you until you suddenly need one and then you turn into a Democrat. A liberal is a conservative who's been through treatment.

QUESTIONS FOR DISCUSSION

1. What do you think it means to have a "civil compact"?
2. What is Keillor trying to accomplish in paragraph 2? How does he integrate this paragraph into the rest of this piece?
3. Why is it significant that the paramedics and EMTs Keillor describes are government employees? How well do you think they are paid? Based on what you learn about them here, do you think they earn their pay?
4. Why do you think Keillor emphasizes the difference between Democrats and Republicans? How do you respond to the distinction he draws?
5. What is the purpose of the examples in paragraphs 4 and 5? Why do you think Keillor gives more space to the story of the young professor?
6. What is Keillor evoking in paragraph 6 when he uses the phrase "We the People"?
7. Do you agree that government programs are the "logical extension" of the spirit that inspires individuals to help one another out?

SUGGESTIONS FOR WRITING

1. Think about what you expect from your fellow citizens in an emergency. Then write an essay in which you address them as your audience and inspire them to do what you think is most important to do in these situations.
2. Write an essay that would inspire people to recognize the importance and dignity of human life. Assume that your audience understands this on some level but has become self-absorbed while getting on with their professional lives.
3. Listen to an episode of *Prairie Home Companion* and then write an essay in which you discuss how Keillor's words enrich, diminish, or complicate your response to "At the Café."

LINKS

■ Within the Book

In "Letter from Birmingham Jail" (pages 488–501), Martin Luther King, Jr. also uses examples of children to inspire a response that suits his motive for writing.

■ Elsewhere in Print

Canning, Peter. *Rescue 471: A Paramedic's Stories*. New York: Ballantine, 2000.

Keillor, Garrison. *The Book of Guys*. New York: Penguin, 1994.

———. *Homegrown Democrat*. New York: Viking, 2004.

———. *Leaving Home*. New York: Penguin, 1992.

Stern, Jane. *Ambulance Girl: How I Saved Myself by Becoming an EMT*. New York: Crown, 2003.

Witcover, Jules. *Party of the People: A History of Democrats*. New York: Random, 2003.

■ Online

www.mhhe.com/motives

Click on "More Resources" then "Writing to Inspire Others."

■ ■ ■

I KNOW A CHILD

Ron Reagan, Jr.

Political conventions provide many examples of speaking to inspire. The delegates who gather every four years at these conventions usually know who the nominee will be and what the party platform will include. The speeches given there serve a double purpose: They reinvigorate delegates who have already been working hard and must continue to work hard until the next election, and they appeal to undecided voters by presenting a positive image and raising questions about the opposition. Unfortunately, by 2004, when the Democrats gathered in Boston to nominate John Kerry to run against President George W. Bush, the major television networks (ABC, NBC, CBS) had reduced coverage of the week-long convention to three hours. Viewers who wished to see more of the convention could do so by watching public television, CNN, and C-Span. But millions of other Americans were content to watch reruns or old movies.

It is therefore important to consider the context of the following speech. It was delivered in person to Democratic delegates in Boston who had already decided to support stem cell research in their party platform, and it was heard elsewhere primarily by Americans who take an interest in public affairs. You must decide for yourself whether the speech itself can hold your attention. But even before he began his speech, the author generated interest because of his identity and context: Ron Reagan, Jr. is the youngest son of President Ronald Reagan, one of the most highly respected Republicans of the twentieth century. His father had died only a few weeks earlier, but his mother, Nancy Reagan, could have been among the audience watching the convention that night on television.

Thank you very much. That's very kind. Good evening, ladies and gentlemen.

A few of you may be surprised to see someone with my last name showing up to speak at a Democratic convention. Apparently some of you are not. Let me assure you, I am not here to make a political speech and the topic at hand should not—must not—have anything to do with partisanship.

I am here tonight to talk about the issue of research into what may be the greatest medical breakthrough in our or in any lifetime: the use of embryonic stem cells—cells created using the material of our own bodies—to cure a wide range of fatal and debilitating illnesses: Parkinson's disease, multiple sclerosis, diabetes, lymphoma, spinal cord injuries, and much more.

Millions are afflicted. And every year, every day, tragedy is visited upon families across the country, around the world. Now, it may be within our power to put an end to this suffering. We only need to try.

Some of you—some of you already know what I'm talking about when I �₅ say embryonic stem cell research. Others of you are probably thinking, that's quite a mouthful. Maybe this is a good time to go for a tall cold one. Well, wait a minute, wait a minute.

Let me try and paint as simple a picture as I can while still doing justice to the science, the incredible science involved. Let's say that ten or so years from now you are diagnosed with Parkinson's disease. There is currently no cure and drug therapy, with its attendant side-effects, can only temporarily relieve the symptoms.

Now, imagine going to a doctor who, instead of prescribing drugs, takes a few skin cells from your arm. The nucleus of one of your cells is placed into a donor egg whose own nucleus has been removed. A bit of chemical or electrical stimulation will encourage your cell's nucleus to begin dividing, creating new cells which will then be placed into a tissue culture. Those cells will generate embryonic stem cells containing only your DNA, thereby eliminating the risk of tissue rejection. These stem cells are then driven to become the very neural cells that are defective in Parkinson's patients. And finally, those cells—with your DNA—are injected into your brain where they will replace the faulty cells whose failure to produce adequate dopamine led to the Parkinson's disease in the first place.

In other words, you're cured.

And another thing—another thing, these embryonic stem cells, they could continue to replicate indefinitely and, theoretically, can be induced to recreate virtually any tissue in your body.

How'd you like to have your own personal biological repair kit standing ₁₀ by at the hospital? Sound like magic? Welcome to the future of medicine.

Now, by the way, no fetal tissue is involved in this process. No fetuses are created, none destroyed. This all happens in the laboratory at the cellular level.

Now, there are those who would stand in the way of this remarkable future, who would deny the federal funding so crucial to basic research. They argue that interfering with the development of even the earliest stage embryo, even one that will never be implanted in a womb and will never develop into an actual fetus, is tantamount to murder.

A few of these folks, needless to say, are just grinding a political axe and they should be ashamed of themselves. But many—but many—many are well-meaning and sincere. Their belief is just that, an article of faith, and they are entitled to it. But it does not follow that the theology of a few should be allowed to forestall the health and well-being of the many.

And how can we affirm life if we abandon those whose own lives are so desperately at risk? It is a hallmark of human intelligence that we are able to make distinctions.

Yes, these cells could theoretically have the potential, under very different ₁₅ circumstances, to develop into human beings—that potential is where their magic lies. But they are not, in and of themselves, human beings. They have

COMPANION TEXT *Remarks at a Benefit for the Juvenile Diabetes Research Foundation*

Two months before the death of Ronald Reagan in 2004, or "Ronnie" as he is called here, former First Lady Nancy Reagan made a rare public appearance to accept an award for her work in encouraging stem cell research. The award was presented by the actor Michael J. Fox in front of a crowd of invited guests attending a tribute to her. This is the speech she made after walking on to the stage and hugging Fox.

There are so many people to thank—I don't think any of us would be here tonight without the hard work of Lucy Fisher and Doug Wick. And thank you Michael . . . I have such admiration for you. Your children must be so proud of you. And James Taylor, wherever you are, I'm a big fan of yours. [*Singer James Taylor walks on stage and gives Mrs. Reagan a kiss.*] And, of course, my old friend Larry King. And I'd also like to add my thanks to Novo Nordisk for making this evening possible.

I'm so grateful to all of you for coming tonight and showing your interest in stem cell research. When Ronnie wrote his letter to the people telling them that he'd been diagnosed with Alzheimer's, I didn't really know or understand what that meant. I really didn't. But—I found out. Those with AD are on a rocky path that only goes downhill. Ronnie's long journey has finally taken him to a distant place where I can no longer reach him. We can't share the wonderful memories of our 52 years together, and I think that is the hardest part. And because of this I'm determined to do whatever I can to save other families from this pain.

And now science has presented us with a hope called stem cell research, which may provide our scientists with answers that have so long been beyond our grasps. I just don't see how we can turn our backs on this—there are so many diseases that can be cured, or at least helped. We have lost so much time already, and I just really can't bear to lose any more.

All of you are here tonight because you believe not just in science but in hope. By supporting stem cell research, everyone here is a caregiver. There are so many people in this country filling the job of caregiver and I want to acknowledge all of the caregivers who right now may be sitting beside a bed or holding a hand. So I accept this award on behalf of each and every one of them. Thank you for this honor. I am very grateful. Thank you very much.

Nancy Reagan

no fingers and toes, no brain or spinal cord. They have no thoughts, no fears. They feel no pain.

Surely we can distinguish between these undifferentiated cells multiplying in a tissue culture and a living, breathing person—a parent, a spouse, a child.

I know a child—well, she must be 13 now—I guess I'd better call her a young woman. She has fingers and toes. She has a mind. She has memories. She has hopes. And she has juvenile diabetes. Like so many kids with this disease, she has adjusted amazingly well. The—the insulin pump she wears—she's decorated hers with rhinestones. She can handle her own catheter needle. She's learned to sleep through the blood drawings in the wee hours of the morning.

She's very brave. She is also quite bright and understands full well the progress of her disease and what that might ultimately mean: blindness, amputation, diabetic coma. Every day, she fights to have a future.

What excuse will we offer this young woman should we fail her now? What might we tell her children? Or the millions of others who suffer? That when given an opportunity to help, we turned away? That facing political opposition, we lost our nerve? That even though we knew better, we did nothing?

And, should we fail, how will we feel if, a few years from now, a more enlightened generation should fulfill the promise of embryonic stem cell therapy? Imagine what they would say of us who lacked the will. 20

No, no, we owe this young woman and all those who suffer—we owe ourselves—better than that. We are better than that. We are a wiser people, a finer nation.

And for all of us in this fight, let me say: we will prevail. The tide of history is with us. Like all generations who have come before ours, we are motivated by a thirst for knowledge and compelled to see others in need as fellow angels on an often difficult path, deserving of our compassion.

In a few months, we will face a choice. Yes, between two candidates and two parties, but more than that. We have a chance to take a giant stride forward for the good of all humanity. We can choose between the future and the past, between reason and ignorance, between true compassion and mere ideology.

QUESTIONS FOR DISCUSSION

1. Why is it useful for Reagan to begin by claiming that his topic is nonpartisan? Does he seem nonpartisan in the speech itself?
2. How would you describe Reagan's word choice? Given his topic, motive, audience, and context, how appropriate are phrases such as "quite a mouthful" and "a good time to go for a tall one"?
3. What assumptions has Reagan made about his audience?
4. How plausible is the scenario Reagan provides in paragraph 7?
5. Why does Reagan emphasize that the research he calls for does not involve fetal tissue?
6. How fairly does Reagan treat people who disagree with him?
7. How important in this speech is the girl to whom Reagan draws attention? Is gender significant in this example?
8. In what sense is this speech "inspiring"? Could it be considered an argument?

SUGGESTIONS FOR WRITING

1. Identify an issue important to one of the nation's political parties, and then imagine that you have the opportunity to speak for ten minutes at that party's convention. Write a speech that would inspire the delegates to renew their efforts on behalf of the cause to which they are already committed to some extent.

2. If you are opposed to stem cell research, consider who else shares this position. Then write an essay directed toward this audience in which you inspire them to maintain their beliefs.

3. Consider the remarks by Nancy Reagan that appear on page 546. Then write an essay in which you compare her voice and her son's.

LINKS

▨ Within the Book

In "Same-Sex Sexuality" (pages 221–238), Joan Roughgarden focuses on scientific research when pursuing another motive for writing.

▨ Elsewhere in Print

Committee on Biological and Biomedical Application. *Stem Cells and the Future of Regenerative Medicine.* Washington, DC: National Academy P, 2002.

D'Sousa, Dinesh. *Ronald Reagan: How an Ordinary Man Became an Extraordinary Leader.* New York: Free, 1999.

Green, Ronald M. *The Human Embryo Research Debates: Bioethics in the Vortex of Controversy.* New York: Oxford UP, 2001.

Kiessling, Ann, and Scott Anderson. *Human Embryonic Stem Cells: An Introduction to the Science and Therapeutic Potential.* New York: James, 2003.

Prentice, David, and Michael Palladino. *Stem Cells and Cloning.* San Francisco: Benjamin, 2002.

▨ Online

www.mhhe.com/motives

Click on "More Resources" then "Writing to Inspire Others."

■ ■ ■

THE STATE OF OUR UNION

George W. Bush

> *On September 11, 2001, terrorists seized planes from four commercial airlines and used them to cause massive destruction. Two of these planes flew directly into the twin towers of the World Trade Center, the tallest buildings in New York City, causing them to collapse. A third plane destroyed part of the Pentagon in Washington, DC. A fourth crashed in rural Pennsylvania, its target unknown. Thousands of people died as a result of these attacks, which stunned the nation and horrified much of the world. A week after the attack, President George W. Bush addressed a joint session of Congress—as millions of Americans watched the live television broadcast—to draw the nation together and provide direction for the future. The transcript of that speech is included here as an example of writing to inspire, given at a critical moment in American history when feelings of shock, sorrow, anger, and anxiety prevailed.*
>
> *The forty-third president of the United States and the son of another president, George W. Bush graduated from Yale University and Harvard Business School. Before becoming president, he worked in the oil industry and served as governor of Texas.*

Mr. Speaker, Mr. President pro tempore, members of Congress, and fellow Americans:

In the normal course of events, presidents come to this chamber to report on the state of the union. Tonight, no such report is needed. It has already been delivered by the American people.

We have seen it in the courage of passengers who rushed terrorists to save others on the ground, passengers like an exceptional man named Todd Beamer. Please help me to welcome his wife, Lisa Beamer, here tonight.

We have seen the state of our union in the endurance of rescuers working past exhaustion. We have seen the unfurling of flags, the lighting of candles, the giving of blood, the saying of prayers—in English, Hebrew, and Arabic. We have seen the decency of a loving and giving people, who have made the grief of strangers their own.

My fellow citizens, for the last nine days, the entire world has seen for itself the state of our union—and it is strong. 5

Tonight we are a country awakened to danger and called to defend freedom. Our grief has turned to anger and anger to resolution. Whether we bring our enemies to justice or bring justice to our enemies, justice will be done.

I thank the Congress for its leadership at such an important time. All of America was touched on the evening of the tragedy to see Republicans and Democrats joined together on the steps of this Capitol, singing "God Bless

America." And you did more than sing; you acted, by delivering $40 billion to rebuild our communities and meet the needs of our military.

Speaker Hastert and Minority Leader Gephardt, Majority Leader Daschle and Senator Lott, I thank you for your friendship and your leadership and your service to our country.

And on behalf of the American people, I thank the world for its outpouring of support. America will never forget the sounds of our national anthem playing at Buckingham Palace and on the streets of Paris and at Berlin's Brandenburg Gate. We will not forget South Korean children gathering to pray outside our embassy in Seoul, or the prayers of sympathy offered at a mosque in Cairo. We will not forget moments of silence and days of mourning in Australia and Africa and Latin America.

Nor will we forget the citizens of eighty other nations who died with our own. Dozens of Pakistanis. More than 130 Israelis. More than 250 citizens of India. Men and women from El Salvador, Iran, Mexico, and Japan. And hundreds of British citizens. America has no truer friend than Great Britain. Once again, we are joined together in a great cause. The British prime minister has crossed an ocean to show his unity of purpose with America, and tonight we welcome Tony Blair.   *10*

On September 11, enemies of freedom committed an act of war against our country. Americans have known wars, but for the past 136 years, they have been wars on foreign soil, except for one Sunday in 1941. Americans have known the casualties of war, but not at the center of a great city on a peaceful morning. Americans have known surprise attacks, but never before on thousands of civilians. All of this was brought upon us in a single day, and night fell on a different world, a world where freedom itself is under attack.

Americans have many questions tonight. Americans are asking, "Who attacked our country?"

The evidence we have gathered all points to a collection of loosely affiliated terrorist organizations known as Al Qaeda. They are the same murderers indicted for bombing American embassies in Tanzania and Kenya and responsible for the bombing of the U.S.S. *Cole.*

Al Qaeda is to terror what the Mafia is to crime. But its goal is not making money; its goal is remaking the world and imposing its radical beliefs on people everywhere.

The terrorists practice a fringe form of Islamic extremism that has been   *15* rejected by Muslim scholars and the vast majority of Muslim clerics, a fringe movement that perverts the peaceful teachings of Islam. The terrorists' directive commands them to kill Christians and Jews, to kill all Americans, and [to] make no distinctions among military and civilians, including women and children.

This group and its leader, a person named Osama bin Laden, are linked to many other organizations in different countries, including the Egyptian Islamic Jihad and the Islamic Movement of Uzbekistan.

There are thousands of these terrorists in more than sixty countries. They are recruited from their own nations and neighborhoods and brought to camps in places like Afghanistan, where they are trained in the tactics of terror. They are sent back to their homes or sent to hide in countries around the world to plot evil and destruction.

The leadership of Al Qaeda has great influence in Afghanistan and supports the Taliban regime in controlling most of that country. In Afghanistan, we see Al Qaeda's vision for the world.

Afghanistan's people have been brutalized; many are starving and many have fled. Women are not allowed to attend school. You can be jailed for owning a television. Religion can be practiced only as their leaders dictate. A man can be jailed in Afghanistan if his beard is not long enough.

The United States respects the people of Afghanistan—after all, we are   20
currently its largest source of humanitarian aid—but we condemn the Taliban regime. It is not only repressing its own people, it is threatening people everywhere by sponsoring and sheltering and supplying terrorists. By aiding and abetting murder, the Taliban regime is committing murder. And tonight, the United States of America makes the following demands on the Taliban:

- Deliver to United States authorities all the leaders of Al Qaeda who hide in your land.
- Release all foreign nationals, including American citizens you have unjustly imprisoned, and protect foreign journalists, diplomats, and aid workers in your country.
- Close immediately and permanently every terrorist training camp in Afghanistan and hand over every terrorist, and every person in their support structure, to appropriate authorities.
- Give the United States full access to terrorist training camps, so we can make sure they are no longer operating.

These demands are not open to negotiation or discussion. The Taliban must act and act immediately. They will hand over the terrorists, or they will share in their fate.

I also want to speak tonight directly to Muslims throughout the world. We respect your faith. It is practiced freely by many millions of Americans and by millions more in countries that America counts as friends. Its teachings are good and peaceful, and those who commit evil in the name of Allah blaspheme the name of Allah. The terrorists are traitors to their own faith, trying, in effect, to hijack Islam itself. The enemy of America is not our many Muslim friends; it is not our many Arab friends. Our enemy is a radical network of terrorists and every government that supports them.

Our war on terror begins with Al Qaeda, but it does not end there. It will not end until every terrorist group of global reach has been found, stopped, and defeated.

Americans are asking, "Why do they hate us?"

They hate what we see right here in this chamber, a democratically   25
elected government. Their leaders are self-appointed. They hate our freedoms—our freedom of religion, our freedom of speech, our freedom to vote and assemble and disagree with each other.

They want to overthrow existing governments in many Muslim countries, such as Egypt, Saudi Arabia, and Jordan. They want to drive Israel out of the Middle East. They want to drive Christians and Jews out of vast regions of Asia and Africa.

These terrorists kill not merely to end lives, but to disrupt and end a way of life. With every atrocity, they hope that America grows fearful, retreating from the world and forsaking our friends. They stand against us, because we stand in their way.

We are not deceived by their pretenses to piety. We have seen their kind before. They are the heirs of all the murderous ideologies of the twentieth century. By sacrificing human life to serve their radical visions, by abandoning every value except the will to power, they follow in the path of fascism and Nazism and totalitarianism. And they will follow that path all the way to where it ends in history's unmarked grave of discarded lies.

Americans are asking, "How will we fight and win this war?"

We will direct every resource at our command—every means of diplomacy, every tool of intelligence, every instrument of law enforcement, every financial influence, and every necessary weapon of war—to the disruption and defeat of the global terror network.   30

This war will not be like the war against Iraq a decade ago, with its decisive liberation of territory and its swift conclusion. It will not look like the air war above Kosovo two years ago, where no ground troops were used and not a single American was lost in combat.

Our response involves far more than instant retaliation and isolated strikes. Americans should not expect one battle, but a lengthy campaign unlike any other we have seen. It may include dramatic strikes visible on television, and covert operations secret even in success. We will starve terrorists of funding, turn them one against another, drive them from place to place until there is no refuge or rest. And we will pursue nations that provide aid or safe haven to terrorism. Every nation in every region now has a decision to make. Either you are with us or you are with the terrorists. From this day forward, any nation that continues to harbor or support terrorism will be regarded by the United States as a hostile regime.

Our nation has been put on notice: We are not immune from attack. We will take defensive measures against terrorism to protect Americans.

Today, dozens of federal departments and agencies, as well as state and local governments, have responsibilities affecting homeland security. These efforts must be coordinated at the highest level. So tonight I announce the creation of a Cabinet-level position reporting directly to me—the Office of Homeland Security.

These measures are essential. But the only way to defeat terrorism as a threat to our way of life is to stop it, eliminate it, and destroy it where it grows.   35

Many will be involved in this effort, from F.B.I. agents to intelligence operatives to the reservists we have called to active duty. All deserve our thanks, and all have our prayers. And tonight, a few miles from the damaged Pentagon, I have a message for our military: Be ready. I have called the armed forces to alert, and there is a reason. The hour is coming when America will act, and you will make us proud.

This is not, however, just America's fight. And what is at stake is not just America's freedom. This is the world's fight. This is civilization's fight. This is the fight of all who believe in progress and pluralism, tolerance and freedom.

We ask every nation to join us. We will ask, and we will need, the help of police forces, intelligence services, and banking systems around the world. The United States is grateful that many nations and many international organizations have already responded with sympathy and with support. Nations from Latin America, to Asia, to Africa, to Europe, to the Islamic world. Perhaps the NATO Charter reflects best the attitude of the world: An attack on one is an attack on all.

The civilized world is rallying to America's side. They understand that, if this terror goes unpunished, their own cities, their own citizens may be next. Terror, unanswered, can not only bring down buildings, it can threaten the stability of legitimate governments. And we will not allow it.

Americans are asking, "What is expected of us?"   40

I ask you to live your lives and hug your children. I know many citizens have fears tonight, and I ask you to be calm and resolute, even in the face of a continuing threat.

I ask you to uphold the values of America and remember why so many have come here. We are in a fight for our principles, and our first responsibility is to live by them. No one should be singled out for unfair treatment or unkind words because of their ethnic background or religious faith.

I ask you to continue to support the victims of this tragedy with your contributions. Those who want to give can go to a central source of information, <libertyunites.org>, to find the names of groups providing direct help in New York, Pennsylvania and Virginia.

The thousands of F.B.I. agents who are now at work in this investigation may need your cooperation, and I ask you to give it.

I ask for your patience with the delays and inconveniences that may accom-   45
pany tighter security—and for your patience in what will be a long struggle.

I ask your continued participation and confidence in the American economy. Terrorists attacked a symbol of American prosperity. They did not touch its source. America is successful because of the hard work and creativity and enterprise of our people. These were the true strengths of our economy before September 11, and they are our strengths today.

Finally, please continue praying for the victims of terror and their families, for those in uniform, and for our great country. Prayer has comforted us in sorrow, and will help strengthen us for the journey ahead.

Tonight I thank my fellow Americans for what you have already done and for what you will do. And ladies and gentlemen of the Congress, I thank you, their representatives, for what you have already done and for what we will do together.

Tonight, we face new and sudden national challenges. We will come together to improve air safety, to dramatically expand the number of air marshals on domestic flights, and take new measures to prevent hijacking. We will come together to promote stability and keep our airlines flying with direct assistance during this emergency.

We will come together to give law enforcement the additional tools it *50* needs to track down terror here at home. We will come together to strengthen our intelligence capabilities to know the plans of terrorists before they act, and find them before they strike.

We will come together to take active steps that strengthen America's economy and put our people back to work.

Tonight we welcome here two leaders who embody the extraordinary spirit of all New Yorkers: Governor George Pataki and Mayor Rudy Giuliani. As a symbol of America's resolve, my administration will work with the Congress and these two leaders to show the world that we will rebuild New York City.

After all that has just passed—all the lives taken and all the possibilities and hopes that died with them—it is natural to wonder if America's future is one of fear. Some speak of an age of terror. I know there are struggles ahead and dangers to face. But this country will define our times, not be defined by them. As long as the United States of America is determined and strong, this will not be an age of terror; this will be an age of liberty, here and across the world.

Great harm has been done to us. We have suffered great loss. And in our grief and anger we have found our mission and our moment. Freedom and fear are at war. The advance of human freedom—the great achievement of our time and the great hope of every time—now depends on us. Our nation, this generation, will lift a dark threat of violence from our people and our future. We will rally the world to this cause by our efforts and by our courage. We will not tire, we will not falter, and we will not fail.

It is my hope that in the months and years ahead, life will return almost *55* to normal. We'll go back to our lives and routines, and that is good. Even grief recedes with time and grace. But our resolve must not pass. Each of us will remember what happened that day and to whom it happened. We will remember the moment the news came—where we were and what we were doing. Some will remember an image of fire or a story of rescue. Some will carry memories of a face and a voice gone forever.

And I will carry this. It is the police shield of a man named George Howard, who died at the World Trade Center trying to save others. It was given to me by his mom, Arlene, as a proud memorial to her son. This is my reminder of lives that ended and a task that does not end.

I will not forget this wound to our country or those who inflicted it. I will not yield, I will not rest, I will not relent in waging this struggle for the freedom and security of the American people.

The course of this conflict is not known, yet its outcome is certain. Freedom and fear, justice and cruelty, have always been at war, and we know that God is not neutral between them.

Fellow citizens, we will meet violence with patient justice, assured of the rightness of our cause and confident of the victories to come. In all that lies before us, may God grant us wisdom, and may He watch over the United States of America.

Thank you.   *60*

QUESTIONS FOR DISCUSSION

1. At the beginning of his speech, Bush draws attention to one of the passengers who died on the plane that crashed in Pennsylvania before it could hit its target—and to the passenger's wife, who was present for the speech. What does he accomplish by this rhetorical strategy?
2. Bush addresses his remarks to his "fellow Americans." Where does he demonstrate that he understands that Americans come from diverse cultural backgrounds, and why is it important for him to do so?
3. In the weeks following the attacks of September 11, the Bush administration worked to forge an international coalition to oppose terrorism. How does this speech contribute to that effort?
4. In paragraphs 20–21, Bush makes a series of demands that are, he states, "not open to negotiation." What is the purpose of making nonnegotiable demands? Do these demands sound reasonable to you as an American citizen? How would they sound to you if you were a citizen of another country?
5. In paragraph 25, Bush claims the attacks of September 11 were inspired by hatred of the freedoms Americans enjoy. How does this claim support his purpose? Do you agree with it?
6. What do you think Bush means when he refers to the "civilized world"? What countries are part of this world? Which ones would be excluded?
7. At the end of this speech, Bush displayed the police shield he refers to in paragraph 56. What role does this shield play in the speech?

SUGGESTIONS FOR WRITING

1. Write an essay that could inspire people to work on behalf of world peace.
2. Write a eulogy paying tribute to the firefighters who died when trying to rescue people from the World Trade Center.
3. Research the charges that Osama bin Laden made against the United States when attempting to justify the terrorist attack of September 11, 2001. Then write an essay that would move readers to care about what you discover.

LINKS

▪ Within the Book

For another example of political oratory, see Martin Luther King, Jr.'s "I Have a Dream" (pages 535–538).

▪ Elsewhere in Print

Bulliet, Richard W. *Islam*. New York: Columbia UP, 1995.

Bush, George W. *A Challenge to Keep: My Journey to the White House*. New York: HarperCollins, 2001.

Goldziher, Ignaz. *Introduction to Islamic Theology and Law*. Trans. Andras Hamori and Ruth Hamori. Ed. Bernard Lewis. Princeton: Princeton UP, 1981.

Kaplan, David. *The Accidental President: How 413 Lawyers, 9 Supreme Court Justices, and 5,963,110 Floridians (Give or Take a Few) Landed George W. Bush in the White House*. New York: Morrow, 2001.

National Commission on Terrorist Attacks upon the United States. *The 9/11 Report: Final Report of the National Commission on Terrorist Attacks upon the United States*. New York: Norton, 2004.

Reich, Walter. Ed. *Origins of Terrorism: Pyschologies, Ideologies, States of Mind*. Washington, DC: Wilson, 1998.

▪ Online

www.mhhe.com/motives

Click on "More Resources" then "Writing to Inspire Others."

▪ ▪ ▪

A HANGING

George Orwell

Born in India when it was still part of the British Empire, George Orwell (1903–1950) joined the Indian Imperial Police after graduating from Eton College. From 1922 to 1927, he was stationed in Burma—an experience upon which he drew for his first novel, Burmese Days *(1934) and for several of his essays, including "A Hanging." Although Orwell is best known for two novels he wrote late in his life,* Animal Farm *(1945) and* Nineteen Eighty-Four *(1949), he is also widely respected for his nonfiction. "Good prose is like a windowpane," he once wrote, and his essays have been praised for their clarity of style. But like his novels, Orwell's essays also demonstrate a strong commitment to social justice. In "Why I Write," Orwell declares, "My starting point is always a feeling of partisanship, a sense of injustice. When I sit down to write a book, I do not say to myself, 'I am going to produce a work of art.' I write because there is some lie I want to expose, some fact to which I want to draw attention, and my initial concern is to get a hearing." Bearing in mind Orwell's motive for writing, consider what "lie" he is trying to expose in "A Hanging."*

It was Burma, a sodden morning of rains. A sickly light, like yellow tinfoil, was slanting over the walls into the jail yard. We were waiting outside the condemned cells, a row of sheds fronted with double bars, like small animal cages. Each cell measured about ten feet by ten and was quite bare within except for a plank bed and a pot for drinking water. In some of them brown silent men were squatting at the inner bars, with their blankets draped round them. These were the condemned men, due to be hanged within the next week or two.

One prisoner had been brought out of his cell. He was a Hindu, a puny wisp of a man, with a shaven head and vague liquid eyes. He had a thick, sprouting moustache, absurdly too big for his body, rather like the moustache of a comic man on the films. Six tall Indian warders were guarding him and getting him ready for the gallows. Two of them stood by with rifles and fixed bayonets, while the others handcuffed him, passed a chain through his handcuffs and fixed it to their belts, and lashed his arms tight to his sides. They crowded very close about him, with their hands always on him in a careful caressing grip, as though all the while feeling him to make sure he was there. It was like men handling a fish which is still alive and may jump back into the water. But he stood quite unresisting, yielding his arms limply to the ropes, as though he hardly noticed what was happening.

Eight o'clock struck and a bugle call, desolately thin in the wet air, floated from the distant barracks. The superintendent of the jail, who was standing apart from the rest of us, moodily prodding the gravel with his stick, raised his head at the sound. He was an army doctor, with a grey toothbrush moustache and a gruff voice. "For God's sake hurry up, Francis," he said irritably. "The man ought to have been dead by this time. Aren't you ready yet?"

Francis, the head jailer, a fat Dravidian° in a white drill suit and gold spectacles, waved his black hand. "Yes sir, yes sir," he bubbled. "All iss satisfactorily prepared. The hangman iss waiting. We shall proceed."

"Well, quick march, then. The prisoners can't get their breakfast till this   5
job's over."

We set out for the gallows. Two warders marched on either side of the prisoner, with their rifles at the slope; two others marched close against him, gripping him by arm and shoulder, as though at once pushing and supporting him. The rest of us, magistrates and the like, followed behind. Suddenly, when we had gone ten yards, the procession stopped short without any order or warning. A dreadful thing had happened—a dog, come goodness knows whence, had appeared in the yard. It came bounding among us with a loud volley of barks, and leapt round us wagging its whole body, wild with glee at finding so many human beings together. It was a large woolly dog, half Airedale, half pariah. For a moment it pranced round us, and then, before anyone could stop, it had made a dash for the prisoner and, jumping up, tried to lick his face. Everyone stood aghast, too taken aback even to grab at the dog.

"Who let that bloody brute in here?" said the superintendent angrily. "Catch it, someone!"

A warder, detached from the escort, charged clumsily after the dog, but it danced and gambolled just out of his reach, taking everything as part of the game. A young Eurasian jailer picked up a handful of gravel and tried to stone the dog away, but it dodged the stones and came after us again. Its yaps echoed from the jail walls. The prisoner, in the grasp of the two warders, looked on incuriously, as though this was another formality of the hanging. It was several minutes before someone managed to catch the dog. Then we put my handkerchief through its collar and moved off once more, with the dog still straining and whimpering.

It was about forty yards to the gallows. I watched the bare brown back of the prisoner marching in front of me. He walked clumsily with his bound arms, but quite steadily, with that bobbing gait of the Indian who never straightens his knees. At each step his muscles slid neatly into place, the lock of hair on his scalp danced up and down, his feet printed themselves on the wet gravel. And once, in spite of the men who gripped him by each shoulder, he stepped slightly aside to avoid a puddle on the path.

It is curious, but till that moment I had never realized what it means to   10
destroy a healthy, conscious man. When I saw the prisoner step aside to avoid the puddle I saw the mystery, the unspeakable wrongness, of cutting a life

----

°*Dravidian:* A member of a race of people living in southern India and Sri Lanka.

short when it is in full tide. This man was not dying, he was alive just as we are alive. All the organs of his body were working—bowels digesting food, skin renewing itself, nails growing, tissue forming—all toiling away in solemn foolery. His nails would still be growing when he stood on the drop, when he was falling through the air with a tenth-of-a-second to live. His eyes saw the yellow gravel and the grey walls, and his brain still remembered, foresaw, reasoned—reasoned even about puddles. He and we were a party of men walking together, seeing, hearing, feeling, understanding the same world; and in two minutes, with a sudden snap, one of us would be gone—one mind less, one world less.

The gallows stood in a small yard, separate from the main grounds of the prison, and overgrown with tall prickly weeds. It was a brick erection like three sides of a shed, with planking on top, and above that two beams and a crossbar with the rope dangling. The hangman, a grey-haired convict in the white uniform of the prison, was waiting beside his machine. He greeted us with a servile crouch as we entered. At a word from Francis, the two warders, gripping the prisoner more closely than ever, half led half pushed him to the gallows and helped him clumsily up the ladder. Then the hangman climbed up and fixed the rope round the prisoner's neck.

We stood waiting, five yards away. The warders had formed in a rough circle round the gallows. And then, when the noose was fixed, the prisoner began crying out to his god. It was a high, reiterated cry of "Ram! Ram! Ram! Ram!" not urgent and fearful like a prayer or cry for help, but steady, rhythmical, almost like the tolling of a bell. The dog answered the sound with a whine. The hangman, still standing on the gallows, produced a small cotton bag like a flour bag and drew it down over the prisoner's face. But the sound, muffled by the cloth, still persisted, over and over again: "Ram! Ram! Ram! Ram! Ram!"

The hangman climbed down and stood ready, holding the lever. Minutes seemed to pass. The steady, muffled crying from the prisoner went on and on. "Ram! Ram! Ram!" never faltering for an instant. The superintendent, his head on his chest, was slowly poking the ground with his stick; perhaps he was counting the cries, allowing the prisoner a fixed number—fifty, perhaps, or a hundred. Everyone had changed color. The Indians had gone grey like bad coffee, and one or two of the bayonets were wavering. We looked at the lashed, hooded man on the drop, and listened to his cries—each cry another second of life; the same thought was in all our minds: oh, kill him quickly, get it over, stop that abominable noise!

Suddenly the superintendent made up his mind. Throwing up his head he made a swift motion with his stick. "Chalo°!" he shouted almost fiercely.

There was a clanking noise, and then dead silence. The prisoner had vanished, and the rope was twisting on itself. I let go of the dog, and it galloped

15

°*Chalo:* Hindi for "Let's go."

immediately to the back of the gallows; but when it got there it stopped short, barked, and then retreated into a corner of the yard, where it stood among the weeds, looking timorously out at us. We went around the gallows to inspect the prisoner's body. He was dangling with his toes pointed straight downwards, very slowly revolving, as dead as a stone.

The superintendent reached out with his stick and poked the bare brown body; it oscillated slightly. "*He's* all right," said the superintendent. He backed out from under the gallows, and blew out a deep breath. The moody look had gone out of his face quite suddenly. He glanced at his wrist-watch. "Eight minutes past eight. Well, that's all for this morning, thank God."

The warders unfixed bayonets and marched away. The dog, sobered and conscious of having misbehaved itself, slipped after them. We walked out of the gallows yard, past the condemned cells with their waiting prisoners, into the big central yard of the prison. The convicts, under the command of warders armed with lathis°, were already receiving their breakfast. They squatted in long rows, each man holding a pannikin, while two warders with buckets marched round ladling out rice; it seemed quite a homely, jolly scene, after the hanging. An enormous relief had come upon us now that the job was done. One felt an impulse to sink, to break into a run, to snigger. All at once every one began chattering gaily.

The Eurasian boy walking beside me nodded towards the way we had come, with a knowing smile: "Do you know, sir, our friend (he meant the dead man) when he heard his appeal had been dismissed, he pissed on the floor of his cell. From fright. Kindly take one of my cigarettes, sir. Do you not admire my new silver case, sir? From the boxwalah, two rupees eight annas. Classy European style."

Several people laughed—at what, nobody seemed certain.

Francis was walking by the superintendent, talking garrulously: "Well, sir, all hass passed off with the utmost satisfactoriness. It was all finished—flick! like that. It iss not always so—oah, no! I have known cases where the doctor wass obliged to go beneath the gallows and pull the prissoner's legs to ensure decease. Most disagreeable!" *20*

"Wriggling about, eh? That's bad," said the superintendent.

"Ach, sir, it iss worse when they become refractory! One man, I recall, clung to the bars of hiss cage when we went to take him out. You will scarcely credit, sir, that it took six warders to dislodge him, three pulling each leg. We reasoned with him. 'My dear fellow,' we said, 'think of all the pain and trouble you are causing to us!' But no, he would not listen! Ach, he wass very troublesome!"

I found that I was laughing quite loudly. Everyone was laughing. Even the superintendent grinned in a tolerant way. "You'd better all come out and

---

°*lathis:* Heavy sticks bound with iron.

have a drink," he said quite genially. "I've got a bottle of whiskey in the car. We could do with it."

We went through the big double gates of the prison into the road. "Pulling at his legs!" exclaimed a Burmese magistrate suddenly, and burst into a loud chuckling. We all began laughing again. At that moment Francis' anecdote seemed extraordinarily funny. We all had a drink together, native and European alike, quite amicably. The dead man was a hundred yards away.

QUESTIONS FOR DISCUSSION

1. Consider the scene Orwell describes in his opening paragraph. How does his description of the weather and the cells contribute toward inspiring sympathy for the prisoner who is about to be executed?
2. Around what type of contrast has Orwell constructed his second paragraph?
3. What role does the dog play in this essay? Why does Orwell describe its presence at the execution as "dreadful"?
4. Why does Orwell consider it significant that the condemned man stepped aside to avoid a puddle?
5. Orwell describes the prisoner's prayer as "steady, rhythmical, almost like the tolling of a bell." Why is he calling attention to the prayer? Do you recognize an allusion in the reference to the bell?
6. How did witnessing this execution affect the men in the essay? How did it affect you?
7. Some critics have claimed that Orwell never witnessed the execution described in this selection. In that case, what is usually considered an "essay" would become a "story." Would that limit its effectiveness? Would your own response change if you considered the piece fiction?

SUGGESTIONS FOR WRITING

1. If you have ever witnessed a disturbing event that you were powerless to stop, narrate the story of that event so that other people will feel as you do about what you saw.
2. For many people, capital punishment is simply an abstract social issue, but an essay or story focused on a specific execution can make people see the issue differently. Identify a social issue that concerns you, and then dramatize it using narration.
3. Research a capital case that is controversial because of the age, race, gender, or intelligence of the person convicted. Incorporate what you discover in a letter to the governor of the state in which the prisoner is held, attempting to move him or her to grant clemency.

Links

■ **Within the Book**

For another example of Orwell's work, see "Marrakech" (pages 633–638).

■ **Elsewhere in Print**

Baird–Murray, Maureen. *A World Overturned: A Burmese Childhood, 1933–1947*. Brooklyn: Interlink, 1998.
Bowker, Gordon. *Inside George Orwell: A Biography*. New York: Palgrave, 2003.
Harvey, Godfrey. *British Rule in Burma, 1824–1942*. 1946. New York: AMS, 1992.
Orwell, George. *Burmese Days: A Novel*. 1934. New York: Harcourt, 1989.
———. *The Lion and the Unicorn: Socialism and the English Genius*. 1941. New York: AMS, 1976.
Prejean, Helen. *Dead Man Walking: An Eyewitness Account of the Death Penalty in the United States*. New York: Random, 1993.
Said, Edward W. *Culture and Imperialism*. New York: Knopf, 1993.

■ **Online**

www.mhhe.com/motives

Click on "More Resources" then "Writing to Inspire Others."

■ ■ ■

AM I BLUE?

*"Ain't these tears in these eyes tellin' you?"**

Alice Walker

> *Alice Walker is best known as the author of* The Color Purple, *which was turned into a popular film by Stephen Spielberg. But Walker is also the author of several other novels—as well as poems and essays, many of which focus on issues of race, family, and gender. In addition to winning the Pulitzer Prize for fiction in 1983, she has received the Lillian Smith Award from the National Endowment for the Arts, the Rosenthal Award from the National Institute of Arts and Letters, and a Guggenheim Fellowship.*
>
> *"Am I Blue?" was first published in 1986 by* Ms. *magazine. In this piece, Walker writes about a stallion named Blue living in a pasture near her home. She describes how his life changed when he was given a companion and how it changed again when that companion was taken away. But as the title suggests, Walker is not interested in the horse alone. You will find that she uses Blue's story to convey feelings about a number of concerns.*

For about three years my companion and I rented a small house in the country that stood on the edge of a large meadow that appeared to run from the end of our deck straight into the mountains. The mountains, however, were quite far away, and between us and them there was, in fact, a town. It was one of the many pleasant aspects of the house that you never really were aware of this.

It was a house of many windows, low, wide, nearly floor to ceiling in the living room, which faced the meadow, and it was from one of these that I first saw our closest neighbor, a large white horse, cropping grass, flipping its mane, and ambling about—not over the entire meadow, which stretched well out of sight of the house, but over the five or so fenced-in acres that were next to the twenty-odd that we had rented. I soon learned that the horse, whose name was Blue, belonged to a man who lived in another town, but was boarded by our neighbors next door. Occasionally, one of the children, usually a stocky teenager, but sometimes a much younger girl or boy, could be seen riding Blue. They would appear in the meadow, climb up on his back, ride furiously for ten or fifteen minutes, then get off, slap Blue on the flanks, and not be seen again for a month or more.

---

*"Am I Blue?" by Grant Clarke and Harry Akst, 1929.

There were many apple trees in our yard, and one by the fence Blue could almost reach. We were soon in the habit of feeding him apples, which he relished, especially because by the middle of summer the meadow grasses—so green and succulent since January—had dried out from lack of rain, and Blue stumbled about munching the dried stalks half-heartedly. Sometimes he would stand very still just by the apple tree, and when one of us came out he would whinny, snort loudly, or stamp the ground. This meant, of course: I want an apple.

It was quite wonderful to pick a few apples, or collect those that had fallen to the ground overnight, and patiently hold them, one by one, up to his large, toothy mouth. I remained as thrilled as a child by his flexible dark lips, huge, cubelike teeth that crunched the apples, core and all, with such finality, and his high, broad-breasted *enormity;* beside which, I felt small indeed. When I was a child, I used to ride horses, and was especially friendly with one named Nan until the day I was riding and my brother deliberately spooked her and I was thrown, head first, against the trunk of a tree. When I came to, I was in bed and my mother was bending worriedly over me; we silently agreed that perhaps horseback riding was not the safest sport for me. Since then I have walked, and prefer walking to horseback riding—but I had forgotten the depth of feeling one could see in horses' eyes.

I was therefore unprepared for the expression in Blue's. Blue was lonely. 5
Blue was horribly lonely and bored. I was not shocked that this should be the case; five acres to tramp by yourself, endlessly, even in the most beautiful of meadows—and his was—cannot provide many interesting events, and once rainy season turned to dry that was about it. No, I was shocked that I had forgotten that human animals and nonhuman animals can communicate quite well; if we are brought up around animals as children we take this for granted. By the time we are adults we no longer remember. However, the animals have not changed. They are in fact *completed* creations (at least they seem to be, so much more than we) who are not likely to change; it is their nature to express themselves. What else are they going to express? And they do. And, generally speaking, they are ignored.

After giving Blue the apples, I would wander back to the house, aware that he was observing me. Were more apples not forthcoming then? Was that to be his sole entertainment for the day? My partner's small son had decided he wanted to learn how to piece a quilt; we worked in silence on our respective squares as I thought . . .

Well, about slavery: about white children, who were raised by black people, who knew their first all-accepting love from black women, and then, when they were twelve or so, were told they must "forget" the deep levels of communication between themselves and "mammy" that they knew. Later they would be able to relate quite calmly, "My old mammy was sold to another good family." "My old mammy was _____." Fill in the blank. Many more years later a white woman would say: "I can't understand these Negroes, these blacks. What do they want? They're so different from us."

And about the Indians, considered to be "like animals" by the "settlers" (a very benign euphemism for what they actually were), who did not understand their description as a compliment.

And about the thousands of American men who marry Japanese, Korean, Filipina, and other non-English-speaking women and of how happy they report they are, "*blissfully*," until their brides learn to speak English, at which point the marriages tend to fall apart. What then did the men see, when they looked into the eyes of the women they married, before they could speak English? Apparently only their own reflections.

I thought of society's impatience with the young. "Why are they playing   10
the music so loud?" Perhaps the children have listened to much of the music of oppressed people their parents danced to before they were born, with its passionate but soft cries for acceptance and love, and they have wondered why their parents failed to hear.

I do not know how long Blue had inhabited his five beautiful, boring acres before we moved into our house; a year after we had arrived—and had also traveled to other valleys, other cities, other worlds—he was still there.

But then, in our second year at the house, something happened in Blue's life. One morning, looking out the window at the fog that lay like a ribbon over the meadow, I saw another horse, a brown one, at the other end of Blue's field. Blue appeared to be afraid of it, and for several days made no attempt to go near. We went away for a week. When we returned, Blue had decided to make friends and the two horses ambled or galloped along together, and Blue did not come nearly as often to the fence underneath the apple tree.

When he did, bringing his new friend with him, there was a different look in his eyes. A look of independence, of self-possession, of inalienable *horse*ness. His friend eventually became pregnant. For months and months there was, it seemed to me, a mutual feeling between me and the horses of justice, of peace. I fed apples to them both. The look in Blue's eyes was one of unabashed "this is *it*ness."

It did not, however, last forever. One day, after a visit to the city, I went out to give Blue some apples. He stood waiting, or so I thought, though not beneath the tree. When I shook the tree and jumped back from the shower of apples, he made no move. I carried some over to him. He managed to half-crunch one. The rest he let fall to the ground. I dreaded looking into his eyes—because I had of course noticed that Brown, his partner, had gone—but I did look. If I had been born into slavery, and my partner had been sold or killed, my eyes would have looked like that. The children next door explained that Blue's partner had been "put with him" (the same expression that old people used, I had noticed, when speaking of an ancestor during slavery who had been impregnated by her owner) so that they could mate and she conceive. Since that was accomplished, she had been taken back by her owner, who lived somewhere else.

Will she be back? I asked.   15

They didn't know.

Blue was like a crazed person. Blue *was,* to me, a crazed person. He galloped furiously, as if he were being ridden, around and around his five beautiful acres. He whinnied until he couldn't. He tore at the ground with his hooves. He butted himself against his single shade tree. He looked always and always toward the road down which his partner had gone. And then, occasionally, when he came up for apples, or I took apples to him, he looked at me. It was a look so piercing, so full of grief, a look so *human,* I almost laughed (I felt too sad to cry) to think there are people who do not know that animals suffer. People like me who have forgotten, and daily forget, all that animals try to tell us. "Everything you do to us will happen to you; we are your teachers, as you are ours. We are one lesson" is essentially it, I think. There are those who never once have even considered animals' rights: those who have been taught that animals actually want to be used and abused by us, as small children "love" to be frightened, or women "love" to be mutilated and raped. . . . They are the great-grandchildren of those who honestly thought, because someone taught them this: "Women can't think," and "niggers can't faint." But most disturbing of all, in Blue's large brown eyes was a new look, more painful than the look of despair: the look of disgust with human beings, with life; the look of hatred. And it was odd what the look of hatred did. It gave him, for the first time, the look of a beast. And what that meant was that he had put up a barrier within to protect himself from further violence; all the apples in the world wouldn't change that fact.

And so Blue remained, a beautiful part of our landscape, very peaceful to look at from the window, white against the grass. Once a friend came to visit and said, looking out on the soothing view: "And it *would* have to be a *white* horse; the very image of freedom." And I thought, yes, the animals are forced to become for us merely "images" of what they once so beautifully expressed. And we are used to drinking milk from containers showing "contented" cows, whose real lives we want to hear nothing about, eating eggs and drumsticks from "happy" hens, and munching hamburgers advertised by bulls of integrity who seem to command their fate.

As we talked of freedom and justice one day for all, we sat down to steaks. I am eating misery, I thought, as I took the first bite. And spit it out.

QUESTIONS FOR DISCUSSION

1. Consider the opening paragraph of this essay, a paragraph that sets the scene but does not mention the horse that provides the focus for the paragraphs that follow. Why does Walker write that the mountains were farther away than they seemed and that an unseen town intervened?
2. Why is it significant that the horse is named Blue? How has Walker attempted to make readers sympathize with him?
3. The title of this essay, which comes from a song popular in the 1920s, can be read in more than one way. How do you interpret it?

4. Walker refers to her "companion" and "partner"; later, she refers to Blue's "friend." Why do you think she has chosen these words when there are other alternatives?
5. Walker writes that she looked into Blue's eyes and found them lonely, grief-stricken, and, eventually, filled with hatred. Do you think an animal can express these emotions? Or do you think that Walker is projecting her own feelings on the horse?
6. Consider the transition between paragraphs 6 and 7, where Walker moves temporarily away from the story of Blue to reflect on other types of oppression. How successfully does she manage this transition? How would the essay change if she kept Blue's story together and added social commentary only in her final paragraphs?
7. Explain the last paragraph of this essay. Is Walker bothered by eating meat? Or is something else upsetting her?

SUGGESTIONS FOR WRITING

1. Write about neglected or abandoned animals in order to inspire people to contribute to your local humane society.
2. Write an essay about racial injustice that would move members of one race to overcome prejudice they have toward another.
3. Write an essay comparing Walker's essay with Annie Dillard's "The Deer at Providencia" (pages 627–630). Both Dillard and Walker have looked closely at a member of another species. How does their point of view differ?

LINKS

■ Within the Book

To see how a scientist writes about animals mating with other animals, see "Same-Sex Sexuality" by Joan Roughgarden (pages 221–238).

■ Elsewhere in Print

Regan, Tom. *The Case for Animal Rights.* Berkeley: U of California P, 1983.
Singer, Peter. *Animal Liberation.* New York: Ecco, 2002.
Spiegel, Marjorie. *The Dreaded Comparison: Human and Animal Slavery.* Pref. Alice Walker. Rev. ed. New York: Mirror, 1996.
Walker, Alice. *By the Light of My Father's Smile: A Novel.* New York: Random, 1998.
———. *The Color Purple.* 1982. New York: Harcourt, 1992.
———. *Horses Make a Landscape More Beautiful: Poems.* San Diego: Harcourt, 1984.

■ **Elsewhere in Print (continued)**

————. *In Search of Our Mothers' Gardens: Womanist Prose.* San Diego: Harcourt, 1983.

————. *Now Is the Time to Open Your Heart.* New York: Random, 2004.

■ **Online**

www.mhhe.com/motives

Click on "More Resources" then "Writing to Inspire Others."

■ ■ ■

9

Writing to Amuse Others

Writing to amuse, like writing to inspire or to persuade, requires that you focus on readers other than yourself. You may enjoy the experience and take pride in what you accomplish, but you cannot settle for amusing yourself alone. Writing to amuse gives you an opportunity to bring pleasure to others. Seize the opportunity, and make the most of it.

If you find pleasure in writing to amuse, it will come from knowing that you succeeded in bringing pleasure to others. Consider what happens when you tell a joke. If people laugh, you feel pleased that you told the joke—and told it well. However, if no one laughs, you probably feel disappointed or embarrassed. An egotist might be so self-absorbed that he doesn't notice that others are not amused by his efforts at humor, but that may explain why he is not funny: He is focusing on himself rather than his audience.

Of course, an audience that is not laughing might still be amused—although this is unlikely in the case of a good joke. In telling some stories and writing some essays, you could be hoping to inspire only a wry smile, as if to say, "I know what you mean; something like that happened to me, too." It is a rare and wonderful piece of writing that can make us laugh out loud. More common, but not necessarily less valuable, is writing that makes us smile at aspects of life about which we have mixed feelings—things that we can enjoy making fun of but would hesitate to abandon altogether. Patricia Volk's essay on technology can make us laugh without deciding to eliminate technology from our lives. Similarly, David Sedaris can make us laugh at an incompetent teacher with disgruntled students without making us feel that teaching and learning are worthless pursuits.

This observation leads us to a basic principle about writing to amuse: Whether designed to produce belly laughs or merely to bring a twinkle of recognition to someone's eye, humor has an element of tension in it. Despite the great range of material that can be considered "comic," one constant feature is that humor always sends a double message: "Take me seriously, but

569

don't take me seriously." People often laugh because of a sudden, surprising shift between the two parts of this message.

Laughter, however, is not always a sign of amusement, any more than amusement is always indicated by laughter. To release an excess of good spirits, you might laugh when you are having fun, even when no one has said or done anything funny. Strictly speaking, laughter is physiological—a motor and intellectual response to many situations. And these situations are not necessarily amusing. Laughter can be inspired in ways that are essentially mean-spirited attempts to deprive other people of their humanity—as, for example, in the once common practice of laughing at dwarves. It can also signal anxiety, as in a nervous laugh, or hysteria, as when someone is emotionally overwrought and cannot stop laughing.

When writing to amuse, your primary object is to make readers enjoy themselves. You can be funny, but you should also be good-humored. This means having sympathy for human frailty rather than a contempt for anyone or anything that seems different from what you are accustomed to. Ridicule is not genuinely amusing, and it lends itself easily to abuse. You should try to laugh *with* rather than *at,* since your purpose is to give pleasure through reconciliation. By helping readers laugh about their failures, you may help them fail less frequently. But by reminding people that failure is not unique, you can make them feel part of a larger community. Humor thus reconciles people to human imperfection.

CONSIDERING AUDIENCE

Almost everyone can be amused, but almost no one can be amused by everything. When writing to amuse, you need to have a good sense of audience. Consider, for example, how you are more likely to tell a joke—and to tell it well—when with a group of friends than when among strangers. This is because you have a sense of what your friends may find amusing—in terms of both subject matter and delivery. But if you try to amuse a group of strangers without determining whether you have any common ground with them, your attempt may fall flat.

The common ground you discover may be psychological, relational, or situational. When writing about how men and women enjoy different kinds of vacations, Jill Conner Browne establishes a psychological bond with other women who think men can be ridiculous. When David Sedaris writes about the interaction between an inept teacher and his students, or when Cindy Chupack writes about the mishaps of dating, they are assuming that readers will have experienced similar relationships. The authors of "Would Hemingway Get into Harvard?" on the other hand, are focusing on a specific situation: taking the SAT writing exam.

The extent to which readers find these pieces amusing will vary. But all of these works say, in effect, "Hasn't something like this happened to you?"

The version of events offered may be an exaggeration; in fact, it often is. The hunting trip described by Browne and the classroom experiences related by Sedaris go beyond what most readers are likely to have experienced—but they evoke memories of similar experience, and that is the common ground in which humor flourishes.

If you misjudge your audience, you may irritate rather than amuse. Make fun of a prominent Republican in a room full of Republicans, and your humor may be received in grim silence; an audience of Democrats might find the same material hilarious. On the other hand, if you are a Republican speaking to other Republicans and make fun of another party member, your humor may succeed because you are perceived as someone who shares common ground—not someone camped on the other side of a big divide.

As you consider your audience when writing to amuse, think of the various factors that contribute to your identity—age, geography, gender, religion, ethnicity, racial identity, social class, and sexual orientation (see pages 382–386)—and ask yourself if there is a topic that would appeal to an audience that shares one aspect of your background. Think also of the activities you enjoy and those you loathe. If you use a cell phone to stay in touch with friends but recognize that there is a potentially comic side to this behavior, then write about it with an audience of fellow users in mind. If you are irritated by frequent calls from telemarketers, then envision an audience that shares this concern as you write. The possibilities are endless. But whatever possibility you pursue, be sure to have common ground with your audience.

THINKING ABOUT SUBJECTS

You are probably wondering by now what types of material are appropriate for humor. Answering this question is like trying to explain why a joke is funny. Part of the problem is that different people laugh at different things, and circumstances can determine whether something seems amusing to the same person on any given day. What seemed funny in the morning could be annoying in the afternoon. Another problem is that much humor is topical or closely related to a specific cultural context, so that what amused people in the past (and inspired various theories about the comic) can provide only a general sense of what is likely to amuse people today. The humor of John R. Alden's "Breakfast at the FDA Café," for example, depends on readers' being familiar with the sort of consumer warnings that are a feature of contemporary American culture. Someone from another era or culture might be baffled by the piece and wonder how anyone could find it funny.

Yet Alden's work reflects one of the oldest theories of humor. Aristotle wrote in his *Poetics* that comedy—like poetry—springs from the pleasure people find in imitation. He argued that this pleasure is instinctive. Whether or not his argument is true, we can observe young children already delighting in imitation when they see someone mimic another person or when they mimic someone themselves. One way to approach "Breakfast at the FDA Café" is to consider how Alden mimics the language of consumer warnings. Similarly, the authors of "Would Hemingway Get into Harvard?" imitate the style of several well-known writers—as well as the kinds of questions and evaluations students get on tests that are rarely fun to take. In a broader sense, other selections in this chapter also involve imitation. When Patricia Volk writes about her frustrations with technology, Cindy Chupack about dating the wrong kind of guy, or Jill Conner Browne about a vacation on which many things go wrong, they are portraying kinds of experience that are familiar to many readers. In cases such as these, the imitation is of behavior rather than language.

UNDERSTANDING PERSONA

David Sedaris demonstrates another feature frequently found in writing to amuse. He establishes a nonthreatening *persona,* a first-person narrator who conveys a particular voice and point of view that may or may not be the author's own. Persona (derived from the Latin word for the masks used in classical theater) is usually associated today with fiction, but the creation of a literary self is also useful when you are writing to amuse. One way to create a persona is to make yourself seem like an average person who is faintly bewildered by whatever you want readers to be amused by. During the 1930s, Will Rogers achieved great fame by cultivating this kind of voice. More recently, Garrison Keillor and Andy Rooney have succeeded with similar voices. Another way to create a persona is to invent an exaggerated version of yourself, emphasizing a quirk of some kind—such as a tendency to procrastinate, to repeat yourself, or to become impatient so that the exaggerated version of this quirk is comic rather than irritating. In *God Save the Sweet Potato Queens* (an excerpt from which appears in this chapter), Jill Conner Browne consistently presents herself as a pleasure-loving woman who is obsessed with men and food—even though she is also a conscientious parent and a hard-working writer. David Sedaris, another highly productive writer, is by no means as inept as he pretends to be in "The Learning Curve."

In presenting themselves as less than perfect, writers like Sedaris and Browne also draw on another Aristotelian principle: that comedy concerns characters who have a "defect." According to Aristotle, "Comedy is . . . an imitation of persons inferior—not in the full sense of the word bad. . . . It consists of some defect or ugliness which is not painful or destructive." Like the characters in a comedy, comic writers often seem to have a flaw we ourselves may have. But they do not truly suffer from it, and this is one reason we can afford to laugh. The incompetence David Sedaris attributes to himself in "The Learning Curve" can be reassuring to anyone who has ever felt disorganized or ill prepared for work, and it is reassuring, in part, because the situation he describes is so improbable: Despite everything that goes wrong in the classroom, it is hard to believe that he was harmed by working with the students he taught (or that students have truly suffered by taking a class with him).

By creating an engaging persona, writers can make readers laugh *with* them rather than *at* them. We may smile at the way Sedaris presents himself, but the principal source of amusement is a problem that is independent of him: classrooms in which learning is not facilitated. We may laugh at this problem, but we also might be moved to fix it.

This leads to another important aspect of writing to amuse: It is often designed as corrective. The assumption behind much comic writing is that if you can make people laugh, they will change their behavior. In this vein, Patricia Volk implies that we would be wise to avoid buying unnecessary gadgets and appliances. And the authors of "Would Hemingway Get into Harvard?" imply that a standardized test should be revised.

THINKING ABOUT PURPOSE

Writing to amuse can, at times, take less friendly forms. In *satire,* for example, the corrective aspect of writing to amuse is readily apparent. The satirist usually assumes a persona that is more likely to seem aloof than affable and may not use the first person at all. The satirist usually directs attention to the flaws of other people rather than to his or her own. The result can be very funny, but it can also be cruel. A basic bond between writer and audience exists even in satire, however. The satirist assumes that someone or some group has departed from behavior that is recognized as acceptable; this presumes that recognized standards exist and that the audience of a satire (if not its butt) believes in the standards that have been violated.

In keeping with its role as a social corrective, writing to amuse often reinforces traditional standards (such as marriage, which provides the happy ending that resolves so many comedies written for the stage). Beneath much humor is the message that people should grow up and stop acting silly, a conservative, responsible message made palatable through laughter.

But humor can also be subversive. As Mikhail Bakhtin, a Russian critic, has argued, comedy records "the defeat . . . of all that oppresses and restricts." For example, the Marx brothers often amused audiences by disrupting proper, pompous socialites. Or to take an example close at hand: Alden challenges government regulations even as he uses them as a source of humor. Although "Breakfast at the FDA Café" pokes fun at health advisories about popular kinds of food and drink, the essay as a whole invites readers to think critically about the role of government agencies in regulating our lives. And David Sedaris presents himself as an agent for change by providing an exaggerated version of the kind of incompetent teaching that should not be tolerated in our schools. Move overtly, Cindy Chupack urges readers who habitually date the wrong people to look at the extent to which they are responsible for the choices they make.

The disruptive potential of humor may be one reason some people are suspicious of it. Convinced that comedy inspired social rebellion, Plato proposed banning comedians from his ideal republic, and Aristotle argued that comedy was like strong wine and, as such, was unsuitable for the young. Once people have begun to laugh at authority, the credibility of that authority is undermined. Dictators do not take kindly to jokes at their expense.

Apparently, then, humor involves a certain amount of tension, because it encourages people to laugh at what, on some level, they think is no laughing matter. Hence, humor can seem to work simultaneously toward both reconciliation and rebellion. The rebellion is against rigid and artificial authority, rules, or behavior, while the reconciliation is aimed at restoring a natural sense of community. Alden assumes that regulations governing the way people are expected to eat have become too rigid. He is rebelling against authorities that insist he eat sensibly. But he is also attempting to reconcile people to what, in fact, many people want to do—enjoy themselves and not worry so much about maintaining a healthy diet.

THINKING ABOUT PATTERNS

The humor of Alden's piece depends on people's recognizing a frequently repeated pattern. The essay would not seem funny if the author were the only person who, when reading a menu, felt torn between eating wisely and dining well. In other cases, comic writers exploit the idea of a repeated pattern much more directly. According to Henri Bergson, a French theorist who wrote an important work on laughter, one of the principal sources of humor is a situation in which people behave mechanically, repeating the same motion or saying the same thing. Once we begin to notice this repetition, it becomes predictable—and we are inclined to laugh when our expectations are fulfilled. For example, students may laugh after noticing that their professor always says "One last thing" at least twice in every class. Cartoons often depend heavily on this principle of predictable repetition: We know that the Roadrunner will always outmaneuver the Coyote, and the Coyote will always be back no matter how many times he falls off the cliff.

In an essay of your own, you could amuse readers by identifying a predictable form of behavior that you have observed in yourself or in others and then showing that pattern in action. Someone who is always ready to party, nap, or shop—or offer unsolicited advice, avoid paying bills, or turn all conversations to memories of his ex-girlfriend—could provide the inspiration for humor once you see the comic potential of behavior that seems unvaried and automatic.

PLANNING YOUR ESSAY

How can you go about writing an amusing essay? Although there is no formula guaranteed to succeed, the following guidelines may help you get started.

First, be aware that your own experience, or the readings that follow, may suggest a variety of topics. But if you're stuck for an idea, try to identify a flaw in the behavior of people you know. The flaw you choose should be easy to observe so that you can count on its being recognized by your audience. When writing about it, do not be afraid to exaggerate.

Second, cultivate an appropriate voice. Address your readers as members of a community who share the same values and have suffered the same problems. Be careful not to make yourself sound superior to your readers or sound as if you would do anyone a real injury.

Third, experiment with wordplay. One of the great sources of humor is the pleasure people derive from unexpected combinations of words. Surprise readers with a pun or a playful variation of a cliché. (An actress of questionable virtue once described herself as being "pure as the fresh-driven slush.") Or you can invent words that are delightful simply because of the way they sound. (For example, Lewis Carroll—the author of *Alice in Wonderland*— invented *jabberwocky* as a word signifying meaningless speech or writing.)

Fourth, use repetition. Although deliberate repetition can serve many rhetorical ends, it can be especially useful when you are trying to amuse. The repetition may take the form of someone's always saying the same thing or always reacting in a predictable way—such as Homer Simpson, who routinely makes foolish choices.

Finally, be aware that a good way to measure your success in writing to amuse is to read a draft of your paper aloud to friends. But you should also ask yourself if there is anyone in whose presence you would be embarrassed to read it. A good-humored paper should be suitable for many audiences. It should produce a smile rather than a sneer. If you are worried that your paper might give offense, you may be writing to ridicule rather than to amuse.

TIPS FOR READING AND WRITING HUMOR

When Reading

- Determine the underlying purpose in writing to amuse. What can the author of a specific piece accomplish by treating the topic in question with humor?
- Consider the self-presentation of the author. To what extent does the author seem to take him- or herself seriously? Is the author willing to be the subject for at least part of the piece's humor, or is the humor achieved strictly at the expense of others?

■ Be alert for exaggerations and consider what is achieved by each exaggeration you note.

■ Note whether the piece makes you feel more light-hearted, and if so, why.

When Writing

■ Choose a topic well suited for your audience by considering what you have in common with them.

■ Consider the extent to which you want to be subversive. If challenging authority or conventional wisdom, determine how far you want to go and how long your audience is likely to accompany you.

■ If using the first person, decide how you want to present yourself. What aspect of yourself do you want to emphasize? What aspects would interfere with your ability to amuse?

■ Experiment with word play.

■ Feel free to exaggerate, but don't let your exaggerations grow so large that your audience will miss the realities behind them.

TECHNOLOGY MAKES ME MAD

Patricia Volk

If you've ever had trouble programming a new television with multiple features or found yourself wondering why your computer can't read the disk on which you carefully saved a paper that's due in twenty minutes, you're likely to understand the kind of frustration that Patricia Volk expresses in "Technology Makes Me Mad," which was first published by The New York Times Magazine *in 1997.*

Formerly an art director at Seventeen *magazine and at* Harper's Bazaar, *Volk has also worked as a senior vice president in the advertising industry. Her essays and short stories have appeared in* The Atlantic, Playboy, The New Yorker, Family Circle, *and* Cosmopolitan, *among other publications. With this background in mind, consider whether Volk may be creating a comic version of herself as you read the following selection.*

First there was breast-feeding. Then there was formula. Now there's patent No. 5,571,084, a microprocessor-controlled breast-pump vest with a programming chip that vacuums out milk for your baby without human contact. Why? So you can answer more E-mail?

Call me a technophobe. Technology drives me nuts. It even makes me lie. I hold for the operator, faking a rotary dial. When you call Metro North for a train from 125th Street to Dover Plains, you get the info in 16 seconds from a person. Take the touch-tone route and it's 5 minutes, 49 seconds.

"Please stay on the line. The next available representative will assist you." Ahhhhhhhh.

True, the electric coffee maker has changed my life. It brews eight perfect cups in five minutes flat and keeps the coffee hot all day. I'll never go back to perk or drip. But the front panel says "2:11 A.M." no matter what time it is. The thing has no buttons. Just a pressure-sensitive panel pressure-insensitive to me. "2:11 A.M. . . . 2:11 A.M." it flashes urgent-green round the clock. I'm thinking of covering it with the millennial cure for everything: duct tape.

In the early 19th century, English workers destroyed two improved stocking frames to thwart labor-saving technology. I'm no Luddite. I love pantyhose. The wheel is O.K., too. So are heated car seats, fetal monitors and ice makers. And what would I do without the phone? See people?   5

The best part of being a technophobe is that you get to blame everything bad on technology, whether it's technology's fault or not—the disappearance of the photobooth, peanut butter and jelly in the same jar, the horrible, unforgivable change in the taste of Hellmann's Real (hah!) Mayonnaise.

But I feel betrayed when my state-of-the-art fridge breaks down. State-of-the-art actually means no one's really sure it works right yet. Regardless of what the accompanying literature says, there's no way you can slice a tomato in my new, improved Cuisinart.

Here's the worst. When I tried removing hair from my legs with a high-tech electronic device, it bit my knee. It wouldn't let go. A machine was whirring on my leg, a mechanical pit bull. Bleeding, I dialed the 800 number. A guy named Bruce talked me down.

"Oh, is it grabbing your knee?" he yawned.

"Uhhhhhhhh. . . ." I tried not to cry.   10

"O.K., now I want you to start by pulling out the plug. . . ."

Bruce offered to pick up all dermatology bills. He sounded as if he'd been talking down bit women all day.

The technology-impaired get a systolic surge when confronting any machine. We cover our reproductive organs when the microwave lights up. The eighth wonder of the world is what prevents electricity from spilling out all over the floor when the sockets are empty. Given the choice, we patronize drugstores that carry six brands of hairnets even though we don't use hairnets. We want to support hairnet availability in a world that's turned to ozone-eating hair spray. Why does Saran Wrap have a longer life expectancy than I do?

We know for a fact that things are made with too many parts. Why else would the dishwasher still work when there are three rubber items on the kitchen floor that never went back in? The Web is where the spider waits. Windows are what you look out. We like our phones black.

Everything good in life, what makes you feel something, has nothing to   15
do with technology—family, a peach, the beach. Pastrami on rye. A deep who-pulled-away-first? kiss.

A Short List of Technology I Could Easily Live Without: TV zappers, the VCR, running shoes that look as if they have pool floats for soles, artificial intelligence, morphing, olestra, miracle-fiber shoelaces that come undone *even when you double-knot*. Recently, every historic place I went in Vienna a man was lurking in the doorway shouting into his cell phone. If these babies are such technological wonders, why do people have to scream into them? The $2 billion Stealth bomber couldn't tell the difference between a mountain and a cloud? The last time I checked, a pilot could.

Past cyberspace, into outer space, I stare at the Sturgeon Moon. It's a full moon, a gorgeous moon. Then I remember—we've left junk up there. Aluminum flagpoles, parachute cloth, lunar rovers. Yup, junk on the moon. Or do I mean technology? "Get wood," an architect once told me. "Plastic only goes downhill."

It's 2:11, coffee time.

QUESTIONS FOR DISCUSSION

1. In her opening paragraph, Volk jokes that a new kind of breast pump will make it easier for nursing mothers to answer more e-mail. Why is this joke funny? What assumption about technology is being challenged here?

2. Paragraphs 2, 3, and 8–12 involve getting "help" over the telephone. In using these examples, what has Volk assumed about her audience?
3. Consider the concessions that Volk makes to technology. Is there any pattern to the goods she admits enjoying?
4. What is Volk implying when she asks, "Why does Saran Wrap have a longer life expectancy than I do?"?
5. What aspects of technology are essential to your own comfort? What would be on your own "Short List of Technology I Could Easily Live Without"?

SUGGESTIONS FOR WRITING

1. Consider occasions when technology has somehow let you down, whether it be your alarm clock failing to go off or your car refusing to start. Choose one specific experience and—however frustrating it may have been at the time—tell the story of what happened to you, making it as funny as you can.
2. Imagine yourself in a school from which technology has suddenly disappeared. Write a humorous essay describing the unexpected difficulties you would encounter.
3. Drawing on your experience with e-mail or online discussion groups, write an essay showing the humorous side of life on the Internet.

LINKS

■ Within the Book

In "Reach Out and Annoy Someone" (pages 251–256), Jonathan Rowe explores another problematic aspect of technology.

■ Elsewhere in Print

Anuff, Joey, and Ana Marie Cox, eds. *Suck: Worst-Case Scenarios in Media, Culture, Advertising, and the Internet.* San Francisco: Wired, 1997.

Barry, Dave. *Dave Barry in Cyberspace.* New York: Crown, 1996.

Heim, Judy. *I Lost My Baby, My Pickup, and My Guitar on the Information Highway: A Humorous Trip down the Highways, Byways, and Backroads of Information Technology.* San Francisco: Starch, 1995.

Levine, Rachel. *Cyberyenta's Old-Fashioned Wisdom for Newfangled Times.* Lincoln: Writers, 2000.

Volk, Patricia. *All It Takes: Stories.* New York: Atheneum, 1990.

———. *White Light.* New York: Atheneum, 1987.

■ Online

www.mhhe.com/motives

Click on "More Resources" then "Writing to Amuse Others."

■ ■ ■

BREAKFAST AT THE FDA CAFÉ

John R. Alden

> *"Everything that's any fun,"* the old joke used to run, *"is illegal, immoral, or fattening."* In this article from a 1991 issue of the Wall Street Journal, *John R. Alden postulates that today we need to add one or two new categories. As you read "Breakfast at the FDA Café," notice how Alden makes a common act—ordering breakfast in a restaurant—a source of humor as well as a social critique.*
>
> *An anthropologist at the University of Michigan, Alden reviews books on diverse topics for* Smithsonian *and* Natural History *magazines.*

"I'll have two eggs over easy, home fries, a blueberry muffin, decaf coffee and the fresh-squeezed orange juice," I told my waiter.

"Very good, sir," he said, and hurried away.

I had just unfolded my paper as he came back with the coffee.

"Here you are," he said. "But before you can have this, our corporate legal department insists that we warn you that recent studies indicate that consumption of three or more cups of coffee a day may increase your risk of stroke and bladder cancer. This is decaffeinated, so I don't need to say that caffeine is addictive and can cause temporary but significant increases in your blood pressure and heartbeat. However, FDA regulations do require me to notify you that the decaffeination process may leave minute traces of carcinogenic solvents in the coffee beans." He poured.

I had nearly finished the front page when he returned with my breakfast.   5

"Your eggs," he said as he put my plate in front of me, "are fried in a polyunsaturated oil high in fat and calories. Eggs that are only lightly cooked may contain salmonella, an organism causing food poisoning, and the National Society for the Alleviation of Allergies warns that many Americans exhibit a mild allergic response to the ova of domestic fowl. Egg yolks contain large quantities of cholesterol, and the American Association of Cardiological Surgeons recommends that people over 40, particularly those who smoke or are more than 10 pounds overweight, limit their consumption to four eggs per week."

I sucked in my stomach.

"Potatoes," he continued, "are a member of the nightshade family, and any greenish patches on their skin may contain traces of an alkaloid poison called solanine. *The Physician's Reference Manual* says solanine can cause vomiting, diarrhea, and acute nausea. However, your potatoes have been carefully peeled, and our supplier has agreed to assume any liability that may arise from their consumption.

"The blueberry muffin contains enriched flour, cane sugar, eggs, butter, blueberries and low-sodium baking powder. The Institute of Alimentary Studies warns that a diet high in processed flour may add to your risk of stomach and intestinal cancer. The Center for Dietary Purity warns that processed wheat flour may be contaminated with up to two tenths of a part per billion of fungicides and rodenticides. It has been bleached and brominated and in cool wet years might also contain minute traces of ergot. Ingested in sufficient quantities, ergot can cause hallucinations and convulsions, arterial spasms, and induce abortions in pregnant women.

"Citizens Against Empty Calories, an independent research organization 10 funded in part by the American Beet Sugar Producers Association, warns that cane sugar is high in calories, low in nutritional value, and one of the principal dietary factors associated with dental cavities.

"Butter, like eggs, is high in cholesterol, a material that studies have identified as playing a potentially significant role in the development of arteriosclerosis and heart disease, particularly in genetically susceptible individuals. If any of your close relatives ever had a heart attack, the Department of Health and Human Services warns that your personal physician might advise you to limit your intake of butter, cream and other dairy products.

"Our blueberries are from Maine. They have not been fertilized or treated with pesticides. However, the U.S. Geological Survey has reported that many Maine blueberry barrens are located on granite, and granitic rock frequently contains measurable amounts of radioactive uranium, radium and radon gas.

"Finally, the baking powder used in these muffins contains sodium aluminum sulfate. Aluminum, some researchers suggest, may be a contributing factor in the development of Alzheimer's disease. The National Institute of Mental Health has not stated a position on this, but it *has* asked us to inform our customers that it will be funding a seven-year, $47 million study examining the association between aluminum consumption and senility syndromes."

He picked up a pitcher. "I have to inform you that our 'fresh-squeezed' orange juice was actually prepared before 6 this morning. It is now 8:30. The FDA and the Justice Department recently sued a restaurant in Georgia (*U.S. v. Mom's Home-baked Café*) for describing three-hour-old juice as 'fresh-squeezed.' Until that case is decided, our legal advisers have required us to get a waiver from any customer ordering a similar product."

I signed the form he handed me, and he stapled a copy to my bill. But as 15 I reached for the glass, he stopped me.

"Excuse me, please. Our salt and pepper shakers are clearly labeled, but corporate policy requires that I repeat the warnings to you verbally. On the salt it says, 'If consumed in large quantities, sodium chloride can be highly toxic, and habitual ingestion of this compound has been shown to cause life-threatening hypertension.' The other shaker says: 'Pepper. Use with extreme caution! The Center for Communicable Disease warns that sneezing associated with careless use of this powder may contribute to the transmission of rhinoviral and influenza-type diseases.' Finally, the Department of Consumer

Safety has determined that the tines of your fork are sharp, and new regulations require me to caution customers to use that utensil with extreme care."

He turned, and with a cheery "Enjoy your breakfast, sir," headed off to the next table. I picked at my meal but couldn't finish it. The food had gotten cold, and somehow I had lost my appetite.

QUESTIONS FOR DISCUSSION

1. What do you think prompted Alden to write this essay? Is he making fun of the FDA's warnings, or is he making fun of something else?
2. Describe the setting Alden chose for this piece. Would he be able to make his point in a different setting?
3. How does Alden use repetition for humorous effect? How does he use exaggeration?
4. Who is likely to enjoy this essay more, an audience of people who take pleasure from dining out frequently or people who are often on a diet? Why?
5. Alden treats the waiter much as a short story writer or a dramatist might. Describe this character and how he sounds.

SUGGESTIONS FOR WRITING

1. Have you ever been annoyed by what seems to be an endless bombardment of often ridiculous health messages, such as fitness requirements, warnings on appliances, and signs on pillows or plastic bags? Write an essay on how you respond to these warnings.
2. Do any of the people you know have a strict sense of what they will or won't eat? Is it ever a challenge to cook for them or to eat out with them? If so, write an essay showing how these people are what they eat—or won't eat, as the case may be.
3. If you have worked in a restaurant, write an essay showing the humorous side of your experience there.

▪ LINKS

▪ Within the Book

If, like Alden, you enjoy eating food that is not necessarily nutritional, you might enjoy "Grub" (pages 60–64) by Scott Russell Sanders.

▪ Elsewhere in Print

Barth, Stephen, David K. Hayes, and Jack D. Ninemeier. *Restaurant Law Basics.* Hoboken: Wiley, 2001.

Downey, Jim, and Tom Connor. *Zeguts Ridiculous Restaurants.* New York: Kensington, 1997.

■ **Elsewhere in Print (continued)**

Hoffman, Ken. *You Want Fries with That? A Collection.* Houston: Winedale, 1999.

Kraus, Scott. *Stuff and Other Junk: FDA Certified Generic Humor.* Valley City: Dutch, 1998.

Lileks, James. *The Gallery of Regrettable Food.* New York: Crown, 2001.

Richman, Alan. *Fork It Over: The Intrepid Adventures of a Professional Eater.* New York: Harper, 2004.

Spitznagel, Eric. *The Junk Food Companion: The Complete Guide to Eating Badly.* New York: Penguin, 1999.

■ **Online**

www.mhhe.com/motives

Click on "More Resources" then "Writing to Amuse Others."

■ ■ ■

THE LEARNING CURVE

David Sedaris

Have you ever taken a class from an incompetent teacher or been supervised by someone who did not understand how to do his or her job? Have you ever felt that you have somehow gotten yourself into a position that was too much responsibility for you? Have any of the activities in a college course ever seemed a little odd? If you can answer "yes" to any of these questions, you should enjoy the following essay by David Sedaris, in which he presents himself as an ill-prepared writing teacher who is desperate to fill up class time.

A former house cleaner who now lives in Paris, Sedaris is a regular contributor to National Public Radio and the author of many humorous essays. "The Learning Curve" is from his 2000 collection, Me Talk Pretty Someday. *Reviewing this collection for the New York Times Book Review,* Craig Seligman advises, *"Not one of the seventeen autobiographical essays in this new collection failed to make me crack up; frequently I was helpless. [. . .] Even the bleakest of them contain stuff you shouldn't read with your mouth full."*

A year after my graduation from the School of the Art Institute of Chicago, a terrible mistake was made and I was offered a position teaching a writing workshop. I had never gone to graduate school, and although several of my stories had been Xeroxed and stapled, none of them had ever been published in the traditional sense of the word.

Like branding steers or embalming the dead, teaching was a profession I had never seriously considered. I was clearly unqualified, yet I accepted the job without hesitation, as it would allow me to wear a tie and go by the name of Mr. Sedaris. My father went by the same name, and though he lived a thousand miles away, I liked to imagine someone getting the two of us confused. "Wait a minute," this someone might say, "are you talking about Mr. Sedaris the retired man living in North Carolina, or Mr. Sedaris the distinguished academic?"

The position was offered at the last minute, when the scheduled professor found a better-paying job delivering pizza. I was given two weeks to prepare, a period I spent searching for a briefcase and standing before my full-length mirror, repeating the words, "Hello, class, my name is Mr. Sedaris." Sometimes I'd give myself an aggressive voice and firm, athletic timbre. This was the masculine Mr. Sedaris, who wrote knowingly of flesh wounds and tractor pulls. Then there was the ragged bark of the newspaper editor, a tone that coupled wisdom with an unlimited capacity for cruelty. I tried sounding businesslike and world-weary, but when the day eventually came, my nerves kicked in and the true Mr. Sedaris revealed himself. In a voice reflecting doubt, fear, and an unmistakable desire to be loved, I sounded not like a thoughtful college professor but, rather, like a high-strung twelve-year-old girl; someone named Brittany.

My first semester I had only nine students. Hoping they might view me as professional and well prepared, I arrived bearing name tags fashioned in the shape of maple leaves. I'd cut them myself out of orange construction paper and handed them out along with a box of straight pins. My fourth-grade teacher had done the same thing, explaining that we were to take only one pin per person. This being college rather than elementary school, I encouraged my students to take as many pins as they liked. They wrote their names upon their leaves, fastened them to their breast pockets, and bellied up to the long oak table that served as our communal desk.

"All right, then," I said. "Okay, here we go." I opened my briefcase and realized that I'd never thought beyond this moment. The orange leaves were the extent of my lesson plan, but still I searched the empty briefcase, mindful that I had stupidly armed my audience with straight pins. I guess I'd been thinking that, without provocation, my students would talk, offering their thoughts and opinions on the issues of the day. I'd imagined myself sitting on the edge of the desk, overlooking a forest of raised hands. The students would simultaneously shout to be heard, and I'd pound on something in order to silence them. "Whoa, people," I'd yell. "Calm down, you'll all get your turn. One at a time, one at a time."

The error of my thinking yawned before me. A terrible silence overtook the room, and seeing no other option, I instructed my students to pull out their notebooks and write a brief essay related to the theme of profound disappointment.

I'd always hated it when a teacher forced us to invent something on the spot. Aside from the obvious pressure, it seemed that everyone had his or her own little way of doing things, especially when it came to writing. Maybe someone needed a particular kind of lamp or pen or typewriter. In my experience, it was hard to write without your preferred tools, but impossible to write without a cigarette.

I made a note to bring in some ashtrays, and then I rooted through the wastepaper basket for a few empty cans. Standing beneath the prominently displayed NO SMOKING sign, I distributed the cans and cast my cigarettes upon the table, encouraging my students to go at it. This, to me, was the very essence of teaching, and I thought I'd made a real breakthrough until the class asthmatic raised his hand, saying that, to the best of his knowledge, Aristophanes had never smoked a cigarette in his life. "Neither did Jane Austen," he said. "Or the Brontës."

I jotted these names into my notebook alongside the word *Troublemaker,* and said I'd look into it. Because I was the writing teacher, it was automatically assumed that I had read every leather-bound volume in the Library of Classics. The truth was that I had read none of those books, nor did I intend to. I bluffed my way through most challenges with dim memories of the movie or miniseries based upon the book in question, but it was an exhausting exercise, and eventually I learned it was easier to simply reply with a question, saying, "I know what Flaubert° means to *me,* but what do *you* think of her?"

As Mr. Sedaris, I lived in constant fear. There was the perfectly under- 10 standable fear of being exposed as a fraud, and then there was the deeper fear that my students might hate me. I imagined them calling their friends on the phone. "Guess who *I* got stuck with," they'd say. Most dull teachers at least had a few credentials to back them up. They had a philosophy and a lesson plan and didn't need to hide behind a clip-on tie and an empty briefcase.

Whenever I felt in danger of losing my authority, I would cross the room and either open or close the door. A student needed to ask permission before regulating the temperature or noise level, but I could do so whenever I liked. It was the only activity sure to remind me that I was in charge, and I took full advantage of it.

"There he goes again," my students would whisper. "What's up with him and that door?"

The asthmatic transferred to another class, leaving me with only eight students. Of these, four were seasoned smokers who took long, contemplative drags and occasionally demonstrated their proficiency by blowing ghostly concentric rings that hovered like halos above their bowed heads. The others tried as best they could, but it wasn't pretty. By the end of the second session, my students had produced nothing but ashes. Their hacking coughs and complete lack of output suggested that, for certain writers, smoking was obviously not enough.

Thinking that a clever assignment might help loosen them up, I instructed my students to write a letter to their mothers in prison. They were free to determine both the crime and the sentence, and references to cellmates were strongly encouraged.

The group set to work with genuine purpose and enthusiasm, and I felt 15 proud of myself, until the quietest member of the class handed in her paper, whispering that both her father and her uncle were currently serving time on federal racketeering charges.

"I just never thought of my mom going off as well," she said. "This was just a really . . . depressing assignment."

I'd never known what an actual child-to-parent prison letter might be like, but now I had a pretty clear idea. I envisioned two convicts sharing a cell. One man stood at the sink while the other lay on a bunk, reading his mail.

"Anything interesting?" the standing man asked.

"Oh, it's from my daughter," the other man said. "She's just started college, and apparently her writing teacher is a real asshole."

°*Flaubert:* Gustave Flaubert (1821–1880), French writer best known for his novel *Madame Bovary.*

That was the last time I asked my students to write in class. From that ₂₀ point on, all their stories were to be written at home on the subject of their choice. If I'd had my way, we would have all stayed home and conducted the class through smoke signals. As it was, I had to find some way to pass the time and trick my students into believing that they were getting an education. The class met twice a week for two hours a day. Filling an entire session with one activity was out of the question, so I began breaking each session into a series of brief, regularly scheduled discussion periods. We began each day with Celebrity Corner. This was an opportunity for the students to share interesting bits of information provided by friends in New York or Los Angeles who were forever claiming firsthand knowledge of a rock band's impending breakup or movie star's dark sexual secret. Luckily everyone seemed to have such a friend, and we were never short of material.

Celebrity Corner was followed by the Feedbag Forum, my shameless call for easy, one-pot dinner recipes, the type favored by elderly aunts and grandmothers whose dental status demanded that all meat fall from the bone without provocation. When asked what Boiled Beef Arkansas had to do with the craft of writing, I did not mention my recent purchase of a Crock-Pot; rather, I lied through my rotten teeth, explaining that it wasn't the recipe itself but the pacing that was of interest to the writer.

After the Feedbag Forum it was time for Pillow Talk, which was defined as "an opportunity for you to discuss your private sex lives in a safe, intellectual environment." The majority of my students were reluctant to share their experiences, so arrangements were made with the audiovisual department. I then took to wheeling in a big color television so that we might spend an hour watching *One Life to Live.* This was back when Victoria Buchanan passed out at her twentieth high-school reunion and came to remembering that, rather than graduating with the rest of her class, she had instead hitchhiked to New York City, where she'd coupled with a hippie and given birth to a long-lost daughter. It sounds farfetched, but like a roast forsaken in the oven or a rescheduled dental appointment, childbirth is one of those minor details that tends to slip the minds of most soap opera characters. It's a personality trait you've just got to accept.

On *General Hospital* or *Guiding Light,* a similar story might come off as trite or even laughable. This, though, was *One Life to Live,* and no one could suddenly recall the birth of a child quite like Erika Slezak, who played both Victoria Buchanan and her alternate personality, Nicole Smith. I'd been in the habit of taping the show and watching it every night while eating dinner. Now that I was an academic, I could watch it in class and use the dinner hour to catch up on *All My Children.* A few students grumbled, but again I assured them that this was all part of my master plan.

Word came from the front office that there had been some complaints regarding my use of class time. This meant I'd have to justify my daily screenings with a homework assignment. Now the students were to watch an episode and write what I referred to as a "guessay," a brief prediction of what might take place the following day.

"Remember that this is not Port Charles or Pine Valley," I said. "This is   *25*
Llanview, Pennsylvania, and we're talking about the Buchanan family."

It actually wasn't a bad little assignment. While the dialogue occasionally falters, you have to admire daytime dramas for their remarkable attention to plot. Yes, there were always the predictable kidnappings and summer love triangles, but a good show could always surprise you with something as simple as the discovery of an underground city. I'd coached my students through half a dozen episodes, giving them background information and explaining that missing children do not just march through the door ten minutes after the critical delivery flashback. The inevitable reunion must unfold delicately and involve at least two-thirds of the cast.

I thought I'd effectively conveyed the seriousness of the assignment. I thought that in my own way I had actually taught them something, so I was angry when their papers included such predictions as "the long-lost daughter turns out to be a vampire" and "the next day Vicki chokes to death while eating a submarine sandwich." The vampire business smacked of *Dark Shadows* reruns, and I refused to take it seriously. But choking to death on a sandwich, that was an insult. Victoria was a Buchanan and would never duck into a sub shop, much less choke to death in a single episode. Especially on a Wednesday. Nobody dies on a Wednesday—hadn't these people learned anything?

In the past I had tried my hardest to be understanding, going so far as to allow the conjugation of nouns and the use of such questionable words as *whateverishly*. This, though, was going too far. I'd taught the Buchanans' Llanview just as my colleagues had taught Joyce's Dublin or Faulkner's Mississippi, but that was over now. Obviously certain people didn't deserve to watch TV in the middle of the afternoon. If my students wanted to stare at the walls for two hours a day, then fine, from here on out we'd just stick to the basics.

I don't know who invented the template for the standard writing workshop, but whoever it was seems to have struck the perfect balance between sadism and masochism. Here is a system designed to eliminate pleasure for everyone involved. The idea is that a student turns in a story, which is then read and thoughtfully critiqued by everyone in the class. In my experience the process worked, in that the stories were occasionally submitted, Xeroxed, and distributed hand to hand. They were folded into purses and knapsacks, but here the system tended to break down. Come critique time, most students behaved as if the assignment had been to confine the stories in a dark, enclosed area and test their reaction to sensory deprivation. Even if the papers were read out loud in class, the discussions were usually brief, as the combination of good manners and complete lack of interest kept most workshop participants from expressing their honest opinions.

With a few notable exceptions, most of the stories were thinly veiled   *30*
accounts of the author's life as he or she attempted to complete the assign-

ment. Roommates were forever stepping out of showers, and waitresses appeared out of nowhere to deliver the onion rings and breakfast burritos that stained the pages of the manuscripts. The sloppiness occasionally bothered me, but I had no room to complain. This was an art school, and the writing workshop was commonly known as the easiest way to fulfill one's mandatory English credits. My students had been admitted because they could admirably paint or sculpt or videotape their bodies in exhausting detail, and wasn't that enough? They told funny, compelling stories about their lives, but committing the details to paper was, for them, a chore rather than an aspiration. The way I saw it, if my students were willing to pretend I was a teacher, the least I could do was return the favor and pretend that they were writers. Even if someone had used his real name and recounted, say, a recent appointment with an oral surgeon, I would accept the story as pure fiction, saying, "So tell us, Dean, how did you come up with this person?"

The student might mumble, pointing to the bloodied cotton wad packed against his swollen gum, and I'd ask, "When did you decide that your character should seek treatment for his impacted molar?" This line of questioning allowed the authors to feel creative and protected anyone who held an unpopular political opinion.

"Let me get this straight," one student said. "You're telling me that if I say something out loud, it's me saying it, but if I write the exact same thing on paper, it's somebody else, right?"

"Yes," I said. "And we're calling that fiction."

The student pulled out his notebook, wrote something down, and handed me a sheet of paper that read, "That's the stupidest fucking thing I ever heard in my life."

They were a smart group.

As Mr. Sedaris I made it a point to type up a poorly spelled evaluation of each submitted story. I'd usually begin with the high points and end, a page or two later, by dispensing such sage professional advice as, "Punctuation never hurt anyone" or "Think verbs!" I tended to lose patience with some of the longer dream sequences, but for the most part we all got along, and the students either accepted or politely ignored my advice.

Trouble arose only when authors used their stories to vindicate themselves against a great hurt or perceived injustice. This was the case with a woman whom the admissions office would have labeled a "returning student," meaning that her social life did not revolve around the cafeteria. The woman was a good fifteen years older than me and clearly disapproved of my teaching methods. She never contributed to Pillow Talk or the Feedbag Forum, and I had good reason to suspect it was she who had complained about the *One Life to Live* episodes. With the teenage freshmen, I stood a chance, but there was nothing I could do to please someone who regularly complained that she'd wasted enough time already. The class was divided into two distinct groups, with her on one side and everyone else on the other. I'd tried everything except leg irons, but nothing could bring the two sides together. It was a real problem.

The returning student had recently come through a difficult divorce, and because her pain was significant, she wrongly insisted that her writing was significant as well. Titled something along the lines of "I Deserve Another Chance," her story was not well received by the class. Following the brief group discussion, I handed her my written evaluation, which she quietly skimmed over before raising her hand.

"Yes," she said. "If you don't mind, I have a little question." She lit a cigarette and spent a moment identifying with the smoldering match. "Who are *you*," she asked. "I mean, just who in the hell are you to tell *me* that *my* story has no ending?"

It was a worthwhile question that was bound to be raised sooner or later. 40 I'd noticed that her story had ended in midsentence, but that aside, who was I to offer criticism to anyone, especially in regard to writing? I'd meant to give the issue some serious thought, but there had been shirts to iron and name tags to make and, between one thing and another, I managed to put it out of my mind.

The woman repeated the question, her voice breaking. "Just who . . . in the stinking hell do you think . . . you are?"

"Can I give you an answer tomorrow?" I asked.

"No," she barked. "I want to know now. Who do you think you are?"

Judging from their expressions, I could see that the other side of the class was entertaining the same question. Doubt was spreading through the room like the cold germs seen in one of those slow-motion close-ups of a sneeze. I envisioned myself burning on a pyre of dream sequences, and then the answer came to me.

"Who am I?" I asked. "I am the only one who is paid to be in this room." 45 This was nothing I'd necessarily want to embroider on a pillow, but still, once the answer left my mouth, I embraced it as a perfectly acceptable teaching philosophy. My previous doubts and fears evaporated, as now I knew that I could excuse anything. The new Mr. Sedaris would never again back down or apologize. From here on out, I'd order my *students* to open and close the door and let *that* remind me that I was in charge. We could do whatever I wanted because I was a certified professional—it practically said so right there on my paycheck. My voice deepened as I stood to straighten my tie. "All right then," I said. "Does anyone else have a stupid question for Mr. Sedaris?"

The returning student once again raised her hand. "It's a personal question, I know, but exactly how much is the school paying you to be in this room?"

I answered honestly, and then, for the first time since the beginning of the school year, my students came together as one. I can't recall which side started it, I remember only that the laughter was so loud, so violent and prolonged that Mr. Sedaris had to run and close the door so that the real teachers could conduct their business in peace.

QUESTIONS FOR DISCUSSION

1. Early in this essay, the author jokes about being mistaken for his father when he is addressed as "Mr. Sedaris." How do you feel when addressed as "Mr.," "Ms.," "Miss," or "Mrs."? Do your feelings change depending upon the age of the person who is addressing you—or the site where the conversation takes place?
2. Most college students would be surprised if one of their teachers asked them to wear orange name tags shaped like maple leaves on the first day of class. Are there any activities or methods from your grade school education that you think could be successfully adapted for the college classroom?
3. If unqualified teachers are sometimes hired at the last minute, why do you think that happens?
4. Of the activities "Mr. Sedaris" eventually organizes for his students, could any of them help you to write well? If so, why?
5. In the courses that you have taken, have any been as ridiculous as the one described here? Have any been a waste of time? If so, why?
6. This essay ends with teacher and students coming together in harmony. Is this conclusion appropriate? What does Sedaris achieve by ending this way?

SUGGESTIONS FOR WRITING

1. If you have ever been in a class taught by a teacher who seemed incompetent, write a humorous description of that teacher's performance from a student's point of view.
2. Sedaris offers a bleak view of how peer review operates in a writing class. If you have ever been disappointed by how other readers responded to your work or by the effort put forth by someone with whom you are collaborating in some other field, write about that experience in a way that makes it seem amusing.
3. Imagine that you are teaching an introductory class in your weakest subject. Write an essay describing your first day in class.

LINKS

■ Within the Book

For a serious piece focused on education, see Elizabeth Kolbert's "Unchartered Territory" (pages 136–145).

■ Elsewhere in Print

Ford, Michael Thomas. *It's Not Mean If It's True.* Los Angeles: Alyson, 2000.
Nagan, Greg. *The Five-Minute Iliad and Other Instant Classics.* New York: Simon, 2000.

■ **Elsewhere in Print (continued)**

Sedaris, David. *Barrel Fever: Stories and Essays.* Boston: Little, 1995.
————. *Holiday on Ice.* Boston: Little, 1998.
————. *Me Talk Pretty Someday.* Boston: Little, 2000.
————. *Naked.* Boston: Little, 1998.
————. *Dress Your Family in Corduroy and Denim.* New York: Little, 2004.

■ **Online**

www.mhhe.com/motives

Click on "More Resources" then "Writing to Amuse Others."

■ ■ ■

RELATIONSHIP RERUNS

Cindy Chupack

If you have ever known anyone who tends to go out with the same kind of person, and each of these relationships runs a predictably unhappy course, or have ever found yourself on a date with someone who reminds you far too much of someone else, then you may be amused by the following selection from Cindy Chupack's The Between Boyfriends Book.

Born in Tulsa, Oklahoma, Chupack earned a degree in journalism from Northwestern University before deciding that she liked writing to amuse. Her humorous essays on dating and relationships have appeared in such periodicals as Glamour, Harper's Bazaar, *and* Slate. *A writer and co-executive producer for* Everybody Loves Raymond, *she subsequently became a writer and executive producer for HBO's* Sex and the City. *When asked about her writing process, she has said that she likes "having time to write and rewrite" and offers the following advice: "I think you should write what you love, not what you think will sell, and take jobs if you like what you'll write about, not for any other reason.* Sex and the City *wasn't a hit when I signed on, and it paid a lot less than* Everybody Loves Raymond, *but I just followed my heart on that one."*

You know you're in the metaphorical summer of your soul mate search when you turn on the charm and all you can find are reruns. Not reruns in the sense that you've actually been out with this particular man before (although my friend Ellen claims she's been dating so long that she was set up with someone a second time, and unfortunately they didn't realize this until they were on their déjà date). But that's not what I'm talking about. I'm also not talking about running into ex-boyfriends because a) recycling is good for the environment and b) ex-boyfriends are too easy to recognize. Relationship reruns are much more subversive. They sneak up on you in the form of a fresh suitor who slowly reminds you of an ex-boyfriend until you realize you've already been there, done that, lived that episode of your life.

I first noticed I was in relationship reruns after I broke up with a guy who, at thirty-two, lived with his parents and didn't have a checking account. (Note: He didn't live with his parents when I met him. He lived with a roommate. . . . who was dealing drugs, and that's why he moved out, and okay, pretty much any way you slice it I look like someone who should not be doling out dating advice.) The point is I did finally break up with him, because he wasn't even looking for his own place, and I didn't want to always have to be the responsible one. A few months later I threw a party for my single friends and their single friends, and somebody's single friend was flirting with me, which was, of course, the whole point of the party. Over cocktails and artichoke dip he told me that he was a screenwriter who house-sits a fabulous home (read: doesn't pay rent), and that his last girlfriend broke up with him because she wanted him to get his own place, and she obviously didn't understand the life of a struggling screenwriter, and did I want to go to lunch some time? All I could think was: "We've been to lunch. I've already dated you." My party epiphany: It's tempting to settle for a rerun when there's nothing else on, but if you recognize some of the lines, and you know how it turns out, why waste your time? Especially if that particular episode of your life was not so great the first time.

It's tempting—it's *always* tempting—to blame men or the lack thereof, to conclude the single ones are all the same, or at least the same type, or several types but you've dated one of each. But after a certain number of rerun run-ins, you have to consider whether *you* might be the one stuck in a rut. Maybe it's true that you get what you put out there (or whom you put out for). Not many women I know would have dated a guy who had no checking account, who had to drive to the phone company to pay his bill in dollar bills, so maybe it's no surprise that I continued to attract others like him. Maybe in order to avoid reruns you have to re-program your VCR (Various Crappy Relationships), get off the couch (unless it's your therapist's), and open yourself up to a new season of men.

QUESTIONS FOR DISCUSSION

1. Chupack has extensive experience writing and producing television shows. Do you detect signs of this background in "Relationship Reruns"?
2. How do you respond to the author's reaction to the screenwriter in paragraph 2? Does she sound as if she is drawing a reasonable conclusion, or is she allowing prejudice to cloud her judgment?
3. Why is it useful for Chupack to establish that both parties in a "relationship rerun" have responsibility if the "show" is a flop?
4. Does the advice that Chupack offers in this piece undercut her ability to amuse?
5. How old do you think you need to be to enjoy a piece like this? How would you describe Chupack's sense of audience?
6. Consider Chupack's definition of a VCR. Is her phrasing appropriate for her topic and audience?

SUGGESTIONS FOR WRITING

1. If you have made some bad choices in terms of the people you date, write a humorous essay that establishes a pattern in these choices.
2. Envisioning an audience of single men in their twenties, amuse this audience by writing about women who might be difficult to build a relationship with, no matter how good-looking they may be.
3. Write a humorous essay focused on something other than dating in which it is tempting to blame either men or women.

LINKS

▪ Within the Book

Gender is also used as a source for humor in "Vacations: His and Hers" by Jill Conner Browne (pages 596–601).

▪ Elsewhere in Print

Chupack, Cindy. *The Between Boyfriends Book: A Collection of Cautiously Hopeful Essays.* New York: St. Martin's, 2003.

Harris, Lynn. *He Loved Me, He Loved Me Not: A Guide to Fudge, Fury, Free Time, and Life beyond the Breakup.* New York: Avon, 1996.

Moore, Myreah, and Jodie Gould. *Date like a Man: What Men Know about Dating and Are Afraid You'll Find Out.* 2nd ed. New York: Perennial Currents, 2001.

Nakamoto, Steve. *Men Are like Fish: What Every Woman Needs to Know about Dating.* Huntington Beach: Java, 2002.

Weingarten, Gene, and Gina Barreca. *I'm with Stupid: One Man. One Woman. 10,000 Years of Misunderstanding between the Sexes Cleaned Up Right Away.* New York: Simon, 2004.

▪ Online

www.mhhe.com/motives

Click on "More Resources" then "Writing to Amuse Others."

▪ ▪ ▪

VACATIONS: HIS AND HERS

Jill Conner Browne

Jill Conner Browne is the leader and spokesperson for the Sweet Potato Queens, a group of southern women who since 1982 have been celebrating the pleasures they find in men, food, shopping, and all manner of fun. At public events such as parades, the Queens attract large numbers of fans, many of them wearing costumes and pretending that they too are Queens—or on the road to becoming one. Although the Queens now make appearances elsewhere, they are most likely to be seen in Browne's hometown of Jackson, Mississippi. When asked by an interviewer for the Jackson Free Press *if she was surprised that her books had brought so many fans to the "Bible Belt," she responded: "I have never thought that Jesus and fun were mutually exclusive. I wasn't brought up that way, so it doesn't surprise me in the least that there are other people that know you don't have to be an atheist to have a good time." (Excerpts from this interview appear on pages 600–601.)*

"Vacations: His and Hers" comes from Browne's book God Save the Sweet Potato Queens, *a collection of essays focused on the joys of being a woman who understands men. As you read this piece, consider how Browne is able to make fun of men without sounding as if she would want to live without them.*

There is a disparity between what we (female types) think is a great vacation and what they (male types) think is a great vacation. Now, me, I think a cruise is just about your perfect vacation. . . .

What I'm saying is that the Queens like vacations that are luxurious and pampering in nature, ones that involve lots of lolling about in lush surroundings. Guys, on the other hand, do not.

The following is an absolute true-life example of what can happen if you give a guy a bunch of money and a travel agent. It should provide all the proof you will ever need to support this ironclad rule: Never Let a Guy Plan a Vacation.

A good friend of mine recently returned (by the skin of his teeth) from a "dream vacation" that cost a gazillion and a half dollars. My friend Bill and his friend Ron put their heads together to figure out the farthest-away place that would cost the most *possible* money and time to reach, and would offer the *worst* accommodations imaginable, where they could go to and try to kill something big. Hmmm. How about Bearplop, Alaska?

So Bill & Ron coughed up big bucks and went to an inordinate amount   5 of trouble to go to this godforsaken place in the nether regions of Alaska in order to hunt moose and grizzly bears. See, this is what the other women and I think qualifies this trip under the stupid category. Who of sound mind would go out of his way to try to have a confrontation with a grizzly bear? A guy, that's who. And clearly, a guy with not enough fiscal responsibility weighing him down. These guys have got that old problem (I never have it myself): You know what I mean, when you get too much money in your checking account, it will start backing up on you. You have to keep it moving freely through there in order to avoid the backup measures to clear it out in a hurry.

Anyway, they have to fly for a couple of days to get to the part of Alaska that has people living in it, before they can head out to their forsaken vacation spot. *Forsaken* may be a misnomer; somebody would have had to live there in order to then forsake it, and I don't think anybody ever has or ever will live where these guys went. And don't you just imagine there's a good reason for that? I mean, look at Gulf Shores and Destin—you can't sling a dead cat without hitting a condo with a thousand people in it. That's because those are desirable locations. Where Bill and Ron went, you could sling a dead cat for a couple of thousand miles and not even hit a gas station or a mobile home park. Which, in and of itself, doesn't sound all bad, but the climate isn't exactly what you'd call a big draw. Y'know?

Wheee! They are on the trek to their final destination, getting on progressively smaller airplanes at each leg of the journey, until finally, it is just Bill and Ron and the pilot in this itty-bitty plane, which the pilot informs them is still too large to fly into where *they're* going. They land on this bald knob on top of a mountain and the pilot tells them to "get out and wait right here 'cause I'll be right back." And, with that, he took off, leaving Bill and Ron on top of the bald knob with no food, no water, no nothing, including no idea when the pilot was coming back. Ostensibly he was going to get yet a smaller plane, but his parting words were no comfort to our intrepid travelers: "There's a tent in that box over there. You guys can put that up for shelter, in case I don't get back." Now, I *gotta* tell you, I'd have been stroking out big time. No way would I have let that guy fly merrily off into the wild blue yonder without my person being on that plane.

So Bill and Ron were stranded on the bald knob, somewhere in Alaska, and several hours later, the pilot returned, circled the knob, and flew away. This was perplexing to our heroes, a radio being high on the list of the things they did not have, along with food, water, shelter, guns, toilet facilities and/or paper. But by and by—ten hours later—the pilot came back and landed, and took Bill away with him, with promises to Ron to "be right back." Happy Ron. "I'll be right back" is my all-time favorite line. And when *I* use it, what I really mean is: "Good-bye! If you're looking for me—I'll be the one that's gone! Just try and catch me! If I ever come back, it will be one chilly day, buckwheat!"

Eventually both made it to their vacation home, and were they ever happy then. "Home" was a Quonset hut on the side of what we in Mississippi would call a mountain or an Alp; the indigenous folk of Alaska liked to think of it as a "hill." Meals would be taken "down the hill." And down the hill it was, too— three hundred feet straight down the hill. You practically had to rappel down three times a day. Meals were then followed by the inevitable climb back up the hill. Now, our boys were both in what I would call really good shape, but nothing they had done here in the relative flatlands had prepared them for this "hill." For the first two days, they threw up whatever meal they had just eaten, getting back up the hill to the Quonset hut.

Remember, they came on this fire drill to hunt, specifically moose and   *10* grizzly bear. A fool's errand, if you ask me, but, of course, nobody did. They hired "major-league hunting guides," who sound an awful lot like garden-variety igmos to me. (But again, that is strictly my totally unsolicited opinion.) In the whole two or three weeks they were stuck off up there in the exact center of nowhere, how many moose and/or grizzly bears do you think they saw? Well, let me put it this way: I saw just as many in my very own backyard. "Hunting" with these wily woodsmen—these very expensive wily woodsmen—consisted of either (1) crashing through the brush, making enough noise to alert every bear and moose within a two-hundred-mile radius, or (2) sitting by themselves on a stump, personally selected for them by their wily woodsmen, for ten to twelve hours at a time. Sure makes me want to take up huntin'. Boy hidee, it just sounds like a bucket o' fun. I envision Bill and Ron off warming stumps, while all the bears and mooses were in the Quonset hut playing cards with the wily woodsmen.

After killing virtually nothing, not even the crazy guy who kept them up all night, every night, for ten nights running, the morning of departure dawned bright and clear. Ron was the first to be extricated. Bill was remaining until early the next morning, and this gave him time to squeeze in one more round of stump sitting. (Ron was so jealous.) Remember, they had to come and go from this Eden in a two-seater—counting the pilot—plane. So Ron bids farewell, happily, to the whole shooting match and starts the air trek back to what passes for civilization in Alaska.

Bill endures one last (he thinks) night and hops up on his last (he thinks) day in the wilds to race out to the woods and sit on a stump. Back from another exciting day of stump sitting, Bill readies himself for pickup. Sure enough, right on time—this will be the first thing to go right the whole entire trip (he thinks)—what does he hear but de plane! *De plane!* And out he runs with all his gear, looking up expectantly, only to see his transport plane circle the area and leave. There is still plenty of time to make his connections, so Bill is fairly understanding about the mountain winds and the difficulty of landing small planes. By and by, he hears the plane again, and once more he trots out expectantly with all his stuff. Again he gets the big flyover. Visualize this process repeating itself all day long—until all hope of connecting flights is dashed. Meanwhile, Ron, who got his happy hiney out the day before, is flying home, solo, with no info on Bill—like is he dead or alive, maimed, lost, did he run off with an Eskimo, or what? Nobody knows and nobody has any way of knowing because there ain't no phones or radios or any other type of communication equipment back at the Quonset hut in paradise.

This also means Bill gets to spend yet another night in the hut. Oh, it was a sad, sad night. We were feeling pretty pitiful. One little lamb lost in the woods. It was a long and lonely night for our Bill, who did confess to lying in bed and actually crying. But the night's sniveling vanished in the morning with the actual landing of the plane!

Oh, happy, happy day! This was in the top three best days of Bill's entire life. He didn't even mind (too much) his stint on the bald knob with a guy who said he was a doctor of some sort and whose conversation revealed him to be the cheapest man in the universe. Doc was living up there in the wilderness, it seems, on account of it only takes about four thousand a year. Well, I don't think we would have to resort to the wilds of Alaska to be complete and total tightwads, do you? I bet you could reside in New York City for under four thousand a year if you lived in a box with no heat or lights or running water. I mean, I think he was a little off the deep end on this frugality thing. Bill even overcame his mild bout of trepidation when he discovered that the tent in the box that could be erected for shelter, in case the pilot was unable to return that night, had been eaten by a bear.

But, as luck would have it, the pilot did, in fact, return for Bill and he did, in fact, make it to the actual airport where they have big airplanes. This brought up another issue. Out in the wilderness, it was either unnoticeable or irrelevant, but in the relative confines of the big airport, Bill could not help but notice that he smelled like a goat, although perhaps that reference is slanderous only to the goat and flattering to Bill. Bottom line: He had not had a shower in a long time and it showed—so much so that he himself could not bear it. And so, as if it made perfect sense, he goes into the men's room— handicapped stall—and strips. The man is completely naked in the men's room at the big airport, trying to de-funk himself with lavatory soap and wet paper towels. Quite a picture, no?

15

Several days late and somewhat scruffy, Bill did make good his return, amid great rejoicing by friends and family, who had no idea whether he would make it back alive or they would be claiming a box containing his stinky remains. All's well that ends well. Alaska is safe once more for the grizzlies and the moose.

If we were going to spend tens of thousands of dollars on a vacation, there would be things called "Sea Goddess" and "Ritz Carlton" figuring prominently. Hell, we could have plastic surgery and recuperate in a fancy hotel for that kind of money. All we can think of is how very glad we are men don't try to make us go with them and how hilarious it is that they seem to think they are pulling something over on us by slipping off on those expeditions without us. We are laughing ourselves sick all the way home from dropping them off at the airport, are we not?

Here is the Queens' ideal vacation: Delbert McClinton's Blues Cruise. Delbert . . . is one of our very most favoritest musicians in the entire world,

COMPANION TEXT *Jill Conner Browne Tells All*

In October 2004, Jill Conner Browne was interviewed by a reporter for her hometown newspaper, the Jackson Free Press. *Here is an excerpt in which she reveals values that motivate her writing.*

You've said that you're a feminist. What does being a feminist mean to you?
When my daughter was first learning to read, in the first grade, they were studying about Martin Luther King and how he was treated. . . . I said [to her], slow down, black men got the vote in this country before women of any color. In my mother's lifetime, women could not vote. In my lifetime, women could not serve on juries. When I was working at Sears when I was 19, a woman could not get a credit card in her own name. You had to have a father, a husband, a brother or a cousin—someone with a penis—to sign for you. . . . I wanted her to get it, that discrimination goes across the board . . . that only when all people are empowered will all people be free. . . . You are a minority, I told her. I think that just like a lot of young black people don't appreciate the struggle that came before them, young women her age have no idea. . . . It's a good thing that they can [take it for granted], but at the same time, we don't want them to take it for granted.

I think I'll be glad when there's no need for the word feminist because it's just a matter of course that you're a person, therefore these things are afforded to you. I think for too long women had to take themselves too seriously, in order to be taken seriously, and I think we've made enough progress now that I think that's what the Sweet Potato Queen is about.

The Sweet Potato Queen seems to have a huge impact on a lot of women's lives. Does that make you feel a sense of responsibility or a sense of empowerment? I feel a very strong sense of spiritual mission about what I do. . . . I always wanted to be five foot two, have long red hair, green eyes, big tits, little feet and be able to sing, and I never got any of it. Growing up, I experienced maybe more than my share of self-loathing because . . . I wasn't anything that I thought I ought to be, that I wanted to be. It took me a long time to accept the gifts that I did have, that God had not ignored me.

Whatever your gifts are, and some did get more than others, but whatever you got, if you lift it up, God will honor it. When I started writing the first book, I did pray that God would use me for good. I always pray before I speak that God would let me say something that somebody needs to hear. Without exception . . . somebody will come up afterward, usually tears streaming, and say, "Your books changed my life." How? They left a job that was killing them. They left a marriage that was killing them, or they're dealing with cancer. My books are in many, many cancer centers all over the country.

I have a message—the humor is the vehicle by which the greater message is delivered, and I believe that God always speaks a language that can be understood. He uses all kinds of people in all kinds of ways. He uses me to talk to people who cuss like sailors 'cause I are one.

What advice would you give to someone who wants to be a writer, young or old? You have to write something first. You can't always be fixing to write or wanting to write. Lots of people say, "I want to write a book." Well, write one. Sit down and write some every day, and you'll have a pile of paper and it'll be a book. You have to get it out of your head and onto paper. When I asked Roy Blount, after he used my piece in his book, I said, "You know, I'd like to do something else with my writing. What should I do?" And he said, "Write. Write a book." There's no trick to it, but you have to do it.

Lynette Hanson

living or dead, and he sponsors a cruise every January and books all the rest of our very most favoritest musicians in the entire world, living or dead, to go on this cruise with him. They all perform just night and day the whole time, so you can be on a cruise, getting waited on hand and foot, basking in the sun, even seeing exotic ports of call if you are so inclined. (But I warn you, the lackeys do not follow you ashore to wait on you hand and foot there.) You can have all this *plus* you get to dance with Delbert and his buddies all night every night. I cannot imagine a circumstance under which you could possibly have more fun unless you happen to own a monkey that I don't know anything about.

For all you Wannabe Wannabes out there who have been clamoring for a Sweet Potato Queen Convention, here's the deal: We're all going on Delbert's Blues Cruise! All you have to do—I'm completely serious—is call this number: 1-800-DELBERT and tell them you want to book yourself and your cohorts for a week of Sweet Potato Queens and Delbert. Don't bother paying your bills before you leave—you won't be wanting to go home, anyway.

QUESTIONS FOR DISCUSSION

1. Browne claims that the story of Bill and Ron is "an absolute true-life example" and that she is "completely serious." Do you believe her? If you think she is exaggerating, what strikes you as improbable?
2. Is there an element of truth to this essay? Do men and women, in your experience, ever have different expectations about vacations?
3. Consider Browne's comment in paragraph 8 about "I'll be right back." Have you heard other expressions used that you have learned not to take seriously?
4. How does Browne use word choice and sentence structure to convey a sense that she is chatting with her readers?
5. Why do you think men enjoy going on vacations without women? Why might women laugh "all the way home from dropping them off at the airport"?

6. How would you describe Browne's sense of audience? Do you feel included or excluded from this audience?

SUGGESTIONS FOR WRITING

1. Browne offers the following rule: "never Let a Guy Plan a Vacation." Imagine a parallel rule: "Never Let a Gal Plan a Vacation." With this second rule in mind, write a humorous essay about a vacation planned by a woman.
2. Part of the humor in this essay involves unexpected problems that occur when traveling. If you have ever had a series of things go wrong when traveling and told yourself, "This will be funny someday," draw on these memories to make them funny now.
3. Based on what you have learned from reading this piece, write an essay defining what it means to be a "Sweet Potato Queen."

■ **LINKS**

■ **Within the Book**

In "As Freezing People Recollect the Snow—First Chill, Then Stupor, Then the Letting Go" (pages 107–115), Peter Stark offers a serious perspective on an outdoor experience that does not go according to plan.

■ **Elsewhere in Print**

Browne, Jill Conner. *God Save the Sweet Potato Queens.* New York: Three Rivers, 2001.

———. *The Sweet Potato Queens' Book of Love.* New York: Three Rivers, 1999.

———. *The Sweet Potato Queens' Field Guide to Men: Every Man I Love Is Either Married, Gay or Dead.* New York: Three Rivers, 2004.

Caperon, Rosemary, et al. *The Unsavvy Traveler: Women's Comic Tales of Catastrophe.* Seattle: Seal, 2001.

Conner, Judy. *Southern Fried Divorce: A Woman Unleashes Her Hound and His Dog in the Big Easy.* New Orleans: Light, 2004.

Dale, Wendy. *Avoiding Prison and Other Noble Vacation Goals.* New York: Three Rivers, 2003.

Leo, Jennifer. *Sand in My Bra and Other Misadventures: Funny Women Write from the Road.* San Francisco: Travelers, 2003.

■ **Online**

www.mhhe.com/motives

Click on "More Resources" then "Writing to Amuse Others."

■ ■ ■

WOULD HEMINGWAY GET INTO HARVARD?

John Katzman, Andy Lutz, and Erik Olson

Do you remember taking the SAT or ACT exams? Did you enjoy preparing for these exams and feel confident that the results would accurately reflect your abilities? However you respond to these questions, you might find the following essay of interest. The writing test it satirizes is now being administered to thousands of students, but the writing samples featured here are fictitious. Hemingway died in 1961, and while Shakespeare seems to have lived a rich and rewarding life, he never had the chance to take the SATs.

Jonathan Katzman is CEO of the Princeton Review, *where Andy Lutz is vice president of research, and Erik Olson is director of publications. The* Princeton Review *claims to help 100,000 students to prepare for the SAT each year, but Katzman thinks that the verbal and math tests are ridiculous. In an interview with* Frontline, *he stated, "The SAT is a scam. It has been around for 50 years. It has never measured anything. And it continues to measure nothing. And the whole game is that everybody who does well on it, is so delighted by their good fortune that they don't want to attack it. And they are the people in charge, because of course, the way you get to be in charge is by having high test scores." With this in mind, you should not be surprised to find that the following essay, first published in* The Atlantic *in March 2004, makes fun of the writing test recently introduced by the makers of the SAT.*

Every year more than a million college-bound high school students spend a Saturday morning taking the SAT. In 2001 the University of California system, led by Richard Atkinson, then its president, threatened to change that by replacing the SAT with a test that measured a student's mastery of advanced high school–level math, did not contain verbal-analogy questions, and included an essay. Since the University of California is the SAT's biggest customer, and has been for more than thirty years, many thought this spelled the beginning of the end for the test.

In the summer of 2002 the College Board announced its plans to change the SAT. The new test will (surprise, surprise) contain several higher-level algebra questions, will no longer contain analogies questions, and will—as part of a whole new section on "writing"—include an essay question. It is scheduled to be administered for the first time in March of next year.

The writing section (which will be scored on a scale of 200 to 800, making 2400 the new maximum score on the SAT), will seem familiar to anyone who has taken the SAT II: Writing test (formerly known as the English Composition Achievement test). In its haste to satisfy the University of California, evidently, the College Board has simply tacked the SAT II test onto the SAT I. Students will have an extra half hour to complete the test, which currently lasts three hours.

To grade the roughly 2.5 million student essays the new SAT will generate each year, the College Board will have to hire thousands of readers (mainly high school teachers), who will generally score each essay in a minute or two.

Students will be asked to respond to a vague, platitudinous quotation with an essay that will be graded on a scale of 1 to 6. Essay readers will be trained to grade "holistically," taking into consideration "development of ideas, supporting examples, organization, word choice, and sentence structure." To receive a score of 6, according to the College Board, a paper must demonstrate "clear and consistent competence," though it may have "occasional errors." More specifically, a grade of 6 will indicate that an essay "effectively and insightfully addresses the writing task," "is well organized and fully developed, using clearly appropriate examples to support ideas," and "displays consistent facility in the use of language, demonstrating variety in sentence structure and range of vocabulary." A score of 1, in contrast, will indicate that an essay "demonstrates incompetence" and suffers from one or more of the following weaknesses: "very poor organization," "very thin development," "usage and syntactical errors so severe that meaning is somewhat obscured." (The full version of the SAT grading rubric can be found at www.collegeboard.com.)

We and our colleagues at The Princeton Review have spent many years training students to take the SAT II, and have carefully analyzed the College Board's essay-grading criteria. To receive a high score a student should write a long essay of three or more paragraphs, with each paragraph containing topic and concluding sentences and at least one sentence that includes the words "for example." Whenever possible the student should use polysyllabic words where shorter, clearer words would suffice. The SAT essay will not be a place to take rhetorical chances. Flair will win no points; the highest-scoring essays will be earnest, long-winded, and predictable.

To illustrate how the essays on the "new" SAT will be scored, The Princeton Review has composed some typical essay questions, provided answers from several well-known authors, and applied the College Board's grading criteria to their writing.

Directions: *Consider carefully the following quotation and the assignment below it. Then plan and write an essay that explains your ideas as persuasively as possible. Keep in mind that the support you provide—both reasons and examples—will help make your view convincing to the reader.*

> "Writing is the most demanding of callings, more harrowing than a warrior's, more lonely than a whaling captain's—that, in essence, is the modern writer's message."
>
> —Melvin Maddocks

Assignment: *In an essay, discuss your opinion of the quotation above. Support your view with one or more examples from literature, the arts, science, politics, current events, or your personal experience or observations.*

Writing, at its best, is a lonely life. Organizations for writers palliate the writer's loneliness but I doubt if they improve his writing. He grows in public stature as he sheds his loneliness and often his work deteriorates. For he does his work alone and if he is a good enough writer he must face eternity, or the lack of it, each day.

For a true writer each book should be a new beginning where he tries again for something that is beyond attainment. He should always try for something that has never been done or that others have tried and failed. Then sometimes, with great luck, he will succeed.

How simple the writing of literature would be if it were only necessary to write in another way what has been well written. It is because we have had such great writers in the past that a writer is driven far out past where he can go, out to where no one can help him.

Reader's evaluation: *Although it displays a solid vocabulary, Mr. Hemingway's essay lacks specific examples and clear topic sentences. Too undeveloped to be good. Grade: 3 out of 6*

"The four stages of life are infancy, childhood, adolescence, and obsolescence." —Art Linkletter

All the world's a stage, and all the men and women merely players: They have their exits and their entrances; and one man in his time plays many parts, his acts being seven ages. At first the infant, mewling and puking in the nurse's arms. And then the whining schoolboy with his satchel and shining morning face, creeping like snail unwillingly to school. And then the lover, sighing like furnace, with a woeful ballad made to his mistress' eyebrow. Then a soldier, full of strange oaths and bearded like the pard, jealous in honour, sudden and quick in quarrel, seeking the bubble reputation even in the cannon's mouth. And then the justice, in fair round belly with good capon lined, with eyes severe and beard of formal cut, full of wise saws and modern instances; and so he plays his part. The sixth age shifts into the lean and slipper'd pantaloon, with spectacles on nose and pouch on side; his youthful hose, well saved, a world too wide for his shrunk shank; and his big manly voice, turning again towards childish treble, pipes and whistles in his sound. Last scene of all, that ends this strange eventful history, is second childishness and mere oblivion, sans teeth, sans eyes, sans taste, sans everything.

Reader's evaluation: *This essay is poorly organized, with only one paragraph (though, to Mr. Shakespeare's credit, the topic sentence does speak to what the rest of the sentences in his one paragraph are about). It is riddled with errors in syntax, incomplete sentences being the most noticeable problem. Although his supporting sentences are vivid in their description, they are vague and general, not true examples. And he unfortunately spells "honor" with the extraneous "u." Grade: 2 out of 6*

"Nothing great will ever be achieved without great men, and men are great only if they are determined to be so." —Charles de Gaulle

The Irish lady can say, that to-day is every day. Caesar can say that every day is to-day and they say that every day is as they say.

In this way we have a place to stay and he was not met because he was settled to stay. When I said settled I meant settled to stay. When I said settled to stay I meant settled to stay Saturday. In this way a mouth is a mouth. In this way if in as a mouth if in as a mouth where, if in as a mouth where and there. Believe they have water too. Believe they have that water too and blue when you see blue, is all blue precious too, is all that that is precious too is all that and they meant to absolve you. In this way Cezanne nearly did nearly in this way. Cezanne nearly did nearly did and nearly did. And was I surprised. Was I very surprised. Was I surprised. I was surprised and in that patient, are you patient when you find bees. Bees in a garden make a specialty of honey and so does honey. Honey and prayer. Honey and there. There where the grass can grow nearly four times yearly.

Reader's evaluation: *Although Ms. Stein's essay is expressive, it's a bit flaky, lacking any semblance of structure, focus, or examples, and using non-standard syntax to boot. Grade: 1 out of 6*

"Whoso would be a man must be a nonconformist."
—Ralph Waldo Emerson

Psychologists use the term "socialization" to designate the process by which children are trained to think and act as society demands. A person is said to be well socialized if he believes in and obeys the moral code of his society and fits in well as a functioning part of that society. It may seem senseless to say that many leftists are oversocialized, since the leftist is perceived as a rebel. Nevertheless, the position can be defended. Many leftists are not such rebels as they seem.

The moral code of our society is so demanding that no one can think, feel and act in a completely moral way. For example, we are not supposed to hate anyone, yet almost everyone hates somebody at some time or other, whether he admits it to himself or not. Some people are so highly socialized that the attempt to think, feel and act morally imposes a severe burden on them. In order to avoid feelings of guilt, they continually have to deceive themselves about their own motives and find moral explanations for feelings and actions that in reality have a non-moral origin. We use the term "oversocialized" to describe such people.

Oversocialization can lead to low self-esteem, a sense of powerlessness, defeatism, guilt, etc. One of the most important means by which our society socializes children is by making them feel ashamed of behavior or speech that is contrary to society's expectations. If this is overdone, or if a particular child is especially susceptible to such feelings, he ends by feeling ashamed of HIM-SELF. Moreover the thought and the behavior of the oversocialized person are more restricted by society's expectations than are those of the lightly socialized person. The majority of people engage in a significant amount of naughty behavior. They lie, they commit petty thefts, they break traffic laws, they goof off at work, they hate someone, they say spiteful things or they use some underhanded trick to get ahead of the other guy. The oversocialized person cannot do these things, or if he does do them he generates in himself a sense of shame and self-hatred. The oversocialized person cannot even experience, without guilt, thoughts or feelings that are contrary to the accepted morality; he cannot think "unclean" thoughts. And socialization is not just a matter of morality; we are socialized to conform to many norms of behavior that do not fall under the heading of morality. Thus the oversocialized person is kept on a psychological leash and spends his life running on rails that society has laid down for him. In many oversocialized people this results in a sense of constraint and powerlessness that can be a severe hardship. We suggest that oversocialization is among the more serious cruelties that human beings inflict on one another.

Reader's evaluation: *Mr. Kaczynski's essay is well developed, displays an impressive vocabulary, and makes good use of supporting examples. He also demonstrates an understanding of how to use simple, compound, and complex sentences. Grade: 6 out of 6*

QUESTIONS FOR DISCUSSION

1. How accurately would a thirty minute essay, written after three hours of testing, reflect your writing ability?
2. What do you think of the way in which these tests are scored?
3. To what extent does the humor of this piece depend upon familiarity with the work of the authors whose styles are parodied within it?
4. Based on these parodies, which author would you most enjoy reading?
5. Why does the final example receive the highest score? Would you like to write like this?
6. This essay was originally titled "Would Shakespeare Get into Swarthmore?" Why do you think it was retitled for this book? Which title do you prefer?

SUGGESTIONS FOR WRITING

1. Choose a writer whom you have been required to study, and then write a parody of this person's style in which you address the kind of subject matter associated with the writer in question.
2. Write a humorous essay about your own experiences when applying for college, financial aid, or a job.
3. Research the "author" of the final essay in this piece, and then write a paper explaining how this parody reflects his views and why it would be ironic for him to receive the highest grade.

LINKS

■ Within the Book

Education is also the subject for humor in "The Learning Curve" by David Sedaris (pages 584–590).

■ Elsewhere in Print

Dentith, Simon. *Parody: The New Cultural Idiom.* New York: Routledge, 2000.

The Harvard Lampoon's Guide to College Admissions: The Comprehensive, Authoritative, and Utterly Useless Source for Where to Go and How to Get In. New York: Warner, 2000.

Hemingway, Ernest. *The Complete Stories.* New York: Scribner, 1998.

Katzman, John, et al. *Cracking College Admissions.* 2nd ed. New York: Princeton Review, 2004.

Shakespeare, William. *As You Like It.* 1599. New York: Washington Square, 1997.

Stein, Gertrude. *How to Write.* 1931. New York: Dover, 1975.

———. *Selected Writings of Gertrude Stein.* New York: Vintage, 1990.

■ Online

www.mhhe.com/motives

Click on "More Resources" then "Writing to Amuse Others."

■ ■ ■

10

Writing to Experiment with Form

Schools across the country have for many years offered courses in "creative writing," which is commonly understood to mean writing fiction, poetry, or drama. The problem with this designation is that, as useful as it has been as an easy reference, it implies that any writing but "fiction," "poetry," or "drama" is *not* creative. Thinking along these lines does serious injustice to the imagination, intelligence, and courage that inform other kinds of writing. Ironically, when we look for a convenient term for writing other than fiction, poetry, or drama, we often fall back on *nonfiction*—defining something in terms of what it is not and, in so doing, using a term that is so broad that it includes writing as diverse as memoir, exposition, and argument. But even if we call a work *non*fiction, for lack of a better term, it does not necessarily follow that the work in question lacks creativity. Anything written and revised by human beings is creative to some extent, since an individual intelligence—working alone or in collaboration with others—has made choices about what ideas to include, how to express them, and how to arrange them.

Nevertheless, a user's manual for a software program is very different from an essay by a writer like Annie Dillard—although both are, strictly speaking, nonfiction. When writers test the boundaries between different genres and take chances on what they say and how they present it, they are engaging in a kind of creative writing that is drawing increasing attention from literary theorists. Such writing is sometimes called "experimental writing" as a way of distinguishing it from creative writing as the term is commonly understood. A writer who is especially interested in creating new patterns can be said to be "writing to experiment with form."

Like any of the other kinds discussed in this book, writing to experiment with form does not exist in a vacuum. When writing to understand experience, inspire readers, or amuse them, writers may experiment with the form their work takes as they seek to capture and convey meaning. All the writers included in this chapter have more than one motive, and you can find evidence of experimentation in chapters focused on other motives. (See, for example, the essays by André Aciman, Peter Stark and Alice Walker in Chapters 1, 2 and 8, respectively.) Moreover, if a work is to have any real value, form cannot be divorced from substance. A serious writer will not try to create a new form and then pour anything at hand into this vessel. Ideally, the form any work takes should be the form it needs; the form gives shape to content that benefits from being shaped in this way.

Of course, new forms are not invented every day. Inventing something both new and useful is a great challenge. Because experimental writing is such a challenge, the writers who undertake it are likely to have both discipline and commitment. There is, after all, a great difference between designing a new form and carelessly scattering thoughts across the page in a way that may look creative but is actually formless. And it is important to understand that you can successfully experiment with form without feeling that it is your responsibility to invent a structure that has never been seen before. Whenever you try something that is new to you, you are experimenting, even if what you are attempting is not necessarily new to your readers.

Flexibility is thus one of the keys to experimenting successfully with form. While you can benefit from trying a ready-made form like dialogue, you should not hesitate to alter it if you find that it doesn't fit comfortably or suit your presentation. Instead of following a predetermined form (like the five-paragraph theme) that dictates what must happen in any given paragraph, you can adopt strategies that work for you and combine them in different ways. In this respect, writing to experiment with form honors a motive especially associated with essays.* The word *essay* comes from *essayer,* which means "to try" in French. By providing an opportunity to test ideas—instead of proving points and employing patterns that are already known—experimental essays follow a distinguished tradition that can be traced back to such writers as Michel de Montaigne and Francis Bacon.

UNDERSTANDING MONTAGE AND COLLAGE

Of the various essays in this chapter, you may find the form of George Orwell's "Marrakech" the most unusual. Orwell is writing what is called a *montage*—from the photographic term used to describe a rapid sequence of related short scenes or the process of making one picture out of many closely arranged images. When experimenting with this form, a writer composes a series of separate scenes and arranges them in a meaningful pattern with no transitions between them. These scenes are like a series of pictures arranged on the wall of an art gallery. The audience is expected to fill in the gaps between these

---

*For a discussion of essays, see pages 295–301.

scenes by reflecting on how each contributes to the meaning of the whole. By experimenting with this form, writers have ample opportunity to play with ideas, but they are also responsible for helping readers understand the nature and meaning of that play. If you study Orwell's essay closely, you will find that his arrangement follows a clear pattern and that certain images reappear in different pictures, helping to unify a work that—at first glance—may seem to be nothing more than a series of unrelated fragments.

The narrative fragments in Geeta Kothari's "If You Are What You Eat, Then What Am I?" may seem to be more closely linked than the scenes in Orwell's essay. But Kothari is also working with montage—in this case to convey how she felt as a child when encountering significantly different kinds of food: the traditional cuisine of her Indian family and American dishes such as hot dogs, tuna salad, and brownies. Familiarity with montage can also help you understand an essay like Luc Sante's "I Was Born." This essay consists of seven short autobiographical sketches offering very different versions of the author's childhood—versions so different that they cannot all be true. It is impossible to read this essay without noticing that the author is contradicting himself. Further, the contradictions are so bold that readers can reasonably assume that the author is aware of contradicting himself and that these contradictory versions of his life must be intended to convey a kind of truth that is independent of factual accuracy—a philosophical truth about the nature of experience and the way in which memories are created.

One way to read Sante's essay is to view it as a montage in which every photograph is of the author and his family wearing a different kind of costume and acting out a different drama. The costumes and scripts may disguise who these people are or reveal truths about what they are like on the inside. Readers are invited to interpret Sante's childhood by comparing startling but different pictures. The form he uses challenges common assumptions about how readers can tell the difference between fiction and nonfiction. It also creates a confrontation between writer and reader: Because it is impossible to read this piece without noticing the major contradictions within it, readers are forced to decide whether to make the intellectual effort necessary for understanding. Some readers are likely to dismiss such work as "weird" and move on to something else; others will be engaged by it. When you decide to experiment with form, you should consider that experimentation involves risks. And the more radical the experiment, the greater the risk.

Writers who enjoy experimenting with form also use *collage* rather than montage. Collage is an art form in which materials not usually associated with each other are pasted together—thus encouraging viewers to see each piece anew and to consider how different pieces play off one another. Whereas montage gives us a series of separate scenes, collage gives us a single surface and invites us to consider the work as a whole. If you see a collage in a museum or read an essay presented as a collage, you can, of course, analyze it by studying its specific components. But its structure indicates that the whole is more important than any of its parts.

The clearest example of collage in this chapter is "Oranges and Sweet Sister Boy" by Judy Ruiz. In this piece, a main narrative runs chronologically from the beginning of the essay to the end, but pasted on (or woven into) this narrative are pictures and pieces of writing that have—so to speak—been cut out of other cloth. A more subtle example of this form is provided by John Berger, who narrates how he traveled to Stockholm to attend the funeral of a close friend, providing information about what he did in that city before the funeral, and what happened there on the day of the funeral, before moving on to an experience that he had with his son a week later. But within this main narrative, Berger loops back to include memories of his friend from time to time as well as brief descriptions of three important paintings. In this case, the paintings are pieces of the collage, as are the memories generated by the author's trip to Sweden.

If you are interested in experimenting with collage, you can decide for yourself how many pieces to paste together and how different those pieces should be. But in making that decision, you should be mindful of the audience for whom you are writing and the context in which you are going to offer this work.

CONSIDERING AUDIENCE

When you experiment with form, you often ask readers to invest more time in your work than they would if you followed a conventional, predictable plan. With this in mind, you should submit a work of experimental writing only when you are confident that your audience is willing to take this trouble. How can you tell? There's no foolproof way for determining in advance how readers will respond to your work; even readers you know well may surprise you at times with responses that, although elicited by the work you shared with them, were influenced by other issues in their lives. Few readers read with the same degree of attention and patience every time they sit down to read. But there are some clues that can help you decide if an audience is likely to be receptive to an experimental essay.

Readers who seem to welcome originality and who seem interested in what *you* think (as opposed to getting you to write what *they* think) may enjoy original form and expression as much as they enjoy original thought. Readers who have already responded to your work with thoughtful comments have demonstrated that they are willing to pay close attention to your work (as opposed to rushing through it to pursue some other activity). Such readers also may be ready to take up the challenge of encountering an unexpected form. And if you see yourself writing primarily for a specific teacher, you can be guided not only by your assignment but also by the amount of emphasis the instructor places on organization. A teacher who stresses the importance of outlining papers in advance is less likely to welcome an experimental essay than is a teacher who encourages you to draft and then see what kind of organization emerges from what you have written.

You should also remember that even intelligent, imaginative readers simply may not have the time to study at length a paper that seems interesting but unconventional. Further, it would be a mistake to assume that instructors who insist on fixed patterns of arrangement are incapable of enjoying originality of form. These instructors might welcome experimental writing if they are not overwhelmed by the need to read large quantities of such material. A heavy workload often explains why teachers and other readers insist that you follow a standard form; when they know how your essay is supposed to be organized, they can appraise its content more quickly. However, readers who have a large, steady diet that seems monotonous might be pleased to be served an unexpected dish. When writing for readers with whom you are already familiar, you should be able to make a fairly accurate guess about how creative you can be. And if you are in doubt, you can easily ask.

You can also imagine yourself writing for readers you have not actually met. For an experimental essay, you might benefit from envisioning an audience of well-educated, open-minded adults like those for whom essays in periodicals like *The New Yorker* and *The Atlantic* seem intended. When you write for an audience of this sort, your actual readers may be willing to assume the role your work implies for them even if they usually see themselves as less sophisticated.

In terms of audience, you should remember as well that writers can be their own audience. Although writing is usually a transaction between different people, it can also be pursued for the writer's own benefit—as is the case, for example, when you freewrite or keep a personal journal. If you are interested in growing as a writer but suspect that the readers you actually know are unlikely to welcome experimental writing, you can do it on your own simply as an exercise or for the sheer joy of it. As you grow, your world will also grow, and the readers you will know next year may be very different from those currently in your life.

CONSIDERING CONTEXT

According to a time-honored tradition, artists should learn the rules before earning the freedom to break them. In art school, this means mastering perspective and learning how to draw from life according to the principles that governed the old masters before painting like an abstract expressionist in bold strokes on a large canvas. This school of thought is well illustrated in *Strictly Ballroom,* an Australian comedy about ballroom dancing. The movie focuses on a young man whose parents were competitive ballroom dancers and who have raised him since early childhood to become a champion dancer. Now in his early twenties, the young man knows all the steps by heart and can dance them perfectly, but he's bored by them and wants to invent dances of his own. The problem is that the world of competitive ballroom dancing is highly structured; all dancers are expected to execute the same steps and to express themselves only in minor variations on these steps, through the music they choose to dance to, and in their costumes. Anyone who invents steps—no matter how good they are—threatens this rigid system. You'll have to rent the movie to see how this conflict is resolved. What's relevant at the moment, however, is this: The young man becomes a superb dancer in part because he *knows* all the steps; this knowledge enables him to improvise and combine moves that would not normally be expected in the same dance routine. He's learned the rules, and now he's ready to break them.

This school of thought has much to recommend it. When you are grounded in tradition and can do what others do, you are well positioned to identify what has not yet been done and then do it. Someone who lacks this kind of knowledge and experience can spend a lot of energy reinventing the wheel—a wheel that's weaker than those already on the road. But does this mean that only the most experienced writers can enjoy experimenting with form? Certainly not. You can experiment whenever the impulse moves you, but you may benefit from honoring two principles.

First, as noted earlier, you should share experimental writing with readers only when you have some reason to believe they'll be receptive to it. When making this decision, it is important to consider *when* you are asking them to read such work. Readers may be more receptive after they have had the chance to become acquainted with you and when they are not especially hurried. Remember that it usually takes longer to read an experimental essay than one that follows a standard form. As a general rule, make this request for readers' time after you have won their confidence or feel confident in your relationship with them. A specific writing assignment may provide a ready-made context for an experiment, but you can also create your own context by looking for a time that works for both you and your readers. Just as you need time to experiment with form, your readers need time to study the results of your experiment. An especially busy part of the semester, for example, may not be the best time for this kind of work.

Second, a college writing course can provide an ideal context for experimenting with form—especially if your instructor encourages revision. As noted earlier, experimentation involves taking risks. Risks become less threatening when you know that you don't have to get everything right in your first draft. Whenever you have the chance to submit more than one draft of an essay for review, you would be wise to seize the opportunity to grow by attempting something you haven't already mastered. Experimenting with form is one way to grow as a writer. And if such an experiment seems overly ambitious for a specific context, you can still experiment with writing by trying out elements of style (such as parallelism and anaphora, discussed on pages 524–525) that would be new for your work.

Because experimenting with form happens most productively when writers feel at ease, the writing that results from this activity often has a personal dimension. All of the works included in this chapter employ the first person, the *I* that helps convey the sense of an individual mind at play. Using the first person also suggests that these writers have given readers their trust and expect trust in return. Annie Dillard invites readers into the privacy of her bedroom at the end of her essay, and Geeta Kothari invites readers into her family's kitchen as well as into other rooms that are important for her. The most personal essay in this chapter may well be "Oranges and Sweet Sister Boy," a work that focuses on the author's history with mental illness and her response to the news that her brother is planning to have a sex-change operation. Because her material is unconventional, Judy Ruiz chose to present it in an unconventional way. Naturally, you can write in the first person without sharing experience as intimate as Ruiz's, but you may feel most at ease when writing in other than first person. (See pages 42–43.) Whether you use the first person or draw directly on personal experience matters less than your willingness to operate in a spirit of trust—trusting yourself by believing that you can grow by trying something new and trusting your readers by believing that they will welcome this kind of growth.

When you experiment with form, you venture into unfamiliar territory and thus take some risks. But if there are risks, there are also rewards: originality of expression and a heightened awareness of what can be achieved through language. Remember, however, that when you write an essay of this sort, you are venturing into the unknown and hope your readers will follow. It is your responsibility to glance back once in a while to make sure that they are still with you. By studying the essays included in this chapter, you will be able to see how other writers have undertaken this kind of adventure without abandoning readers in a literary wilderness.

TIPS FOR READING AND WRITING EXPERIMENTAL NONFICTION

When Reading

- Consider what the author has gained by experimenting with form. How does the form used relate to the author's topic and purpose?
- Consider the audience for which the work was originally composed, and imagine that you are a part of that audience.
- Identify the parts of the work that you understand, and then use this understanding to improve your comprehension of what you do not yet understand.

When Writing

▨ Be sure that your audience is willing to make an extra effort to understand what could be said more conventionally.

▨ Choose a topic that is unconventional or an experience that involves some kind of loss or fragmentation—something that is not, by definition, straightforward or easy.

▨ If uncertain how to begin, draft a straightforward narrative and then experiment by rearranging its components or breaking up the narrative by inserting other elements into it.

▨ Use related images to unify what may not seem unified at first glance.

ET IN ARCADIA EGO°

John Berger

When inspired to write about a friend or relative who has died, writers face the chal-
lenge of how to make that person come alive once again through words—alive as a
particular individual, not just as a person who is defined by a single role: grandmother,
brother, friend, and so on. Grief, guilt, or sentimentality can sometimes lead to eulo-
gies about perfect human beings. The perfect, however, is rarely human. How, then,
can a writer pay tribute to the deceased without exaggerating authentic feeling or
ignoring genuine quirks? This is the challenge that John Berger faced when writing
about a fellow artist who was his friend for fifty years, and he meets this challenge by
experimenting with form: He incorporates references to art within a series of sketches
that combine to form a portrait.

John Berger is a British artist, art critic, essayist, novelist, and screenwriter who has
chosen to live most of his life in a remote part of the French Alps where he enjoys close
contact with the rhythms of rural life while remaining deeply informed by what is hap-
pening in the world at large. Assessing Berger's achievement in an article for The New
York Times Book Review, *Robert Boyers writes, "To read Mr. Berger over the last thirty*
years has been to feel oneself in the presence of an intelligence utterly unmoved by
literary or political fashion and unfailingly committed to its own clear vision of what is
decent and important, in art and in life." The following essay, first published by Harper's
in August 2004, provides you with an opportunity to enter Berger's world.

Scandinavia is sparsely populated, and when its inhabitants live closely
side by side or come together to form a crowd, they resist becoming a mass.
In the strict physical sense of the term, they remain incoherent. This reluc-
tance to merge, or this need to remain separate, is not a simple expression of
individualism, for the same people are in other ways obedient, civic-minded,
and conventional. The Calvinist conscience may have something to do with
it. But there is something else too, which is not in the least Calvinist. They all
inherit a certain ideal of a wayward happiness, an ideal sustained by a shared
memory, partly invented, partly true, of childhood summers, of sun and water
and of days that never end. All cultures invent their own Arcadia, but this arcadia is closely connected with the region's climate and geography. Its winters
are intolerably long and dark, and annually the two months of summer, with
their more or less white nights—depending upon the exact longitude—are
like a physically earned reward, and are like a declaration of innocence.

°*Et in Arcadia Ego:* Latin for "I, too, am in Arcadia" or, in this context, "Even in Arcadia, there
am I" (indicating that death lurks even in a place of pastoral tranquility).

As I write these words, I suddenly think of the paintings Sven made ten years ago on the island of Belle-Isle, off the coast of Brittany. Naked bodies, surf, saltwater sluicing off rocks, a sparkling sunlight touching everything, no end in sight. They are, in fact, images of that wayward happiness and those childhood summers.

In the Scandinavian summer, people of all ages take off as many clothes as their self-respect permits, so that the three innocences of sunlight, water, and rewarded bodies can touch.

I came to Stockholm to attend his funeral.

We were friends during fifty years and we did many things together. We mended roofs. We cooked. We collaborated on books. We traveled. We mixed cement. We went to demonstrations. Sometimes we read the same book in the same week so as to discuss it. What Sven was politically has not yet been named—maybe it will be in the next twenty years when the world transformations taking place are better understood. For want of a better term, he accepted being called anarchist. Had he been labeled a terrorist today, he would have shrugged his shoulders. 5

He had a trundling walk, as if his torso were riding a camel. He spoke rather slowly and his voice was exceptionally reassuring—the voice of a man whispering to you in confidence that a cease-fire has been announced. Meanwhile, when he insisted upon a point, when he became intransigent, and when he still had hair, it stood on end. His long bony fingers ended in particularly large fingertips, which somehow promised that he could distinguish quality blindfolded. And this also reassured both women and men.

Although thin and tall, he swam with the ease and grace of a porpoise.

On the day before the funeral, I went to the National Museum in Stockholm, to look at paintings we had once looked at together. There was a Berthe Morisot landscape he particularly liked. It's painted like the inside of a dress, he said, the inside of a dress touching the skin!

The summer of exactly forty years ago was the first time I lived for several months in Sven and Romaine's house in the Vaucluse. Their daughter Karin had just been born. The house, with two fig trees, surrounded by cherry and apricot orchards, was primitive, there was no electricity and no tap water. There was collected rainwater for washing in, and the drinking water we fetched from a fountain in the village. The cooking we did on a hearth in the kitchen. At midday when it was hot the chickens came into the kitchen for shade. There were also two dogs. Romaine worked outside, chiseling local stone and making sculptures. She was often covered with white dust. Sven painted in a kind of upstairs shed. The one luxury of the four-roomed house was a library—a room lined with books belonging to Sven—where I worked. All the money we had was kept in a bowl on the mantelpiece above the hearth in the kitchen. Everywhere the sound of cicadas and at night the screech of

In the Bois de Boulogne, by Bethe Morisot.

owls. It was not at all Scandinavian, but Sven brought his arcadia with him, and in July and August we paid the price, since more and more visitors came and did not want to leave. They slept in the grass or put up tents.

Sven and I cooked and served the evening meal. We had only enamel   *10* plates because they were easier for stacking and did not break. People had to sit on the stones Romaine would one day sculpt or the removed seats from a Citroën 2cv. The guests came from Paris, Germany, London, Stockholm. They were scientists, professors, doctors, art historians, architects, and they all believed—such was Sven's presence, welcome, and sleight of hand—that they had fallen (by accident) into Paradise.

Seven visitors have been here since midafternoon. We hear another car-load coming along the dirt-track which leads to the house. The house had formerly belonged to an old peasant who, when he was dying, gave it to Sven to cheat the State. I look at my watch. We'll have Menu C tonight, Sven says to me confidentially. I'll light the fire, you go!

Menu C means that I drive to the public rubbish dump in Cavaillon and pick out the still edible vegetables and fruit, thrown away when the market closed. Before leaving the kitchen I take money from the bowl to buy bread.

Simeon in the Temple,
by Rembrandt.

In the National Museum was a Rembrandt which I'd never seen before and which wasn't there when we went round the museum together. The subject is Simeon, the old man, presenting the infant Jesus in the Temple. Soon he will say his famous Nunc Dimittis.

My wanting to try to do a drawing of the painting had nothing, however, to do with words. I simply wanted to look closer at the way the swaddled child was lying like a fish across the old man's outstretched forearms, with the thumbs and eight fingers of the two hands almost but not quite touching.

Sven was a full-time painter for more than sixty years, and during that time he sold fewer paintings than any other artist I've ever known. As a result, he faced considerable material difficulties. He always lacked money. Most of his life he lacked what the most modest painter would think of as a proper studio. And, except by a few friends, he was unrecognized. Nevertheless, scarcely a day passed when he did not pick up a brush, pastel, or pen to work, and on many days he worked until the hours counted no more, and he stepped into the innocence of that season where nature can be taken by surprise.

I always had the impression Sven didn't choose his subjects; it was they who placed orders. His subjects became his patrons: a coastline, a cherry

15

orchard, a river crossing a city, a range of mountains, the gnarled branches of a vine, the face of a friend.

During the last few years, when he was suffering from advanced Parkinson's disease, his patron, on every day he felt strong enough, would be a plate of fruit which he arranged with his long trembling fingers on the corner of a table in the flat where he lived with his family in the center of Stockholm. Of these fruit he made still lifes, scarcely larger than postcards, using oil sticks.

He considered it a waste of time to talk of his difficulties because he believed in Providence. He counted on happy accidents (of course you have to recognize them when they happen, he points out), the example of Pissarro, who had a heart of gold as well as being a great painter, unexpected encounters (a question of keeping your eyes open, most people don't), and natural mystery. This is why on his last, very small, still lifes the colors speak to one another. It is also why he lived without resentment. He could become angry but he personally resented nothing. And when he listened to Bach, his belief in Providence was deeply confirmed.

Those who disapproved of Sven thought him pigheaded. He never retracted, he never openly changed an opinion. He continually edged forward. Even during the final months when, unassisted, he could only move forward twenty centimeters by twenty centimeters, and five meters was an impossibly long distance, he continually edged forward, or else he rested, with his eyes shut, until he found the strength to do so. Others disapproved of him because he devoted his whole life to art, and they saw he was not a genius. For them, the nobility of that persistence passed unnoticed.

He died, alone, of a heart attack, a few meters away from the table where *20* he arranged the little plates of fruit for his still lifes. It was the longest day of the year, the twenty-first of June, 2003. When his body was discovered, the days were already getting minimally shorter.

The funeral was to take place at 2:00 P.M. in a southern suburb called Skogskyrkogården. We decided to take the metro and eat a sandwich there before going to the designated chapel. After half an hour's wait a train arrives and we climb in. All the men are in shorts and the women have bare shoulders. It is very hot. Through the coach, as it rocks on its way with all its windows open, wafts a tolerance for clumsy love, inelegance, missed opportunities, freckled backs, strange murmurs, sweaty hair, hot feet, and life as it is.

Where we arrive there are two flower shops and a cemetery which appears to go on forever. We each buy a rose to place on the coffin. There is nowhere to buy anything to eat. For that we have to take the metro back to the last station, which is at the beginning of the cemetery.

This is what we do. More flower shops, and in front of them a complex of modern flats, built around a lawned square. By the entrance to this inner square I spot a sign announcing a restaurant, with an arrow. We follow it, hoping to find a sandwich. Many tables and a self-service counter. A menu of boiled hake with white sauce and boiled potatoes. A big display of sweet cakes and colored pastries like toys, from which to choose a dessert. Coffee. Tea. Apple juice or what they call *small beer* (2 percent alcohol). Many of the people in the waiting queue have sticks. Everything in the canteen is white, glossy white—like a white metal drawer for cutlery. And there is a faint smell of rubber tubing. Three more clients arrive in wheelchairs. The man behind me, as I hesitate about what to drink, says: Small beer is better than nothing!

A few minutes later I notice a man and a woman in white uniforms wearing plastic gloves and carrying drip-feed bottles, and I put two and two together. We are in the canteen for flats which are reserved for old people who, thanks to the medical aid on the spot, still manage to live by themselves. And the canteen, which is available to them for their meals, is also open to the public.

Each one has chosen to sit at a different table. They preserve their inde- 25 pendence like passengers in a station waiting room. Their common destination is behind the florists across the road.

They keep their eyes lowered, studying what is on their plates. To watch day by day the evident solitude of each of the others is probably harder to bear than one's own solitude. The one exception is the small-beer man who wanders from table to table, repeating: Another hot day! and then, grinning, decides to join us at our table just as we are on the point of leaving so as not to be late for the funeral.

Outside the air is as hot as a panting horse's breath, and the cemetery and its stillness extend as far as the eye can see.

After the funeral, the hundred or so people attending were invited to a buffet meal in the garden, outside the building in which Sven had been allotted a municipal studio. At one moment I left the garden and opened the door I remembered on the ground floor. The studio was uncannily tidy. The tidiness bespoke his absence. There was nothing on the easel. A number of canvases were visible instead of being face to the wall; the strong ones looked stronger, and the weaker ones looked desolate. What astounded me most, however, was the large reproduction pinned at eye level to the wall which was facing the easel. It was the Rembrandt Simeon.

I rejoined the family and guests drinking wine in the garden, and asked about the reproduction, but nobody was sure when Sven had acquired it and pinned it there. It is thought to be the last painting Rembrandt worked on.

The day after the funeral we drove north toward the archipelago on an 30 old Yamaha 550cc. bike which a Swedish friend had lent me. The archipelago, with its abundance of islands, straits, sounds, peninsulas, and bays, somehow copies the topography of Memory, and thus easily lends itself to being the dream site of legendary childhoods. These childhoods contain nautical skills and a familiarity with sailing that are not dreamlike, and it's through these practices, through the tying of knots, the trimming of sails, the beaching of boats, the skills of using a tiller, that the arcadian dream feeds off a traditional reality. Come to the archipelago and every man over fifty-five puts on a cap which pretends he was once a sea captain.

On the bike we were heading north for the island of Furusund, which is three km long and about one km wide.

At the southeast corner of the island there's a landing stage, a shop, a cafe, and many fair-haired, bare-legged giants—both women and men—who lick ice creams very slowly, read the sky, fill up their launches with petrol, carry their towels to take showers because they've been swimming far out at sea, and let their toddlers in life jackets pace the decks of their boats unaccompanied.

It is late afternoon. Beside us a sea captain in shorts has offered an ice cream to a young boy whom I noticed playing with a football. He has very smart feet.

I saw a moose this morning, says the boy to the captain.

I doubt it at this time of year.   35

I did.

How many branches did it have?

I didn't have time to count—it ran off.

At this point the two of them stop and look toward the water. A ship has appeared sailing north along the channel between Furusund and Yxlan.

The scale of this ship is unfathomable. She is taller than four forests placed   40
one on top of the other. She passes silently, as if her improbability has been able to pierce the visible but not the audible. She will arrive in Helsinki tomorrow morning just after the sun has lit up a four-story yellow building there, before which she will dock.

How did your moose get on the island? asks the sea captain.

It swam, replies the boy, must have swum.

Moose move around in herds. They are not loners, and they don't swim in the sea.

Then this one must have been lost. I saw him between the trees, he was an old one.

I join the people, the children, and the dogs on the quayside. All of them   45
are standing and looking up with astonishment at the improbably large and silent white ship, an astonishment which is habitual, for the same ship or sister ship passes every evening at the same hour.

I traveled on this line fifteen years ago. And I drove a bike off the ship by the four-story yellow building in Helsinki. I was writing a novel then, and I incorporated the ship into the story. I described her as the vessel which transports the dead across the Styx.°

If we knew how our stories risk to catch up with us, would we write differently? I think not. But at that moment on the ship, I, as storyteller, was the decider of destinies. I was the navigator. I might even have been invited onto

---

°*Styx:* In Greek mythology, the river that separated the living from the dead.

Et in Arcadia Ego, by Nicolas Poussin.

the captain's bridge! Whereas now on the island of Furusund I look up at the same ship passing and feel as small as everyone else. The few passengers on deck look down at us from something like the height of a suspension bridge. And only I know that Sven is on board.

I walk between some birches, listen to the special sound the leaves of trees make when they are growing beside saltwater. Then I return to the café.

Is the weather going to stay the same? the boy is asking the captain.

Yes, it'll be fine tomorrow.

Tomorrow I'm going to look for the moose before the sun's up.

The white ship has passed the northern point of Furusund and has vanished.

A week later in the Haute-Savoie, I'm cooking fish on a wood fire out-side and my son, Yves, brings me a glass of wine to drink and holds out a bowl of olives. It's getting dark and my eyes are sore from the smoke, so I feel for a couple with my fingers without looking, and pop one into my mouth. As I spit out the stone and try to define the flavor—sharp, bitter-black, Greek—a thought crosses my mind. From now on I taste olives for Sven too.

Et in Arcadia ego.

And suddenly, rubbing my eyes, I remember: Sven and I first met by chance and swapped addresses in a large Poussin exhibition in London where, among many others, the painting *Et in Arcadia ego* was hanging. The canvas

50

55

shows a shepherdess and three arcadian shepherds, brought up short by a tomb, which is the last thing they were expecting to come upon there. One of them is reading out the inscription on the gravestone to the others.

Wonderful! Sven said with his hair standing on end. Everything in the painting leads the eye to the shadow of the arm of the one who's reading the words! You see? This shadow here! And he pointed.

QUESTIONS FOR DISCUSSION

1. What do you think it means to be able to invent your own arcadia and to be able to carry it with you?
2. Consider how Berger uses white space to separate the sections of this essay. What is your response to the shift from paragraph 3 to paragraph 4 and from paragraph 8 to paragraph 9?
3. What does Berger achieve by interrupting the story of his visit to the National Museum in Stockholm and locating another memory within that narrative?
4. What do the three sentences in paragraph 20 convey to you?
5. Berger devotes four paragraphs to a scene set in a cafeteria reserved for old people. Why do you think he gives this cafeteria, and the people within it, so much attention?
6. How do you interpret the dialogue between the sea captain and the boy who claims that he saw a moose? What does this dialogue contribute to the essay as a whole?
7. What does it mean to "taste olives for Sven"?
8. What role do the paintings play in this essay? Why are they arranged in the sequence in which they appear? Why is the final painting, which provides the essay's title, especially significant?
9. When writing about the loss of someone they loved, some writers become sentimental. Does Berger?
10. How do you interpret the last two paragraphs of this essay? Why do you think Berger chose to conclude by showing Sven excited by the painting reprinted on page 624?

SUGGESTIONS FOR WRITING

1. Taking the metro to Sven's funeral, Berger describes an atmosphere filled with "a tolerance for clumsy love, inelegance, missed opportunities, freckled backs, strange murmers, sweaty hair, hot feet, and life as it is." Write an essay in which you convey tolerance for several aspects of "life as it is," thinking in particular of the inelegant and sweaty things from which some people might turn scornfully away.
2. Write a tribute to someone you loved that establishes how this person was rooted in a specific culture.
3. Write an essay about a painting that makes your hair stand on end.

Links

■ Within the Book

For another view of how life can be lived both simply and passionately, see Annie Dillard's "Living like Weasels" (pages 82–85).

■ Elsewhere in Print

Andrews, Per. *Stockholm: City of My Dreams.* Trans. Jennifer Baverstom. Iowa City: Penfield, 2000.

Berger, John. *About Looking.* 1980. New York: Vintage, 1991.

———. *Here Is Where We Meet.* London: Bloomsbury, 2005.

———. *Selected Essays.* New York: Vintage, 2003.

———. *Ways of Seeing.* 1972. New York: Vintage, 1995.

Cooper, Elizabeth, and Charles Dempsey. *Nicolas Poussin.* Princeton: Princeton UP, 2000.

■ Online

www.mhhe.com/motives

Click on "More Resources" then "Writing to Experiment with Form."

■ ■ ■

THE DEER AT PROVIDENCIA

Annie Dillard

> *Drawn from the same collection as "Living Like Weasels," (pages 82–85), "The Deer at Providencia" focuses on an encounter with wildlife in the Amazon. Dillard traveled there as a tourist, and her response to what she witnessed strikes the other tourists in her group as inappropriate. As you read, try to understand why Dillard cannot offer the conventional response expected of her. And be prepared for what may seem like a sudden shift in direction once she returns home from her trip.*
>
> *Dillard has been praised for having "a mystic's wonder at the physical world." As you read the following essay, you will find that she pays close attention to the physical world but does not pretend to understand everything she observes. And as you work on your own writing, you might benefit from advice that Dillard offers writers in another of her essays, "Write Till You Drop": "One of the few things I know about writing is this: Spend it all, shoot it, play it, lose it, all, right away, every time. Do not hoard what seems good for a later place in the book, or for another book; give it, give it now. The impulse to save something good for a better place is the signal to spend it now. Something more will arise for later, something better. These things fill from beneath, like well water. Similarly, the impulse to keep to yourself what you have learned is not only shameful, it is destructive. Anything you do not give freely and abundantly becomes lost to you. You open your safe and find ashes."*

There were four of us North Americans in the jungle, in the Ecuadorian jungle on the banks of the Napo River in the Amazon watershed. The other three North Americans were metropolitan men. We stayed in tents in one riverside village, and visited others. At the village called Providencia we saw a sight which moved us, and which shocked the men.

The first thing we saw when we climbed the riverbank to the village of Providencia was the deer. It was roped to a tree on the grass clearing near the thatch shelter where we would eat lunch.

The deer was small, about the size of a whitetail fawn, but apparently full-grown. It had a rope around its neck and three feet caught in the rope. Someone said that the dogs had caught it that morning and the villagers were going to cook and eat it that night.

This clearing lay at the edge of the little thatched-hut village. We could see the villagers going about their business, scattering feed corn for hens about their houses, and wandering down paths to the river to bathe. The village headman was our host; he stood beside us as we watched the deer struggle. Several village boys were interested in the deer; they formed part of the circle we made around it in the clearing. So also did four businessmen from Quito who were attempting to guide us around the jungle. Few of the very different people standing in this circle had a common language. We watched the deer, and no one said much.

The deer lay on its side at the rope's very end, so the rope lacked slack to   5
let it rest its head in the dust. It was "pretty," delicate of bone like all deer, and thin-skinned for the tropics. Its skin looked virtually hairless, in fact, and almost translucent, like a membrane. Its neck was no thicker than my wrist; it was rubbed open on the rope, and gashed. Trying to paw itself free of the rope, the deer had scratched its own neck with its hooves. The raw underside of its neck showed red stripes and some bruises bleeding inside the muscles. Now three of its feet were hooked in the rope under its jaw. It could not stand, of course, on one leg, so it could not move to slacken the rope and ease the pull on its throat and enable it to rest its head.

Repeatedly the deer paused, motionless, its eyes veiled, with only its rib cage in motion, and its breaths the only sound. Then, after I would think, "It has given up; now it will die," it would heave. The rope twanged; the tree leaves clattered; the deer's free foot beat the ground. We stepped back and held our breaths. It thrashed, kicking, but only one leg moved; the other three legs tightened inside the rope's loop. Its hip jerked; its spine shook. Its eyes rolled; its tongue, thick with spittle, pushed in and out. Then it would rest again. We watched this for fifteen minutes.

Once three young native boys charged in, released its trapped legs, and jumped back to the circle of people. But instantly the deer scratched up its neck with its hooves and snared its forelegs in the rope again. It was easy to imagine a third and then a fourth leg soon stuck, like Brer Rabbit and the Tar Baby.

We watched the deer from the circle, and then we drifted on to lunch. Our palm-roofed shelter stood on a grassy promontory from which we could see the deer tied to the tree, pigs and hens walking under village houses, and black-and-white cattle standing in the river. There was even a breeze.

Lunch, which was the second and better lunch we had that day, was hot and fried. There was a big fish called *doncella,* a kind of catfish, dipped whole in corn flour and beaten egg, then deep fried. With our fingers we pulled soft fragments of it from its sides to our plates, and ate; it was delicate fish-flesh, fresh and mild. Someone found the roe, and I ate of that too—it was fat and stronger, like egg yolk, naturally enough, and warm.

There was also a stew of meat in shreds with rice and pale brown gravy. I   10
had asked what kind of deer it was tied to the tree; Pepe had answered in Spanish, "*Gama.*" Now they told us this was *gama* too, stewed. I suspect the word means merely game or venison. At any rate, I heard that the village dogs had cornered another deer just yesterday, and it was this deer which we were

now eating in full sight of the whole article. It was good. I was surprised at its tenderness. But it is a fact that high levels of lactic acid, which builds up in muscle tissues during exertion, tenderizes.

After the fish and meat we ate bananas fried in chunks and served on a tray; they were sweet and full of flavor. I felt terrific. My shirt was wet and cool from swimming; I had had a night's sleep, two decent walks, three meals, and a swim—everything tasted good. From time to time each one of us, separately, would look beyond our shaded roof to the sunny spot where the deer was still convulsing in the dust. Our meal completed, we walked around the deer and back to the boats.

That night I learned that while we were watching the deer, the others were watching me.

We four North Americans grew close in the jungle in a way that was not the usual artificial intimacy of travelers. We liked each other. We stayed up all that night talking, murmuring, as though we rocked on hammocks slung above time. The others were from big cities: New York, Washington, Boston. They all said that I had no expression on my face when I was watching the deer—or at any rate, not the expression they expected.

They had looked to see how I, the only woman, and the youngest, was taking the sight of the deer's struggles. I looked detached, apparently, or hard, or calm, or focused, still. I don't know. I was thinking. I remember feeling very old and energetic. I could say like Thoreau that I have traveled widely in Roanoke, Virginia. I have thought a great deal about carnivorousness; I eat meat. These things are not issues; they are mysteries.

Gentlemen of the city, what surprises you? That there is suffering here, or that I know it? 15

We lay in the tent and talked. "If it had been my wife," one man said with special vigor, amazed, "she wouldn't have cared *what* was going on; she would have dropped *everything* right at that moment and gone in the village from here to there to there, she would not have *stopped* until that animal was out of its suffering one way or another. She couldn't *bear* to see a creature in agony like that."

I nodded.

Now I am home. When I wake I comb my hair before the mirror above my dresser. Every morning for the past two years I have seen in that mirror, beside my sleep-softened face, the blackened face of a burnt man. It is a wire-service photograph clipped from a newspaper and taped to my mirror. The caption reads: "Alan McDonald in Miami hospital bed." All you can see in the photograph is a smudged triangle of face from his eyelids to his lower lip; the rest is bandages. You cannot see the expression in his eyes; the bandages shade them.

The story, headed MAN BURNED FOR SECOND TIME, begins:

"Why does God hate me?" Alan McDonald asked from his hospital bed.

"When the gunpowder went off, I couldn't believe it," he said. "I just couldn't believe it. I said, 'No, God couldn't do this to me again.'"

He was in a burn ward in Miami, in serious condition. I do not even know if he lived. I wrote him a letter at the time, cringing.

He had been burned before, thirteen years previously, by flaming gaso- *20* line. For years he had been having his body restored and his face remade in dozens of operations. He had been a boy, and then a burnt boy. He had already been stunned by what could happen, by how life could veer.

Once I read that people who survive bad burns tend to go crazy; they have a very high suicide rate. Medicine cannot ease their pain; drugs just leak away, soaking the sheets, because there is no skin to hold them in. The people just lie there and weep. Later they kill themselves. They had not known, before they were burned, that the world included such suffering, that life could permit them personally such pain.

This time a bowl of gunpowder had exploded on McDonald.

"I didn't realize what had happened at first," he recounted. "And then I heard that sound from 13 years ago. I was burning. I rolled to put the fire out and I thought, 'Oh God, not again.'

"If my friend hadn't been there, I would have jumped into a canal with a rock around my neck."

His wife concludes the piece, "Man, it just isn't fair."

I read the whole clipping again every morning. This is the Big Time here, every minute of it. Will someone please explain to Alan McDonald in his dignity, to the deer at Providencia in his dignity, what is going on? And mail me the carbon.

When we walked by the deer at Providencia for the last time, I said to Pepe, with a pitying glance at the deer, "*Pobrecito*"—"poor little thing." But I was trying out Spanish. I knew at the time it was a ridiculous thing to say.

QUESTIONS FOR DISCUSSION

1. What details inspire sympathy for the deer tied up in the village? Why does Dillard inspire sympathy for a deer that she did not attempt to rescue?
2. Dillard makes a point of describing the lunch she enjoyed the day she saw the deer. How do you respond to knowing that she enjoyed eating warm fish roe as well as a stew of what seems to be deer meat—and that after lunch she "felt terrific"?

3. Why do the men in her group disapprove of her response to the deer? What are they failing to understand about her?
4. Why do you think Dillard keeps a picture of a burn victim on her mirror at home?
5. What relation does the story of Alan McDonald have to the story of the deer at Providencia? What has Dillard achieved by placing these two stories together?
6. Why is it significant that most of this essay is set in a village called "Providencia"?

SUGGESTIONS FOR WRITING

1. Imagine that you are one of the villagers who witnesses four North Americans having lunch in Providencia when their tour pauses there. Write an account for people in a neighboring village in which you describe the behavior of these visitors.
2. Toward the end of her essay, Dillard writes, "Will someone please explain to Alan McDonald in his dignity, to the deer in his dignity, what is going on? And mail me the carbon?" (*Carbon,* in this case, refers to carbon paper, a once common way of making a duplicate copy when using a typewriter.) Experiment with form by writing a letter in three parts, in which you explain first to McDonald, then to the deer, and finally to Annie Dillard what you think they most need to understand about what Dillard calls "The Big Time."
3. Think of things that either bother or please you. Choose two that apparently have nothing in common and then try writing about them both. Without comparing them directly or explaining why you feel they are somehow connected, try to help readers see how understanding one element makes understanding the second easier.

LINKS

▪ Within the Book

Dillard's essay raises questions about the nature of suffering. "Am I Blue?" (pages 563–566) by Alice Walker also encourages readers to reflect on how people make animals suffer.

▪ Elsewhere in Print

Dillard, Annie. *For the Time Being.* New York: Knopf, 1999.
———. *The Living.* New York: Harper, 1992.
———. *Tickets for a Prayer Wheel: Poems.* Columbia: U of Missouri P, 1974.
———. *The Writing Life.* New York: Harper, 1989.

■ **Elsewhere in Print (continued)**

MacDonald, Theodore, Jr. *Ethnicity and Culture amidst New "Neighbors": The Runa of Ecuador's Amazon Region.* Boston: Allyn, 1999.

■ **Online**

www.mhhe.com/motives

Click on "More Resources" then "Writing to Experiment with Form."

■ ■ ■

MARRAKECH

George Orwell

Like "A Hanging" (pages 557–561), "Marrakech" shows how George Orwell (1903–1950) was concerned about the consequences of colonialism. In his essay "Why I Write," he identifies "political purpose" as one of the "four great motives for writing," the others being "sheer egotism," "aesthetic enthusiasm," and "historical purpose." By "political purpose," he explains that he means, "Desire to push the world in a certain direction, to alter other peoples' idea of the kind of society they should strive after." And he goes on to note, "The opinion that art should have nothing to do with politics is itself a political attitude."

A city in North Africa, Marrakech was a popular destination for American and European tourists when Morocco was ruled by the French; it still attracts many travelers. The following essay, first published in 1939, the year the Second World War began, presents a series of scenes of how the city looked during the colonial era. Orwell provides no transitions between these scenes, expecting his readers to see for themselves how each "snapshot" relates to another. As you read, consider what the scenes have in common.

As the corpse went past, the flies left the restaurant table in a cloud and rushed after it, but they came back a few minutes later.

The little crowd of mourners—all men and boys, no women—threaded their way across the market-place between the piles of pomegranates and the taxis and the camels, wailing a short chant over and over again. What really appeals to the flies is that the corpses here are never put into coffins, they are merely wrapped in a piece of rag and carried on a rough wooden bier on the shoulders of four friends. When the friends get to the burying-ground they hack an oblong hole a foot or two deep, dump the body in it and fling over it a little of the dried-up, lumpy earth, which is like broken brick. No gravestone, no name, no identifying mark of any kind. The burying-ground is merely a huge waste of hummocky earth, like a derelict building-lot. After a month or two no one can even be certain where his own relatives are buried.

When you walk through a town like this—two hundred thousand inhabitants, of whom at least twenty thousand own literally nothing except the rags they stand up in—when you see how the people live, and still more how easily they die, it is always difficult to believe that you are walking among human beings. All colonial empires are in reality founded upon that fact. The people have brown faces—besides, there are so many of them! Are they really the same flesh as yourself? Do they even have names? Or are they merely a kind of undifferentiated brown stuff, about as individual as bees or coral insects?

They rise out of the earth, they sweat and starve for a few years, and then they sink back into the nameless mounds of the graveyard and nobody notices that they are gone. And even the graves themselves soon fade back into the soil. Sometimes, out for a walk, as you break your way through the prickly pear, you notice that it is rather bumpy underfoot, and only a certain regularity in the bumps tells you that you are walking over skeletons.

I was feeding one of the gazelles in the public gardens.

Gazelles are almost the only animals that look good to eat when they are   5
still alive, in fact, one can hardly look at their hindquarters without thinking of mint sauce. The gazelle I was feeding seemed to know that this thought was in my mind, for though it took the piece of bread I was holding out it obviously did not like me. It nibbled rapidly at the bread, then lowered its head and tried to butt me, then took another nibble and then butted again. Probably its idea was that if it could drive me away the bread would somehow remain hanging in mid-air.

An Arab navvy° working on the path nearby lowered his heavy hoe and sidled slowly towards us. He looked from the gazelle to the bread and from the bread to the gazelle, with a sort of quiet amazement, as though he had never seen anything quite like this before. Finally he said shyly in French:

"*I* could eat some of that bread."

I tore off a piece and he stowed it gratefully in some secret place under his rags. This man is an employee of the Municipality.

When you go through the Jewish quarters you gather some idea of what the medieval ghettoes were probably like. Under their Moorish rulers the Jews were only allowed to own land in certain restricted areas, and after centuries of this kind of treatment they have ceased to bother about overcrowding. Many of the streets are a good deal less than six feet wide, the houses are completely windowless, and sore-eyed children cluster everywhere in unbelievable numbers, like clouds of flies. Down the centre of the street there is generally running a little river of urine.

In the bazaar huge families of Jews, all dressed in the long black robe and   10
little black skull-cap, are working in dark fly-infested booths that look like caves. A carpenter sits cross-legged at a prehistoric lathe, turning chair-legs at lightning speed. He works the lathe with a bow in his right hand and guides the chisel with his left foot, and thanks to a lifetime of sitting in this position his left leg is warped out of shape. At his side his grandson, aged six, is already starting on the simpler parts of the job.

I was just passing the coppersmiths' booths when somebody noticed that I was lighting a cigarette. Instantly, from the dark holes all round, there was a frenzied rush of Jews, many of them old grandfathers with flowing grey

---

°*navvy:* A workman employed in excavation.

beards, all clamouring for a cigarette. Even a blind man somewhere at the back of one of the booths heard a rumour of cigarettes and came crawling out, groping in the air with his hand. In about a minute I had used up the whole packet. None of these people, I suppose, works less than twelve hours a day, and every one of them looks on a cigarette as a more or less impossible luxury.

As the Jews live in self-contained communities they follow the same trades as the Arabs, except for agriculture. Fruit-sellers, potters, silversmiths, black-smiths, butchers, leatherworkers, tailors, water-carriers, beggars, porters—whichever way you look you see nothing but Jews. As a matter of fact there are thirteen thousand of them, all living in the space of a few acres. A good job Hitler isn't here. Perhaps he is on his way, however. You hear the usual dark rumours about the Jews, not only from the Arabs but from the poorer Europeans.

"Yes, mon vieux, they took my job away from me and gave it to a Jew. The Jews! They're the real rulers of this country, you know. They've got all the money. They control the banks, finance—everything."

"But," I said, "isn't it a fact that the average Jew is a labourer working for about a penny an hour?"

"Ah, that's only for show! They're all moneylenders really. They're cun-   15
ning, the Jews."

In just the same way, a couple of hundred years ago, poor old women used to be burned for witchcraft when they could not even work enough magic to get themselves a square meal.

All people who work with their hands are partly invisible, and the more important the work they do, the less visible they are. Still, a white skin is al-ways fairly conspicuous. In northern Europe, when you see a labourer plough-ing a field, you probably give him a second glance. In a hot country, anywhere south of Gibraltar or east of Suez, the chances are that you don't even see him. I have noticed this again and again. In a tropical landscape one's eye takes in everything except the human beings. It takes in the dried-up soil, the prickly pear, the palm tree and the distant mountain, but it always misses the peasant hoeing at his patch. He is the same colour as the earth, and a great deal less interesting to look at.

It is only because of this that the starved countries of Asia and Africa are accepted as tourist resorts. No one would think of running cheap trips to the Distressed Areas.° But where the human beings have brown skins their pov-erty is simply not noticed. What does Morocco mean to a Frenchman? An orange-grove or a job in Government service. Or to an Englishman? Camels, castles, palm trees, Foreign Legionnaires, brass trays, and bandits. One could prob-ably live there for years without noticing that for nine-tenths of the people

---

°*Distressed Areas:* Parts of Britain especially hard hit by economic depression.

the reality of life is an endless, back-breaking struggle to wring a little food out of an eroded soil.

Most of Morocco is so desolate that no wild animal bigger than a hare can live on it. Huge areas which were once covered with forest have turned into a treeless waste where the soil is exactly like broken-up brick. Nevertheless a good deal of it is cultivated, with frightful labour. Everything is done by hand. Long lines of women, bent double like inverted capital L's, work their way slowly across the fields, tearing up the prickly weeds with their hands, and the peasant gathering lucerne for fodder pulls it up stalk by stalk instead of reaping it, thus saving an inch or two on each stalk. The plough is a wretched wooden thing, so frail that one can easily carry it on one's shoulder, and fitted underneath with a rough iron spike which stirs the soil to a depth of about four inches. This is as much as the strength of the animals is equal to. It is usual to plough with a cow and a donkey yoked together. Two donkeys would not be quite strong enough, but on the other hand two cows would cost a little more to feed. The peasants possess no harrows, they merely plough the soil several times over in different directions, finally leaving it in rough furrows, after which the whole field has to be shaped with hoes into small oblong patches to conserve water. Except for a day or two after the rare rainstorms there is never enough water. Along the edges of the fields channels are hacked out to a depth of thirty or forty feet to get at the tiny trickles which run through the subsoil.

Every afternoon a file of very old women passes down the road outside   *20* my house, each carrying a load of firewood. All of them are mummified with age and the sun, and all of them are tiny. It seems to be generally the case in primitive communities that the women, when they get beyond a certain age, shrink to the size of children. One day a poor old creature who could not have been more than four feet tall crept past me under a vast load of wood. I stopped her and put a five-sou piece (a little more than a farthing)° into her hand. She answered with a shrill wail, almost a scream, which was partly gratitude but mainly surprise. I suppose that from her point of view, by taking any notice of her, I seemed almost to be violating a law of nature. She accepted her status as an old woman, that is to say as a beast of burden. When a family is travelling it is quite usual to see a father and a grown-up son riding ahead on donkeys, and an old woman following on foot, carrying the baggage.

But what is strange about these people is their invisibility. For several weeks, always at about the same time of day, the file of old women had hobbled past the house with their firewood, and though they had registered themselves on my eyeballs I cannot truly say that I had seen them. Firewood was passing—that was how I saw it. It was only that one day I happened to be walking behind them, and the curious up-and-down motion of a load of

----

°*five sou . . . farthing:* A sou is a former French coin; five sou equaled a centime, or a hundredth of a franc. A farthing is a former British coin worth a quarter of a penny.

wood drew my attention to the human being beneath it. Then for the first time I noticed the poor old earth-coloured bodies, bodies reduced to bones and leathery skin, bent double under the crushing weight. Yet I suppose I had not been five minutes on Moroccan soil before I noticed the overloading of the donkeys and was infuriated by it. There is no question that the donkeys are damnably treated. The Moroccan donkey is hardly bigger than a St. Bernard dog, it carries a load which in the British Army would be considered too much for a fifteen-hands mule, and very often its pack-saddle is not taken off its back for weeks together. But what is peculiarly pitiful is that it is the most willing creature on earth, it follows its master like a dog and does not need either bridle or halter. After a dozen years of devoted work it suddenly drops dead, whereupon its master tips it into the ditch and the village dogs have torn its guts out before it is cold.

This kind of thing makes one's blood boil, whereas—on the whole—the plight of the human beings does not. I am not commenting, merely pointing to a fact. People with brown skins are next door to invisible. Anyone can be sorry for the donkey with its galled back, but it is generally owing to some kind of accident if one even notices the old woman under her load of sticks.

As the storks flew northward the Negroes were marching southward—a long, dusty column, infantry, screw-gun batteries, and then more infantry, four or five thousand men in all, winding up the road with a clumping of boots and a clatter of iron wheels.

They were Senegalese, the blackest Negroes in Africa, so black that sometimes it is difficult to see whereabouts on their necks the hair begins. Their splendid bodies were hidden in reach-me-down khaki uniforms, their feet squashed into boots that looked like blocks of wood, and every tin hat seemed to be a couple of sizes too small. It was very hot and the men had marched a long way. They slumped under the weight of their packs and the curiously sensitive black faces were glistening with sweat.

As they went past, a tall, very young Negro turned and caught my eye. 25 But the look he gave me was not in the least the kind of look you might expect. Not hostile, not contemptuous, not sullen, not even inquisitive. It was the shy, wide-eyed Negro look, which actually is a look of profound respect. I saw how it was. This wretched boy, who is a French citizen and has therefore been dragged from the forest to scrub floors and catch syphilis in garrison towns, actually has feelings of reverence before a white skin. He has been taught that the white race are his masters, and he still believes it.

But there is one thought which every white man (and in this connection it doesn't matter twopence if he calls himself a socialist) thinks when he sees a black army marching past. "How much longer can we go on kidding these people? How long before they turn their guns in the other direction?"

It was curious, really. Every white man there had this thought stowed somewhere or other in his mind. I had it, so had the other onlookers, so had the officers on their sweating chargers and the white N.C.O.'s marching in the ranks. It was a kind of secret which we all knew and were too clever to tell; only the Negroes didn't know it. And really it was like watching a flock of cattle to see the long column, a mile or two miles of armed men, flowing peacefully up the road, while the great white birds drifted over them in the opposite direction, glittering like scraps of paper.

QUESTIONS FOR DISCUSSION

1. What is Orwell implying when he writes, in paragraph 8, "This man is an employee of the Municipality"?
2. What does Orwell accomplish by exploring aspects of Marrakech overlooked by the average tourist?
3. In paragraph 17, Orwell writes, "All people who work with their hands are partly invisible." Why are the laborers in Marrakech "partly invisible"? Are they seen by some people but overlooked by others? Are there "partly invisible" people in the United States today?
4. Orwell is well known for political novels such as *1984* and *Animal Farm*. Is there a political message in "Marrakech"?
5. Why do you think Orwell draws attention to storks and "great white birds" in paragraphs 23 and 27, respectively? How do you respond to this final scene?
6. The essay is divided into five sections. Do the sections come together to make a whole? Is there a pattern to the arrangement of scenes Orwell describes? Are there any images that help tie the scenes together?

SUGGESTIONS FOR WRITING

1. Choose a place you know well, and write an essay composed of a series of scenes showing what that place is like. Without stating a specific thesis, arrange your scenes in a pattern that will help readers understand the vision you are sharing with them.
2. If you share Orwell's concern about social injustice, write a series of scenes that convey different aspects of a specific problem.
3. Write an essay exploring what a writer can accomplish by using the form Orwell has used in "Marrakech." What possibilities does it open? Does it pose any risks?

■ LINKS

■ Within the Book

The harmful effects of colonialism motivated the Declaration of Independence (pages 481–484) by Thomas Jefferson.

■ **Elsewhere in Print**

Fernea, Elizabeth Warnock. *A Street in Marrakech*. Garden City: Doubleday, 1975.

Orwell, George. *Animal Farm: A Fairy Story*. 1945. New York: Signet, 1996.

———. *Down and Out in Paris and London*. 1933. New York: Harcourt, 1983.

———. *Homage to Catalonia*. 1938. New York: Harcourt, 1987.

———. *1984*. 1949. New York: NAL, 1989.

———. *The Orwell Reader: Fiction, Essays, and Reportage*. Ed. Richard H. Rovere. New York: Harcourt, 1956.

Porch, Douglas. *The Conquest of Morocco*. New York: Knopf, 1983.

■ **Online**

www.mhhe.com/motives

Click on "More Resources" then "Writing to Experiment with Form."

■ ■ ■

IF YOU ARE WHAT YOU EAT, THEN WHAT AM I?

Geeta Kothari

> *A member of the English Department at the University of Pittsburgh, Geeta Kothari writes both fiction and nonfiction. When discussing her anthology* Did My Mama Like to Dance? *and why she writes about her own mother, Kothari offers a comment about her motive for writing that may help you to understand the organization and purpose of the following essay: "I feel an urgency to record the pieces of our life together, while understanding that no matter how hard I try, there will be things left unspoken or unasked."*
>
> *"If You Are What You Eat, Then What Am I?" was first published in 1999 by* The Kenyon Review, *one of our country's most prestigious literary magazines. As its title suggests, the essay explores the role of food in shaping identity. In the case of Geeta Kothari, who is an Asian American, the foods that shaped her childhood were either Indian or American. As an adult, she now reflects on what she valued and what she took for granted as she ate at her family's table. As you read this essay, consider what Kothari achieves by dividing it into sections and how these sections relate to one another.*

To belong is to understand the tacit codes of the people you live with.
—MICHAEL IGNATIEFF, *Blood and Belonging*

I

The first time my mother and I open a can of tuna, I am nine years old. We stand in the doorway of the kitchen, in semidarkness, the can tilted toward daylight. I want to eat what the kids at school eat: bologna, hot dogs, salami—foods my parents find repugnant because they contain pork and meat byproducts, crushed bone and hair glued together by chemicals and fat. Although she has never been able to tolerate the smell of fish, my mother buys the tuna, hoping to satisfy my longing for American food.

Indians, of course, do not eat such things.

The tuna smells fishy, which surprises me because I can't remember anyone's tuna sandwich actually smelling like fish. And the tuna in those sandwiches doesn't look like this, pink and shiny, like an internal organ. In fact, this looks similar to the bad foods my mother doesn't want me to eat. She is silent, holding her face away from the can while peering into it like a half-blind bird.

"What's wrong with it?" I ask.

She has no idea. My mother does not know that the tuna everyone else's   5
mothers made for them was tuna *salad*.

"Do you think it's botulism?"

I have never seen botulism, but I have read about it, just as I have read about but never eaten steak and kidney pie.

There is so much my parents don't know. They are not like other parents, and they disappoint me and my sister. They are supposed to help us negotiate the world outside, teach us the signs, the clues to proper behavior: what to eat and how to eat it.

We have expectations, and my parents fail to meet them, especially my mother, who works full-time. I don't understand what it means, to have a mother who works outside and inside the home; I notice only the ways in which she disappoints me. She doesn't show up for school plays. She doesn't make chocolate-frosted cupcakes for my class. At night, if I want her attention, I have to sit in the kitchen and talk to her while she cooks the evening meal, attentive to every third or fourth word I say.

We throw the tuna away. This time my mother is disappointed. I go to   10
school with tuna eaters. I see their sandwiches, yet cannot explain the discrepancy between them and the stinking, oily fish in my mother's hand. We do not understand so many things, my mother and I.

II

On weekends, we eat fried chicken from Woolworth's on the back steps of my father's first-floor office in Murray Hill. The back steps face a small patch of garden—hedges, a couple of skinny trees, and gravel instead of grass. We can see the back window of the apartment my parents and I lived in until my sister was born. There, the doorman watched my mother, several months pregnant and wearing a sari, slip on the ice in front of the building.

My sister and I pretend we are in the country, where our American friends all have houses. We eat glazed doughnuts, also from Woolworth's, and french fries with ketchup.

III

My mother takes a catering class and learns that Miracle Whip and mustard are healthier than mayonnaise. She learns to make egg salad with chopped celery, deviled eggs dusted with paprika, a cream cheese spread with bits of fresh ginger and watercress, chicken liver pâté, and little brown-and-white checkerboard sandwiches that we have only once. She makes chicken *à la king* in puff pastry shells and eggplant Parmesan. She acquires smooth wooden paddles, whose purpose is never clear, two different egg slicers, several wooden spoons, icing tubes, cookie cutters, and an electric mixer.

IV

I learn to make tuna salad by watching a friend. My sister never acquires a taste for it. Instead, she craves

> bologna
> hot dogs
> bacon
> sausages

and a range of unidentifiable meat products forbidden by my parents. Their restrictions are not about sacred cows, as everyone around us assumes; in a pinch, we are allowed hamburgers, though lamb burgers are preferable. A "pinch" means choosing not to draw attention to ourselves as outsiders, impolite visitors who won't eat what their host serves. But bologna is still taboo.

V

Things my sister refuses to eat: butter, veal, anything with jeera. The baby-   *15*
sitter tries to feed her butter sandwiches, threatens her with them, makes her cry in fear and disgust. My mother does not disappoint her; she does not believe in forcing us to eat, in using food as a weapon. In addition to pbj,° my sister likes pasta and marinara sauce, bologna and Wonder Bread (when she can get it), and fried egg sandwiches with turkey, cheese, and horseradish. Her tastes, once established, are predictable.

VI

When we visit our relatives in India, food prepared outside the house is carefully monitored. In the hot, sticky monsoon months in New Delhi and Bombay, we cannot eat ice cream, salad, cold food, or any fruit that can't be peeled. Definitely no meat. People die from amoebic dysentery, unexplained fevers, strange boils on their bodies. We drink boiled water only, no ice. No sweets except for jalebi, thin fried twists of dough in dripping hot sugar syrup. If we're caught outside with nothing to drink, Fanta, Limca, Thums Up (after Coca-Cola is thrown out by Mrs. Gandhi)° will do. Hot tea sweetened with sugar, served with thick creamy buffalo milk, is preferable. It should be boiled, to kill the germs on the cup.

°*pbj:* Peanut butter and jelly.
°*Mrs. Gandhi:* Indira Gandhi (1917–1984), prime minister of India 1966–1977 and 1980–1984.

My mother talks about "back home" as a safe place, a silk cocoon frozen in time where we are sheltered by family and friends. Back home, my sister and I do not argue about food with my parents. Home is where they know all the rules. We trust them to guide us safely through the maze of city streets for which they have no map, and we trust them to feed and take care of us, the way parents should.

Finally, though, one of us will get sick, hungry for the food we see our cousins and friends eating, too thirsty to ask for a straw, too polite to insist on properly boiled water.

At my uncle's diner in New Delhi, someone hands me a plate of aloo tikki, fried potato patties filled with mashed channa dal and served with a sweet and a sour chutney. The channa, mixed with hot chilies and spices, burns my tongue and throat. I reach for my Fanta, discard the paper straw, and gulp the sweet orange soda down, huge drafts that sting rather than soothe.

When I throw up later that day (or is it the next morning, when a stom-   20
achache wakes me from deep sleep?), I cry over the frustration of being singled out, not from the pain my mother assumes I'm feeling as she holds my
hair back from my face. The taste of orange lingers in my mouth, and I remember my lips touching the cold glass of the Fanta bottle.

At that moment, more than anything, I want to be like my cousins.

VII

In New York, at the first Indian restaurant in our neighborhood, my father orders with confidence, and my sister and I play with the silverware until the steaming plates of lamb biryani arrive.

What is Indian food? my friends ask, their noses crinkling up.

Later, this restaurant is run out of business by the new Indo-Pak-Bangladeshi combinations up and down the street, which serve similar food. They use plastic cutlery and Styrofoam cups. They do not distinguish between North and South Indian cooking, or between Indian, Pakistani, and Bangladeshi cooking, and their customers do not care. The food is fast, cheap, and tasty. Dosa, a rice flour crepe stuffed with masala potato, appears on the same trays as chicken makhani.

Now my friends want to know, Do you eat curry at home?   25

One time my mother makes lamb vindaloo for guests. Like dosa, this is a South Indian dish, one that my Punjabi mother has to learn from a cookbook. For us, she cooks everyday food—yellow dal, rice, chapati, bhaji. Lentils, rice, bread, and vegetables. She has never referred to anything on our table as "curry" or "curried," but I know she has made chicken curry for guests. Vindaloo, she explains, is a curry too. I understand then that curry is a dish created for guests, outsiders, a food for people who eat in restaurants.

VIII

I have inherited brown eyes, black hair, a long nose with a crooked bridge, and soft teeth with thin enamel. I am in my twenties, moving to a city far from my parents, before it occurs to me that jeera, the spice my sister avoids, must have an English name. I have to learn that haldi = turmeric, methi = fenugreek. What to make with fenugreek, I do not know. My grandmother used to make methi roti for our breakfast, cornbread with fresh fenugreek leaves served with a lump of homemade butter. No one makes it now that she's gone, though once in a while my mother will get a craving for it and produce a facsimile ("The cornmeal here is wrong") that only highlights what she's really missing: the smells and tastes of her mother's house.

I will never make my grandmother's methi roti or even my mother's unsatisfactory imitation of it. I attempt chapati; it takes six hours, three phone calls home, and leaves me with an aching back. I have to write translations down: jeera = cumin. My memory is unreliable. But I have always known garam = hot.

IX

My mother learns how to make brownies and apple pie. My father makes only Indian food, except for loaves of heavy, sweet brown bread that I eat with thin slices of American cheese and lettuce. The recipe is a secret, passed on to him by a woman at work. Years later, when he finally gives it to me, when I finally ask for it, I end up with three bricks of gluten that even the birds and my husband won't eat.

X

My parents send me to boarding school, outside of London. They imagine   30
that I will overcome my shyness and find a place for myself in this all-girls' school. They have never lived in England, but as former subjects of the British Empire, they find London familiar, comfortable in a way New York—my mother's home for over twenty years by now—is not. Americans still don't know what to call us; their Indians live on reservations, not in Manhattan. Because they understand the English, my parents believe the English understand us.

I poke at my first school lunch—thin, overworked pastry in a puddle of lumpy gravy. The lumps are chewy mushrooms, maybe, or overcooked shrimp.

"What is this?" I don't want to ask, but I can't go on eating without knowing.

"Steak and kidney pie."

The girl next to me, red-haired, freckled, watches me take a bite from my plate. She has been put in charge of me, the new girl, and I follow her around all day, a foreigner at the mercy of a reluctant and angry tour guide. She is not used to explaining what is perfectly and utterly natural.

"What, you've never had steak and kidney pie? Bloody hell."   35

My classmates scoff, then marvel, then laugh at my ignorance. After a year, I understand what is on my plate: sausage rolls, blood pudding, Spam, roast beef in a thin, greasy gravy, all the bacon and sausage I could possibly want. My parents do not expect me to starve.

The girls at school expect conformity; it has been bred into them, through years of uniforms and strict rules about proper behavior. I am thirteen and contrary, even as I yearn for acceptance. I declare myself a vegetarian and doom myself to a diet of cauliflower cheese and baked beans on toast. The administration does not question my decision; they assume it's for vague, undefined religious reasons, although my father, the doctor, tells them it's for my health. My reasons, from this distance of many years, remain murky to me.

Perhaps I am my parents' daughter after all.

XI

When she is three, sitting on my cousin's lap in Bombay, my sister reaches for his plate and puts a chili in her mouth. She wants to be like the grownups, who dip green chilies in coarse salt and eat them like any other vegetable. She howls inconsolable animal pain for what must be hours. She doesn't have the vocabulary for the oily heat that stings her mouth and tongue, burns a trail through her small tender body. Only hot, sticky tears on my father's shoulder.

As an adult, she eats red chili paste, mango pickle, kimchee, foods that   40
make my eyes water and my stomach gurgle. My tastes are milder. I order raita at Indian restaurants and ask for food that won't sear the roof of my mouth and scar the insides of my cheeks. The waiters nod, and their eyes shift—a slight once-over that indicates they don't believe me. I am Indian, aren't I? My father seems to agree with them. He tells me I'm asking for the impossible, as if he believes the recipes are immutable, written in stone during the passage from India to America.

XII

I look around my boyfriend's freezer one day and find meat: pork chops, ground beef, chicken pieces, Italian sausage. Ham in the refrigerator, next to the homemade bolognese sauce. Tupperware filled with chili made from ground beef and pork.

He smells different from me. Foreign. Strange.

I marry him anyway.

He has inherited blue eyes that turn gray in bad weather, light brown hair, a sharp pointy nose, and excellent teeth. He learns to make chili with ground turkey and tofu, tomato sauce with red wine and portobello mush-rooms, roast chicken with rosemary and slivers of garlic under the skin.

He eats steak when we are in separate cities, roast beef at his mother's 45 house, hamburgers at work. Sometimes I smell them on his skin. I hope he doesn't notice me turning my face, a cheek instead of my lips, my nose wrin-kled at the unfamiliar, musky smell.

XIII

And then I realize I don't want to be a person who can find Indian food only in restaurants. One day my parents will be gone and I will long for the foods of my childhood, the way they long for theirs. I prepare for this day the way people on TV prepare for the end of the world. They gather canned goods they will never eat while I stockpile recipes I cannot replicate. I am frantic, disorganized, grabbing what I can, filing scribbled notes haphazardly. I regret the tastes I've forgotten, the meals I have inhaled without a thought. I worry that I've come to this realization too late.

XIV

Who told my mother about Brie? One day we were eating Velveeta, the next day Brie, Gouda, Camembert, Port Salut, Havarti with caraway, Danish fontina, string cheese made with sheep's milk. Who opened the door to these foreigners that sit on the refrigerator shelf next to last night's dal?

Back home, there is one cheese only, which comes in a tin, looks like Bakelite, and tastes best when melted.

And how do we go from Chef Boyardee to fresh pasta and homemade sauce, made with Redpack tomatoes, crushed garlic, and dried oregano? Mac-aroni and cheese, made with fresh cheddar and whole milk, sprinkled with bread crumbs and paprika. Fresh eggplant and ricotta ravioli, baked with marinara sauce and fresh mozzarella.

My mother will never cook beef or pork in her kitchen, and the foods 50 she knew in her childhood are unavailable. Because the only alternative to the supermarket, with its TV dinners and canned foods, is the gourmet Italian deli across the street, by default our meals become socially acceptable.

XV

If I really want to make myself sick, I worry that my husband will one day leave me for a meat-eater, for someone familiar who doesn't sniff him suspi-ciously for signs of alimentary infidelity.

XVI

Indians eat lentils. I understand this as absolute, a decree from an unidentifiable authority that watches and judges me.

So what does it mean that I cannot replicate my mother's dal? She and my father show me repeatedly, in their kitchen, in my kitchen. They coach me over the phone, buy me the best cookbooks, and finally write down their secrets. Things I'm supposed to know but don't. Recipes that should be, by now, engraved on my heart.

Living far from the comfort of people who require no explanation for what I do and who I am, I crave the foods we have shared. My mother convinces me that moong is the easiest dal to prepare, and yet it fails me every time: bland, watery, a sickly greenish yellow mush. These imperfect imitations remind me only of what I'm missing.

But I have never been fond of moong dal. At my mother's table it is the last thing I reach for. Now I worry that this antipathy toward dal signals something deeper, that somehow I am not my parents' daughter, not Indian, and because I cannot bear the touch and smell of raw meat, though I can eat it cooked (charred, dry, and overdone), I am not American either.   55

I worry about a lifetime purgatory in Indian restaurants where I will complain that all the food looks and tastes the same because they've used the same masala.

XVII

About the tuna and her attempts to feed us, my mother laughs. She says, "You were never fussy. You ate everything I made and never complained."

My mother is at the stove, wearing only her blouse and petticoat, her sari carefully folded and hung in the closet. She does not believe a girl's place is in the kitchen, but she expects me to know that too much hing can ruin a meal, to know without being told, without having to ask or write it down. Hing = asafetida.

She remembers the catering class. "Oh, that class. You know, I had to give it up when we got to lobster. I just couldn't stand the way it looked."

She says this apologetically, as if she has deprived us, as if she suspects that   60
having a mother who could feed us lobster would have changed the course of our lives.

Intellectually, she understands that only certain people regularly eat lobster, people with money or those who live in Maine, or both. In her catering class there were people without jobs for whom preparing lobster was a part of their professional training as caterers. Like us, they wouldn't be eating lobster at home. For my mother, however, lobster was just another American food, like tuna—different, strange, not natural yet somehow essential to belonging.

I learned how to prepare and eat lobster from the same girl who taught me tuna salad. I ate bacon at her house too. And one day this girl, with her houses in the country and Martha's Vineyard, asked me how my uncle was going to pick me up from the airport in Bombay. In 1973, she was surprised to hear that he used a car, not an elephant. At home, my parents and I laughed, and though I never knew for sure if she was making fun of me, I still wanted her friendship.

My parents were afraid my sister and I would learn to despise the foods they loved, replace them with bologna and bacon and lose our taste for masala. For my mother, giving up her disgust of lobster, with its hard exterior and foreign smell, would mean renouncing some essential difference. It would mean becoming, decidedly, definitely, American—unafraid of meat in all its forms, able to consume large quantities of protein at any given meal. My willingness to toss a living being into boiling water and then get past its ugly appearance to the rich meat inside must mean to my mother that I am somehow someone she is not.

But I haven't eaten lobster in years. In my kitchen cupboards, there is a thirteen-pound bag of basmati rice, jars of lime pickle, mango pickle, and ghee, cans of tuna and anchovies, canned soups, coconut milk, and tomatoes, rice noodles, several kinds of pasta, dried mushrooms, and unlabeled bottles of spices: haldi, jeera, hing. When my husband tries to help me cook, he cannot identify all the spices. He gets confused when I forget their English names and remarks that my expectations of him are unreasonable.

I am my parents' daughter. Like them, I expect knowledge to pass from   65
me to my husband without one word of explanation or translation. I want him to know what I know, see what I see, without having to tell him exactly what it is. I want to believe that recipes never change.

QUESTIONS FOR DISCUSSION

1. Why, as a child, was Kothari disappointed with her parents?
2. Consider the last sentence in paragraph 11: "There, the doorman watched my mother, several months pregnant and wearing a sari, slip on the ice in front of the building." Why is the sari significant? What is Kothari implying about the doorman?
3. According to Kothari, her mother would not use "food as a weapon." What does it mean to use food as a weapon? Can you give an example from your own experience?
4. If you are what you eat, what kind of person is Kothari?
5. In what sense has Kothari become her "parents' daughter"?
6. Why does Kothari "want to believe that recipes never change"?
7. What does Kothari accomplish by dividing her essay into separate, numbered sections?

SUGGESTIONS FOR WRITING

1. According to the quotation from Michael Ignatieff with which Kothari prefaces her essay, "To belong is to understand the tacit codes of the people you live with." Without defining or explaining the codes of the people you live with (or have lived with), write an experimental essay showing these people behaving in ways that you were encouraged to emulate.
2. Write a series of scenes in which you show yourself eating foods you like or are expected to eat. Arrange these scenes in a pattern that will help readers understand how your tastes have evolved.
3. Visit a restaurant that serves a kind of food you have never had before. Order a variety of dishes and then explore what you have learned from this experience.

LINKS

■ Within the Book

For another essay about the relationship between food and identity, see "Grub" by Scott Russell Sanders (pages 60–64).

■ Elsewhere in Print

Ignatieff, Michael. *Blood and Belonging: Journeys into the New Nationalism.* New York: Farrar, 1994.

———. *The Warrior's Honor: Ethnic War and the Modern Conscience.* New York: Metropolitan, 1998.

Jaffrey, Madhur. *An Invitation to Indian Cooking.* Hopewell: Ecco, 1999.

Jhabvala, Ruth Prawer. *Heat and Dust.* New York: Harper, 1975.

Kothari, Geeta, ed. *Did My Mama Like to Dance?: And Other Stories about Mothers and Daughters.* New York: Avon, 1994.

Mukherjee, Bharati. *Jasmine.* New York: Grove, 1989.

Seth, Vikram. *A Suitable Boy.* New York: Harper, 1993.

■ Online

www.mhhe.com/motives

Click on "More Resources" then "Writing to Experiment with Form."

■ ■ ■

I WAS BORN

Luc Sante

As a child, Luc Sante moved four times between Belgium and the United States be-
fore his family settled in New York. Reflecting on this experience, he told an interviewer
for the New York Times, *"For me, going back and forth between Belgium and the*
United States when I was a kid, I had the feeling not only of traveling in space but also
traveling in time." Elsewhere, he describes himself as an "outsider" because he grew up
"being both an immigrant and having no ethnic community to belong to as a Belgian—
there aren't many of us Belgians running around." In addition to writing about his search
for identity, Sante also writes social history and popular culture, and his awards include a
Grammy for best album notes.

In the following selection from The Factory of Facts *(1998), Sante experiments with*
autobiography by trying out different versions of his past—thus testing the boundaries
between fiction and nonfiction. When you read "I Was Born," you will find that these
different versions cannot all be true if truth is determined by factual accuracy. Consider
what information seems likely to be accurate and what other kinds of truth are
conveyed by this experiment with form.

I was born on May 25, 1954, in Verviers, Belgium, the only child of Lucien Mathieu Amélie Sante and Denise Lambertine Alberte Marie Ghislaine Nandrin. Following the bankruptcy of my father's employer, an iron foundry that manufactured wool-carding machinery, and at the suggestion of friends who had emigrated earlier, my parents decided to move to the United States in search of work. We arrived at Idlewild Airport in February 1959 and moved in with my parents' friends in Summit, New Jersey. Prospects were not as bright as they had been depicted, and that November we sailed back to Belgium, but the situation there was no better, and early in 1960 we re-emigrated. Several more such trips occurred over the next few years, spurred by momentary hopes, by the Cuban Missile Crisis, by the illnesses and deaths of my maternal grandparents. At length my parents decided to remain in America, at least until the time came when they could retire to Belgium.

I was born in 1954 in Verviers, Belgium, the only child of Lucien and Denise Sante. Following the bankruptcy of my father's employer, an iron foundry that manufactured wool-carding machinery, and at the suggestion of my mother's brother, René Nandrin, my parents decided to move to the Belgian Congo, where my father was to take up a position as local field director for a palm-oil concern. In February 1959, we arrived in Coquilhatville, on the banks of the Congo River, and moved into a company-owned villa in the European district. Suddenly we had servants and a chauffeured car. On the other hand, I came down with a succession of ailments aggravated by the climate and spent most of my time in bed. Barely a year later the Belgian government announced that the Congo would be granted its independence that June, and my parents' friends and colleagues began to show signs of alarm, sending prized possessions, for example, back to their families in Belgium. Emotions had risen to a point of panic by late May, when the first general elections were held. My parents and their friends dismissed their servants, fearing treachery. My father barricaded my mother and me inside the house and would himself not leave without a loaded revolver on his hip. Violent incidents began occurring, most of them in the south of the country, but some close enough that my father, over my mother's protests, sent us home. He followed a little over a month later, when fighting had become widespread; his employer turned over local control to native African managers. Connections made in the Congo led my father to a job with the Ministry of Commerce, and we moved to Berchem-Ste.-Agathe, a suburb of Brussels, where I recovered and later found I had a surprising aptitude for competitive cycling.

I was born in 1954 in Verviers, Belgium, the only child of Lucien and Denise Sante. Following the bankruptcy of his employer, an iron foundry that manufactured wool-carding machinery, my father tried to find another job, but without success. After depleting their savings and selling our house in Pepinster, as well as most of the major household possessions, my parents moved into a succession of progressively smaller and dingier apartments, finally winding up in a single room in Seraing, an industrial suburb of Liège, where my father got a barely remunerative stint as nightwatchman in a warehouse. We endured two years of this as a family. My mother became chronically ill, probably due to stress as much as to bad food and lack of heat, and consequently I was taken in by my cousins in the country. They, too, were feeling the pinch of the economy, however, and palmed me off on other relatives, who in turn passed me along after a while. I spent three years being thus shunted around, until the Christian Brothers admitted me as a hardship case at their boarding school in Liège in the winter of 1964. By then my mother had been hospitalized full-time and my father had retreated into a vigilant and apparently unbreakable silence. At the school I was constantly victimized by the other pupils, most of them offspring of well-to-do families. Finally, at thirteen, I snapped. I set a fire that consumed the dormitory and took the lives of five boys.

I was born in 1954 in Verviers, Belgium, the only child of Lucien and Denise Sante. My father's employer, an iron foundry that manufactured wool-carding machinery, miraculously escaped the effects of the recession of 1958 and the collapse of Verviers's textile industry by a rapid and timely change to the manufacture of radiators. My father, who had worked his way up to junior management from the labor ranks, devised a streamlined method of cooling molds that earned him a succession of promotions, ultimately to the top seat. By 1964 we had sold our row house in Pepinster and moved into a villa in a parklike setting on the heights of the "boulevard" district of Verviers. I grew up fast and was quickly bored by the provincial life around me. I barely maintained passing grades at St. François-Xavier, the local Jesuit *collège,* and would surely have failed and been expelled had it not been for my parents' social and political prominence. As it was, I was taking clandestine excursions—longer and longer ones—out into the world: to Amsterdam, to Paris, to London, to Majorca. I took every drug I could get my hands on, and I was possibly a father several times over; I was adept at vanishing when matters came to a head. My parents' threats to cut off my allowance became steadily more credible until, in the spring of 1971, I bribed the manager of the Place Verte branch of the Générale de Banque and withdrew my entire trust fund in cash—or nearly entire; I left a token five hundred francs. I flew to Marrakech, where I lived for eight months in a hotel frequented by members of British rock groups, until a run-in with one of the Berber chieftains who controlled the hashish traffic from the Rif caused me to fear for my life. I snared a series of van rides that took me to Goa, on the Indian Ocean, where I dwelt in a permanent cloud of dope in a waterfront flat. When my money ran out, I relocated to the beach. I contracted scabies and syphilis, but I didn't care.

I was born in 1954 in Verviers, Belgium, the only child of Lucien and Denise Sante. Following the bankruptcy of my father's employer, an iron foundry that manufactured wool-carding machinery, my parents decided to emigrate to the United States, on no more firm a basis than a visit to the U.S. pavilion at the 1958 Brussels World's Fair. We arrived at Idlewild Airport in February 1959 with eight suitcases, my father's prewar memories of high-school English, and the name of someone's cousin who apparently lived in Long Island, New York, which my parents thought was a town. A taxi driver who knew some French took us to a hotel in Manhattan, which turned out to be a clip joint. We lost three of our suitcases before fleeing to another hotel, respectable enough but commensurately expensive. My parents combed telephone books in search of the cousin, but to no avail. They applied for help from the Belgian consulate and were turned away with frosty finality. They spent days on complex and indeterminate errands, looking for chimeric friends of relatives of friends, my father trying to look for jobs in his field without much idea of where to start. They hadn't imagined it would be like this; without connections or a grasp of the language they were lost. The money was rapidly dwindling, too; already there was not enough left for passage back to Europe, and soon they would no longer be able to foot the hotel bill. On the advice of the chambermaid, a kind woman from Puerto Rico— communication between her and my parents, conducted around a tongue none of them possessed, was comically histrionic—my parents relocated to a

5

dank hostelry near Herald Square where the rooms were lit by fluorescent tubes. We lived on rolls and hot dogs. My mother made me sleep wrapped in a chiffon scarf to protect me from the cockroaches. My father took his watch, of a decent but undistinguished Swiss make, to a pawnshop, where he was given five dollars in return. Our suitcases, minus their contents, followed, and soon my parents' overcoats and their extra pairs of shoes went as well. They were beginning to consider applying to a church for assistance but were hindered by their pride. One day, when it seemed no other option remained, a man who lived down the hall from us offered my father a job. He was to deliver a manila envelope to an address in Newark; he would be paid fifty dollars. He accepted with alacrity and set off. That night, after I had fallen asleep, while my mother wept with fear at having heard nothing from him, two men in dark suits came to our room and took us away. They were FBI agents. My father had been arraigned for interstate traffic in narcotics; the house to which he made his delivery had been under surveillance for several weeks. My mother was held as a material witness in the Essex County Women's Correctional Facility. I was kept in a wing of Juvenile Hall for four days, in the course of which I repeatedly wet my bed and was punished by being deprived of food. Then I was sent to a foster home, with a large and strict Irish-American family in Irvington. My inability to speak English enraged the father, who would take me into the vest-pocket back yard and beat me with a razor strop. I was moved to another foster home, and then another and another—I lost count. I had no news from my parents. After a while I couldn't remember their faces.

I was born in 1954 in Verviers, Belgium, the only child of Lucien and Denise Sante. Following the bankruptcy of my father's employer, an iron foundry that manufactured wool-carding machinery, and with the knowledge that there were no other jobs to be had, a combined result of the collapse of the centuries-old Verviers textile industry and of the recession of 1958, my parents decided to go for broke. They sold our row house in Pepinster and the bulk of its contents, and we set off by train for Biarritz, the beautiful city in France fronting on the Bay of Biscay and backed against the Pyrenees. The trip was glorious; we laughed and sang songs and pointed out the window at the spectacular scenery. When we got there my parents checked into a modest hotel, left me with sandwiches and a pile of comics, and went to the casino. My father's plan was to parlay the stake amassed from selling off their possessions into a small fortune at the baccarat table. It didn't work.

I was born in 1954 in Verviers, Belgium, the only child of Lucien and Denise Sante. Following the bankruptcy of my father's employer, an iron foundry that manufactured wool-carding machinery, my parents sat on the floor. Dust accumulated. Things fell and were not picked up. Mold grew on the potatoes in the cellar. The milk solidified. The electricity was cut off. Neighboring boys threw stones that broke the windows, and cold air blew in.

COMPANION TEXT   *The Great Forgetting*

One of the past lives Sante creates is set in the Congo (also known as Zaire) when it was still a Belgian colony. The treatment of Africans by the white rulers, especially when the Congo was exploited for the personal enrichment of King Leopold II of Belgium, was so brutal that it inspired international outrage and Joseph Conrad's Heart of Darkness *among other literary works. When the Congo gained its independence in 1960, most of the Belgium population fled within a year. The following text comes from the conclusion of* King Leopold's Ghost *(1998), a history designed to keep the world from forgetting the harm that was done to that country.*

History lies heavy on Africa: the long decades of colonialism, several hundred years of the Atlantic and Arab world slave trade, and—all too often ignored—countless centuries of indigenous slavery before that. From the colonial era, the major legacy Europe left to Africa was not democracy as it is practiced today in countries like England, France, and Belgium; it was authoritarian rule and plunder. On the whole continent, perhaps no nation has had a harder time than the Congo in emerging from the shadow of its past.

    When independence finally came to the Congo, the country fared badly. Like most other colonial powers in Africa, Belgium was taken by surprise by the demand for self-rule that swept across the continent in the 1950s, igniting mass demonstrations in Leopoldville in 1959 that were bloodily suppressed by the Force Publique. Until then, Leopold's heirs had thought independence might come, but decades hence. Some Africans were being trained for that distant day; but when pressure grew and independence came in 1960, in the entire territory there were fewer than thirty African university graduates. There were no Congolese army officers, engineers, agronomists, or physicians. The colony's administration had made few other steps toward a Congo run by it's own people: of some five thousand management-level positions in the civil service, only three were filled by Africans.

Adam Hochschild

First insects, then rodents, and eventually birds arrived to make their homes with us. Soon snow covered the dust, and then soot covered the snow. We grew increasingly warm as we slept.

QUESTIONS FOR DISCUSSION

1. When you compare the different versions of Sante's past, are there any elements that seem consistent?
2. In your opinion, which version seems the most probable and which the least?

3. Of the versions in this piece, the fifth is the longest by far. Why do you think this one is so detailed?
4. Can you detect any pattern to the sequence in which Sante has arranged these seven versions of his early life?
5. Consider the final version of Sante's childhood. How well does it serve as the conclusion for this work as a whole?

SUGGESTIONS FOR WRITING

1. Write a fictional account of your childhood in which you imagine what your life would have been like if something quite different from what actually transpired had occurred.
2. Imagine several different versions of your life ten years from now. Write a series of scenes, arranged from least desirable to most desirable, in which you describe future possibilities for yourself.
3. Write a series of short narratives, each beginning with the same information but then taking a different direction. Then arrange these narratives in a pattern that will help readers make sense of them.

LINKS

■ Within the Book

For a more straightforward example of autobiography, see Itabari Njeri's "Life with Father" (pages 71–75).

■ Elsewhere in Print

Hochschild, Adam. *King Leopold's Ghost: A Story of Greed, Terror, and Heroism in Colonial Africa.* Boston: Houghton, 1998.

Muniz, Vik, Luc Sante, and William J. Mitchell. *Making It Real.* New York: Independent Curators, 1997.

Sante, Luc. *Evidence.* New York: Farrar, 1992.

———. *The Factory of Facts.* New York: Pantheon, 1998.

———. *Low Life: Lures and Snares of Old New York.* New York: Farrar, 1991.

Singer, Barnett, and John Langdon. *Cultured Force: Makers and Defenders of the French Cultural Empire.* Madison: U of Wisconsin P, 2004.

■ Online

www.mhhe.com/motives

Click on "More Resources" then "Writing to Experiment with Form."

■ ■ ■

ORANGES AND SWEET SISTER BOY

Judy Ruiz

Judy Ruiz, a poet, essayist, and writing teacher, begins the following essay by announcing that her brother has become her sister—that he has, in other words, become a transsexual. This is hardly the kind of news most people expect to receive when a relative calls them on the phone, and Judy Ruiz decided to write about this unusual experience in an unusual way. As you read, you will find that she has included blocks of text printed in a font different from the one used for most of the essay. Pay close attention to them and see if you can determine how they help Ruiz convey her response to her brother's news.

When asked about what can be achieved by writing essays like "Oranges and Sweet Sister Boy," Ruiz told an interviewer for Creative Nonfiction: *"Most ideally, creative nonfiction ends up saving the people of the world, those of us who have forgotten who we are, those of us who are on fire, those of us who must have stories. Stories are something that people like. Except for the really long, boring ones that leave the reader saying huh or duh after the first sentence; but you have to read them too—if they come to you—because there might be a perfect blue pearl hidden in the middle or near the end, some little sentence that will save you as you scramble around for your own salvation. That scrambling around is pretty much a full-time job."*

I am sleeping, hard, when the telephone rings. It's my brother, and he's calling to say that he is now my sister. I feel something fry a little, deep behind my eyes. Knowing how sometimes dreams get mixed up with not-dreams, I decide to do a reality test at once. "Let me get a cigarette," I say, knowing that if I reach for a Marlboro and it turns into a trombone or a snake or anything else on the way to my lips that I'm still out in the large world of dreams.

The cigarette stays a cigarette. I light it. I ask my brother to run that stuff by me again.

It is the Texas Zephyr° at midnight—the woman in a white suit, the man in a blue uniform; she carries flowers—I know they are flowers. The petals spill and spill into the aisle, and a child goes past this couple who have just come from their own wedding—goes past them and past them, going always to the toilet but really just going past them; and the child could be a horse or she could be the police and they'd not notice her any more than they do, which is not at all—the man's hands high up on the woman's legs, her skirt

---

°*Texas Zephyr:* A long-distance passenger train.

up, her stockings and garters, the petals and finally all the flowers spilling out into the aisle and his mouth open on her. My mother. My father. I am conceived near Dallas in the dark while a child passes, a young girl who knows and doesn't know, who witnesses, in glimpses, the creation of the universe, who feels an odd hurt as her own mother, fat and empty, snores with her mouth open, her false teeth slipping down, snores and snores just two seats behind the Creators.

News can make a person stupid. It can make you think you can do something. So I ask The Blade question, thinking that if he hasn't had the operation yet that I can fly to him, rent a cabin out on Puget Sound. That we can talk. That I can get him to touch base with reality.

"Begin with an orange," I would tell him. "Because oranges are mildly intrusive by nature, put the orange somewhere so that it will not bother you—in the cupboard, in a drawer, even a pocket or a handbag will do. The orange, being a patient fruit, will wait for you much longer than say a banana or a peach."

I would hold an orange out to him. I would say, "This is the one that will   5
save your life." And I would tell him about the woman I saw in a bus station who bit right into her orange like it was an apple. She was wild looking, as if she'd been outside for too long in a wind that blew the same way all the time. One of the dregs of humanity, our mother would have called her, the same mother who never brought fruit into the house except in cans. My children used to ask me to "start" their oranges for them. That meant to make a hole in the orange so they could peel the rind away, and their small hands weren't equipped with fingernails that were long enough or strong enough to do the job. Sometimes they would suck the juice out of the hole my thumbnail had made, leaving the orange flat and sad.

The earrings are as big as dessert plates, filigree gold-plated with thin dangles hanging down that touch her bare shoulders. She stands in front of the Alamo while a bald man takes her picture. The sun is absorbed by the earrings so quickly that by the time she feels the heat, it is too late. The hanging dangles make small blisters on her shoulders, as if a centipede had traveled there. She takes the famous river walk in spiked heels, rides in a boat, eats some Italian noodles, returns to the motel room, soaks her feet, and applies small Band-Aids to her toes. She is briefly concerned about the gun on the nightstand. The toilet flushes. She pretends to be sleeping. The gun is just large and heavy. A .45? A .357 magnum? She's never been good with names. She hopes he doesn't try to. Or that if he does, that it's not loaded. But he'll say it's loaded just for fun. Or he'll pull the trigger and the bullet will lodge in her medulla oblongata, ripping through her womb first, taking everything else vital on the way.

In the magazine articles, you don't see this: "Well, yes. The testicles have to come out. And yes. The penis is cut off." What you get is tonsils. So-and-so has had a "sex change" operation. A sex change operation. How precious. How benign. Doctor, just what do you people do with those penises?

News can make a person a little crazy also. News like, "We regret to inform you that you have failed your sanity hearing."

The bracelet on my wrist bears the necessary information about me, but there is one small error. The receptionist typing the information asked me my religious preference. I said, "None." She typed, "Neon."

> Pearl doesn't have any teeth and her tongue looks weird. She says "Pumpkin pie." That's all she says. Sometimes she runs her hands over my bed sheets and says pumpkin pie. Sometimes I am under the sheets. Marsha got stabbed in the chest, but she tells everyone she fell on a knife. Elizabeth—she's the one who thinks her shoe is a baby—hit me in the back with a tray right after one of the cooks gave me extra toast. There's a note on the bulletin board about a class for the nurses: "How Putting A Towel On Someone's Face Makes Them Stop Banging Their Spoon/OR Reduction of Disruptive Mealtime Behavior By Facial Screening—7 P.M.—Conference Room." Another note announces the topic for remotivation class: "COWS." All the paranoid schizophrenics will be there.
>
> Here, in the place for the permanently bewildered, I fit right in. Not because I stood at the window that first night and listened to the trains. Not because I imagined those trains were bracelets, the jewelry of earth. Not even because I imagined that one of those bracelets was on my own arm and was the Texas Zephyr where a young couple made love and conceived me. I am eighteen and beautiful and committed to the state hospital by a district court judge for a period of one day to life. Because I am a paranoid schizophrenic.
>
> I will learn about cows.

So I'm being very quiet in the back of the classroom, and I'm peeling an orange. It's the smell that makes the others begin to turn around, that mildly intrusive nature. The course is called "Women and Modern Literature," and the diaries of Virginia Woolf are up for discussion except nobody has anything to say. I, of course, am making a mess with the orange; and I'm wanting to say that my brother is now my sister.

Later, with my hands still orangey, I wander in to leave something on a   *10* desk in a professor's office, and he's reading so I'm being very quiet, and then he says, sort of out of nowhere, "Emily Dickinson up there in her room making poems while her brother was making love to her best friend right downstairs on the dining room table. A regular thing. Think of it. And Walt Whitman out sniffing around the boys. Our two great American poets." And I want to grab this professor's arm and say, "Listen. My brother called me and now he's my sister, and I'm having trouble making sense out of my life right now, so would you mind not telling me any more stuff about sex." And I want my knuckles to turn white while the pressure of my fingers leaves imprints right through his jacket, little indentations he can interpret as urgent. But I don't say anything. And I don't grab his arm. I go read a magazine. I find this:

> "I've never found an explanation for why the human race has so many languages. When the brain became a language brain, it obviously needed to develop an intense degree of plasticity. Such plasticity allows languages to be logical, coherent systems and yet be extremely variable. The same brain that thinks in words and symbols is also a brain that has to be freed up with regard to sexual turn-on and partnering. God knows why sex attitudes have not been subject to the corresponding degrees of modification and variety as language. I suspect there's a close parallel between the two. The brain doesn't seem incredibly efficient with regard to sex."

John Money said that. The same John Money who, with surgeon Howard W. Jones, performed the first sex change operation in the United States in 1965 at Johns Hopkins University and Hospital in Baltimore.

Money also tells about the *hijra*° of India who disgrace their families because they are too effeminate: "The ultimate stage of the *hijra* is to get up the courage to go through the amputation of penis and testicles. They had no anesthetic." Money also answers anyone who might think that "heartless members of the medical profession are forcing these poor darlings to go and get themselves cut up and mutilated," or who think the medical profession should leave them alone. "You'd have lots of patients willing to get a gun and blow off their own genitals if you don't do it. I've had several who got knives and cut themselves trying to get rid of their sex organs. That's their obsession!"

Perhaps better than all else, I understand obsession. It is of the mind. And it is language-bound. Sex is of the body. It has no words. I am stunned to learn that someone with an obsession of the mind can have parts of the body surgically removed. This is my brother I speak of. This is not some lunatic named Carl who becomes Carlene. This is my brother.

So while we're out in that cabin on Puget Sound, I'll tell him about LuAnn. She is the sort of woman who orders the in-season fruit and a little cottage cheese. I am the sort of woman who orders a double cheeseburger and fries. LuAnn and I are sitting in her car. She has a huge orange, and she peels it so the peel falls off in one neat strip. I have a sack of oranges, the small ones. The peel of my orange comes off in hunks about the size of a baby's nail. "Oh, you bought the *juice* oranges," LuAnn says to me. Her emphasis on

---

°*hijra:* Males of indeterminate gender because of the nature of their bodies or the way in which they live.

the word "juice" makes me want to die or something. I lack the courage to admit my ignorance, so I smile and breathe "yes," as if I know some secret, when I'm wanting to scream at her about how my mother didn't teach me about fruit and my own blood pounds in my head wanting out, out.

> There is a pattern to this thought as there is a pattern for a jump-suit. Sew the sleeve to the leg, sew the leg to the collar. Put the garment on. Sew the mouth shut. This is how I tell about being quiet because I am bad, and because I cannot stand it when he beats me or my brother.

"The first time I got caught in your clothes was when I was four years old and you were over at Sarah what's-her-name's babysitting. Dad beat me so hard I thought I was going to die. I really thought I was going to die. That was the day I made up my mind I would *never* get caught again. And I never got caught again." My brother goes on to say he continued to go through my things until I was hospitalized. A mystery is solved.

He wore my clothes. He played in my makeup. I kept saying, back then, that someone was going through my stuff. I kept saying it and saying it. I told the counselor at school. "Someone goes in my room when I'm not there, and I *know* it—goes in there and wears my clothes and goes through my stuff." I was assured by the counselor that this was not so. I was assured by my mother that this was not so. I thought my mother was doing it, snooping around for clues like mothers do. It made me a little crazy, so I started deliberately leaving things in a certain order so that I would be able to prove to myself that someone, indeed, was going through my belongings. No one, not one person, ever believed that my room was being ransacked; I was accused of just making it up. A paranoid fixation.

And all the time it was old Goldilocks.

So I tell my brother to promise me he'll see someone who counsels adult children from dysfunctional families. I tell him he needs to deal with the fact that he was physically abused on a daily basis. He tells me he doesn't remember being beaten except on three occasions. He wants me to get into a support group for families of people who are having a sex change. Support groups are people who are in the same boat. Except no one has any oars in the water.

I tell him I know how it feels to think you are in the wrong body. I tell him how I wanted my boyfriend to put a gun up inside me and blow the woman out, how I thought wearing spiked heels and low-cut dresses would somehow help my crisis, that putting on an ultrafeminine outside would mask the maleness I felt needed hiding. I tell him it's the rule, rather than the exception, that people from families like ours have very spooky sexual identity problems. He tells me that his sexuality is a birth defect. I recognize the lingo. It's support-group-for-transsexuals lingo. He tells me he sits down to pee. He told his therapist that he used to wet all over the floor. His therapist said,

15

"You can't aim the bullets if you don't touch the gun." Lingo. My brother is hell-bent for castration, the castration that started before he had language: the castration of abuse. He will simply finish what was set in motion long ago.

I will tell my brother about the time I took ten sacks of oranges into a school so that I could teach metaphor. The school was for special students—those who were socially or intellectually impaired. I had planned to have them peel the oranges as I spoke about how much the world is like the orange. I handed out the oranges. The students refused to peel them, not because they wanted to make life difficult for me—they were enchanted with the gift. One child asked if he could have an orange to take home to his little brother. Another said he would bring me ten dollars the next day if I would give him a sack of oranges. And I knew I was at home, that these children and I shared something that *makes* the leap of mind the metaphor attempts. And something in me healed.

A neighbor of mine takes pantyhose and cuts them up and sews them up   20
after stuffing them. Then she puts these things into Mason jars and sells them, you know, to put out on the mantel for conversation. They are little penises and little scrotums, complete with hair. She calls them "Pickled Peters."

A friend of mine had a sister who had a sex change operation. This young woman had her breasts removed and ran around the house with no shirt on before the stitches were taken out. She answered the door one evening. A young man had come to call on my friend. The sex-changed sister invited him in and offered him some black bean soup as if she were perfectly normal with her red surgical wounds and her black stitches. The young man left and never went back. A couple years later, my friend's sister/brother died when s/he ran a car into a concrete bridge railing. I hope for a happier ending. For my brother, for myself, for all of us.

My brother calls. He's done his toenails: Shimmering Cinnamon. And he's left his wife and children and purchased some nightgowns at a yard sale. His hair is getting longer. He wears a special bra. Most of the people he works with know about the changes in his life. His voice is not the same voice I've heard for years; he sounds happy.

My brother calls. He's always envied me, my woman's body. The same body I live in and have cursed for its softness. He asks me how I feel about myself. He says, "You know, you are really our father's first-born son." He tells me he used to want to be me because I was the only person our father almost loved.

The drama of life. After I saw that woman in the bus station eat an orange as if it were an apple, I went out into the street and smoked a joint with some guy I'd met on the bus. Then I hailed a cab and went to a tattoo parlor. The tattoo artist tried to talk me into getting a nice bird or butterfly design; I had chosen a design on his wall that appealed to me—a symbol I didn't know the meaning of. It is the Yin–Yang, and it's tattooed above my right ankle bone. I supposed my drugged, crazed consciousness knew more than I knew: that yin combines with yang to produce all that comes to be. I am drawn to androgyny.

Of course there is the nagging possibility that my brother's dilemma is   25
genetic. Our father used to dress in drag on Halloween, and he made a beautiful woman. One year, the year my mother cut my brother's blond curls off, my father taped those curls to his own head and tied a silk scarf over the tape. Even his close friends didn't know it was him. And my youngest daughter was a body builder for a while, her lean body as muscular as a man's. And my sons are beautiful, not handsome: they look androgynous.

Then there's my grandson. I saw him when he was less than an hour old. He was naked and had hiccups. I watched as he had his first bath, and I heard him cry. He had not been named yet, but his little crib had a blue card affixed to it with tape. And on the card were the words "Baby Boy." There was no doubt in me that the words were true.

When my brother was born, my father was off flying jets in Korea. I went to the hospital with my grandfather to get my mother and this new brother. I remember how I wanted a sister, and I remember looking at him as my mother held him in the front seat of the car. I was certain he was a sister, certain that my mother was joking. She removed his diaper to show me that he was a boy. I still didn't believe her. Considering what has happened lately, I wonder if my child-skewed consciousness knew more than the anatomical proof suggested.

I try to make peace with myself. I try to understand his decision to alter himself. I try to think of him as her. I write his woman name, and I feel like I'm betraying myself. I try to be open-minded, but something in me shuts down. I think we humans are in big trouble, that many of us don't really have a clue as to what acceptable human behavior is. Something in me says no to all this, that this surgery business is the ultimate betrayal of the self. And yet, I want my brother to be happy.

It was in the city of San Antonio that my father had his surgery. I rode the bus from Kansas to Texas, and arrived at the hospital two days after the operation to find my father sitting in the solarium playing solitaire. He had a type of cancer that particularly thrived on testosterone. And so he was castrated in order to ease his pain and to stop the growth of tumors. He died six months later.

Back in the sleep of the large world of dreams, I have done surgeries   30
under water in which I float my father's testicles back into him, and he—the brutal man he was—emerges from the pool a tan and smiling man, parting the surface of the water with his perfect head. He loves all the grief away.

I will tell my brother all I know of oranges, that if you squeeze the orange peel into a flame, small fires happen because of the volatile oil in the peel. Also, if you squeeze the peel and it gets into your cat's eyes, the cat will blink and blink. I will tell him there is no perfect rhyme for the word "orange," and that if we can just make up a good word we can be immortal. We will become obsessed with finding the right word, and I will be joyous at our legitimate pursuit.

I have purchased a black camisole with lace to send to my new sister. And a card. On the outside of the card there's a drawing of a woman sitting by a pond and a zebra is off to the left. Inside are these words: "The past is ended. Be happy." And I have asked my companions to hold me and I have cried. My self is wet and small. But it is not dark. Sometimes, if no one touches me, I will die.

Sister, you are the best craziness of the family. Brother, love what you love.

QUESTIONS FOR DISCUSSION

1. What is the purpose of the blocks of text included in paragraphs 2, 5, 8, 10, and 13?
2. In paragraphs 4, 5, and 19, Ruiz imagines how an orange could help her brother. Why would anyone consider the orange to be "a patient fruit"? How do oranges relate to her brother's situation and her own?
3. What does Ruiz reveal about her own experience in the process of responding to her brother's call? Why is she comforted to discover that her brother used to wear her clothes?
4. Ruiz tells her brother that people from dysfunctional families have "very spooky sexual identity problems"? Is this a fair response to her brother? Is it reasonable to assume that someone who has undergone a sex change did so as the result of a sexual identity "problem"?
5. Although she reports making a serious effort to empathize with her brother, Ruiz also writes, "I try to be open-minded, but something in me shuts down. I think we humans are in big trouble, that many of us don't really have a clue as to what acceptable human behavior is." Do you have a clue? How would you respond if someone close to you chose to have a sex-change operation?

SUGGESTIONS FOR WRITING

1. Think of someone who is relatively close to you and yet very different from you. Write an essay in which you explore what draws you together and what keeps you apart.
2. Consider occasions in your life when you have received important news. Write an essay conveying how this news inspired diverse feelings and

memories. Like Ruiz, experiment with including blocks of memories and other responses in your principal narrative.

3. Imagine that for some compelling reason you must spend a week living as a gender different from your own but still living your life as regularly as possible. Although your body has changed, you feel like essentially the same person on the inside. With this situation in mind, experiment by writing a series of collagelike scenes (see pages 610–612) describing events or encounters in the course of that week.

LINKS

■ Within the Book

In "Levi's" (pages 55–58), Marilyn Schiel also writes about the relationship between siblings of different gender.

■ Elsewhere in Print

Boylan, Jennifer. *She's Not There: A Life in Two Genders.* New York: Broadview, 2003.

Brown, Mildred C., and Chloe A. Rounsley. *True Selves: Understanding Trans-sexualism.* San Francisco: Jossey-Bass, 1996.

Califia, Pat. *Sex Changes: The Politics of Transgenderism.* San Francisco: Cleis, 1997.

Colapinto, John. *As Nature Made Him: The Boy Who Was Raised as a Girl.* New York: Harper, 2000.

Fausto-Sterling, Anne. *Sexing the Body: Gender Politics and the Construction of Sexuality.* New York: Basic, 2000.

Ruiz, Judy. *Talking Razzmatazz: Poems.* Columbia: U of Missouri P, 1991.

■ Online

www.mhhe.com/motives

Click on "More Resources" then "Writing to Experiment with Form."

■ ■ ■

Appendix: Documenting Sources and Avoiding Plagiarism

When you document sources that you have drawn upon for a paper of your own, you increase your credibility with readers and provide them with additional information that may be helpful to them. Your credibility is enhanced by demonstrating that you have undertaken research and kept track of where you acquired the material you have integrated into your paper. And documentation gives readers interested by your work a sense of where they can continue to read about the topic you have addressed. Properly documenting sources is especially important in academic discourse. At stake is nothing less than your personal integrity and your responsibility to your audience.

Failure to provide documentation where it is necessary means that you have not only discarded two important benefits, it also means that you may be considered guilty of plagiarism. Most colleges and universities have strict policies regarding plagiarism. If you pass off another person's ideas as your own, you violate the trust of your audience and can be subject to serious penalties—such as failing the class in which you submitted the work in question.

The first step to properly documenting sources is to keep an accurate record of the works you consult and what ideas, facts, opinions, or quotations come from which source. In the case of print publication, you will need to record the author, title, and date of a source—as well as additional information (such as the page number, the publisher of a book and the journal title and volume number for a scholarly article). For an online source, you will need to record the accurate URL, the date you were able to retrieve it, and the date when it was first posted or last updated.

Here is a list of the kinds of material you will need to document when incorporating research into a paper of your own.

- Direct quotations
- Paraphrases of quotations
- Ideas and opinions that come from other writers
- Specific data or facts that are not common knowledge

◼▨◼▨◼ AVOIDING PLAGIARISM

Plagiarism is defined as deliberately passing off someone else's language or ideas or other original material as your own without acknowledging the source you used.* It has also been defined as "intellectual theft" and "fraud"— theft because the plagiarist is taking something that belongs to someone else, and fraud because the plagiarist is deceiving others. It has become an increasing problem because of the ease with which material can be cut and pasted from the Internet. Someone who assembles a paper by cutting and pasting unacknowledged work by others—or even goes so far as to download a whole paper found online—is almost certain to understand that unethical (and possibly illegal) conduct is in question.

But there are other kinds of plagiarism that can happen simply because a writer does not fully understand academic expectations for the proper use of material obtained through research. For example, while most students know that a direct quotation should be documented, some think that they can use material (without documenting it) simply by changing the wording. But plagiarism occurs if the wording is too close to the original and ideas follow in the same sequence. Here is an original passage from an essay written by Susan Sontag and published in the *New York Times Magazine.*

> The pictures taken by American soldiers in Abu Ghraib, however, reflect a shift in the use made of pictures—less objects to be saved than messages to be disseminated, circulated. A digital camera is a common possession among soldiers. Where once photographing war was the province of photojournalists, now the soldiers themselves are all photographers—recording their war, their fun, their observations of what they find picturesque, their atrocities—and swapping images among themselves and e-mailing them across the globe.

The following paraphrase requires documentation:

> The photographs from the Iraq war are different than the war photography of previous wars. Rather than items taken and selected by photojournalists, these photos were taken by the perpetrators themselves, via digital camera, and meant to be sent anywhere across the world as messages.

Although the wording is different, the paraphrase conveys the same ideas as the original in the same sequence, and there is no reference to Sontag, so the author could be charged with plagiarism. To rectify the problem, the author needs to cite Sontag (according to one of the documentation styles discussed later in this appendix).

However, not all ideas are as distinct as Sontag's. Many ideas that you include in an essay might be common knowledge and so not need to be docu-

---

*This definition is modified from the Council of Writing Program Administrators' statement "Defining and Avoiding Plagiarism."

mented. Of course, what is "common knowledge" is determined by your rhetorical situation—your purpose, audience, and context. If you were writing a proposal in an engineering course, for example, certain equations and facts would be common knowledge to engineers. However, in a similar proposal for the general public, you would need to explain and document equations and facts that a layperson might not know.

For an interactive tutorial on avoiding plagiarism, go to www.mhhe.com/motives and click on "Research" then "Avoiding Plagiarism."

■■■■■ STYLES OF DOCUMENTATION

As you proceed with any project in which you draw upon the work of other writers, you need to employ a single documentation style, and the documentation style you use may vary from one course to another. Different disciplines use different documentation styles. For example, each discipline in the natural sciences has its own documentation style. And the *Chicago Manual of Style* is often used by scholars and editors in a range of fields. A list of relevant handbooks can be found on pages 40–41. Your professor will usually tell you what documentation style to use when giving you an assignment. If not, you should ask.

This appendix introduces you to two of the styles most frequently required for work by college students: MLA style and APA style. It concludes with a student essay with MLA-style documentation. Additional information about documentation can be found by going to the book's website, www.mhhe.com.

For software that will help you format your citations, go to www.mhhe.com/motives and click on "Research" then "Bibliomaker."

Modern Language Association (MLA) Documentation Style

The Modern Language Association (MLA) style is generally used for essays and published work in literature, the arts, and the humanities.

MLA In-Text Citations

The MLA allows for using footnotes or endnotes to document sources. (For an example, see pages 403–409.) But it recommends using parenthetical citations in the text of your work whenever you use a quotation, idea, statistic, or fact that you obtained elsewhere. These citations include the author's (or authors') last name, followed by the page where the material in question can be found. Leave a space between the author's name and the page number, but do not separate them with punctuation or abbreviate the word *page*. If you mention the author's name when introducing the material you obtained from him or her, you should give only the page number, because including the author's name would be redundant.

Here are some examples showing how the same source can be cited, depending on how it is being introduced or used. In this case, the book being referenced is *King Leopold's Ghost,* by Adam Hochschild. (See page 669 for the bibliographic form for citing this work.)

Standard Citation

> Central African sculpture influenced artists such as Picasso because "the human face and figure are broken apart and formed again in new ways and proportions that had previously lain beyond the sight of traditional European realism" (Hochschild 73).

The period follows the parenthetical citation.

Citation When Author's Name Appears in the Text

> Hochschild argues that in central African sculpture "the human face and figure are broken apart and formed again in new ways that had previously lain beyond the sight of traditional European realism" (73).

Because the author's name appears shortly before the quote, it is not repeated in the parenthetical citation.

Citation When More Than One Work by the Same Author Appears in the Bibliography

> Hochschild argues that in central African sculpture "the human face and figure are broken apart and formed again in new ways that had previously lain beyond the sight of traditional European realism" (Ghost 73).

A key word from the work's title is added if the bibliography includes more than one work by the author in question. In this case, the author's name appears in the text. If the author's name appears in the parenthetical citation, a comma separates his or her name from the shortened title: (Hochschild, Ghost 73).

Long Citation

> Discussing the sculpture that was brought back to Europe from the Congo, Hochschild argues:
>
> > It is easy to see the distinctive brilliance that so entranced Picasso and his colleagues at their first encounter with this art at an exhibit in Paris in 1907. In these central African sculptures some body parts are exaggerated, some shrunken; eyes project, cheeks sink, mouths disappear, torsos become elongated; eye sockets expand to cover almost the entire face; the human face and figure are broken apart and formed again in new ways and

> proportions that had previously lain beyond the sight of traditional European realism. (73)

When a quotation takes more than four lines of text, it should be set off as a block, indented ten spaces (or one inch) from the left margin. Quotation marks are not used, because they would be redundant: The indention indicates quotation. In this case, the period ends the sentence because the page number is clearly linked to the quotation.

Indirect Quotation

> In a letter about his work to end colonial abuse in the Congo, E. D. Morel confides that his "home life is reduced to microscopic proportions" (qtd. in Hochschild 210).

The abbreviation *qtd.* stands for "quoted." In this case, the reference to E. D. Morel establishes who wrote the words in question. The reference to Hochschild establishes where the quotation was found.

Citation from the Internet

> Although the Social Security Program is likely to continue in some form, the retirement age at which people will be eliigle for benefits may well increase to seventy (Sullivan).

When there are no page numbers, paragraph numbers, or screen numbers supplied within a text that you retrieve from the web, you provide the author's last name and readers will understand that this is an online source when they refer to your list of works cited. If such numbers are provided, conclude with that information—for example, (par. 6). But do not add them if they are not already in the source.

MLA Works-Cited List

At the end of a paper using MLA-style parenthetical citations, you should add a bibliography that provides additional information about the sources you used. This bibliography is called "Works Cited" and should include all sources cited but no sources that you did not cite. The entries in this list are arranged alphabetically according to the authors' last names. When an entry takes more than one line, additional lines should be indented five spaces (or one-half inch).

Book with One Author

> Hochschild, Adam. <u>King Leopold's Ghost: A Story of Greed, Terror, and Heroism in Colonial Africa</u>. Boston: Houghton, 1998.

When a book has a subtitle, include it (preceded by a colon) after the title. MLA-style calls for identifying commercial publishers by choosing a key word from the company's name. In this case, Houghton Mifflin becomes Houghton.

Following this principle, Random House becomes Random, and Alfred Knopf becomes Knopf (because words like "House" and "Alfred" are less specific).

Book with More Than One Author

> Pope, Jr., Harrison, Katherine A. Philips, and Roberto Olivarda. The Adonis Complex: The Secret Crisis of Male Body Obsession. New York: Free, 2000.

When a book has more than one author, give the last name first only for the first author because this last name determines where to place the entry alphabetically in the list of works cited. Follow the order in which the authors are listed on the title page. A title like "Jr." or "III" follows the last name.

Edited Book

> Busby, Mark, and Dick Heaberlin, eds. From Texas to the World and Back: Essays on the Journeys of Katherine Anne Porter. Fort Worth: Texas Christian UP, 2001.

The editors' names take the place of an author's name, and they are identified as editors by the abbreviation *eds.* For a book with only one editor, use the abbreviation *ed.*

Reprinted Book

> Cather, Willa. The Professor's House. 1925. New York: Vintage, 1990.

This work was first published in 1925, but the text used was published in 1990. Omitting the date of original publication would give the impression that the book was first published in 1990. The 1925 edition cannot be cited unless that is what was actually used. Citing the date of first publication along with the date of the reprint tells readers that this book was attracting readers sixty-five years after it first appeared; it also establishes exactly which edition was used in case variations appear from one edition to another.

Translated Book

> Godelier, Maurice. The Enigma of the Gift. Trans. Nora Scott. Chicago: U of Chicago P, 1999.

The translator's name appears immediately after the title. When citing material published by university presses, use the abbreviations *U* for University and *P* for Press. The University of Chicago Press becomes U of Chicago P; Oxford University Press becomes Oxford UP; the University Press of Virginia becomes UP of Virginia.

Work with a Group or Organization as Author

> National Parent Teacher Association. National Standards for Parent/Family Involvement Programs. Chicago: National PTA, 1997.

Credit the organization, group, commission, association, or corporation as the author if its individual members are not identified on the title page.

Article in a Scholarly Journal

> Friedrich, Paul. "Tolstoy, Homer, and Genotypical Influence." Comparative
>   Literature. 56 (2004): 283–299.

The volume number precedes the year of publication, which appears within parentheses. Issue numbers are not necessary when a journal's pages are numbered consecutively throughout the year (so that each issue begins with the page number that would follow from the last page in the previous issue). If each issue of a journal begins with page 1, then add the issue number after the volume number, separating the two by a period (22.2).

Article in a Magazine

> Hilton, Isabel. "Royal Blood." New Yorker 30 July 2001: 42–57.

Include the issue's date immediately after the magazine's title. In this case, the citation is for a magazine published weekly, so the day of the month is placed before the month. (In the case of a monthly magazine, give only the month and year: Feb. 2002.) Abbreviate the names of months except for those that are only three or four letters long: May, June, and July. The MLA calls for the use of the following abbreviations: Jan., Feb., Mar., Apr., Aug., Sept., Oct., Nov., and Dec.

When a magazine article begins on one page and is continued elsewhere in the magazine (not on the next page of text), give the page where the article begins and add the mathematical symbol for plus: 17+.

Article with No Author

> "New Fuel for the Culture Wars." The Economist 28 Feb. 2004: 24–28.

When there is no author, the title is the first item in the citation. In this case, you alphabetize by the title.

Editorial in a Periodical

> "Down and Dirty in the Gun Debate." Editorial. New York Times 27 Feb.
>   2004: A26.

The word *editorial,* capitalized and followed with a period, comes after the title.

Letter to the Editor of a Periodical

> Campell-Orde, John. Letter. The Atlantic Mar. 2004: 14–16.

As with editorials, the word *letter* directly follows the title. If there is no title for the letter, just include the author's name.

Article in an Anthology

> Yaeger, Patricia. "White Dirt: The Surreal Landscapes of Willa Cather's South."
> Willa Cather's Southern Connections: New Essays on Cather and the South.
> Ed. Ann Romines. Charlottesville: UP of Virginia, 2000. 138–55.

In this case, the citation indicates that the article by Yaeger was first published in the anthology edited by Romines. If a scholarly article was reprinted in an anthology (after being first published elsewhere), you need to provide information about the original publication as well as the anthology in which the work was located.

> Cushman, Ellen. "The Rhetorician as an Agent for Social Change." College Composition and Communication 47 (1996): 7–28. Rpt. in On Writing Research:
> The Braddock Essays 1975–1998. Ed. Lisa Ede. Boston: Bedford, 1999.
> 372–89.

Note that two sets of pages are given: the pages in the journal issue where the piece originally appeared and the pages in which the piece can be found in the anthology that was consulted. Note also that the abbreviation *Rpt.* stands for "reprinted."

For an essay or nonscholarly article that was originally published elsewhere, you may simply add the year of original publication (followed by a period) between the title of the piece and the title of the anthology in which you found it.

> Stark, Peter. "As Freezing People Recollect the Snow, First the Chill, Then the
> Stupor, Then the Letting Go." 1997. Motives for Writing. 5th ed. Ed. Robert
> K. Miller. New York: McGraw-Hill, 2006. 107–115.

An Entire Internet Site

> International Virginia Woolf Society. Ed. Melba Cutty-Keane and Alan C.W.
> Chong. 31 Aug. 2002. 11 Apr. 2005 <http://www.utoronto.ca/IVWS/>.

Begin with the underlined name of the site, and then add the name(s) of the editor(s) who maintain the site if available. Provide the date when the site was published or last updated followed by the date when you were able to retrieve it.

The publication date establishes how recent the material is; the access date establishes how recently you were able to retrieve it. Providing an accurate URL is essential. Locate the URL within angle brackets.

An Anonymous Source Published Online by a Sponsoring Organization

> Alternatives to Food Irradiation. 8 Aug. 2002. Organic Consumers Assn. 5 Sept.
> 2001 <http://www.purefood.org/irad/Alertnatives.cfm>.

Begin with the underlined title of the source you used; include the name of the sponsoring organization or institution after the date of access.

A Home Page for a Course

> Warren, Martin. Issues in English Studies. Course home page. 16 Apr. 2003.
> Dept. of English, University of St. Thomas. 10 Apr. 2005 <http://
> www.stthomas.edu/english/issues>.

Begin with the instructor's name followed by the course title. Add *Course home page* (without italicizing or underlining) followed by the academic department and the name of the school where that department is located.

Magazine Article Available Online

> Starobin, Paul. "The Accidental Autocrat." <u>Atlantic Online</u> March 2005. 10 Apr.
> 2005 <http://www.theatlantic.com/prem/200503/starobin>.

Give the issue date, followed by a period, and then provide the date of access.

Newspaper Article Available Online

> Markon, Jerry. "Va. Colleges May Bar Illegal Immigrants." <u>Washington Post</u> 25 Feb.
> 2004. <u>washingtonpost.com</u> 27 Feb. 2004. <http://www.washingtonpost.com/
> wp-dyn/articles/A6936-2004Feb25.html>.

Include the newspaper title after the article title, followed by the date of original publication.

Email

> Hadley, Destiny. "Re: Production Questions Arising." Email to author.
> 1 Mar. 2004.

After the subject line of the email, indicate that the source is an "Email to author."

Posting to a Newsgroup

> Peter, Frank. "CFP Islam and the Dynamics of European National Societies."
> Online posting. 26 Feb. 2004. 27 Feb. 2004. <http://www.h-net.org/search>

After the title of the post, indicate that the source is an "Online posting." Otherwise, treat it the same as you would an Internet source.

American Psychological Association (APA) Documentation Style

The style of the American Psychological Association (APA) is generally used for papers and published work in psychology and the social sciences, such as education, sociology, and anthropology.

APA In-Text Citations

Like the MLA, the APA encourages writers to use parenthetical citations instead of footnotes or endnotes for documentation. Like the MLA, the APA also expects writers to document quotations, ideas, statistics, and facts that are not common knowledge. The most significant difference between the two styles of parenthetical citation is that, unlike the MLA, which calls for the author's last name and the page number, the APA calls for the author's last name and the year in which the author's work was published. There are two reasons for this: Social scientists want to see immediately how current the research being cited is, and writers in the social sciences often cite entire studies as opposed to specific passages. But when a specific passage is cited, APA-style parenthetical citation can incorporate a page reference in addition to the author's name and the year of publication:

> Good teaching requires integrity and emotional commitment (Palmer, 1998).

Or:

> Palmer (1998) argues that good teaching requires integrity and emotional commitment.

Or:

> Palmer believes that education is fostered through the creation of a "community of truth" (1998, p. 128).

APA-Style Reference Lists

APA-style bibliographies are titled "References"; they include information about the sources cited in the article or book, and these sources are arranged in alphabetical order by the authors' last names. APA style observes rules for capitalization and punctuation that are quite different from those of the MLA:

- Only the first word of a book or article title (and the first word of the subtitle if there is one) is capitalized. All other words appear in lowercase (unless the word would be capitalized when it is not part of a title, in which case the capital is retained).
- Article titles do not appear within quotation marks.
- The main words in a journal title (unlike an article or book title) are all capitalized.
- Books and journal titles are italicized as are some punctuation marks.

Moreover, the APA calls for using different kinds of indentation in bibliographic entries, depending upon whether a writer is submitting "copy manuscript" or "final manuscript." Copy-manuscript indentation should be used when an article or book is submitted to a publisher; final-manuscript style should be followed by students submitting a paper to a college or university professor. The following examples are indented in final-manuscript style.

Book with One Author

> Palmer, P. J. (1998). *The courage to teach: Exploring the inner landscape of a teacher's life.* San Francisco: Jossey-Bass.

First and middle names are indicated only by initials. Only the first word in the title and subtitle is capitalized. A colon separates the title from the subtitle. When the state of publication is unclear, add it after the city: Bakersfield, CA, but not San Francisco, CA.

Book with Two or More Authors

Belenky, M. F., Clinchy, B. M., Goldberger, N. R., & Tarule, J. M. (1986). *Women's ways of knowing: The development of self, voice, and mind*. New York: Basic Books.

Place last name first for all authors, and use the ampersand (&) instead of "and."

Translated Book

Mauss, M. (1990). *The gift: The forms and reason for exchange in archaic societies* (W. D. Halls, Trans.). New York: Norton. (Original work published 1922)

In this case, the English translation was published long after the work was published in its original language.

Article in a Scholarly Journal

Connors, G. L., & Walitzer, K. S. (2001). Reducing alcohol consumption among heavily drinking women: Evaluating the contributions of life-skills training and booster sessions. *Journal of Consulting and Clinical Psychology, 69,* 447–456.

Capitalization of journal titles differs from capitalization of book and article titles. Quotation marks are not used around the article title. If citing from a journal in which each issue begins with page 1, add the issue number within parentheses immediately after the volume number: *27*(3).

Article in a Magazine

Denny, M. (2001, May). The rewards of chance. *Natural History, 110,* 75–82.

The month is inserted after the year. In this case, the magazine is published monthly. If citing from a magazine published weekly, add the day listed on the issue: (2002, March 14).

Article in an Anthology

Delacour, J. (1996). A model of the brain and the memory system. In H. L. Roitblat & J. Meyer (Eds.), *Comparative approaches to cognitive science* (pp. 305–327). Cambridge, MA: MIT Press.

A period follows the article title but not the book title. In this case, the anthology has two editors. When an anthology has a single editor, use the abbreviation *Ed.* instead of *Eds.*

Web Site

> *Eating Disorders Awareness and Prevention Home Page* (September 6, 2001).
> Seattle: Eating Disorders Awareness and Prevention, Inc. Retrieved
> September 10, 2001 from http://www.edap.org/

When an author is not identified, begin with the title followed by the date of posting or the most recent update. (In the above example, words after the first one are capitalized because they are part of a name that would be capitalized outside a title.) Provide the name of the sponsoring organization even if this repeats information in the title. Provide the date you used this site, and conclude with the URL (which is not followed by a period). When an author is identified, use the following pattern: author/date/title/city of publication/ sponsoring organization/date of access/electronic address.

Article from an Electronic Version of a Printed Journal

> Deangelis, T. (2002, March). Promising treatments for anorexia and bulimia
> (Electronic version). *Monitor on Psychology, 33*(3). Retrieved March 15,
> 2004, from http://www.apa.org/monitor/mar02/promising.html

If you are citing the electronic version of an article that also appears in print, note that it is an electronic version after the title.

Posting to a Newsgroup

> Sufian, S. (2004, February 14). Mental disability in Iraq. H-Disability Discussion
> Group. Message posted to http://www.h-net.org/~disabil/

Include the title of the post followed by the title of the group.

■■■■ SAMPLE STUDENT RESEARCH PAPER IN MLA STYLE

The following paper demonstrates MLA-style documentation and also shows how to organize an argument according to classical arrangement (see pages 459–460). Rebecca wrote her argument in response to an assignment that urged students to address a local or statewide issue that concerned them and to imagine, as their audience, people who were in a position to act upon what the argument proposed. Completing this assignment at a university in Minnesota, she decided to address the governor of Minnesota, the state's education commissioner, the speaker of the house, and the minority leader of the house. You will find that she reaches out to this audience at two points in her argument and that she uses statistics that are likely to impress government officials. As you read, be alert for how Rebecca anticipates potential objections to her proposal and tries to establish how it is reasonable.

For another sample of a student paper in MLA style, visit www.mhhe.com/ motives and click on "Research" then "Sample Paper in MLA Style."

Schmoll 1

Rebecca Schmoll

Professor Miller

English 252

20 Apr. 2005

Abstinence-Only Is Not the Only Way

There is an epidemic going on with today's youth that demands action.

After declining in the early 1990s, the rate of sexually transmitted diseases

in Minnesota has been on the increase for the past five to seven years,

jumping nearly 19% in the year 2002 alone (Marcotty, Diseases). According

to data released by the state Health Department in May of 2004, "sexually

transmitted diseases continued unabated in 2003 among teenagers and

young adults in Minnesota" (Marcotty, Diseases).

Minnesota's Health Department also reports that, since 2002, the

number of new diagnoses of chlamydia, gonorrhea, and syphilis increased

by six percent, with the majority of increases occurring in 15–24 year olds.

Seven out of every ten chlamydia cases and half of all gonorrhea cases

were reported among adolescents and young adults (Marcotty, Diseases).

Other STDs such as herpes and HPV (Human Papillomavirus), both incurable,

are also showing significant increases among youth. Between 15% and

20% of youth, nationwide, will become infected with herpes by the time

they reach adulthood and 28% to 46% of young women under the age of

25 are infected with HPV (Tracking). What is even more alarming is the

number of people who are unaware that they have been infected with

an STD. Only 20% of people with herpes know that they are infected,

while 75% of women and 50% of men with chlamydia have no symptoms at

all (Tracking).

Double space between date and title and between title and first paragraph

Introduction establishes the problem.

Author has two works cited, so this work is identified with short title, "Diseases."

Facts relevant as background.

Schmoll 2

Additional background.

Teenagers and young adults are more likely than any other age group to engage in unprotected sex. A 1995 Minnesota Student Survey indicated that 31% of sexually active 9th grade females and 43% of sexually active 12th grade females reported that they did not use a condom the last time they had intercourse. This same survey reported that 54% of students are sexually active by their senior year, a number that has not decreased in recent years (Minnesota School 12-2).

Parenthetical documentation shows an online source with separate chapters and pages.

According to the Center for Adolescent Health and Development at the University of Minnesota, teen pregnancy in Minnesota is also part of the sexual epidemic among youth. A sexually active teen that does not use contraception has a 90% chance of getting pregnant within one year (Work 7). Each year there are 9,440 teen pregnancies in Minnesota. Of these, 57%

Page number indicates that this electronic source included pagination.

Significance of background.

result in live births and 28% in abortion (Grow). Nationally, 4 in 10 teenage girls become pregnant at least once before the age of 20 (Work 3).

The financial aspect of STDs in our country is just as alarming as the actual diseases. In 1994, the direct and indirect costs of the major STDs and their complications were estimated to total almost $17 billion annually (Tracking). As the number of STDs has increased in recent years, it can be assumed that the cost of STDs today is even higher than the $17 billion in 1994.

Certainly no one argues that this is an important issue among youth that needs to be addressed. There is, however, opposition in how to address it. While I commend you leaders of Minnesota on implementing new academic standards in Minnesota, the new standards do not require any sort of curriculum guideline for teaching health. Rather, the method of sex education, either abstinence-only or comprehensive sex education, which teaches both

Appeal to audience.

Schmoll 3

abstinence and contraception, is left up to each individual school district. Since

districts are required to develop their own assessments, none of which are

reported to the state, there is no accountability to ensure students have

learned what they have been taught in health class.

Minnesota's greatest effort, thus far, in preventing STDs and pregnancy

among youth has been ENABL (Education Now and Babies Later), the state's

$5 million abstinence-only sex education program taught to 45,500 Minnesota   *Author establishes that the current system is not working.*

junior high students. But according to an independent study commissioned

by the Minnesota Department of Health, it isn't working. The study revealed

that "sexual activity among junior high students at three schools where the

program was taught doubled between 2001 and 2002—a pattern similar to

that exhibited by kids statewide—and that the number who said they would

probably have sex during high school nearly doubled, as well" (Marcotty,

State).

In response to the study, Minnesota's Health Department recommended

broadening the program to include more information about contraception.

And they are apparently not the only ones. Part of a follow-up study on

ENABL included a survey of the parents of students in the program. An

overwhelming 77% of parents felt it was best both to promote abstinence

and teach about contraception, while only 20% felt abstinence-only was the

best approach (Minnesota Education 64).

In response to ENABL's expensive and apparently ineffective solution   *Author's proposal: statewide standards for comprehensive sex education.*

to preventing teenage sex, as well as the alarming increases in sexually

transmitted diseases and pregnancy among Minnesota teens, I propose that

Minnesota's new Academic Standards be further changed to include statewide

standards in Health Education that promote comprehensive sex education.

Schmoll 4

Teen's sexual beliefs, attitudes, perceived norms, and confidence strongly correlate to their sexual and contraceptive behavior, all of which can be strengthened through education (Work 14). In many aspects, our society tries to raise knowledgeable individuals who know all the facts so that they can make informed decisions. Why should sex education be any different? Abstinence should by all means be a part of sex education as it is the only sure way to prevent pregnancy and sexually transmitted diseases. Students should be made thoroughly aware of this and know the consequences of not abstaining from sex. However, they should also learn how to protect themselves once they do become sexually active. This includes being taught the proper use of condoms, where teens can get condoms and other forms of birth control, as well as how they can get tested for STDs. They deserve *all* the facts.

Comprehensive sex education programs are effective because they cover an array of subjects and start educating children in grade school with age-appropriate lessons. Concepts include human development, relationships, sexual behavior, and sexual health. According to Pardini, "Children in primary grades, for example, might be taught about inappropriate touching. Fourth graders are introduced to the human reproductive system. In middle school, students begin learning about contraception, and in high school, about the responsibilities and consequences inherent in sexual relationships."

By far, the greatest benefit of comprehensive sex education is that it teaches abstinence along with contraception options. A program such as this can thoroughly educate youth without encouraging premarital sex. By continuously pressing the benefits of abstinence, students are still learning that it is the best way to protect themselves. However, by

Margin annotations:

Support for proposal.

Author makes a concession likely to please opposition.

Source introduced in text.

Quote expands author's proposal.

Schmoll 5

providing students with contraceptive information, they will be prepared

when they do decide to become sexually active. In fact, a 2001 Surgeon

General report found that the abstinence-only approach increases the

chance that youth will neglect to use condoms or other contraceptives

when they do become sexually active—putting them at a higher risk for

disease and pregnancy than kids who were taught contraception practices

(Sex Ed).

    Teaching comprehensive sex education goes beyond high school

graduation in that it prepares students who remained abstinent in high

school, if they become sexually active once in college. A recent study,

by the American Psychological Association, found that more than sixty

percent of college students who had pledged virginity during their middle

or high school years had broken their vow to remain abstinent until

marriage (Brody). If college students such as these decide years after their

abstinent-only education to become sexually active, they may lack the

resources and knowledge to protect themselves from STDs and pregnancy.

The ignorance and lack of proper sex education of students such as these

can be reflected in two quotes from anonymous college students: "I just

don't see AIDS as being much of a threat to heterosexuals, and I don't

find a lot of pleasure in using a condom," says a male college student.

"I have an attitude, it may be wrong, that any guy I would sleep with

would not have AIDS," says a female college student in explaining

why she doesn't insist that her partner use a condom (Strong 300).

Certainly comments like these illustrate the need for comprehensive

sex education that teaches proper protection as well as the true facts

about STDs.

Additional support for proposal.

Quote illustrates author's point. Documentation shows that it is from a printed source.

Schmoll 6

Another benefit to comprehensive sex education is that it stresses the

fact that sex and its consequences should be taken seriously without using

scare or shame tactics, used in abstinence-only programs. In 1991, the video

Additional support.

"No Second Chance," which discusses AIDS and teaches abstinence, shows a

student asking the school nurse, "What if I want to have sex before I get

married?" The nurse responds with, "Well, I guess you'll just have to be

Author uses another printed source with page numbers.

prepared to die" (Levine 106). Another scare or shame tactic used in

abstinence programs is a pledge to virginity, intended to make one who

breaks the pledge feel shameful. Aside from making a person feel bad upon

breaking a virginity pledge, these pledges typically delay the onset of sexual

activity by approximately 18 months, and youths who made one are more

likely to have unprotected sex after breaking it than youth who never pledged

their virginity (Brody).

Argument turns to refuting oppositional claims.

Comprehensive sex education programs are based on factual information,

where abstinence-only programs have recently been shown to give false

information. A congressional report released in November 2004 found that teens

taking abstinence-only courses are frequently receiving "medically inaccurate

or misleading information, often in direct contradiction to the findings of

government scientists" (Connolly A6). Several million youth have participated

A newspaper article is identified by section as well as by page.

in numerous federally funded abstinence-only programs since they began in

1999. Thirteen of the most commonly used curricula were reviewed in the

report, revealing that 11 of the 13 programs, used by 69 organizations in

25 states, contained "unproved claims, subjective conclusions, or outright

falsehoods" (Connolly A6). Among the misconceptions cited: touching a

person's genitals can result in pregnancy, HIV can be spread via sweat and

tears, and condoms fail to prevent HIV transmission as often as 31% of the

Schmoll 7

time in heterosexual intercourse. According to federal researchers, condoms are 97% effective at preventing pregnancy and STDs when used correctly and consistently (Connolly A6).

Another example of abstinence-only supporters giving misleading information can be found in an article that claims youth need to know that if they choose to become sexually active, they have a one in four chance of contracting an STD by the age of 21 (Wallace). While it is true that 1 in 4 sexually active teenagers will contract an STD by adulthood, this article leaves out the fact that if condoms are used correctly, a teenager will have less than 3% of a chance of being one of the 25% of teens with an STD. Comprehensive programs give the whole truth about all aspects relating to sex, unlike abstinence-only programs, which give only partial facts or in some cases completely inaccurate information.

Refutation continues.

Unfortunately, the majority of today's teens do not consider oral sex "sex" and therefore see no problem with it. Comprehensive sex education clearly defines what constitutes sexual activity, something abstinence-only education fails to do. A study in the Journal of Pediatric Psychology revealed that in 2003, 40% of teens have engaged in oral sex and more than 25% of those teens have had three or more oral sex partners (Prinstein, Meade, and Cohen). While it may seem unfathomable, children as young as 12 are having oral sex; it's happening on school buses, school bathrooms, and after school when parents have not yet arrived home from work. Psychologist Wayne Warren says, "I see girls, seventh and eighth graders, even sixth graders, who tell me they're virgins but they've had oral sex 50 or 60 times. It's like a goodnight kiss to them" (qtd. in Prinstein, Meade, and Cohen).

Citation for a work with three authors.

Citation indicates quote comes from other source.

Schmoll 8

Oral sex referred to as a goodnight kiss may seem shocking, but it's not to the teens that are doing it. Teens surprisingly think of oral sex as less intimate than kissing and often consider it a routine part of dating. Ashley, a 14-year-old girl who started having oral sex at age 11, says, "Girls don't have to sleep with their boyfriends, but boys will say, 'Give me a blow job, or I'll break up with you'" (Lanzendorfer). Deborah Roffman, a sexuality educator, asserts that "middle-school girls sometimes look at oral sex as an absolute bargain—you don't get pregnant, they think you don't get diseases, you're still a virgin, and you're in control since it's something that they can do to boys (whereas sex is almost always described as something boys do to girls)" (qtd. in Remez). These teens are in most cases unaware that they can still contract STDs from oral sex, something comprehensive sex education teaches.

Supporters of abstinence-only programs claim that to teach abstinence along with contraception information provides a mixed message: "Don't do it, but if you do, protect yourself" (Brody). This is certainly a valid claim if this were the way comprehensive sex education programs were taught. However, comprehensive sex education's approach is to neither encourage premarital sex nor discourage it. Rather, it focuses on instilling the fact that abstinence is the only 100% effective way to protect oneself from STDs or pregnancy. When this is the focus, it does not become a mixed message to also inform students about contraception.

Advocates of abstinence-only education defend their programs by citing studies showing that teens who have sex have higher rates of depression compared with teens that are not sexually active. The National Longitudinal Survey of Adolescent Health conducted a study of 6,500 adolescents that produced alarming results: 25.3% of teenage girls who were sexually active

Author makes another concession.

Additional refutation.

Schmoll 9

reported being depressed all, most, or a lot of the time compared with only

7.7% of teenage girls who were not sexually active (Rector, Johnson, and

Noyes). This same study found that 8.3% of sexually active teenage boys were

depressed compared to 3.4% of teenage boys who were not sexually active

(Rector, Johnson, and Noyes). Outcomes such as these have been proven in

many studies and are excellent reasons for teens to abstain from sex.

Depression is an issue that should be talked about as it can be a consequence

of having sex. Because comprehensive sex education programs aim at

educating students on a variety of issues relating to sex, issues such as

depression are discussed as well as the possible negative effects sex can have

on a teenage relationship. The difference is that comprehensive sex education

does so in a manner that is not meant to scare, but simply inform.

    Advocates of abstinence-only programs also claim that teaching

Additional
refutation.

contraceptive practice encourages or intrigues students to become sexually

active. However, research has repeatedly shown that "comprehensive,

factually accurate sexual education" does not increase the sexual activity of

youth (Work 13). One high school health educator insists that teaching

contraceptive practices aids in the delay of sexual activity. Part of her

lesson on birth control involves students observing her rolling a condom

onto a test tube. But she also tells them, "if you are considering having

sex, don't just think about how it will feel to do it. Also think about how

you'll feel standing naked in front of someone else, or how you'll feel if

you break up the next day" (qtd. in Pardini). In this way, sex becomes real,

forcing kids to seriously question their emotional readiness and physical

capability of protecting themselves, not intriguing them to go out and

have sex.

Schmoll 10

A final concern with sex education in schools, which is not specific to abstinence-only supporters or comprehensive sex education supporters, is that sex education belongs in the home. Supporters of this idea believe that sex education is a topic to be discussed according to the parents' particular values. In an ideal world, children could learn all they need to know about sex from their parents. But there are two problems associated with this idea, both of which can be solved by teaching comprehensive sex education in the schools. While a majority of students wish they could feel comfortable about talking to their parents about sex, many parents find it hard to discuss this topic. They may not know all the facts or be embarrassed, but whatever the reasons, studies show that only half of parents talk with their children about sex. While some students may benefit from learning sex education from their parents, we as a society cannot leave behind the children whose parents do not talk about sex with them. By teaching it in the school, we can ensure that every student is knowledgeable on the subject. Also, students are influenced by what they see and observe in school. If students are hearing about or in some cases even participating in sexual acts on school grounds, it makes sense that students learn the actual facts about these events in that same school atmosphere. And parents usually have the final say in whether they allow their child to be present in health class when sex education is being discussed.

In addition to Minnesota educating more knowledgeable students, there would be other benefits to implementing new health standards that include comprehensive sex education. Changing sex education from being locally determined to statewide determined would ensure that any Minnesota child will know the benefits of abstinence as well as the proper use of

Additional refutation.

Argument turns back to benefits.

Schmoll 11

contraception. It would also be a step in making comprehensive sex education

a national standard. Minnesota was not the only state to implement a program

like ENABL. Ten other states tried identical or similar programs having

comparable outcomes. None of the programs demonstrated evidence of long-

term success in delaying the initiation of sex or in reducing other sexual risk-

taking behaviors. Also, adding statewide academic standards for health would

show students that Minnesota views learning how to take care of one's body

as important as math, science, and reading.

    I urge you as leaders of Minnesota to consider implementing statewide

health academic standards that include comprehensive sex education. The

increase in STDs and pregnancy among youth as well as the number of

sexually active teens show an important need for it. If more than half of

teenagers are sexually active by the time they reach their senior year,

obviously abstinence-only programs do not help the majority of students.

Therefore it makes sense that a sexuality education program be put into action

that addresses both abstinence and contraceptive use. A comprehensive sex

education method gives youth the greatest access to the information they

need to make informed choices, while educating them not only about sex, but

about human development, relationships, and communication. Comprehensive

sex education teaches abstinence as the only true way to prevent STDs and

pregnancy, clearly defines what constitutes sexual acts, thoroughly describes

facts about STDs and pregnancy, and teaches the proper use of contraceptives.

Comprehensive sex education educates youth on every aspect relating to sex,

so no matter when they decide to become sexually active, they will have the

knowledge and confidence to make the safest choices possible.

Conclusion addresses the audience and reestablishes proposed solution.

Schmoll 12

Works Cited
starts new
page.

1″

Works Cited

Brody, Jane. "Abstinence-Only: Does It Work?" <u>New York Times</u> 1 June 2004.

Sources are
alphabetized.

7 Nov 2004 <http://www.religiousconsultation.org/News_Tracker/

abstinence-only_does_it_work.htm>.

1″

Connolly, Ceci. "Kids Get Dose of False Data with Abstinence Programs,

½″
Congressional Report Says." <u>Star Tribune</u> 2 Dec. 2004: A6.

Grow, Doug. "'Saving' the Sexually Naive." <u>Star Tribune</u> 5 Mar. 2004. 6 Nov.

2004 <http://nl.newsbank.com/>.

Author's
last names
come first.

Hauser, Debra. "Five Years of Abstinence-Only-Until-Marriage Education:

Assessing the Impact." 2004. Advocates for Youth. 7 Nov. 2004

<http://www.advocatesforyouth.org/publications/stateevaluations/>.

Lanzendorfer, Joy. "Kids Aren't Having Casual Sex, They're Having Oral Sex."

Electronic
sources
include post
date and
retrieval
date.

<u>North Bay Bohemian</u> 17 Oct. 2002. 7 Feb. 2005 <http://

www.metroactive.com/papers/sonoma/10.17.02/sex-0242.html>.

Larson, Lisa. "Minnesota's New K-12 Academic Standards and Assessments."

June 2004. 6 Nov. 2004 <http://www.house.leg.state.mn.us/hrd/

issinfo/ssk12stan.pdf>.

Levine, Judith. <u>Harmful to Minors: The Perils of Protecting Children from Sex.</u>

New York: Thunder, 2002.

Home page
given when
URL is too
cumbersome.

Marcotty, Josephine. "Sex Diseases Continue to Rise." <u>Star Tribune</u> 11 May

2004. 6 Nov. 2004 <http://nl.newsbank.com/>.

"State Sex Ed Not Working, Study Finds: Sexual Activity Increasing Despite

Abstinence Emphasis." <u>Star Tribune</u> 4 Jan. 2004. 6 Nov. 2004 <http://

nl.newsbank.com/>.

Entries
without
authors
alphabetized
by title.

<u>Minnesota School Health Guide.</u> "Chapter 12: Sexuality and Reproductive

Health." St. Paul, 1996. Minnesota Department of Health. 6 Nov. 2004

Schmoll 13

<http://www.health.state.mn.us/divs/fh/mch/schoolhealth/

guide/chap12.pdf>.

Minnesota Education Now and Babies Later (MN ENABL). "Evaluation Report

1998–2002." St. Paul, 2003. Minnesota Department of Health. 6 Nov. 2004

<http:// www.saynotyet.com/report.htm>.

"New Minnesota Academic Standards at a Glance." Minnesota Department

of Health. 6 Nov. 2004 <http://www.mnschoolhealth.com/article/

pubs/040130151046-825499/040202090143-262938/

fmnschoolhealthcompa.pdf>.

Pardini, Priscilla. "Abstinence-Only Education Continues to Flourish."

Rethinking Schools 17.2 (2002/2003). 7 Nov. 2004 <http://

www.rethinkingschools.org/archive/17_02/Abst172.shtml>.

Prinstein, Mitchell J., Christina S. Meade, and Geoffrey L. Cohen. "Adolescent

Oral Sex, Peer Popularity, and Perceptions of Best Friends' Sexual

Behavior." Journal of Pediatric Psychology 28.4 (2003): 243–49. 7 Feb. 2005

<http://jpepsy.oupjournals.org/cgi/content/full/28/4/243>.

Rector, Robert E., Kirk A. Johnson, and Lauren R. Noyes. "Sexually Active

Teenagers Are More Likely to Be Depressed and to Attempt Suicide."

3 June 2003. The Heritage Foundation. 7 Feb. 2005 <http://

www.heritage.org/Research/Family/cda0304.cfm>.

Remez, Lisa. "Oral Sex Among Adolescents: Is It Sex or Is It Abstinence?"

Family Planning Perspectives 32.6 (2000). 7 Feb. 2005 <http://

www.agi-usa.org/pubs/journals/3229800.html>.

"Sex Ed: The Threat of 'Abstinence-Only'." Star Tribune 11 Jan. 2004. 6 Nov.

2004 <http://nl.newsbank.com/>.

Strong, Bryan. The Marriage and Family Experience. Belmont, CA:

Thomson, 2001.

When date of posting is not available, provide the date of access.

URLs are broken after slashes.

Schmoll 14

"Tracking the Hidden Epidemics: Trends in STDs in the United States." 6 Apr.

    2000. U.S. Centers for Disease Control and Prevention. 6 Nov. 2004.

    <http://www.cdc.gov/ nchstp/dstd/Stats_Trends/

    Trends2000.pdf>.

Wallace, Marian, and Vannessa Warner. "Abstinence: Why Sex Is Worth the

    Wait." 5 Sept. 2002. Concerned Women for America. 6 Nov. 2004

    <http://www.cwfa.org/articles/1195/CWA/family>.

Weller Health Education Center. "STD Epidemic." 7 Feb. 2005 <http://

    www.wellercenter.org/STD PreventionProgram.htm>.

"A Work in Progress v. 2: Building a Minnesota State Plan for Teen Pregnancy,

    Prevention, and Parenting." Minnesota Organization on Adolescent

    Pregnancy Prevention and Parenting. 6 Nov. 2004 <http://

    www.mnstateplan.org/StatePlan.pdf>.

Acknowledgments

Text Credits

ANDRÉ ACIMAN. From "Lavender." Copyright © 2003 by André Aciman. Reprinted by permission of the author.

JOHN R. ALDEN. "Breakfast at the FDA Café," originally in *The Wall Street Journal* 1991. Reprinted by permission of the author.

AMERICAN FEDERATION OF TEACHERS. "Charter School Results Repeatedly Delayed," August 17, 2004 press release reprinted by permission of the American Federation of Teachers.

FREDERICK W. BASSETT. "Noah's Nakedness and the Curse of Canaan: A Case of Incest?" *Vetus Testamentum* 21 (1971): 232–237. Reprinted by permission of *Vetus Testamentum*.

AARON BELKIN AND MELISSA S. EMBSER-HERBERT. "A Modest Proposal: Privacy as a Flawed Rationale for the Exclusion of Gays and Lesbians from the U. S. Military," *International Security*, 27:2 (Fall 2002), pp. 178–197. Copyright © 2002 by the President and Fellows of Harvard College and the Massachusetts Institute of Technology. Reprinted here as "Privacy and the U.S. Military."

KEN BELSON. "Saved, and Enslaved, by the Cell." *The New York Times,* October 10, 2004. Copyright © 2004 by The New York Times Company. Reprinted by permission.

JOHN BERGER. "Et in Arcadia Ego." Copyright © 2004 by *Harper's Magazine*. All rights reserved. Reproduced from the August 2004 issue by special permission.

LAWRENCE I. BERKOVE. "Fatal Self-Assertion in Kate Chopin's 'The Story of an Hour'" from *American Literary Realism,* 32:2 (Winter 2000): 152–158. Copyright © 2000 by the Board of Trustees of the University of Illinois. Used with permission of the University of Illinois Press.

KATHERINE BOO. "The Best Job in Town," *The New Yorker,* July 5, 2004. Copyright © 2004 by Katherine Boo. Reprinted by permission of International Creative Management.

SUSAN BORDO. Excerpts from "Beauty (Re)discovers the Male Body" from *The Male Body* by Susan Bordo. Copyright © 1999 by Susan Bordo. Reprinted by permission of Farrar, Straus, and Giroux, LLC.

ANNIE BOURNEUF. "Machen Sie Platz: The Re-rebranding of Berlin." Copyright © 2003 by *Harper's Magazine*. All rights reserved. Reproduced from the January 2004 issue by special permission.

SARAH BOXER. "Torture Incarnate, and Propped on a Pedestal." *The New York Times,* June 13, 2004. Copyright © 2004 The New York Times Company. Reprinted with permission.

Gloria Naylor. Reprinted by permission of Sterling Lord Literistic, Inc. Reprinted with permission of the author as "Meanings of a Word."

ITABARI NJERI, "Life with Father" from *Every Goodbye Ain't Gone* by Itabari Njeri. Originally appeared in *Harper's Magazine,* January 1990. Copyright © 1990 by Itabari Njeri. Reprinted by permission of Miriam Altschuler on behalf of the author.

GEORGE ORWELL. "A Hanging" from *Shooting an Elephant and Other Essays* by George Orwell. Copyright © 1950 by Sonia Brownell Orwell and renewed by Sonia Pitt-Rivers. Reprinted by permission of Harcourt, Inc.

GEORGE ORWELL. "Marrakech" from *Such, Such Were the Joys.* Copyright © 1953 by Sonia Brownell Orwell and renewed in 1981 by Mrs. George K. Perutz, Mrs. Miriam Gross, and Dr. Michael Dickson, Executors of the Estate of Sonia Brownell Orwell. Reprinted by permission of Harcourt, Inc.

CYNTHIA OZICK. "She: Portrait of the Essay as Warm Body" from *Quarrel and Quandry* by Cynthia Ozick. Copyright © 2000 by Cynthia Ozick. Used by permission of Alfred A. Knopf, a division of Random House, Inc.

WES PITTS. "Photo Exorcism," *PC Photo Magazine,* June 2003. Reprinted by permission of *PC Photo Magazine.*

NANCY REAGAN. Remarks Made at a Gala Tribute to Nancy Reagan. Reprinted by permission of Nancy Reagan.

RON REAGAN, JR. "I Know a Child." Speech to the Democratic National Convention, 2004. Reprinted by permission of Ron Reagan, Jr.

ADOLPH L. REED, JR. "Majoring in Debt" by Adolph L. Reed, Jr. Reprinted by permission from the January 2004 edition of *The Progressive.* www.progressive.org.

GENE RICE. "The Curse That Never Was (Genesis 9:8-27)." *The Journal of Religious Thought,* 29.1 (Spring/Summer 1972) 5–27. Reprinted by permission.

GARY RIVLIN. "Bet On It: How the Slot Machine Was Remade and How It's Remaking America." *The New York Times,* May 9, 2004. Copyright © 2004 by Gary Rivlin. Reprinted by permission of the New York Times Co. All rights reserved.

TIM ROGERS, "Tough Break" originally appeared in *American Way Magazine,* March 15, 1994. Reprinted by permission of the author.

JONATHAN ROWE. "Reach Out and Annoy Someone," *The Washington Monthly,* November 2000, pp. 35–37. Copyright © 2000 by Washington Monthly Publishing LLC, 733 15th Street, NW, Washington, DC 20005. www.washingtonmonthly.com Reprinted by permission of the publisher.

JOAN ROUGHGARDEN. "We, Like Sheep" from *Evolution's Rainbow: Diversity, Gender and Sexuality in Nature and People* by Joan Roughgarden. Copyright © 2004 by the Regents of the University of California Press. Reprinted by permission. Reprinted here as "Same-Sex Sexuality."

JUDY RUIZ. "Oranges and Sweet Sister Boy" originally appeared in *Iowa Woman,* Summer 1988. Reprinted by permission of the author.

SCOTT RUSSELL SANDERS, "Grub" from *Wigwag,* June 1990. Reprinted by permission.

LUC SANTE. "I Was Born" from *The Factory of Facts* by Luc Sante. Copyright © 1998 by Luc Sante. Used by permission of Pantheon Books, a division of Random House, Inc.

MARILYN SCHIEL, "Levi's." Copyright © 1991 by Marilyn Schiel. Reprinted by permission of the author.

ERIC SCHLOSSER. "Why McDonald's Fries Taste So Good" from *Fast Food Nation: The Dark Side of the All-American Meal* by Eric Schlosser. Copyright © 2001 by Eric Schlosser. Excerpted and reprinted by permission of Houghton Mifflin Company. All rights reserved. First published in *The Atlantic Monthly.* Reprinted here as "The American Flavor Industry."

DAVID SEDARIS. "The Learning Curve" from *Me Talk Pretty One Day* by David Sedaris. Copyright © 2000 by David Sedaris. By permission of Little, Brown and Company, Inc.

DEBORAH SOLOMON. "Questions for Joan Roughgarden: Same-Sex Selection," *The New York Times Magazine,* May 9, 2004. Copyright © 2004 Deborah Solomon. Reprinted by permission of The New York Times.

PETER STARK. "As Freezing Persons Recollect the Snow—First Chill, Then Stupor, Then the Letting Go" from *Outside,* January 1997, pp. 69–71. Copyright © 1997 by Peter Stark. Reprinted by permission of the author.

STUART TAYLOR, JR. "Racial Profiling: The Liberals Are Right," *National Journal,* April 24, 1999: 1084–1085. Copyright © 1999 by National Journal Group, Inc. All rights reserved. Reprinted by permission.

PATRICIA VOLK. "Technology Makes Me Mad" originally from *The New York Times,* September 28, 1997. Reprinted by permission of the author.

ALICE WALKER. "Am I Blue?" from *Living by the Word: Selected Writings 1973–1987.* Copyright © 1986 by Alice Walker. Reprinted by permission of Harcourt, Inc.

MATT WELCH. "The Pentagon's Secret Stash: Why We'll Never See the Second Round of Abu Ghraib Photos," *Reason Online,* April 2005. Reprinted with permission.

BARBIE ZELIZER. "Conveying Atrocity in Image" from *Remembering to Forget* by Barbie Zelizer. Copyright © 1998 by Barbie Zelizer. Reprinted by permission of University of Chicago Press.

Photo Credits

Page 91 Michael Rougier/Time & Life Pictures/Getty Images **Page 121** Royalty Free/Corbis **Page 159** Sajjad Hussain/AFP/Getty Images **Page 169** David H. Wells/Corbis **Page 181** Royalty Free/Corbis **Page 182** Royalty Free/Corbis **Page 183** Royalty Free/Corbis **Page 196** Courtesy of Mesa Verde National Park, Colorado.

Neg. no. CO-MV45-001 **Page 205** Joe Raedle/Getty Images **Page 222** Royalty Free/Corbis **Page 227** Michael Yamashita/Corbis **Page 275** The Michael Ochs Archive **Page 291** Ron Wurzer/Getty Images News **Page 292** Lawrence A. Martin/GreatBuidings.com **Page 314** Britt Erlanson/The Image Bank/Getty Images **Page 331** Joel Gordon **Page 339** Bettmann/Corbis **Page 343** Steve Vacceriello/nonstick **Page 344** Paolo Curto/Getty Images **Page 347** *Left* Bettmann/Corbis **Page 347** *Right* "Gordon Hanson, 1954," George Platt Lynes. © The Estate of George Platt Lynes. Courtesy of Vance Martin Photography & Fine Art, San Francisco **Page 350** The NeXT block logo is a registered trademark of NeXT Software, Inc., registered in the U.S. and other countries and used with permission. The use of the NeXT block logo does not necessarily reflect NeXT's approval or disapproval of viewpoints represented by the author. McGraw-Hill's publication has not been authorized, sponsored, or otherwise approved by NeXT Software, Inc. NeXT is not responsible for the accuracy or any representation made herein. **Page 353** Courtesy of IBM. IBM is a registered trademark of International Business Machines Corporation **Page 353** Courtesy of UPS **Page 355** Jan-Peter Boening/ZENIT **Page 361** NARA **Page 362** NARA **Page 364** NARA **Page 365** *Top* Courtesy of the Trustees of the Imperial War Museum, London **Page 365** *Bottom* NARA **Page 366** Corbis **Page 367** Courtesy of the Trustees of the Imperial War Museum, London **Page 368** Courtesy of the Trustees of the Imperial War Museum, London **Page 370** Graham Morrison/AP Photos/Wide World Photos **Page 371** Jean-Marc Bouju/AP Photos/Wide World Photos **Page 373** AFP/Getty Images **Page 375** Getty Images **Page 376** Ali Jasim/Reuters/Corbis **Page 619** Bridgeman Art Library **Page 620** Kavaler/Art Resource, NY **Page 624** Erich Lessing/ Art Resource, NY

Index to the Readings by Rhetorical Strategy (Mode)

Definition

Analysis

Argument

Index of Authors, Titles, and Subjects